Dennis Potter's death in 1994 deprived British television of its most controversial figure. Potter was a prolific writer of genius. Yet while his subversive television plays, such as *Pennies from Heaven* and *The Singing Detective,* scandalized and delighted the nation, they also made him the butt of the tabloids, who nicknamed him 'Dirty Den' for his 1989 serial *Blackeyes*.

Humphrey Carpenter, Potter's official biographer, is already well known for his candid lives of Benjamin Britten and Robert Runcie. He has interviewed everyone who came close to Potter, and has had exclusive access to Potter's archives, including the many unmade television and film scripts. Carpenter portrays a very different Potter from the aggressive public image: a deeply shy and reclusive man, who was psychologically as well as physically scarred by the illness which struck him down at the age of twenty-six. Potter was a man with a vast interest in sex but also a terrible loathing of it, thanks to an appalling experience he suffered in childhood.

Potter has been a man much gossiped about, both in his lifetime and after his death. Carpenter's remarkable new biography establishes the extraordinary truth behind the rumours; describes Potter's strange, obsessive relationships with women such as Gina Bellman, who played Blackeyes; and gives a vivid portrait of the backstage dramas and fights behind Potter's screen triumphs.

Humphrey Carpenter is the acclaimed biographer of J. R. R. Tolkien, W. H. Auden, Ezra Pound, Benjamin Britten and Robert Runcie. He is married with two children and lives in Oxford.

Dennis Potter
A Biography

—

HUMPHREY CARPENTER

faber and faber

First published in 1998
by Faber and Faber Limited
3 Queen Square London WC1N 3AU
This paperback edition first published in 1999

Photoset by Agnesi Text, Hadleigh
Printed in England by Mackays of Chatham plc, Chatham, Kent

© Humphrey Carpenter, 1998

Humphrey Carpenter is hereby identified as author of this
work in accordance with Section 77 of the Copyright,
Designs and Patents Act 1988

A CIP record for this book
is available from the British Library

ISBN 0-571-19721-3

2 4 6 8 10 9 7 5 3 1

Contents

——

PART THREE: 1976–1986
Now that I've got the power

PART FOUR: 1986–1994
The ending is sooner than I thought

No biography!

In Dennis Potter's last work for television, *Cold Lazarus*, the dying writer Daniel Feeld struggles to make his final wish clear to friends gathered around his hospital bed. Eventually, out come 'the last two words the mortal Daniel will ever speak'. He almost screams them: '*No biography!*'

One might assume this to have been Potter's own last wish. Yet he did consider allowing his biography to be written in his lifetime. In 1987, not long after the screening of *The Singing Detective*, Angela Lambert of the *Independent* wrote to him saying that he and she 'had a surprising number of things in common – we were contemporaries at Oxford . . . both lifelong socialists . . . [and have] spent most of our working lives in journalism and television'. Could she begin work on a biography of him?

Potter replied that her suggestion caused 'an instinctive recoil, and yet also, perhaps, an astonishment that someone of your abilities should want to do such a thing! It is flattering, and it is threatening: and I don't yet know how to react.' He suggested that they had 'lunch or a drink or something', adding that 'meeting people always makes me ill at ease, so be warned'.

A few weeks later, he telephoned Lambert and arrived at her flat, 'complaining about the stairs (seventy-five and no lift),' writes Lambert,

and gratified to find that I had – or so he claimed – laid in two bottles of his favourite wine (a Côte du Rhône Paul Jaboulet Aîné, I seem to remember). He and I and my partner demolished those in the space of an hour or so, after which DP asked if I had any food in the flat. I said I could knock up a spaghetti bolognese but not much more than that. He then suggested that he should take us both out to dinner. He was very brilliant and caustic over the meal, and all three of us got fairly drunk. I can remember very little of what he said, except that at one point he looked at me and said, 'You've still got nice arms anyway!' (They were very brown as I'd just returned from a long stay in France.)

He insisted on paying for dinner, and left us in the Earl's Court Road, jumping into a taxi to go back to his Great Titchfield Street flat.

A few days later, on 24 August 1987, Potter wrote to Lambert, 'I have thought and thought all over again about this flattering and threatening biography question: the answer has to be No. I'm very sorry, especially as I enjoyed meeting you, and have no doubts about your ability. But there it is – the door won't open, for more than my boot is jammed against it.'

Seven years later, facing death, he knew that a biography would soon be written. His daughter Sarah recalls:

Towards the end – I think late May [1994], when he was fading fast but still very lucid – Judy [Daish, Potter's agent] was down, and we were talking about various work things that were unresolved, and what was going to happen. And the question of the biography was one that had to be discussed. I think Dad's feeling on it at the time was that he wasn't particularly comfortable with the idea, but he certainly wasn't going to try to block anything, because he knew it was going to happen, and Judy talked about Fabers [Potter's publishers] and what they wanted, and Dad said, 'Fine, who are the candidates?' And there were a few names I can't remember.

Reviewing Michael Holroyd's life of Lytton Strachey in *The Times* twenty-six years earlier, Potter had written:

Biography is in some ways the most brutish of all the arts. It shifts about uncomfortably in the strangely uncertain middle ground between deliberate assassination and helpless boot-licking – two activities which are in themselves frequently interchangeable . . . The Judas kiss, of course, is part of the necessary equipment of any competent biographer and hindsight expressed in a decorous prose is a horribly effective and very one-sided weapon.

Elsewhere that year he wrote of 'the whorish clutches of incompetent biographers', and in a 1969 review he asked, 'How do you make that final, crucial leap from the pile of external events . . . into the hidden tangles of the mind . . . ?' Many years later, he said, 'I despise biographies. They're hidden novels.' He added that he was not 'interested in the sort of criticism that tries to make links between the work and the life . . . I think it's invalid and impertinent. Biographical criticism doesn't really discover anything.'

Yet he had admired Holroyd's book, and had described Robert Gittings's life of Keats as 'a glowing, generous, rewarding and extremely enjoyable exercise, formidable in scholarship and yet always eminently readable'. The same year, 1968, he admitted that, for some while, he had 'played with the idea' of writing a biography of his literary idol, William Hazlitt, observing, with a biographer's eye, 'He was the type of manic depressive who was able to use even the black moments to reach deep down into himself and find an extremity of meaning or experience which could be communicated to others.' He noted that it was exceptionally difficult to separate Hazlitt's life from his works: 'He used himself, used up himself, in so unique a fashion.' Was Potter here dropping hints about his own literary personality?

Many of his plays, most notably *The Singing Detective*, contain some element of autobiography. But he often issued warnings about this: '*The Singing Detective* played with the autobiographical genre. It pretended to be autobiographical because that's a very powerful way of writing. One thinks, "Oh, this must be the truth", and of course it isn't.' He told an interviewer in 1990, 'I'm a reclusive character and I don't expose myself. I appear to.'

For thirty years, his works played hide-and-seek with the facts of his life. At times he even seems to have been setting a trap for his biographer: 'I do not believe what writers say about themselves,' he wrote in 1983, 'except when they think they are not saying it about themselves . . . the masking of the Self is an essential part of the trade.' In a 1975 article he remarked upon the connection between writing and lying: '*Telling stories* is a popular description of both arts.' He admitted that he could even be dishonest about the meaning of his plays: 'What I say about them and what they are are not necessarily the same thing.' And in his (unfilmed) movie adaptation of *The Singing Detective*, the autobiographically based hero says, at one moment, 'That's what it's about. My book. My life. Sex. Sex and lies.'

Yet there was an extraordinary honesty in most of what he said about himself. He rarely wrote letters, and when he did, they were carefully planned and almost formal, revealing no more than he had intended. He never kept a diary. However, despite his reclusive nature, he rarely refused a request for an interview, and spoke with extraordinary candour to journalists and broadcasters about intimate experiences and feelings, culminating in his television interview with Melvyn Bragg when he was dying. Although he, rather than the interviewer, tended to set the agenda for these conversations, and he usually spoke about only what he chose to, he never falsified information about himself, and rarely made errors of fact. 'Several times, publishers have written to me saying, "Will you write your autobiography?" and I say, "No,"' he remarked four years before his death. In fact the accumulated interviews amount to something approaching an autobiography. And though he did not make his most private utterances in front of the microphone or the reporter's notebook, these are found where they should be, in his plays.

I was not on the list of possible biographers that he considered on his deathbed. I never met him, and the idea of writing his life occurred to me only after he had died. The project would have seemed attractive to almost any biographer; Mark Lawson, interviewing Potter in 1993, shrewdly observed that one day he would make the perfect biographical subject, because his life was spun out of so many powerful themes: class, religion, sex, politics and illness. Moreover, Potter was for many years the almost unchallenged king of British television drama, beginning his career as a hero of the Left and ending it as an enemy of the tabloids – other good causes for discovering the man behind the image. But it was also a book I wanted to write for more personal reasons.

I had been watching his plays since *Vote, Vote, Vote for Nigel Barton*, broadcast in 1965 when I was nineteen, and in 1969 I had been particularly struck by the now almost forgotten *Moonlight on the Highway*, the first play in which he makes the connection between Thirties popular songs and sexual innocence. Indeed, the references to childhood sexual abuse in this play even then seemed to me autobiographical, and began to make me curious about his early life.

Thirties popular songs have an almost inexplicable grip on me, too, though not, as far as I am aware, for sexual reasons. For some years I ran a Thirties-style dance band, giving 'historically authentic' performances, as they say at the more serious end of the music business. Indeed, my band, Vile Bodies, actually played a small part in one Potter project: we recorded some of the songs on the album from his 1988 serial *Christabel*. His two masterpieces, *Pennies from Heaven* and *The Singing Detective*, both touch a significant nerve in me, because of the way they use songs with which I, too, am obsessed.

But beyond Mark Lawson's list of themes, and that musical empathy, lies another, deeper attraction to me. A friend, reading the first draft of this book, commented that Potter seemed to 'lead his life outside in, showing in a very public way the parts that other people hide'. This is true; yet I gradually came to realize that this apparent self-exposure was both perfectly genuine and, at the same time, a carefully calculated performance, done with a cool eye for effect.

He himself was acutely aware of this. He once said, of the character of Arthur Parker, hero of *Pennies from Heaven*:

You meet people sometimes who seem utterly authentic; their eyes will moisten, the structure of their speech implies they really believe something, and for those minutes or seconds they might. But you have no idea *what* they believe because you have nothing to go on. They leave you anchorless. They are very difficult people to work out. They may be self-deluding or extremely self-knowing, but they have a paintbrush in their hands and they paint the scenery in around them to fit whatever it is they momentarily feel.

I am sure that Potter, albeit unconsciously, was here drawing a self-portrait. This means that he poses a special challenge for biography. With such a subject, the book has to become a game of hide-and-seek. I have hugely enjoyed responding to that challenge, that invitation to pursue the 'real' Dennis Potter through the tangled forest of his extraordinary life.

PART ONE: 1935–1962

Listening to myself

——

CHAPTER I

Painting the Clouds with Sunshine

━━━

Dennis Potter's capacity for making up his own life story was never more obvious than when he talked or wrote about his childhood in the Forest of Dean. Two people have suggested that he was exaggerating its unusualness. Roger Smith, who was at Oxford with him and later commissioned his first television play, recalls:

I went to the Forest, expecting some weird, wonderful world which I knew nothing about. But I recognized it immediately. We drank at the miners' club, and had a smashing time, singing songs and having a knees-up. And it was just like my relatives, not at all the cut-off part of the world Dennis had made it out to be.

Gareth Davies, who directed the Nigel Barton plays and other early Potter scripts, recalls a trip there to look for locations for *A Beast with Two Backs*:

I'd heard scurrilous things about the Forest of Dean, babies with two heads in the attic, and all that sort of thing. But when I started wandering around it, talking to the miners and going down one or two of those funny coal-pits, I realized that these people weren't even remotely like the characters in Dennis's plays. They weren't dour and shut in. There was a lot of humour. And I felt much the same atmosphere as the South Wales mining communities, which I knew well.

But both Smith and Davies went there in the late Fifties and Sixties, when the Forest had changed. And even then, Graham Wale, a young cousin of Potter, visiting it from his London home, reacted quite differently: 'It was like a dream, another world – it was so different.'

Potter's fullest description of the Forest comes in his first book, *The Glittering Coffin*, a survey of the state of Britain, written in 1958 when he was twenty-three:

The Forest of Dean is hilly and relatively isolated, bounded by the Wye to the west and the broader valley of the Severn to the east. The people of this district are conscious of the unique identity of their birthplace, and speak a dialect so forceful and individual that, at times, it might almost be another language. Mining of one sort or another has gone on here for centuries, and the majority of the working population have always been coalminers. The sense of community has been a real characteristic of this region, and is expressed in the strange 'free miners' gales' [places where coal may be mined] and the tremendous inter-village rivalry. These villages are ugly for the most part, yet set against woods and fields and the distant prospect of the Welsh mountains or, to the north, the Malvern Hills . . . Occasionally, the great black sores of the pits erupt out of the surrounding green.

At the other end of his working life, speaking to Melvyn Bragg in his final interview, Potter called the Forest 'a heart-shaped place between two rivers, somehow slightly cut off from them, [from] the rest of England and Wales'. He told Bragg it had been, in his childhood, 'a strange and beautiful place, with a people who were as warm as anywhere else, but they seemed warmer to me'; but elsewhere he called it 'enclosed, tight, backward', even 'suffocatingly in-turned'.

To the casual observer, Forest of Dean people had, and have, more in common with the emotional Welsh than the reserved English; but Potter usually disclaimed any such affinity. 'As a border person I always hate the Welsh,' he told Bragg, and on *Desert Island Discs* he said, 'I . . . hated the Welsh with a passion which even to this day [1977] makes me want to amend the Race Relations Act to exclude the Welsh.' Yet this 'hatred' was only a joke, and he added, 'I must admit they were like us in many ways.' The heroes of two of his plays are Welsh: Willy Turner in *Where the Buffalo Roam* and Francis Francis in *Lipstick on Your Collar*.

The geographical isolation of the Forest led to the preservation, until the age of television, of a dialect that often used ancient forms of English. '"Thee" and "thou" is the most common way of saying "you",' Potter explained to Graham Fuller, who was interviewing him for the book *Potter on Potter*. 'You would say, "Where'st thou going, old butty?" instead of "Where are you going, pal?" or whatever. It's a very old English. You would say "highsht" for "hist", meaning "listen carefully", and "surry" – "Where'st thou been, surry?" – from "sirrah", of course.'

Potter's mother, who at the time of writing still lives in the Forest, in her late eighties, quotes another common expression: '"How bist, o' butty?" You don't hear that now,' she adds. 'They'd say "This is my butty" – his mate at work.' Her son-in-law, Eddie Thomas, a Londoner now living in the Forest, explains, 'I think originally the coalface was only about a metre high – so when your mate was crawling along in front of you, all you saw was his bum, his butt. And this is where the American "buddy" has come from. Because Forest miners went to America, and "butt" went over too, and became "bud".'

To Bragg, Potter spoke of 'those rather ugly villages in beautiful landscape'. Even today, with much new housing, most Forest villages still have an untidy, unfinished look about them. There are few ancient parish churches or picturesque cottages, for the majority of settlements originated as illegal squatting.

From Norman times, Dean was designated a Royal Forest, and the only people allowed to live there were a handful of the king's keepers. The villages grew up behind their backs. Berry Hill, where Potter and his father were born, and where his mother still lives, is a typically careless-looking, unofficial Forest straggle of small houses, just outside the small town of Coleford. It sprawls across open ground on the north-western side of the hilly plateau that, densely wooded with oak and beech, has always been the Forest's heart.

In Potter's second book, *The Changing Forest* (1962), he describes a comedian in the local working men's club cracking a joke about Berry Hill: 'The last place God made – and then him had to apologize.' Potter's mother ascribes this joke to her father, a Londoner: 'The first time he came here he said it was the last place God had made and He got tired before He had finished!'

Under the Normans, Royal Forests were chiefly places of hunting for the sovereign and those whom he chose to benefit; later, they supplied shipbuilding timber for the navy. Dean was rich in this, and in coal seams and iron ore, and from early times the local people were granted privileges of mining. According to local historian Humphrey Phelps,

The Free Mining Rights were established in the reign of Edward I (1272–1307) as a reward for the part played by the miners at the Siege of Berwick-on-Tweed, where they are alleged to have undermined the fortifications. To become a free miner [in the Forest] a man had to be born within the Hundred of St Briavels [the old administrative boundary of the Forest] and to have worked for a year and a day in an iron or coal mine within the Hundred.

The Gaveller, on behalf of the Crown, regulates the award of gales . . . and collects the dues from the free miners.

However, the chief authority on the Forest, Cyril E. Hart (who was a Forester himself, and Her Majesty's Senior Verderer of the Forest) is less definite in his 1953 book *The Free Miners of the Royal Forest of Dean*. This mentions the Free Miners' role as siege tunnellers, which they performed on a number of occasions, but says that they were already emancipated and allowed to mine on their own account by the first half of the thirteenth century – that is, before Edward I came to the throne. They were at the same time near outlaws, squatting in the Forest without right of abode, stealing the king's timber and deer, and also valuable specialists – miners and military engineers – providing a useful supply of coal and iron ore. Hart gives the impression, indeed, that the miners had had their privileges from time immemorial and were allowed to go about their lives as a special race, mostly un-molested by Crown officials.

Free Miners were – indeed, still are – allowed to open a new mine anywhere they wanted in the Forest, without permission, providing that the Gaveller (the monarch's representative) was informed, and that they paid the appropriate due once the working had begun. Hart emphasizes that their livelihood was carried on 'in an atmosphere of remoteness and secrecy'. Their Laws and Privileges stated that no stranger was to be allowed to 'come within the mine and know all the privities'. Twentieth-century Forest miners have been equally secretive. Eddie Thomas takes visitors to a coal-working near the Potter family home, only recently abandoned, where a notice nailed to a tree drily warns: 'TRESPASSERS WILL NOT BE PROSECUTED. NEXT OF KIN WILL BE INFORMED.'

By the nineteenth century, so many miners, charcoal burners and iron-ore prospectors were scraping a living in the Forest that eviction was no longer practical, and freeholds and leases for dwellings were being granted. In the 1850s more than two hundred coal-pits were being worked. The Free Miners were now permitted to lease or sell their gales to 'foreigners' who had money to develop larger coal-workings, and a network of railways began to snake along the valleys to the pits. But most of the lines were confined to coal and other freight, and the Forest remained a separate territory, aloof from the remainder of Gloucestershire, the county to which it nominally belongs.

'Foreigners' were regarded with hostility, while the outsiders themselves thought it a strange place, with wild ways; across the Severn in Bristol they joked that the Foresters were so intermarried that they were half-witted. There were reports of policemen being murdered, and it was said that in 1889 the villagers of Ruardean became so worked up by the spectacle of two dancing bears, displayed by a band of Frenchmen, that they hit and stoned them to death, and the owners were lucky to escape with their lives. As late as 1905, a woman was accused in court of being a witch.

Because the Forest was officially uninhabited until the 1800s, no parish churches were built there for a long while, and the Dissenters were the first to fill the religious void. Gradually, Nonconformist chapels appeared, and their preachers attempted to impose moral order on communities where couples rarely bothered to get married, and arguments were settled with sticks and fists.

Nonconformity was the religion of the working man, and in the Forest, as in neighbouring Wales, it helped to foster Radicalism and the will to improve the social system. With no squire to answer to, the Forester was fiercely independent. As Potter put it, 'All the villages were mining villages, and therefore are not English country villages – there were no squires . . . It isn't like, say, the Sussex village . . . It's both more democratic and more powerful in its emotions . . . '

It was a society in which men did virtually all the earning, with almost no employment for women. The wives were up before dawn to light the fires and feed their men before the miners set off on their walk to the pits. There was, of course, plenty of coal, and many households kept a pig for its meat. But life was near the poverty line.

For the men, work underground was hard and dangerous. The Forest coal seams were free of gas, but if a collier survived rockfalls, he was likely to fall prey to silicosis, even in the twentieth century; it claimed the life of Potter's grandfather as late as 1950. Free Miners gave their pits names that joked ironically about conditions and prospects: Croesus, Pluckpenny, Little Scare, Strip-and-at-it, Rainproof, Small Profit, Work or Hang.

Although 'o' butty' means 'old friend', or 'old mate', in the larger coal-pits the 'butty man' was the foreman of each gang, who took the money from the owner and paid his fellow miners. By the early 1900s, there were several of these bigger pits, which penetrated deep to previously inaccessible coal. But 'foreigners' were still rare, and

Foresters rarely left to see the outside world. Winifred Foley, who was born two decades before Dennis Potter, describes an old crippled man who had never left the village saying, 'Doosn't thee fret for I, me booy; I bain't tired o' round 'ere yet.' She comments, 'The Forest was that sort of place. As my father once said, "Nobody wants to come 'ere if they can 'elp it; but once they do settle down you'd atter shoot 'em to get 'em to muv."'

*

Three of Dennis Potter's four great-grandfathers were Forest miners: Edward Potter of Shortstanding, Richard Hawkins of the Lonk (adjacent to Berry Hill), and Thomas Howells, who had his own 'level' (coalmine) at Readypenny, as well as being an innkeeper at Joyford. His son Walter was killed working in it, and Dennis's father Walter was named in memory of him.

The male Potters of this generation could not read, and Edward was not able to write his name on his son George's birth certificate – there is an 'X' for his mark. George would ask his better-educated children to read to him. One of them, Dennis's aunt Eunice, who still lives in the Forest, remembers doing this for her father, and says he was quite content to be illiterate.

Dennis's maternal grandmother, Jane Hawkins, was born in the Lonk in 1868. 'My mother was a Forester,' says Dennis's mother. 'In fact we bought the ground where she was born and all. Of course the old place is pulled down.' In her early teens Jane left Berry Hill to get a job in London. Potter told Bragg that she 'went into service . . . [as] a skivvy and a drudge, a servant in a London house – and met a Fulham plumber and married him – had . . . the usual eleven, twelve kids and all that . . . ' The plumber was Christopher Wale, two years her junior, who eventually became a master builder and what we would now call a developer, building or improving houses and then selling them. Later, he lost a lot of money and had to revert to plumbing.

There had been members of the Wale family in Fulham and neighbouring Hammersmith since at least the mid-eighteenth century. Christopher's grandfather, James Wale, was the Beadle, Bellman (town crier) and Parish Constable of Hammersmith in the 1840s, and each Christmas he composed a set of doggerel verses for the coming year, circulated in the parish as an almanac – the nearest Dennis Potter gets to a writer among his forebears. Graham Wale thinks that the family may be descended from the baronial Wales of Northamptonshire, landowners since the Conquest, 'but Dennis wouldn't have wanted that sort of ancestry at all!'

Christopher Wale and Jane Hawkins married in London in 1891, and eventually had eleven children. The penultimate of these, Margaret Constance ('Mag') Wale, Dennis's mother, was born in 1910 in Hammersmith, which was then still almost rural in character. 'As kids,' she recalls, 'we used to be able to play in the street, with the great barge ropes from the Thames – skipping from one side of the street to the other. The bigger girls would turn the rope, and we'd jump. And in the summer holidays we'd push off over Hammersmith Bridge, to Barnes Common and Richmond Park for the day. It was very pleasant. I wish I could walk across that bridge again.'

Mag was sent to St Paul's Church of England School on Hammersmith Broadway. She proved to be musical – 'I had piano lessons from when I was seven till I was fourteen' – and good at schoolwork – 'I was top of the school. I've got a silver medal, which was only given once a year.' She left school at the age of fourteen, and found work in Fuller's bakery: 'I was in the bakery – my sister as well – until I married.' In Potter's 1980 play *Blade on the Feather*, the old spy Jason Cavendish recalls, 'Fuller's used to make the best macaroons. Before they built the Hammersmith Flyover in front of their factory, and moved the whole caboodle to some Godforsaken place in Scotland, or wherever.'

Mag had to hand over most of her earnings to her parents: 'You had to pay your board. There was six of us children still at home.' Her father spent a lot on drink: 'He drank – I'm going to be honest! He wasn't an abusive man, but he liked his drop of Scotch.'

Potter told Bragg that 'my mother used to come down to the Forest of Dean to visit her mother's family with her mother, and one weekend she met . . . my dad'. Elsewhere he said, 'My mother came to the Forest of Dean on a weekend charabanc trip to visit her strangely spoken and flushless-toileted relatives.' Mag says she was 'eighteen or nineteen' when she made this trip to Berry Hill and met Dennis's father: 'Walt Potter was friends with my cousin. And I was in that cousin's house, and he came there.'

Walter Edward Potter had been born in Berry Hill in 1906, the second child of George Thomas Potter, coalminer, and Mary Jane

Howells. In his 1993 MacTaggart Lecture at the Edinburgh Television Festival, Potter said that his mother was

duly impressed by my father's ever-shy little smile, gentle little delicacies, sparkling well-polished shoes and, most importantly of all, perhaps, the way he sang 'I'm Painting the Clouds with Sunshine', with an emphatic if hardly necessary double stamp-stamp of those same well-polished feet to mark each otherwise wistful chorus. Jesus, my throat narrows. You are not supposed to talk like this in our country.

At which point in the lecture, Potter started to sing the song himself:

> When I hold back a tear
> To let a smile appear
> I'm only painting
> The clouds
> With sunshine . . .

Coreene Wilks, who was brought up in Berry Hill alongside Dennis Potter, compares the characters of his parents: 'You didn't get near her. I liked her, but I'd go so far as to say I *loved* Mr Potter. She'd give you the time of day, but he'd chat for ages and ages.' Dennis's cousin Graham says the same about Potter's father: 'Walt was a lovely man. I used to struggle to understand his speech, but he was lovely, gentle. There was a profoundness, sometimes, in his simplicity. He'd start to tell a joke, and burst out laughing, and never tell you the punchline!' Graham's father – Mag's brother Sidney – says that Walt was always genial 'unless he'd had a bit too much cider', in which case he would get excited 'and his eyes would flash'.

Though able to read and write, Walt Potter did little of either. Dennis told Graham Fuller, 'I once said, in a would-be casual aside in an interview many years ago, that my father had only read one book in his life, and that, I think, was by Hall Caine.* Such a remark, in an English class situation, appears to imply some kind of condescension or patronizing contempt, which was not the case at all.'

Walt had become a coalminer as soon as he left school at fourteen. 'My father . . . started work at the Waterloo pit,' writes Potter in *The Changing Forest*. 'He was very young . . . ' Waterloo was at Lydbrook, a few miles from Berry Hill. Later, Walt signed up for work at Cannop,

---

* Hall Caine (1853–1931), friend of Dante Gabriel Rossetti and author of many popular novels.

one of the biggest Forest mines, half an hour's walk from his home.

'I got engaged to Walt when I was twenty-one,' recalls Mag. But three years of the Depression had to pass before they could afford to marry – a white wedding, on 7 July 1934, at St Paul's Church, Hammersmith. A honeymoon was out of the question, and Walt took his bride back at once to Berry Hill. Mag recalls, 'I can always remember my mother saying to Walt, "Don't forget, you're taking her down to a hornets' nest!"'

*

There was no house for the newly married couple, and no money, since at that time the collieries were able to give the men only two days' work a week, and they had to draw the dole. Mag's mother's sister let her and Walt have two rooms in her cottage – 'one up, one down, and a share of the kitchen'. Mag says she was 'very homesick the first few months'.

She became very conscious of being a Londoner among Forest people. 'I used to be afraid to go by two or three women, because they would be talking, you know, and when you'd gone by they'd look. I've got over that, but I don't feel I belong, and I've been here sixty years.'

In *The Changing Forest*, Potter writes that it was 'an entirely male-dominated society. The women stayed at home . . . confined by the cooking on big open grates, cleaning the metal fenders, drawing water from the wells or village spout, getting in the tin baths from the back kitchen walls, and sending their children to Sunday School with clean shoes and big white handkerchiefs.' There was 'occasional wife-beating and more frequent drunkenness'.

On the days when there was work at Cannop – and nights, for mining continued during the hours of darkness – Walt would walk over there with the other men on his shift. 'Dad used to take a tin flask of cold water, flung over his shoulder,' says Potter's sister June, 'and on the other there was his tommy bag, a cloth bag with his food in.' As the Forest coal-seams were free of gas, the men would work under-ground with a candle in a jam jar, and if returning home in the dark would use this to light their way along the steep, densely wooded paths.

'You could tell miners for two reasons,' says Eddie Thomas. 'One, they would have blue marks all over them, which is where they'd had cuts, and the coal got under their skins. And, two, they walked down the middle of the road. I think it was a form of independence.' 'And their hobnail boots used to ring,' adds Mag Potter. 'You could hear them going down Joyford Hill, coming home from the shift, their hobnails sliding on the stone.' Later, 'a fellow got a bus, and they started riding there. And they'd all be on the corner there by the shop, waiting for the bus, doing the colliers' squat. Always squatted on their heels, didn't sit on the ground.' Potter writes in *The Changing Forest* that Dean miners 'squat on the backs of their heels . . . whenever they have to wait'.

He observes that each village had its 'chapel . . . like a warehouse with tall, thin windows and a heavy door . . . Rugby football, brass band, choir and pub: that's the old Forest.' In *The Glittering Coffin* he records that Berry Hill

has had a rugby side since the 1890s, and in its ramshackle wooden Institute building you can find photographs of the renowned teams of the past, many of them with huge moustaches, ordinary trouser belt to hold up their knee-length trousers, and even heavy pit-boots on their feet. The miners used to go straight from a Saturday morning shift on to the rugby field . . . Every village had its own side, which it entered for the Forest of Dean Combination Cup.

Walt Potter was not in the Berry Hill rugby fifteen, but he played the euphonium in the village band. Potter writes that the Globe, the Berry Hill pub, was 'the place for the band and rugby players to gather after practice or a game . . . a pair of antlers at the top of the room, and lots of pictures of former rugby teams squatting before their cups, and concert parties leering back at the camera . . . long tables and split benches'. Walt would generously buy rounds that he could not afford, and then stagger home, humming a band march, to his waiting wife – the women did not go to the Globe.

By the autumn of 1934, only a few months after the Potters' wedding, Mag's aunt needed the two rooms for her daughter, who was getting married. There seemed to be no other accommodation, so Mag packed her clothes and went back to London until Walt could provide her with another home. 'And of course I was pregnant,' she says.

Walt came up to London for Christmas, and then managed to get two other rooms, in a house belonging to Mag's uncle, Will Hawkins – again, it was one up, one down, and use of kitchen. 'It was then called Brick House,' says Mag (it is now named Tokamena Cottage), 'because most places were built with stone around here, and it was brick.' Here, on 17 May 1935, she gave birth to her first child.

CHAPTER 2

He always had this way
with language

Mag Potter recalls that her son was born during a great frost:

The District Nurse used to come every day for two weeks [for antenatal care], but she lived at Cannop, where the pit was – quite a way. And it was the 17th of May, 1935, and that morning was the worst frost they'd had in years. Even oak trees were cut down with the frost. And Walt had to go to get the nurse for me. He'd gone off on his bike, and he was so worried he didn't put enough clothes on, I suppose. And he got chilled in the stomach – all the lining of his stomach went, it was a question of live or die with him for the week, and he had to go to bed on the Saturday in his mother's house next door. So I never saw him, you see, while I was in bed with the baby, with Dennis.

Was it a difficult birth? 'Eight and three-quarter pounds,' Mag answers, 'hard enough work for me!' 'Mum thought he was an ugly baby!' adds Dennis's sister June. Mag admits this: 'His nose had got flattened in the birth. And he was born red-headed. I thought he was Wale-featured, but there was none of my family red-headed.' The ginger hair came from Walt.

They gave him three names, Dennis Christopher George. Dennis was 'for himself – though I don't know why we chose that,' says Mag – and Christopher and George after his two grandfathers. June Potter was born a year later, in June 1936. 'I have a sister who is thirteen months younger than I am,' Dennis said on *Desert Island Discs*, 'and people used to think we were twins.'

Choosing his records on that programme, he mentioned that the song 'Roses of Picardy' always touched him, 'always pours out of me things that are so deep that you can't express them. And I found out why much later, when my mother told me that in fact she used to sing this to me when I was very small.' This was a rare memory. Usually he had little or nothing of this sort to say about his mother.

'We were poor,' he recalled bluntly of his early childhood. 'We didn't have a flush lavatory, we didn't even have a sink – you used to empty a bowl on to the garden.' The earth closet stood at the bottom of the garden: 'The lavatory had a long split wooden seat half the size of a park bench, built high over its smelly cargo, and for light a tiny window about the size of an average book.' Next to it stood 'a thick stone-walled pig's cot'.

He explains in *The Changing Forest* that life in these 'two up, two down' houses centred on the ground-floor back room, the kitchen with its 'big fireplace of four-barred iron grate, fronted by a long brass fender and set off with a mantelpiece cloaked in a brown tassle-frilled mantel-cloth'. In Walt's parents' cottage, next door to Brick House (and now called Holmdale), 'a grey streak of phlegm stained the bars of the grate, slightly luminous like the path a slug has made on its morning slither across a concrete path: silicosis spit'. The spitter was Walt's father George, who had 'a rattle in his chest as if the mechanism which wound him up was beginning to break down, dust in its wheels'. In *The Singing Detective*, Marlow's mother – a London girl – is particularly disgusted by her father-in-law's habit of spitting into the grate of his Forest cottage. 'How can anybody eat with *that* going on?' she snaps, causing a bitter argument to break out. Her husband (very much a portrait of Walt) fails to stand up for her.

The Forest families would cram into the kitchen, leaving the ground-floor front room to show off to visitors. 'The Front Room has always been a holy of holies,' writes Potter, 'a shrine to respectability rather than a place of retreat. If I was very good as a small boy my grandmother would sometimes ask me if I would like to sit with her awhile in the Front Room – this was an honour qualified by "but doosn't thou touch nothing, bless your little golden yud".' Asked if there were 'books in the house' during his childhood, he answered: 'No. Sankey's *Sacred Songs and Solos*; there was one romance novel; and there was *Red Star* and *My Weekly* – these were women's magazines. But that was about the extent of the literature available in the early days.'

The Sankey hymn book was revered almost as much as the Bible, and was carried 'up the hill . . . twice . . . on a Sunday, sometimes three times to Salem Chapel'. Berry Hill had two chapels: 'one a Methodist outpost, Zion, and the other a "free church", Salem . . . Zion and Salem, Salem and Zion, twin guardians of the village, not above a great deal of jealousy for each other'. Zion was grander and bigger, with a balcony, and was favoured by the shopkeepers and other more prosperous members of the community. Salem, more modest, was where the Potter family went.

Potter emphasized that neither of his parents was particularly religious; 'they just, in their matter of fact way, assumed a basic Christian background, unexamined and possibly unfelt'. They seem not to have minded when he drifted away from religion in adolescence.

Salem was often so full that young Dennis and June, with 'clean shoes, clean hanky', would have to perch on the windowsill. The congregation did not have enough money to pay a minister. 'The preacher at Salem was a sort of a cousin, just a lay preacher, that's all,' says Mag Potter. Dennis wrote:

At Salem, nearly all the so-called 'visiting speakers' came only from as far as some of the nearest villages . . . They were usually men who worked in the local pits, and in other circumstances and different times some of them would surely have become writers, poets or actors . . . They had a tremendous and sometimes unfortunate range of imagery.

In *The Changing Forest* he quotes the family story of a Salem preacher of a bygone generation who was so small of stature that, in order to see over the edge of the pulpit, he had to stand on a wooden box:

While reaching up on tiptoe, lunging out his arms to make a particularly dramatic point, the margarine box at last gave way with a splintering, blasphemous crack, and Emmanuel fell into ignominy, below the level of the pulpit. A moment's horrified pause, and his head appeared once more in view, shakily above fingers clutching at the dark oak. 'Be not afeared!' he announced with great dignity, 'for 'tis I.'

Potter's cousin Tony Baldwin, who grew up in Berry Hill, recalls him telling this and other comic tales about local characters: 'Dennis would latch on to them all – some old miner, or a preacher. He always knew who'd got up to the most mischief.'

Asked what kind of doctrine was preached in Salem, Potter said it was 'fundamentalist but not in that American, charlatan way . . . It was a bit like Methodism, but slightly less structured than that.' The hymns made at least as much impression on him as the doctrine – 'Sankey's *Sacred Songs and Solos* . . . exactly 1,200 hymns in a little floppy, orange-covered book . . . They were about crossing the Jordan and meeting people on the other side, or "Come hail or storm or flood". They were both simple and dramatic.' In his last work for television, *Cold Lazarus*, there is a scene of Forest children singing a typical Sankey hymn:

> I am thinking today of that beautiful land
>   I shall reach when the sun goeth down;
> When through wonderful grace by my Saviour I stand,
>   Will there be any stars in my crown?
>
> Will there be any stars in my crown,
>   When at evening the sun goeth down?
> When I wake with the blest in the mansion of rest,
>   Will there be any stars in my crown?

Potter told Melvyn Bragg that this hymn 'makes me laugh, and yet it tugs at me'.

As well as the chapel services, there were Bible classes for the children, held 'in the red tin hut of Berry Hill Silver Prize Band'. In a 1977 radio programme, Potter recalled

the sound of the village band at rehearsal in the band hut . . . A group of small children would hover at the door, staring at the gleaming instruments, the big drum, the puffing cheeks . . . These giants, with leather straps for the heavier instruments, could outdo the Pied Piper of Hamelin when it came to collecting a throng of entranced infants . . . My father was in the band, and he used to practise in the front room at home. This gave me the opportunity, now and again, to sneak in, and puff a mixture of air and spit into the mouthpiece – to produce nothing more grand than a tiny raspberry of sound, which was just loud enough to provoke instant retaliation: 'Thou leave thik instrument alone!'

The band gave concerts, played at rugby matches, and marched round the village behind the chapel banners. Then the musicians would retire to the Globe, leaving the children sitting on the wall outside, swinging their legs and listening to the miscellany of sacred and secular music that emerged raucously from the pub – 'Bread of Heaven', 'The Old Rugged Cross' and 'I'm Forever Blowing Bubbles'. And Walt Potter and his cousin Wilf Baldwin would get to their feet, with 'the most endearing of expressions', and give a rendition of

'Painting the Clouds with Sunshine', stamping their feet in unison at the end of each chorus.

*

Dennis learned to read before he went to school, probably at Salem: 'My feeling is that words began to make sense and take shape via things like Sankey's *Sacred Songs and Solos*.' Then came the parables in the New Testament, which, in his imagination, seemed to be set in the Forest:

As a child – aged four, five, six or seven – it is natural to see the surrounding landscape as the landscape one reads about. So I thought of the big ponds near the pit where Dad worked as Galilee. The Valley of the Shadow of Death was a lane descending between overhanging hedges where you tended to want to whistle – but I was a timid child anyway, and the Forest itself was a labyrinth of old oaks and beeches and ash trees. The words both of those hymns and the Bible, and fairy stories, too, fitted very happily into that landscape.

Encouraged by 'the imagery of those evangelical hymns' and 'the wonderful language of the Bible', seemingly riddled with local references, he began to feel an impulse to 'see words make sense in sequence' – tentatively, to write:

I was sitting on the windowsill, looking down at the garden sloping down towards the earth closet at the bottom, and watching the rain run in rivulets down the path. I remember trying to write something about the rain, but the images came in the shape of a hymn, because that was my experience of how you put words together. My mother probably thought it was a complicated form of blasphemy.

Elsewhere he said, 'I remember . . . [on] a wet day . . . writing a hymn. And . . . my mother taking it from me with some worry . . . and saying, "What sort of boy are you going to turn into?" . . . But . . . I knew that the words were chariots in some way.' His mother does not remember the incident, but says he was 'writing things all the time' in childhood. In one interview, he said he had 'difficulty in answering questions about why or what and when did you become a writer. Because I cannot think of the time really when I wasn't in one way or another.' He told Angela Lambert, 'As I child I'd always thought of myself as a writer . . . '

Asked if it was expected that Forest boys would follow their fathers down the pit, he said, 'It was an assumption that you certainly made as a child. Every father would say, I think, to every son, "Whatever I do, you're not going down there." But that was a kind of bravado against the implacable economic facts of the time. You just simply assumed that that was where your path lay.'

As he grew, he began to explore the Forest landscape. It was 'a place to collect birds' eggs and build secret cabins in the thickest parts of the wood, to climb trees and search out and occupy abandoned quarries or old, disused pits, smelling with stale, silvery mud caked over the rusted rails'. Walking along the Forest tracks, he experienced 'the rushing and exhilarating feeling of space and height, air and beauty', in contrast with the 'tightness and stifle' of village life. But there could be no protracted escape: 'Your business is known, your troubles are known, your family is known, your weaknesses are known,' he writes of Berry Hill life. Above all, there was 'the strong feeling of being "a Forester", something complex and unique, something that outsiders were rarely expected to understand'. Maybe he would never have become curious about the world beyond the Forest if his mother had not been 'a Londoner, bringing occasional uncles with outlandish Fulham or Hammersmith tongue, who did not say "thee" and "thou"'.

*

'I was four years old when the Second World War began,' Potter said in his MacTaggart Lecture, 'and it took me until I was ten before I finally won it, with a little help from Rockfist Rogan, Tommy Handley and Mr Harris at Salem Chapel.' These three figures – the boys' adventure-comic hero, the radio comedian, and the chapel preacher – marked the boundary of his imaginative world in early childhood.

The war enlarged it a little; he remembered munition dumps in the thickest parts of the wood, Italian prisoners-of-war guarded in a camp near Berry Hill, and 'soft-booted Americans' who begat 'a few hybrid Foresters'. Walt Potter, being a miner, was classed as having a 'reserved occupation', so was not called up. Indeed the Forest coal was now much in demand because of the war effort: 'It took World War II to give my father a full week's work – you know, I think the first full week's work he had was in 1940.' Meanwhile the Potters acquired their own (temporary) house.

One of Walt's sisters was married to the caretaker at Dean Hall, a big house a few miles from Berry Hill. He was called up for war service, and Walt's mother and father moved in with her, leaving Walt,

Mag and the children to occupy their cottage, at least for the time being. 'But there still wasn't much room,' says Mag: 'We had evacuees – my own family, luckily, my sister and sisters-in-law in turn, and all through the war we lived with those in Gran's house.'

It was now that Mag discovered she had a talent as a musical entertainer. 'Until the war came, I couldn't play a note by ear. But we used to go and have a drink then, in the club, and there was a piano there, and somebody told me to play. I said "I can't!" But all of a sudden the penny dropped. If there was a tune, I could play it.' She quickly became a regular 'turn' at the Berry Hill Club, a long low building near Salem Chapel, sometimes singing as she played. Walt was proud and delighted; Dennis recalled how he would 'shout "order, order", and glare round with quite venomous hostility at those who dared to make the slightest or most unavoidable sounds during "Bless This House" or "The Lost Chord". Quite right, too.' When Dennis's cousin Tony Baldwin watched *Pennies from Heaven* more than thirty years later and heard the songs, 'I said to myself, "That's Dennis's mum."'

The wireless brought the day's popular songs into Dennis's life. In 1978, as *Pennies* was being screened, he recalled

lying in bed, and the wireless downstairs, and these songs drifting up the stairs . . . sounds that you can never quite place and locate, because they pre-date your full consciousness of yourself; so that I'm sure that Al Bowlly and Lew Stone and all these sounds were drifting up the stairs – they do something to me, and that must be the reason.

*

He began formal education 27 May 1940, a fortnight after his fifth birthday, being enrolled at Christchurch School, which stood next to a Victorian parish church at a crossroads half a mile from his house. His sister June recalls that the Vicar of Christchurch, Canon Wyndham-Jones, used to fill the brim of his hat with coins to give the poorer among the local children: 'He'd shake its brim and call out, "Pennies from Heaven!"'

Potter described the school as 'one-storeyed, ramshackle', with windows 'too high for a child to look out', and remembered that it 'had a bucket to catch the wet from the rotting roof. And five more buckets at the bottom of the sloping yard as "toilets". We were only coalminers' kids, you see.' Iris Hughes, who taught him there, and still lives in Berry Hill, agrees that it was all under one roof, 'but there was a separate Infant Department, and a Junior Department. There would have been three teachers in the Infants and four in the Juniors. And the head, Mr Gwilliam, was a teaching head. It was quite a large school – those four classes would have been in the region of about 140 children in all.'

Miss Hughes was very young, but mostly Potter was 'taught by teachers who had taught my father'. Tony Baldwin, who arrived at the school at about the same time as his cousin Dennis, says that 'Miss Wakefield, one of the infant teachers, was our first encounter with terror. She used the cane – and she'd throw a wooden blackboard duster at you so it would clip the side of your head.'

Potter entered Iris Hughes's class when he was seven, in 1942. She recalls him as 'always nicely dressed. But there were only two children in his family. When you had five or six boys, clothes got torn.' He was possibly thinking of Miss Hughes when he said, in a 1976 radio programme: 'There was a young woman who taught us six- and seven-year-olds with such sweet grace, so wondrous a smile, such lovely eyes, that naturally I fell in love for the very first time. Certain fairy tales, at her lips, were full of mysterious tensions and secrets I had to wait years and years to unravel.' If Miss Wakefield contributed to the character of the witch-like teacher in *Stand Up, Nigel Barton* and *The Singing Detective*, Potter might have had Iris Hughes in mind when he invented Eileen in *Pennies from Heaven*, the sweet-natured teacher who tells the story of Rapunzel to her class of Forest children. Yet of the former, Potter said: 'I didn't really know any such person as that . . . The character in the plays is more like the witch in *The Wizard of Oz* . . . a caricature.'

'He was a very quiet boy,' Iris Hughes says of him, emphasizing that he was less ebullient than his sister June. 'He didn't shine as a youngster. I'm not going to say he wasn't capable. He coped with his work. But he never came to the surface. He was more of an introvert. He didn't really stand out in any way.' She adds that the curriculum would have given him little chance for individuality. Gloucestershire schools at that date used the Parents' National Education Union method, by which the teacher read out lessons to the class, and the children stood up, one by one, and repeated each passage. Tony Baldwin corroborates this: 'We didn't get to use many books. It was mostly blackboard stuff.'

Iris Hughes explains: 'Books weren't available. There were no libraries – no library van, and no library books at school. Sometimes the children shared a book, sitting in pairs. And they always looked forward to Christmas, because there were annuals.' Potter remembered that the school did have one 'big locked cupboard of books – *real* books (!) – and how to break into it after hours was for me an avid but wholly secretive preoccupation'.

His mother says that, in her own Hammersmith childhood, 'we always had books at home'. 'But *we* didn't,' chips in June. 'Whether it was general of all Forest children, I don't know. But we had no books, only Christmas annuals and so on. There were no books that you could go and select to read. And we didn't have library books – not until we went to London. My Granch, my dad's dad, couldn't read or write. He used to look if there was any pictures in the paper.' So might Dennis's early reading have been of the newspaper? 'Yes,' says his mother, 'he used to read the paper.'

Iris Hughes says that the seven-year-old Dennis 'never looked robust. He wasn't a toughie.' She recalls recently meeting one of his classmates, who said, 'He was a funny boy at school. Never mixed with us, did he? You know we used to try to climb up those trees at playtimes. Never old Dennis. You could say, "Come on, Den, let's see what you can do." But no, he'd stand well back.' Potter himself told Bragg that 'as a child, without question, I know for a fact, and there's no argument about this, that I was coward. A physical coward.' A journalist noted in 1992, 'Potter says that he was a cowardly child, "a slight, spindly redhead who was too clever for his own good". He used his intelligence to transform himself from a victim into the class comedian. "I probably would have been a bully", he adds, "if I'd had the chance to be."' He said that he did climb trees, 'but only when I was alone'.

Tony Baldwin disagrees with his cousin's claim to have been a coward: 'Dennis would die rather than give in. He'd pick fights with chaps who'd have dusted him up.' But others who were at school with him at Christchurch accept Potter's estimate of himself. 'We used to be all one big gang, fooling around and climbing the trees – but not Dennis,' says Horace Wilks, whose wife Coreene, at the school too, remembers Dennis as 'very puny'. Olwen Birch describes him as 'a nervous boy', and Horace Wilks adds, 'He'd have a game of rugby, and kick around, but just to make the team up. If we'd have had any fights, I don't think Dennis would have got involved. No, Dennis was no bully. If anybody had started anything, he'd have run home.' At home, 'June was the boss,' says Dennis's mother. June agrees: 'Yes, I was when we were very small. I know Dennis didn't like fisticuffs and things like that. He only ever had one fight, to my knowledge, and then they just pulled each other's hair.'

*

Opinion differs about his ability in class at Christchurch. 'At school, he was well above me – he was very brainy,' says Horace Wilks. Olwen Birch remembers him as an 'awfully clever boy', and Potter himself said, 'I was clever, which is a curse in a working-class village. It set me apart and I used to wander off a lot on my own.' But, when asked if his cousin was particularly able at school, Tony Baldwin says,

He was and he wasn't. He was usually in the top three or four in the class [of about thirty to forty children], but he wasn't the top. There were smarter kids than him, who could see him off.

But he always had this way with language. He was always spluttering out long words, always dealing with words. He was a debater, too. He would always debate to score his point. He would use long words – but in a way that meant, even if you didn't know them, you wouldn't misunderstand him.

Horace Wilks agrees: 'We never knew what he meant. But he'd never say, "You're illiterate."'

Potter himself said that language had held an attraction for him since childhood: 'I love the sound of words. "Elbow" was my favourite word and "elastic" and "slither". I used to say them over and over again to myself in bed.' He was frightened by his glibness with words: 'It's a gift and a vice. You can be trapped into using it.'

By the time he reached the top of the school, his verbal dexterity was winning him approval. Olwen Birch says that he became 'the favourite of the headmaster, Mr Gwilliam, because he was so brilliant', and Potter himself remembered, in *The Glittering Coffin*,

the humiliating moment at school, at the primary school with the decaying classrooms, when the headmaster had gathered together the two top standards – the nine- and ten-year-olds – to read out one of my compositions, and had called me out in front of them all and given me sixpence for something that 'no boy in the whole of England could have done so well'. In my rage and misery at being identified as 'different' in the sense that no working-class schoolboy wants to be different, I stayed behind after the final bell and wrote 'shit' on the blackboard so that I could be a hero again at the subsequent 'inquest'.

He also recalled that sometimes, when the teacher left the room, 'she would say, "Come out to the front, Dennis, and tell a story." That was meant as a reward, or a compliment: it was, of course, a punishment.'

His mother says she 'knew he was very bright'. Horace Wilks believes she put pressure on him to shine at school: 'We used to get a football, and play Joyford against Berry Hill. That was Dennis, Tony [Baldwin], and a few more. Dennis would come for about a couple of hours, then he'd have to go and do his studying. He was always home early, to do his homework. His mother was pretty strict on him like that.' Tony Baldwin agrees: 'His mother drove him.' But she denies this, and says the motivation came from Dennis: 'I had no trouble getting him to do his homework.' Potter himself writes of 'the times I had refused to play football in the streets outside because I wanted to read'.

He recalled that his father 'was very proud of the fact that I seemed to be bright and could draw and write. He used to put some of my drawings up on the mantelpiece, and then tear them up if he thought I was getting too uppity.' Walt himself had some talent with words and pictures: 'He . . . would almost casually describe the colour of the sky and how he felt that day. And he would always draw an apple or something on the white margins of the newspaper.' He also encouraged Dennis in music:

I used to tinkle on the piano, and I played in the village brass band . . . when I was ten . . . a baritone, which is a size down [i.e. smaller] from the euphonium. When I was being taught by the conductor, as a ten-year-old, he said, 'Just imagine, ol' butt', tha's got a bit a' backy on tha' tongue, and try and spit it out', which as a ten-year-old who had had an illicit Woodbine – ! I think that was about the closest to musical perfection I ever achieved.

Although his parents might have been pleased with his progress at school, the environment was essentially hostile to the development of the mind. In *The Glittering Coffin* he describes the typical working-class home as one where 'reading is rather "soft"; homework a waste of time ("School ends at four o'clock – you don't get paid for overtime, son"), and legitimate academic ambitions shade into something dangerous, being regarded as pretentious and "uppity".'

No one objected, on the other hand, to an interest in politics. On *Desert Island Discs*, Potter recalled being asked, at about the age of seven, what he wanted to be: 'I used to say, either a great writer or prime minister.' Tony Baldwin recalls that 'all Dennis's early arguments were about politics. He would stand in the middle of a group of miners, as Red as could be, and he'd get them arguing so they didn't know what they believed in.' Berry Hill was firmly socialist: 'I was brought up to regard "tory" as the dirtiest of all oaths, and the Royal Family as useless, miserable wasters. Sir Winston Churchill is remembered today [in the Forest] more as the man who once ordered the troops to South Wales than the great war leader intoning about the beaches.' (It was in 1921 that Churchill, as Secretary for War, had sent troops to the Valleys in response to a mining strike.)

Despite Potter's precocious talent for political argument, Tony Baldwin 'always thought he was going to be an actor. He was always involved in the little plays we'd do at school or chapel – invariably he was the star.' Horace Wilks explains that these performances were part of the Anniversary Sunday ceremonies in the Forest chapels: 'You used to dress up in your best suit, say your bit of poetry, or sing. Everyone had to have a go.' In *The Changing Forest*, Potter mentions 'Anniversary Day ... crinkling with new dresses ... where the children sing and recite three times in one day'.

He also became an actor in what he called 'the perpetual melodrama of the classroom', learning to protect himself from tougher boys with 'strategic comic turns, and fantasies labyrinthine to pull in my companions, forcing them to lower their fists ... ' One incident stuck particularly in his mind.

A 'few weeks before my ninth birthday', he was suddenly moved one day to pull 'a daffodil out of its pot on the classroom table, breaking the stem in doing so'; he then carried 'the damaged bloom home in strange triumph'. Perhaps it was a reaction to being treated as teacher's pet, an impulsive attempt to behave like one of the tough boys. Next morning, the teacher demanded to know which 'evil boy' was the vandal. Finding himself blushing and twitching with anxiety, Dennis got to his feet and found that 'a story came almost unbidden to the lips'. He put on 'fine show of reluctance' about revealing the culprit, but eventually pretended to do so, naming 'an odd, rather portly child from Standard 4, the oldest class'.

This boy – whom Potter, in this account, calls 'Isaac Holt' – was fetched, and cross-examined; and then it was that Potter began to discover how successful a story-teller he had been:

'Please, Miss,' volunteered a girl in pigtails, 'I saw Isaac with the daff outside the bread shop.' She paused for the slightest moment, then added the clinching detail of her own lie. 'Him said as a' was goin' to plan' n,' Miss.' A hiss of relief or pleasure came from the rest of the class. Voice after voice now gave chase, released from the leash by the girl's corroboration . . . Miss at last rephrased her question in the proper manner: '*Did* you take it, Isaac?'

He dropped his head. 'Yes, miss,' he said to my complete incredulity. Moreover, he now obviously believed that he *had* taken it . . . He did not seek me out later to thump me. The lie had so enveloped him that he saw no choice but to accept it as the truth, really the truth.

And I discovered in one precocious leap, back there in childhood, what people are like when they sense drama in the air. They want to shape it, control it, entertain themselves with it . . .

Potter used this incident in *Stand Up, Nigel Barton*, and in *The Singing Detective*, where the breaking of the daffodil is replaced by young Philip Marlow defecating on the teacher's desk. When recounting the version of it quoted here, in *New Society* in 1975, he added that the tale itself might be a lie; and he refused to say whether it was. But on a television programme in 1987 he confirmed that it was true, and gave the other boy's name as Abraham.

*

The year that this incident took place, 1944, saw a radical reform in the British education system. A new Education Act, piloted by the Education Minister R. A. Butler (a liberal-minded Conservative), raised the school leaving age from fourteen to fifteen, and greatly increased the provision of free places for high-quality secondary education. Potter was one of the first beneficiaries.

Prior to 1944, children at Christchurch School had gone on, at the age of about ten, to the big council school at Five Acres on the other side of Berry Hill. The majority would remain there until they were fourteen, then leave school altogether. A lucky few – about half a dozen out of a class of thirty – would be handpicked by the head-master, and given special coaching to prepare them for a scholarship examination. If they won a scholarship, they would go to Bell's Grammar School in Coleford. Otherwise they would leave school with the others. Bell's provided free places for the scholarship winners, but children from affluent homes could by-pass the scholarship system, and (if they passed a fairly simple entrance examination) take up fee-paying places at the grammar school. The Butler Act changed all this. At 'eleven plus', all children would now sit an examination (testing both intelligence and attainment), and, on the results of this, a percentage of them would be awarded free places in grammar schools – a much higher proportion than under the old scholarship system.

The Butler Act was not without its injustices, as Potter realized by the time he came to write *The Glittering Coffin* in 1958: 'Out of every hundred working-class children, sixteen manage to pass the selective examination, while only five stay on through the grammar-school course and spread themselves in the sixth form, and by the university stage only two survive the drastic weeding.' Nevertheless the Act hugely increased the chances of a grammar-school place for a child like himself from a poor working-class home; and, whatever the odds, a university education became far more possible than before.

The war ended in May 1945 and Walt Potter's parents returned to their house. Walt, Mag, Dennis and June found themselves crammed into one small back bedroom, with Walt's mother making it clear that she wanted the house to herself. 'It was all unpleasantness,' says Mag. 'And there were no houses. We tried and tried, but there were no houses. And I went to the local councillor – he was our grocer, as it happens – and asked him whether there was any chance of us getting a council house. But he said, "I can't make any promises." So I said, "Right – then we go." So we went to London.'

CHAPTER 3

Something foul and terrible

Walt Potter hoped to go to London with Mag and the children and get a job there, but wartime regulations had not yet been repealed, and permission for him to leave Cannop mine was not granted – 'He couldn't get out of the pit,' says Mag.

It was not quite Dennis's first trip out of the Forest. 'Most Forest miners never had a holiday in their lives away from home,' he writes in *The Changing Forest*, but for the children there were Sunday School outings to the Malverns and Porthcawl, and June says they had already been to London to visit her mother's family. Now, 'We went up there hopeful that we could find something to live in, but it was almost as bad [as the Forest]. There were no flats, no houses to rent. It was a rough old time.' They had to lodge in Mag's father's house, 56 Rednall Terrace, Hammersmith. This street of terraced houses, which has now vanished, stood at what is now the London end of the Hammersmith Flyover. Ironically, in view of what happened there to Dennis Potter, the site is occupied by the West London Magistrates' Court.

Mag's father had retired, and her mother was dead. Mag's unmarried sister Florence was living there, looking after her father, and so was Ernest, the one brother who had not married, though when Mag and the children arrived he was still in the army. Also (Mag recalls) 'there was a woman with two rooms upstairs, a sub-let place'; so the arrivals from the Forest had to cram in with the rest of the family, sharing bedrooms and even beds as necessary.

Mag managed to feed and look after her children on what Walt sent her. 'The pits were working full time then,' she says, 'and he used to keep me.' Some weekends, he would come up to London to see them. But the division of the family seems to have disturbed Dennis. In *The*

Singing Detective, the young Philip Marlow, transplanted from the Forest to Hammersmith, asks his mother: 'Why can't our Dad come wi' us . . . ? Why do him have to stay back whum [home]?' She replies, 'Because they won't let him out of the pit,' but this is not the whole truth; the marriage has collapsed.

June recalls that 'Dennis said to me, when he was dying, and he was talking about the past, didn't I find it odd that Mum took us two and Dad didn't come? He said to Mum, "Was that a separation?" And Mum said, "Well, no." But he must have seen it as a separation – though I didn't.' Her mum insists, 'Well, it wasn't! There was no separation. Oh no, never.'

Dennis also missed the Forest. He writes in *The Glittering Coffin*:

I remember that the first time I left the Forest of Dean for any length of time (for a few months, in fact, thanks to a housing shortage when I was ten years old, weedy and shyly precocious, but determined to become a miner) I cried all through a hot, noisy London night, cried with the kind of sick passion of those who love a place almost as much as they love a person.

Elsewhere he said, 'I couldn't believe that people lived like this. I so longed for the Forest of Dean that I just couldn't bear to be where I was.'

Dennis and June were enrolled at St Paul's Primary School in Hammersmith, where their mother had been a pupil. Dennis felt an outsider there because of his speech: 'Although most of the kids at school had been evacuees during the war and had been to the country-side, they hadn't been anywhere like the Forest of Dean, and when I'd say things in this uncouth "thee–thou" language they'd look at me strangely.' In his first attempt at fiction, *The Country Boy* (written in about 1958), he describes the mockery and name-calling he experienced at school because of his accent: '"Here, miss!" . . . On that first dreadful morning in this place, six weeks back, the class had bellowed with unforced laughter when he had said the two words.'

But there were advantages to Hammersmith. He could now get books from the local library. Favourites included Richmal Crompton's 'William' series. And there was the cinema:

When we lived in London I used to go to what is now called the Hammersmith Odeon – that huge cinema on Hammersmith Broadway – but it was then the Gaumont [it is now the Labatt's Apollo]. I thought it was a palace, and I was impressed that the films were shown continuously, so you could come in in the middle. People *did* come in in the middle, and watch until it came round again, and then they'd clap up their seats and say, 'This is where we came in.' But I just sat there the whole time, if I could!

I can clearly remember the first time I went to the Gaumont, when I was ten. It was some time between VE Day and VJ Day. The second feature was a Dagwood Bumstead and Blondie film, and *Tarzan* was the main feature. Outside the cinema they'd put up the names in eight- or nine-foot letters, and I thought it meant they could only ever show those films, and that they'd put those letters up in honour of the greatest films ever made! Then, again in 1945, I saw *State Fair*, in colour on a huge screen, with Dana Andrews, the pig and Dick Haymes singing in the swingboats at the funfair. In fact I used a song from it, [Rodgers and Hammerstein's] 'It Might as Well be Spring', in *The Singing Detective*. I thought seeing that film was the most wonderful experience anyone could possibly ever have. The cinema was an art-deco, Thirties kind of place. I remember it had two big pyramids of light: the transparent curtains used to rustle open and then the projector beam would go *boing!* and hit the screen, laced with blue tobacco smoke. And you would see the organist, and the tip of a great, white, gleaming Wurlitzer – I think it was a Hammond Organ actually – rising like a demigod out of the pit. The totality of that experience was something I will never forget.

He described himself in the cinema in childhood as 'a grim little boy who used to hoot at all the mushy kissing'. Some of the films gave him nightmares:

When I saw *The Count of Monte Cristo* I didn't sleep for a week because of that man with his tangled beard in the next cell, who'd been in prison all his life and scraped little holes in the wall. The terror of that affected me deeply. I'd wake up covered with sweat, thinking I was in that cell. Films have the effect of totally occupying your sensibilities.

There may be an echo of this in the prison scenes in Potter's own *Casanova*.

Real life in London could be as frightening as the cinema. 'I can remember once,' says June, 'Dennis and I were going through one of those subways in Hammersmith Broadway, with toilets in. And a man came out the gents' toilet and grabbed Dennis. And I was screaming. He didn't get him in the toilet, mind. I didn't know what he was going to do – I was still only barely nine. Dennis managed to pull himself away.' June did not know that what nearly happened in that public lavatory was taking place at home.

*

Potter's first explicit mention of this comes in a 1983 preface to the published texts of three of his plays, where he writes:

I don't know whether it was too obvious 'cleverness', examination salted, which ensured my early isolation, or whether, as I now dare to think but not inspect, something foul and terrible that happened to me when I was ten years old, caught by an adult's appetite and abused out of innocence.

He spoke of it again in his 1993 MacTaggart Lecture, where he said that 'at the age of ten, between VE Day and VJ Day, I had been trapped by an adult's sexual appetite and abused out of innocence'. Victory in Europe Day was on 9 May 1945, and Japan surrendered on 15 August.

By the time he made this disclosure, he had spoken of it to his own children. His daughter Sarah says:

I remember something being talked about when I was, I think, a teenager, and Mum asking Dad, 'Do you think you should be saying this?' And Dad said something like, 'This is our family – they should know about it.' And I think it was beginning to be talked about or speculated about, on account of what he was writing. Then it was more and more openly talked about. The first time we knew about it, we weren't told who it was – that came later.

When asked who was the abuser, Sarah says, 'Uncle Ernie.'

Ernest Wale, aged forty in 1945, had worked as a bricklayer until the war. He came home in uniform not long after Mag, Dennis and June had arrived at Rednall Terrace, and Dennis had to share a bed with him. 'I think it happened late at night, on a handful of occasions,' says Sarah, 'after Uncle Ernie had come in from the pub – it was when he got drunk. Dad would wake up, and Ernie would have put his [Dennis's] willy in his mouth. And then would be crying about it.'

When asked about the abuse in 1992 by a journalist, Ginny Dougary, Potter, without specifying exactly what had happened, or who had done it, said, 'In the scale of things it was, I suppose, the smallest – what is the word they use? – interference. It was the drink, you know, and it didn't happen all that often.'

Ernie was known by at least some members of the family to be homosexual. June says that he had 'attempted suicide in 1941, and because that was then illegal, he was sent to a prison hospital for a couple of weeks. After that he was called up for the army, and served in the Orkneys.'

No one knows his motive for the suicide attempt, but it is assumed that his homosexuality was getting him into trouble or causing depression. His younger brother Sidney says Ernie put his head in the gas oven. He had once tried to interfere sexually with Sid, who fended him off. Sid's son Graham Wale says, 'Ernie came to stay with us when I was thirteen or fourteen, for a week, and I had to sleep downstairs, even though there were two beds in my room. I wasn't told why.'

Mag says she had no idea that Ernie was interfering with Dennis. 'Oh God, I'd have killed my brother. You don't think that such things can happen. Especially in your own family. But I didn't know at the time. Dennis didn't say a word.' June agrees: 'Oh, he never mentioned it – no, never.' They knew nothing about it until Dennis began to disclose it nearly forty years later.

In the MacTaggart Lecture, Potter spoke of his feelings once the abuse had begun: '*Why–Why–Why?* The . . . desperately repeated question I had asked myself without any sort of answer, or any ability to tell my mother or my father . . . ' He told Ginny Dougary, 'I knew instinctively, of course, that it was wrong, that I was being invaded and abused and assailed.' Dougary questioned him further:

Did he tell anyone about the abuse? 'No, I had enough inner decorum not to tell my mother until later,' he replies . . . Inner decorum? 'I couldn't talk about it,' he says. 'You don't know the circumstances, the house and the sense that I had, that it would be like throwing a bomb into the middle of everything that made me feel secure. So – ' His voice fades away.

He admitted to Dougary that the abuser had been 'someone very close to home', but did not name Uncle Ernie.

In 1993 Mark Lawson tried to get him to speak about it:

He said he found that impossible . . . There had been an article last year [Dougary's], which had more or less outed one of his dead relatives as the abuser, and he wanted to say no more about it. OK, I said, but why had he left that strange trail in the 1983 preface ('something foul and terrible that happened to me when I was ten years old . . .')? Had it not been the act of someone wanting to confess?

'I don't know why I did that. Because it is something which, if I approach too directly, I start to squirm. It's obviously there in my consciousness, and is there in the work, if people want to see it. A lot of the characters are the abused, the helpless ones.'

In the 1983 preface, he speculates that the abuse might have caused not merely his introspection but, eventually, his illness: 'Certainly, with a kind of cunning shame, I grew for long into someone too wary, too cut off, too introspective, too reclusive, until, finally, as though out of the blue, or the black, too ill to function properly.' He told Ginny Dougary, 'It did deeply affect me. In adolescence, there were feelings of anxiety because it's the child that assumes guilt. My imagination was totally invaded and swamped and warped for a while and, maybe, who knows, for ever.' To her, he added, 'It might have made me homophobic but it didn't, thankfully. Not that I'm – well, I'm 100 per cent heterosexual.'

He also suggested to Dougary, 'It has probably made me more alert to the kinds of behaviour that hide behind apparently placid exteriors.' And in the MacTaggart Lecture he said:

If anyone cares to look, really look, at my work over the years, they would not take too long to see how the great bulk of it is about the victim, someone who cannot explain, cannot put into the right words, or even cannot speak at all. But I do know, without doubt, that the nearer writing approaches self-therapy, the worse it becomes.

In another interview, he suggested that, while the sexual abuse was a central fact in his life, it was possible to exaggerate its importance:

I mean I was sexually assaulted when I was ten years of age. That is true, I was. A lot of things can be traced to that, but to trace *everything* to that is absolute nonsense. People endure what they endure and they deal with it. It may corrupt them. It may lead them to all sorts of compensatory excesses in order to escape the nightmare and the memory of that. But it is a footnote, or a sidenote. It's important but it's not *that* important, because still you're left with your basic human strivings and dignity and talent.

*

Although he said nothing of the abuse to his mother, after some weeks he managed to get himself away from his uncle. 'I wouldn't eat,' he tells Graham Fuller in *Potter on Potter*, 'I wanted to go back to the Forest of Dean.' Giving homesickness as his reason, he asked to leave London and return to Berry Hill, where he could stay with his father and grandparents. His mother let him go; she and June remained in London.

'He must have done a bit more at Christchurch School,' says June, 'getting ready for his eleven plus.' His teacher Iris Hughes has no recollection of his returning to the school from London, but this must have been the case, since the following summer (1946) he passed the examination, shortly after his eleventh birthday, and began at Bell's Grammar School in Coleford in September. In *The Changing Forest* he writes that 'it was . . . thought rather amusing and cissy to go to the grammar school'; but others from Christchurch went with him, including Tony Baldwin.

The Butler Education Act had heralded a wave of other social reforms, which were now being achieved by the post-war Labour government. Looking back in 1994, Potter described it as 'one of the great governments of British history – those five, six years of creating what is now being so brutally and wantonly and callously dismantled was actually a period to be proud of, and I'm proud of it'. Coal was nationalized during 1946 (though not the Free Miners' pits in the Forest, which were subject to rules and inspection, but were left independent). In *The Changing Forest*, Potter recalls his father's optimism about what the new National Coal Board might achieve, and a sense of 'things are going to be different from now on'. It was his 'first genuine emotional and mental involvement with adult talk and hopes of politics'.

Edward Bell's Grammar School had been founded in 1570; in 1876 it moved from Newland, the village with the largest parish in Gloucestershire, to three acres of land at the top of Lords Hill, overlooking the town of Coleford. By 1949 it was a co-educational Voluntary Controlled Grammar School, with more than three hundred pupils. (Following another reorganization of the education system in 1968, Bell's closed in 1968, and a golf club and hotel now occupy the site.)

Tony Baldwin recalls that, at first, he and Dennis were in different classes at Bell's: 'He started off in the A-stream, whereas I was in the B-stream for the first year and then joined him in A. But he was by no means the top there, by no means outstanding. He was generally in the top seven or eight in each class.' Baldwin says that staff included a science master who was 'a sadist, that's what you'd call him now. And the headmaster was free with the stick. On the other hand there were softies, like our English teacher – Dennis and I would wreck his classes. The chap simply couldn't teach. And if there was mayhem, Dennis was in the thick of it.' Potter himself recalled one classroom incident:

I have this particularly strong image of Form 2A at Bell's Grammar School in Coleford, when the teacher left the room for a rather prolonged period, and seeing this thirteen-year-old, startlingly attractive black-haired girl, cheekily going to the front, and to the desk, and picking up a twelve-inch ruler, and beating out with enormous vigour 'Twelfth Street Rag' at the top of her voice – and all the signals, the sort of adolescent sex, flaring up at the sight of this pretty girl doing 'Twelfth Street Rag'. I can never hear 'Twelfth Street Rag' without being reminded of some of the great joys of life.

Emlyn Richards, who taught handicrafts at Bell's, remembers Potter, at the start of his teens, as 'a person who knew what he wanted, self-confident and a bit of a leader. He was recognized by the English teacher as a boy with something different.'

At the end of Dennis's second year at Bell's, his mother and sister returned from London to the Forest. New council houses were now being built, but there was still nothing available for the Potters, so the entire family had to squeeze once more into Walt's parents' house. 'We moved back to the Forest in the summer of 1947,' says June, 'and I started at Five Acres Secondary School that September.' She had passed her Eleven Plus in London, but Gloucestershire would not provide a grammar school place for her.

She recalls that her brother was now 'always writing and thinking about plays', in particular a play he wanted to put on at Salem Chapel:

Dawn Wilson, one of our cousins who used to go to chapel, was going to play his mum because she'd got red hair, and I was going to play the sister – and he'd work all this out. He never did put it on, mind, but he was, even in those days, into thinking about plays.

I used to see some of his stories. 'Mac of the Islands' was one he wrote but I can't remember what it was about now. I used to write stories too but my talent didn't come.

He had had few chances to see plays – an occasional show at the Lyric Theatre, Hammersmith, when the family was in London, and per-formances by the Coleford Amateur Dramatic Society. He also recalls, in *The Changing Forest*, being 'impressed and bewildered by a version of *Wuthering Heights* put on by a touring "ham" company' in the YMCA hut (a kind of village hall) at Berry Hill. Also, 'there was a cinema in Coleford . . . and when I was very young they were showing heroic war films. I saw one film about aeroplanes. I don't remember its name, but I remember afterwards, getting on the bus, I wanted to be a pilot.'

He was also excited by the radio. In September 1946 the BBC opened its new Third Programme, extending the range and quality of broadcast plays (as well as classical music and talks); but Potter was more drawn to the Light Programme and Home Service, as he recalled in the MacTaggart Lecture:

You could hear a play that made the back of your neck tingle as well as a dance band that made your foot tap, a brow-furrowing talk about something I'd never heard of, as well as an I-say-I-say-I-say music-hall routine, or even (and how bizarre) a ventriloquist's dummy as well as a not wholly dissimilar newsreader.

I would not dispute for one wayward whistle or crackle that the BBC of my childhood was not paternalistic and often stuffily pompous. It saw itself in an almost priestly role. But at a crucial period of my life it threw open the 'magic casement' on great sources of mind-scape at a time when books were hard to come by, and when I had never stepped into a theatre or a concert hall, and would have been scared to do so even if given the chance.

Of course, the characteristic media ploy of separating the 'popular' from the 'serious' . . . had already begun with the split between the Home Service and the Light Programme. But such a parting of the ways was nothing like as rigidly mapped out as it is nowadays . . . On the old Light Programme you could suddenly, maybe reluctantly, collide with a play or a discussion or an embryonic drama-documentary. The now totally pervasive assumptions of the market-place . . . had not by then removed the chance of being surprised by something you didn't know, or – better still – by something you didn't know that you knew.

Although the radio widened his mental horizon, it also contributed to his awareness of the limitations of life in Berry Hill. In a 1977 broadcast he recalled a day during his first winter at Bell's:

It was already cold; the air was like splinters of glass against your raw cheeks. When people spoke in the streets – and in the Forest they always did – their breath pumped out in fine clouds, which looked as though they could be frozen solid and then snapped off, giving one a pocket-full of greetings to take home and warm in front of the grate.

There was a man a few houses down from us, whose particular, small eccentricity was to walk up the hill on the very outside edge of the pavement, rather as though he was on a tightrope. I passed him, and spoke. 'Hello, o'butty,' he said, blowing out his cheeks with the cold. 'Warm enough for thee'?' ''Tis that.' And as I went on, a noise made me half stop, and look back. The man had stopped dead still on the pavement, on the edge of the pavement, exactly as though he was going to wobble and fall off the tightrope, and plunge all of two inches to his death on the rocks below. The noise was a sharp tin-tack rattle in his chest, the silicosis rattle.

Not an unfamiliar sound to Forest of Dean children at that time; my own grandfather, who lived with us, was to die of the same disease . . . My father worked at Cannop pit, a huge black pile in the middle of the woods, and most of the men I knew, the fathers of my friends, were coalminers. But this man's face was changing colour as he fought, literally *fought* for breath. I hovered, uncertainly, not sure what (if anything) to do. He was blue with more than cold.

'Thou go on,' he gasped out at last, annoyed at being observed. So I went on up the hill, obscurely ashamed, and yet also full of revulsion. I was clever . . . I knew I could 'get on', as the phrase goes. And with the necessary impertinence and confusion of the very young, destined to go up the ladder by the usual combination of accident and examination, I wanted somehow, some time, to get away from this place and these people, and this suffocatingly close, interned culture of gossip and chapel and pit-talk and brass band and rugby team and – oh, there was a long list. The tin-tack rattle in the chest became another sort of sharp rattle in my cocky little head.

*

Graham Fuller put it to Potter that he had written very little dealing with the problems of adolescence. 'No, I haven't,' he answered. 'I don't know why that is and I don't know if it's significant.' He gave a rare glimpse of his pubescent self on *Desert Island Discs*. Choosing 'My Happiness' by the Pied Pipers, a hit song of the post-war years, he explained:

Whenever I'm tempted to say I wish I was very much younger again, I think of being thirteen, sitting in the sheltered bus-stop in Cinderford . . . watching this young man whistling 'My Happiness', oh, lugubrious! I'm thinking, 'Is that what sex and love – is that what it's all about?' And if you listen to it – oh God! – it still tugs at you, it still makes you feel, you know, 'Have I combed my hair? Have I got a pimple?' You know, all that . . . I suppose it's pre-masturbation music.

Puberty had to be experienced at very close quarters with his family:

We lived in a four-roomed cottage, semi-detached. There were six of us: my parents, my grandparents, my sister June and myself. June and I had to share our parents' room. When we were fourteen and thirteen it was just two steps across from our bed to their bed. And we were already in puberty. It was insufferable for my mother. All the more so because the front room downstairs remained unused. Except for occasions, some Sundays when somebody with a suit came.

In *Vote, Vote, Vote for Nigel Barton*, Nigel says, 'There was only a sort of curtain between their [his parents'] half of the room and the place where we kids slept.' But June says that in real life there was no dividing curtain.

Potter spoke of this sharing of bed and bedroom on many occasions, as if it had been in some way traumatic; for example, in a 1968 article: 'Even when I was fourteen (in 1949) I was still sleeping with my thirteen-year-old sister, two short steps from the bed in the same narrow room where my mother and father slept.' On another occasion, repeating his description of this scene, he added, 'I still dream about it, you know, that moment of knowing.' He did not explain what sort of 'knowing' he meant.

Asked what she felt and feels about it, June writes:

About all sharing the same bedroom, as children we had no particular thoughts on it, as it seemed to be the norm round here when an extended family lived in a two-bedroomed cottage. Of course it must have been awful for Mum and Dad, but as children – and in those days thirteen–fourteen-year-olds *were* children – we would not even have thought about their plight.

In the other bedroom were Dennis's grandparents: 'Here, most of the time, my silicosis-ridden, illiterate grancher was painfully coughing up years of coal-dust into a huge pink po under the bed.' As in *The Singing Detective*, the old man's spitting was exasperating Dennis's mother. 'I could count the times of losing my temper – only about three or four times in my life,' she says, 'but we had a falling out [with her in-laws].' June adds, 'My granch [grandfather] used to spit in the fire, which must have been objectionable to my mum.' 'It was,' her mother agrees. June continues, 'But I accepted it – because he'd got silicosis, poor old thing.' Her mother shows no such sympathy: 'Oh, it was vile! Used to put me off!'

In an early attempt at a novel, *Wedding Night*, Potter describes the hero's Forest grandmother as a 'sanctimonious, Guinness-swigging and gossipy old cow'. He gives no portrait of his grandfather, who died in February 1950, aged seventy-two, of broncho-pneumonia brought on by silicosis. About eight months earlier, Dennis and his parents and sister had left Berry Hill. 'We took Dad as well that time,' says June.

They returned to Hammersmith, squeezing once more into 56 Rednall Terrace, where Ernie and his sister Flo were still living with their father. Mag took a job at Fuller's bakery, where she had worked before her marriage, and Walt found a job there in the maintenance department, later taking other manual work. 'My father became a builder's labourer,' said Potter, 'plumber's mate, all sorts of odd things. He couldn't stand it . . . '

Wedding Night portrays the narrator's father as helplessly miserable in London, and his mother as ruthlessly determined to keep the family there. 'Dad was almost literally shattered – choked,' says the narrator.

He saw me as his only ally, I'm sure. Mum hated him for it . . . and I think she hated me for the same reason . . . He said – or tried to say – that the road which joined up places, the road from [the Forest] to London he meant, never seemed to join up their skies, their moons, their dawns and sunsets . . . it knocked the stuffing out of him . . . He was helpless, absolutely helpless.

Dennis himself, however, was much happier than on the previous stay in London. Uncle Ernie seems to have made no further attempts on him, and he began to cultivate 'close-up acquaintance with a football team [Fulham] that took upon itself the task of restoring some of that sense of identity which the removal van had dislodged'. He remained devoted to Fulham Football Club for the rest of his life, a passion that reached its climax in 1975 when he went to Wembley to watch them play in the FA Cup Final (they lost 2–0 to West Ham).

The move to London meant yet another change of school. June, once again, got the poorer deal: 'The only one Mum could get me in was in Fulham, and it was an awful school. They thought I was very clever, but it was because the others were thick. But Dennis luckily got into St Clement Danes School. And that school got him on, brought him out.'

CHAPTER 4

Mr Amelot thinks I ought
to go to Oxford

St Clement Danes School, known as 'Danes', had grown out of the charitable activities of the Holborn Estate in central London. Founded in 1862 as the Holborn Estate Commercial Grammar School, it had originally been situated on the site of the present London School of Economics, near St Clement Danes Church in the Strand. The clearance of this overcrowded slum-ridden area led to the school being moved out to west London, where in 1928 new buildings were opened in Ducane Road, Hammersmith, next to Hammersmith Hospital and, beyond that, the sinister towers and battlements of Wormwood Scrubs Prison. (Nowadays, a little up the road, stands the BBC Television Centre.)

Since the 1944 Education Act, all places at Danes had been free, but the boys – it was single sex – wore uniforms, purchased at D. H. Evans in Oxford Street. There were a few distinguished Old Danes, among them the conductor Sir John Barbirolli, but sport rather than academic work was the chief preoccupation. About forty members of staff were in charge of almost eight hundred pupils, under the headmastership of J. McGill Clouston, a slightly absurd figure, inclined to malapropisms. Potter wrote in 1959, 'Grammar-school sixth forms are predominantly middle class.' But Bob Christopher, who became one of his best friends at Danes, says, 'Most of us were from working-class homes.'

As a late arrival in the school, in September 1949, aged fourteen, Potter did not at first attract much attention. One of the masters, Jack Harvey, describes him as 'confident and a good mixer – full of fun. He wasn't a games-player, but he mixed in well with everyone.' Tim Neal, who taught modern languages, recalls him as 'a very pleasant, friendly sort of chap – he had this noticeable West Country accent'. This aroused some ridicule at first; Bob Christopher recalls other boys saying in mock West Country tones, 'Ar, Percy Potter be 'ere, 'e be.' They gave him the nickname 'Perce', which stuck, even among his friends. 'I never called him Dennis, and neither did anyone else,' says Christopher. Maybe because of this, he rarely talked about the Forest while at Danes, even to close friends. But Christopher says he soon became 'quietly popular' in the school, and was soon recognized as 'a bit special'.

He seems to have felt comfortable there from the start: 'None of the almost suffocatingly close Forest of Dean atmosphere persisted at all. That turned me very much to academic work.' He came first in his form in the end-of-year examinations, and chose to specialize in maths and science at Ordinary ('O') Level, equivalent to today's GCSEs. Meanwhile academic success began to give him a feeling of difference from the rest of his family: 'a kind of complicated shame about the way you speak, the fact that there are no books in the house'. Elsewhere he said of this:

Teachers love to get their hands on a bright and pliant child, and they do not consciously give wing to the invisible worm that flies in the night, bringing the blight of an especially English type of betrayal deep into the oh-look-at-me! folds of the most precocious bloom. You are first made to feel a little different, and then you *want* to be different.

These are among the very few remarks he made in adult life about his secondary schooling. He kept virtually silent about his time at Bell's and Danes, even when talking to his own children, giving the impression that he had gone almost directly from the village school to Oxford. Roger Smith, a close friend in Oxford years, says, 'He never talked about his grammar schools at all.' Gareth Davies, who directed the Nigel Barton plays, agrees that there often seemed to be a veil over this: 'I never quite worked out what Dennis's school background was. Sometimes it seemed to be have been entirely in the Forest of Dean, and other times he seemed to have gone to grammar school in Hammersmith. You wouldn't get him to talk about it – it just occasionally slipped out.'

In his second year at Danes (1950–51) he began to do well athletically. 'Although not an outstanding player in games,' noted Clouston the headmaster, 'he has a keen interest in them, especially in cricket.' He also made a mark on the school stage, being cast as

Merrythought in Beaumont and Fletcher's *The Knight of the Burning Pestle*. The review in *The Dane* gives the impression that he was already a school character: 'The irrepressible Merrythought . . . was delightfully portrayed by D. C. G. Potter, with an infectious gaiety that only Potter could bring to the part.'

He began to take part in the school debating society, giving the impression – according to another teacher, Philip Gush – that he was 'rather left wing'. The headmaster noted, 'He is extremely sensitive to the wrongs and injustices of the world as he sees them, but is able to conduct discussions and arguments with good humour and a growing tolerance of the opinions of others . . . ' According to Bob Christopher, who was in the fifth form with Potter, he now definitely envisaged a career in politics:

Perce was fourteen or fifteen, and we were in an English lesson taken by John Bilsborough, a thoroughly pleasant man. He returned our marked homework to us – an essay on life in the year 2000. I imagined we'd all written fanciful science-fiction-type stuff. Without precedent, Bilsborough explained that he was going to read one of the essays out loud to us. Perce, of course, had written it: 'Good morning, this is the BBC Home Service, here is the seven o'clock news. There was uproar in the House of Commons last night when the Prime Minister, Leader of the Labour Party, the Right Honourable Dennis Potter . . . '

There was uproar in the class, and ribald shouts, but they soon became quiet and the essay was read. It was clever, cynical, and genuinely funny. Basically, the news was much the same as it always is – same old problems, same old statements. But he built into it the names of some of the boys, allocating to them positions (in the year 2000) that reflected their aptitudes as schoolboys.

In the summer of 1951 he sat his O levels in English language and literature, French, maths, physics and chemistry, and did particularly well in English language – he was awarded the upper-fifth form prize for the best result in that subject. Yet he decided not to specialize in English (or science) in the sixth form, but picked subjects more in tune with his political ambitions. 'At the end of his preparation for . . . Ordinary Level,' wrote Clouston, 'it became evident that his main interests were not in the field of natural science, and he entered a VIth form wherein his main subjects – economics, economic history, geography and the British Constitution – were in harmony with his interests. Here his abilities have found full scope . . . '

He struck Jack Harvey, who was beginning to teach him the British Constitution, as 'brilliant – we didn't know what to do with him, but Oxford or Cambridge seemed on the horizon, though Danes usually didn't get Oxbridge places, and the ones we did get were usually on account of games'. Potter says the same, 'I used to be first in every subject, it was always going to be Oxford or Cambridge.'

Asked on *Desert Island Discs* if a particular individual had encouraged him to aim for Oxbridge, he answered, 'Yes, a teacher in the first year of sixth form, who really did it. He slapped down Plato's *Republic* – in translation, of course – and said, "Read that. I think you ought to go to Oxford."' This was René Amelot, who taught him economics. Half French, over six feet tall and broadly built, he was also the Danes careers master. 'I went home,' recalled Potter, 'and said, "Mr Amelot thinks I ought to go to Oxford." And the instinctive quick response (which is quite understandable) from my mother was, "We can't afford it, you can't possibly go there." But I knew that I could.' Elsewhere he recalled, 'They said, "You must try for Oxford" – and that seemed to me the way out.'

Jack Harvey says that he had now developed 'a tremendous way with words. He wrote an essay on the causes of inflation that was so good I told everyone I couldn't have done it better myself. He read very widely.' Bob Christopher agrees: 'He really did shine in the sixth form. We all got on well with each other, but Perce was easily the most articulate and persuasive. He seemed to have read so much, remembered so much, thought about things I'd hardly heard of. He wasn't cocky or loud and he didn't seem to be a swot.'

He was back on stage in December 1951, in *The Importance of Being Earnest*. 'The Garden Scene', wrote the school theatre critic,

was, of course, most noteworthy for the Canon Chasuble of D. C. G. Potter, and for the Miss Prism of R. E. Allen. In a comedy part, Potter, with his irrepressible high spirits, is very soon on good terms with his audience. Not for him the muted subtleties of Wilde. He is not to be contained within the mere singular designation, Canon. He lets fly with a whole comic battery, and brings the house down – and all, on this occasion, in spite of an atrocious wig that apparently denied the efforts of the make-up department . . . If Potter had not already brought the house down, Allen, as Miss Prism, would eventually have done so.

Roger Allen, who played Miss Prism, says, 'Dennis was very easy to act with. He didn't take over. I used to ham a bit, and forget my lines and ad lib., but I don't think Dennis ever did – he was more mature than me. As Canon Chasuble he was dourly funny.'

His first published writings appeared in the school magazine in July 1952. One was a report on an Easter walking holiday in the Lake District, which blended comedy with social observation:

Later that day Keswick was spread at our feet as we climbed the lower Latrigg; it seemed a shame that a large housing estate should extend itself over the valley, as an ink-stain on a white tablecloth – but people must be housed . . . Throughout the tour rain was an almost unknown element, a strange and miraculous feature, especially as Stevens was pessimistic enough to wear a sou'wester like a trawlerman and Christopher often struggled manfully in a cape bound to impede progress . . .

The other described an economics and politics course for sixth-formers which he had attended at a college in Hertfordshire:

We had six lectures, and all were very interesting, particularly the ones on coal, by an ex-Bevin boy on the staff; the United Nations, by the head of the Foreign Office U.N.O. Department; and the work of a film director, by Charles Frend, of Ealing Studios, whose films include *Scott of the Antarctic* and the coming naval epic, *The Cruel Sea*.

After each lecture we went to Discussion Groups to thrash out agreements, or, more likely, disagreements, before returning to the lecture room to submit the unfortunate lecturer to a barrage of questions.

But the social side was just as important, for we had the opportunity to meet people with different backgrounds and ideas to ourselves. Informal dances were held, and one sing-song was a great success, particularly when we managed to convert the others to sing 'eight for the Queen's Park Rangers' (I still think it should be Fulham!) in 'Green Grow the Rushes, Oh!'

Bob Christopher went with him to watch Fulham play at Craven Cottage on many Saturdays.

During 1952, Dennis's mother decided to shift the family once again, because at last she had found a house in Berry Hill, a large cottage called Spion Kop, with a big garden, just off the road down to Joyford. She, Walt and June moved back, and Walt signed up at Cannop colliery once more. 'It had more dignity than what he'd been forced to do in London,' said Dennis. But he was finding it difficult to communicate with his father: 'My . . . journey from grammar school to Oxford . . . slightly intimidated him.' Walt was so much in awe of

Dennis's achievements that he used to quieten noisy, cursing drinkers in the Berry Hill club with 'Hush, mind, our Dennis is here.' Not that Dennis had returned with the family. 'My parents soon went back to the Forest,' he writes, 'but . . . a smell of freedom wafted off the print of textbooks, and I stayed on . . . with the London relations.'

In the autumn of 1952, the beginning of his final year at school, he was made a prefect. 'Potter is a person of complete integrity of mind and character,' wrote Clouston in a testimonial to accompany his application to Oxford. 'He is a School Prefect and is meticulous in the performance of his duty . . . In my opinion, Potter is a person adapted in the highest degree for University education in the widest sense and at the highest level. I have rarely had a pupil of whom I could say this with greater confidence.'

He became involved in drama outside school, serving on the committee of the Hammersmith Drama Festival, while in February 1953 (the term before A levels) he took the title role in a school production of *Noah* by André Obey. Kaye Barnes, wife of the head of modern languages at Danes (and mother of the novelist Julian Barnes), says, 'I can see Dennis to this day, on the platform, dressed in some funny loose-hanging beige thing, and his arms upraised, and calling upon God. He was absolutely marvellous. And the Forest of Dean accent seemed to fit Noah perfectly.' The *Dane* reviewer was equally impressed: 'D. C. G. Potter . . . played magnificently the exacting role of Noah. As a feat of memory alone his performance was superb. That he was able also to convey the profounder aspects of the play and to stir our minds and hearts is beyond praise.'

He sat the Oxford scholarship exam in March, tackling papers on politics and economics, geography, English government and economic history, and general papers. He did not win a scholarship, but was offered a place as a commoner at New College, to read philosophy, politics and economics (PPE). A commoner is a fee-paying under-graduate, whereas a scholar has some or all of the fees covered by the scholarship. However, in practice at this time, fees for all under-graduates whose families could not afford them were paid by state scholarships, provided by the government, and the difference between commoner and scholar was merely one of status, and not a significant difference at that. Potter had also sat for, and won, the Hume Lloyd Scholarship in Economics at University College, London, but Amelot firmly advised him to opt for Oxford.

44

'I am pleased to accept your offer of entrance to New College as stated in your letter of the 24th March,' he wrote to the Tutor for Admissions at the college. He had not yet taken A levels; passing these would exempt him from most of Responsions, the university's entrance exam, but there were no 'grades' in those days – simply pass, fail, and distinction – so he had little to worry about. In the event he achieved passes in all four subjects, and Bob Christopher thinks he was awarded a distinction in economic history. His letter to New College continued, 'Regarding Responsions, I have taken up the study of Latin, and will take the examination before October 1955, the date at which I applied for entry and by which time my national service will have been completed.' Since he did not have Latin O level, it would be necessary to pass this part of Responsions before Oxford would admit him.

Earlier in the school year, he had been asked to edit the first ever 'literary supplement' to *The Dane* – 'its aim is to encourage literary and creative work among boys at all stages of the school', explained the magazine. The supplement appeared at the end of his final term. 'Our aim', Potter wrote in his editorial, 'has been to choose contributions in which the writer has used his own eyes or imagination, and his own voice . . . As far as possible we have excluded imitations of the classics and the comics, preferring what is first hand and vigorous.' He himself contributed an essay on 'Modern Poetry':

Writing this article, I find it difficult not to fall into what I am assured are terrible errors: lack of originality and that ridiculousness which may overcome the unsuspecting schoolboy when he attempts a treatise on such weighty subjects . . . The only claims I can make are that I read modern poetry, and that I enjoy much of it, and that I wish to get others interested in at least trying some of the best poetry written today . . .

The poet of today faces many problems . . . How can he penetrate the barrier of contempt and indifference set up by a public saturated with popular newspapers, Hollywood films, radio and television?

He said that 'the two poets I have found the easiest to get on with are C. Day Lewis and W. H. Auden'. He thought Auden 'very much a poet of the modern world . . . aware of the contemporary dilemmas . . . He has something to say about the times we live in, and he says it freshly. Do not ignore him.'

There were no signs of Auden's influence in the thirty-five-line poem that he contributed to the supplement. Called 'The Artist', it begins:

Beauty is like the transcendent God
whom earthly pilgrims never attain;
for as in the cradle man seems to lurk
behind the façade of infancy,
the greatest beauty ever gained
hints at a glory yet to be,
however wondrous the artist's work.

But (the poem goes on) if the artist cannot attain pure beauty, its 'bright beam' nevertheless sparkles within him. His 'purpose and tragedy' will be the endless search for it, and sometimes, 'after a particular piece of work', he will experience a visionary moment when

the mind clears suddenly before the sun
and tall towers of beauty are bared
into naked actuality.
That moment is all, the time for which
he lives: eternity.

It is clear that he is writing from experience, and already regards himself as an artist. Thirty years later, he described how in adolescence he had believed 'that Art had a capital initial in the shape of the gable of a house which had been carefully and tightly built to lock out the crass, the crude, the ignorant, and most of those who made noises in the street'.

Yet something was already tugging him away from this élitist view of art. On 2 June 1953 the Coronation was watched in the streets of London by thousands of people – including Potter himself, who camped out all night in the Mall with Bob Christopher and Mike Stevens – and on television by a record audience of 20 million. Though he mentions television in his list of popular media when discussing modern poetry, until now only a few households owned sets. The Coronation woke people up to TV. Forty years later, Potter recalled, 'I was in the sixth form when I first saw television, so that I saw it at the very moment when I was thinking: what am I about? This thing sitting in people's living rooms. I thought: how wonderful this could be . . . ' And he wrote in his MacTaggart Lecture, 'I first saw television when I was in my late teens. It made my heart *pound*. Here was a medium of great power, of potentially wondrous delights, that could slice through all the tedious hierarchies of the printed word and help to emancipate us from many of the stifling tyrannies of class and status and gutter-press ignorance.'

Returning to Berry Hill many times over the next few years, he would see TV sets beginning to invade and erode the culture of the Forest:

Those early grey-faced, tall nine-inch sets – almost antique pieces now – were the most expensive, most beautiful and by far the most exciting things to be brought into the house . . . the bow-tied announcers and women in evening dresses . . . so the Front Room became, however reluctantly, a room for use. The little screen found its place amongst the cumbersome best furniture and the heavily flowered, deep-bordered wallpaper. And, of course, when the family began to watch, furniture got moved around, a few superfluous things were slung out, a giant change in domestic habits was being made . . . a minor revolution was finally consummated when supper was eaten in the room to the pale flicker of the Lime Grove light.

*

National Service had been introduced immediately after the Second World War, requiring all male school-leavers to undertake two years' military training, though this could be postponed until they had left university. The majority, like Potter, preferred to get it out of the way first. He was enlisted under the National Service Act and posted to the Royal Army Ordnance Corps on 17 September 1953. Writing to New College, he gave his number and rank as '22920071 Pte D. Potter'.

In 1977, on his first trip out of Britain (at the age of forty-two), he was reminded by the queues for the US Immigration desks at John F. Kennedy Airport of 'a place long buried in the darkest part of my soul . . . the reception area at Blackdown Camp in Aldershot on the first day of my National Service'. He was 'so shocked by the Army, my only thought was how could I survive'. Tony Baldwin, who was already doing National Service, met him on leave at Berry Hill:

Dennis was having a rough time with his drilling. The bullying was amazing – the drill sergeants couldn't bash a whole squad of about thirty lads into shape, so they'd pick on two or three unfortunates. Dennis was one of them. He couldn't tie up a shoelace, so he was an absolute gift to the sergeants. He had no dress sense at all – he could just about put on a tie, but getting it in the middle was beyond him, and as to bulling [polishing] his boots, he almost cried when I did it for him. I suppose he had to put up with eight to ten weeks of that. I told him, 'Get through this and it'll get better.' It already had for me – I got a stripe, and they put me into administration.

Potter's sister June recalls that when he was doing National Service he begged the family to write to him with any news of home, however trivial, and his daughter Sarah says it was the anxiety of army life that first drove him to smoke. 'I regret the day . . . in National Service that I was persuaded to take that cigarette,' he once admitted. 'I did stop for ten days in 1959, and I nearly died!' And, in 1977, he said, 'Nobody has yet been able to demonstrate to me how I can join words into whole sentences on a blank page without a cigarette burning away between my lips.'

He was rescued very quickly from Blackdown Camp. Ministry of Defence records show that, after only two weeks, on 1 October 1953, he was 'Transferred to the Intelligence Corps'. To New College, he gave his address as 'Intelligence Corps Centre, Maresfield Park Camp, nr Uckfield, Sussex'.

It was at Maresfield that Potter first met Kenith Trodd, who would play an enormous part in his life. 'I can't pinpoint our first meeting,' Trodd says. 'You were in huts – dormitories – and I wasn't in the same one as Dennis. But we were in the same squad.' Brian Gibson, who directed Potter's *Blue Remembered Hills*, says, 'I remember Dennis telling me that Trodd was always getting the squad into trouble, because he always had his hat on wrong, or something like that.' Michael Grade recalls being told by Potter that he always tried to stand next to Trodd when the platoon was being inspected, because Trodd's kit would be in such disarray that it distracted the officer from Potter's own failings. 'Dennis said it was the only time that Ken had been utterly indispensable to him.'

Kenneth Trodd – as his first name was still spelt in National Service days – was almost Potter's twin, having been born eleven days after him, on 28 May 1935, in Southampton:

My father had been a crane driver, and by studying he had converted himself into a maintenance electrician, working at Fawley refinery, which was a big step up. I was at King Edward VI School in Southampton, an old foundation. My family was just me and a sister adopted when I was about eight – my mother had a miscarriage, and I think was advised not to have more children. 'Trodd' is, I think, a Jutish name, associated with that part of the country, but I've never gone in for family trees.

Trodd looks Celtic rather than English. 'Yes, people say that, but I don't have any family-tree insight into it – though perhaps my indiscriminate attention to all things Irish may be a clue.'

Like Potter, he came from a Nonconformist background – a far less tolerant one:

My mother was a Southampton girl (her surname was Pitfield), and she and my father met at the Plymouth Brethren church, across the road from where she was brought up. I think they were both converts; they were both very ardent about it, but my mother with much more guilt and uncertainty. I have a strong, searing memory of her, when she was pregnant, dragging me around icy Southampton, depositing tracts through doorways of random people. And often these were scraps of Scripture written out in her own handwriting.

Did he have Potter's sense of being a clever child in an unintellectual environment? 'Yes. I passed the Eleven Plus – the first sheep-and-goats separation – and, almost as soon as I arrived at the grammar school, was put into the "S" (Special) stream, for able pupils. And yet I was a rebel in that situation from the word go. I was bolshie, and led various rebellions, and had a thoroughly iffy time at school, despite being a success academically.'

Compared to Clement Danes, there was little in the way of drama at King Edward VI:

There was an Essay Club, in which I was quite prominent. It met in members' homes, but I couldn't face being host when my turn came – I was ashamed of the relative working-classness of our way of life. Also we lived out at Fawley, in a council house, and it was a long journey to school, and that, too, separated me from the other boys. Like Dennis, I became aware of a dichotomy: the world of school, which was opening me up, and the world of home, where I had to continue to be ostensibly loyal to religious fundamentalism.

Yet Trodd was never baptized: 'The Plymouth Brethren still practised total immersion as the rite of passage for adolescents, but I was never pressured into doing it.' He agrees that, within the terms of the Plymouth Brethren, his parents were quite liberal. 'There was another, more extreme branch of the Brethren, called the Exclusives, and various family friends drifted from them or back again; but my parents were always in the regular Brethren.' Nevertheless the dichotomy between home and school was so great that 'when I got a scholarship to Oxford, the first my mother knew about it was when she read it in the *Southern Evening Echo*'. Why did he not tell her?

Because I don't know how to express celebration, how to rejoice. And I think what that relates to – and there may be a connection with Dennis here – is the horror of discovering the falsity of the rejoicing that the Plymouth Brethren had offered. It makes you suspicious of any other kind of expression of positiveness or allegiance. Once you've had that experience of the world being an irreconcilable dichotomy, you are always aware of false hope, false enthusiasm, false value – even when it's not false at all.

There was, however, one form of celebration that Trodd discovered and accepted:

When I was about six, my mother got friendly with a neighbour who was one 'of the world'. There was smoking in that house, and some drinking, and phonograph records. One was by Lew Stone's band – a maudlin item called 'The Red Maple Leaves'. I made a connection between the music in this alien house – where I shouldn't have been – and a world of drama and emotion, which was more rewarding than that of fundamentalism and primitive hymns. The Lew Stone figure obviously epitomized the more rewarding and exciting world . . . Lew Stone was my adopted imaginative background.

At first Trodd was simply listening to the dance music of the day – the recordings by Lew Stone and other bandleaders which preserved the style of the Thirties into the early war years. But he continued to be mesmerized by these recordings into adulthood, so that it became a nostalgic fixation: 'I can remember biking round the record shops to look at their old stock.'

Trodd experienced no encouragement to academic work from his parents, nor (in his case) did a schoolmaster pick on him and groom him for success; so why did he work hard and get to Oxford? 'You got out on a tide that was moving that way.' Yet, compared with the young Potter and his dreams of political fame, he was not ambitious: 'I've always loathed the notion of ambition, of planning one's life – it was somehow dirty, discreditable. My particular take on left-wing ideas was that ambition was something you didn't go in for.'

Though they were now in the Intelligence Corps, Potter and Trodd found that life at Maresfield consisted of 'more square-bashing'. In early November 1953 they were transferred to the Joint Services School for Linguists at Bodmin in Cornwall, where they were to learn Russian, with the Cold War in mind. Trodd says that they were taught 'mostly by slightly sad Russian émigrés – I remember a rather beautiful woman, and an older man, who was pathetic; he couldn't cope with the unruly class'.

Three months later, Potter wrote to New College:

As a private in the Intelligence Corps, I have been on a Russian language course since early November, and since this course is designed to get its students up to GCE (A) Level in a year, the first few months allow little time for anything else in the way of other studies. Consequently, I abandoned my Latin studies, and am now about to take them up again.

He later recalled the Bodmin course: 'Five hours' Russian, non-stop each day, with one hour's weapon training tacked on.' He passed A-level Russian the following May. Quite apart from lifting him above the herd during National Service, his knowledge of Russian proved useful in his plays in later years. A surprisingly large number of them include Russian-speaking characters, or other references to the language and its literature.

The future actor Joe Melia, then an eighteen-year-old bound for Cambridge, was also on the Bodmin course. 'Dennis came across to me as very original,' he says. 'He was very enthusiastic about proper theatre (the rest of us only bothered with radio comedy and American films).' Melia gathered that Potter came from the Forest of Dean, but was told nothing about his London schooling – 'Was Dennis at grammar school in Hammersmith? I never knew about that.' At this stage, however, Potter did not put any emphasis on his origins. 'The other thing I remember', says Melia, 'is that he was a wonderful mimic. We had a sergeant major with a speech impediment. He didn't exactly stammer, but he would fluff, and Dennis used to have us in stitches, doing an impersonation of him.' In contrast, Trodd, in those days, struck Melia as 'religious'.

Potter achieved 82 per cent at A-level Russian, and was therefore graded by the army as a Russian Linguist Group A Class II. Trodd explains the consequences of this:

They were running a superior Russian course at Cambridge, and a small proportion at Bodmin were creamed off for that. (Michael Frayn, a year or two before, had gone on it.) But neither Dennis or I were selected for it. We didn't get quite high enough marks in the Russian exam, and also we weren't officer material – because the people who went on the Cambridge course became second lieutenants. Another possibility was to get posted to Germany, and we didn't get that either. But of the ones left behind, we were probably the two most literate – the two boys bound for Oxford.

They stayed on at Bodmin until August 1954, attending a

translators' course, and were then sent back to Maresfield. On 3 January 1955, Potter wrote to New College:

The amount of work that I have been called upon to do during these two years of National Service has far exceeded what I expected. I have studied the Russian language to 'A' level and above from 'scratch', and now I hear that next week I shall be commencing yet another course which will demand private study, etc. . . .

Joe Melia says that at Maresfield, after the Bodmin training, they were set to translate Soviet pamphlets, 'which we found very boring'.

Melia was eventually sent to an RAF base near Birmingham, to transcribe and translate intercepted radio conversations between Warsaw Pact tank commanders. Trodd and Potter had a more colourful posting: to the War Office in London. 'I think we may have done some scheming to get there,' says Trodd. 'We were the only two in our batch to be selected for it.'

Arriving there during May 1955, he and Potter were allocated to different departments – 'Dennis was in MI3(D) and I was adjacent in MI3(C).' They were to wear civilian clothes except on pay day, and Potter was able to live with his family in Hammersmith – though during these months his Wale grandfather died, and he moved in with a sister of his mother's, Nell. His uncle Sidney says that 'Nell found Dennis very studious – he'd go up to his room to work on a Friday night and she wouldn't see him all weekend.'

With the death of their father, Ernie and Flo left Rednall Terrace, and went to join Mag and Walt at Spion Kop in Berry Hill. 'Flo was a scream,' says Tony Baldwin. 'At a Christmas party she sang songs like I've never heard. She was tall, thin, with grey hair, very mannish, very London. They were rugby songs – raucous stuff! Ernie was quieter, and took a back seat.' Dennis's mother was, of course, still ignorant of what Ernie had done. 'If I'd known,' she says, 'I would never have allowed him to live with us.' Ernie worked as a bus conductor in the Forest until his health began to fail. When he won £4000 on the football pools he paid off the mortgage on Spion Kop. He was still living there in the Sixties. 'I can remember Uncle Ernie very well,' says Potter's daughter Jane. 'He was a very nice bloke, but my brother Robert was never left with him on his own.'

Potter said that the use at the War Office of young men who had been studying Russian 'wasn't entirely trivial . . . at that point, at the height of the Cold War, just after the Berlin airlift, there could have been another world war at any moment'. He described his duties there:

MI3 dealt with the Soviet Army, where it was, where it had been: where it was going. The information came in, partly in code, partly overt. There was an incredible amount of crap. We had to read documents, soldiers' letters and all the Russian military newspapers, because, as with all newspapers, someone would make a mistake and reveal the name of a place or person.

He worked in a 'huge office with . . . the majors and the colonels and a service sergeant who was like a sort of office administrator'. The officers 'had all been fighting soldiers. They were called – comically – intelligence officers.' He particularly recalled one of them bellowing: 'Pottah! . . . How do you spell "accelerator"? I've been all through the blasted X's in this bloody dictionary.' But mostly he was bored:

God! those long afternoons in summer, when you could hear the clock on Horse Guards Parade strike every quarter-hour, and it would be stiflingly hot and all those nerds would have their tightly furled umbrellas and their bowler hats on. And having to go through that ridiculous 'permission to speak – SAH!' routine every time you opened your mouth. That little phrase seemed to me to sum up the whole of English life at that time.

Ministry of Defence records state that Potter was 'Discharged on termination of whole-time National Service' on 9 October 1955. He took Latin Responsions at Oxford in June 1955, and failed – a blow, because he was to go up to New College in October. He wrote to the college, pleading to be allowed take Responsions again after matriculating, because he was 'rather concerned about requesting the Ministry of Education to postpone my state scholarship for yet another year . . . and there is a natural feeling of frustration about kicking one's heels for another twelve months. If it is at all possible, I beg to be allowed to come up this October . . . ' The college replied that the university regulation could not be waived, and consequently Potter now faced an empty year – and the anxiety of having to attempt the Latin exam again. Meanwhile Trodd took up his scholarship at University College, Oxford, in October 1955, to read English. His tutor, P. C. Bayley, found him brilliant but difficult: 'He looked like a hungry animal that you could never give enough food to.'

Potter took a temporary job at the Meredith & Drew biscuit factory in Cinderford, where (as he writes in *The Changing Forest*) 'men would be trundling heavy tubs of dough from under the mixing blades to a long waiting hall of shrouded tubs to await fermentation and manufacture'. Meanwhile, says his mother, he 'taught himself Latin, more or less'. He finally passed Latin Responsions the month after his twenty-first birthday, June 1956, and was therefore able to tell New College that he would be arriving in October on a state scholarship which would cover his fees and living expenses.

In *The Glittering Coffin* he recalls the night before he left the Forest:

I had gone to the Berry Hill Working Men's Club at home, with my mother and father, to have a 'farewell' drink and underline the importance of the occasion. People kept coming across to our table, between the radiogram and the bar, to wish me luck. 'I'd always like to see a bloke from round here getting on, ol' un'.' Pumping hands. Free drinks. 'Thou go all the road, butty. Only don't forget where tha come from, oot?' Jokingly – I think. And my stomach was starting to move with excitement. I looked down the long, wood-and-stone building, at the county rugby team on the wall, at the old men with their bread and cheese, and attempted to take in the whole atmosphere of stale, slopped beer and eye-smarting cigarette smoke, the hum of conversation and the occasional cackle of laughter. 'S'all this tinned food', the ashen-faced man sniffed, blue coal scars clear on the bridge of his nose, 'there's him and her out scratching for a living when they've got enough, and no time for something proper to yut, so it's tinned this, and tinned that. Gives her boils. She's got boils on her arms and boils on them groite legs of hers.' Gulp, and a maliciously timed pause. 'And I'll bet she's got boils up her arse', at which all laughed and joined in. Warm and safe.

But, to my shame, I realized that more than anything I wanted to get away from it all, more than ever before that I was glad to be going, glad to be taking this heaven-sent passport to the world of – what? I wasn't sure, but I knew it was a world where I should be happier, a world where my books were not muddles, where I wasn't on the defensive when putting forward my opinions and value judgements. At that moment of change, I wanted to take a different path, wanted to struggle out of the carefully wrapped cocoon of loyalties and sentiments. A potential Joe Lampton,* without the remorse.

* Hero of John Braine's novel *Room at the Top*.

CHAPTER 5

Plunder about

'I remember that when I first arrived at New College,' Potter wrote two years after the event, while still an undergraduate,

wearing a dark suit and white shirt, with plastered-down hair and eight pounds in cash, nervous as hell but determined to conform until I could claim my freedom, take my bearings and generally be able to relax over coffee with some other newcomers, I found my room at the top of a long winding stone flight of stairs and began to unpack. Standing by the windows, I could see Holywell Street way below, and hear about five clocks spacing out the autumn evening. It was impossible not to feel both moved and strangely excited, nervously energetic . . . Now, I thought . . . it would be all right to read poetry or listen to the Third Programme, to take the edge out of my accent and the shyness out of my manner.

And so, when I threw up the window and leaned out over Holywell, the air I breathed seemed clearer, freer and more challenging. I couldn't wait to get my hands round the slim stem of a glass of sherry.

There came a knock at the door. The party seemed to be beginning already.

However, the person who came in wasn't an undergraduate. He was too old. But he had a collar and tie, and a confident manner. 'Just popped in to see if you had arrived and that everything is all right,' he said, looking round the room and not quite at me. I was momentarily unsure how to respond, but he went on, 'Had a good journey up, sir?' and I realized that this was my 'scout', the person who would make my bed and clean my shoes.

He called me 'sir' in a fresh way; not the way a shopkeeper calls you 'sir', either automatically or with menacing deference, but in a way which reflected an assumed difference in status, in a class way in other words. I suppose that this was my first embarrassment, my first stab of guilt or conscience, call it what you will. The man was much older than I was, old enough to be a parent of mine in fact, and yet he was supposed to clean my shoes, make my bed, and be deferential. The dangers and anomalies of my position became immediately clear; when faced with the choice, despite my frustrations with some of the norms of working-class life, I could but choose that world in preference to any other.

This decision, to remain loyal to his class roots, affected the whole of his Oxford career – indeed, the remainder of his life.

Alan Coren, who came up to Wadham College in 1957, remembers hearing that Potter had asked his scout not to call him 'sir'. Coren's own scout told him that Potter was 'the talk of the scouts'.

The encounter with his scout left Potter feeling that 'we are plonked down with a bank balance into what still appears to be an essentially medieval establishment'. The bank balance was a decent one; besides paying his tuition fees, the Ministry of Education gave him a substantial maintenance grant of £308 per annum. 'Money wasn't a problem,' says Trodd. In *The Glittering Coffin*, Potter observes that the pre-war Oxford social life – 'champagne parties, coloured waistcoats and cavalry twill' – had given way by the mid-Fifties to 'earnest, hard-working young people on state grants, eating their lunches in Joe Lyons' or Woolworth's'. All the same, 'many of the conversations in Christ Church's Peckwater quad could have taken place fifty years ago, and some of the lectures in Schools did'.

New College in 1956 was still (Potter said later) 'at least more than two-thirds public school, and of the Winchester and Eton kind of public school'. Strikingly, he decided to mix with these people rather than to socialize with other young men from poorer homes: 'The few other grammar-school boys were creeps, adopting as many mannerisms of Oxford as they could and distancing themselves from their past. I took to being aggressive and making an issue of it.' He also decided to leave his accent untouched: 'I do not wish', he wrote later in his time at Oxford, 'to speak with a different accent, or cut any of the ties that keep me to the Forest of Dean.'

These decisions made, 'things seemed to become possible at once. I knew I was on the make, and suddenly I knew it was easier than I'd dared hope . . . There was plunder about.' He looked round for the 'supremely intelligent beings', who supposedly populated Oxford – and soon realized that no such people existed. 'My assumption when I went up was that everyone was going to be so much better, brighter, more intelligent,' and 'what . . . shocked me about Oxford when I got there was how easy everything was'.

But what was to be his field of operation? Three weeks into term, the Suez crisis broke. 'For the first time in years,' observed the editorial in the undergraduate magazine *Isis*, 'Oxford has thrown off its legendary apathy; protest meetings, whitewashed slogans, debates, lobbying groups to London – only the most cynical have deliberately remained aloof.' Potter later referred to the sending in of British troops by the Conservative Prime Minister Anthony Eden as 'the Suez abomination'.

The (all-male) Oxford Union Society was packed that week, with everyone hoping for a debate on Suez. Instead, they got the advertised one: 'In the opinion of this House, the modern man does not require religious belief in order to be moral.' *Isis* reported that, from the floor, 'Mr Denis [*sic*] Potter (New College) made an excellent maiden speech'; and the other undergraduate weekly *Cherwell* agreed: 'For the motion, there were three delightful minutes of wry comment from Mr Dennis Potter.'

He had another chance a month later, when the Union debated the motion 'that the Trade Union movement now includes powerful influences that effectively harm the political and economic life of the country'. *Cherwell* reported: 'Mr Dennis Potter . . . spoke of the broader aspects of Union activity, and the paradox that it is only within the Union that men can be in the fuller sense free. Mr Potter is undoubtedly the season's best bag.'

*

His first term ended a few days after this, and he had to make the difficult, temporary transition back to the Forest, the first of many.

He describes it in *The Changing Forest*:

I had to change buses at Cinderford . . . The early winter dark . . . would mean crumpets and talk in my big ugly room in New College . . . I found a place to get a hot cup of coffee and warm myself. The Telebar. During the day, the juke-box can be seen right up against the window . . . A teenager with a leathery, fur-collared jacket and carefully dishevelled haircut had just succeeded in getting his coin to drop with a clatter into the sleek fat belly of the machine. The grill-like, concave strands at the back began to revolve, and the arm came over with a click, hovered for a moment, a snake-headed bird, then, as if making an intelligent, considered choice, pounced swiftly on to the tiny black disc whirred into place by the machine, crushing it until it screamed with protest.

> *I'm ev-er so lone-ly bay-bee lone-ly bay-be*
> *I-I could diiie!*

Sex, sex, sex. Sing to it, call for it, yearn for it. 'I got the UUUUUUrge for you, UUUUUUrge for you.' 'What will the teacher do, what will the teacher say, if she only knew, we were making love, mak-ing love, making lo-o-o-ve, making love.'

Under the ironic social observation, one glimpses the lonely young twenty-one year old.

Walt was now anxious that Dennis should not become 'uppity'; he must 'speak to every conceivable person' in Berry Hill, otherwise Walt would say, disapprovingly, 'That's Oxford, that's bloody Oxford.' Consequently Dennis kept his distance from his father, and 'began asking [him] questions through my mother'. He found himself 'willy-nilly being pulled away in a contradictory series of shame and scorn, pride and bewilderment, from the tight, warm mesh of sometimes stunted, often vivid alternative values into which I had been born and bred'.

Returning to Oxford, he found these feelings described by someone else who had experienced them, in a book published during his second term. *The Uses of Literacy: Aspects of Working-Class Life*, which became an immediate bestseller and was reprinted three times that year (1957), was by a Yorkshireman in his late thirties, who had been brought up in a working-class family in Leeds, and was now a lecturer at Hull University. Potter wrote in *The Glittering Coffin* that Richard Hoggart's name had become 'something of an incantation' in under-graduate left-wing circles.

Hoggart's thesis was that the old-style working-class life, with its strong family ties and exuberant culture, was swiftly giving way to a more pallid, commercialized lifestyle. 'The fact that illiteracy . . . has been largely removed', he wrote, 'only points towards the next and probably more difficult problem.' Hoggart was better at describing the old order than anatomizing the new; his portrait of working-class women shopping in Leeds rang truer than his sketches of the juke-box society of the mid-Fifties, and he steered clear of politics. Potter probably perceived at once that much more could be written, from first-hand experience and observation, about the new mass culture and its dangers.

Roger Smith, who became friends with Potter at Oxford, says that his 'intellectual mentors' in those days 'were Hoggart and Raymond Williams – *Culture and Society*. But he wouldn't touch Marx.' *Culture and Society 1780–1950*, by the left-wing critic and novelist Raymond Williams, was published in 1958. Potter makes passing references to Williams in *The Glittering Coffin* and *The Changing Forest*, but Williams does not seem to have been nearly so influential on him as was Hoggart.

He was back at the Union in his second term, where the motion was 'that this House envies the uneducated their pleasures'. *Cherwell*, the undergraduate weekly, reported that 'speaking against the motion . . . Mr Dennis Potter (N[ew] C[ollege]) said that education was a good thing. Mr Kenneth Trodd (Univ[ersity College]) proclaimed the truism that "rubbish is rubbish".' At another debate that month, 'Kenneth Trodd (University) made the best of the floor speeches.'

Trodd says that his own first year at Oxford, before Potter had joined him, had been fairly quiet; whereas Potter sprang into prominence almost at once: 'I think I skulked about. Maybe I needed the stimulus of Dennis. Because I was always that bit behind him in the things I did.'

Trodd recalls that they took no interest in the cinema: 'We all went to the Scala in Walton Street, but I certainly never had any inclination that I would get into show business. I was being encouraged to think of myself as an academic.' Potter, meanwhile, was on the stage again. In his first term he appeared in the New College entry for 'Cuppers', the annual play competition, and then took part in a combined New College and Worcester College production of Ibsen's *Rosmersholm*, directed by Charles Lewsen (later to appear in *Stand Up, Nigel Barton*). 'The most memorable performance was the producer's Brendel,' wrote the *Isis* reviewer, adding, 'Dennis Potter's radical, and Gwen Nuttall's housekeeper, despite the youthful appearance of the players, were always in the right key.'

Potter's role in this play about sexual and political radicalism was a small one: Peter Mortensgaard, the editor of a left-wing newspaper, who appears only in the second of the four acts. The future professional actor Jonathan Cecil, son of Lord David Cecil and then a New College undergraduate, recalls that Potter's acting at Oxford was 'rather good, though he had only one performance, which was verging on hysteria. His voice on stage was rather high-pitched and strangulated.'

A review of Potter's performance in a New College production of Pirandello's *Man, Beast and Virtue* in his third term, in which he played Paolino, a manic private tutor hell-bent on covering up his affair with a sea captain's wife, confirms Cecil's recollection. 'His interpretation, basically sound, is still ragged at the edges,' wrote the reviewer; 'he boils over once or twice too often, sometimes without motive.' He was also cast as the Clown in Nevill Coghill's Oxford University Dramatic Society production of *Dr Faustus*, at the Playhouse, in March 1957. *Isis* described it as 'a bad production of a good play', and made no mention of Potter's performance.

Trodd's tutor at University College, Peter Bayley, was then the University's Junior Proctor, and recalls Potter being summoned before himself and the Senior Proctor for drunken behaviour in the King's Arms pub after a play performance. When challenged by a university 'Bulldog' (policeman), Potter had given a false name, which resulted in a reprimand and a fine. But it did nothing to stop his swift progress into the public eye.

At the end of his second term, he received a 'Collections' report from one of his tutors, the young historian Keith Thomas, who was then at All Souls but doing some teaching for New College in British Constitutional history, 1660–1914. 'Mr Potter wishes to read modern history in place of PPE,' wrote Thomas, 'and I strongly recommend that he be allowed to do so . . . He is a very intelligent person capable of first-class work. If he reads history I think he may well do extremely well at it.' Sir Keith Thomas (as he now is) recalls that his New College pupils 'used to come in a class, and Dennis was the one I became aware of soonest, because he was very conspicuous – I knew nothing about his background, but he was a great drawer of attention to himself, very egocentric, and he clearly had a chip about something, though it wasn't clear precisely what'.

Potter did not abandon PPE for history, perhaps because his academic work was less important to him than his determination to become 'conspicuous', as Thomas puts it. In his third term, he joined the staff of *Isis* as an 'editorial assistant'. The editor was Stephen Hugh-Jones of New College, a former scholar of Eton who was in the Labour Club at Oxford. Hugh-Jones recalls that he first approached Potter after hearing him speak at the Union. Despite their different backgrounds, they immediately became friends. 'If anyone says Dennis had a chip on his shoulder, that's not true,' says Hugh-Jones. 'He was very happy – though he liked to make a certain noise about being working class.' Jonathan Cecil agrees: 'I remember him sounding off about the abolition of the aristocracy. It was only afterwards that he discovered I was an Old Etonian and the son of Lord David Cecil. He was amazed that I had been interested rather than offended. But then I was pretty anti-Eton myself.'

In *The Glittering Coffin*, Potter writes that he would like to see 'the great "public schools" of England . . . used as Civil Defence Corps billets, for the pointlessness of the one would add pungency to the anachronism of the other'. In 1960, shortly after leaving Oxford, he said that the public schools were 'very, very amusing' but 'must be got rid of'. Yet it was hard to take this issue seriously when, as a result of Suez, so many – perhaps the majority – of undergraduates, whatever their social background, regarded themselves as at least moderately left wing. A very large number had joined the University Labour Club. In *The Glittering Coffin*, Potter notes that by 1958 it had 'a membership . . . hovering between one thousand and one and a half thousand', which made it 'by far the largest socialist student body in the country'.

Isis was run from a 'small and untidy office next to the Alfred Street gymnasium and opposite the "Bear Inn"'. Potter's first article for the magazine, 'Changes at the Top', appeared in the middle of his third term. This is how it begins:

At twenty-five past three in the afternoon the morning shift would crunch down the road that drooped through the village, their work over for the day. 'Evenings' came back at half-past eleven at night, and the others at six in the mornings, so this was the only returning shift you could see properly, and it was accordingly always something of an event in the day. The ponderous and out-of-step clamp, clamp, clamp of steel-toed pit boots could be heard minutes before the men came by, and I was able to rush to the wall, eager to see the coal-black faces, the corduroy trousers hitched and string-tied just below the padded knees, and the helmets shaped rather like those worn by the Nazi soldiers in my weekly copy of the *Champion* (the comic everyone seemed to take to supplement the *Daily Herald* or the *Daily Mirror*). For me, and, I suspect, for the adults as well, those returning, grimy men up from the bowels of the earth had a peculiar glamour that inevitably disappeared when the pale, scrubbed faces and collars and ties came out later in the evening; anyway, most people came to the door when this shift passed, including the miserable-looking whippets, tails curved to a taper under their trembling tube-thin bodies.

My grandfather had silicosis after more than fifty years working at the coal face, yet he would always try and come to the wall, breathing so heavily that I was never quite sure whether he was laughing to himself, or humming some old tune. He could neither read nor write, nor remember the time before he went down the pit, so all his conversations were on this one theme, and he constructed elaborate pieces of invective about some event that had happened years before. He would invariably greet the first man by with a set question, and a little formalized dialogue would take place:

'And how's him been, butty?' ('him' was the pit manager. This was occasionally rephrased as 'the bastard', but without any particularly violent connotation, being used merely as an accepted and perfectly natural description).

'Not too bad today, ol' un.' Pause. 'And how's your chest?'

'Middlin', middlin', butty.'

Only something as exciting as a severe accident at pit-bottom or a sudden change in the weather would upset the pattern of this conversation. The men were never very eager to stop and talk, since in their homes the tin baths had already been unhooked from the back-kitchen walls, and kettles would be boiling, ready for the scrub.

It is only when remembering the normal events of the past that even I fully realize the incredible changes that have taken place in the coal industry during and since the war . . .

The article goes on to detail these changes, the benefits of nationalization – though Potter's style now becomes rather hollow after this vivid word-painting. The Coal Board, he says, has 'engaged in a heavy investment programme . . . even in the smallest mines'; production has increased; 'our coal is cheaper than any other in Western Europe'; and 'the British miner . . . has gained a lead in efficiency and effort over his European counterparts'. There have also been 'amazing and sweeping changes in morale, habits and outlook' which have made Orwell's *The Road to Wigan Pier* obsolete, 'a piece of *history*'. The National Coal Board 'is to be congratulated on making a genuine effort to get to terms with the mining communities . . . [It has] kept to a very substantial degree the good will of the miners.' The article ends:

The morning shift still comes home at twenty-five past three, but not with black faces and steel-tipped boots. Pigeons and whippets are now rare pets; television aerials finger from the roofs; there has been only one fatal accident this year in my father's pit. Admass, of course, has seen to it that some of the changes have actually been for the worse, and I prefer the old whippet to Elvis Presley's 'Hound Dog'. But it is a strange thought that NCB of all organizations is mostly responsible for the thinly attended and faintly apologetic shuffle still called 'May Day Demonstration', an unrecognizably anaemic descendant of the long, hungry marches of the Thirties.

'Admass', the advertising-driven affluent society, was a concept much in the left-wing air this year, thanks to *The Hidden Persuaders*, a best-selling study by an American author, Vance Packard, of the sub-liminal influence of advertising on a susceptible public. Packard argued that society was being 'influenced and manipulated – far more so than we realize', by unscrupulous advertisers, who 'try to invade the privacy of our minds'. Potter cannot have been unaware of the book, though he does not acknowledge it in his own invective against advertising.

Kenith Trodd says of Potter's decision to expose, indeed flaunt, his family background as he does in the *Isis* article, 'I remember thinking, when we had both got to Oxford, that Dennis had better credentials than me – we were both working-class boys, but being a miner's son was more glamorous.' Potter himself wrote in 1963 that, soon after his arrival at Oxford, 'some unsuspected pride in my own class and back-ground made me deliberately seek to bring my own tensions out into the open. And then they didn't matter half so much.'

Later, he admitted that there had been a considerable element of self-conscious posing in his emphasis on being a miner's son. On *Desert Island Discs* in 1988 he said, 'There's nothing more terrifying than a young man on the make. And of course I was feeling these things, but at the same time I was manipulating the very feelings that I was in a sense enduring. Therefore I went out of my way [to say] "My father is a miner." Which of course is a slightly more complicated sort of betrayal.'

Two weeks after his article about the Forest miners appeared in *Isis*, he contributed to the magazine an exposé of electoral malpractice in university politics – a bold step for a first-year undergraduate. Among his allegations was that, in the Junior Common Room elections at University College (where of course Trodd was his informer), Conservative undergraduates from other colleges had been infiltrated in order to vote illegally. He also threw in a gratuitous insult to the future Labour MP and broadcaster Brian Walden, then an under-graduate at Queen's College – even though they were of the same political persuasion, Potter described Walden as 'a rather virulent and not very pleasant socialist'.

In the 1983 preface which first disclosed the sexual abuse, Potter writes of the emergence of a more aggressive side to his personality at Oxford: 'The pale, timid and precocious child, not too badly bullied, remained clever, and added aggression to a secret and misplaced arrogance.'

*

In his first summer vacation from New College, he stayed in London and worked on a 'depressingly busy W. H. Smith news-stall' in Kensington – depressing because to sell popular magazines made him feel 'slightly criminal'. Before returning to New College, he played rugby for Berry Hill – the first time he had reached the heights of the village team; he admitted that it was 'in difficulties (else I wouldn't have got into the side)'. He recalled being 'sick with fear and pride before my first game, for the whole village would replay the match throughout the next week'. The club's logbook recalls his performance on the field: 'October 5th, 1957: Dennis Potter, in his last game before returning to Oxford University, dribbled the ball over the Tedworth line, but lost possession . . . ' Tony Baldwin, who was in the team too, describes Dennis's performance – on and off the field:

We used to call him Ginge. If it was a wet day, he'd start the game by wallowing away like a whale, all over the field. So then he couldn't get any wetter or muddier. But then he was like that. When he came to my twenty-first birthday party, he fell down in the back doorway, so, being Dennis, he had to go and roll all over the lawn as well, so he was absolutely filthy.

The rugby field inflicted a minor injury on him. 'I was . . . once kicked rather savagely in the knee when playing rugby for Berry Hill against another Forest of Dean side . . . and it hurts when I keep it bent for very long.' He wrote this in 1961, the year before his psoriatic arthropathy began. The left knee was the first place it affected.

It was during one of his vacations in 1957 that he went, with a crowd of friends from Berry Hill, to a dance at Lydney, on the south side of the Forest. 'At Lydney . . . Town Hall . . . on a Saturday night,' he writes in *The Changing Forest*,

the young people crowd into the dance, taking a rubber stamp on the hand so that they can go out and return without paying again . . . A scratch dance band from the Forest, faces sweating against the pink light, syncopates a top-twenty number . . . I dislike going to dances, always saddened by the boy-trying-to-meet-girl endemic loneliness, competitive loneliness, of such affairs.

Two girls from Potter's part of the Forest, Margaret Morgan and Noreen Tye, were among the crowd that particular evening, and Noreen describes what happened next: 'There was a band called Squiz Bailey – Cyril Bailey was his name – and I think it was them playing. I remember particularly that we were sitting up on the balcony, looking down, and Dennis Potter and a couple of mates (I presume) came up the stairs. And he spotted us sitting there, and his eyes went to Margaret. And he started talking to her, and that's where it all began.'

Sarah Potter describes her mother's appearance at this time: 'Very slim build, about five feet three, quite dainty, very pretty. Brown hair, green eyes – the smoky green that Dad often described. She was a lot shorter than him – he was six feet.' Sarah's elder sister Jane says that her mother was engaged to someone else, 'but Dad stole her away, though the first time he came to call at her house, her mother said, "Doosn't go out with thik, him's got red hair."' Potter himself said that he had been instantly entranced by Margaret's 'green eyes, the flick of her hips, whatever, whatever, whatever. I decided that this was the person I wanted and that was it.'

Despite their Welsh surname, the Morgans had lived in the Coleford area of the Forest as long as anyone could remember – Margaret's paternal grandfather had kept a smallholding and a quarry. She was one of nine children. Her father had been a miner, invalided out of Cannop pit, where he had known Walt Potter slightly. She was born on 14 August 1933, a year and nine months before Dennis Potter. Like the rest of her family, she failed the Eleven Plus and left school in her mid-teens. She worked for a while as cashier in Pont & Adams's grocery in Coleford, then took an office job at Carter's factory near by, which made Ribena. 'We had a lot of fun at Carter's,' says Noreen Tye, who worked alongside her there. 'She used to pull faces at me, and we used to giggle. She was a really lively, intelligent girl.'

'We weren't a bad-looking family,' says Margaret's sister Mavis, who emphasizes that it was Margaret, rather than Dennis, who was regarded as a matrimonial 'catch' in the Forest. Noreen Tye says:

He was so young-looking – I thought, 'He seems a bit young for Margaret.' But I think she was probably quite intrigued with him, because he was at Oxford. And it seemed to develop from the moment they met that night.

After that, when he was home from Oxford, Margaret and I used to go to the Feathers Hotel in Lydney before going on to the dance, and Dennis used to join us there. He used to write her beautiful letters from Oxford – so descriptive – and she used to show them to me. They were beautiful.

None of the letters has survived.

June thinks Margaret was Dennis's first girlfriend, though at one time he took to going to church because there was a girl in the choir whom he fancied. 'But he never told her. And Margaret was the first girl he ever brought home.' She guesses that till then he had been 'too shy'. The year after he met Margaret, he wrote: 'I . . . construct elaborately exhausting, and perhaps even exhaustive, sexual fantasies (and then blush when I meet a girl) . . . '

On *Desert Island Discs*, he described his first date with Margaret, at the cinema:

You know, left arm, as it were, creeping round her shoulder, and seeing how far down the other arm it could go. Cigarette (as usual) in the other hand. And she had these luminous green eyes, and they swivelled at my cigarette smoke, and she was obviously irritated by it. And . . . I didn't have my glasses on in the cinema, because I was scared of not looking my best, so I couldn't actually see much of the film, and I was concentrating on her. And I thought, like a young fool, in a way – and yet I'm glad I did think it – that we were going to have a song . . . 'our song' . . . and it's 'Smoke Gets In Your Eyes'.

Sarah Potter says:

Although Dad had made his choice, I think at the beginning Mum wasn't that interested in him. But he pursued her, and won her over. She was attracted by his gentleness and shyness. He was awkward – he'd always tread on her toes when they were dancing. But there was clearly something that she was very drawn to.

I think, from what Dad said, one of the reasons he was so taken with her was that she was very at ease in all sorts of company. And *he* wasn't. He drew quite a strength from her in that respect. She was very open, very warm – if she was talking to you now, she'd touch you on the arm, draw you in, because of her warmth. In other words she was all the things that he wasn't.

*

At the beginning of his second year at Oxford, he moved into lodgings at 104 Divinity Road, off the Cowley Road in east Oxford. He also became editor of *Clarion*, the journal of the Labour Club. A year later, *Isis* reported, 'When he took over *Clarion* . . . it had very nearly been shut down by the E[xecutive] C[ommittee] because of its low circulation. Potter savaged the contents and the format and doubled the circulation.' Unfortunately all copies of the magazine from the period of his editorship seem to have disappeared, though we know from a mention in *The Glittering Coffin* that he persuaded the Labour politician Richard Crossman to write for one issue. He was helped by another undergraduate, the Labour MP Maurice Edelman's daughter Natasha, who describes working with Potter as 'like being in a room with electricity'.

He also became joint features editor of *Isis*, and, to the first issue of the 1957 Michaelmas term, contributed an article on the Wolfenden Report on Homosexual Offences and Prostitution, which had just been published. Noting that 'nearly 40 per cent agree with the recommendation that homosexual behaviour between consenting adults in private should no longer be a criminal offence', and that 'public opinion is slowly but surely advancing to the acceptance of a rational attitude', he continued:

Inevitably the natural reaction of all of us who find the thought of homosexual behaviour repulsive or difficult to comprehend will be a troubled one . . . Homosexuals tend to bring forward all kinds of defences to justify this pattern of living, whether from the facts of history or the claims of the strength and beauty of this type of relationship. Under the burden of a savage criminal law, these defences have often seemed to border on the hysterical, while the homosexual has become an increasingly sympathetic figure in the novel.

The article gives no hint that he had been an unwilling juvenile victim of a homosexual act. After his initial statement of repulsion and incomprehension, he showed a detached curiosity:

. . . one is struck by the paucity of evidence and the narrowness of its scope. Wouldn't it have been worthwhile to have called together research sociologists, psychiatrists and psychologists to sift more evidence in the Kinsey manner, and assemble known facts from the vast literature on sexual behaviour? . . . it is scandalous that there is no permanent research institution with the task of exploring the complexities and problems of sex and the social order.

Then he turned to the Wolfenden committee's findings on prostitution. He agreed that 'these wretched women had to be cleared from the streets as far as was possible', but doubted that prison sentences would do any good. He regretted that the report did not devote much space to discussing the legalization of brothels:

If trading in sex is admitted to be inevitable, there is surely a great deal to be said for a legal and regulated trade rather than the kind of squalid black market that now exists. True, the thought appears particularly appalling in an English setting, thanks to our lack of rationality towards sex, and one can almost imagine some great grey establishment floating off the Bayswater Road with brown Ministry of Health posters on its whitewashed walls.

A week later he wrote his first *Isis* report on the Union, which had been debating the motion 'that this House has confidence in the Conservative Party'. Potter clearly had none; he cited the 'horrifying picture of tweedy women and debs' mums howling for blood' given by one speaker against the motion, Anthony Howard (a former President of the Union, now doing National Service), and mocked the Tory participants in the debate.

Two undergraduates wrote to *Isis* to complain of his anti-Tory bias, observing that 'your correspondent is a member of the Labour Club Committee'. Potter replied in his next Union report, 'I have been accused of undue political bias in this column, but anyone who could make a presentable case for the Conservative arguments from the floor is welcome to try – without being rude, that is.' This time he was equally abusive to speakers on both sides. The following month, *Isis* reported that, in the Labour Club elections, Ken Trodd had been returned unopposed as chairman, and Potter was one of two candidates for secretary (he was unsuccessful).

He acted again in the New College entry for 'Cuppers', taking the part of the author in Ionesco's *The Shepherd's Chameleon* – a one-acter about a harassed playwright. John Fuller (the future poet), who was the stage manager, says, 'Dennis played the part like a troubled left-wing writer, which we realized later wasn't what Ionesco himself was like at all.'

Also in the cast was Roger Smith, who had come up to New College this term, and quickly became friends with Potter (whose first television play he would later commission). 'In some senses, I have rather a similar background to Dennis,' he says.

I was born in 1937 in south-east London, the Old Kent Road. My father was a progress chaser in factories. Later we lived in Sydenham, and I went to a school called Henry Thornton's, where the painter Tom Phillips was – it was a strange gathering of rather able people. But I was unusual at the school for getting into Oxford. I did Russian during National Service too. It was in the army that I met my first public schoolboy.

Smith says that, like Potter, he had few working-class friends at Oxford, preferring the company of the public schoolboys: 'They were far more radical than the majority of the grammar schoolboys, who were just *grateful* to be at Oxford, which I couldn't stand. Ironically the Old Etonians tended to belong to the Left.'

Smith took over Potter's old rooms in the Holywell building of New College, and first came to know him during the 'Cuppers' production. 'Dennis was a bit uncontrolled on stage,' he says. But Jonathan Cecil 'overheard two girls in the audience who were obviously very impressed by Dennis – they were saying: "Who is he? He looks so poetic, so passionate."' Cecil continues:

Dennis's appearance at this time certainly was quite startling. He was tall and rather Celtic-looking, with a shock of red hair and (like so many redheads) very pale skin. He had a fine-boned build, and his voice was very pleasing, with its definite Forest of Dean burr, which he wasn't making any attempt to suppress – except possibly when he was acting (he didn't go in for the 'proletarian' style on stage; it hadn't yet come into fashion). As to clothes, I think he probably favoured corduroys. There would usually be rather a bright tie, probably red to make his political affiliation clear. He looked 'artistic' but not in the dowdy sense; I'd say he was poetic-looking, a classic left-wing poet.

In late November 1957 a scandal burst upon Oxford, with Potter at the centre of it. This was the *Cherwell* front page story:

'FILTHY SMEAR' SHOUTS WALDEN IN UNION RIOT
Potter Alleges Corruption

The President of the Oxford Union, Brian Walden (Queen's and Nuffield) is to sue Dennis Potter (New College) for what he described in the Union on Thursday night as 'a gross and grave libel'.

Potter, in an article written for *Isis* but not published, accused Walden of trying to influence the forthcoming elections. Potter alleges that he was summoned to an interview by Walden who gave him information reflecting upon Rudolf D'Mello (Pembroke), who is expected to be a candidate for the presidency, intending that it should be published.

The issue was raised during Private Business, when Stephen Hugh-Jones, last term's editor of *Isis*, asked Walden whether he had given Potter an interview in which he made charges against one of the candidates standing for the presidency next term.

Commenting that 'it was the most disgusting question I have ever heard', Walden denied the charges. 'The facts', he said, 'are entirely and absolutely different.'

Walden's version was that Potter had asked to see him to get his comments on the candidates. He had not seen Potter's draft article for *Isis*, but he gathered that Potter had put words into his mouth. *Isis* had dropped the article on legal advice, but as the contents had become widely known, Walden intended to sue. 'Walden's statement in his own defence brought an ovation from the House,' the *Cherwell* report continued,

but Kenneth Trodd (Univ.) rose unconvinced. He asked for a full discussion of these charges at next week's debate . . .

Potter was then called to the dispatch [*sic*] box. 'Either the president or myself', he said, 'are lying.' According to Potter, the interview had taken place at Walden's request, and for three-quarters of an hour, Walden had discussed the age, sex life, and morals of Rudolf D'Mello (Pembroke), the treasurer. Walden had said that D'Mello was 'the worst candidate in the history of the Union'.

'I don't care if I am concerned in a libel action,' Potter declared, 'but I will do anything to prove the truth of this article.'

After Potter's death, Stephen Hugh-Jones, writing in *The Economist*, recalled how he, Potter and Trodd had hatched the plan to accuse Walden at a late-night session in Trodd's digs – and he had ended up uncomfortably sharing a bed with Potter: 'Planning done, the hour was late, their lodgings far, and transport non-existent. Trodd invited his visitors to stay, but wisely took the sofa himself, offering them half-shares of an uncapacious bed.'

As well as carrying the front page story, *Cherwell* ran an interview with Walden in which he said, 'I would have liked to have got my hands on Potter's throat . . . I am a poor man but if I have to sell everything I have I will pull his bluff and get that apology in the courts if necessary.' The *Isis* editorial (by the current editor, Robert Symmons) commented:

If Potter is in the right, he did his duty to the Union Society by bringing this matter forward; if the accusations are untrue, Walden has behaved properly in treating them seriously . . . Potter, at any rate, if his accusations are true, appears to have acted in an entirely disinterested way for the benefit of the Society, for he had nothing to gain personally, and everything to lose, by making them.

The editorial mentioned that the affair had got 'into the national Press'; there had been reports in the *Daily Express* and the *News*

Chronicle, and on the BBC's regional radio news, and the *Oxford Mail* remarked that the Union had not seen such uproar since the 'King and Country' debate before the war.

The Union now appointed a three-man tribunal to examine Potter's allegations against Walden, and this decided that both parties were in the wrong: 'We cannot wholly divorce the fault on Mr Potter's side from that on Mr Walden's,' states the Union minute book, observing that 'the sooner the affair is forgotten the better'. But Potter came out of it untarnished. Peter Jay, who had come up to Christ Church from Winchester, and had joined the Labour Club, says, 'Dennis had this capacity for making people feel that what he thought was not merely right, but an expression of moral truth.' Kenneth Baker, future Tory cabinet minister, then a Magdalen undergraduate, observes, 'We [the Tories] said, "That's how it always happens in the Labour Party." While Dennis and Brian were at fisticuffs, we, on the other hand, just sat back and indulged in discreet electoral malpractice!'

Walden evidently harboured little resentment against Potter,* since the final debate of that term was on the motion 'that Truth is never put to the worst in a free and open contest'. Participants included Walden himself, Alan Brien, and Potter, making his first Union appearance as a 'paper' (advertised) speaker. Unfortunately *Isis* did not report on the debate, so there is no knowing what was said.

At the end of that term, Potter's economics tutor at New College, Peter Wiles, wrote a 'Collections' report which took account of Potter's increasing fame – the Union story had now reached *The Sunday Times* and *Observer*:

Like an experimental machine made of glass: every emotion, thought and emotional thought (for he doesn't distinguish) can be watched forming & expressing itself. He is an endless spectacle.

General level alpha beta. Would rise to alpha treble minus if fewer libel cases, left-wing views, proctorial imbroglios, amateur dramatics, social inferiority complexes, etc., etc.

Pointless as it now seems, the Potter–Walden affair had the immediate result of making Potter famous throughout the university. The first *Isis* of the next term, on 22 January 1958, ran a comic New Year Honours, in which he was given 'life-membership of the Union

---

* Though he declines to discuss the Walden–Potter affair today.

Society'. The magazine also announced that he had become its assistant editor. Lewis Rudd of Magdalen (later a television executive) was now the editor. 'My stuff was absolute crap,' says Rudd. 'He was a much better writer than me.'

Potter's first signed contribution in his new role was the opening article in a series of *Isis* forays against 'Top People' (a current catchphrase, from the advertising slogan 'Top People Read *The Times*'). He chose to attack the trade unions, which he said were failing to resist the Labour Party's dilution of its principles as it struggled to regain power from the Conservatives, who had been in office since 1951. The influence of Hoggart was visible here and in his next *Isis* article, which attacked women's magazines for their limited picture of the world – Potter observed that they excluded 'such sordid things as politics or hydrogen bombs'. He had now called for a Labour Club petition for nuclear disarmament; this became a referendum to be distributed to every undergraduate. 'I took the forms round New College,' Potter writes in *The Glittering Coffin*, 'and although a few bloodies were provoked into their usual startled braying, the heartening thing was the revelation of the serious approach and genuine argument offered by many undergraduates . . . ' Soon after the referendum – in which only half the forms were returned – he wrote in *Isis*, 'I have never been ashamed to admit that I want to make a career in politics.'

In the summer term of 1958, at the end of his second year, he became editor of *Isis* (chosen for the job by his predecessor, Lewis Rudd). His first editorial attacked the Fleet Street journalists who had been hanging about Oxford in the hope of picking up stories about the nuclear referendum – it was being alleged that a Soviet spy ring was behind it:

Anyone who has had the slightest contact with national newspaper reporters has been left appalled by their standards . . . Oxford seems to suffer a high 'news value' . . . and always this 'news' is inflated or distorted . . . Undergraduates cannot help taking themselves seriously when Fleet Street is so ridiculous.

Yet he was not exactly spurning Fleet Street himself. Four days after this issue of *Isis* was published, the *New Statesman* carried an article by him headed 'Base Ingratitude?'

The article was concerned with his complicated feelings about 'being a coalminer's son . . . among the dreaming spires'. After satirizing the attitudes of fellow undergraduates ('"Now look," initial finger eagerly jabbing, "simply by being a member of New College you cannot possibly be a member of the working classes"'), he went on:

At home, my parents grew away as I grew up; not their fault or mine . . . By now, my father is forced to communicate with me, much of the time, with an edgy kind of shyness, possibly tinged with contempt as well as admiration, rarely flashing into the real stuff except when one of us is angry or inebriated.

Sometimes, he said, he wished he had 'left school at fifteen'.

Then came a passage that astonished his Oxford friends:

When I leave Oxford, I am going to get married to a girl from home, with exactly the same background as myself, the daughter of a man invalided out of the pit at which my father works, although she had her life determined differently at the age of eleven, thanks to a criminally stupid education system . . .

When my girl first came up to Oxford to meet some of my friends, it was something of a strain for both . . . She must have felt like I once felt as a private in the officers' mess.

The article ended with Potter asking whether 'the ingratitude of the miner's son at Oxford' was, or was not, 'some kind of betrayal'.

One of Potter's New College contemporaries, David Cocks (now a barrister), says that before this *New Statesman* article appeared he had liked Potter hugely. However, the 'private in the officers' mess' remark completely misrepresented the way that Margaret Morgan had been treated when Dennis brought her to Oxford. It began to make Cocks feel that Potter was opportunistic, exploiting other people to his own ends. Roger Smith agrees: 'He'd set up this thing about Margaret in what I felt was an offensive way. And I can see why David Cocks and the others got pissed off.'

Trodd suggests that Potter's speedy decision to marry Margaret was

one way of not dealing with the difficulties of being a scholarship boy at Oxford. It was a problem all we working-class undergraduates had: getting a girlfriend at Oxford meant, by definition, getting a posh one – there must have been some girls from grammar schools, but I don't remember any. So to get a sexual relationship, you had to cut through the class problem. But Dennis foreclosed this by marrying a back-home girl.

Roger Smith recalls:

When he was editor of *Isis*, Dennis took on a really very attractive upper-middle-class girl called Dinah, and she was a knockout, and fancied him. And he was terrified. And that was one of the reasons he got married to Margaret, I think. Dinah used to sit on the table in the *Isis* office, swinging her legs – terrific legs – with slightly crumpled stockings, loose, which just made you want to take them off. But his reaction was puritan. And he rushed back to the Forest and got married.

Jonathan Cecil recalls Dinah too: 'She seemed to be demented about Dennis, and he couldn't cope with this at all.'

Potter's 'miner's son at Oxford' image was now beginning to irritate other undergraduates from grammar schools. Lewis Rudd observes sarcastically, 'Dennis . . . was always The Only Person With a Humble Background at Oxford.' John Fuller agrees: 'We all thought Dennis protested too much.' The writer Alan Garner, who had come from a Cheshire rural working-class background, and was now reading classics at Magdalen, met Potter briefly and found his aggressive stance on class 'obnoxious'.

Potter knew he was causing offence. In a memorable passage in *The Glittering Coffin*, he writes, 'Talking about class in highly personal terms is a shocking and embarrassing thing for an Englishman to do. There is a kind of pornography about the subject, an atmosphere of whispered asides and lowered eyes. It is too much like small boys discussing sex in the school playground.'

Two days after the *New Statesman* article had appeared, Potter received a telegram: 'REGARDING YOUR LETTER [*sic*] IN NEW STATESMAN PLEASE TELEPHONE ME AT BBC SHEPHERDS BUSH 1244 AS SOON AS POSSIBLE – JACK ASHLEY'. Ashley, the future Labour MP, was then a producer in the BBC's Television Talks department. Potter telephoned, and was invited to take part in a forthcoming series of documentaries, *Does Class Matter?* Although in an *Isis* article a few weeks earlier he had sneered at television – 'everyone is looking at the telly . . . No conversation, apart from occasional grunting and noddings' – he accepted Ashley's invitation, thereby making his first contact with the medium to which he would devote his life.

CHAPTER 6

Probably one of the leaders
of the next generation

▰

Potter appointed Roger Smith as his news assistant on *Isis*, and Trodd as the political correspondent. However, Trodd's first article for him was on popular music, under the title 'Smoke Gets In Your Eyes?' In retrospect, it looks like a manifesto for *Pennies from Heaven*, twenty years later.

Trodd began by describing the average undergraduate's contempt for Tin Pan Alley: 'We may have heard a song or two which stayed in the mind . . . but, as one of Noël Coward's drawing-room layabouts remarked, "cheap music can be so potent".' Trodd admitted that some 1958 hit songs were meaningless, but argued that

many Pops communicate *genuine* emotion, and encapsulate the tang, the 'atmosphere' of their mood and period to a degree which seems to contradict the shoddiness of their raw materials . . . In the Thirties, the image was largely middle class, evening dressed . . . The dance bands which marketed the tunes were based on smart West End restaurants . . . one of Lew Stone's best-selling records was called simply '10.30 Tuesday Night'. The songs' milieu was supra suburban, their ideal the cosy wedded bliss of the folks who live on the hill . . .

Trodd concluded that, for all their triviality, popular songs were 'one use of literacy which is not entirely abuse'.

Two undergraduate members of the Labour Party, William Miller and Paul Thompson, who had contributed to an *Isis* issue on nuclear disarmament, were now being questioned by the authorities. They had been on the National Service Russian course and worked at the Admiralty, and were suspected of having breached the Official Secrets Act by supplying information on Cold War strategy for the *Isis* articles. Potter wrote in *Isis* that there are many disturbing things about this case ... People who were on the Russian course were interviewed, and apparently one of the questions was, 'And what did *you* do to stop this article being published?' I was on the Russian course. Let's all spy on each other.

By the time the next issue of *Isis* appeared, on 7 May 1958, Miller and Thompson had been charged by the Special Branch. Potter opened the issue with a short, bleak editorial headed 'Defence Fund':

Incredible though it seems, events have lurched beyond the reach of balanced comment ... Obviously the two people charged have the prior claim to our attention ... A committee is now in busy and approved existence to help them. They feel, and the *Isis* staff feel, that so far as we are concerned, this case must not be made into a political issue (difficult, and almost impossible, but necessary) ... All that is needed for the time being is money, and needed badly ... Some people have been spirited enough to send us money already. Thank you. May we be sent more, please, as soon as possible?

The following week, Potter announced that letters of support for the accused men had been received from J. B. Priestley, John Berger, Kenneth Tynan, Christopher Logue, Doris Lessing, Enid Starkie and other prominent supporters of the new Campaign for Nuclear Disarmament; but the captain of the University Boat Club thought Miller and Thompson ought to be strung up. 'We're so glad that we lost the Boat Race,' was Potter's riposte. The defence fund eventually reached £541. Miller and Thompson went on trial at the Old Bailey during the summer vacation, and were given three-month prison sentences.

Meanwhile Trodd, in *Isis*, was laying into the monarchy, describing the Royal Family as 'a prop to the pink-tinted pillars of the dry-rotting Establishment'. The proprietors of the magazine, the local printing firm the Holywell Press, added a notice dissociating themselves from this article, and appended a similar disclaimer later in the term to an *Isis* exposé of Freemasonry. Potter later claimed that, during his term as editor, he was warned by the Proctors that 'medieval wrath would descend upon us if we produced any more articles like the now infamous "Frontier Incidents" [the article that had led to charges against Miller and Thompson], or gave, in their own words "propaganda against the West"'. On the other hand he had decided that the first Union debate report under his editorship should be by a well-known Conservative undergraduate, Adrian Berry (whose family owned the *Daily Telegraph*). It elicited a letter to *Isis* complaining of Tory bias; to which Potter belligerently responded, 'We are glad that our readers are not satisfied.'

Berry had just founded another Oxford magazine, a satirical weekly called *Parson's Pleasure* (he soon handed it over to Richard Ingrams and Paul Foot). In its first issue (27 May 1958) it commented on Potter's editorship of *Isis*: 'The present editor seems resolved to turn it into a more literary version of *Tribune*, employing for the purpose the techniques of distortion and near mendacity which he attacks so fiercely in the popular press and a collection of writers of obscure talent but obvious political bias.' The issue of 10 June included an 'exposé' of *Isis* and its editor by another Oxford Tory, Humphry Crum Ewing, who made a shrewd assessment of Potter's character:

The show is run ... by the first *Isis* man to succeed in looking like a journalist since Philip French [later a BBC producer and film critic]. But of course 'beneath that rugged exterior beats a heart of – '. He's a sensitive youth is Dennis Potter. His frequent displays of histrionics are not the product of a domineering megalomaniac, but of a slightly hysterical, soft-centred, anxiety-complex-ridden Make-Gooder with a winning way with his underlings.

Meanwhile Potter's *Isis* editorial of 4 June denied that he and his friends were simply being Angry Young Men – a fashionable label of the time, in the wake of John Osborne's 1956 play *Look Back in Anger*:

'Are you going all angry this term?' someone asked. 'All these attacks, the Bomb, the Monarchy, the Establishment, and so forth, bit of a gimmick, isn't it?' NO! Maybe the big emotional orgies have disappeared, as Jimmy Porter raves [in Osborne's play], but a great greyness has blanketed all the rest – Admass, a diluted Welfare State, a sense of shame and disillusion, contempt for authority, a widespread desire to emigrate or cheat ... a feeling of the flatness and bleakness of everyday England ...

We have seen people a little older than ourselves shed many of their ideals, and make too many concessions. Happy little copywriters ...

Brize Norton H-bombers fly over the dreaming spires and the new Woolworth's, and the Conservative women dedicate themselves to restoring full capital punishment, or even the cat. Doesn't it all make you sick? Or does it make you certain of the need to be awake and articulate, pompous perhaps, but *alive*?

Despite Potter's denial, this was the language of Osborne's hero.

Jonathan Cecil says of his first encounters with Potter, 'I thought, "My God, here's a man actually talking like the character in *Look Back in Anger*."'

Potter was now hoping to succeed Trodd as chairman of the Labour Club. According to *Isis*, he had an unusual manifesto: the Club should not 'drift along with constituency-type electoral harangues', but should redirect its energy into such things as performing Brecht, holding a films evening, and achieving 'some recognition of the political importance of literature'. He said he wanted to have 'dictatorial powers' over the Executive Committee, and added, 'I'd rather ruin the Labour Club in an exciting way, than carry on yawning.' Not surprisingly he was defeated by a more conventional candidate. *Parson's Pleasure* wondered why he had scuppered his chances so clumsily.

At the end of his term editing *Isis*, he would, by tradition, nominate his successor; but on 14 June 1958 *Cherwell* reported that Potter and the entire staff of *Isis* had been sacked by the proprietors. Potter claimed that the Holywell Press had wanted to set up a panel of censors to vet all articles, to be chaired by Hugh Trevor-Roper, Professor of Modern History. 'Meanwhile,' continued *Cherwell*,

Potter is moving his left-wing platform to *Clarion* [the journal of the Labour Club], which will appear fortnightly under his editorship. He has refused to edit next week's *Isis*. 'I would willingly have done so if Whitford, the managing director of the Press, had allowed me to attack his policy in an editorial.'

He described Whitford's attempts to get him to increase coverage of university sport as 'ridiculous'. Ken Trodd was quoted too: 'We've had arguments with Whitford over every article we've wanted to put in this term.'

The Holywell Press now printed its own version of events in *Isis*, alleging that Potter had 'dismissed himself by the well-tried method of "staging a walkout"'. They regretted that under Potter's editorship *Isis* had attacked traditional institutions and become 'definitely left wing'. (John Fuller, who served as the magazine's literary editor that term, says that Whitford was also annoyed because Potter had turned a portrait of his father to face the wall.)

Once again the national press picked up the story. *Time & Tide* observed that, under Potter's editorship, *Isis* had become 'exactly the kind of magazine which must be produced at Moscow University'. There was an article and letters in the *Spectator*, and a *Daily Express* reporter wrote:

Mr Hugh Trevor-Roper, Regius Professor of Modern History, sat at home last night awaiting an apology from undergraduate Mr Dennis Potter. Unless the twenty-three-year-old miner's son makes a public withdrawal of 'violent and hysterical' attacks he has made in print on the professor, he faces being sent down.

He seems to have made the apology, but he took his revenge in *The Glittering Coffin*, where he described Trevor-Roper as one of 'a long line of notable Oxford oddities . . . hollow figures'.

He made a second appearance in the *New Statesman* on 21 June to give his own version of the *Isis* affair:

The Oxford undergraduate magazine *Isis* is, by the decision of its middle-aged proprietors, to cease being a radical and serious weekly . . . Last week the directors . . . decided to make a break with tradition, and refused to accept the nomination of any member of this term's staff as the next editor. They also informed me, as editor, that they were disgusted and offended with the socialism which had marked *Isis* of recent years, and that this drift must be halted . . .

Somewhere lurks that growing fear of vigour and rebellion that is coming to stain this sterile, conformist society of ours . . . The managing director of the press that produces *Isis* has been quoted in the newspapers as saying that he is 'for this country as it stands', a peculiarly repulsive statement . . .

Isis used to be a preserve for smart young men in gaily coloured waist-coats – bright, cynical, full of gossip and puerile chatter . . . Suez, however, was a shock . . . For the first time many undergraduates realized that politics was much too important a thing to be left to the government . . . *Isis* inevitably caught this mood . . .

With Brize Norton bombers carrying H-bombs flying over the changing Oxford skyline, and the hideous new Woolworth's like an overgrown juke-box squatting in the Cornmarket, *Isis* was not out of tone. It had to shout, and the fact that it has been muffled is a shameful comment on the fears and prejudices of those who refuse to see what is happening around them.

*

During that summer term, on 16 May 1958, a BBC film crew had come to New College to film Potter for *Does Class Matter?*, with Jack Ashley producing and the Labour MP Christopher Mayhew as interviewer. Ashley says he took quickly to Potter – 'There was an unspoken rapport' – and Mayhew was hugely impressed by him:

I thought he was brilliantly intelligent, spiky, ambitious. And these things were so obvious as to be almost endearing – they made you want to help him. His conversation was the real thing (I never went for his written prose style). He was an obvious choice for our Class series, and proved a good television interviewee, though he was very nervous, very keen to do well.

The interview, for which Potter was paid three guineas, was to appear in the second programme in the series, entitled 'Class in Private Life'. (The first had examined 'Class Boundaries', money, education, job and accent.) In an opening voice-over, Mayhew spoke of people who were experiencing the problems of spanning the class gulf, and went on, 'Let's have a look at some of these people – starting at New College, Oxford.' Potter was seen walking across the quadrangle, while Mayhew said, 'Here one of the undergraduates is a miner's son from the Forest of Dean, Mr Dennis Potter. In Mr Potter's life we see the problem of social class in its modern setting.' Mayhew then interviewed a strikingly self-assured and confident-looking Potter, in his college rooms:

MAYHEW: Mr Potter, you are very much aware of class at Oxford?

POTTER: Yes, I am. For example, if you take the first week of coming up for the new term and also the first week of the vac[ation] in leaving Oxford, I think then the tensions become most obvious to myself. I mean, when I first came up to Oxford, for example, I was very happy to do so. I wanted in fact to enter into this new way of life and to leave my own background, and when I did come up I looked around my New College room, very big and comfortable and happy, and then there was the inevitable knock on the door, and the scout, that's the college servant, came in and he called me 'sir', in a way not like the shopkeepers call you 'sir', if you know what I mean, but with more deference than that. In fact I felt for the first time what it was like to be called 'sir' from a position of – of a class position, in fact. And it was this, not only with the relationship with the scout, which I personally found embarrassing, because I wanted him to think in fact that I was not from the working classes. I wanted to make it quite clear that my insecurity, which I did feel, should not be conveyed to the college scout. Similarly with Hall – I mean, the first evening in college one goes in a dark gown, there's silver, there's a Latin prayer from the high table, and long tables with people opposite you talking about the relative merits of two European cities, or something – an accent, in fact, that was completely different, that's startling in its difference, and it makes you feel uncomfortable.

MAYHEW: Do you want to become classless, Mr Potter?

POTTER: No. Well, I did at one stage, I think, like most people from the working classes want to get away from the working class, but I certainly want to keep a sense of identity, as it were, with that background.

MAYHEW: Do you tend to get together a bit, then, with people in your own position?

POTTER: Well, I think initially, yes, this is inevitable. The trouble in a place like New College is that 75 per cent of the undergraduates, I should say, are from the public schools, and they greet each other in a way that seems – that this, in fact, is just a continuation of their way of life, as it were. Whereas you see the *other* people – you can see them somehow, it's just perhaps the way they lower their eyes in a conversation, or something. You recognize that they're like you, and you talk to them.

MAYHEW: What about your home, then, Mr Potter?

POTTER: Well, tensions exist at home just as much as at Oxford, only in this sense, of course, they are far more urgent, far more personal of their kind, because family relationships are at stake, long-term personal relationships. I mean, by now my father is forced to communicate with me almost, as it were, with a kind of contempt, now and again. It is inevitable. I mean, he does everything he can possibly do to get through to me, and I to him, but it is just that our circumstances make this communication rather difficult. I mean, he is likely to ask me a question through my mother, for example. And a little thing like the allocation of radio time – it might seem small, petty. If I want something on which is likely to be – in fact very often is – very different from what the rest of the family want, then, well, this is likely to spotlight the tensions far more than any [sic]. The little petty things like that. I mean, I have a row with my sister, inevitably, over whether we should have something like *Life with the Lyons** on, or not. And, well, I – it's at times like this that I think, oh, darn, why does one have one way of life, and you just can't come to terms with it ever again?

There's a new kind of classlessness which I am now, thanks to being at Oxford, quite incapable of ever wanting. And I thought that I could keep these two worlds apart, neatly, almost callously. There's home, and there's Oxford. Both have their tensions, but I always kidded myself that

* A comedy show on the BBC Light Programme.

I have a certain kind of ability, and I can get through without bothering too much about the tensions. I can overcome them, in fact. But it is impossible, in fact, to change from one way of life to another without dragging a lot of people with you. In particular, when I felt it in its most personal and important [*sic*], was with my girlfriend from Gloucestershire, and she's got exactly the same background as I have. Her father was a coalminer, and her whole family background is exactly the same as mine, except that she left school at fifteen. Her whole life was determined differently, at the age of eleven, by one silly little exam. Well, when she came up to Oxford, I could see the tensions between her and my friends. My friends at New College, by some chance, happen to be people who went to Winchester, Rugby and Eton. They are very nice people. I am now at ease with these people, but she wasn't. And they weren't at ease with her. And it was this division between the two which only I could somehow see properly, and I could see both sides, as it were. I felt torn. For the first time I didn't have – to say – use one language at Oxford and one language at home. I never talk about Oxford at home, for example, because somehow one would be using a qualitative kind of language. One would be saying that Oxford was better or something. And I rarely talk about home at Oxford, simply because you can't just communicate a whole medium of experience which people haven't got, for the most part.

Later in the programme, Mayhew spoke to Richard Hoggart, who had seen the interview with Potter, and called it 'most moving' in its depiction of the 'tensions and stresses' he had experienced himself. Yet later, in *Stand Up, Nigel Barton*, Potter's *alter ego* Nigel suggests that his performance in front of the camera in a similar interview had a degree of glibness and artificiality: 'All the time . . . I was – well, sort of *calculating*.'

*

About a month before transmission, a reporter from the popular Sunday newspaper *Reynolds News* asked Ashley for a transcript of the programme. Ashley let him see it, and on 3 August the paper carried the headline 'MINER'S SON AT OXFORD FELT ASHAMED OF HOME: THE BOY WHO KEPT HIS FATHER SECRET'. The reporter had called on Margaret Morgan, who told him, 'Dennis is very sincere. I'm a socialist like he is, though I'm not sure that it would be a good idea to have one of his Oxford friends as best man at our wedding. He wouldn't be quite in place down here.' Walt Potter was quoted as saying, 'There's no snobbery in Dennis. I don't think he has grown apart any more than any son does who is away for a few years. He's still got the old Forest twang and he plays in the rugby team when he comes home.' Jack Ashley had allegedly told the reporter, 'Potter should not have tried to conceal his background. I made it clear at Cambridge that I was not ashamed of my origins.'

In *The Glittering Coffin*, Potter calls the *Reynolds News* story 'humiliating and painful . . . nasty', and writes, 'I shall never forget the moment when I came down the stairs in stockinged feet that Sunday morning to hear my mother reading out that headline to the assembled household, or the momentary bewilderment on my father's face as he turned to me.' He protested to Mayhew and Ashley about the disclosure of the interview in advance of screening, and Mayhew sent him a telegram: 'JACK ASHLEY AND I SHARE YOUR STRONG RESENTMENT REYNOLDS ARTICLE AND DENY REMARKS ATTRIBUTED TO US STOP CONSIDER ARTICLE WILL BE COMPLETELY DISCREDITED WHEN ACTUAL INTERVIEW SHOWN STOP PROTESTING TO EDITOR.'

Does Class Matter? was transmitted on 25 August 1958. The next *Isis* described the Potter interview as 'a rare bright spot in a glum series'. Potter summarizes the reviews in *The Glittering Coffin*:

Philip Phillips of the *Daily Herald* went to town with a bit of misplaced moralizing – 'the things education can do for a lad! . . .' Thank God, the *Observer* and the *Listener* were generous enough to see the dilemmas I was attempting to describe, while the *Universities & Left Review* commented that 'it seems to be a minor art of television producers to milk off just the exact amount of information and personality they require in a specific situation so that not an atom more peeps through. What is needed to make a general point is extracted; the germ of the human being is discarded. That is why it's so refreshing when an occasional individual slips unseen through the producer's net – as happened in this case with Dennis Potter. Considering how little time he was allowed, and how complex and important the problem he was trying to describe, this was a rare achievement.'

A BBC Audience Research Report on the programme came to the same conclusion: 'Of those interviewed, the Oxford undergraduate made the most favourable impression . . .' Compared to the other wooden interviews in the series, Potter's contribution does indeed stand out for its candour and clarity.

He decided to issue a writ for libel against *Reynolds News*, and a BBC solicitor met the paper's lawyer, who agreed that the headline had been 'inaccurate and possibly defamatory', and that there had been further inaccuracies in the article. *Reynolds* printed an apology, and paid Potter's legal costs 'with an immediate generosity' (he writes in *The Glittering Coffin*) 'which restored my considerable respect for what is undoubtedly the best "popular" Sunday newspaper'.

Meanwhile Mayhew had asked Potter to help him write a book based on the series. 'I couldn't possibly have written it by myself,' he explains. 'I was far too busy combining Parliament with working at the BBC. I put it to Dennis that, with all the material from the series, it would be an easy task for him to help me do it.'

On 15 July 1958 Mayhew wrote to the publishers George Allen & Unwin, 'The book is going well and I have every hope that we shall finish it by the end of September – Dennis Potter is putting a tremendous amount of work into it.' But six weeks later, Mayhew told the publisher, 'I am sorry to say that work on the book is progressing terribly slowly. Dennis Potter is sending me stuff pretty regularly; but it will need a lot of work doing on it . . . At the same time, my ideas for the book are getting rather more ambitious.'

In October, Mayhew wrote to Potter:

I knew that the BBC were going to offer you a job. If you have not already heard – the Director-General [Sir Ian Jacob] rang up himself immediately after your interview with me was broadcast and made the suggestion that you might be taken on the staff! I am sure I ought not to have told you this, so don't let anybody know. As you already know perfectly well, it is a hard job in every sense, TV broadcasting. But if you have something to say, there is simply nothing to compare with it – neither writing, sound radio, public speaking, nor anything else.

However, Mayhew soon decided that the book collaboration was not working. 'The trouble was, Dennis kept sending me reams and reams of his *own* views on class – about fifty thousand words of it in all – whereas he was supposed to be editing other people's contributions to the series.' He wrote to Potter in late November saying he was thinking of calling the project off. Potter replied on 30 November:

Dear Christopher,

Thank you for your letter, and for your warm remarks about my coming marriage and future prospects. Yes, I am feeling pretty content with the world – and, on the smaller but personally satisfying level, have just been elected Chairman of the University Labour Club and the Union Standing Committee. Of course, I am up to my neck with work for both Schools and my book [he was writing *The Glittering Coffin*] but term ends on Friday, which will be something of a relief!

I cannot hide the fact that I was terribly disappointed and rather bewildered to find that you are thinking of abandoning your book. That feeling was inevitable I suppose – spending so long on it, neglecting academic work and so on, and I really do care that people should think about 'class', since it obviously exists. Honestly, my disappointment is not over failing to see my name in print – I really *don't* care about that, and would be happy to see it appear without my name attached to it at all.

But perhaps you have been too kind to say that the stuff I sent you was either not good enough or completely out of tune with what you wanted. This thought has been growing with me, I'm afraid – please tell me if it is so, since I am beginning to have all sorts of doubts about the thing I am writing at the moment for Gollancz. I would gladly rewrite the whole lot for you if necessary – you only have to say so, and I won't mind, since at least I'll know what went wrong . . .

If you do decide to drop your book . . . could you let me have some of the stuff back for use in a chapter for the Gollancz book? I would have to know this as soon as possible, since it is well under way and has to be finished in a month . . .

The Glittering Coffin had come into existence because one of Potter's articles had caught the eye of John Gross, then a young editor with the left-wing publishing house of Victor Gollancz; the firm had recently had a huge success with *The Outsider* (1956), a polemical book by twenty-four-year-old Colin Wilson, and Gollancz seems to have been looking for a successor. 'V.G. was always urging me to find new unattached authors,' says Gross.

Not easy, because even in those days most writers had agents; but I used to look at student magazines, and something or other by the unknown Dennis Potter (in *Isis*, perhaps) caught my eye. I showed it to V.G., who said, 'Get hold of him, go down to Oxford, take him to lunch' – an unusual occurrence – it was a firm where junior staff weren't exactly encouraged to run up expenses.

So I got in touch, and I went to Oxford, and we had our lunch – at the Mitre. We were wary of each other. He obviously thought, on principle, that I was some kind of London smoothie; I'd by this time read a second article by him, with a jeering remark in it about David Cecil which had irritated me. Still, we kept a conversation going – I'm afraid I can't recall any of the details – and at the end he agreed to write a 'state of the nation' book (which he'd already had in mind).

I reported back encouragingly, and he was signed up. The actual commissioning was done by V.G.: I was only twenty-one or twenty-two at the time, and would never have been allowed to commission anything off my own bat.

London publishers did not usually commission books on the state of the nation from undergraduates; but Gollancz no doubt envisaged Potter as yet another Angry Young Man, and therefore potentially commercial.

Potter wrote to Gross from his parents' house on 14 July 1958:

I have been busy attempting to gather together the ideas I would wish to use . . . The enclosed skeleton is very rough . . . I can send you a specimen chapter . . . within three weeks if necessary, but would very much like a reply of some kind if possible, if only because Allen and Unwin have also made me a very good offer (to which I have yet to reply – I will not do so until I have heard from you). I am pretty sure that I could produce something that would please you, and am eager to begin.

He sent a chapter to Victor Gollancz in person on 21 August, adding, 'I could finish the whole book by October or November, but would need some kind of advance to avoid spending the rest of the long vac. in a local factory.'

On 29 August, Hilary Rubinstein, one of the directors of Gollancz, wrote saying they liked the chapter and wanted to commission the book (Gross had left the firm to go to America). Privately, Rubinstein did not care for it at all: 'I took quite a powerful dislike, and, if I'd had a vote, would have turned *The Glittering Coffin* down. I thought it meretricious and over the top – and never cared for Potter's later work, either.' But Victor Gollancz was keen to go ahead, and the firm offered an advance of £100 on delivery. Potter agreed, and added, 'I would also appreciate any advice you may care to give about a novel I have been working on since February, initially for the "prize first novel competition" offered by a firm of publishers.'

*

This novel may have been *The Country Boy*, of which the opening chapters survive among Potter's papers. It begins:

David knew that in fact the long, dull brick wall which enclosed nearly a third of Long Church Lane had been built high to protect people from the knot of railway lines below, but, sometimes, he had to think that some owner of allotments and trees had put up the wall to protect his incredible patch of green from pavement dust and blown newspapers. For green-ness filled David's mind at that time. They called him 'a country boy' at school, despite his white face and slight, nervous appearance. The Fulham kids named him so because his speech gave him away. Swede and turnip speech. But, the new-comer found it impossible to explain, he came from a hilly, green and lovely certainly, yet coalmining part of England, on the borders of Wales. The Forest, the land on its own. Not just 'the country'.

David misses the Forest, but this is nothing to the sense of disloca-tion felt by his miner father Harry, whose London-born wife Mary has brought him and the children back to her native Fulham and 'locked him up in its dank, excessive nothingness and gardenless, butty-less, green-less acres of squatly horrible streets'. Harry protests, 'I didn't want to come, and doosn't thou forget it. Only you had to row with Our Mam.' An argument rages between the parents, watched silently by Mary's mother, in whose house they are living, and overheard by David in his makeshift bedroom, with the radio as a background:

The radio, still on, was playing late dance music, with a fuzzy, airless sound, sentimental in its throb-throb-throbbing syncopation. None of the three in the tiny oblong kitchen appeared to be taking any notice of it. Yet for all of them the tune, 'Tip-toe Through the Tulips', was later to be heard with a faint, unknowing depression, a feeling of stifled discontent. Tip-toe sounded in words of the country, and, the way it was played, plonk ploink, of neon, of street lights that made fair people look near to corpses. At any moment now putrid tears would drip out around the bleary edges of Harry's eyes. 'That's the beer,' Mary would say, too gruffly, nearly right.

The argument between David's parents becomes vicious, with the weeping Harry calling his wife 'arsehole' and threatening to go back to the Forest, to which she responds, 'Well go back then. And good riddance. You great baby.' The eavesdropping, homesick David reminds himself that this is the father who can

draw an apple with a pencil on the white edges of the newspaper so good that you might almost want to pick it from the page . . . and he always described things or events by knocking together ideas of their colour, or the way the light smacked against their sides or what the sky felt like at the time. This was the only time that he was genuinely articulate, and when David loved him most. The boy had a vague sense of the unused, unusable delicacy within his father . . . Now David could hear the other Harry, horse-like, blundering, loud-mouthed and stupid.

As for David himself, at school in Fulham he is 'called "Ginge",
because his hair was copper coloured', and is 'not very popular, largely
because he was too bright and too private in class, but also because he
reacted so sullenly to the continual playground baiting about the way
he talked . . . They told him he was a turnip, a swede, a yokel, Farmer
Giles.' During scripture lessons, he imagines the biblical landscape as
the Forest:

The Dead Sea, the dead sea, was the huge dreary pool near the pit where
his father worked, edged with reeds, stones and barren-looking trees,
roots twisting back to the surface to escape the poisoned earth. Yea, though
I walk through the valley of the shadow of death: trees arched at the
winter-black tops above the gouged-out lane descending swiftly to
Bradbrook's Farm, an overhung, shadowy, stumbly lane where people
walked quickly, whistling.

For the rest of the class, scripture is an excuse for horseplay. When
the class rebel, Michael Murray, is told by Mrs Williams ('the old
teacher with a grizzle hovering on her face') to pick a passage from the
Bible and read it aloud, he chooses some Old Testament lines about
'whoredoms' and 'breasts', and the children burst into ribald laughter.
Potter later used this in *Stand Up, Nigel Barton. The Country Boy*
breaks off abruptly with the narrator's theft of the teacher's daffodil,
which he blames successfully on another boy.

*

On 31 December 1958, Potter told Hilary Rubinstein that he needed
'another nine or ten days (at the outside)' to finish *The Glittering
Coffin*. 'The first half is with a don at Oxford who has kindly
described it as "exciting" . . . I . . . will definitely get the book to you
by then – since I badly need that £100!' This was his third and last year
at Oxford, and his final examinations loomed. Trodd had decided to
postpone them by a year. 'Most people take Schools in three years,'
noted *Parson's Pleasure* ironically, 'but Mr Trodd wanted, as he
modestly put it, "to make sure of my First".'

Potter's tutor Peter Wiles now noted, in his end-of-term report, that
he and Potter had 'made a verbal agreement he'd work hard enough to
get a Second only. A pity in a way, as he . . . would certainly get a First
with work.' Wiles added that Potter 'really believes that everyone who
disagrees with him is a crook', and prophesied: 'Probably he is one of

the leaders of the next generation: he has the energy, the initiative, the idealism, the egocentricity . . . '

Potter reciprocated Wiles's admiration. 'I was lucky enough to have tutors of the calibre of Peter Wiles and Anthony Quinton,' he writes in *The Glittering Coffin*,

who never attempted to impose any illiberal 'discipline' upon my activities, took some interest in my extra-academic activities, and edged me towards some understanding of the relevance of their subjects to wider issues. Mr Wiles seems to believe in the validity of education through provocation, and once allowed an economics tutorial to move into a discussion of the relevance or otherwise of 'committed' literature to the condition of our society. But he is unfortunately not typical of the system.

He was less kind when, reviewing a television appearance by Quinton in 1978, he recalled philosophy tutorials with him at Oxford:

I sat opposite him, then as now, thinking about various unmentionables as a great cataract of words flowed out of the armchair in which he appeared to repose . . . Philosophy . . . had developed into an elaborate structure which seemed designed to prevent you saying anything whatsoever which wasn't already a tautology. It was utterly impossible to believe that its endlessly masticated propositions had any bearing upon the shape of one's own life.

Quinton, however, remembers Potter as one of his brighter pupils, 'lively, interested, with not enough skins'.

The *Isis* editor for Michaelmas term 1958 was, after all, the man Potter had chosen, Nicholas Deakin, who had been his assistant editor. Deakin's first choice of subject for the regular 'Isis Idol' column – a pen-portrait of some prominent junior member of the university – was Potter himself. The article made one interesting disclosure: 'He confesses to being, as he puts it, "right-wing about sex", and his veneration of monogamy and the family *almost* led him to Catholicism when in the army . . . ' It also observed: 'To the undeserving charlatan he can be terrifyingly rude and those who witnessed the tirade which reduced a *Daily Express* reporter to feverish splutters wonder at the paradoxical "soft streak" in his dealings with pettier antagonists.'

Potter was still living in Divinity Road, and at the beginning of the 1958 Michaelmas term Roger Smith joined him: 'Dennis dragged me out there. It was the grimmest little boarding-house.' It was now that he took Smith on a visit to the Forest. 'His mother was just the same as one of my aunties,' says Smith, 'one of those rather tough, bright,

London working-class women. If you asked me what the basis of Dennis's parents' marriage was, I have no idea, because his father was utterly unlike her. He would mumble away in a corner – though Dennis's description of him was always based on the image of the noble working man.'

In November, Potter was back at the Union, as a star speaker, proposing the motion 'that this House has no confidence in Her Majesty's Government'. The *Isis* report on the debate was by Peter Jay:

Dennis Potter spoke with a devastating combination of conviction and information . . . In a slashing peroration he denounced the Tory chrome-plated coffee-bar civilization; and with withering irony he juxtaposed the opportunity state's values of efficiency and liberty-to-be-imposed-on-by-advertisers with the appalling realities of old-age poverty, stagnation, unemployment, emigration, boredom, ITV and Selwyn Lloyd [the Conservative Foreign Secretary]. He was received with a great ovation.

Parson's Pleasure was more sardonic: 'Dennis Potter . . . proposed the motion in his now familiar "sincere" frenzied manner.' The motion was defeated, but *Cherwell* judged Potter's speech 'fiery and convincing', and described him 'sweeping back his revolution-red hair'.

He was running again for chair of the Labour Club, and this time he won by a landslide. *Cherwell*, reporting this triumph, added, 'Congratulations to Dennis Potter. On January 10th he marries his childhood sweetheart. "We have been engaged for two years," he tells me, "so now I've found a flat and my future looks secure I've decided there's no point in waiting any longer."' This was just before he heard that the Mayhew book was off, though he seems to have been confident of a BBC job after leaving Oxford.

Noreen Tye remembers Margaret saying, 'I'm not buying anybody any Christmas presents this year, because we've got to really save to get married.' The wedding was at Christchurch, Berry Hill, on 10 January 1959 (Salem Chapel was not licensed for marriages). Roger Smith was best man, Margaret's sister Mavis was bridesmaid, Ken Trodd was among the guests, and the reception was in the Berry Hill Club. The couple then set off for Oxford and Dennis's penultimate term.

They moved into a flat at 64 Hill Top Road, just around the corner from Divinity Road. Roger Smith moved with them. 'They had the flat upstairs, and I had a room downstairs, in the flat of two weird gays who pretended they weren't.' Margaret took a job in one of the town shops. 'Mum wasn't fazed by Oxford, or by having to live there while he was studying,' says Sarah Potter. 'I remember Dad mentioning his pride in having her with him.'

Potter's New College friends speak very warmly of her. Stephen Hugh-Jones thought Margaret 'extraordinarily impressive – a really *good* and nice person, which is not the usual sort of impression people make on you when you (and they) are in their twenties'. Jonathan Cecil agrees: 'Margaret seemed a lot older than us eighteen-year-olds (I was one of the first non-National Service undergraduates at New College). In fact she was rather maternal. She seemed to have no self-consciousness or shyness, and wasn't at all thrown by us supposedly clever young things.'

John Fuller became editor of *Isis* for the spring term of 1959, and signed up the newly married Potter for a weekly column, called simply 'Potter'. In the first, he contemplated emigrating – 'there seems to be less smugness, less suffocation and more purpose in the ethos of the younger nations' – but admitted that he could not live anywhere but Britain: 'Love of place is something so fundamental that it must be divorced from the claims of jingoistic nationalism or sophisticated insularity.' In his second column he sneered at the 'shabby dishonesty' of a group of advertising men from top agencies who had been recruiting in Oxford.

He said much the same when invited to address the university Liberal Club: 'Attacking ferociously Jimmy Porter's cry, "There aren't any good brave causes left", Potter tried to analyse what is wrong with England. Our fault lay in too much emphasis on material prosperity . . .' This invitation to speak came from Paul Foot, the club's president. 'I knew Dennis pretty well at Oxford,' says Foot. 'I hated him at first, because Richard Ingrams and I distrusted all ideologues, and I was still a Liberal – all my family were Liberals. But I heard Dennis speak in the Union in my second week there – a quite exhilarating experience. His invective was magnificent. And by the end of my first year at Oxford, I'd come round to Dennis completely.' Ingrams recalls Potter telling the Liberal Club audience that 'whenever he saw a Rolls-Royce he spat at it!' He repeated the remark in *The Glittering Coffin*: 'I . . . spit on a parked Rolls-Royce.'

Foot noticed a peculiarity about his manner when speaking at the Union:

You had all these public schoolboys pretending to be cabinet ministers, at the age of nineteen – and he was completely different. For a start, he had a very broad Gloucestershire accent, and he was utterly vitriolic, so different to the stuff you normally heard there – wonderful rant, a chapel rhetoric. But there was an amazing thing about how he spoke. As he was going into a rant, he would almost laugh at himself ranting. For example, he might use an expression like 'the cash-register society' – the typical sort of phrase that was being used by the Left at the time. But before he said that, he would give a little giggle – as though he was constantly looking at himself, and saying, 'What an absurd figure this is.'

Potter himself touches on this acute self-awareness in *Stand Up, Nigel Barton*, when Nigel goes into a rant about how the working class can see through the speciousness of politicians – and then stops, with the remark, 'Oh God, there I go again. Listening to myself.'

The novelist Margaret Forster, who was an undergraduate at Somerville College in 1959, describes the 'incredible popularity' Potter had achieved by then in the Oxford political world:

My Somerville chums, card-carrying members of the Labour Party all, talked endlessly about him – this brilliant working-class boy, Dad a miner, etc., who was a firebrand, etc., etc. They'd seen/heard him at the Labour Party Group meetings held on Sunday mornings in Somerville. 'You must come,' they said, 'just to see Dennis.' I was deeply suspicious of all this gush and refused at first. I recall looking out of my window, ground-floor library block, and seeing this amazing procession walking through the college – Dennis leading, and literally a horde of hangers on trotting behind. He looked so desperately ordinary to me and – this is very politically incorrect – shabby and deprived, but even at that distance his energy was striking – the way he walked, hands in pockets, very fast, talking all the time, though of course I couldn't hear what he said. Maybe I'd imagined he'd look like Heathcliff or someone but his frailty, in spite of the psychic and physical energy, also struck me. He was so thin, and pale (well, redheads are and he was sort of sandy) and looked underfed and had that pasty sort of skin.

I went, eventually, to hear him and was actually quite impressed. Can't remember a word he said but I liked his sarcasm and his, in general, sardonic manner. His voice carried surprisingly well and was pleasant to listen to, especially compared to the pukka tones of his acolytes.

Forster, the daughter of a fitter at the Metal Box factory in Carlisle, adds, 'Being working class at the end of the Fifties, and being in any way prominent in Oxford life, was *the* thing – both Dennis and I exploited it to the full – instead of being embarrassed by our class, or concealing it, we flaunted it, to great effect, realizing how special it made us (how disgusting!).'

Parson's Pleasure (4 March 1959) was scathing about the new 'Potter' column:

Isis have been silly enough to allow Dennis Potter to adorn their pages this term with weekly gibberish. Every week with monotonous regularity we see his clever little eyes peering at us from the top of his page and the dirty typescript frieze with his name repeated four and a half times. As if we didn't know! Under the frieze, the same old stuff. That's the trouble – read one Potter article and you've read the lot.

He was certainly writing on the same subjects as two years earlier – class, the Admass culture, the decline of trade unionism – and even using the same phrases.

He was probably also the author of an 'Isis Idol' portrait of Trodd, which appeared this term:

Ken Trodd once wanted to be a dance-band leader . . . He places Lew Stone well above Hugh Gaitskell [the leader of the Labour Party] in the distinctly bizarre hierarchy of those he respects . . . On the virulent *Isis* of last summer . . . he put in a tremendous amount of work, and was in reality the assistant editor, despite the usual frequent and heated rows with Dennis Potter.

This shows that rows were already a fundamental part of their relationship.

The article suggested that Trodd had not yet achieved his potential because of 'a self-created gloom about his own value and purpose'. For example, he had 'made a couple of excellent paper speeches in the Union and then left in disgust when he had poked his finger through the cardboard quality of that little world'; whereas Potter was now a candidate for the Union presidency. But, as in the Labour Club election, Potter's Union manifesto suggested that he had less interest in politics than the arts – he told *Cherwell* he wanted Union debates on 'theatre, films and so on – and I'd like one on the future of the novel'. The reporter noted that he wanted to become a 'writer and politician'.

His determination that the Labour Club should perform Brecht came to fruition this term, with a production of *The Caucasian Chalk Circle*. 'A lot of people have heard of but few have ever seen any of [Brecht's] work,' the producer, Christopher Williams of New College, wrote in *Cherwell*. Potter had neglected to obtain the Proctors' permission for the production, and was fined ten pounds, but the performances were allowed to go ahead.

He was to play Azdak, the rascal who becomes a judge, and Margaret Forster was cast opposite him as Grusha. 'We didn't exactly get on, though we should have done,' writes Forster.

He seemed to me to both ignore me – never, I thought, meeting my gaze/look straight on – and to try to dominate, not just me but the entire proceedings. What Dennis said *went* – it was as simple as that. He upstaged everyone shamelessly and because the producer was not strong-minded he got away with it. But at least he was never pompous or pretentious – I liked his not exactly frivolous or flippant but near to it approach – he fooled around a lot.

Forster adds that when they met again twenty years later, Potter wrote to her alleging that he had fallen in love with her during the Brecht production, but she had refused to have anything to do with him. She believes this was 'total rubbish, a fantasy he thought up later', but does recall that when her boyfriend and future husband Hunter Davies, already working in journalism, came to see the play, 'Dennis was horrible to him – really cutting and superior.' Forster says she met 'Dennis's shop-assistant girlfriend' – unaware that they were already married. 'She was attractive, pleasant, cheerful and I thought Dennis bloody lucky to have her. He was very offhand with her, a bit patronizing I thought, but she didn't seem to mind – I thought she had his measure. She just laughed and said, "He's different on his own."'

In the Brecht, Potter and his producer cast another Somerville undergraduate as the Governor's Wife – Hugh Gaitskell's daughter Julia. 'Gaitskell came to our play, with Mrs G.,' recalls Margaret Forster, 'and Dennis and I were introduced. Dennis was wonderfully arrogant (so, probably, was I) and not in the least impressed. Nobody fazed him – I liked that.' He was probably thinking of Julia when he wrote in *The Glittering Coffin*:

I have heard the elegantly and expensively perfumed daughter of a prominent Labour politician say, in a gorgeously posh Cheltenham accent, that of course 'our Party' hasn't lost touch with 'ordinary people'! I did not know whether to be more annoyed about the error of fact or the proprietary tone which was used to describe the huge organization of the Labour Party in terms of some smart club.

Julia McNeal, née Gaitskell, says, 'This could have been me, though

I didn't go to Cheltenham.' She adds that, whatever Potter might have felt about her father, he was always polite to her.

The Brecht production was reviewed flatteringly in *Isis*, but less so in *Cherwell*:

Technically, practically everything was wrong in the Labour Club's production . . . Dennis Potter (playing Azdak) was ineffective until he had stopped squawking . . . But, far outweighing these quibbles, was the exhilaration of the play . . . Roger Smith did an admirable sketch of a bawdy corporal, and once Dennis Potter had assumed judicial robes, they proved very sly, very rascally, and most refreshing. He had a tendency to over-act.

Paul Foot in *Parson's Pleasure* was scathing:

Readers of *Isis* and *Cherwell*, if such there be, might form the erroneous conclusion that this production was worth seeing. In fact it was a ludicrous farce. Spotlights shone on bare boards. Grotesque music drowned the vocalists. Absurd military figures stumbled on stage, shouted, and stumbled off again . . . Potter ranted. But he was on a stage, not a platform, and the same technique is not applicable . . . That Margaret Forster managed to give a sincere performance amidst this shambles is a great tribute to her ability.

(Reading this review today, Paul Foot says, 'I'm hideously distressed and embarrassed about it. In those days I had no knowledge of Brecht at all.')

T. C. Worsley, sent to Oxford by the *New Statesman* to review the production, agreed with Foot that it was amateurish, but allowed that 'the three main parts were very well handled: Mr Dennis Potter, as Azdak, and Mr Roger Smith, the Ironshirt Corporal, acted with real vigour and conviction, while Miss Margaret Forster was beautifully cast as Grusha.'

A few days before this review appeared, Potter wrote to Hilary Rubinstein at Gollancz apologizing for not yet having delivered *The Glittering Coffin*: 'I have been – and still am – ill, unable to take tutorials or do anything . . . marriage, financial worries, the Labour Club, Brecht play, Schools, my book and a weekly column in *Isis* have all been too much.' Nevertheless he sent them the finished book shortly afterwards. Rubinstein read it and told Potter, 'A lot of the writing, if you will forgive me saying so, is a bit slapdash . . . The manuscript will . . . be gone through by our chief office editor.'

Potter went on writing for *Isis* until a matter of days before his final examinations. 'I was too involved with other things to get more than a Second,' he said years later, and recalled one of his tutors ironically pointing out an advertisement which said, 'Why not read for a degree in your spare time?' Nevertheless his last report from Peter Wiles was as enthusiastic as ever: 'I'm proud to have failed to teach him anything. A cross between Jimmy Porter and Keir Hardie, he goes his own way. He can't dominate me, so he just lets me ramble on. Do I not belong to a Doomed Class *and* an Older Generation?'

Trodd got a First. 'I then stayed on a fifth year, doing a B.Litt., which I never finished.' He edited *Isis* in the spring term of 1960 – ending his term of office as explosively as Potter by protesting publicly against the proprietors once more breaking the tradition of the outgoing editor appointing his successor. This time they had chosen the future broadcaster David Dimbleby.

CHAPTER 7

I was drowning

Potter's *Does Class Matter?* interview did not instantly get him a job at the BBC, but he applied for one of its general traineeships for graduates. These had been instituted in 1954, with the aim of recruiting 'men and women of first-class all-round quality . . . between the ages of twenty-one and twenty-five inclusive'. Successful candidates were given about two years' training, in the form of 'attachments' to various programme departments, after which they were expected to find permanent jobs within the BBC. Although applications for the traineeships were invited 'from the universities and elsewhere', the majority of successful candidates so far had been from Oxbridge (and male). They had included, in the first year, Alasdair Milne, also from New College, a future Director-General. There were usually about eight hundred applicants for a handful of places.

During his last months at Oxford, Potter got through to the final round, when he had to face a three-man panel consisting of P. H. Newby (Controller of the Third Programme), Stuart Hood (Head of Television News), and a representative of the Appointments Department. Newby recalls that Potter's style in the interview was combative:

Potter, looking rather farouche, came in and challenged our authority to make decisions about his future – which of necessity we had to do, because that was the nature of the operation. We had in front of us recommendations from Oxford – including one from his Moral Tutor – and the Moral Tutor was a very well-known figure, whose name I forget, who said, 'If you appoint Dennis Potter to a traineeship, you will be taking a very great risk indeed. But I think it is on balance probably a risk that is worth taking.' So we discussed Potter, in the expectation that he would be a 'stirrer up' rather than a contributor. And Stuart Hood and I agreed that, yes, it was a risk worth taking. And so he was appointed.

His BBC traineeship began on 6 July 1959. At first, he commuted into London from Croydon, where he and Margaret had taken a flat at 13 Dunheved Road North, Thornton Heath. 'As a general trainee,' he recalled, 'I went first into radio, Bush House and all that. So you were thrust in front of a microphone almost straight away doing little talks about football and . . . goodness knows what, to an unknown and probably non-existent audience.' After four months of overseas broadcasting, he went, in November 1959, to the Lime Grove television studios and the BBC's flagship current affairs programme *Panorama*. (He once said that he had also worked on *Tonight*, the early-evening magazine, but though he was interviewed on it about *The Glittering Coffin*, and in 1961 did some research for it in a free-lance capacity, he was not attached to it while a trainee.)

At *Panorama*, he was immediately given two items to set up for the edition of 23 November: the actor James Robertson-Justice defending falconry (against accusations that falcons attacked racing pigeons); and a discussion about the possible return of the birch, between a right-wing MP and a civil servant. Robin Day chaired it – his first appearance on the programme – and he recalls 'a red-haired young man just down from Oxford, by the name of Dennis Potter. With his already keen sense of the dramatic, he effectively arranged a fearsome birch to have before us on the table.'

Potter had ordered the birch from a firm that still made them. But the editor of *Panorama*, Michael Peacock, judged the item 'not a startling one', largely because of Potter's inexperience. Potter himself presumably proposed the next item on which he worked, 'Closing of Pits in the Forest of Dean', for *Panorama* on 30 November. He went with a producer and reporter (James Mossman) to stay at the Speech House Hotel in the middle of the Forest, and they made a thirteen-minute film. It included an interview with an anonymous ex-miner who was in fact Walt Potter. He had now left the pit and become a cleaner at a bus garage; he told Mossman he could 'see the red light' for the coal-pits, 'and in my opinion they won't last much longer'. Peacock says he thought this piece was 'good social colour' but did not have the sense from it that Potter was going to make a good television journalist.

His final *Panorama* assignment was to research a thirteen-minute filmed report on 'Paperbacks' for Christmas week. It was produced by Jack Ashley; Richard Hoggart appeared in it (presumably at Potter's suggestion) and the presenter was Robert Kee, who found Potter 'a very sympathetic, rather shy, intelligent young person who felt a bit disappointed with the sort of work he was being given to do at the Beeb, and wondering if he really wanted to stay on'.

Potter wanted to do a *Panorama* item about the deplorable power of advertising, but Peacock told him that polemic was not in *Panorama*'s brief. 'I couldn't in the end make much of him,' Peacock recalls, 'so I sent him back to Grace [Wyndham Goldie, Assistant Head of Talks, Television] who had sponsored him in the first place. He was clearly intelligent, clearly had something going for him, but he was not a journalist. A nicer class of person altogether.'

Potter seems to have harboured no bitterness against Peacock – when Peacock was chosen as the first Controller of BBC2 in 1963, he described him as 'not the kind of person to bungle such an opportunity'. But when he became a TV reviewer he often sneered at the dullness of *Panorama*.

Next, he was sent on attachment to the documentary film producer Denis Mitchell, who was then editing the last programme in *The Wind of Change*, a trilogy on Africa, to be called *Between Two Worlds*. Mitchell had begun as a radio features producer, and his distinctive style of TV documentary depended heavily on a soundtrack of 'real people talking', to which he then matched images. In 1977 Potter described him as

one of television's great innovators . . . His films brought the densities of thought, the nuances of ambiguity and the stretch of tension between sound and picture which made so much else seem so ploddingly literal and predictable. He has always been an author, not a bystander. A dramatist, and not a snoop . . . by far the most talented and humane documentary-maker television has yet produced . . .

For his part, Mitchell thought Potter 'first and foremost a literary man', who felt more at home with scripts than interviewees.

He already wanted to make his own documentary, a film about the changing culture of the Forest of Dean, and Mitchell championed this cause. During January 1960 Potter drafted two outlines, which Grace Wyndham Goldie approved. She allocated a budget of £600 and a producer, Anthony de Lotbinière, who would film with Potter in the Forest from 15 February to 2 March. Meanwhile, during February, *The Glittering Coffin*, delayed by a printers' strike, was finally published.

*

The dying Potter told Melvyn Bragg that *The Glittering Coffin* had been 'a kind of metaphor for the condition of England. Typical young man's title, you see, typical piece of that sort of humbugging, canting rhetoric, which young men – bless their hearts – specialize in.' In another interview he said, 'It had everything I felt about Oxford, London, class, plus a bit of opportunism thrown in . . . I wanted then to be a Labour MP.'

This admission is made at the beginning of the book:

I think I ought to begin this scattered, highly impressionistic and youthful description of a few of the social and political problems of present-day Britain with the damaging but necessary admission that I should very much like to make a career in politics . . . I only make the admission that one of my most deeply felt ambitions in life is to become a competent Labour Member of Parliament because honesty and youthful arrogance, as well as the intensely political nature of this book, demand it.

He referred to this passage on *Desert Island Discs* thirty years after it was written: 'I didn't actually say my ambition was to be a Labour cabinet minister, or even Labour prime minister, but of course it was. I was already being political, in discreetly modifying a public statement of ambition!'

The Glittering Coffin is based on the numerous articles he had written for *Isis*, with many passages reused almost word for word. The dominating topic is Labour's abandonment of socialist principles: 'the pin-striped ethos of the Labour Party, stinking as it does with the green-gabled, tea on the vicarage lawn atmosphere of neat suburban homes and well-mannered conversation over garden fences'. He attacks the trivial escapism of women's magazines and the 'appalling rigidity' of the nuclear deterrent, and writes at length about the Admass juke-box-and-television society and its impact on socialism and working-class culture.

The book takes its title from a passage on this subject in the third chapter: '. . . it is obvious that all the chrome and comfort is not going to lead us very far towards socialism. It is going to preclude so many forms of vitality, and help create a dead land, grey in its values, ambitions and pleasures, its people buried in a huge coffin, a glittering coffin.'

As Hilary Rubinstein remarked, the book (even after editing at Gollancz) looks slapdash. It does not seem to have been planned, and tends to meander or jump from one topic to another. Its best passages are autobiographical, especially those about Potter's Forest childhood, from which he was now able to distance himself – he writes, 'It seems at times as if even my boyhood belongs to somebody else.' He portrays Oxford vividly, too, but St Clement Danes School receives no mention.

By comparison, the argumentative sections are verbose and shrill, but always radiate passionate conviction – 'It is impossible to be young in a dead land' is a typical phrase. Potter is also a shrewd analyst of contemporary trends. Of the Conservative Party's use of an advertising agent, he writes, 'We must teach people to read so that they can understand the jingles. The Prime Minister, Harold Macmillan, is sold on the hoardings by the Mayfair agents of Colman, Prentis and Varley – hold him up to the light, not a stain! shining bright! Ninety per cent of the housewives of Merthyr Tydfil cannot tell him from the real thing, etc., etc.' Prophetically, he fears that 'the Welfare State is to dwindle to an end', looks gloomily at the prospect of an England 'with people, houses and streets coming to look the same . . . [and] our culture . . . flattened out into a kind of syncopated, monotonous form of substitute living', and guesses at the role that television will play in this future era: 'The new people's capitalism, prosperously acquisitive and beamed on to a seventeen-inch screen via a multitude of different channels, will perhaps satisfy enough consciences to end once and for all the moral fervour and passion of socialism.'

Yet he also perceives that there are positive possibilities in television, at least in the hands of the BBC:

The one institution of power and influence in this country which attempts to make points of contact, albeit from a stuffy and remote area of 'superior' culture, is the BBC . . . We can only hope that [it] does not lose its nerve, for it is one of the few means by which a valuable, yet 'popular' level of programmes could make points of contact. Its opportunities are still immense, and its responsibilities are onerous . . .

And he quotes 'the comments of Angus Wilson, who claims that "society today is deeply in need of nourishment, no people more so than the passive, semi-articulate audiences of radio and television. It would be disastrous if the creative writer through disdain or alarm or laziness failed to contribute his particular riches to that audience."'

Despite swingeing criticisms of Labour in *The Glittering Coffin*, Potter still puts his allegiance firmly with it, and the book ends with rhetoric worthy of a Labour Party Conference:

England could have become all the things she tends now to claim for herself, and her role may yet be a tremendous one: shall we be able to see here, once again, the long flow of a profound social revolution, a revolution aimed at discovering man again, rather than burying him still deeper in his glittering coffin? . . . Before the lid finally closes, or the Bomb eventually drops on London, let us please begin to think again, and to think hard and long.

Since he had finished the book in April 1959, Labour had lost the General Election for the third time in succession (on 8 October), and Victor Gollancz himself had suggested that Potter should add a post-script about this, to be printed at the front. Potter agreed, and in it he speaks of 'the anger and contempt so many of us feel about the drift and decay that ruined Labour's electoral opportunity'.

Reviewing *The Glittering Coffin* in the *Manchester Guardian* in February 1960, Anthony Howard dubbed Potter 'Unlucky Jim', and called the book 'an almost indecent exposure of conscience'. But he conceded that 'Mr Potter is at least superbly honest.' Kenneth Allsop in the *Daily Mail* called it 'as heartening and galvanizing a book as I have read', and Douglas Brown in the *News Chronicle* described it as 'a challenge to every smug convention. It re-creates a vision, which is the desperate need of the hour.' The anonymous *Times Literary Supplement* critic called the book 'refreshingly devoid of stale language. But [Potter] often weakens his case by attacking so many diffuse targets.' Similarly Alisdair MacIntyre in the *New Statesman* wished 'he had written a less untidy and rambling book . . . But *The Glittering Coffin* survives all its second-hand mishmash of thoughts . . . by reason of the nagging integrity which keeps the social problem alive in Mr Potter's writing.'

The first printing sold quickly, and Gollancz swiftly reprinted, adding press comments and the slogan 'They've sat up!' to the book jacket. Potter was interviewed about it on BBC Television's *Tonight*, and was invited to take part in a 'younger generation' edition of radio's

Brains Trust, chaired by Shirley Williams, during which he forecast a twenty-first century dominated by 'twenty-one-inch television screens in every room and the constant throbbing of commerce'.

During the years that followed, Potter's Oxford friends and admirers mostly treasured their copies of *The Glittering Coffin* (in the usual Gollancz yellow-paper wrapper); but Potter himself claimed, a year before his death, that he had lost his own copy, telling an interviewer that he squirmed at the mention of it, and that it was written by 'a young man on the make'. If he had re-read it, he would have discovered that his twenty-three-year-old self had anticipated this rejection. 'I am making sure,' he had said in the opening chapter,

that some pain and embarrassment may be caused to the kind of person I might easily become when I have gone down from Oxford and started to earn my living. It is all too easy to shine with the gloss of idealism and purpose when amongst the chiming towers, dark gowns and coffee cups of Oxford, and I know that the personal stresses have yet to come. When they do crowd in on me, this book will be there to read and wince over, there to remind me of what I once believed and hoped. I trust it will prove to be too vigorous to allow me the usual gracious and always so damnably logical shuffle away from the demands of belief and commitment, too uncompromising and too passionate to be shelved with the usual flabby nostalgia of the middle-aged for the supposed glories of carefree youth.

*

By the time Potter and Anthony de Lotbinière returned from the Forest, their film had been given the title *Between Two Rivers*, a nod in the direction of Denis Mitchell's *Between Two Worlds*. Lotbinière has said of Potter, 'I was absolutely the antithesis of everything [Dennis] was . . . I'd been to Cambridge and in the army . . . My voice wasn't exactly his voice. But we worked together very well.'

Potter had been fascinated by the experience of filming, and of attempting to get the truth on to the screen: 'That was my first meeting with film cameras and with the BBC at work, as it were – as opposed to television cameras in the studio in the discussion programmes and what have you – and it, well, it fascinated me, the process fascinated me, and the lies fascinated me, and the way in which it failed to deal with what I knew to be there.'

Lotbinière – who stayed at Spion Kop with the Potters during the filming – explains that Dennis had decided to show his birthplace and its inhabitants 'in two lights, one from his Oxford perspective when he [had] rather despised them, the other from coming back when he realized their full value. So all this had to be done in the film.'

The Potters' first child, Jane, was born in January 1960, and *Between Two Rivers* begins with her christening. 'Jane is my daughter,' explains Potter's off-screen voice,

and in a way this film is about her and about myself, for I brought her down from London, where she was born, to be christened in the Forest of Dean where I grew up.

It's a story of my discovery of things here to respect, and of my anxiety about the kind of Forest of Dean she will see as she grows older.

In the opening shots, we see Margaret, and Potter's mother and father, watching as the Vicar of Christchurch baptizes the baby. Then comes a sequence in which Potter describes the Forest and its miners: '. . . the green Forest has a deep, black heart beneath its sudden hills . . .' The camera pans over the hamlets that cluster around Berry Hill, visits Salem Chapel for a glimpse of the Sunday School, and shows the Globe pub, the band marching through the village, and the interior of the Club, with Dennis's mother playing the piano. 'Mum always played the piano at weekends and pub harvest festivals,' he explains, 'and sometimes people would clap as she came into the club room – then I'd sit listening, blushing with triumph. And perhaps afterwards Dad's friends would come crowding into our house for a party.' There is a brief glimpse of Walt Potter and his neighbour Wilf Baldwin, in the crowded sitting room at Spion Kop, singing 'Painting the Clouds with Sunshine' and stamping their feet in rhythm.

'Soon, though, I went to the local grammar school in Coleford,' continues the narration, 'and almost imperceptibly began to grow away from this tight and secure world.' We see a boy struggling to do his homework in a crowded living room with a blaring television. Potter explains that he now started to feel a 'confused exasperation' with his family:

I began to read with a gluttonous desperation, eager to discover new ideas and revel in insights and feelings I had never dreamt of before. Everything I saw began to take on depressing and drab colours. The Forest came to narrow and constrict itself around me. The fortress became a prison. Even at home with my own parents I felt a shamefaced irritation with the tempo of a pickle-jar style of living.

Here we see Walt Potter eating at a table, with a pickle jar prominent beside him. The commentary continues:

I felt as much remorseful hate as love for the miners squatting for the bus, measuring them by their dirty caps and mufflers. I loathed the thought of lives and minds warped by the dirt . . . I could see no virtues in grubbing in the earth for a living . . . I couldn't stand the old, old men muttering inanely to each other . . . And I writhed under the gossip of village life, where it seemed to me nothing I did could possibly escape ignorant and sometimes vicious comment. Even the parties which had excited me collapsed under the boring, repetitive chatter . . . God! the talk, talk, talk about nothing.

This is accompanied by more shots from the party at Spion Kop, with close-ups of talking mouths. 'Rising sound of excited and un-intelligible chatter,' states the script, and we hear a speeded-up tape-recording of voices, which climaxes in high-pitched gibberish. Lotbinière admits that this part of the film worried him: 'I found it fractionally distasteful, simply because I'd become great friends with [Dennis's] father and mother.'

Potter's narration continues: 'These hands and faces seemed all wrong to me – crippled from the inside. I couldn't imagine a poem meaning anything to them, or these people meaning anything to a poet.' On the soundtrack, an actor's plummy voice intones lines by Byron, and we hear a few bars of Beethoven's Ninth Symphony. 'And I thought then that this miserable pile of dull villages could not, just could not, possibly be reconciled with great art, vital emotions, and classical music. Oh, I wanted to escape! I yearned to get away.' We see images of drab streets, and a fish-and-chip shop.

Potter himself now appears for the first time, his breath steaming in the cold as he walks down a village street in a heavy overcoat. Talking in a relaxed but forceful way to the camera, he explains that, 'by process of examination and accident', he did get away, to Oxford, where he could 'relax and spread myself in what seemed to me to be a far more fertile and richer world than the Forest of Dean'. Now he has returned, 'with a shiny new degree', and, looking at the community again, 'I find myself wondering'. He says he has now come to admire the way of life of the older Forest people – we are shown an elderly couple in their traditionally furnished house – and is glad that modern times have brought a better standard of life to the community. 'But I get worried when the synthetic and canned take over so completely.'

We cut to shots of the Telebar in Cinderford, the Espresso Grill in Lydney, and other samples of the juke-box culture. An advertisement hoarding proclaims 'Let This Site Sell For You', and a British Railways poster offers 'Paris 112 shillings from Lydney'. Potter's cousin Tony Baldwin appears, saying that, when he gets married, he will be leaving the Forest: 'I think the social life here is too narrow . . . I want to reach the new middle classes . . . We want to be progressive.'

The film shows other examples of change bringing decay: the old pubs being replaced by modern roadhouses, Salem Chapel shorn of most of its congregation, and the Berry Hill rugby team and band no longer enjoying the support of the whole village. A bunch of teenagers discussing Elvis Presley records in the Coleford coffee bar is contrasted with the older people enjoying a sing-song at the Berry Hill Club – but the numbers are dropping here too, explains Harvey Harris, the club secretary. The documentary concludes with Potter declaring (over pictures of derelict cottages) that he wants his daughter Jane

to know something of this land between the two rivers . . . before it's beaten down by the world of pop and U and Non-U, seventeen-inch screens and double-your-money. Only a quarter of a mile from my parents' house, Joyford has become a dead village: the chapel has closed and the people have gone. I don't want my child to know a Forest as derelict as this. I don't want her to be blind to the strengths of this community, for then the forest will be a graveyard, not a fortress.

Transmission of *Between Two Rivers* was scheduled for 3 June 1960 at the peak time of 9.25 p.m. The *Radio Times* gave it the star billing for that day, printing a photograph of Potter. Anthony de Lotbinière has suggested that the programme was a precursor of the highly successful BBC series of documentaries *One Pair of Eyes*, which began in 1967, in which an individual was invited to interpret a landscape or subject very personally (Lotbinière directed and produced many of them himself). But Potter had tried to fit three different programmes into the half-hour: a portrait of the Forest as he had known it in childhood, an account of his adolescent revulsion followed by his adult reappraisal of its way of life, and his concern about the encroachment of Admass on traditional working-class society. Not surprisingly, many people, especially in the Forest, failed to perceive the programme's abrupt changes of direction, and some of those who took part in the programme were deeply offended by the scorn that

Potter appeared to be pouring on the Foresters, including his own parents. One of the participants, Tony Baldwin, points out that 'ordinary people didn't do documentaries in those days. And a lot of home truths came out. People's reaction was horrendous.'

In later years, Potter himself admitted that the programme had been largely a mistake: 'I was what, twenty-three, -four, and it was about my own background, and it trapped me into . . . I trapped myself into making premature judgements about things that actually were terribly dear and tender to me . . . I was embarrassed by the tenderness of them, and therefore the embarrassment had to be expressed in rhetoric and the rhetoric was phoney . . . ' When asked (in this 1987 interview) if he felt that, to some extent, he'd betrayed his parents in *Between Two Rivers*, he answered, 'Yes, I did.' He also realized that his own performance in the film was largely a pose: 'I was trying to describe some of [my] feelings . . . but . . . accuracy wasn't enough. Posturing comes in.'

He said it had made him aware of the dishonesty of television as a medium for factual reporting:

Documentaries don't tell the truth, as I saw myself when I made one. They show you what is there, but they don't mediate it through the truths of all the complications, all the inner subtleties of why this person is like that, why that person is like this. Documentary is . . . simply observing behaviour, with a voice-over telling you what you're supposed to think. Whereas fiction, drama, films, plays, all avoid that form of dishonesty – or *can* avoid it. They don't usually, I know. But that's what drama's for, to tell truths.

*

The BBC had been searching for some time for the right type of television programme about books. While *Between Two Rivers* was being edited, Grace Wyndham Goldie noted that she had been 'discussing some ideas with Dennis Potter and these might have something very valuable to contribute . . . His notions were primarily concerned with a book programme of a non-intellectual kind which would hit the kind of young audience which reads, on the whole, paperbacks.' She had suggested to the two producers drawing up proposals for the programme, Stephen Hearst and Christopher Burstall, that they incorporate him into their plans.

He worked with them during the summer of 1960, and by the autumn had decided to resign from the BBC staff in order to be employed by the new programme in a freelance capacity. The Television Training Officer noted on 22 August:

Dennis Potter is at present a general trainee who will be resigning from the Corporation at the end of September. We should like him to receive a letter of contract for his services on the new book programme which would include research and script-writing. We would like him to be paid for a week's work per fortnight – the programme will be transmitted fortnightly and we would expect him to spend a maximum of five days by arrangement with the producer on each programme. It would seem most convenient that he should be paid at the end of each fortnight . . . Something in the region of £20/£30 per fortnight's payment . . . would seem to us to be reasonable.

His BBC file also contains a handwritten note stating that he was resigning 'because he is publishing a book in December with political bias'.

It was a bold move to give up the security of a BBC career and salary at the age of twenty-five, with a wife and small child to support. When asked many years later why he had done it, he said, 'Because I was still writing things, and I would be called in front of [BBC] people saying, "You know, you realize you mustn't do this." And I thought, "Oh, my goodness, what do they mean I can't do this?" And I was aware that I would not be able to write about politics. So I resigned after a year.'

His 'book . . . with political bias', *The Changing Forest*, was commissioned in the spring of 1960, and Potter intended to deliver it to the publishers 'about mid-August', but this proved to be wildly over-optimistic – he was still working on it a year later. The author and journalist Mervyn Jones explains how it originated:

Clancy Sigal, an American living in England, had written a book about a Yorkshire mining village – a kind of sociological portrait. And the success of this gave him the idea of a series of similar books about different aspects of Britain, to be called 'Britain Alive'. He sold the idea to Secker & Warburg, and Fred Warburg said there might be some criticism of the editor being an American, so Clancy asked me to be the co-editor. We drew up lists of possible writers and subjects – not just places, but things like the trade union leaders and the Brigade of Guards. In the end the series ground to a halt, because we couldn't get enough of the writers we wanted. But one person we managed to sign up was Dennis Potter. One knew about *The Glittering Coffin* and his origins in the Forest of Dean. He didn't seem very keen, but he agreed to do it.

We had a session with him, in Clancy's flat. He was a lean, hungry-looking young man, tall, skinny, red-haired, a striking figure. Very defensive, was the first thing I thought about him – very much 'How am I going to get on with these people?' The discussion didn't go well. He didn't want us to edit the book in any way; and he said he didn't want to write about himself, or about real, identifiable people whom he knew in the Forest – 'They won't like it,' he said. In the end we talked him round.

Potter had mentioned in *The Glittering Coffin* that he intended his next book to be 'a detailed study of the breakdown of a distinct regional identity' – meaning its breakdown as a result of Admass. *The Changing Forest* is such a book, a 40,000-word account of the encroachment of the affluent society on Berry Hill, which, 'almost every time I return', was becoming 'less distinct and more like the rest of the country'.

He sees 'new, well-designed council houses everywhere . . . My village has easily trebled in size with whole new roads of aerial-topped, flush-doored, nicely painted, flat-windowed buildings with cars outside them . . . ' The growing influence of television worries him: 'The external culture comes from the telly, and mostly from commercial television: on the whole, I think, television that is dreary, repetitive, sordid, commercial and second-rate'.

The Changing Forest is less bombastic than *The Glittering Coffin* and written with a lighter touch, though once again it lacks a clear shape, and seems to have been poured out at Potter's usual high speed. Two decades later, he observed that his first two books had been written 'with the ardently youthful skill of a tyro fresh out of Oxford who could pronounce upon the condition of his culture and his nation without knowing much of any real significance about himself'.

Compared with its predecessor, *The Changing Forest* attracted very little attention, and sold poorly. The newspaper for which Potter was then working, the *Daily Herald*, printed a review by John Diamond, Labour MP for Gloucester, who was not very enthusiastic: 'Rather too large a part of the book is taken up with the author's personal reactions to change. But . . . the book is enlivened with very human incidents and very human stories.' The anonymous *TLS* reviewer was cooler: 'There is . . . rather too much word-painting of the old times of the author's youth . . . and rather too little serious examination of what the future actually has in store . . . The repetitiveness of the author's style makes continuous reading difficult.' Certainly he had not yet found what he was later to describe as 'your own "voice", the one you have to delve as deeply as possible into yourself to find and attend to'.

The BBC fixed his fee as part-time researcher and writer for the new TV book programme at the rate of £16.10s a week, but he soon found he was working for it full time, so this was increased to £22. In mid-September 1960, Grace Wyndham Goldie noted that he was 'working very well on the series'. The title *Bookstand* was agreed on, and Goldie wrote in the *Radio Times* that it would be popular in flavour and visual in approach. The first forty-minute edition was broadcast live at 4.10 p.m. on Sunday, 16 October 1960. Potter was billed as 'script associate', with 'dramatic sequences directed by John McGrath'. The presenter was Dick Taverne, then a young barrister and Labour candidate for Putney.

Taverne explains that Potter did not write the linking script, only the dramatized excerpts from novels. The two of them got on fairly well: 'Dennis was very suspicious of me as a Gaitskellite, but we established a fairly close rapport. The BBC high-ups wanted *Bookstand* to consist of well-known literati talking about serious literature, but we were trying to make it speak to non-book-readers. It was Dennis's first attempt on television to get through to a more popular audience.'

Hearst says that Potter worked from home, coming into the office only to deliver his scripts. By this time he and Margaret and the baby (having lived briefly in Chiswick) had moved to 11 St Paul's Mansions, Hammersmith, just across the road from his mother's family home in Rednall Terrace, and a short journey from Lime Grove. They rented a top-floor flat, overlooking the noisy traffic of Hammersmith Broadway and (at the back) an all-night bus garage. Margaret's sister Mavis was appalled: 'We had to climb all these stairs, to the top floor. Margaret had a dreadful time carrying Jane and her push-chair up and down. She and Dennis didn't have any money, and Frank [Mavis's husband] and I lent them some to tide them over.' Jane Potter recalls her father 'singing "One Man Went to Mow" as a lullaby when we were living there, and I think the highest he said he ever got to was three hundred, because I wouldn't get to sleep'.

John McGrath, who was working on *Bookstand* too, had been at Oxford with Potter and had similar working-class roots. At university, he had been suspicious of him, regarding him as a 'columnist' whose opinions were designed chiefly to catch the eye. But now they became friends, and McGrath liked what Potter was writing for the programme:

We'd have a meeting in the office next door to Lime Grove, with Stephen Hearst, to agree which novel or novels to dramatize – we'd all have read half a dozen – and which bits of them to use. And then Dennis and I would go off and work out what actors we needed. His scripts were very workmanlike and economical. Given that the maximum time was about four and a half minutes, there could be nothing too experimental. But we tried things (I did some of the adaptations myself, especially the ones that were to be on film). I think we both learned a huge amount. There was no videotape, and film was expensive, and took time; so we learned about the studio – how to make a studio sing.

The first edition of *Bookstand* included 'acted scenes' from John Wain's *Hurry On Down*, Iris Murdoch's *Under the Net*, Kingsley Amis's *That Uncertain Feeling* and Stan Barstow's *A Kind of Loving*. Potter's best man Roger Smith appeared in the programme as a 'man in the street' talking about a novel: 'I had to speak about *Under the Net*. The book wasn't a favourite of mine, but it was a favourite of Dennis's, so I said it was a favourite of mine. Then there was an extract from it – a couple of actors.' Asked what he thought of Potter's work for the programme, Smith says, 'I don't think he read much, frankly – he never admitted to any literary influences at all.' McGrath agrees: 'I don't think his heart was in the *Bookstand* job. I thought what he really wanted to do was go off and be an MP, or write polemical articles. But he never did the work with any scorn.'

On 30 October (the programme was broadcast fortnightly) viewers saw his dramatizations of excerpts from *King Mob* by Christopher Hibbert and *Absolute Beginners* by Colin MacInnes. Later in the series he tackled, among others, Henry James's *The Turn of the Screw*, *Three Weeks* by Elinor Glyn (done as a silent film), William Cooper's *Scenes from Married Life* and Dashiell Hammett's *The Glass Key*. None of his *Bookstand* scripts seems to have survived, but his increasing skill at matching pictures to words, and honing his natural verbal exuberance to the needs of the medium, is demonstrated by a voice-over he wrote for the edition of 5 March 1961. This was to accompany still photographs illustrating a collection of stories called *Out West*:

Out West is the story of the hopeful ones, reaching out to the frontiers, dwarfed by the ringing emptiness of the land and its threats of danger . . . the bleak toughness of all explorers, all outcasts and all beginners, knotted together by their hope and their utter insignificance in this uncharted country . . . These are the classic scenes of the *Out West* story, the traditional settings which were often drab, boring, suburban. Towns where you could safely take snaps. But men still carried guns.

Potter may have voiced this script himself, since after this sequence of photographs he was seen interviewing an expert on American history. In another programme, he talked about travel writing to James (now Jan) Morris, who had just written on Venice. (Morris remembers the interview, and was not particularly struck by Potter on this occasion, but recalls going to his home some years later: 'I remember talking about Welshness with him – he'd been brought up not to like the Welsh very much. Even then, he seemed to be terribly ill and frail.') Paul Foot saw Potter conduct a *Bookstand* interview and thought, 'He isn't very good at this' – sensing that Potter wanted to do the talking rather than listen to someone else.

Stephen Hearst says that the *Bookstand* team were 'a happy lot who learned a good deal from each other', though Potter 'had a tremendous distrust of anyone who was in charge. Conspiracy theory was always quickly in his mind.' Audience figures for the first five editions were good, rising from 1.5 to 2 million – much better than for the rival ITV book programme – but Hugh Carleton Greene, who had succeeded Sir Ian Jacob as Director-General, disliked the dramatizations; in particular he thought that Potter's version of part of Albert Camus's *The Outsider*, broadcast in February 1961, was 'quite unworthy' of the book. An article in *The Times* said much the same, adding, 'It is better to overestimate than to underestimate an audience's patience, taste and intelligence.' Meanwhile Stephen Hearst told Grace Wyndham Goldie that Potter would need to find some other work while the programme had its summer break, otherwise 'he may be forced to take a full-time job with the *Daily Herald*'.

Greene continued to complain about the dramatizations, and Stuart Hood, now Controller of Programmes, Television, agreed that they were 'a waste of time and money'. During the summer break it was decided to cut the programme to half an hour and eliminate the scripted excerpts. Potter would no longer get regular work from it.

The disappearance of his regular BBC income came just as his and Margaret's second child, Sarah, was born in July 1961, in the Hammersmith flat. 'Since it was a home confinement,' Potter wrote to Secker & Warburg, for whom he was just completing *The Changing Forest* (much later than he had intended), 'I more or less abandoned all my work for a week or so!' The Hammersmith Flyover was now being built outside their windows. 'I live on the top floor of a block of flats on a bloodshot-eye level to the thing,' Potter wrote a few months later.

Only a few yards of exhaust-laden air separates us from The Start Of A New Age, as Transport Minister Marples threateningly called the thing . . . For months and months they have been building [it] – pneumatic drills, monstrous creaking cranes, shouting foremen, acetylene burners, bulldozers, portable radios, and all the other things which more than justify a tea-break.

I spent a little time leaning out of the window, in a vain attempt to foment a strike, when our second baby was born in July, but she came into the world while a grotesque new machine was dropping concrete girders into position with all the gentility of a front-row rugby forward bearing down on a tiny full-back.

John McGrath says the disturbance caused by the flyover works was 'awful, a nightmare', and that it added to the considerable strain Potter was obviously experiencing: 'I did feel Dennis was doing too much – I felt a tension about him. He was already married (unlike most of us), having children, earning his living, and trying to write a book. We were all uptight, but Dennis seemed to have a greater tension.' Asked about the Potters' lifestyle at home, McGrath says, 'The impression I got was that Dennis was trying to re-create, amid trendy London, a sort of working-class kitchen-based life, from his childhood – and was succeeding. He rejected fashionable living. And Margaret was very private, and retreated from his work.' Certainly, Potter tried to give Jane and Sarah something of the flavour of his own childhood: 'Whenever I wished to be tender with my children, when they were very small, I would say "thee" and "thou", as my father did to me.'

When *Bookstand* came on the air again in October 1961, Hearst had left to make documentaries, and Christopher Burstall was in sole charge. He was keen that Potter should still contribute. But, as Potter explained in a letter at the beginning of that month, he was now heavily committed elsewhere: 'They've given me a "series" to work on at the *Herald* . . . '

*

He had had his first article published in the *Daily Herald* while still on a weekly wage from *Bookstand*. On 4 November 1960 the paper's front page flagged '*As I See It* by Dennis Potter – See page 2'. This was a daily guest opinion column, and Potter's article was a light piece about freshmen at Oxford:

Oxford and Cambridge, in their attitudes and insularity, are ultimately two of the most depressing institutions we have . . . And where would I go if I had to choose all over again? Oxford, of course. The process of rejection, the discovery of what a sterile thing 'Tradition' can be, was, maybe, worth half the money the State spent on me.

The *Daily Herald* had begun in 1911 as a strike sheet produced by London print workers. Between the wars it became a high-quality left-wing paper, owned by the Trades Union Congress; but it needed frequent injections of cash from the TUC and the Labour Party, and eventually the mass-market newspaper and magazine group Odhams Press bought half the shares. Circulation dipped alarmingly in the Fifties, and shortly before Potter joined the staff the paper had been taken over by the *Daily Mirror* group, headed by Cecil King and his editorial chief Hugh Cudlipp. They appointed as editor the political journalist John Beavan, who embarked on a policy of supporting Labour in general but criticizing it whenever he disagreed with party policy. Hugh Gaitskell was soon protesting that the *Herald* no longer gave adequate support to the party: 'If . . . you still want to help us . . . show at least as much friendliness to Labour as the *Daily Telegraph* does to the Tories . . . Don't make our job more difficult by publishing offensive and ill-informed articles . . . '

Potter said that, when he joined the *Herald*, he presumed 'in my innocence' that it was still 'a Labour newspaper . . . Jesus Christ!' The pro-Labour content was now limited to a guest column written by Michael Foot, Barbara Castle, and other prominent members of the party, and Foot says that John Beavan was even trying to axe this. The news coverage tended towards the sensational. Headlines in the first issue to which Potter contributed included 'Ex-Vicar Ran Off With Farmer's Wife', 'Her Wedding Night Confession', and 'Wrestler Told Girl: "I'll Cut You Up"'. The features and arts reporting were skimpy. David Nathan, who was then the paper's theatre critic, describes its overall style as 'pretty fish-and-chippy'.

The day after Potter's piece on Oxford had appeared, Saturday, 5 November 1960, the *Herald* carried this item on its front page:

GROUP 60 REPORTS

A team of Oxford graduates are touring Britain looking at the social scene with the candid eye of youth. They call themselves GROUP 60. This week they are making their first report to Andrew Mellor. The subject – WHY ARE FEWER PEOPLE WATCHING SOCCER? *For a new, clear view read the* Daily Herald *next week.*

The following Friday, 9 November, one of the paper's inside pages carried the headline SHODDINESS IS STRANGLING SOCCER. This was 'A Group 60 Report presented by Andrew Mellor' (a regular writer for the *Herald*). The story carried photos of the group: 'Kenneth Trodd, 25, Robin Blackburn, 21, Perry Anderson, 21, Roger Smith, 22, Nigelfred Young, 22, Dennis Potter, 25.' Mellor explained:

They call themselves Group 60 because their self-allotted task is to take a close new look at the 1960s. They are six young men, all under twenty-six, who recently graduated from Oxford, and are now touring Britain to survey the social scene with the candid eye of youth.

'Why are fewer people watching soccer today?' is the first question Group 60 set out to answer. Members of the group put the question to scores of people up and down the country . . . Here is their report.

The report – which gave no indication of who had done what research – stated that because of 'new tastes and habits . . . dissatisfaction with cramped, dirty grounds, defeats abroad, dull games, allegations of bribery and the grey miseries of the British mid-winter, the pull of football is slackening'. One passage has the Potter touch:

We found similar responses wherever we went. In a bacon-roll-and-bottled-coffee café in Deptford High Street, London, for example.
It was no more than a small room crowded with teenagers.
An enormous juke-box quivered out the 'glamour' – 'Tell Laura I Love Her.'
'If you want to know why we don't go to football, it's *that!*' said Jimmy Clarke, pointing at the huge, glistening creature.

Despite the fanfare, this seems to have been Group 60's sole appearance in the *Herald*. Trodd has only a slight recollection of it – 'Dennis and I, along with Roger Smith, formed some kind of writers' group, called Group 60' – but Smith remembers more:

Group 60 was Dennis's idea. We set out to interview youth. We went off – Ken and I and the others (we must have been the only people who went in and out of Liverpool and never discovered the Beatles playing at the Cavern) – and Dennis stayed at home. We did all the leg-work, and he did the article. And then *he* got the regular job with the *Herald*.

As Potter recalled it, when the *Bookstand* job came to an end he joined the *Herald* as a feature writer 'on August Bank Holiday 1961'. In fact he had started earlier that month, but his first piece as a staff writer, another 'As I See It' column on 12 August 1961, was about the Bank Holiday and the British attitude to it:

There is a deep capacity for uninhibited enjoyment buried under the placid and hag-ridden exterior of the British male . . . Those of the status-ridden classes who skulk behind their privet hedges can have no inkling of the joys of a summer at Southend, for instance. I was there this time last year, and didn't mind the puddles or the rising price of fat, sticky rock.

I saw a man who looked like a parody of the Lord's Day Observance Society gradually disintegrate before the long cackle and sparkle of a Southend Saturday.

In no time at all he was knocking back Guinness like the stevedore in the advertisement, and tried to kiss a middle-aged Sunday School teacher, who disengaged herself to sing the chorus of 'Eskimo Nell'.

The swilling music in the pubs has been rubbed round inside the barrel of a pint glass then held up to dry by the hearty warm blasts of a hundred throats in full throttle . . .

He had been taken on as a feature writer, and his first true feature assignment (published four days later) was to report on the rise of Britain's new betting shops, made legal the previous May. He interviewed 'Sid on the Railings, a Hammersmith Broadway bookie's runner with a face the colour of damp sawdust', who was still managing to make a living, and he spoke to several betting-shop proprietors:

George Graham's shop along the Fulham Palace Road was doing very well at lunchtime. And Mrs Flo Steel, of Wandsworth Bridge Road, reported that business was on the up and up . . .

Birmingham Central Police Station gave the same story. 'There have been 326 licences for betting shops issued here,' a desk sergeant added, 'and the old runner is being pushed out.' . . .

I put all this to Sid, still on the Rails [*sic*].

'All right, all right,' he said. 'I'll get another job, on the old sandwich boards. I'll carry a message for me profession.' He took his roll-up out of his mouth, and winked.

'*Prepare to meet thy doom.*'

Though the main *Herald* office, in Long Acre, Covent Garden, was a purpose-built piece of art deco, the features staff worked in adjacent buildings – 'cobwebbed attics in the middle of long corridors which went on and on like a spiked story', as Potter put it. There, 'I sat next to the *Herald's* theatre critic, David Nathan, who chivalrously protected me from requests to write readers' letters, and even the next day's horoscope when the old man called Daphne, or something, was absent on unforetold illness.' Elsewhere he told this story in more detail:

The first day I went into work, there was this old journalist and he said, 'Oh, shit, I've got to be Ariadne today.' He was this astrologer, supposedly. And there was this other old guy, writing the readers' letters. I said, 'What address do you use?' He said, 'If it's controversial, I always put: The Upper Richmond Road.' I said, 'Why?' He said, 'Because it's a bloody long road.'

This was not the kind of journalism to which *Isis* had accustomed him. 'He wasn't what you would call a born journalist,' says Nathan.

We were a bit suspicious of him at first. We had worked our way up through lowly positions, and we thought the only way to get into Fleet Street was to work on provincial papers – as I had. Here Dennis was, undoubtedly ex-working class, but also one of the glittering Oxford graduates. Also it was a fairly heavy drinking crowd. And he was never one of the lads, one of the habitués of the Cross Keys. I got on with him very well, though.

Potter admitted, 'I didn't enjoy the conviviality of office life very much.'

He wrote another 'As I See It', which appeared on 19 August, this time about naughty seaside postcards – he noted that the buxom women were being replaced by jokes about flying saucers. He contributed his first book review (of *England, Half English* by Colin MacInnes) on 28 August; and on 2 September 1961 he was back with a feature about gypsies, suggested by a report that a local council was digging a moat around common land to keep them out. This mixture of opinion pieces, reviews and features became his diet for the remainder of the year, with his byline appearing in the *Herald* every few days.

Occasionally he became seriously interested in his subject-matter; for example, when he went to meet Michael Flanders, the entertainer in a wheelchair whose *At the Drop of a Hat* was a current West End hit:

Flanders caught polio . . . 'They gave me only a few hours to live,' he told me, as if talking about another person, 'and for about five years nothing more was demanded of me than that I should *live*. That I should attempt the long grind of returning to "normal" life. My target then was merely independence.'

He explained that, once you had had to create the drive to return to 'independence', then the impetus continued into other fields . . . 'Most of the work I've done is as easy with a wheelchair as without. In a way, the wheelchair has almost been a help. I've had to concentrate on the things I can do. I haven't frittered my energies away.' . . . I left feeling very, very small indeed.

But mostly he hated the work: 'I was full of disappointment: I was drowning on the *Daily Herald* and various guilts were bubbling and slowly seeping through.'

David Nathan says that the paper did not seem to know how to use him. 'They wanted him for the big series but these take time to prepare. On a paper, then as now, if you didn't fit into the formula you didn't get used a lot. I had a definite beat, Dennis didn't.' Potter also began to perceive the paper's dishonesties, as over 'the self-motivation courses run by bodies like the Dale Carnegie Institute, which I covered as a newspaper reporter at one of their so-called free sessions. The *Herald* wouldn't use the article because Dale Carnegie was advertising in the paper.'

By the beginning of 1962, 'I hated every second of it'. He sensed that a dramatic change would happen within himself: 'I knew something physical was going to happen, and it did.'

PART TWO: 1962–1975

Hide and seek

CHAPTER 1

Ring the bell and shout 'unclean'

He was 'already very pale, and I had some odd patches on my neck and on my arm, but I didn't know what they were'. At the beginning of March 1962 he went to Lincoln, to write a *Daily Herald* feature about a key by-election. 'Teams of canvassers are out in the acres of streets,' he wrote, 'and, in a cold, snow-laden wind from the East Coast, I have been following them, reluctantly discovering a new way to see an old city.' He did indeed seem reluctant, harping on the cold weather ('the air . . . bruising one's face is so cold that it seems made of frosted glass'), turning in some lacklustre prose ('the little streets slope wildly, yet with an ancient grace'), and interviewing only one of the candidates, a local man who was standing as an independent in favour of conscription. He did not even mention that Labour had selected someone he knew very well, Dick Taverne – who was to win with a big majority. Nor did he refer to the fact that he was now a prospective Labour candidate himself.

He had been selected by the constituency party in East Hertfordshire in 1962, soon after joining the *Herald*. Ron Brewer, who was the full-time Labour agent there, recalls that Potter had first offered himself as a candidate in Essex: 'He'd been on a selection conference at Harlow. They chose a local man, but somebody recommended Dennis to us. I don't think we'd heard of him before, but, as far as I can remember, he walked straight through the selection process for our constituency.'

It was therefore striking that his report on the by-election at Lincoln seemed to show no interest in politics. But he was beginning to feel strangely ill. 'My nails were all pitted,' he recalled of the Lincoln visit. 'I couldn't sleep. I was pale and losing weight. I felt that there was a sea change going on in me.'

His next *Herald* article, which appeared on Friday, 16 March, was a review of a book on Hitler. Then he was sent to cover a Young Conservatives' Conference at the Friends' Meeting House near Euston Station in London. 'I hated being there. I hated having to file that copy. I remember I went to get up from the press table, and I couldn't. I looked down, and my left knee [site of his old rugby injury] was the size of a soccer ball, bulging out against my trousers.' He managed to leave the building, but 'when I was crossing the road outside, my legs locked again. I was sweating with panic.'

In fact his medical records show that the onset of illness was not as sudden as this. He wrote nothing for the *Herald* after 16 March, so was presumably already ill by that time, but he did not visit his doctor in Hammersmith, Dr D. R. Jones of Bridge Avenue, until more than a month later, on 24 April. On that date, he told the doctor that his left knee had been painful and swollen since Christmas, and said he had been feeling unusually tired as well. His right knee and other joints were now beginning to be affected, and there was a rash on his scalp and neck. Dr Jones prescribed him aspirin and a painkiller.

These had no real effect, and the *Herald* now wanted him back. Since he was still immobile, he was told to work from home, standing in for the paper's television critic, Alan Dick, who was on a week's holiday – he could watch the programmes in his flat and phone in his copy late at night. (These were the days before television critics could be sent videotapes in advance of transmission.) Potter's first TV column appeared on Monday, 7 May 1962, under the heading 'Too Tough for a Sheriff':

Bad men die with their boots on, scowls frozen into their evil faces. The heroes, holsters slung low on the hip, stride out on the side of the angels.

'Folks must have their heroes,' muses *Wagon Train*'s Chris Hale, 'whether they are real or not.' A dangerous comment from a television cowboy.

But the good old BBC, introducing gore with the gushing good taste of its woman announcer, stolidly claims that *Wagon Train* is 'mainly based on historical facts'.

Last night's episode – the first of the new series captured from the other channel with a faster-on-the-draw cheque book – featured guest star Joseph Cotton as pioneer hero Captain Dan Brady.

He sought to return to the West he had known in the old days when 'all I had to worry about was the plains, the buffaloes, the Indians and the good God'.

So we had bags of nostalgia, buckets of sentiment and plenty of tension. Nothing broke the golden rules of the ritual, predictable yet exciting, the most productive folklore of all time.

With *Bronco*, *Laramie*, and *Wagon Train* now on the BBC the best tele-cowboys are not interrupted by the claims of striped toothpaste and detergents. You can count the corpses in peace.

But one fact ate like a maggot into this enjoyment.

The whole evening of BBC Television was grimly dominated by a *Meeting Point* marking Christian Aid Week, with a fact-filled documentary called 'Bread for my neighbour'.

Nearly a year later, after watching dozens more, he told his readers that he was an addict of westerns: 'I have a gluttonous appetite for tales of the purple sage and blazing guns. Indeed, I've seen so many cowboy films that I could draw a detailed street map of, say, Dodge City . . . These yarns have the essential simplicity and brutally satisfying finality of all the best folklore.'

It also appeared, during his trial week as *Herald* TV critic, that he was already hooked on *Emergency – Ward 10*, which had just returned to the screen: 'Addicts must have been half hoping that the programme's long absence would wean them from the habit. But they had about as much chance of escaping as a bug in boiling water.' The series was 'a heady pill of concentrated hokum, guaranteed to anaesthetize the credulous. But harmless in small doses.' He was an aficionado, too, of the new BBC programme *Z Cars*, which he judged 'undoubtedly supreme' among the popular series. 'It thrives on superb camera work, earthy dialogues [*sic*] and characters who have not been cut out of stiff cardboard.'

Z Cars had recently been created by Potter's former *Bookstand* colleague John McGrath and the writer Troy Kennedy Martin. McGrath explains that they 'were watching an American cop series, and we asked ourselves why *we* couldn't do something with a cop in a car. We set it up with Elwyn Jones, Head of Drama Documentaries. Troy kind of story-edited the whole thing, and I wrote for it a bit – and for a time I had to direct a live fifty-minute episode every other week!' In 1974 Potter wrote:

When Troy Kennedy Martin, Allan Prior and John McGrath launched the first *Z Cars* on to our screens the exhilaration of the scripts was instant and seminal. Along drab streets and dark alleys, in noisy tenements and asphalt playgrounds, Barlow and his men tangled inconclusively with the petty thieves, the flashier criminals, the drunks and feckless casualties of a familiar city and managed to turn the conflict into resonant and sometimes moving drama. This, you were made to feel, is how it is: an authenticity so close to the ground that the headlights showed the cracks in the paving stones.

In his Thursday piece during his first week as TV critic in May 1962 he turned to comedy, specifically the face of 'the under-rated Sid James', declaring, 'It is a kind of electronic concoction of boiled cabbage and old fag ends – the best comic face in the business, squeezing in a rusty-nailed voice into the bargain.' In contrast, the 'aloof Peter Dimmock', presenter of *Sportsview*, 'somehow manages to reduce the tingling passion of sport to the teatime comments of a retired insurance clerk'. Potter ended the week by praising a BBC adaptation of *Wuthering Heights*: 'Last night on BBC, that talented producer Rudolph Cartier did his best to squeeze it down to the niggardly dimensions of the TV screen. What a task that is! . . . The howl of the wind against the windows, the muted pain of Claire Bloom as the wretched Cathy, and the hunted misery of Keith Michell as Heathcliff, made this a more than adequate offering of a great work.'

At the end of the week working from home, Potter was still unable to walk, and he was sent to the rheumatology clinic of the West London Hospital in Hammersmith. On 24 May a doctor there noted that the diagnosis was still uncertain, but the most probable explanation was rheumatoid arthritis. He recommended that Potter should be admitted to the hospital for further investigation. There was a shortage of beds, but on 3 June one was found for him because, the hospital noted, 'he was unable to carry on with his job'. In hospital, as much attention was paid to his rash as to his swollen joints, and after further tests it was decided that he probably had psoriatic arthropathy.

He later wrote that it had taken some time to diagnose his illness, 'because of the weird swiftness of it . . . [it] just invaded every joint – bang! My jaws, fingers, knees, hips, ankles, toes . . . Shortly after that, just as quickly, overnight, my skin went. And I thought, "Well, this is it, then." . . . It was like one of the plagues of Egypt!'

His illness does indeed appear in the Old Testament, as 'Zaraath', the Hebrew word generally translated as 'leprosy', which seems to have been used in biblical times for any scaly or ulcerated condition of the skin. When Naaman, captain of the host of the king of Syria, took the advice of Elisha and washed seven times in the sulphur-rich waters of the Jordan to rid himself of Zaraath (2 Kings 5:1–14), he was probably suffering from what we would now call psoriasis. The ancient Greek writers divided cutaneous diseases into *psora*, meaning 'itch', and *lepra*, meaning 'scale', and psoriasis was clinically described and differentiated as a separate entity in Persia in the eighth century BC, but not until the mid-nineteenth century did Western medicine clearly distinguish between leprous and psoriatic disorders.

Psoriasis affects about 2 per cent of the population. Unlike leprosy, it is non-infectious, an auto-immune malfunction in which the body produces new skin cells at an abnormally rapid rate. These push their way to the top of the skin, forcing its dead surface to flake off like the scales shed by a snake. An attack is likely to be triggered by emotional stress or trauma, but susceptibility to psoriasis is passed on genetically, and when Potter was admitted to hospital in June 1962, it was noted that he had 'a family history suggestive of psoriasis'.

Asked if the illness runs in the family, Potter's mother says, 'Yes. My grandfather – that's where it's come from. I don't know how long before that. But my grandfather on my father's side, the Waleses, must have had it, because my mother used to say he had some kind of a –' June chips in, 'Leprosy kind of thing.' Mag Potter continues, 'But it must have been psoriasis.' This grandfather died when her father, Christopher Wale, was only nine; she does not know whether his psoriasis was arthritic, though in 1986 Potter told an interviewer that his great-grandfather 'suffered from a crippling arthritic disease'.

Mag Potter continues, 'My father was – not like Dennis – but very dry-skinned. If he took a shirt off, you'd almost see powder flying.' She herself began to experience it mildly in her seventies: 'I've got it – yes. A little patch here on the head.' Dennis's first cousin, Graham Wale, suffers from it mildly as well, and says it comes on when he is under stress.

Mag says that Dennis had a mild attack of it in his late teens: 'The first I remember of Dennis showing any sign of it was when he did his National Service. He came home on his first leave and he said, "What's that on my back?" He'd got a couple of little patches, but it seemed to go.' This was probably *psoriasis vulgaris*, or common plaque psoriasis, which affects more than 90 per cent of psoriasis sufferers, usually appearing on the scalp, lower back, shoulders, knees and elbows. The psoriatic patches, which look like small discs or plaques, can start as a small spot and then enlarge, joining up with other patches to cover quite a large area of the body; however, there are always places where the skin looks normal. In a typical attack, the patches may spread quickly but will then reduce and disappear altogether for a while.

About 5 to 10 per cent of psoriasis patients suffer, as Potter did, the further complication of arthritis. Psoriatic arthropathy, as this condition is known, may take different forms: mild arthritis and severe psoriasis, or vice versa. At first in Potter's case the arthritis was the dominant factor. The doctors at the West London Hospital gave him a course of cortisone injections, which at first eased his joints, so that he could soon walk about the ward 'without undue discomfort'. But his spirits were very low. Writing six years later, he vividly recalled being 'in the first and so most irrationally terrifying grip of an illness which still flickers hotly at my limbs, and . . . also walled up in a near-suicidal depression which apparently had more to do with biochemistry than the more attractive lures of self-judgement'. His old schoolfriend Bob Christopher visited him, and remembers 'Dennis saying that he had had the song "Happy Days Are Here Again" going interminably round his head'.

Ron Brewer, the Labour agent for East Hertfordshire, was another visitor, and they discussed whether Potter should continue as candidate. Potter had thought: 'Well, if I'm going to be forced to give up too much, it's going to be so dreadful that I shall become utterly depressed and beaten. So I hung on to the candidacy.'

After three weeks, on 27 June, he was discharged from hospital, but his case was kept under review as an out-patient. A fortnight later, a doctor at the rheumatology clinic noted that 'his psoriatic arthritis has relapsed to some extent since his discharge. He is having considerable pain in the right jaw, and there is inflammation of the right knee and both metatarsal regions. The psoriasis has also flared to some extent.' Injections continued, and he was advised 'to rest as much as possible at home'.

The *Daily Herald* now decided, on the strength of his stand-in week as television critic, to give him that job on a regular basis, and on 23 July he started to write the paper's Monday to Friday TV column. Again, he began with a lowbrow programme, ITV's American crime series *Sunset Strip*:

'Boy, in this business you meet the craziest people,' mumbled a visiting cop, unmoved by mere death.

This alarmingly zany episode was set in America's cocktail belt, where feeble-minded matrons slim to a bouncing one-sy, two-sy, touch your toes, three-sy, four-sy, waistline goes.

Boy, in this business you see the craziest things.

At first, he maintained this pose of intellectual detachment, writing of *Coronation Street*, 'Strange that in this slick, neon-lit age, we should find solace in the gossipy vindictiveness of old ladies in hair nets.' But he made a beeline for sports programmes, with the excuse that 'television reaches its peak with sport. It can catch an event as it happens and this urgent feeling of immediacy goes well with the muscular action and unpredictability of most sports.' In a later *Herald* review, he admitted, 'I respond to soccer with an intense if entirely unreasonable passion . . . ' One Saturday, he told his readers that he would not be watching television but going to the Cup Final.

His style in these early reviews was sometimes overwrought; he described Peter Dimmock's screen smile as 'the bared but hesitant grin of a guest at an upper-crust house party agreeing to a devilish game of whist', and the soap opera *Compact* as 'fleeting shadows in a polished plate-glass window . . . as harmless as a mousetrap without cheese . . . as giddy as a cut-rate marriage bureau on the first day of spring'. But he wrote with unaffected admiration of *Morecambe and Wise*, Tony Hancock and *Maigret*, and was delighted by the first episode of *Dr Finlay's Casebook*: 'The strength of this programme lay in the almost casual accumulation of background details. Compared with the shiny surface of Dr Kildare's world, this was a neat little study in social history.'

After a month as full-time TV critic, he was invited to write a *Herald* opinion column on the state of British television. He observed that, though 'the gogglebox' had been attacked so often for shoddiness and bad taste, there were now 'splendidly worthwhile' programmes, which were the work of 'new men' in the BBC and ITV. 'They do not yet get enough credit for what could yet turn out to be the most significant cultural revolution of our times.'

He now had to start campaigning as a Labour candidate. It was hard, unglamorous work. His agent Ron Brewer explains that East Hertfordshire 'was a county constituency, with four urban and two rural districts, which made life very difficult – if Dennis made the most brilliant speech in one place, it wouldn't be reported in the other local newspapers. So we had to try to make an impact everywhere.' They slogged around the village halls in Brewer's car, and Potter found himself addressing every kind of group; they never forgot their visit to the Buntingford Women's Co-operative Guild, where an old lady knitted non-stop while Potter spoke. However, Brewer says Potter's speeches 'caught his audience by their sheer honesty, language and wit'.

In Potter's third month as television critic, the *Herald* announced the start of a weekly column in which he would single out special programmes or important issues in television. In the first (8 September 1962) he reported on 'the overworked drama departments of both channels', which he said were in turmoil: 'There is a war of attrition raging. On one side there are those who want to be cautious and take plays and ideas direct from the theatre. On the other are the revolutionaries who want to shake things up a bit. They are eager to inject new forms, fresh techniques, bolder themes into the TV play . . . '

Five years later, in his introduction to *The Nigel Barton Plays*, Potter described this war in more detail. Television drama had begun (he wrote) as 'small-scale "naturalism"', a studio version of 'third-rate theatre', in which the only excitement for the viewer was likely to be 'a desperate actor wordlessly opening and shutting his mouth while waiting for a prompt'. As a result, by the mid-Sixties the TV play seemed unlikely to survive. But there were those in television (Potter continued), like Troy Kennedy Martin, who were campaigning for bold experiment and the abandonment of 'all drama which owes its form or substance to theatre plays'.

The main thrust of his *Herald* TV column in 1962 continued to be populist and anti-highbrow. In September he attacked the pretensions of the BBC arts series *Monitor*, concluding, '"Culture" . . . has become too suspect for too many people. TV can help, must help, break down these false barriers.'

The following month he told his readers that both the BBC and ITV were planning late-night satire shows: 'I hope these new programmes will get away with murder. The "new" humour, whether sick or savagely satirical, is at least pungent and provocative – qualities desperately needed on the TV.' The BBC's *That Was The Week That Was* started on Saturday, 24 November 1962. Potter reviewed it the following Monday, calling it 'wildly funny, dubiously improper'. He added that it was 'written by a variety of people with chips rather than pips on their shoulders'. He was soon writing for it himself.

*

David Nathan, in his role as the *Herald*'s arts reporter, had been sent to interview Ned Sherrin and David Frost, the producer and linkman of *TW3*, as the new show soon became known. 'On the way there,' says Nathan,

I saw something in the paper which struck me as worth a comment. I mentioned it to Ned and he said, 'Yes, write it.' Well, I hadn't done anything like that before but I did and they used it the following week. Then I got another idea and I wrote that. And then Ned asked if I knew Dennis and he suggested that as a lot of people writing for the show seemed to operate best in pairs we might do the same. Dennis thought it was a good idea. We were both desperately short of money at the time – the *Herald* didn't pay very well. So we started writing sketches.

Nathan adds that he and Potter had already tried jointly writing a television serial about students, but it had come to nothing. Sherrin, on the other hand, does not recall knowing of Potter before Nathan came to him, and thinks the collaboration was entirely Nathan's idea.

Potter seems to have regarded their *TW3* contributions as of little importance in his career – 'Around this time I also did a few sketches with David Nathan' was as much as he said about it. In fact he and Nathan wrote a great deal of material, for *TW3* and at least one other programme, and Potter learned much in the process.

Nathan, who had left school at fifteen and worked his way to Fleet Street through journalism in his native Manchester and elsewhere in the provinces, says that they would write the sketches in the *Herald* office or at his own house in Wembley Park, the Potters' Hammersmith flat being too cramped and noisy. 'I would be at the typewriter, and Dennis would be pacing the room.' They agreed at the outset to take joint credit and equal payment, whatever their individual contributions to each sketch. 'It didn't seem very important,' says Nathan. 'We were just a couple of journalists making a few quid on the side in a new and exciting programme.'

The first sketch to be accepted by Sherrin, performed by David Frost, William Rushton and Lance Percival in the edition of 5 January 1963, was a collage of comments that had been made over the years about Clement Attlee, Labour Prime Minister from 1945 to 1951. This showed that, when he was in power, Attlee had been dismissed as a nonentity, but now, on his eightieth birthday, he was being hailed as one of the great prime ministers.

Nathan recalls he did the research for this sketch, using the *Herald* cuttings library. Sherrin says that the scripts 'used to turn up done on different typewriters, and my theory was that they each wrote them in turn, but then David told me that he tapped them all out – on an office machine as well as his own. I must have met Dennis by then, but I don't have any clear memory of it, though of course I became very much aware of him later.' Nathan says it was he rather than Potter who rang Sherrin to suggest ideas. He also occasionally went to Lime Grove to meet the *TW3* team. Neither he nor Potter was there for rehearsal or transmission – 'unless there was a party'.

The second Nathan–Potter sketch, shown a month later, mocked Canon John Collins, the left-wing Anglican who was Chairman of the Campaign for Nuclear Disarmament; their script jibed at his ideological inconsistencies and tendency to make a fool of himself. Three weeks later the duo wrote an ingenious squib about the pop singer Adam Faith, who had given evidence that week to a British Medical Association committee investigating teenage sex. The Nathan–Potter version of the proceedings begins:

CHAIRMAN: Never having been teenagers ourselves, Mr Faith, we have called you here to ask your advice and views on the problems of young people in Britain today. Perhaps for a start, you could tell us your qualifications. For the record, of course.

FAITH: (*talking rather than singing, no musical accompaniment*) I may be young and I still go to school. When it comes to chicks I'm no poor little fool. I'm a man, yay yay yay, I'm a man. Yu-huh-huh.

CHAIRMAN: Quite so, Mr Faith, quite so. This is precisely the kind of information we wanted from you.

REST OF COMMITTEE: Rhubarb, rhubarb.

WOMAN MEMBER OF COMMITTEE: (*with giggle*) Very charmingly put, if I may say so, Mr Faith.

CHAIRMAN: We are deeply concerned about the apparent instability of young people's relationships.

FAITH: I know that love is blind, don't you know it, don't you know it? And I know that love's unkind, don't you know it, don't you know it?

Faith's 'evidence' to the committee continues in this fashion, and at the end the committee members, 'greatly moved', mob him like pop fans.

Potter had already discovered that pop songs could be used ironically on screen.

The Nathan–Potter duo was even-handed politically. 'We weren't trying to keep any political balance – it was just what amused us,' says Nathan. They wrote a sketch purporting to show that the Conservatives had as lengthy a record of nationalization as Labour, and a spoof of a South African government film promoting tourism (Frost introduced it by saying that it was, of course, 'in black and white'); also a monologue for Millicent Martin as a Christine Keeler lookalike – the Profumo affair was beginning to destabilize the Tory government. On the other hand they also mocked the *New Statesman*, in a sketch featuring three earnest-minded left-wing readers poring over the lectures advertised on its back page: 'Here's a must for Thursday – *Pleading and Proof in Classical Hindu Law . . .* '

There were three Nathan–Potter sketches about Potter's *bête noire*, Admass, of which the best was a monologue for the eve of Mother's Day. Delivered by Kenneth Cope, it encapsulated the advertising industry's concept of a typical mother:

What is a Mum?

A Mum lives with a Dad and 2.4 children in a rented house where the neighbours notice her washing on the line. A Mum relies upon secret ingredients and instant cake-mixes. She has kids with dirty teeth who regularly shout, 'Don't forget the Fruit Gums, Mum.'

A Mum is full of faith. She thinks every washday is a miracle . . . She buys disinfectants that make her clean round the bend . . . She is so flaming ignorant that she can't tell Stork from butter – or even Stork from margarine. She thinks a Free Gift is something she doesn't have to pay for.

A Mum, in short, is a snob who buys plastic flowers and floor polish containing real lavender. She solves emotional problems with Horlicks, and on Mother's Day this idle, ignorant, tasteless and irresponsible lump of girdle-encased margarine fat has the cheek to turn round and expect *us* to buy *her* a bleeding present!

Nathan says that he contributed 'only one line' to this piece – and that the original idea came from Jack Rosenthal, who was writing for *TW3* too.

Potter received fees ranging from ten to thirty guineas for his share in each sketch accepted by *TW3*. This increased his earnings substantially, and in May 1963 he and the family moved from Hammersmith to a quiet suburban address in north London not far from David

Nathan and his wife, a small rented furnished house at 15 Fairway Avenue, Kingsbury, NW9.

*

Meanwhile he was conducting much of his Labour campaign in East Hertfordshire as if it were a *TW3* sketch. Ron Brewer laughs at the memory of him addressing a United Nations Association meeting in Bishop's Stortford, and referring in his speech to Cecil Rhodes, who had been born there, as 'a cheap crook from this town'. Brewer also preserves the menu of the same town's Civic Dinner and Dance on 22 March 1963, at which Potter caused a sensation.

Jean Brewer, Ron's wife, recalls that the evening got off to a sticky start with the Brewers and Dennis and Margaret Potter discovering that they were underdressed – the rest of the top table were in evening clothes. The first toast was to be proposed by the constituency's Tory MP, Sir Derek Walker-Smith, a baronet and QC whom Brewer describes as 'rather pompous'. The seat had been Tory 'since time immemorial', says Brewer, and at the dinner Walker-Smith, who had had a majority of ten thousand at the 1959 Election, made a speech that Brewer and Potter found patronizing and complacent. 'And Dennis said to me, out of the corner of his mouth, "I'm going to have a go at him." Well, when it was his turn, he took the rise – I can remember him referring to Walker-Smith's "sonorous Victorian tones". At first, this caused quite a bit of laughter at the top table, until everyone saw Walker-Smith's reaction. And then the laughter froze, as if somebody had thrown a switch.'

Jean Brewer recalls that the guests began to bang their cutlery against their plates in protest at Potter. 'Afterwards, we went down into the bar, and were standing in a group, talking, and the barman came out from behind the bar, poked Dennis in the back, and said, "I found your speech offensive." We gaped. So Dennis looked him up and down, and said, "You're a bit offensive yourself." Margaret and I went into the ladies and hung on to each other!'

Ron Brewer was delighted at his candidate's behaviour – though he adds, 'We weren't intimate friends – he wasn't a man to whom it was easy to get close.' He and Jean found Margaret a much warmer personality. On one occasion, she stood in for Dennis at a campaign meeting. 'We met her at the station,' says Ron Brewer, 'and we scarcely recognized her, because her hair had been dyed quite a brassy blond, which made her look barmaidish. She said Dennis wanted that, which rather surprised me.'

Writing his TV column that spring, Potter continued to castigate the BBC Drama Department for the 'shrieking banality' of many plays, which were often ruined by plodding realism – 'so damned "authentic"'. For example, Rhys Adrian's *Too Old for Donkeys*, set on Euston Station, was 'too drab', and James Saunders's *Just You Wait*, about bus crews, was 'dismally authentic'. Two notable exceptions, both on ITV, were Harold Pinter's *The Lover*, which Potter found 'infuriating, enthralling, disturbing and then wildly funny . . . a fascinating experience', and Granada's adaptation of *War and Peace*, which side-stepped realism by using a narrator, convincing Potter that 'the simple, naturalistic, tediously "authentic" drama is not the only way of liberating the TV play'.

In June 1963 he admitted to his readers that the obligation to watch the screen for 'more than twenty hours a week' was wearing him down. The next month he wrote:

Watching *Emergency – Ward 10* while actually in hospital, as I did last night, is an uncanny situation.

Shimmering on the screen is the mythical, glamorized world of godlike doctors and nubile, toothpaste-smiling nurses.

But the real world of bedpans and squeaking tea trolleys around one is far less like the cover of a glossy film magazine . . .

His psoriasis, in remission for a while, had flared up again, and the dermatologists at the West London Hospital were now trying 'the new occlusive technique' of anointing his skin and then covering it in polythene bags, creating a small-scale greenhouse around his body.

TW3 returned in September after a summer break, with a Nathan–Potter sketch about a striptease club trying to get on the Shakespeare quatercentenary bandwagon – 'The Hey Nonny Nude Show'. Their other contributions that autumn included two further monologues on the 'What is a Mum?' model, this time dealing with subjects close to Potter. 'What is a smoker?' begins the first.

A smoker is a patriot who collectively pays enough taxes in a year to buy an American warhead or individually to provide a car for the Minister of Labour.

But all he wants is the right cigarette at the right price and at the right size. In return he gets a hacking cough and is never lonely . . .

A smoker . . . mistakes the hot cancerous tar in his lungs for the healthy trickle of a cool mountain stream . . .

These were allusions to two cigarette slogans, 'You're never alone with a Strand', and 'Consulate, cool as a mountain stream'. A month later came a sketch called 'What is an invalid?', with the surely auto-biographical line: 'He takes cigarettes to calm his nerves and linctus to cure his cough.'

A few weeks before this sketch was written, a dermatologist decided to refer Potter to a psychiatrist. The referral note explained that having to make public appearances as a political candidate while suffering from psoriasis was causing him 'distress'. An appointment was made for mid-October, at Charing Cross Hospital, and Potter was driven there by Ken Trodd.

Trodd was then working as a university lecturer in Nigeria and Ghana, and was paying a summer visit to London. He returned to England in the summer of 1963, with another university job in mind. 'I can't remember Dennis telling me very much about why he was going to the psychiatrist,' says Trodd. 'He was obviously troubled.'

The psychiatrist, Dr John Randell, found Potter hostile. 'This man confused the date of his first appointment,' Randell noted,

and was rather indignant. He is an assertive red-headed Gloucestershire political journalist, son of a miner, who has an Aneurin Bevan resentment of privilege and the Establishment . . . He has psoriasis and rheumatoid arthritis [*sic*] and is somewhat disabled by this complaint. He is a prospective Labour candidate but for the moment feels little enthusiasm for this role.

I had the impression that he was basically a cycloid and prone to swings of mood; for example, when he was at Oxford he edited *Isis* and was prominent in the Labour movement, and I suspect that he did all this on the crest of a hypermanic wave. Now he is somewhat depressed with typical symptoms of that pattern.

Dr Randell judged Potter's depression severe enough to prescribe an antidepressant, and to contemplate giving him ECT (electro-convulsive therapy) if this had no effect. His record of the consultation with Potter continues, 'There is quite a serious psycho-sexual problem and a family history of attempted suicide.' Potter's sister June says of this, 'Uncle Ernie was the only one on both sides of the family to attempt suicide. So I think that was a bit of hyperbole on Dennis's part.'

Potter's daughter Sarah recalls her father saying years afterwards that the visit to Randell had been 'a total waste of time, because apparently the psychiatrist went through Dad's various symptoms, and then said, "And what were your feelings towards your male friends at Oxford?" And I think at that point Dad just stopped the session and said, "Forget it – you're on the wrong track."'

In 1990 Potter mentioned the consultation to an interviewer:

In 1962–63, when I was first in hospital and desperately ill, I asked to see a guy who was attached to the hospital. And the dermatologist said, 'Oh you mean Freud and all that stuff.' I said, 'No, I just feel I need to talk to someone.' I had about three meetings which I found both useful and threatening. What was useful about it was the very fact that I had the appointment enabled me to talk about some of the things that were troubling me. And that was like a turning point, acknowledging I was in desperation was important. That was before I had written any of these plays, and it may well have been that, had I not acknowledged I was *in extremis*, I would never have written at all.

It is not clear what 'psycho-sexual problem' Randell believed he had discovered. If Potter told him about being abused by his uncle, he may have thought that it was – as Sarah's recollection suggests – a case of repressed homosexuality. On the other hand, on one of his brief trips back to England while teaching in Africa, Ken Trodd had found himself listening to a confession from Potter that suggests a very different sort of problem.

'I was staying in a friend's house in Putney,' says Trodd,

and I know that that's where Dennis told it to me. And he was then going to go back to tell Margaret, so I was being used as a sort of rehearsal. I don't remember it being an extremely long conversation. He said that he wanted to tell me that during a period – I don't remember whether he specified how long, but I sensed some years, though not a vast number of years – he'd had sex with an enormous number of prostitutes.

Trodd was struck less by the confession itself than by the self-conscious manner in which it was delivered: 'He'd decided that he wanted to try something out on me. It was sort of intended. I don't think it was that we were just there, that afternoon, had a drink, and up it came. He'd made up his mind.'

Around this time Roger Smith listened to the same confession:

It was in about 1963, something like that, and Dennis and Margaret had rented a furnished house in north London, on one of those terrible estates. And I'm sure it was before I joined the BBC in 1964. And he said he had this terrible confession to make, that he felt badly about. So then he started talking about all the various whores that he'd had. I wasn't shocked. As somebody who would be terrified to go with whores, I felt, wow, this is very impressive. But I couldn't believe it, because it was at a time of great sexual liberation. In the Fifties you never had any hope of sex with women, even at Oxford. But suddenly in the Sixties they didn't say no any more! So why bother with the whores?

Smith does not recall that Potter gave any details of these sexual encounters, but Trodd remembers him describing one incident:

He said that one of the things that had brought him to his senses was the fright, one evening when he was doing a knee-tremble with a girl down some basement steps, caused by a policeman coming along and shining his light down, trying to apprehend them. Dennis, rapidly disconnecting and buttoning himself up, rushed up the steps, kneed the policeman in the groin, and ran away. And one of his main concerns about that incident was that he already had a sense of himself as a public figure. So clearly it had happened quite imminently before he told me the story.

Trodd gathered that 'he wanted to end all this, in a total way, by telling Margaret. And telling me was a way of rehearsing.' But nobody knows if he did tell her, or if, for the time being, it did end.

Others thought there might be secrets in his private life. Paul Foot, who had known Potter at Oxford, joined the *Daily Herald* in 1964 and sometimes glimpsed him in and around the office. Foot says, 'I think he saw a lot of young women. It was generally the gossip around the *Herald* – that he would be seen in pubs with young women who were not his wife. I remember seeing him one day in the Coach and Horses, the *Private Eye* pub, and there was a young woman with him. He was plainly wishing he hadn't been seen with her by someone who knew him.' Potter's political agent Ron Brewer remarks, 'I think Dennis was capable of flirting or having an affair – just from little things which he said. The kind of things that one says over a jar in the pub.' His *TW3* collaborator David Nathan is of the same opinion, but emphasizes that the Potters' marriage did not seem to be under threat:

I don't think Dennis was particularly faithful sexually, but the marriage struck me as being indissoluble – that whatever he got up to from time to time (and I have no direct evidence that he got up to anything), it was insignificant compared with the strength of the marriage. And I didn't know whether Margaret knew or not. *I* didn't know for certain. But a couple of things he said made me think that possibly he was not above having the odd fling elsewhere.

But this was the alleged Swinging Sixties with its sexual revolution that was always somewhere else, so I didn't take any moral high ground. And I think Dennis had a deep, deep regard for Margaret – a high regard for her qualities. She was staunchly loyal, totally supportive, and I think he recognized these qualities and responded to them. He may have been unfaithful in another respect, but he was totally committed to her, and I can't imagine any circumstances in which they would have split up.

Sarah Potter says of the stories of her father going with prostitutes, 'I'm not saying it didn't happen, because I don't know – I really don't. But there was never any question of his wanting to sever the link with Mum. In the end she was always the rock, and he did recognize that.' Her sister Jane agrees: 'Mum and Dad certainly had rows, and some of those were spectacular. But they were very open about everything with each other, and with us. And they were in love.'

It is of course impossible to discover, thirty-five years later, whether Potter did buy the services of prostitutes and, if so, how often. It is conceivable that the whole story was a fantasy, or at least a considerable exaggeration, inflated from a few actual experiences. What is clear is that the confessions (whether real or fabricated) answered some psychological need within him. It could be argued that they were a kind of exhibitionist sexual act in themselves. And they do appear to be closely linked to his illness.

It is widely recognized that an individual's state of mind can play a large part in triggering a psoriatic attack. Potter was aware of this. 'My disease is to some extent psychosomatic,' he would tell journalists later in his life. 'If you suddenly find yourself covered in lesions or scales or what have you, your normal tendency is to believe that there is something in you that is responsible. Especially if you are a Protestant.' He believed that, although 'psoriatic arthropathy is a genetic condition', it had been triggered because 'I had reached such a low point that . . . the affliction was also a release'. He specifically mentioned his unhappiness at the *Daily Herald* – 'paralysis became more than a metaphor for how I felt about my job' – and his discomfort at trying to be a popular journalist: 'My condition was genetic, but it felt psychological. I knew that I had lost touch with something, and that the soapbox words were no longer capable of restoring enough of what had been half-unknowingly jettisoned.' But a wrong turn in his career could have been righted without too much difficulty. The confessions suggest that there was a more profound self-loathing.

Certainly he associated psoriasis with a feeling of pollution. 'I've talked to dermatologists about this,' he said towards the end of his life. 'Your skin is your outer self – your boundary between you and the world – and inevitably you feel part of that leper syndrome, you know, "Ring the bell and shout 'unclean'."' He was alluding to *The Singing Detective*, where the psychotherapist tells Marlow: 'The temptation is to believe that the ills and the poisons of the mind or the personality have somehow erupted straight out on to the skin. "Unclean! Unclean!" you shout, ringing the bell, warning us to keep off, to keep clear.'

In Potter's 1985 television adaptation of Scott Fitzgerald's *Tender is the Night*, he puts a similar thought into the mind of a female psoriasis patient, Hannah, who is talking to the psychiatrist Dick Diver (the words are not in Fitzgerald's novel):

HANNAH: If I knew what I had done to deserve this I could accept it with equanimity . . .

DICK: You use the word 'deserve'. As though your illness were a punishment.

HANNAH: It is. It *is* . . . The poisons in my mind have broken out upon my skin.

Roger Smith sees it this way too: 'Actually what Dennis was was this kind of biblical man in torture. His whole illness was biblical – the scales, the skin falling around him, and he couldn't walk. This was someone who was suffering the most terrible kind of guilt.'

CHAPTER 2

Vote, Vote, Vote for Dennis Potter

Despite having become cult viewing for a vast audience, *That Was The Week That Was* did not complete its second series. The BBC took it off the air at the end of 1963, on the specious grounds that it might prejudice the General Election, due the following autumn. In his *Herald* column, Potter wrote that Hugh Greene, the Director-General, had 'slaughtered' the satire show, and called it an act of 'wanton destruction'.

He also reported continuing turmoil in the BBC Drama Department: 'The current shortage of writing talent has reached crisis point. BBC drama boss Sydney Newman confesses that he would "go down on his knees" before a fresh new writer.' A month later, on 22 February 1964, he reported that 'two young men' had been charged with the responsibility of improving the single plays:

They are James McTaggart [*sic*], as executive producer, and Roger Smith, as script editor, both currently involved in the tiny but unorthodox *Teletale* series on alternate Friday nights.

McTaggart thinks 'naturalism' – the kind of dreary authenticity which duplicates the very grease on the fish-and-chip paper – has had its day.

Smith, who has to find the new plays, said, 'We're talking with a lot of writers to see what can be done about changing the form and contents of the TV play.'

Among those writers was Potter himself.

Sydney Newman, who had been Head of Drama at the Canadian Broadcasting Commission, had arrived in London in 1958 to head the ITV series *Armchair Theatre* at ABC Television. He began to commission the newly fashionable 'kitchen sink' type of play from writers such as Harold Pinter, Alun Owen, Clive Exton and Bill Naughton. 'I am proud', he said in January 1963, the month in which he had transferred to the BBC as Head of Drama, 'that I played some part in the recognition that the working man was a fit subject for drama, and not just a comic foil in a play on middle-class manners.' At the BBC, Newman divided the enormous Drama Department into a Drama Group comprising three sections – Plays, Series and Serials – and launched *First Night*, a Sunday-night single-play slot which was to showcase new writers (it would go out in opposition to *Armchair Theatre*). Newman's staff included a number of 'story editors' who were to find these writers.

One of them was Roger Smith, who after leaving Oxford in 1960 had begun to write for television – he had a play called *Our Ted* accepted for Granada's *Younger Generation* series, and he recalls how this led to work at the BBC:

Troy Kennedy Martin, whom I'd met through John McGrath, asked me to write for an experimental BBC play series called *Storyboard*. I adapted a Raymond Chandler story for it, called *I'll Be Waiting*, and Jimmy MacTaggart directed it. Elwyn Jones, who was really running BBC drama then, offered me a scriptwriter–adapter contract, and I then wrote and adapted stories for a play series called *Studio 4*. That led to another play series called *Teletales*, for new directors off the BBC training course, and Ken Loach directed his first television play for it – a play of mine called *Catherine*, which was based on the break-up of my marriage [to Caroline Seebohm, later an important figure in Potter's life]. One of the actors in it was Tony Garnett. When Jimmy MacTaggart was asked by Sydney Newman to become producer of the play series which became *The Wednesday Play*, he insisted that I should be the story editor. A little later, I brought in Tony Garnett and Ken Trodd as assistant story editors.

Smith describes MacTaggart as 'a Scottish middle-class ex-National Service paratrooper about five or six years older than me. He was no great rebel, but terrific in what he allowed to happen. He was very open to ideas. And we cared about making *television* drama. The old idea of television drama at the BBC was to take a West End play, pencil out "Curtain" and put "Fade to black". But Jimmy wanted to *use* the studio.' Ken Trodd describes MacTaggart as 'the brake on our wildness – a bit older, more of a BBC person, who had Scottish restraint; and yet he knew this was a cutting edge and he had to encourage us'.

Smith is enthusiastic about Sydney Newman: 'Sydney I liked,' says

Smith. 'He was outrageous, he was commercial, he did his office hours, he had a bar in his office – you felt, this is the grown-up world, this is showbiz. Sydney gave us *carte blanche* to make something popular of the new *Wednesday Play* slot, and I said, "We're going to go and find new writers." We had a year to do it. And Dennis was one of the very first I went to.'

Trodd emphasizes the desperate hunger for new writers:

The quantity of plays we were making was amazing, and this meant that you could risk some failures – try out new talent, give it a chance. Tony Garnett used to say that, with a new writer, you should regard the first commission as an investment in the second – you weren't very likely to find the first one winning through. And the commissioning ratio was prodigally generous. You could commission ten and make one.

The story editors were able to commission plays themselves, without anyone else's approval. 'That was the dream time,' says Trodd wistfully.

Potter's own accounts of the beginning of his career as a television playwright, given to interviewers over the years, make little mention of Roger Smith, and imply that he chose to become a creative writer because his journalistic work and political ambitions had become unfeasible through his illness. For example:

What I wanted to do, or what I *thought* I wanted to do – to have a political career, to be a public man – wasn't possible. But all of a sudden, there was a whispering seduction within that despair, saying, 'Now you can do whatever you choose. Now you don't have to go out and fend in that way, with those people, about those things . . . It was a crisis point, an either–or situation: either you give in, or you survive and create something out of this bombsite which you've become – you put up a new building.

But the fact is that, when Smith approached him with the proposal, his position at the *Daily Herald* was still secure, and his psoriatic arthropathy was relatively stable – there is no record of his seeking medical attention in the early part of 1964.

He gave some acknowledgement to Smith in a 1969 *Times* article:

Roger Smith . . . was a notable exception to the 'company man' story editor who so afflicts writers. He persuaded people that they actually *could* write, out of their own experience . . . Several other writers were, like myself, persuaded to treat the television play as a serious vehicle for their ambitions. But . . . he [has] left the BBC unsung and since uncelebrated.

Potter admitted to Melvyn Bragg that his first television plays had been written in a 'burst of energy', but usually he liked to make out that his early scripts had been the product of the sickbed: 'I was depressed and ill and in pain, and I found that my writing was a pass out of it.' To Bragg, he said, 'through illness . . . I reinvented myself, quite consciously, as an act'. And in his MacTaggart Lecture: 'I had the opportunity [through psoriasis] of reassembling myself from what I hesitate to call scratch. I had the chance of making myself up all over again.' He liked to say that psoriasis was the 'strange, shadowy ally' on which he had founded his writing career. Yet he did once admit that illness was the trigger rather than the cause: 'As a child I'd always thought of myself as a writer . . . The illness was the propellant, but it would have happened anyway, only more slowly.'

Smith explains why he approached Potter: 'Dennis was already writing for *TW3*, and I went to anybody who might have a story. I used to say, "I know how to do it; you give me the story, and I'll tell you how to put it down." And Dennis already had the idea for *The Confidence Course*, or was writing it as something else – maybe as a novel (he wouldn't have thought about the stage). And I said, "Do it for television."'

A BBC memo from Smith to Copyright Department, dated 18 February 1964, stated that he wished to commission *The Confidence Course*, an original TV play, from Dennis Potter, at seventy-five minutes, with a target delivery date of 1 April 1964. The memo noted that Potter's agent was Roger Hancock of 8 Waterloo Place, Pall Mall. On 16 March, Copyright informed Smith that Potter had now signed a 'Guild Agreement' for the play, at a fee of £600, half payable immediately and half on acceptance. On 19 June, Smith's secretary told Copyright that the script had been accepted. Roger Hancock, the younger brother of the comedian Tony Hancock (whom David Nathan had got to know while writing theatre reviews in the provinces) had been engaged by Nathan to negotiate his and Potter's *TW3* contracts. 'I wasn't a close friend,' Hancock says. 'Dennis used to complain to me, "You're non-political", and I'd say, "Totally. I just want to do the deals for you."'

Potter said he felt little hesitation in accepting Smith's invitation to write a play: 'The experience of watching television for two years nearly, and writing those silly little pieces in a silly little newspaper, was such that I (like millions of people, no doubt) felt, well, I can do better than this . . . '

David Nathan says that the play began as another collaboration:

After *That Was The Week*, Dennis was intent on more interesting work and he started to write a play called *The Confidence Course*. He intended we should write it together, operating as we had with the sketches. So I was at the typewriter, because I typed faster than Dennis, and he walked up and down and we wrote dialogue between us. But every line I contributed was taken out . . . So I said, 'Come on, Dennis, this is your play, why don't you go away and write it?'

The Nathan–Potter collaboration did, however, continue for a while. The two wrote a little material for the successor to *TW3*, called *Not So Much a Programme* . . . , which was broadcast from November 1964 to April 1965, though by the end of the series Potter had dropped out. Nathan says, slightly bitterly, 'Nothing Dennis wrote about his background takes account of our collaboration. He was so dismissive that it seemed he was ashamed of it.'

*

Potter said that *The Confidence Course* was 'really about the self-motivation courses run by bodies like the Dale Carnegie Institute, which I covered as a newspaper reporter at one of their so-called free sessions. The *Herald* wouldn't use the article because Dale Carnegie was advertising in the paper.' However, when the play caused trouble with the Carnegie organization, the BBC noted that Potter's knowledge of it had been gained not as a newspaperman, but while reporting on it for the radio news programme *Ten O'Clock* (his piece was not used).

Potter recalled of the Carnegie session:

A group of people gathered together in a hotel conference room – some of them were planted, I believe. The speakers were hustling and bustling people up to the front, where they'd let them speak for three minutes, then describe how they could have done it better, how they should impress people – standard pop psychology. They'd show you how to have a better memory by blindfolding somebody who would recite a list of twenty objects that they'd just seen. I thought this was so theatrical an attempt to pull certain kinds of social skills out of people – and phoney . . .

What interested me was why those people were there, what sort of anxiety had brought them to that hotel. But something deeper was worrying me about it, and that was this so-called confidence factor. This was about self-functioning at a time when I was beginning to feel that I couldn't self-function. The people running it were saying, 'We can give you confidence.'

The Confidence Course begins like a *TW3* sketch, with the course director and his lackeys waiting in a hotel conference room for their customers. 'I got soaked through coming here tonight,' complains one of the confidence men. '*And* I carried half a ton of pamphlets . . . Some of the *Personal Dynamism* got a bit soggy at the edges.' There is also an invisible narrator, who sets the scene and comments on the gullible individuals who sign up for the course: 'A few more people are coming . . . Each one looking for something purchasable called CONFIDENCE, knowing themselves failures of one sort or another, but unwilling to acknowledge the need for a psychiatrist.'

The narrator is Potter's first step away from naturalism. Nearly thirty years later he wrote, 'So-called naturalism is by far and away the dominant mode, and easily the most characteristic syntax of television grammar. But one of the troubles of supposedly showing things-as-they-really-are . . . is how difficult it then becomes . . . not to make people feel deep in their souls that this is also more or less the way things have to be.'

While Potter was writing *The Confidence Course* in the spring of 1964, Troy Kennedy Martin delivered an onslaught against naturalism in television drama, in the theatre journal *Encore*:

Television drama at the moment is going nowhere fast . . . It can and will destroy itself unless a breakthrough in form is made . . . Not an art set-up like the Langham Group [a BBC think-tank of television writers and directors, which was trying to develop forms of television that made more use of images] but a working philosophy which contains a new idea of form . . . Something which can be applied to mass audience viewing. Something which can re-create the direction, the fire, and the ideas which TV used to have . . . The key to this revolution lies in taking a long look at naturalism to find out why it was, and is, the wrong form for drama for the medium . . . The new drama will . . . relate, directly, man's relation to God . . . and to himself. It will be much more personal in style . . .

Martin recommended such radical techniques as the 'wild editing of random objects', which he said could 'stimulate a very personal kind of meaning like pictures seen in the fire'.

Among the responses to this in the next issue of *Encore* was one from Potter, in his role as *Herald* TV critic. He praised the vigour of Martin's argument, but said he was wary of eccentric visuals, and argued that conventional storytelling could still convey experience successfully, providing the dialogue is good enough and the writer genuinely has something to *say* . . . What you want to say still comes first . . . The sort of didacticism we need, passionately concerned to present all sorts of evidence, constantly infiltrating all our defences, is ideally suited to the narrative method. The writer can attack from all sides at once, out of a mosaic of objects, details, moods, memories and conversations. Pictures in a real fire, pictures ablaze.

The Confidence Course avoids visual trickery and, in form, is a conventional one-act play; yet it takes another bold step away from naturalism when, after the other customers have arrived, a strange figure comes up the corridor. 'Name doesn't matter,' he snaps. 'It's Hazlitt, actually, 1778–1965.'

In hospital during 1962, Potter had discovered the writings of William Hazlitt, and felt an immediate affinity. In his teens, he had 'probably dipped into one or two of the essays without feeling particularly impressed'. Now,

I was fortunate enough to be the beneficiary of a deviant volume in an otherwise orthodox hospital welfare trolley. Tucked almost shamefully away on the bottom layer was a well-worn, orangey-brown collection of Hazlitt's essays, which I took with a graceless reluctance designed less to pull myself out of a hole than to fend off the formidable trolley-pusher, who had Good Deeds shining on her face like a badly applied cosmetic.

Like Potter, Hazlitt came from a radical and Nonconformist background. He worked as a newspaper reporter but was also a painter. His portrait, with hair brushed back and a suspicious scowl, makes him look a little like Potter, and though his skin was normal his unpopular opinions, expressed in journalism and essays, earned him the wounding nickname 'Pimpled Hazlitt'. He had an obsession with young girls which made him write a self-exposing book, *Liber Amoris*, and he eventually died of stomach cancer.*

Reading the essays in hospital, Potter 'responded eagerly and almost immediately' to Hazlitt's angry abuse of those he despised. Six years later he remarked that Hazlitt 'could use invective with such viperish skill that his victims might well have examined themselves in a hand mirror to see if the venomous prose had erupted into discoloured flesh or broken skin. A quirky, pungent, obsessive, honest and extremely

---

* In 1992, Potter told two film producer friends, John Roberdeau and Robert Michael Geisler, that he was contemplating writing a stage play (with music) about Hazlitt and *Liber Amoris*.

forceful writer who alienated most of his friends [and] exposed himself
without mercy . . . ' He could have been saying all this about himself;
and there is definitely self-portrayal when he remarks, elsewhere, that
Hazlitt

was an odd combination of very progressive . . . and quite reactionary. He
would prefer an old book to a new book, an old thing to a new thing; you also
see that, though I think to a lesser degree, in someone like George Orwell. I
am interested in the tension in oneself between an instinct that cherishes order,
tradition and discipline, and what, in general terms, might be called a con-
catenation of right-wing emotions underneath or interlaced with radicalism,
where your mind tells you other things. This tension – which I think is evident
in Hazlitt and Orwell – is intrinsically dramatic, because it means you're on
your guard against the facile optimism and brutal idealism of the Left, even
though intellectually you respect and indeed share in it; at the same time, you
pay due attention to the things that would normally be called 'right-wing'.

He chose Hazlitt's essays as his book on *Desert Island Discs* in 1977:
'They are so wide, and he's so brilliant and so provocative, still, that
they would never cease to feed me.'

With Hazlitt installed uneasily in the audience, the confidence course
proceeds. 'Aren't we getting friendly?' chirps the director. 'We're not a
collection of isolated and lonely individuals now, are we?' A spinster
secretary is persuaded to spit out her sexual jealousies, and a man with
a stutter is ritually humiliated by the director. Meanwhile Hazlitt
squirms with distaste at the lies that are being peddled. 'There is something too excitable, too dangerous about him,' observes the narrator.
'Look – he bites his knuckles. He giggles from time to time. He sucks
in his breath, like someone watching a cup tie.' Eventually he
interrupts, ranting against Admass like Potter in the Oxford Union:

HAZLITT: It is, of course, a gigantic conspiracy. We, as human beings, are all
the time and everywhere being mocked and tortured by poster-big images
of the Ideal Family, the Ideal Girl, the Ideal Husband . . . An arbitrarily
defined Perfection assails us *all the time*. Even a pimple on a young girl's
face becomes a symbol of sin and depravity . . . They could get together
tomorrow to make *hairlips* beautiful . . . Your syrupy gospel of success
has nothing to do with it . . .

The course director responds on behalf of Admass: 'Without it modern
industrial society would collapse . . . Are people in this country better
fed now than ever before? . . . And have they more leisure, more cars,

more washing machines, more vacuum cleaners . . . ? . . . And can all this have *nothing* to do with the ad men?'

For a while, Hazlitt is subdued by this; indeed, sometimes he seems not to be Hazlitt after all:

HAZLITT: When old Hazlitt died, you know, he rolled over on one side and whispered to his few remaining friends, 'Well, I've had a happy life.' . . . He died in *terrible* pain. Of a cancer of the stomach . . . I'd like, after cancer and whatnot, to say, 'Well, I've had a happy life.' But happiness is not chalked up there. It doesn't have anything to do with success . . .

To die is only to be as we were before we were born . . . The worst life can do to *you* (*to audience*) is that we shall die. And after this short, fretful, feverish being, after vain hopes and idle fears, sink to final repose again . . . And you, who suffer now, who are timid and shy and beaten down and impotent . . . you have no hope of a cure.

The director's response to this paraphrase of Hazlitt's 1821 essay 'On the Fear of Death' is to bundle the man out of the room, telling the audience not to be upset: 'I have to be ruthless sometimes. You see, any business that sets out to help the weak and life's failures –' He stops short, horrified that he has revealed his true attitude to his customers; and they respond to his sneer by trooping out of the room, leaving – as the narrator observes – the director realizing that he too is a failure.

For a first play, *The Confidence Course* is remarkably confident, though Hazlitt is an enigma. His aggressive ranting switches abruptly to quivering terror, and when the director and his staff eject him he fights like a child, kicking and biting. Roger Smith describes him as 'a weirdo', but Potter may have been portraying the apparently contradictory elements in his own personality.

*

As soon as Smith had received *The Confidence Course*, he commissioned a second script from Potter, named in a memo dated 23 June 1964 as *Vote, Vote, Vote for Nigel Barton*.

In 1969 Potter recalled that this play originated out of a conversation he had had with Smith outside a BBC lift, 'about my experiences as a parliamentary candidate'. The target delivery date for the second play was 14 August 1964, less than two months ahead. Potter's fee for the script went up to £650.

A few days after this contract was signed, Potter dropped a hint about it in his *Daily Herald* column: 'Although I cannot give details, I know of a new young TV dramatist who is writing a play for the BBC which uses speeches from Nye Bevan and Sir Oswald Mosley.' He went on holiday at the end of August, and returned to a different newspaper job. On 15 September the *Daily Herald* became the *Sun*, and Potter began work as one of its leader writers.

The new paper, still a broadsheet, was twice as big as the *Herald* and put much more emphasis on photo-coverage. Potter described it many years later as 'the fairly decent pre-Murdoch *Sun*'. Television was reviewed on the back page by Adrian Mitchell.

It is impossible to say which leaders Potter wrote, in the two weeks he worked on the *Sun*, though, in his book on Potter, W. Stephen Gilbert suggests that 'Put a kick into soccer again' (on the decline of football) and 'Not a stain! Shining bright' (the church turning to advertising), on 16 and 17 September 1964, may be his work. He can hardly have been keen on expressing his opinions anonymously, but he was soon able to escape. A General Election had been called for 15 October, and the *Sun* gave him leave of absence to fight the campaign.

Later in his life, Potter used to tell interviewers that he had had to use a walking stick by the time of the election, and was 'deeply ashamed of the psoriasis, which had spread over his hands and neck'; but his election agent Ron Brewer recalls his being in relatively good health during the four-week run-up to polling, and the photograph in his election pamphlet shows a well-looking young man with unmarked skin.

The pamphlet was called *Purpose in Politics*. Ron Brewer says the title was cribbed from a book by Harold Wilson, and describes Potter's manifesto as 'exquisitely written (it is the only one I have kept from more than thirty years of electioneering)'. It begins:

At 9 p.m. on Thursday, October 15th, it will all be over!

All the leaflets, the posters, the slogans, the charges and counter-charges will be swept away. You will by then have decided who is going to govern our country for the next four or five years.

Of course, many of you will already have decided how to use your vote. And come rain or shine, hell or highwater, you will stick to it.

All of us carry around a mixture of principle, prejudice and habit which shapes our political decisions. Sometimes indeed, the habit has hardened into a crusty shell that repels any argument, any thesis, any fact which upsets any cherished assumptions.

But consider this fact: *If we had merely kept up with the rest of Western Europe since 1951 our national income this year would be one-third more than it is. Another £8000 million to spend on the things we so obviously need.*

Again, we endure unchecked speculation in the price of land. No rational person can find such a situation completely tolerable – particularly with tens of thousands homeless. No society can be proud of having spawned Rachmanism. And yet the Conservatives propose to do nothing about this ugly blot on our consciences. You may also be unhappy about the fact that thousands of our children are crammed into ludicrously over-crowded classrooms. That there is a teacher shortage. That would-be teachers are being turned away from training colleges through lack of resources . . .

For a few paragraphs more, Potter churns out the official Labour policies: 'More schools. More houses. Better roads. Steady economic growth. A rational defence system not based on pretence and jingoism. An end to the land racket. A genuine incomes policy. A less stupid and discouraging tax system.' Then comes a passage of surprising candour:

A Labour Government won't give us all we want. It will inevitably make mistakes. It may even occasionally fail to live up to its ideals. Only 'con-men' promise paradise – and only fools pretend that it has already arrived.

But I honestly believe that Labour can and will bring back a sense of purpose into our national life . . .

Later, Potter recalled that electioneering had disillusioned him about politics. 'Watching the glad-handing,' he told Joan Bakewell in 1976, 'there would be so much acid in the stomach, so much self-disgust!' He claimed that his candidature had appealed to the 'very strong streak of charlatanry in me' rather than to his inner convictions. But Ron Brewer remembers him as naïve rather than cynical: 'I don't think he'd ever done any electioneering. So a lot of it was an eye-opener to him.'

In one village, nobody would answer the door; afterwards they discovered they had been mistaken for Jehovah's Witnesses. Dick Taverne, who came to help Potter canvass in Bishop's Stortford, recalls the racism they often encountered on doorsteps: 'Dennis would say, "I'm the Labour candidate", and the woman at the door would answer, "Well, we're Labour, we're all for keeping the blacks out!"' Potter remembered this too, adding that he would 'get a sharp kick on the ankle' from Brewer if he attempted to argue against racism, 'which was fair enough, because his job was to get the vote'.

On Friday, 16 October 1964, the main headline in Potter's own paper, the *Sun*, was: 'It's victory for Labour – and a new man for No. 10 – [Harold] Wilson.' But in East Hertfordshire there was no change. Potter had increased the Labour vote by nearly four thousand, but Sir Derek Walker-Smith easily held on to the seat for the Tories. 'I never knew whether Dennis was disappointed or not,' says Ron Brewer.

He may have been, since two weeks after the election his general practitioner put him back on the antidepressant he had been prescribed by the psychiatrist. Sixteen years later he told an interviewer that he had been 'crushed, mentally and physically' by the campaign, to the extent that he was 'too weak to return to work and resigned from the *Sun*, forestalling the sack'. He said much the same to Joan Bakewell: 'That election just crippled me. As soon as I do anything too physical the consequences are very rapid. I never went back to the paper. I knew then I'd never hold down a job.' And he told Melvyn Bragg, 'Politics . . . seemed the door, until I actually stood as a candidate. By then, of course, illness had descended and I had a walking stick and . . . I was drowning actually, drowning . . . '

Yet the psoriatic arthropathy was still in remission this autumn, and though the campaign had undoubtedly exhausted him, it would not have been physically impossible for him to continue in politics. In a 1987 interview, he gave the impression that the search for self-expression, rather than illness, had been the deciding factor: 'I had thought that I was going to be a politician . . . because that seemed to be the access to what it was I wanted to say. In fact it isn't and wasn't.'

*

The *Sun* gave him three months' salary, and he returned to *Vote, Vote, Vote for Nigel Barton*, which was two months overdue, finishing it by Christmas.

During the election campaign, he had told Ron Brewer that he was writing a play about it all. And years later he said, 'I wrote [*Vote, Vote*] because I thought, "I must get something out of this election campaign." My former agent in the constituency said, "Bloody hell, Dennis, you're the only candidate I've had who has recycled his own speeches." '

The play takes its title from the First World War song 'Tramp, Tramp, Tramp, the Boys are Marching', which was used for a political campaign in America ('Vote, vote, vote for Billy Martin'). It opens with a filmed sequence showing the death on the hunting field of the Tory MP for West Barset. Once again, Potter is writing in his *TW3* manner – the 'horsey group' who witness the accident are much more concerned about the 'poor bloody horse' than its rider.

In his introduction to *The Nigel Barton Plays*, he admitted that *Vote, Vote* had 'some purely farcical elements and some deliberately, even grotesquely, overdrawn comedy', switching between this and 'the journalistic norm of allegedly straight political reportage'. Only after these genres have been established, showing 'the world of politics as it is represented to the television viewer', does the play 'move towards the experience of politics as it might genuinely be felt by the candidate himself'.

From the Tory's death, we cut to a television newsreader announcing the by-election that it has caused. Nigel Barton is watching the news in his smart flat – no working-class kitchen here – and is appalled to learn that, having stood unsuccessfully as Labour candidate in the recent General Election, he must now go through it all again. Like Potter, he is a young journalist, and his wife Anne, who is middle class, has mixed feelings about his candidacy: 'Every time I grin at a fool or shake hands with an oily alderman you're hovering in the background, being all pure and disapproving.'

We cut to a village hall. The campaign has begun, and Nigel is waiting to address a local women's group (Ron Brewer says that this scene is lifted almost verbatim from his and Potter's visit to Buntingford):

CHAIRMAN: And if we could *just* have the minutes of the last meeting, please.

(*She turns simperingly to* NIGEL, *who wants to shrink away.*)

It won't take a jiffy, Mr – ah – Barton.

NIGEL: (*drags nervously on his cigarette*) Oh, that's OK.

SECRETARY: Minutes of the meeting of the Wattingford Labour Women's Group . . . Apologies were received from Miss Ennis, and from Mrs Hughes on account of her husband's illness. (*She looks up, inquisitively, tongue licking out over dry lips.*) Gall bladder, wasn't it, Mrs Thompson?

(MRS THOMPSON *is a battleaxe. She is knitting, but pauses to nod with relish.*)

MRS THOMPSON: Inflamed.

SECRETARY: Nasty that. And there were present nine members. Not counting Mrs Hughes or Miss Ennis. A raffle was held, the jam sponge being won by Mrs Baker. Then Miss Birrell read to us from her bird book.

(NIGEL *exchanges agonized, hostile glances with his agent. Zoom in to agent,* JACK HAY, *who pulls a face and shrugs helplessly. He is a man who enjoys pretending to be cynical.*)

HAY: (*to us*) I daren't laugh, you see. It might set him off giggling. Which would never do. A parliamentary candidate – like a magistrate sentencing a teenage trollop – must never, ever *giggle*. I'm his agent, you see. (*Winks.*) It's my job to know these little things . . .

Potter uses Hay much as he had employed Hazlitt in *The Confidence Course*, as the voice of reason in a mad world – though Ron Brewer says it is also a portrait of himself: 'I'm noted for those asides. Somebody will say something, and I will turn it into some kind of joke. Being an idealist, working for a party of idealists, you need some kind of defence.'

After attempting to make his political speech to the Wattingford ladies, Nigel is left alone with Jack, sadly contemplating a photograph of the recently dead Labour left-winger Aneurin Bevan. 'Now there was a speaker for you!' he observes, and we cut to archive film of Bevan addressing an anti-Suez rally in Trafalgar Square. This use of documentary material – together with Jack Hay's asides-to-camera, and several flashbacks and flash-forwards – keeps the play away from studio-bound realism. 'My own attitude', Potter writes of this in the introduction to the Barton plays,

is that the television play is as flexible as the whole thing around it, and I would rather work on the assumption that it does not exist in its own right at all . . . The TV play can plunder at will, for it takes its zest and colouring and technical proficiency from the news, documentaries, sports, entertainments and sermons which surround it.

He explains that Hay's direct-to-camera monologues were meant to evoke a party political broadcast (Gareth Davies, who directed the play, used a special lens to come in exceptionally close to Hay's face). Anne taunts Nigel with lacking socialist ideals: 'You are more deeply upset by a bad review of a Brecht play than a Labour by-election defeat.' In reply, Nigel sneers at the middle-classness of Anne's parents –

they showed their disillusionment with the 1945 Labour Government by 'switching from the *New Statesman* to *The Economist*. Very moving, that. Heart-rending.' Stung by this, Anne snaps that not everyone has Nigel's advantage of being born in a working-class home. 'The advantage!' he shouts back at her. 'You silly bloody cow!'

Alone in his office, Jack Hay recalls that, at the previous October's General Election, Nigel 'seemed to me to be a fine candidate. Dishonest in a way that reeked of sincerity. Evasive in a way that seemed embarrassingly frank. Upright when creeping. And dignified when at his most stupid. A potential cabinet minister if ever I saw one.' (These are the terms in which Potter, for the remainder of his life, sneered at his own abandoned political ambitions.) And we see Nigel at a public meeting, dealing deftly with tricky questions. 'See what I mean?' Hay remarks to camera. 'A splendid candidate. The sort of bloke I'd never buy a second-hand car from!'

Anne now complains that Nigel is talking political slogans in his sleep, and he answers in phrases repeated from Potter's *Isis* articles and *The Glittering Coffin*:

NIGEL: Well . . . my dad often used to talk about politics when he was in bed with our Mam.

ANNE: How do you know?

NIGEL: I've told you. There was only a sort of curtain between their half of the room and the place where we kids slept.

(*A momentary spasm of disgust crosses her face.* NIGEL *stares at her.*)

But we didn't wipe our snotty noses in our sleeves . . . Unlike you, I was head over heels in love with the *idea* of Oxford before I ever got there. (*Scornful*) I couldn't wait to get my hands round the slim, cool stem of that first glass of sherry. 'Sweet or dry?' they say. As if I knew the difference . . . There was a time when everything at home disgusted me – magazines being called books, books being called muddles, every discussion degenerating into a *personal* argument . . . Then when I *got* to Oxford – when I grew up a bit – and came to know what it felt like to be torn out by the roots and educated into – into *suave* – treachery – well, I started reversing everything. (*His face momentarily contorts in hatred.*) I threw the sherry back into the smug face that gave it to me.

After we have seen Nigel and Hay canvassing – being mistaken for Jehovah's Witnesses, and encountering doorstep racism, which makes

Nigel physically sick – Hay sets him his next electioneering task: to write letters of condolence to recently bereaved Labour voters: 'It's the personal touch that counts. Grief therapy. And it's standard practice for keen candidates.' When she hears about this ploy, Anne is disgusted. Nigel threatens to leave her, and she sneers that he is no longer any good in bed: 'This blasted by-election has made you impotent as well as crooked.'

Jack drags Nigel off to canvass an old people's home, where he meets a series of senile old men, helpless in their hospital-style beds – one of them, an amputee, begs repeatedly and pathetically for an artificial leg. (It is the first occurrence in Potter's work of the hospital-as-hell motif.) Then comes the climactic sequence – the Council dinner, closely based on the evening at Bishop's Stortford. Nigel responds furiously to the speech by the Tory candidate, Captain Archibald-Lake, whom he describes as 'antediluvian'. With the old amputee's words echoing in his head, he scorns the Tory's platitudes about the 'Opportunity State', and goes on to cite the predicament of his ageing father:

My father has been a coalminer for thirty-five years ... My father could draw an apple on the white margins of a newspaper which was so good, so ripe, so perfectly rounded and shaded, that you *ached* to pluck it off the page. When he describes things from the past, he remembers the colour the sky was, the way the sun glinted and glistened on the buckles and buttons of the village brass band ... But his talents, so long unused, are now unusable ... That's why I object to the cretinous lies which have been spouted here tonight ... Do we *have* to sell our political parties like the fourteenth brand of dog food now on the market? Can't even Captain Archibald-Lake, bless his patriotic heart, see the shameful hollowness of his own miserable half-baked and scarcely literate platitudes?

The guests react by banging their cutlery 'in a great thunderous tide of barracking', and it is now that Nigel turns to the guffawing Archibald-Lake and 'gives the two-fingered salute at its most emphatic'. The script instructs that press cameras should flash, 'Colonel Bogey' be played on the soundtrack, and the action should freeze on Nigel's V-sign.

After the dinner, Hay complains that he has 'never been so humiliated in my life', but Anne compliments Nigel on having behaved honestly at last: 'I have lived with you for five years and I didn't know what you were capable of . . . You know very well how the Labour Party loves a rebel. So it's up to you to go in there and get things done.'

In the original version of the play (preserved in the BBC's Written Archives), Nigel has now lost the by-election. 'I mean,' comments Hay, 'would *you* vote for a candidate who went like this to his opponent?' He repeats the V-sign, and Nigel who is seen in two-shot standing next to him, says:

I'll have the last laugh anyway. If laugh it is. (*He turns to us.*) Because if you object to the tone or content of this – ah – documentary, folks, the only thing you can do is *write to your M.P.* (*Very savage*) And the best of British!

Ken Trodd calls this last speech 'explosive', and guesses it was the principal cause of the trouble that was to come.

*

While Potter was completing *Vote, Vote, Vote for Nigel Barton*, the BBC scheduled *The Confidence Course* for transmission. It was to be shown on 24 February 1965, as part of BBC1's new midweek series, *The Wednesday Play*.

The Confidence Course was telerecorded (from television cameras on to film) in Studio 4 at the BBC's Television Centre in Wood Lane on 9 and 10 February 1965, with Gilchrist Calder directing. Ken Trodd describes Calder as 'an old-timer television director, but of a good kind'. Dennis Price was cast as the course director and Hazlitt was played by the comedian Stanley Baxter. This was probably at Potter's suggestion, since he often proposed (but rarely got) comedians for leading roles in his plays – he wanted Tony Hancock to play Jack Hay in *Vote, Vote*. Jon Amiel, who directed *The Singing Detective*, calls this 'Dennis's penchant for red-nose casting'.

Roger Smith previewed *The Confidence Course* in the *Radio Times*: 'Dennis Potter, the author, would not appear to be lacking in confidence. At twenty-nine he has already made his mark in a number of fields – leader writer, television critic, parliamentary candidate, and now a television playwright.'

The telerecording of the play has not survived. Reviewers were fairly kind. Adrian Mitchell wrote in the *Sun*: 'Dennis Potter is already well known as a passionate critic of apathy and the forces which exploit it. The same passion was the driving force in his play . . . It was sometimes a powerful parable . . . [and] would have been even more terrifying if the direction throughout had been less prosaic.' Richard Sear in the *Daily Mirror* thought the play was overloaded with ideas:

This was former television critic Dennis Potter's first play for the medium and he credited the box with more than it can at present take . . . He crammed some three or four plays into one, filling the screen with telling phrases and rich prose. In doing so his characters talked too much about too much . . . Yet, as a first play, it was full of promise and original thought.

Frederick Laws in the *Listener* was 'considerably puzzled' by the inclusion of Hazlitt, and thought the narrator unnecessary, but concluded: 'Potter's wit, eloquence, and tough-mindedness make him a most welcome recruit to television drama.'

Vote, Vote, Vote for Nigel Barton was to be telerecorded a month after *The Confidence Course* had been transmitted. Tony Garnett wrote to the BBC Copyright Department:

This play is about a by-election and we think it is very important to the play that all the details of the campaign should be accurate. Having recently stood for parliament, Dennis is an expert and has agreed to stay with the director [Gareth Davies] . . . Would you arrange with his agent . . . the appropriate technical adviser's fee.

Potter was paid £75 for this.

Gareth Davies, a genial Welshman who had been an actor and theatre director, and had recently been trained in television direction by the BBC, thought *Vote, Vote* 'a splendid piece, and Dennis and I got on very well together (his thing about hating the Welsh was only a joke). This thing of him being paid extra to spend time with me before was just one of the ways we had of getting round the system and giving a writer some decent money.' In fact, after attending early rehearsals, Potter kept out of Davies's way. 'I would talk on the telephone to the people making them,' he said later of his early plays, 'and I would go to read-throughs and make some comments – I would then just hope for the best.'

Ken Trodd describes Davies's direction of *Vote, Vote* and other early Potter plays as somewhat crude but full of energy: 'The vivacity was in proportion to the gawkiness. There was a lack of conscious artistry, or technical sophistication – not that there were many technical resources for Gareth to use. The energy came from the script and the actors (Gareth was an actors' director) and from very little else. And so you got Dennis raw, really.' Davies himself says, 'Coming from the theatre, I was always brought up to respect the text.' Certainly his productions never distorted Potter's ideas, which, as Trodd remarks, are always expressed in the scripts with great clarity: 'Dennis doesn't give masses of camera instructions, but there is so much resonance in the words – the dialogue and the directions – that they're bound to come alive as he planned it.' Brian Gibson, who directed two later plays (*Where Adam Stood* and *Blue Remembered Hills*), agrees:

Some writers give you innumerable descriptions of everything in the room, what the shot should be, almost what film stock you should be using. Whereas Dennis didn't do that at all. But the world he'd created, when photographed intelligently, would become somewhat magical. With many other writers, the script reads well, but when you really start working with it, there isn't very much there. There was a profound spirit to Dennis's work, which imbued everything with something extra.

Keith Barron, who had been cast as Nigel Barton, explains the method by which plays were recorded for television in the Sixties and Seventies:

It was like the theatre. You rehearsed for at least a couple of weeks in a church hall, then you went into the studio and rehearsed with the cameras for two or three days. On the last day, it was terrible: you broke for supper, and *then* – and only then – the actual recording started, at about seven o'clock, and they attempted to do the whole thing in one go, as if it was a theatre performance.

Barron, a young Yorkshire-born actor who had not had a leading television role before, had seen *The Confidence Course*, and was 'totally gripped' by it.

I was very curious to know who had written it. When Gareth approached me about the Nigel Barton part, he put me in a room with Dennis's handwritten script, and as I read it, I could totally *see* it. Dennis didn't come as much to rehearsals as writers usually do, but I talked to him in the Club at Television Centre, and he seemed very unassuming, very quiet, in those days.

Potter thought Barron 'ideal' for the role of Nigel, and was delighted with the 'superb intelligence and drive' of Davies's production. He also commended John Bailey for his performance as Jack Hay (the role for which he had wanted Tony Hancock) – he called Bailey 'an actor whose glittering yet almost dead eyes seemed to express to perfection whatever pain there was in the part – and then a great deal more besides'.

However, after the telerecording of *Vote, Vote* on 14 April 1965 it became apparent that there had been a technical problem: a broken screw in one of the two telerecording machines had made half the rolls of film unusable. 'Gareth phoned and said, "Don't get your hair cut – every second reel has got a wobble,"' recalls Keith Barron. The cast reconvened for two days in early June to re-record the flawed footage, greatly increasing the cost of the production.

Meanwhile an untitled play was commissioned from Potter by another of the *Wednesday Play* story editors, Tony Garnett, on 20 April, with a target delivery date of 1 August. Potter's fee was now £750. The following month he was paid that amount again for yet another play, *Alice*, which was evidently already completed. Already, he was showing himself capable of turning out scripts at great speed.

*

On his return from Africa, Trodd had applied for several British university jobs, and was offered one at Keele:

But in the meanwhile I had had a drink with Roger Smith, who was already in the BBC. And Roger said, 'Why don't you come and join me? I can't stand these fuckers I'm having to work with.' And I said, 'But is there a job?' Roger said, 'Oh, I'll see what I can do.' And, after I'd pestered him, he eventually came through with an offer of three months as an assistant script editor, on trial. So I said no to Keele, and realized I had burnt boats, and had got to make it work at the BBC.

Trodd describes himself, Roger Smith and Tony Garnett as 'young Turks invading an essentially stuffy, theatre-based milieu. Garnett coined a phrase that we wanted to give *them* (the management) the courage of *our* convictions.' Potter described the *Wednesday Play* team as 'its own little force within this huge stadium called the BBC', and Keith Barron says that the series already had a reputation for being excitingly radical: 'Everyone knew they had to stay in on Wednesday nights to see what it would be this week.'

Trodd arrived at the BBC a few weeks before *Vote, Vote* was recorded – 'but I don't remember seeing it in the studio'. It was billed for transmission on Wednesday, 23 June 1965. 'But by that time,' writes Potter, 'a few highly charged whispers about the "dangerous" nature of the play had begun to drift round and round the rubbery, anonymous and appropriately circular corridors of the hideous new

BBC Television Centre.' He had written in the *Daily Herald* that the Centre, opened in 1960, was 'a terrifying building – a factory from science fiction. A seemingly endless sequence of doors opens out on to endless circular corridors. Offices are banked on top of each other with no identity except in the use of numbers. You can smell the soft-rubbery smell of a bureaucracy . . . '

In fact the nervousness about *Vote, Vote* began only the day before transmission, when James MacTaggart happened to mention to Michael Bakewell, then Head of Plays in the BBC TV Drama Group, that Potter's script 'had a go' at politicians. Bakewell gathered that Sydney Newman, their boss, had not seen the play, and warned him about it. Newman saw the recording, was alarmed, and asked Paul Fox, Head of Current Affairs, to view it and give an opinion. Fox watched it and wrote an urgent memo to Huw Wheldon, Controller of Programmes – it was now already Wednesday, the day of transmission. 'The play', wrote Fox,

is very nearly a documentary. It says this in almost its final line . . .

I am sure that Conservative Central Office will take offence at this portrayal of a Conservative image that is today perhaps not quite so common . . . I am sure the Labour Party will take offence at this portrayal of an unprincipled agent. Furthermore, on a time basis, the Tory is on for about seven minutes – looking a buffoon – the Labour man is on for nearly sixty minutes: a bit starry-eyed, but basically the good guy.

In my view, because of the documentary nature of this play and the present, near pre-Election atmosphere, the parties' complaints would be difficult to rebut.

Harold Wilson was expected to call a General Election soon, with the hope of increasing Labour's majority, but in fact the Election was not held until April 1966, when more Labour members were indeed returned to Parliament.

Wheldon saw the play as well, and agreed with Fox. At 9.25 that evening, viewers of BBC1 were told: 'In place of the advertised *Wednesday Play* we are broadcasting *With Love and Tears*, a play by Colin Morris, which was first seen on BBC2. We hope to broadcast the *Wednesday Play*, *Vote, Vote, Vote for Nigel Barton*, at some future date.' The BBC Press Office issued a statement by Wheldon that he and Sydney Newman had 'decided that the production as a whole was not yet ready for transmission . . . The play is therefore postponed . . .

When we transmit [it], or whether we transmit it, will depend on further work and further consideration.'

Trodd takes up the story:

My memory is that around midday that Wednesday we were told there was a problem, and it might not be broadcast. They couldn't find Dennis, and I said, 'I know where he is.' I knew he was doing a live *Woman's Hour* over at Broadcasting House. I left a message, and at the end of that broadcast, around three o'clock, he rang me, and I said, 'You'd better come over here.' Dennis arrived in Sydney's palatial office, and Dennis and Roger and I and Garnett sat there being plied with drinks. Sydney was a Canadian Jew who looked like Joseph Stalin, and like Joe he could be very avuncular. It was clear to me that his agenda was to use all his avuncular charm to keep the lid on what could be very explosive. So there we were, being schmoozed!

After about an hour, Dennis said to me, in a kind of aside, 'I do think I ought to go home, and I ought to ring Margaret first, so can we go up to your office and do that?' So we got outside Sydney's office, and Dennis said, 'Have you got the telephone directories?' And he phoned every newspaper in Fleet Street. And the following day, *his* account rather than the BBC's was in the press.

Next morning's *Sun* carried a lengthy article on the cancellation, which did indeed reflect Potter's feelings rather than the official Corporation line:

Mr Potter had just finished broadcasting on *Woman's Hour* when he was told the play was off. He went at once to Television Centre . . . Mr Potter said, 'I'm very disappointed, but not altogether surprised.' . . . Actor Keith Barron, who had the title role, said last night, 'I am bitterly disappointed. I thought it a splendid play which was truthful and unlikely to upset anyone.'

In his *Sun* television column, Adrian Mitchell wrote that the cancellation was 'highly disturbing'. Other papers carried their own versions, the *Daily Telegraph* merely stating that the play was 'about politics'.

Roger Smith recalls his own anger with Newman over the cancellation: 'I had a terrific row with Sydney, and said I was resigning, and he said, "Don't be ridiculous, you're leaving anyway." It was true – I hadn't let them renew my contract. They wanted me to stay, but I wanted to go. I was knackered – working on *Wednesday Plays* week after week after week would have been enough for anyone.' James MacTaggart used to say he often woke in the night, covered in sweat, hands clenched, wondering where he would get a script to put into production the very next week, so great was the speed at which the series used up plays.

Potter's own recollection of the crisis meeting was of being asked by one BBC executive if he was 'some kind of fascist', while Sydney Newman 'appeared to be so troubled by the play's outrageous implication that some party politicians were from time to time on nodding terms with overt cynicism that he asked me why I wanted "to shit on the Queen"'.

Michael Bakewell emphasizes that 'we were all anxious that the play *should* get on. And it was a familiar battle. Nearly all of the *Wednesday Plays* were contentious. On the whole, management were very sympathetic to what we were doing, and Huw Wheldon was – in theory – on our side, though being Huw it often got complicated! But I remember we very much wanted to commission more work from Dennis.'

Trodd and Garnett were despatched to see Potter about rewriting parts of the play. They had a long journey, for Potter had just moved his family out of London to a remote corner of East Anglia. His mother, who was with them when Margaret first saw the house, recalls that she had not been consulted: 'We got in the car – we were going to Norfolk. "Oh," he told Margaret, "there's a lovely walled garden!" But when we got there, Margaret's face fell. The bedrooms were a stables. Oh, Margaret's face when she saw that!' This was the Old Club House, Northrepps, near Cromer. Jane says, 'Dad was always daydreaming about places we might live in. And he had rented this cottage, which he said was going to be idyllic, romantic, by the sea. But it was like a barn, very cold, very damp, a weird little place.'

By this time the Potters had a small car, which Dennis drove erratically. 'It took him ages to get through his test,' says Sarah. 'Mum used to say, "For an intelligent man, you do the most amazing things." We were all in the car once and he missed his turn off a roundabout, so he stopped and *reversed* around it!' Jane agrees that his driving was terrifying, and Mervyn James, a family friend in later years, says, 'Toad of Toad Hall wasn't in it.' Margaret did not learn to drive until the Seventies, when the state of Dennis's hands made it almost impossible for him to take the wheel.

A BBC secretary wrote to Potter at the new Norfolk address, 'I see you've moved again – before I had time to come and see the new baby!' The Potters' third and last child, Robert, had been born in

March 1965. Margaret conceived again some time later, but the pregnancy was terminated because of fears that the drugs Potter was taking for his illness might cause deformity in the child.

Potter had hated the north London suburbs; many of his plays satirize the prim stuffiness of life in that land of privet hedges and ding-dong door chimes. But Sarah Potter says that the move to Norfolk also 'highlighted how reclusive Dad was becoming, caused by illness, and not knowing in which direction he was going'. In later years, he would sometimes blame the reclusiveness on his psoriasis: 'I used to be able to get on with all sorts of people at Oxford, and then suddenly out of a clear blue sky along came this illness, which knocks you into reclusiveness, and people become alien creatures teetering on their stilts and coming at you.' Yet at the time of his move to Norfolk, the psoriasis was in remission, and Trodd believes that the reclusiveness was fundamental to Potter's personality. 'He is not a gregarious person,' Trodd told a journalist in 1986. 'He doesn't know, doesn't want to know and never will know, many people. He does not require society in that general way people do.'

Potter himself spoke about this in 1988: 'I do have a very reclusive temperament which occasionally bursts out. You know, reclusiveness and shyness are not the same thing, fortunately. But I like – always have liked – being on my own for long periods. It's sometimes difficult to arrange in marriage! But within, the concept of being on my own is attractive to me.' Since he had left Oxford – where, as the psychiatrist suggested, he seems to have been on something of a manic high – he had shown no sociability, choosing to write his *Bookstand* scripts at home rather than in the office, and not drinking with other staff on the *Herald*. Illness now gave him the excuse for a natural inclination.

Trodd went to Norfolk with Tony Garnett to discuss with Potter what might be done about *Vote, Vote*:

I remember that on the way we stopped to buy presents for Dennis's kids. But when we arrived at the cramped little house, we were treated like shit – as BBC bureaucrats, though we felt we were on Dennis's side. I can remember Dennis saying, 'Have you brought any drink?' And we'd only brought sweets.

He'd set up a scenario by which he was going to make us feel like bureaucratic hoods. I don't think Garnett (who was never a big Potter enthusiast) could understand it at all, but I could see that this was Dennis structuring the event, putting us both in a role – and we could only respond to it by playing to Dennis's agenda. And this agenda was his price for the banning: not so much that we would discuss what the revisions of the text would be, for the reshoot; but he wanted another commission. And that was *Stand Up, Nigel Barton*. He told us he wanted to write a companion piece. So obviously that was agreed to. And Dennis always had a way – and this is very, very political – of using a humiliation or a defeat to achieve a higher ground.

In his introduction to the Barton plays, Potter says that the rewriting he now had to undertake (for an additional £100) disfigured *Vote, Vote* 'in a few important ways'. First, 'some of the savagery of Jack Hay's cynicism had to be muted'. In particular, a passage was inserted where Hay reveals to Nigel the background to his cynicism:

NIGEL: You *ooze* cynicism from every pore, Jack. All this smart chat makes me want to throw up.

HAY: (*suddenly, venomously*) And how the hell do you think it makes *me* feel?

(NIGEL *stares at* HAY, *shocked.* HAY *grins uncomfortably.*)

Sorry old boy. The mask slipped.

NIGEL: Why keep it there in the first place? . . . Why the cheap jokes?

HAY: Cheap! Listen, Nigel, my old man used to keep me from school on Empire Day so I wouldn't have to wave those little blood-coloured flags. We were the richest country in the world at the time, so I'm told. Half the bleed'n atlas red, and my old man bow-legged with malnutrition! We kids nearly died laughing.

NIGEL: (*eager*) And?

HAY: And I've been laughing ever since. You're the one that was sick – not me! Put a few sniggers between yourself and the world, Nigel. You don't bruise so easy that way.

NIGEL: Jack, I never realized that you –

(HAY, *embarrassed, interrupts* NIGEL *quickly. He doesn't want* NIGEL *to get too close.*)

HAY: One day, when you're on the Front Bench, you'll look back on all this as the time when you finally grow up. (*Sniff.*) Even angry young men eventually kiss the Queen's white gloved hand, you know.

Potter regretted having to add this passage: 'It takes the edge off the savagery. It sounds and looks as evasive: moreover, it came over as basically untrue.' However, Ron Brewer says the story about Empire Day comes from his own childhood, 'though I have no recollection of telling it to Dennis!' Potter also added some lines for Mrs Morris, an elderly Labour supporter, who tells Hay, 'Nobody could dare to be as cynical as you pretend to be without knowing what it is to believe and to hope.' Hearing this, Hay 'rolls his eyes', says the script, 'but not convincingly. He is moved.' Potter was afterwards ashamed by this direction: 'So poor Jack Hay (God forgive me!) had to be kitted out like Rigoletto. His benumbing, politically degenerate cynicism was, visibly, to gurgle out of a broken heart.' Yet he did not cut this or any of the rewrites out of the play when Penguin published it in 1967, explaining that he wanted the published text to record 'what was actually shown on the screen'.

There were a few other softenings of Hay's lines, but nothing was done to correct the overall political bias pointed out by Paul Fox. In the introduction, Potter writes contemptuously of the 'stupidity' of the BBC executives, which had allowed him to deal with the letter of their objections without really altering the spirit of the play. But he did not mention making one major change which softened the play's impact – a rewritten final scene, set after the Council dinner but before the voting, in which Nigel rejects Jack's cynicism and appeals to the audience: 'Ladies and gentlemen, polling day tomorrow – Tomorrow you have the chance to use your vote. It is perhaps the greatest privilege you possess. I ask you to use it . . . Vote – vote – vote – for Nigel Barton.' Potter modified this, in the published text, with the direction: 'His final appeal to "vote" is both ironic and anguished. He is temporarily broken.' But the tone is still very different from the sneering end of the original script.

*

The rewrites were finished and approved by Sydney Newman during July 1965. It was also agreed that the 'companion piece', as Potter called it, Stand Up, Nigel Barton, would be shown a week before the revised play. This, too, would subtly soften the impact of Vote, Vote, presenting it as a second chapter of Nigel's story rather than letting it stand alone as an anti-political tract.

In 1988, Potter recalled that Stand Up, Nigel Barton was based on a novel: 'I was sort of midway through a novel – I'd been playing with the idea, and . . . I turned it into a television play.' Among his papers is a foolscap notebook containing twenty-five pages of narrative, written in the early Sixties (it also includes some Nathan–Potter *TW3* material), which reworks his earlier attempt at an autobiographical novel, *The Country Boy*.

Headed *Part One: Wedding Night*, it begins:

I'm getting married tomorrow. I, David Reginald Blake, take thee, Patricia Anne Thomas – but I've already taken her, so to speak. We've already worshipped each other with our bodies, even though we remained aware of the discomforts of the front-room floor and the perils of *coitus interruptus*. The clergyman has a fat face and spectacles and I shan't like repeating all those words after he has said them. But I expect that we shall both be entranced by the ritual, and both sets of relatives will be pleased.

I am very, very nervous.

About sex. About time. And responsibility, and all the sad grey habits which coil into the full stop of 'they lived happily ever after'.

Tomorrow night, I'd like to talk. It's a small, cold bedroom at this time of year, but we can leave the gas fire on. Plenty of light – street light – gets through the curtains and car headlights make patterns on the ceiling. Sometimes a man whistles in the street below. There's no reason why we shouldn't talk.

Will she listen to me, all through the night? Once before, like this, but not quite like this, I tried to talk, but she put her breast to my lips. No: I must be more truthful. She put her hand up to my mouth. If I'd gone on talking she would just have laughed. Her teeth look very bright and sharp in the dark.

The wedding (like Potter's own) takes place on a cold wintry day, and the narrative continues:

'Her teeth look bright and sharp in the dark.'

Only last night he had written the words, feeling the ache of disloyalty but also the exquisite pleasure of what, in one form anyway, was the last complete caesura of absolute privacy. He had written the words on a piece of lined paper. 'I, David Reginald Blake, take thee –' When he read it back to himself he laughed out loud and tore the paper into long, thin shreds.

Now, today, shaking cold hands at the laborious reception, he felt ashamed of what he had written, knowing that he had yet again gone so far as to put down on paper the temporary but recurring delusion which made him treat his own life as a novel in progress.

David is a freelance television scriptwriter. Patricia, whom he met at Oxford, has middle-class parents. On the wedding night, in their top-floor flat in Chiswick, they lie in bed:

David twisted his head away and kissed his bride on the top of her sleek, long blond hair. There was perfume at the parting.

'She's got long blond hair. I never cared for long blond hair. She's got long blond hair. But that's my weakness now.'

Pat pursed her lips again, consciously a parody of the provocative, orange-lipstick female.

'Well. He's got a long blond thing. I never cared for a long blond –'

'No, honey.' There was that irritation, that petulance, in his voice once more. Pat was annoyed, pulling her hand away.

'What's the matter with you!'

'Nothing.'

'You used to like me to say – dirty things. You said it helped you to come.'

David tossed his head, acknowledging that she was right but that the circumstances were not the same. And what did she mean, *dirty*?

They were married now, after all.

After all, they were married now.

He tried once more. 'Darling,' he said, 'don't take umbrage. I know I seem a bit funny tonight, in every way. I don't think I'd be very good at love-making tonight. I'm not even sure that I want it all that much.'

'Thank you very much.'

'Oh ho-ney. Don't be silly. I want *you*. Of course I want you. But can't you see –' he broke off, and began again with a greater urgency, shifting in the bed so that the spring twanged faintly beneath them like the bell of a submerged church. 'Look, I want you in another way as well. Sometimes, somehow – I can't really put it properly – we are just touching each other's bodies, penetrating each other, only in one sense. Very nice. But we keep on evading each other, too.'

'Jesus Christ!' she said, her annoyance bursting out in a way that she still (despite David) accepted as blasphemous. She simply wanted him to make love to her.

They both lay back and looked at the ceiling.

Shall I put my hand on her breast? Shall I pretend to be the hurt lover?

It's not a question of pretence, though. Perhaps I had too much of the whisky and, simply because I can't get, keep, an erection, I – No. I want to talk about things, like we should have done and haven't.

David begins to talk, about his childhood in 'the Wodene' (the Forest), and about the move to London and his father's misery there. Eventually they do make love, but

the tension still clutched at his joints, and his calf muscles stood out as in a piece of amateur sculpture . . . Tonight, this night of commitment and consummation, he was perversely haunted by inexplicable parallels with the final destruction of his parents' marriage and the old tyranny which places can have over insecure and emotional personalities.

Before the draft ends, we learn that the move to London broke up his family: 'He would always love his mother and he was sure that he would always hate her too: far from forgetting her, that small, pinched-in face with the slow grey eyes stayed in his mind as surely as ever, even though he had not seen her since that first full year of the peace in 1946. The year the family had last been one.'

A list of headings in the *Wedding Night* notebook indicates that one of the later episodes in the novel was to be called 'Nightmare: the Uncle'. David's sexual difficulties (which recall Nigel Barton's impotence) are not explained, but possibly Potter intended to link them with abuse in childhood.

Stand Up, Nigel Barton owes more to Potter's earlier attempt at a novel, *The Country Boy*, with its vignettes of his schooldays, than to these *Wedding Night* chapters. He writes, in his introduction to *The Nigel Barton Plays*:

I think [*Stand Up, Nigel Barton*] is a much better play [than *Vote, Vote*] although, perhaps, just a trifle too confusing in structure. It was built that way in order to attempt to illustrate the difficulties and complexities which can beset anyone moving across the minefields of class in this country. 'Environment' is here the crucial factor, but where the central character (Nigel Barton) has moved on and 'up', this becomes translated into 'memory'.

The usual way to present memory on screen (he goes on) is in flash-back, but this rarely works well on television, probably because of the 'crabbed dimensions of the screen', and in any case it 'has degenerated into a stylistic cliché'. He explains that he chose instead the method of 'chipping the play up into swiftly moving fragments', alternating without preamble between present and past.

Stand Up, Nigel Barton opens in a mining village. The script suggests that the setting is 'probably South Nottinghamshire', where the film sequences were shot, and the actors' accents in the BBC recording are north country rather than Forest of Dean; but Potter tends to write Forest dialect for them. Nigel is walking up the road with his father Harry, who is on his way to a shift at the pit; Nigel inclines towards the verge but Harry insists (like the Berry Hill miners) on trudging along the middle, despite the blaring horn of a passing motorist.

Nigel comments that his dad is one of 'the good old solid types of yesteryear', but Harry does not want to be patronized: 'Clever sod, ent ya? I expect they think the sun shines out of your bum down at Oxford.' Nigel corrects him: 'One says "up" at Oxford. You come "down" when you finish there.' Harry affects amazement – 'Does *bloody* Oxford move up and down the *bloody* map?' – and they both start to laugh.

As they reach Harry's workplace, Nigel casts his glance at the looming slag-heap, and observes to himself, 'There but for the grace of God and the Eleven Plus . . . ' The slag-heap dissolves to Nigel 'sitting upright, arms folded, in small school desk in fairly shabby classroom'. We are back in Nigel's schooldays, and Potter specifies that all the children in the play must be 'played by adults, imitating childish manners and movements in horribly precise style'. Potter said he had chosen this device – later used more spectacularly in *Blue Remembered Hills* – so as to communicate 'the excitement, the zest, the terror, the anxiety' of childhood without the sentimental feelings likely to be aroused by child performers. It was, of course, another deliberate assault on naturalism.

Nigel as a child is being commended for good behaviour by his teacher in the village school, Miss Tilling. Like Jack Hay, she addresses the camera to tell us: 'Clever children from common homes like his have to be, shall I say, separated from their – ah – backgrounds.' This cues to another Oxford scene, in Nigel's college rooms, as he tells his scout not to call him 'sir'. Nigel, too, talks directly to the viewer, on the subject of the extravagances of Oxford: 'Don't worry folks. You're paying for it!'

Back in the village school, it is the turn of George Pringle, the class comic, to read aloud from the Bible. As in *The Country Boy*, he has chosen the *risqué* passage from Ezekiel about 'whoredoms in Egypt', and amid the cackles of the class we return to Oxford for a glimpse of whoredom at a party in someone's college rooms. Potter later felt that the Oxford scenes – especially the party – were 'stilted and pointlessly over-mannered' compared with the rest of the play.

Nigel arrives amid the intertwined couples, looking very out of place in a dark suit. He is congratulated for a 'nice piece in *Isis*', and encounters Jill Blakeney, a judge's daughter, whom he already knows as a would-be *Isis* contributor:

JILL: You're very stiff and formal and (*giggles*) and –

NIGEL: *(stiffly)* And proletarian? How horrible for you!

(JILL *laughs and flicks briskly at his shoulder.*)

What are you doing?

JILL: Knocking off that chip, darling.

NIGEL: I like it there. It might be profitable one day.

Jill suggests seductively that Nigel can be 'my very own Andy Capp', but Nigel reacts furiously – 'Get stuffed! You silly flaming cow!' – and stalks out of the party. Another guest comments, 'You have to be very careful with these sons of the workers. They like their women to be very prim and proper, or on their backs with their mouths shut.'

Back in Nigel's schooldays, Miss Tilling has sent naughty George Pringle to the headmaster for a caning. She calls out, 'Stand up, Nigel Barton! . . . Come and read to us the Sermon on the Mount.' As Nigel is reading obediently, Pringle returns, duly caned, just in time to see Miss Tilling cooing over Nigel. We cut to Oxford, where Nigel is trying out a hired evening suit he will wear while speaking at the Union. There is a knock at the door, and to his surprise it is Jill, high on tranquillizers, who laughs at the hired clothes – 'not exactly a cloth cap' – and comes out with an abrupt suggestion:

JILL: Shall we make love?

(*He stops abruptly in his tracks, all brakes squealing. She laughs.*)

NIGEL: Don't make fun of me, Jill. Don't be a bitch!

JILL: Of course not. You can do it in your dinner-jacket if you'd rather.

'He hits her hard,' says the direction. Whereupon we cut to Nigel's parents by their coal fire.

Mrs Barton accuses her husband of envying Nigel's achievements, and denies that her son is being disloyal to his class roots: 'Our Nigel's one of us, and always will be.' We see Nigel in his schooldays being set upon by Bert, the school bully, who taunts, 'You're a *good* little boy, aren't you?' Left sobbing, Nigel lashes out at his schoolfellows – 'You – dirty – rotten – horrible – lot! *Bastards*!' – and on the soundtrack we hear a Sixties pop song by the Animals, 'We've Got to Get Out of This Place'. Gareth Davies says the song was used 'to bring the play into the

Sixties, whereas its natural habitat was the Fifties – the period of Dennis's childhood'.

We are now at the Oxford Union, where Nigel gives a barnstorming speech mocking the class system. Then we see him at home in the vacation, drinking at the working men's club with his father, and enduring further mockery about Oxford, this time from another miner. We go back to the Union, where Nigel's speech alludes to 'the almost suffocating warmth and friendliness' of his working-class background; and then to the working men's club, where the resident comic – none other than the grown-up George Pringle – is telling a funny story about a visitor to the village who mistook a family's privy for their house (Potter includes this story in *The Changing Forest*, where it is ascribed to Cyril Baglin, real-life comic at the Berry Hill Club).

At the Union again, the speakers are having an after-debate supper in the President's office, and an Oxford alumnus, Norman Conrad, invites Nigel to take part in a television documentary on class. In the working men's club, everyone is singing 'The Old Rugged Cross' – but, at Oxford, Nigel has been hauled up by the Proctors for singing the same hymn drunkenly in the King's Arms, and for giving a false name to them. 'Now I've done it! I've really gone and done it!' says Nigel guiltily; and with these words we are back at school, and he is agonizing over his impulsive destruction of the teacher's pot plant on the classroom windowsill (presumably an attempt to prove that he is not a good little boy after all). He manages to blame the crime on George Pringle, and is commended by the teacher for being 'so truthful'.

This word is echoed a moment later, for the TV interview on class has now been filmed, and Nigel tells Jill he was 'truthful' in all that he said on camera:

NIGEL: But all the time . . . I was – well, sort of *calculating*.

JILL: (*smiling*) You don't say!

NIGEL: Am I that sort of person then?

JILL: Most of the time. It's built in.

NIGEL: You make me sound like some sort of cripple. I always thought that I gave the impression of being – extraordinarily – *sincere*.

JILL: Oh, darling!

NIGEL: I used to tell lies at school to get off scot free. I found it gave me – a sort of – *power*. Words could be manipulated. You could defend yourself. Take control of events, instead of being chopped up into little pieces of raw flesh. (*Morosely*) I ought to become a politician, I suppose.

With this he launches into a rhetorical speech about how the working class can see through the rottenness of politicians – but then abruptly stops with the striking remark, 'Oh God, there I go again. Listening to myself.' (Unfortunately the first half of this scene, which includes these lines, was cut.) Jill kisses him, but he now agonizes about the TV interview: 'I talked about my own father and mother! I *used* them, Jill. I damn well, bloody well, *used* them!'

At the Bartons' home, a reporter whose newspaper has seen an advance copy of Nigel's TV interview comes to ask Harry Barton if he thinks that Nigel is ashamed of him. Harry throws him out. At Oxford, Nigel is still confronting the falsity of his own performance in the interview: 'I was acting it up a bit, over-dramatizing. I wouldn't mind a job on the old telly, see. Of course I put in a few highly coloured observations. Hard eyes snapping at the camera. Like they all do . . . Or, more like, I wasn't dramatic and soul-searching *enough*.' Jill protests that he should calm down, but he goes on:

Sorry. Sorry. I can't uncoil. I can't wind down . . . Restless! I'm restless all the bloody time, Jill . . . I don't feel that I *belong* anywhere in particular. I despise this place, and I am no longer equipped to remember where I came from. I despise politics, yet I want things to change. I'm sick of personal tensions, yet I have to exploit them to get any energy, to keep any ambition.

Jill tells him he is 'like a performing animal. It all comes too smoothly.'

We now see the Barton parents watching the broadcast of Nigel's interview on class, while he sits alongside them. (Potter said that this was dramatic licence; he was not at home when *Does Class Matter?* was shown.) Harry is outraged by Nigel's on-screen remarks about feeling alienation from him, and he storms off to the club; but then we see Nigel following his dad up the street. Mollified, Harry tells Nigel he can come with him: 'But Nigel . . . I be walking in the middle of the road, mind!' They trudge away from the camera, and as the play ends we again hear the song 'We've Got to Get Out of This Place'. The final direction states, 'Nigel looks across at his father, but they are separated by a mutual anxiety.'

Nearly thirty years after *Stand Up, Nigel Barton* had been written,

Graham Fuller asked Potter if it had been meant to atone for offending his father in *Does Class Matter?* and *Between Two Rivers*. Potter answered: 'In retrospect it does look like it . . . but . . . using the guilt as a dramatic device is not discharging it. There is no way you can discharge guilt.' He added that his father had watched *Stand Up, Nigel Barton*, 'and he was very proud of it'. The play's real achievement was not its portrayal of class guilt but its subtle examination of Nigel's self-consciousness, which recalls David in *Wedding Night* treating 'his own life as a novel in progress'.

Potter recalled that, as he wrote *Stand Up*, his adrenalin had surged from the knowledge that both social groups portrayed in the play would be watching – 'both coalminers and Oxford dons'. This was the great attraction of television: 'If I wanted to write both for my parents and the people I grew up with, and the people I was now moving amongst, there was only one medium capable of that.' Television could vault over 'the hierarchies of our print culture'. True, much of it was trivial and mundane, 'but if something is working it can be extraordinarily powerful because it sits right in the middle of that mundaneness'. And if television was the chief *modus operandi* of his enemy Admass, 'the voice of the occupying power', then to hijack it for the opposition was doubly effective, because 'the resistance ought to take place within the barracks as well as outside'.

*

Stand Up, Nigel Barton was shown on Wednesday, 8 December 1965. Reviews were enthusiastic, but Nancy Banks-Smith, who was now the TV critic of the *Sun*, was puzzled by one aspect: 'The women were weird. The witch, a bitch and a fool. The schoolmistress was a nightmare to frighten little children with. The girlfriend a tart on tranquillizers. And Mum – well, Dennis Potter is the co-author of the satire "What is a Mum?" – and he hasn't changed his mind.'

Gareth Davies says he raised this point with Potter: 'I said, "When are you going to write a good part for a woman?" And he said, "Women are boring, they don't achieve things."' In 1993 Graham Fuller asked him, 'Do you think the accusations of misogyny against you have ever been justified?' He answered, 'In some part they may be justified. If you come up with English working-class male ideas about women, then traces of that – no, more than traces – a lot of that is going to cling to you for a long time.'

On Monday, 13 December 1965, two days before *Vote, Vote* finally reached the screen, an interview with Potter by Barry Norman appeared in the *Daily Mail*:

Mr Dennis Potter, being an atheist, said, 'I think the Gods must be with me at the moment.' He was very careful about the plural for he is a good atheist.

And, religious questions aside, he seems to be right. Clearly, somebody is with him. Mr Potter, aged thirty, a miner's son and an Oxford graduate, stands at present like a study in suspended animation – poised to hurtle, or be hurtled, through a doorway marked 'Success'.

Behind him, last Wednesday, is *Stand Up, Nigel Barton*, for my money one of the best plays the BBC has presented this year. Ahead, next Wednesday, is the sequel . . . which, if it lives up to expectation, should put him in the forefront of TV playwrights . . .

He is a tall, red-haired and far less prickly man than one would expect from his work . . . Of *Vote, Vote*, he said, 'I only had to make a few changes. The BBC's list of required alterations whittled down in the end to piddling things.' . . .

At the end of the play Nigel Barton tires of the 'skulduggery' of electioneering. Dennis Potter has tired of it too.

'I won't stand for Parliament again. I've got four offers, actually, to have my name put forward but I haven't even replied to them.'

Writing, he thinks, is the thing for him. And perhaps a move back to the Forest of Dean where he came from. 'I've finished with the class thing now. I hope so, anyway. And I think I can return to the Forest of Dean on my own terms.'

He has crossed what he calls the 'tightrope' between the classes into the classlessness of the writer. And that's quite a journey in itself.

On the night of transmission, thanks to an almost unbelievable piece of programme planning, *Vote, Vote* was preceded by a party political broadcast, given by the leader of the Conservative Party, Edward Heath. When he learned that this was to happen, Potter 'spent some time on the telephone vainly trying to get the opening titles dropped so that we could go straight from Mr Heath's toothy valedictory smile into the play itself'.

Adrian Mitchell, reviewing *Vote, Vote* in *The Sunday Times*, observed that Heath might have been a character in the play. 'Mr Potter is not a promiser or a rumbler,' wrote Mitchell admiringly. 'He is a genuine lightning manufacturer.' Julian Holland in the *Daily Mail* noticed the juxtaposition too:

We must be growing up. Immediately after Mr Edward Heath has picked his way through fifteen minutes of questioning in a party political broadcast, the BBC puts on a play about electioneering that includes lines like 'Have you ever once seen a party political broadcast which is even remotely honest?' . . . Potter is not a subtle writer. He makes his points with a propagandist's sledgehammer . . . But he *makes* points. And he *is* very funny. And his plays have an old-fashioned narrative gaiety that is now rare.

James Thomas in the *Daily Express* said the play would make anyone want to hurl their hat in the air; it was 'one of the best irreverent digs at the current political scene ever seen on the usually over-timid box . . . Superb performances . . . But definitely the writer's play.' Nancy Banks-Smith called it 'enormously better than *Stand Up, Nigel Barton* . . . The play started slowly, continued jerkily. Half-a-dozen scenes could have been lifted whole from *That Was The Week That Was* . . . And then suddenly, the smiling stopped and the screaming started . . .' Only Mary Crozier in the *Guardian* suggested that the writing inclined too much to caricature: 'Mr Potter makes everything a bit bigger or blacker or funnier than life and in this sense he came out last night as a political cartoonist who I hope will one day write a consistently brilliant political satire.'

When it was announced, a few months later, that the Barton plays had won awards from the Society of Film and Television Arts (later BAFTA), and from the Screenwriters' Guild and the Guild of Television Producers and Directors, Potter began to feel reasonably secure in his new career: 'For the first time, I thought I could manage. We would be able to survive.' He describes the award ceremony: 'Earl Mountbatten stood up in front of the band . . . and proffered me his hand to shake. In return, I got a misshapen chunk of metal . . . A toast was called for us all . . . I raised my champagne glass. "You don't toast yourself!" hissed a very big, very powerful TV executive . . . "No? That", I thought, "is what *you* bloody think!"'

CHAPTER 3

A nice play for Christmas

Looking back at them, John McGrath observes that the Barton plays 'weren't characterized by imagination – they were drama documentaries. The basic thrust was polemic rather than creative. Dennis's creative side hadn't yet really displayed itself.' In fact even before they were transmitted, a more 'creative' play by Potter had been shown.

The Wednesday Play returned after its summer break on 13 October 1965 with *Alice*, which seems to have been written on Potter's own initiative and then offered to the BBC, rather than commissioned. It opens in a compartment of a Victorian train, with the elderly Charles Lutwidge Dodgson (Lewis Carroll) being recognized by one of his former child friends, who is now a grown woman travelling with her fiancé. Dodgson responds stammeringly, 'with absolutely dead voice and expression', rejecting this unwanted reminder of his past: 'It is of n-no consequence.'

We now see Dodgson many years earlier, as a young Oxford don, hurrying through Christ Church, muttering 'I'm late' like the White Rabbit. But he pauses to smell a white rose on a bush, and an old gardener remarks that it is a pity the flower will fade and die within a few weeks; Dodgson answers pointedly, 'It h-h-happens to all things, you know . . . The little g-g-girl on your knee grows into a mature woman.'

In the Deanery at Christ Church, Mrs Liddell, the Dean's wife, is pleased when she hears Dodgson is to photograph her youngest daughter Alice, remarking that 'as regards the photographic camera he is becoming very distinguished', but is disconcerted when Alice casually mentions that Dodgson '*loves* me, of course'. Meanwhile Dodgson, conducting a tutorial, is outraged when his pupil makes a *double entendre*. This exposes Dodgson's own private turmoil: 'Every m-man suffers blasphemous thoughts. Unholy thoughts, which torture with their hateful presence the f-fancy that fain would be p-p-pure.' He recommends mental arithmetic as an 'ally' against these nameless temptations, and sets the undergraduate a comic mathematical puzzle to solve by next week: 'C-consider this, if you will. Four times five is twelve. Four times s-six is thirteen. Four times s-seven is f-fourteen. Four times eight is f-f-fifteen. Will I ever get to t-twenty? Tell me next week – a question of s-s-scales, Thornton.' The undergraduate leaves, and Dodgson picks up a framed photograph of the child Alice, saying to it, cunningly, 'You don't get to twenty that way, little elfin locks.'

He has been invited to join Alice, with her sisters and mother, on a river picnic. While Dodgson rows, he gazes adoringly at the child, and she suddenly resents this and splashes water in his face. Yet, when told by her mother to apologize, she does so flirtatiously, kissing Dodgson on the cheek and offering him 'my prettiest handkerchief to dry your face'. Asked to tell a story, Dodgson describes Alice at the Mad Hatter's Tea Party, which we now see, with actors in masks as the Wonderland characters.

Back in Dodgson's college rooms, an ingratiating jeweller is showing him a musical box which plays 'Twinkle, Twinkle, Little Star' – 'A little something for a little someone, eh, sir?' Dodgson instructs that it should be inscribed 'To Alice, with love from the Mad Hatter'. Meanwhile in the Deanery, Mrs Liddell is burning his letters to Alice. Nevertheless she allows Dodgson to photograph Alice in his rooms, where he tells her meaningfully, 'I like you exactly as you are.'

Three years later, Dodgson presents Alice with the finished copy of her 'adventures', but is distressed to realize that her interest in boys is awakening. The Dean, attempting to discuss college business with him, finds him suffering from some nameless agony: 'How much can a m-m-man endure?' he cries out. A further three years pass, and, at another picnic, though Alice does her best to console him, it becomes painfully clear to Dodgson that she has grown too old for their relationship to continue.

Peter Black in the *Daily Mail* thought the play old-fashioned and uncertain, and felt that Dodgson, played by George Baker, had 'scarcely emerged' as a credible character, while Deborah Watling's performance had reduced Alice to 'a sturdy and precocious nymphet'.

However, the anonymous *Times* reviewer found *Alice* 'sad, sometimes painfully embarrassing'.

Potter's chief source for the play was probably Florence Becker Lennon's *The Life of Lewis Carroll* (1962), which takes a Freudian approach to Dodgson/Carroll, and assumes that he was in love with Alice. In an interview, Potter described Dodgson as 'that haunted soul, who didn't stutter when talking to little girls but was done for as soon as they reached puberty . . . that tied-in, repressed, strange, playful, tormented, yet joyously inventive man'. This was the nearest Potter came to explaining why he had written *Alice*. In fact he had returned to the type of hero (or anti-hero) he had begun to explore in *The Confidence Course*.

Like Hazlitt, Dodgson is estranged from, and fiercely critical of, the rest of society (there is much in the play about his fury with Dean Liddell's attempts to modernize the college). In Dodgson's case the estrangement arises largely from his guilt about his irregular sexual feelings, which of course imply the possibility of child abuse such as Potter himself had experienced. This guilt breeds both anger and creativity – makes him both 'tormented' and 'joyously inventive'. In 1983 Potter – speaking of his film *Dreamchild*, largely a reworking of *Alice* – said: 'I'm fascinated, with Dodgson, how considerable art can come from repression.'

*

In his 1967 introduction to the Barton plays, Potter makes no great claim for their achievement, remarking that they suffered from 'the conveyor-belt aspects of television' with its 'need to fill so many hours every night of the week, every week of the year'. If he ever reached his full potential as a writer, it would happen only 'out of the reach of television executives and the television conveyor belt'. Yet that belt was of his own making. His decision to try to make a living solely from television plays meant that, in the future, he would have to write very prolifically indeed.

Roger Smith emphasizes that, even after four of his plays had been shown (*The Confidence Course*, *Alice* and the two Barton plays), 'Dennis was only *one* of the *Wednesday Play* discoveries – we didn't think we'd found *the* great television writer.' On the other hand, as Trodd remarks, 'Nobody else was writing anything like as much as him. I'm sure if you look at a checklist of *Wednesday Plays*, I have no doubt that there would be no other writer who had as many entries, or even half as many as Dennis.'

It is true that Potter's output of ten scripts for the *Wednesday Play* (and its successor, *Play for Today*) between 1964 and 1972 was roughly twice that of any other writer who contributed to the series during that period – with one exception. Five plays each were written by Tom Clarke, Julia Jones, and Simon Gray; Hugh Whitemore wrote four; and Jim Allen, John Hopkins and Simon Raven each contributed three. The exception was David Mercer.

Seven years older than Potter, Mercer had had his first television play, *Where the Difference Begins*, screened by the BBC in 1961. Based on his own working-class background (he was the son of a Yorkshire engine-driver), it has similarities to *Stand Up, Nigel Barton* in its portrayal of old-style socialism confronting a younger generation. Mercer's most popular play was *A Suitable Case for Treatment* (1962), the blackly comic story of Morgan Delt, who reacts to being cuckolded by imagining that he is a gorilla (it was later filmed, with David Warner in the title role, as *Morgan*). Later scripts included *And Did Those Feet* (1965), a Gothic comedy about the twin bastard sons of a decaying aristocrat, and *Let's Murder Vivaldi* (1968), a four-hander about sexual betrayal. Potter reviewed one of Mercer's plays, *In Two Minds* (1967), a case history of a schizophrenic, in the *New Statesman*, calling it 'terrifying . . . compellingly written', and ten years later he wrote of Mercer's 'cadences of speech and thought and mocking passion which make him unique among English dramatists'. Mercer died three years after this, in 1980.

The *Wednesday Play* that made the greatest impact of all was written neither by Potter nor Mercer, and was as much a director's as a writer's achievement. On 3 November 1965, between the screenings of *Alice* and the Barton plays, came Nell Dunn's portrait of working-class girls in Battersea, *Up the Junction*, directed by Ken Loach, who had been another grammar-school boy at Oxford. Trodd recalls this being made in the teeth of opposition from BBC executives, on account of its sexual explicitness. A year later the *Wednesday Play* audience was stunned by Loach's even more brilliant film of Jeremy Sandford's devastating exposure of the official treatment of the homeless, *Cathy Come Home*, shown on 16 November 1966. The superbly researched script, and Loach's ability to conjure lifelike performances out of his largely amateur cast, made millions of people aware, literally overnight, of an acute social problem.

'Ken Loach represented everything that Dennis didn't,' says Trodd, another direction, another campaign altogether. I can remember thinking very clearly, 'I want to be in both camps.' Not that Dennis was yet anywhere near proposing I should become his exclusive producer. But Dennis's was another drift altogether from Loach's street-cred, 16-millimetre film style – which was very, very exciting. Dennis, on the other hand, turned everything that television had already done into a kind of whipping-boy, inhabited it in a kind of anarchic way for his own purposes. And he didn't really want to leave the studio and go out to film. His early plays are rooted in the conventions of television – but in order to be able to destroy them for his own purposes.

Gareth Davies agrees: 'Dennis believed, in those days, in the concentrated use of that studio space. He thought that to go filming for television was a mistake. It was essentially a theatrical approach, but I think it suited his work very well. My own view is that his work lacked clarity and drive once it became filmic.'

Potter's resentment of Loach is evident in a 1966 article, in which he sneers at 'BBC drama producers and story editors who think that the studio is insufferable, that the filmed documentary, especially with pop music and a wildtrack of real people being inarticulate about real things, is the norm, and *Up the Junction* the greatest thing since *Hamlet* and Mickey Mouse'. Elsewhere, he scoffed at 'the increasingly fashionable, hand-held camera style distortions of those in search of an allegedly delinquent generation'. He felt strongly that social injustice should be tackled by 'journalism and the essay and political polemic' rather than art. (He hardly knew Loach personally; in 1980 he told an interviewer, 'I've scarcely exchanged the time of day with Loach.')

Despite these feelings, he relished the ideological conflict between the *Wednesday Play* and the BBC bosses. In 1968 he wrote that the series stood out 'like a big, black, aching tooth in a smooth mouthful of plastic dentures', and in his MacTaggart Lecture, he portrays MacTaggart, Garnett, Loach and Trodd holding a council of war in their offices on the fifth floor at Television Centre, which he compares to Hell in *The Divine Comedy*:

Jimmy MacTaggart and his bushy-tailed acolytes used to sit around somewhere in the Fifth Circle talking . . . about the evident iniquities of the BBC management, the tapeworm-length persistence of BBC cowardice . . . [a] threat to the very existence of the single play. You can imagine how much greater our indignation would have been had we known at the time that we were sitting slap in the middle of what later observers were to call the Golden Age of television drama.

He also suggested in the lecture that there was a Kafkaesque aspect to the building and the organization that inhabits it: 'A walk along the corridors of the Television Centre will always bring you back shaken but not stirred to where you started.' But Potter also admits, in the lecture:

I was exceptionally fortunate to begin my career in television at a time when the BBC was so infuriatingly confident about what public-service broadcasting meant that the question itself was not even on what would now be called the agenda. The then ITV companies shared much more of this ethos than they were then willing to acknowledge. Our profession was then mostly filled with men and women who mostly cared about the programmes rather than the dividend.

Michael Bakewell emphasizes that, even when *Vote, Vote, Vote for Nigel Barton* was in trouble, the members of the BBC Drama Group were determined that Potter should keep writing for them: 'We were keen that he should have a three-play contract.' Potter's agent Roger Hancock signed such a contract in January 1966; he was to receive £800, £850 and £900 for the three scripts. By this time, Potter had already completed another play, *Message for Posterity*, and had handed it to the BBC.

The idea for this had been offered the previous spring, in the form of a detailed synopsis. Usually, however, Potter did not plan his plays in advance, as he told Graham Fuller:

POTTER: I never have a plot. I don't have a schema . . . I either have one image, or I may have a sense of where the image has got to be, and then find that it hasn't got to be there at all, which is always the best feeling. Then I write – and I write extremely intensely, hour upon hour until I'm exhausted, because I'm frightened of losing it when I'm doing it. I hate starting it, too. I hate the *process* . . .

FULLER: Do you always write in a linear fashion, from scene one?

POTTER: From the starting point to page 17 or so, yes. Then I usually destroy all those pages and start again . . .

FULLER: Are you a copious rewriter?

POTTER: Only when I'm in difficulties. Normally I write very fast.

Ken Trodd says, 'I doubt if he ever laboured very long at a draft of anything. He might throw some of it away, and he might do a draft before showing me, or whoever was producing, the second one. But I think the actual speed of writing was secretly very high.'

In 1983 Potter said about his creative process:

There are writers . . . I presume, who work out everything before they sit down to put the words in order. For me . . . writing . . . is more like pulling and pulling and pulling on a string that already has its weights attached, or dipping a thimble again and again into a pool that was already there. The effort, the curiosity, the surprise or the anxiety are each strong enough so to fill the mind that there is no room for 'thought' . . .

I do not mean that one is a mindless automaton when crossing the t, dotting the i, or curling the comma: what, you say, will she say *now*? Why did he do *that*? He doesn't mean this, does he? No, they wouldn't look at each other, surely? Well, not with their eyes, anyway – and so on, and so on. Questions, musings, doubts – very concentrated thoughts, in their way – occupy a writer every moment that he or she is writing. A speech has to be torn up, a scene expanded, a silence explained. The mind feels very busy, and yet also oddly passive, almost as though *waiting*.

To Graham Fuller, he explained:

It doesn't feel like making an argument. It doesn't feel like having a purpose. It feels like something you knew but didn't know you knew. It feels like dreaming . . . The intensity of the experience is such that you are almost receiving what you're writing. Of course, you're shaping it at the same time, and then you add to it also. It's an odd thing, knowing that a scene has got to come to an end, or that you've got to make a turn. You don't know what it's going to be, just that you *must* – then it's done. It's being on a trip. It's being subject to it as well as controlling it.

David Mercer said almost exactly the same in 1964: 'I don't know what my next play will be like, or about, and shan't know until I am at least halfway through it. The first impulse springs from an accumulation of images, tensions, fragments. The only rational problem is to find that cohering thread which will lead to an overall statement.'

Yet, despite this fluency and this feeling of 'dreaming', Potter emphasized: 'I think writing is very difficult full stop. If anyone says it's easy, I say to them, here's a clean pad of paper: now go away and produce three thousand words by tonight. I'm always in a state of terror when I start writing. My stomach's going like a laundromat: it's like crossing the Niagara Falls on a tightrope.'

Message for Posterity begins with a parliamentary committee choosing the artist James Player to paint the portrait of the retired Tory leader Sir David Browning. Player is an elderly diehard socialist. 'Painting the portrait of a Pope or a Prime Minister', he tells a pair of reporters, 'is no different from painting a fat bluebottle on a scrap of rotting meat. The important thing is to *attack*.'

Meanwhile old Browning, in his grandiose country mansion ('Eastrepps', a variant on Potter's Norfolk address when he wrote the play, Northrepps), is dozing aimlessly in front of the television. Scraps of his favourite programme, *The Black and White Minstrel Show*, jostle in his memory with his wartime speeches, but he wakes abruptly when a newsreader, announcing that the portrait has been commissioned, quotes Player's 'bluebottle' remark. At home, Player is savouring the remark himself, and recalling (as Potter did of Churchill) that Browning 'once sent the troops into the Welsh Valleys to break up a miners' strike. The fascist swine!'

When he and Browning meet, they are initially amused by each other. However, Player soon tires of Browning's calculated insults, and determines to make the portrait as cruel as possible: 'Little pink and blue veins all broken like an Ordnance Survey map on his bulbous, pickled shallot of a snout. Flesh the colour of old putty, with pink rims to his little pig eyes. Hee! Hee! Hee!' Browning passes out during a sitting, but Player ruthlessly props up his body and works on at the painting, muttering, 'Do it, keep on doing it, with the gentle, precise detachment of a botanist recording the foliage of an extinct plant. For posterity, James.' Browning's manservant discovers his master apparently dead, and shouts for help. Browning's granddaughter (a typical Sixties swinger) rushes in, gasping, 'Let me try.' Potter's direction reads, 'Clara adminsters the "Kiss of Life", a beautiful young girl with lips to a senile old man. Deliberately, symbolically ugly.' Browning regains consciousness, but while the ambulance is summoned Player runs amok, smashing ornaments and glass cases. But the ambulance men arrive before he can do serious harm, and in the last scene Browning, in his hospital bed, learns that Player has been confined in an asylum. 'We always win in the end,' Browning mumbles to himself. 'Always win – in the end.'

By the end of his life, Potter was inclined to dismiss *Message for*

Posterity as a failed satire about Graham Sutherland's ill-fated portrait of Churchill, allegedly destroyed by Churchill's wife because it was so unflattering: 'There was an evasion going on; the main character should have been called Churchill . . . Really it was a remnant of soap-box political rhetoric.'* Browning is certainly handled satirically in the first part of the play. Yet the balance gradually shifts, so that Browning's sense of history is contrasted with Player's heartless exploitation of the old man, and his wild destructive rampage. The ending implies that old-style socialism cannot really change anything; the most it can do is to cause havoc. This may seem a big ideological step for Potter to have taken in the fourteen months since he had been a Labour candidate, but Player's 'Smash it all up!' is only a more melo-dramatic expression of the impotent rage in Nigel Barton's V-sign. If the old order is to be dislodged from power, it will not be through politics.

Asked if he would describe *Message for Posterity* as a naturalistic play, Potter answered: 'Yes, basically it was. And if you start writing like that you are pulled . . . to the outsides instead of the insides of the head.' Though there are some mildly non-naturalistic passages (the flashbacks to Browning's wartime speeches), the greater part of the play is in West End style, dependent on dialogue rather than images – we never even glimpse the portrait taking shape. Potter is not at home in this wordy genre, and does indeed seem unable to get at the 'insides' of his characters. In particular, the relationship between the two old men is never adequately developed.

Gareth Davies, who was to direct once more, says he never liked *Message for Posterity.* 'The original spark was fine, a good intellectual idea, looking for the metaphor in that painting. But I don't think Dennis ever developed it.' Trodd wonders if the writing of the original synopsis had not used up all Potter's interest in the subject: 'We used to discourage writers from doing synopses, because the risk was the energy that ought to have been kept for the actual writing might be exhausted.' And the critic Philip Purser shrewdly spotted that there was too much planning in *Message for Posterity,* calling it 'the result of thinking up a play rather than one insinuating itself'.

---

* However, shortly before his death, Potter allowed the BBC to remake *Message for Posterity*. It was shown on BBC2 on 29 October 1994, with Eric Porter as Player and John Neville as Browning.

Nevertheless *Message for Posterity* was accepted as a *Wednesday Play*, and Potter immediately received another BBC commission from Trodd, who was currently story editor for a BBC2 series, *Thirty Minute Theatre*. Around this time, Trodd changed the spelling of his first name: 'I received a letter which mistakenly spelt it "Kenith", and a girlfriend picked it up and said, "Oh, that's how you spell it – as in zenith", and I said, "All right, we'll keep that."'

Trodd observes of *Thirty Minute Theatre*:

The brief of that series was repellent to me, because it was a live studio performance, which meant it *was* 'theatre', and I'd already developed the ideology, along with Roger Smith and Tony Garnett, of disliking the theatrical element in what was essentially a non-theatrical medium. So I set about getting all the people that were already writing for the *Wednesday Play* to do things for that series, and others. I got a script from Raymond Williams, and another from Simon Gray – he adapted a short story of his own, and it was the first piece of drama he'd ever written.

Potter himself remarked that 'the half-hour play is cripplingly difficult for the television writer – the form constantly degenerates into the shape of a mere anecdote, the mood is temptingly similar to after-dinner conversation and the sort of money you get for taking such risks could be more easily earned by being priggish in the back pages of small left-wing magazines'. He added that writing for *Thirty Minute Theatre* was further restricted by the fact that it was live: 'A "live" play is severely restricted in the number of sets which can be used, in the time-scale manoeuvrability of the actors and even in the range of camera movements.' Nevertheless his script, *Emergency – Ward 9*, was finished very quickly, and broadcast on Easter Monday, 11 April 1966, with Gareth Davies directing.

This short play – which in retrospect looks like a trial run for the hospital strand of *The Singing Detective* – recalls Potter's observation, in the *Daily Herald* three years earlier, that 'watching *Emergency – Ward 10* while actually in hospital' had exposed the falsity of the soap opera, in comparison with 'the real world of bedpans and squeaking tea trolleys'. Though set in a 'ramshackle London hospital', it does not aim at documentary realism, but is a comic parable, revolving around three patients.

Padstow, a young schoolteacher and Nonconformist lay preacher, is in the next bed to the elderly working-class Flanders, and begins by pitying the old man, in terms that identify him as a typical middle-class liberal: 'Paper boy at seven or eight, left school at thirteen, all his life either in rotten old factories or looking for work . . . Wife dead. Children fled to Orpington in Ford Anglias.' Padstow is equally condescending towards an African patient, Adzola, who 'glides up and down the ward' looking like a 'story-book chieftain'. He comments on Adzola's 'marvellous grace', and tells Nurse Angela, 'I feel that Matron ought to pad behind him with a ceremonial fly-swat.' She replies, 'A deodorant would be more to the point', which shocks Padstow with its racism, but this is nothing to old Flanders's reaction: 'See that nigger! . . . He walks down the ward as though he owns the bleedin' place . . . Don't understand why they let all these niggers abuse the National Health what we fought for.'

Padstow unsuccessfully attempts to talk Flanders out of this attitude – 'We're all one human family, you know' – but all he gets is mockery for his Christian beliefs. Flanders then causes trouble by addressing Adzola as 'Sambo', and Padstow tries to apologize on his behalf, but is dismayed by Adzola's response. 'I don't take no notice of a thing like him,' says the African. 'He's a very *common* man. Working class . . . I'm my own boss, I am. He's just scum. I've just got me a new E-type, man, and that man there, he's got *nothing*, you know that? Nothing!' Padstow now hears Flanders weeping, and assumes this is because he had rebuked him for the 'Sambo' incident. The truth, however, is that the old man has wet his bed: 'If there's a heaven, Mr Padstow, then I've gone and shot my bolt good and proper.' As the play ends, Flanders notices that Padstow has put his hands together in prayer. 'Put in a word for me, will you, mate?' he asks pathetically.

Mocking the woolly-liberal conscience and poking fun at what we would now call political correctness, *Emergency – Ward 9* shows that everybody's value system is vulnerable. Potter had been shocked by the racist attitudes he encountered when canvassing, yet he presents the old man's prejudices as the inevitable result of his upbringing, and thus scarcely more blameworthy than Adzola's materialistic class prejudice or Padstow's naïvely literal belief in heaven.

Trodd says that, while the 'propaganda' for *Thirty Minute Theatre* alleged that there was 'more vitality' in live performances, and that actors greatly enjoyed them, the opposite was true – some performers suffered appalling stage fright before transmission, while cameras and stage-hands were frequently visible on screen. 'Dennis's *Emergency –*

Ward 9 nearly went astray because Terence De Marney, who was playing the old man, Flanders, lost his way in a long speech. And there was nothing we could do to help.'

Nancy Banks-Smith in the *Sun* took the play as Potter had meant it:

Thank goodness for Dennis Potter. A loaf of fresh bread in the stale wilderness of Bank Holiday Monday viewing . . . Potter is that remarkable newish playwright who wrote that two-fisted dramatic attack *Stand Up, Nigel Barton* and *Vote, Vote, Vote for Nigel Barton*. Well hip hip hoorah for Dennis Potter and *Emergency – Ward 9* on BBC2 last night. It made *Emergency – Ward 10* look like perjury, an offence against the whole truth.

The play was recorded during transmission, and repeated the following year, but the recording had been made on the newly available electronic videotape system, and to save costs it was eventually wiped and the big, expensive reels of two-inch tape were reused.

Potter's speed of writing *Emergency – Ward 9* suggests that he was already making himself work to a precise timetable. 'When writing flat out,' he explained at the end of his life,

seriously no-nonsensing with anything else whatsoever, I always set myself certain targets per day in terms of page numbers, and if a page or two are lost in one day's difficulties or interruptions, they have to be made up during the next twelve-or-so-hour session. I also reckon on the basis of a minute a page when calculating the length of a script, and lay the work out accordingly in longhand on an A4 writing book. In a sort of print costive enough to drive its first reader (my daughter Sarah [then his typist]) mad, not on the basis of illegibility but in anxieties about the true nature of the person who has composed it in so appallingly neat, clear and orderly a fashion.

*

A mere two months after the transmission of *Emergency – Ward 9*, he delivered to the BBC another of the scripts commissioned under the three-play contract, called *Where the Buffalo Roam*. He was still waiting for *Message for Posterity* to be put into production; there were difficulties over casting, and possibly some nervousness about the implicit caricature of Churchill. Meanwhile *Where the Buffalo Roam* was scheduled for transmission on 2 November 1966, with Gareth Davies as director and Kenith Trodd as story editor.

Young Willy Turner, the working-class 'hero' of *Where the Buffalo Roam*, is supposed to be attending literacy classes at a rehabilitation centre – he is on probation for knocking another boy's teeth out. But his mother can scarcely get him out of the house, so lost is he in fantasies of being the toughest cowboy in town. 'Call me Shane,' he tells her. 'That's all I want. Just – call – me – Shane.' In the opening moments of the play there is almost subliminally fast cutting between Willy's fantasy of himself in cowboy gear, in a western shoot-out, and the drab reality of his family's terraced house in Swansea. (The original script specifies that the play is set in London, but Gareth Davies, directing again, 'thought the language could be freed up if we went to Wales'.) Willy's cowboy fantasy initially seems pathetic, but we soon learn from his widowed mother and curmudgeonly grandfather that his father used to beat him up for stammering and cowardice.

Where the Buffalo Roam begins as a witty, fast-moving exploration of a fantasist's evasions. As Willy comes downstairs to breakfast, the cowboy song going round his head battles with, and eventually vanquishes, the music of *Housewives' Choice* on the kitchen radio. Similarly the bus taking Willy into the centre of Swansea suddenly seems (to him) to be in the Arizona desert. But the pace of the script soon slows, and the dialogue becomes so predictable that one senses a tired writer struggling to keep up a daily quota. 'A cowboy film is full of action – unlike most films nowadays,' remarks the probation officer, with unintended irony, in the midst of an interminably wordy scene in which the only events have been the lighting of a cigarette and the pouring of a cup of tea.

Potter later said, of his reliance on dialogue in his early scripts:

When I first started writing plays I found it almost impossible to make people touch each other, and that was evidence of something in me that I wasn't aware of. I do remember just looking at a page and trying to make people move across the room and touch each other. I found that an appallingly difficult thing to do. The verbal relationships were easier.

He does not manage to prepare us for Willy's transition from harmless daydreamer to murderous psychopath. We suddenly find that the boy's imaginary gun has (inexplicably) become a real one, and he shoots his mother, his grandfather and a policeman before being gunned down himself by a police marksman.

Willy's creation of an alternative personality is an exaggerated version of Potter's own strategy for survival in childhood. 'In those days,' he writes in a 1975 article, 'I protected myself with strategic comic turns, and fantasies labyrinthine to pull in my companions, forcing them to lower their fists.' Indeed, by the time he wrote *Where the Buffalo Roam*, he felt that fantasy had become his method of survival. 'I am aware that I am living a fictional life in a way,' he remarks in *Potter on Potter*.

When my illness first hit me . . . I thought, 'The only way I can save my life is to invent my life.' I hope I'm not being immodest, but I think there is a certain emotional power in my work . . . And I think that power is actually the result of the contest between my real self and my invented self. My invented self overcomes my illness . . . and keeps me sane. Well, sort of sane.

Where the Buffalo Roam, transmitted on 2 November 1966, with Hywel Bennett as Willy, had mixed reviews. The most enthusiastic was by Nancy Banks-Smith in the *Sun*:

This is the play he has written twice before for the *Wednesday Play* series, *Stand Up, Nigel Barton*, *Vote, Vote, Vote for Nigel Barton* and now, virtually, *Stick 'Em Up, Willy Turner*. They are all about a young man's attempts to escape an unbearable and inescapable home background. Perhaps Potter just keeps rewriting his own *Hamlet* . . .

If I were looking for faults I would say there were some lumps of uncooked psychology in the play which made it too much like a classic case history . . . But let all that go. Potter is a pretty astounding playwright. If he goes down much farther into Hell, I doubt if television can follow him. And that will be an irreplaceable loss.

*

Potter had now abandoned the experiment of living in Norfolk; he later told an interviewer that neither he nor Margaret could 'warm' to it. In the summer of 1966 he made the move that he had foreseen when talking to Barry Norman ('I can return to the Forest of Dean on my own terms'). The family's new address was 69 Allasten Road, Lydney, the town on the edge of the Severn estuary where he and Margaret had met a decade earlier. Jane says the house was 'a tiny bungalow'.

In October, the journal *New Society*, for which Potter sometimes reviewed books, asked him to go to the South Wales village of Aberfan, where a slag-heap had collapsed on to a school playground, killing over a hundred children. 'Mothers and fathers queue outside Bethania Welsh Congregational,' he wrote, 'to identify and weep over the soiled bodies of their children. Nothing nor nobody, curse nor prayer, God nor Coal Board, can now assuage the awful grief and anguish of this pitiful place . . .' Describing the cause of the disaster in *New Society*, he used a curious image:

The collapsed slag heap looks weirdly, wickedly voluptuous as you see it from a distance, for it sprawls into the village like a reclining female monster, a wanton negress shifting awkwardly on smelly hams. The sense of outrage and impotent disgust seems to coil itself into the very walk of those who approach the defilement, their gumboots slip-slopping on the slime . . .

When he wrote this, he had just finished a Christmas script for *The Wednesday Play*, based on the Cinderella story. Trodd explained to the BBC Copyright Department:

This [is] to be our Christmas show . . . a version of the fairy tale, probably set in a contemporary princeling state (such as Monaco). Dennis Potter intends to adhere to the values and implications of the original story . . . [He] is having to write it to a very specific and early deadline. The notion is an experimental one and does not, as far as we are concerned, come within the agreed programme of his three-play contract.

Trodd formally accepted *Cinderella*, ensuring that Potter would be paid in full – 'Garnett and I made a rule that we never withheld the second-half fee' – but had serious doubts about the script: 'I found it very gawky. My memory is that Prince Charming had a club foot. I remember that as the sticking point.' Similarly, Lionel Harris, who was to be the producer, had 'grave doubts about its suitability as Christmas fare'. Harris referred it to Gerald Savory, a former West End playwright who was now Head of Plays. 'My dislike of it went further,' Savory told Huw Wheldon, 'and I immediately decided against doing it.' Potter was told that 'so much work needed doing on it, that it could not possibly be ready for this Christmas'.

At this point, on a visit to Television Centre, Potter ran into the journalist Hunter Davies, husband of Margaret Forster, who was himself writing a *Wednesday Play* (*The Playground*, transmitted in May 1967). He told Davies what had happened, and Davies wrote it up in his Atticus column in *The Sunday Times*:

The BBC commissioned Dennis Potter to do them a nice play for Christmas . . . He handed it in last week. Prince Charming turns out to be a sexual degenerate, who on the stroke of midnight does something rather nasty to Cinderella . . . There is a scene with Prince Charming and a prostitute on a gravestone . . .

Naturally enough, Mr Potter says he wasn't trying to give offence. He believes that as fairy tales can worry children, adult versions of them should as well . . . However . . . the BBC don't like it . . .

Potter gave Davies a sketch of his financial situation: 'Mr Potter is now about on the top rate for a TV playwright – he gets £900 a play . . . Last year he made in all £5000, but this included advances on stuff not yet finished. He says his rate of three TV plays a year is too much. One play should be enough, but you couldn't live on that . . . What happens in the long run with *Cinderella* might decide him once and for all to give up television. "Nothing definite has happened, but if it's shelved for good, I just won't bother to send them any more."'

When he had read Davies's article, Gerald Savory observed to Huw Wheldon that Potter was 'yelling to the press' just as he had over *Vote, Vote, Vote for Nigel Barton*. But he invited Potter to come and discuss what might be done about *Cinderella*. 'I asked him if he minded if I spoke frankly,' Savory reported to Wheldon after the meeting,

and he replied that there would be no point in doing otherwise. I said that I found the satire heavy-handed and the humour rather 'sniggering' . . . I assured him . . . that I was not a monarchist, nor a purist, nor prurient . . . He told me what he was trying to get at in the play but I told him that, in my view, he hadn't written what he had really intended.

Potter was deeply hurt; he told Savory it was his 'best play to date', and that he had not been able to write anything else since it had been rejected. Savory agreed to read it again.

Fleet Street was now splashing the story. In the *Sun*, Nancy Banks-Smith wrote, 'The BBC knew the theme and treatment beforehand. They could also have guessed that, being a Potter play, it would be good – and – startling.' In the tabloids, there was criticism of unnecessary censorship, though it was also reported that Mary Whitehouse of the National Viewers' and Listeners' Association had congratulated Savory on his decision. In several papers, Potter was given space to explain the meaning of the play: 'I wrote it for grown-ups. My Prince Charming has problems because his sexual relations with other girls have been difficult. The trouble is he idolizes girls.' He was also quoted as saying, 'If I can arrange my career so that I never have to write plays for BBC TV again then I intend to do so.'

Two weeks after Christmas, Savory wrote to Potter that a third reading had left his mind unchanged. There is no reply from Potter in the files. Nearly thirty years later, he was inclined to agree with Savory:

It wasn't very good. The scenes weren't really worked out. I don't think the script survives anywhere. Prince Charming in it was an emotional cripple, ugly and twisted in some way . . . There was also a bit too much bravado going on in it; I hadn't digested it . . . I was annoyed with the BBC at the time [for rejecting it] . . . But it's best forgotten.

In fact the script – or, at least, a script – of *Cinderella* does survive among Potter's papers, neatly handwritten in a hardback notebook. Its jokes about television and sex are so mild that it is hard to see what the fuss was about, though certainly it is one of Potter's weakest scripts, and would have been panned by the reviewers. On the other hand it is the first Potter play to use Thirties songs as counterpoint to angst about sex.

The setting is 'a minuscule European monarchy situated midway between Windsor and Zenda', the date 'vaguely, early Thirties: or colour-supplement nostalgia solidified and slightly soured'. In the opening scene, the King and Queen are playing snakes and ladders under the cynical eye of the bored Prince Charming; when he makes a mildly risqué joke, the Queen warns him, 'Mrs Whitehouse may have bugged the room.' Later, the royal couple watch a party political broadcast by the Prime Minister – a spoof of Harold Wilson, with pipe and Yorkshire accent: 'Let me say at once, this is not the old dis-credited policy of Stop–Go. (*Sucks on his pipe.*) This is the new policy of Stop. Full stop.' Meanwhile Prince Charming is wandering listlessly through a graveyard, where he encounters a gum-chewing girl with a transistor radio:

PRINCE CHARMING: Do – do you – ah – feel like – cheering me up?

GIRL: (*cautious*) Howdya mean, like?

(*In a paroxysm of humiliating frankness the* PRINCE *gestures at a stone angel.*)

PRINCE CHARMING: There's something s-s-sexy about – graveyards, don't you think?

(*Pause.*)

GIRL: (*menacing*) Howdya mean, like?

PRINCE CHARMING: (*gabbling*) Oh I've heard about this place all right. I've heard, don't you worry. A fine and private place. What do you think I'm doing here? What do you think you're doing here? I'll pay, you know. I can pay. Oh, I can afford it all right.

GIRL: (*brightening*) Can yer?

PRINCE CHARMING: (*desperate*) Yes.

GIRL: (*matter of fact*) All right. If you want to.

(*They stand looking at each other. The* PRINCE *is full of a passionate degradation.*)

PRINCE CHARMING: W-where – do we – you know – ?

GIRL: (*laugh*) Where do you think, lover boy? Down behind one of them bleed'n tombstones. We shan't disturb them as is underneath, that's for sure.

PRINCE CHARMING: (*to himself*) Decay below and corruption above.

GIRL: It's three pounds for a short time. (*Hard grin*) The music is free.

She switches on her radio, which plays 'Ah, Sweet Mystery of Life'.

At the palace, a Thirties-style dance band and crooner are rehearsing for the ball, and the presumably post-coital Prince Charming is behaving very strangely, muttering to his father, 'Slime and putrescence . . . Betrayal in the glitter of adulterous eyes. Fornication in graveyards. Lust. Black, blind lust.' The ball begins, with the crooner chanting, 'Wrap Your Troubles in Dreams' and 'As Time Goes By', but the Prince lurks on the sidelines, with a twisted face, groaning, 'Sex. Sex. Sex.'

Meanwhile Cinderella, left at home by her father and the Ugly Sisters, refuses to believe in the Fairy Godmother:

CINDERELLA: No, not 'magic'! How *can* I accept it.

FAIRY GODMOTHER: Tell me – do you or do you not believe in Christianity, my dear?

CINDERELLA: The BBC is not neutral as regards religion. This is official policy as expressed by a former Director-General. So of course I believe in Christianity. (*Pause*.) In a mild *Meeting Point* sort of way . . .

FAIRY GODMOTHER: So believe in your Fairy Godmother! . . . After all, they can always discuss it in the next *Epilogue* or something.

Cinderella's magical transformation is achieved in an instant, the Fairy Godmother observing that this 'would not have been possible in the days of continuous recording'. When she arrives at the ball and pairs off with Prince Charming (who seems to have forgotten his sexual hang-ups), the crooner sings a 1942 Rudy Vallee hit, 'My Time Is Your Time'. The bandleader pulls down a pantomime song-sheet, and the entire cast sings the refrain –

> My time is your time
> Your time is my time
> We just seem to synchronize
> And sympathize

– as Big Ben strikes midnight, and the song is taken up by a 'chorus of angels, ascending and ascending and ascending'.

In 1993 Potter said of *Cinderella*: 'The only scene I recall was set in a very long room, with the ugly Prince Charming slavering and shuffling his way towards the shoe-fitting of the most beautiful girl; there was something sexually repellent about it.' No such scene appears in the surviving script (neither does Prince Charming's club foot, recalled by Trodd), so there may have been at least one other version.

During the row over *Cinderella*, Potter told one reporter, 'I have never written for ITV. However, I hope to write plays for ABC TV and Rediffusion next year [1967].' Sure enough he wrote another pantomime, *Rumpelstiltskin*, for Rediffusion, the ITV company then serving London, though Trodd thinks it may date from 1968, when Rediffusion had already screened a Potter play, *The Bonegrinder*. Like *Cinderella* it uses pre-war songs, played by a live band, and Rumpelstiltskin's 'theme' song is a 1939 hit, 'The Man with the Mandolin'. Sexual angst is once again the theme: the 'strange little man' is tortured with lust for Griselda, the beautiful woodcutter's daughter. 'All the flamin' time it happens,' he tells her,

shrivelled old men and cripples . . . They see these gorgeous butterflies around them . . . click-clack-clicking along the hard pavement on their spiky high heels, their hips swaying . . . There's nothing for you to say, my dear. You can have all the dreams that are going. The world is *made* for you. Straw will always turn into gold for people like *you*!

Reluctantly, Griselda agrees to sleep with him if he will save her life – but of course his name is discovered and she is absolved. Potter's agent Roger Hancock recalls that 'Dennis was talking about getting Diana Dors to play the girl', but not surprisingly *Rumpelstiltskin* was never made.

CHAPTER 4

Much too raw

Message for Posterity finally reached the screen, with Gareth Davies directing, as the *Wednesday Play* on 3 May 1967. The Churchillian role of Browning had been given to Joseph O'Connor, who had played Old Jolyon in the BBC's hugely successful *Forsyte Saga*, and the painter was played by Patrick Magee, whose creaking voice had inspired some of Samuel Beckett's best work. Reviewers mostly treated the play as a comment on the Graham Sutherland portrait of Churchill, while a panel on *Late Night Line-Up* argued as to whether it was about the impotence of art, the invulnerability of the Establishment, or the pathos of ageing radicalism.

Potter had now begun to write television reviews for the *New Statesman*, then being edited by Paul Johnson, though the invitation seems to have come from the arts editor, Nicholas Tomalin. (He was paid £20 per review.) His columns show that he was still smarting from the rejection of *Cinderella*.

The first, on 17 February, observed that 'the hitherto lively *Wednesday Play*' was 'in danger of slow destruction-by-memo'. After sniping at other BBC programmes, he went on, 'I regret having to present my credentials as a television critic in such a sour fashion, but I think it was Nabokov who pointed out that people usually bare their teeth when they are first introduced. Benevolent days will follow, but there is more than enough to bite on at the moment . . . '

In subsequent weeks he bit on a P. G. Wodehouse series ('I longed for a healthy belch of wind to blow down the striped awnings on the summery lawns; better, far better, to recoil from the authentic stench of life than suffer the distant aroma of stale cucumber inside Lord Emsworth's tent'); on the clerical sitcom *All Gas and Gaiters* ('If the scriptwriters have been warned off making jokes about the Almighty they could at least achieve a passable approximation by working in a few oblique references to the transcendental Huw Wheldon'); and on the cowardice of BBC executives: 'There is at the moment the acrid whiff of battle in the Corporation's Drama Department, where scripts – and the elementary rights of their authors – are being strenuously fought over before the plays ever reach the rehearsal rooms.' Indeed by the end of April he seemed to be in despair about the whole of television, which 'has become for so many of us something that we turn on like tap water'.

Gareth Davies observes, 'Dennis never appeared to be nervous of BBC management; he was always ready to bite the hand that fed him – snap, at the wrist! Tremendous!' But Nicholas Tomalin was now complaining that his reviews were too abusive. 'We all know,' he wrote to Potter,

that a lot of broadcasters are toffee-nosed middle-class idiots, we know that a lot of pop programmes are shit, and we know that BBC executives are spineless idiots. This isn't news . . . I want you to watch some programmes outside your BBC drama experience, and try to establish what the interesting elements are . . . be a proper television critic instead of someone who apparently just doesn't like television, and keeps on smashing a wordy fist into it.

There is no reply from Potter in the files, and his next review seems to be an ironic riposte to Tomalin, since it devotes the entire column to praising *The Black and White Minstrel Show*.

Potter had told Tomalin that he had just finished another play, and it was sent to Trodd at the beginning of May 1967. 'Dennis Potter has delivered us the first draft of a play called *The Rivers of Babylon*,' Trodd told Copyright, 'and we would like to regard this as the second submission under his three-play contract.'

Though *The Rivers of Babylon* was offered to the BBC, it is divided into three 'acts', as were Potter's early plays for ITV – the 'intervals' being the commercial breaks. Its theme is once again sexual anguish, and the treatment of this subject is now passionately serious. Indeed the play is a gripping dramatization of the confession that Potter had made to Trodd and Smith.

Act One opens in 'a sleazy, rather badly lit street in a run-down area of Birmingham'. Lennon and McCartney's 'Can't Buy Me Love' plays behind the titles, and we see a young girl, Carol, walking away from us 'with the deliberate sexual exaggeration of the experienced tart'. The music stops in mid-chord as the camera moves in on a man who is watching her: 'About thirty. His name is Ronnie Wills. His eyes have a dark ominous glittering.' He stares at the departing girl and quotes 'with cold, unemotional precision' from the Bible: 'The dog is turned to his own vomit again: and the sow that was washed to her wallowing in the mire.'

Ronnie starts to follow Carol, his face 'contorted with an unusual, almost psychotic intensity', as he mutters between his teeth, 'Bitch! Bitch! Dirty bitch!' Seeing him, she waits provocatively. He lights a cigarette with shaking hands, muttering again:

RONNIE: He – pitch – he that toucheth – pitch – shall be – (*He drags hard on cigarette.*) Defiled!

(*He flings cigarette away, hitches up his shoulders and strides decisively after the prostitute. As he gets alongside, he momentarily measures his stride with hers.*)

CAROL: Hello, then darling? Where did you spring from?

(*No reply.*)

(*Coyly*) Ooh. The nasty man doesn't like Carol, does he?

(*He looks at her with a slight smile, lengthens his stride and, without a word, walks on in front of her.*)

She calls after him – 'Don't you want a nice time, darling?' – but he strides on, and we hear, very muted, the voices of Sunday School children singing:

> We're marching to Zion,
> Beautiful, beautiful Zion,
> We're marching to Zion,
> Beautiful city of God.

The sound 'fades to nothing, like the weakening of a resolve', and Ronnie turns to Carol ferociously:

RONNIE: All right! All right! How much is it? Where do we go?

CAROL: Here! Hold on a minute –

RONNIE: (*still gabbling*) How long can I stay then? Where do you –

CAROL: You're very eager, entcha? It's just round the corner, love . . . I have lots of men like you, so don't worry about it. Most of my clients are married men looking for a bit on –

RONNIE: Shut up.

CAROL: (*startled*) Wha? . . .

RONNIE: (*quietly*) You dirty rotten cow.

CAROL: (*angry*) What did you say!

RONNIE: I said you are (*spits out the words*) a *dirty rotten* cow!

(*She physically recoils from the blast.*)

CAROL: A flaming nutter! Get off! Gettaway from me!

(*He advances on her, speaking with a terribly deliberate, slowly measured precision.*)

RONNIE: You corrupt and degenerate and degraded little tart –

(*She shrieks and backs away.*)

Quiet!

CAROL: Get off!

RONNIE: You filthy, blasphemous, worm-ridden, disgusting little trollop –

(*Slow mix from his hot, sick, ranting face to –*)

SCENE TWO. INTERIOR. DAY.
A small chapel full of bright-faced children.

The children are singing 'All Things Bright and Beautiful', and the camera picks out one of them, evidently the young Ronnie. His face slowly mixes to that of his adult self, in the corner of a railway carriage, with his wife Amanda, 'an attractive woman in her late twenties'. Staring out of the window, Ronnie declares that England is 'a disgusting mess . . . Full of memory and gangrene.' They are returning to London from Birmingham, where Ronnie has been interviewed for a newspaper job, having lost his position on the *Globe*. He fulminates against the women's magazine Amanda is reading: 'Pages and pages of puerile chatter about the sick glories of swinging London and its tarty little boutiques – matchstick models posing open-mouthed for foul-mouthed photographers . . . ' Then suddenly 'a look of tender gentleness comes on his face', and he leans across and touches her:

RONNIE: (*gently*) I'm sorry.

(*She looks up.*)

... Amanda, darling, I –

AMANDA: Yes?

RONNIE: I – it's – I – (*His nerve fails him.*)

AMANDA: (*concerned*) Ronnie – what's the matter?

(*He sinks back, defeated and inarticulate.*)

RONNIE: Just that – I'm – sorry, my love. So very, very sorry.

Failing to make his confession to her, he stares moodily out of the window, the train wheels seeming to him to be repeating the same word over and over again: 'E-vil E-vil E-vil E-vil E-vil.'

The train plunges into a tunnel, and 'the shrieking whistle becomes the awful shriek of a woman'. We are in the room of another prostitute, 'cringing, cowering . . . near naked', flattening herself against the wall as Ronnie gropes towards her from the end of the bed. In her fear she calls on the name of the Virgin Mary – she is an Irish girl – and Ronnie is shocked by the blasphemy. He pays her extra, 'because of the trouble', and storms out, snarling, 'You filthy and depraved creature.' Greedily, she counts the money and feels the lump around her eye, remarking, 'Eight pounds ten and a shiner. He could have half killed me for another two pounds.'

Another glimpse of the hymn-singing children carries us to Ronnie's and Amanda's flat, where Ronnie is in full tipsy spate in the company of friends, trying to reminisce about the chapel-going days of his working-class childhood. The others keep interrupting, and when Amanda ticks him off for being tedious, Ronnie suddenly flares up in fury: 'Shut up! Shut up! You stupid – !' There is an embarrassed silence, and Amanda sits rigid and white-faced. Ronnie apologizes, and is soon chortling with manic laughter at his own jokes, while the others watch him anxiously. Then he seems to subside into himself, muttering the words of the psalm: 'By the rivers of Babylon, there we sat down, yea, we wept when we remembered Zion.' Recalling the words on the chapel banner in his boyhood, 'Bring Up a Child the Way He Should Go', he begins to sob uncontrollably: 'Oh help me! Help me somebody! Please help me!'

Act Two begins in the out-patients' department of a big old London hospital, where Ronnie is waiting to see a psychiatrist. He attempts to flout the no-smoking rule, upsets an old man with his ceaseless babble of talk, and is paralysed with terror when his name is finally called. As he arrives in the consulting room, we flashback to his encounter with another prostitute, which we will see intermittently during his interview with the psychiatrist, Dr Childs, who asks why Ronnie has requested to see him:

RONNIE: Because my doctor, my ordinary, normal, talkative, friendly doctor, recommended that I should come to see you, Dr Childs.

DR CHILDS: Yes. But *why* have you come to see me, Mr Wills?

RONNIE: Oh, for God's sake.

DR CHILDS: (*drily*) I hope not. I'm afraid I'm not a priest.

RONNIE: You're not much of a comedian either.

(DR CHILDS *smiles a broader smile.*)

DR CHILDS: *Touché.*

Ronnie admits that he has made a fool of himself by crying in front of friends, and Childs responds, 'If that is all, then you are wasting my time . . . Everybody is entitled to cry once in a while.' Timidly, Ronnie suggests that it may be 'a question of – ah – morality', and Childs answers, 'Moral judgements are not *my* business.' Ronnie gets angrily to his feet, protesting, and we cut to the preacher in the chapel, reciting Psalm 137 ('By the rivers of Babylon . . .') to a congregation of one – the child Ronnie: 'If I do not remember thee, let my tongue cleave to the roof of my mouth . . . Happy shall he be, that taketh and dasheth thy little ones against a stone.'

In the consulting room, Ronnie, 'his face contorted with anger', is asking Childs, 'Do you mean to tell me that there is no such thing as wickedness? . . . I *know*, you see. Deep down in my heart I know that there is such a thing as wickedness and that there are some judgements which cannot be evaded or twisted into a medical formula.' We flashback again to the prostitute's room, where the lightbulb goes out, and Ronnie, terrified of the dark, moans to himself, 'Black. Black. Black. Black as pitch.' The woman lights a sheet of folded newspaper, but Ronnie cries out, 'We shall burn to a cinder! Burn! Burn!'

She gets a candle alight, and haggles with Ronnie over money:

PROSTITUTE: Have you got – fi– six pounds, darling? You won't regret it.

RONNIE: You all say that.

PROSTITUTE: Oh, so you know all about it, do you? (*Leers*) This sort of thing is your hobby, is it?

RONNIE: I count them.

PROSTITUTE: You count what?

RONNIE: The number of women I've had. I've paid for. (*He laughs, uncomfortably.*)

PROSTITUTE: And how many's that, Ronnie?

(*He hangs his head.*)

Come on – don't be shy. You don't have to be shy with me, do you?

RONNIE: (*hoarse*) Ninety-seven.

PROSTITUTE: Blimey! It's a wonder you're not worn right out!

RONNIE: (*sharply*) Don't let me have to wash your mouth out, will you!

PROSTITUTE: (*puzzled*) 'Ere! What the hell's up with you?

(*Suddenly, with a violent switch of mood, he begins to jig round the candlelit room.*)

RONNIE: Ninety-seven! Ninety-seven! Ha-AH! (*He stops abruptly and takes out his wallet.*) OK. Ninety-eight. Here's a fiver for you.

She steps out of her dress, and Ronnie takes off his jacket, 'moving slowly, like somebody under water'. They move out of frame, and the bed begins to creak. 'Cut rhythmically', directs Potter, 'between the flickering, smoking, wax-dripping candle and the grotesque shadows.' Over this is superimposed the preacher, still quoting from the psalm; then 'Shadows, candle, creaking, the preacher', and Ronnie crying out, as he climaxes, 'Bitch! Bitch! Bitch! Bitch!' After orgasm, he retches.

In the consulting room, he is highly amused by Childs's reassurance that he can 'take your time . . . there's no hurry' – since this is what all the prostitutes say. Unwillingly, he tells Childs about his obsessive need for prostitutes, and Childs asks if he has discussed it with his wife. 'Amanda?' responds Ronnie in absolute horror. 'Tell my wife I've bought the hips and thighs and breasts of a hundred different women!

Tell her that! I'd sooner go and hang myself!' Childs asks if it is really a hundred, and Ronnie answers, giggling, 'Well, almost. Two to go . . . Ninety-eight, doctor. I've had ninety-eight of them . . . What do you think of that? Eh?' Childs asks 'what happened after number ninety-eight' to make Ronnie seek help. Ronnie answers, 'What happened *to* number ninety-eight you mean!' He slumps in his chair and declares, 'I cooked her goose for her all right, the evil creature! . . . I punished her, doctor. Punished her.'

Act Three begins with a 'loud crash of melodramatic B-movie-type soundtrack music'. Ronnie and Amanda are watching a TV thriller in which the police are investigating the murder of what Ronnie calls 'another little slut'. He snaps off the programme: 'Trash! Trash! It's all bloody trash, written by degenerates for degenerates!' Amanda protests that she was enjoying it, and they begin a row, Ronnie quickly provoking Amanda to walk out on him. As the door slams, he switches on the radio, and (as in *Cinderella*) we hear Tony Bennett singing 'Wrap Your Troubles in Dreams'. Ronnie 'whirls round the room like a drunk at a dance, even singing some of the words'. Then he drops to his knees, uttering a prayer: 'O dear Lord God, great cleanser, all-potent creator . . . look down upon me now and wash, wash, wash, wash my dirt away . . . '

Once again we glimpse the children in the chapel, then mix back to Ronnie, who is still on his knees, but in suddenly changed mood. 'The dog is returned to his own vomit again,' he mutters hoarsely to himself, and we hear him retching in the prostitute's room, as in Act Two. We see the woman complaining that he has not paid her, and when she claws his face he begins to beat her up, banging her head against the wall, and sobbing 'Har-*lot* – Har-*lot* – Har-*lot*'. The preacher's voice is heard again, apparently justifying this violence: 'Happy shall be he that taketh and dasheth thy little ones against the stones.'

Amanda returns, and Ronnie, now 'artificially chirpy', denies that he is praying: 'I'm not a little kid any more. Going to chapel with a clean white hanky, threepence for the collecting box and a shine on my best Sunday shoes.' He spurns Amanda's attempts to talk about their problems, even though she assures him, 'I love you more now than I have ever done.' We then glimpse him retreating down the stairs from the room where we assume the prostitute lies dead or injured, then cut to Dr Childs telling him, 'I *can* help you. There is no reason to doubt it. If the drugs I am going to prescribe for you do not help – as I am sure they will – then there are other things we can do. You do not *have* to be so afflicted.' He gives Ronnie a prescription for tablets, which require the avoidance of alcohol and cheese; otherwise he will experience 'a quite intolerable pain in the head'. Ronnie starts to object, and is silenced:

DR CHILDS: I do not care for the word 'conscience'. If John Bunyan had come into my care, Mr Wills, the world would not have got *Pilgrim's Progress*. He would have been complacent, content and full of drugs. But for fourteen years he was a very sick man. I am here, at this time and in this place, concerned with chemicals far more than with conscience or the gloom which can afflict a man when he sees the moon sailing through the clouds.

RONNIE: Don't talk to me like this!

DR CHILDS: I have diagnosed you, Mr Wills, as a manic depressive.

RONNIE: You've *what*?

DR CHILDS: Your treatment need not go unalleviated. You have thought about suicide?

(RONNIE *nods, looking down.*)

But you won't do it. I am sure of that. Your case is not even a particularly severe one. You can be helped, and I will help you . . . It may take some time, of course. And you may feel, at the end of it, you are left with less insight into the human condition. The choice is entirely yours . . . If you do not let me help you . . . you may find yourself confessing to all sorts of crimes which you have persuaded yourself that you have committed.

In the flat, Amanda protests that Ronnie is 'growing cold again . . . I shouldn't have given you time to put up those damned shutters.' In response, he admits that he *was* praying:

RONNIE: All my life I have been conscious of – a God. A monster spread-eagled on a cloud, looking down and breaking its toys. (*Pause.*) Look at the world. There is no adequate explanation for its miseries. Napalm scorching the skin off hungry babies. Men ripping fingernails from their prisoners . . . Silly old ladies screaming with cancer . . . (*Bitterly*) But the psychiatrist – he's a fool, incidentally . . . he's given me (*searches in his pockets*) a tiny bottle of little blue tablets (*places small bottle on coffee table, with a hard clack*) and a tiny bottle of little pink tablets. (*Puts out second small bottle.*)

AMANDA: You'll take them, won't you?

(*He starts to laugh.*)

Ronnie! You'll take them! You'll do as he says! . . .

RONNIE: OK. OK. I'll take them. I could never write a *Pilgrim's Progress* anyway. Not in a million years . . . (*He carefully selects his tablets and puts them on his tongue.*) . . . Every sane person knows that, give or take a few cripples, the world is a fine and splendid place. With big white angels guarding every precipice.

(*He swallows. A long, careful silence. No camera movement. No movement from* RONNIE *or* AMANDA. *He suddenly buries his face in his hands. The end.*)

*

During May 1967, Trodd read *The Rivers of Babylon* and returned it to Potter as unmakeable. 'The pain was much too raw, on the nose, and not entertaining,' he says about it today. Did he feel that the subject-matter would make it unacceptable to the BBC? 'No. I don't think I was ever the pre-censor of anything. I just remember thinking, this reeks of Dennis's unassimilated pain, and creatively it doesn't work. It exposes a wound without really making the wound into art.'

Potter himself wrote in 1984, 'It is essential to understand . . . that writing is not a displaced form of personal therapy, and is at its worst the nearer it tries to come to that condition.' In 1990 he said, 'The closer writing approaches to therapy, the worse it becomes . . . So you've got to have that ruthless discipline about whether you're doing this to ease and soothe . . . as a balm to your own soul . . . I've destroyed lots of things where I felt that was happening . . . "just letting it out" is one of the definitions of bad art.'

Once again, Trodd arranged for Potter to be paid for the rejected script. (Yet another commissioned play, *See You in My Dreams*, had been delivered to the BBC in June 1966, paid for, and assigned a project number, but it was never made, and has now disappeared.) Trodd does not think that the rejection of *Rivers of Babylon*, following that of *Cinderella*, caused a particular crisis for Potter: 'I don't remember feeling, "Dennis is going through a bad patch, and may not survive as a writer, be able to pay the mortgage." We were paying him quite regularly.' Nevertheless the two consecutive rejections must have caused Potter some worry, for, at the age of thirty-two, he was buying an expensive house.

His sister June and her husband, Eddie Thomas, a telephone engineer, were living in Ross-on-Wye, just to the north of the Forest of Dean. Foresters traditionally thought of Ross as the nearest 'posh' town, regarding it with a mixture of distrust and envy. June and Eddie had a flat in Morecambe Lodge, Archenfield Road, on the edge of Ross – a handsome three-storey late Victorian stone mansion originally built for the town's chemist, which was then in multiple occupancy and had been for sale for two years. 'Dennis came over to Ross, and saw the house,' June says. 'It was expensive – the average was about £2000 in those days, and it was £5,900. That worried Margaret – double the price of a normal property. But they bought it.' Sarah says of 'Morecambe', as the Potters called the house for short, 'There were six bedrooms – it was pretty big. Mum said she knew as soon as she went through the front door that it had a friendly feel. It was in a terrible state, but they fell in love with it.' Jane recalls, 'We didn't have carpets for about a year – things were done when Mum and Dad could afford them.'

Roger Smith was puzzled by Potter's rather grand choice of home: 'Dennis remained resolutely working class in his taste and attitudes. Yet he moved to this sort of rectory in Ross.' The Potters furnished the house in contemporary style, and had bookshelves fitted to almost every alcove. 'When I grow up . . . I be going to have *books*,' says the young Marlow in *The Singing Detective*. 'On shelves, mind.'

A few months after settling there, Potter described Ross as 'a prosperous, placid little market town quietly festering amidst acres of greenery and full of angry little minis with WILSON MUST GO stickers doing their little bit to increase the number of road accidents'. His new home was only a few minutes' drive from Berry Hill, and he later regretted that he had not become closer to his father during the remainder of Walt's life:

When I started writing Dad was still alive – I was living about ten miles away on the edges of the Forest of Dean – and I think he got to the stage where he was shy with me: he would lean on the door-jamb when I was in the middle of something and say, 'Bist thou all right, old butt?' And I'd say, 'Yes, thank you, Dad.' I wanted to carry on writing. 'Are you sure you're all right, now?' 'Yes, thank you, Dad.' And he'd hover a bit and say, 'Well, good to see thou at work.' It's too late, but if only I could now say, 'Come on in. Just let me put my pen away. Let us talk.'

Despite Nicholas Tomalin's warning, Potter's *New Statesman* column continued to pour scorn on the BBC. He praised it sarcastically for repeating more than thirty programmes in one week: 'Writers, actors and singers get half their original fees again . . . The conveyor belt rolls on and on: the repeats at least throw back echoes of excitement from the belly of the clanking machinery.' And he sneered at what he called 'Peeping Tom television': '*Man Alive* has taken to advertising in *The Times* agony column for people willing to confess in front of the cameras. It doesn't matter too much what you confess . . .'

Tomalin had now had enough, complaining that most of the time Potter was 'writing about yourself rather than about television'. He said he was replacing him as *New Statesman* TV critic, though 'I should like you to review books for me'. Potter was able to scorn this offer, since he had just been invited, far more lucratively, to review books for *The Times*. Meanwhile he had finished another play.

*

He had been intending to write 'two companion plays – one about childhood and one about old age'; so Trodd noted on 16 June 1967. The first already had a title, *Blue Remembered Hills*. But by mid-September the linked youth-and-age scripts had been postponed – the BBC gathered that Potter had a 'National Theatre commitment'.

Little is known about this. An 'autobiographical stage play' was commissioned from Potter during 1967 by Kenneth Tynan, in his capacity of literary manager at the National (then based at the Old Vic). Potter told the literary editor of *The Times,* Michael Ratcliffe, in a letter in December 1967, that it was 'a play with obvious perils, being entirely and openly autobiography, not even disguised with a fictitious name'. But if he actually wrote it, it has disappeared, and eventually the National cancelled the contract.

It was agreed by the BBC that, for *Blue Remembered Hills*, he should substitute another play, *A Beast with Two Backs*, for which he would be paid £1,200. It was the first play he had written since settling at Ross-on-Wye, and the first to be set unambiguously in the Forest of Dean. Read or seen in isolation, it looks like a grim portrait of his native territory in Victorian times. Looked at in the context of the rejection of *The Rivers of Babylon*, *A Beast with Two Backs* reveals itself as a more sophisticated attempt at the same theme, the destructive conflict between the teachings of religion and the desires of the flesh. The historical setting means that *A Beast* is more sophisticated than *The Rivers of Babylon*, but it lacks the earlier play's passionate confessional pain.*

Growing out of a story Potter had known since childhood – the supposed bear-killing incident at Ruardean, near Berry Hill – *A Beast* opens in the Forest of Dean woodland, 'thick, damp, alien', with 'rocks in weird shapes' poking up through the trees. Through this tangle lopes a 'shuffling, shambling bear', accompanied by its owner, an elderly itinerant Italian, Joe. 'He talks to the bear only as a means of talking to himself,' states Potter. 'He loves and hates the beast. The bear is what he sees in the mirror.'

They are both heading for a village, where in the pub the 'village idiot', Rufus, is being made to earn his cider by dancing on a table, and is being taunted sexually by the men and Nelly the barmaid:

NELLY: What'll you give Nelly for a drop, Rufus?

(*He stops twitching and gurgling on the table top and seems to concentrate all his attention on her. She leers at him provocatively. The idea of 'sex' seems, momentarily, to crash through to the idiot . . .* RUFUS's *hands, still unco-ordinated, grope down towards his fly-buttons . . .*)

Doesn't thee get *that* out, mind Rufus! Else I'll snip'n off!

WILL: Snip it off! Snip it off!

(*General laughter and ribaldry. Back to* RUFUS, *whose hands cannot complete their task and have fled back up to his idiot face.*)

The hysteria is interrupted by Rufus's uncle Ebenezer, the local preacher, who thrashes him for this display of indecency. We mix from Rufus's 'terrified, idiot face' to that of the bear, as it and Joe continue their descent to the village. A stone crashes down near them, and they are taunted by a gaggle of local boys – 'Bloody I-talian . . . bloody foreigner' (Potter is recalling the Foresters' reaction to Italian prisoners of war in the Forties). Also looking on are two of the adult villagers, Micky, a family man, and Rebecca, the local slut, who have been copulating adulterously in the undergrowth. Micky is suddenly smitten

---

* However, Clive Goodwin, who became Potter's agent shortly before *A Beast with Two Backs* was made, referred to the play as an 'itchy fantasy', a description which Ken Trodd regards as highly appropriate, and with resonance for some of Potter's later work.

with guilt about his wife and child, whereupon Rebecca tells him that he has made her pregnant. When he refuses to accept responsibility, Rebecca threatens to 'tell it at Zion on Sunday'. In response, Micky picks up a rock and crashes it down on her head.

Joe and the bear have now arrived in the village, where the bear is falsely accused of having injured a child. On the hillside, Rufus the idiot stumbles into the dying Rebecca, and tries to comfort her. Ebenezer, in pursuit of his nephew, discovers him bending over her, assumes that it is Rufus who struck her down, and strangles her lest she survive to identify her assailant.

In Zion chapel on Sunday morning, Ebenezer tells his congregation that they must confront their wickedness, 'the beast that is buried under your own skins'. Interpreting this literally, they pursue and destroy the bear, believing it to be Rebecca's killer, while Ebenezer, having failed to summon the nerve to smother the supposedly guilty Rufus to death, hangs himself.

*

A Beast with Two Backs was delivered to the BBC in September 1967. Unlike its two predecessors, it was accepted for production. The following month, the first of Potter's book reviews was printed in *The Times*. Discussing Arthur Koestler's *The Ghost in the Machine*, Potter accepted the author's argument that mankind's irrational behaviour is the consequence of mental biology, but rejected Koestler's conclusion that this should be cured by mind-altering drugs. Potter proposed to erect a sign: 'Every man has an inalienable right to his own biochemistry.'

Biochemically, he himself was once again in poor shape. Two weeks after this review was published, his doctor at Ross-on-Wye noted that his psoriasis was 'very extensive and at the moment very severe', while the arthritis had led to 'deformity of the joints in the hands'. Various medicaments were having little effect, and he referred Potter to Dr Ernest Fairburn, a dermatologist at the Birmingham Skin Hospital. Dr Fairburn saw him during November, and noted that, while 'emotional stress' undoubtedly exacerbated the psoriasis, he did not feel that this was 'a factor of major importance' in Potter's case. He told the Ross doctor that local medication (ointments and suchlike) was unlikely to have more than fleeting success, but hoped that a drug called Methotrexate might prove effective. Potter was admitted to the Skin Hospital for trials in late November.

While there, he reviewed a new biography of Ibsen by Michael Mayer, using the imagery of his own illness:

There have been some studies of famous writers and artists which read a little like out-patient dossiers – lending support to the mechanistic but degenerate thesis that 'creativity' itself is but kindred to, say, a raw psoriatic rash which itches deep into infancy, bits of the bleeding flesh of childhood caught under hard adult fingernails. In such dreary circumstances biography can become a gargoyled extension to the path-lab rather than the last legitimate sanctuary for 'great men' or even (antique concept) heroes.

After trials, Dr Fairburn decided not to prescribe Methotrexate for the time being, since some success was being achieved once again with the 'occlusive treatment', applying a steroid ointment and then covering most of Potter's body with polythene. On 4 December, Potter wrote to Margaret:

My darling,

A few words. I so much enjoyed your visit – and you looked so very pretty in a deliciously surprised & wide-eyed sort of way – and I have been feeling so good over the past few days, that I simply want to get a few thoughts & hopes down on paper. You must put up with the bad writing – my polythene gloves feel slippery and awkward. When I saw you and talked to you I felt a huge blaze of joy inside: those moments underlined both how much you have come to mean to me, and the inexpressible misery of my life over these recent times.

The important thing to realize now is that I need *never ever* get so bad again. No more hours of clawing at raw flesh. No more unsightly weals. No more skulking behind doors with my heart pounding when somebody calls. No more piles of dead skin funnelled into a bloody ashtray or swished down the sink in some hotel room. No more heaps of white confetti splattering every room of the house – I can hardly go on: the release is *so* great, so marvellous.

And think of the effect of the change on my mood and disposition!

Yes, I can and do promise a different style and temper of life for all of us. I shall do my very level best to make up for all the grey years and the black patches. I shall work, but also discipline myself into relaxation. I shall fill the lives of you and Jane and Sarah and Robert with warmth, safety, comfort, love and joy.

OK – so this sounds dreamlike, impossibly Utopian, too-good-to-be-true. But I mean it & will prove it. I haven't had much chance to be a whole human being for years now, but those qualities which have carried me through – and they *are* qualities – will now be released in full for better things.

Most of all, to love *you*.

To love, love, love you, with all my being. You have been an angel to me, the most wonderful wife a man could ever have hoped for. I cannot tell you what you mean to me, but perhaps I will be able to *show* you, my darling.

O God, I look forward to seeing you and holding you and feeling your hands on my smooth, clean body. I am almost choking with joy.

I adore you, and always will, for ever and ever.

Dennis

After his discharge from the Birmingham hospital, the 'occlusive treatment' was continued at home, with Margaret's brother Brian coming to the house to help her anoint Dennis and cover him with the polythene ('Uncle Brian and Auntie Jean did loads for us,' says Jane). By January 1968, the Ross doctor noted that 'fairly acute episode' of psoriatic arthropathy had subsided, though the psoriasis was still 'fairly bad on his feet'.

Despite his promise to Margaret that he would learn to relax, he was now working more furiously than ever, completing another full-length play, *The Bonegrinder*, continuing his *Times* book reviews, and, during January and February, standing in for two months for Nancy Banks-Smith as the television critic of the *Sun* from Tuesday to Friday each week.

He had to fill twice the amount of space that the *Daily Herald* had given him a few years earlier, but he was in sparkling, manic form in the *Sun* columns. He described the winner of an ITV glamour competition as 'a face worthy to launch a thousand fish-fingers', and suggested that Jimmy Saville, presenter of *Top of the Pops*, had been 'discovered, fully grown, in the bulrushes . . . He has the total innocence of the great mystics.'

Signing off at the end of February, he remarked, 'Now I can get back, as a playwright, on to the other side of the screen. Time to put down the little hard balls and climb back among the coconuts. Critics? Ah, what do they know!' But the *Sun* still wanted him, and in March he began a series of Monday columns on anything he chose, describing himself as 'a purveyor of instant opinions, a merchant of the transient'. In his second column, he revealed a personal taste in music:

Whenever the cold winds blow too bleakly through my mind I like to listen to some elderly and rather scratchy recordings of Al Bowlly.

Bowlly was the big crooning swoon on the wireless round around the time I was cutting my first milk teeth. So for me his throatily-velvety version of

'You May Not Be an Angel' has the lingering flavours of chewy rusks, cod-liver oil and National Dried Milk . . . And stumbling across a lethal old song can sometimes be as uncomfortable as coming upon an Oxfam appeal in the middle of some lush colour supplement.

Ken Trodd says that, until a few years earlier, recordings of pre-war dance bands had been 'like *samizdat* material – the fans had collected the old 78s, but the notion of the stuff being reissued on an LP was a breakthrough'. Such a reissue, of recordings by Al Bowlly with Lew Stone and his band, was made by Decca on the Ace of Clubs label during 1964, and Potter seems to have bought it. Trodd thinks this was 'off his own bat', and though Trodd himself was working on a book about Lew Stone (who was then still alive) he does not recall discussing Bowlly–Stone records with Potter at this juncture.

Potter's *Sun* column on 25 March 1968 mentioned the recent London demonstration against the Vietnam War:

I see that Tariq Ali, a demonstration leader, has claimed after the Grosvenor Square shindig that the cops were out to get him as a ringleader, but his friends protected him. Oh, come, come. Policemen are no more perceptive in these complicated questions than are their horses.

If indeed they were out to get Tariq the explanation is far, far less sinister.

All some of them saw was a wog with long hair and a big mouth. Reason enough to rough anybody up, surely?

This was the language of Alf Garnett, the working-class racist in Johnny Speight's TV sitcom *Till Death Us Do Part*. Three months earlier, Potter had mentioned this character and his attitudes in a *Sun* television review of a programme on the growth of Black Power in Britain:

After years of bullying exploitation and arrogant insolence from his self-appointed masters the black man is at last answering back in like coin. It is a vicious reply, dangerously soaked in similar prejudice . . . There are moments when I have to recognize . . . in myself a faint, mocking echo of the filth expressed by racialists everywhere. Alf Garnett makes articulate the buried feelings we are ashamed to acknowledge as our own.

On 20 April 1968, Enoch Powell made a notorious anti-immigration speech, and Potter devoted the whole of a *Sun* column to it, calling it a 'stupid, nasty and wantonly racialist harangue', and saying he hoped it would lead to Powell's political downfall: 'If the day ever comes when he once again holds high office in this land I, for one, shall be hopping on the boat. I am a red-head, you see. One of a minority distinguished by colour.' Yet he went on:

I, too, fear the stranger. Instinctively – and primitively – I do not 'like' people with black skins.

I once found myself in a bar in London's Ladbroke Grove which was entirely filled with West Indians. I sat with my drink in the middle of a noisy, alien throng. A stupid, stiff grin on my face, a little knot of obscure resentment or even fear tightening in the pit of my stomach . . .

There is . . . a sense in which all civilized politics is a conspiracy of the decent, a valiant attempt to hold back the hobgoblins who prance on the perimeters of our fragile reason.

Powell's real and unforgivable crime is that he punctures that 'conspiracy' at one of its most vulnerable points. Of course, emotion will then seep to the surface like pus from a boil. Of course, the letters of support will come in by the truckload. It will always be so when a clever man deliberately drops a barbed hook into deep, dark waters. Powell should be bitterly ashamed of himself.

In his next *Sun* column, he wrote angrily about the sudden closure of Ross-on-Wye County Primary School, which his two elder children had been attending, because the building was unsafe: 'Two little girls learning how to read and write. They could have been buried under rocking timber and decrepit old stones.' He alleged that no proper provision had been made to prevent 'the education of 550 or more children being brought to a standstill'. So he and Margaret were now sending Jane and Sarah to 'another primary school in our town' where 'the children wear straw hats and blue knickers and have a Latin inscription on their blazers . . . A private school, of course . . . I couldn't stand the apathy and neglect any longer.' What of the other children? 'I feel both anger and shame,' he claimed. 'We are thinking of selling up and moving somewhere more civilized.'

Sarah Potter says this change of school was a success: 'We went to St Joseph's Convent, which was a couple of hundred yards up the road from Morecambe, a lovely little school, Roman Catholic – it was a very happy time for us. Dad was sometimes amused at the Catholic indoctrination, but he didn't mind it.' Later they sat the Eleven Plus and went back into the state system, at Ross Grammar School. By that time, Potter's doctor at Ross had withdrawn from the National Health Service; Potter, wishing to remain with him, became a private patient;

but he did not mention this further retreat from socialist principles in his *Sun* column.

On Monday, 13 May, he asked *Sun* readers if they would be watching the play on ITV tonight:

Millions of people will, many millions. But when I think now of all those glazed eyeballs, all those multiplied ears, all those duplicated smiles or snarls or yawns, I can feel the adrenalin flopping about inside like I was a Tory candidate looking at a polling booth.

That's because I wrote the play, you see.

The title is very appetizing: *The Bonegrinder*. But tonight between 8.30 and 10 o'clock it will be my limbs on the rack.

He told his readers that he knew of one television playwright who hid behind an armchair while his work was being shown. 'I simply chain-smoke and tremble at the back of the kneecaps, listening to the dialogue and pretending not to know what is going to happen next. "Oh, this is good," I hiss through my lying teeth. "This is very good. Very, very good." "Yes," says my wife with a heavy sigh.'

He had calculated that 'many, many more people will see my play tonight than have seen *The Mousetrap* in its entire sixteen-year run'. But for him there would be no sense of occasion:

As the final credits zip up on the electronic tube the sense of anti-climax is paralysingly complete. The pictures flow on as easy as tapwater . . . A play which has taken months to write, characters who have leapt up gibbering in your mind when you are trying to sleep, ideas which have simmered feverishly in your blood like a virus – all used up, all at once, all gone.

All wasted? I don't know. But at one minute past ten tonight I know very well that I shall be feeling rather dejected. For the anti-climax – which is a sort of exhaustion – inevitably breeds self-doubt and pessimism. Were those *really* my lines? Those banal, boring, weary little exchanges flopping out of the hired set squatting so malignantly in the corner of the room?

The real irony, the genuine comedy, is that as a dramatist I am afflicted with the ambitions of a ravening wolf. So six years of sometimes intense physical pain, through plaster casts and plastic occlusive dressings and injections and hospital beds and mouthfuls of steroids, I have literally been sustained by one overriding, overwhelming and no doubt intrinsically ludicrous idea: the conviction that one day I will write a masterpiece.

No, not tonight's play, though.

He explained that he could say this with detachment because

suddenly, gloriously, incredibly and (to others) quite incomprehensibly I have been given back my health. On Thursday a specialist in Birmingham acknowledged that something peculiar had happened. Something psychogenic, as he put it. Or mind over body, joy over pain, defiance over despair.

All at once I stopped taking such a heavy daily dose of steroids that I might have, should have, collapsed. It was stupid and arrogant. But worked!

And now the National Theatre has commissioned me to write a play. And now I have my first film script* all lined up. And now the BBC have agreed that I should write a Life of Christ as a TV play.

All the perspectives shift. I no longer get a hot stab of pain when I turn my head. I am filled with big, bright bubbles of exuberance and gratitude.

Happiness is a terrible thing to try to communicate in a newspaper column. You aren't used to it are you? But sorry, I cannot hold it back.

Why, I might even enjoy that play on ITV tonight. But don't ask me at one minute past ten. Any time but that.

Potter was later unable to remember exactly why *The Bonegrinder* was written for ITV rather than the BBC: 'I think that was immediately after *Cinderella* and there was some peevishness going on somewhere. But also I think I had been approached to do something and I was just filling the slot.' It was commissioned by Rediffusion (the London commercial franchise-holder) and networked in the series *ITV Playhouse*. It takes its title from the 'Fee, fie, foe, fum' nursery rhyme, which ends 'I'll grind his bones to make my bread'. The 'giant' smelling the blood of an Englishman is Sam, an aggressive US merchant seaman, his victim George King, an uptight London bank clerk with a dried-up marriage, who gazes furtively at mini-skirted girls' legs. 'Uncle Sam meets King George, right?' observes Sam.

Realizing that the highly respectable George is attempting to pick up a woman while his wife Gladys is away from home, Sam blackmails him, invading his house and mocking George's values:

SAM: R-E-S-P-E-C-T-A-B-I-L-I-T-Y . . . Yessir, respectability. That's the only code of English people like you. Not God. Not country. Not Love. Privet hedges and tea cups and – and – chatting over the fence with your neighbours and mowing the lawn and wearing clean white shirts and not being late for work . . . Why did I get in here in the first place? Eh? Because, dear old George, because I had caught you with your pants down. Because you were scared stiff, *old boy*, after being found out at your timid whoring.

* Probably *The Sins of the Fathers*, which will be discussed later.

When Gladys returns, she eggs on George to murder Sam with the coal hammer – and then calls the police to arrest him. 'Daddy always said that the worst thing a gentleman could do, an English gentleman,' she tells George, who is slumped on the floor in horror as the play ends, 'was to *let the side down*. Get up, George! Get up!'

The Bonegrinder is the first of many Potter plays in which a sinister, not altogether human visitor intrudes into a suburban ménage – a useful device for exposing the turmoil (usually sexual) which lies beneath apparent respectability. These 'visitor' plays require the performers to achieve a deft balance between comedy and the grotesque, and the Rediffusion production of *The Bonegrinder* mostly missed this – the director, Joan Kemp-Welch, took the text at a snail's pace. Consequently the critics were dismayed.

Philip Purser in the *Sunday Telegraph* regarded the play as a serious piece of anti-Americanism; he thought it 'unbelievably vulgar and spiteful . . . Dennis Pooter – I mean Potter – only hates that poor little Englander [George] because he fears that is what he is himself'. In the *Sun*, Nancy Banks-Smith did her best for Potter, but had to admit, '*The Bonegrinder* didn't work. Or not for me.' Peter Black in the *Daily Mail* thought it 'queer and unbalanced', and Stanley Reynolds in the *Guardian* wrote: 'The great virtue of Potter as a playwright is that he goes around gaily ripping the bandages off emotional sores . . . But last night the sores were not worthy of that much examination.'

In his next *Sun* column, Potter responded mock-abjectly to the critics: 'Their scornful unanimity was so appalling that I hardly dare to look in the shaving mirror in case some gibbering monster spits back at its own hideous reflection.' He freely admitted to 'complete and utter failure . . . one of those emotions which can cripple a human being, be he a carpenter, or a cobbler or a writer'. But he laughed at Purser's review – 'I hope he enjoyed the ads in between the acts' – and reported that his physical condition had not relapsed:

It's still true. I can open jars again. And hold a pen in a proper grip. And on Thursday I wriggled all my toes in the bath. A month ago they were stiff, purple-looking, useless slabs of meat stuck on the end of my foot. On Friday I *ran* again. Friday was also my thirty-third birthday – and I hadn't *run* since I was twenty-seven. So the critics didn't hurt one little bit. How could they?

No, that's not quite true. Peter Black in the *Daily Mail* and Stanley Reynolds in the *Guardian* squeezed a few tears through all those big bright bubbles of joy. Both of them always write without spite, and both of them can write like angels when the mood takes them. And like all gifted critics, they have that ability to halt you in mid-stride and make you reassess what you have done.

*

Potter concluded this *Sun* column about the critics' reaction to *The Bonegrinder* by asking himself:

Why be so extreme? Why insist on being perpetually at risk, like a psychotic acrobat condemned for ever to walk along a thin, twanging wire high above a tiny circle of smelly sawdust?

I cannot easily answer those so sensible, so reasonable, so moderate questions. Even this column is willy-nilly turning into a weekly exercise in self-exposure. I find that in my writing I can only use myself, use up myself. So when I die I want to be completely emptied and completely exhausted.

There was another exercise in self-exposure the following Monday, when, still in manic mood, he told his readers about his most recent trip to London:

As soon as I got out of the train at Paddington, I was determined to enjoy myself . . . And . . . it began to pour with rain . . .

Part of the time I was looking for this girl I knew from way back. Somewhere in Fulham to be more precise. But I couldn't find the street . . .

I got tight and walked into a fat milk machine in Gloucester Road. I had champagne and a gypsy dish in a Hungarian restaurant – but it looked like a toad that had been run over by a tractor.

I got wet. A beautiful actress kissed me, a trifle too absent-mindedly, I thought. A friend put his arm round my shoulder and borrowed a fiver. 'I like your jacket,' he said. 'Did you get it in some sort of a sale?'

A policeman asked to look in my bag at two o'clock in the morning.

I counted five people talking to themselves. Saw a man running down the Bayswater Road with a model aeroplane.

And I stood outside Parliament and laughed, laughed, laughed . . .

Oh, I had a good, good time all right. And spent every penny, stretched every muscle, broke a few personal taboos and forgot to ring home.

Just as well. One of the kids had earache, apparently. Miserable little blighter.

During this month, May 1968, there had been massive student demonstrations against the authorities in Paris and other European cities. 'Even in Britain the Establishment is defied,' stated the *Sun*. 'For the students of Paris . . . it is one of those intoxicating moments of history . . . when no institution and no faith seems sacred and nothing seems impossible.' Though they were a generation older than the rioting students, many of Potter's circle were now declaring solidarity with them, and were moving much further to the left. It was into the midst of this political shift – the first since Suez twelve years earlier – that Potter, believing himself cured of his illness, now stepped.

'In the last month I have started coming up to London more frequently,' Potter told readers of *New Society* on 5 June,

seeing people I have not seen for a year or so, catching up on busy metropolitan chatter . . . Most of the flats or houses into which I ventured had Vietcong flags . . . And posters of Che Guevara on the walls . . . And almost all of them had copies of the first issue of the *Black Dwarf* fluttering about the place, the new left-wing fortnightly which has high hopes of not degenerating into another *Tribune*.

The previous autumn he had attended a fund-raising meeting for *Black Dwarf* (named after an early nineteenth-century radical journal), held in the Kensington flat of Clive Goodwin, a former actor, TV producer and magazine editor turned playwrights' agent, who had now acquired Potter as a client from Roger Hancock. Trodd describes Goodwin as 'a trendy social-butterfly figure, a kind of Tynan stand-in – he used to present arts programmes on television now and then. He started the agency, and people flocked to it.' The agent in Potter's first novel *Hide and Seek* (1973) is a portrait of Goodwin – 'not the brightest of creatures, though . . . he is usually able to hide this big hole in his mind with his trendy patter and strategic placing of the latest fashionable phrase or concept'.

Potter described the *Black Dwarf* meeting in another *New Society* article:

It was an odd, uninspiring occasion, relieved by lethal sniping . . . and the sensible late arrival as well as early departure of Kenneth Tynan. I wouldn't have missed airing some of my class prejudices for a lifetime's subscription . . . Gloomily we forked out our money . . . sipped our pretty drinks, talked about Harold [Wilson] and dispersed without fervour into the damp chill of the huge, complacent city.

The first issue, published during June 1968 under the slogan 'Help us to attack the system', was jointly edited by a group including Tariq Ali, Clive Goodwin, David Mercer and Adrian Mitchell. The first front page carried the slogan 'WE SHALL FIGHT – WE SHALL WIN – PARIS LONDON ROME BERLIN'. Tariq Ali recalls:

We had set up *Black Dwarf*, and of all Clive's clients the only one who hated the project was dear old Dennis. When we wrote to him and asked him for money, he refused, and said, 'You're a bunch of gesturing nincompoops' – which we printed on the back of the paper!

Vote, Vote, Vote for Nigel Barton had been fantastic, and had a big impact on all of us, which was why we were so keen to involve him. But he in his strange way was quite committed to the Labour Party, so anything which challenged that hegemony of Labour he couldn't stand – and we challenged it all the time. Another side of him was that he was very English, and his insularity meant that he could not be very moved by the war in Vietnam, which was sad, because virtually everyone was.

Potter reviewed the first issue of *Black Dwarf* in *New Society*:

If the list [Paris London Rome Berlin] had been compiled out of, say, Oldham and Cardiff and Rochdale and Glasgow, the contents might have had more scalpel-like relevance . . . The familiar old, tired old phrases pile up like cobblestones, except that you cannot even throw them . . . We need a paper like the *Black Dwarf*, arrowing in on specific targets with specific facts for its weapons. But it needs, too, an aggressive gaiety, a cool irony, a cynicism tempered by bold optimism, a rumbustious vulgarity, a sense of the surrounding hypocrisy and the wit to draw on the real experiences of its contributors and supporters . . .

My own literary agent is a member of the editorial group . . .

So was Roger Smith, who went to Paris to observe the riots, and wrote an article for *Black Dwarf* calling for 'struggle, under the banner of Marxism . . . the creation of international revolutionary parties of the world's proletariat . . . This is the only way to the true proletarian revolution, to the overthrow of capitalism'.

Ken Trodd recalls: 'Roger joined the Workers' Revolutionary Party (it was called the Socialist Labour League then), and Tony Garnett joined that too, with a number of actors. But a lot of people fellow-travelled, and I suppose that's what I did. They were keen to get me in, but I never joined. And Dennis wouldn't come in either.' Roger Smith confirms this:

I joined the Socialist Labour League in November 1968 – the first of the media recruits. Ken is basically right, but I don't remember Dennis being targeted as a serious possibility. We used to have meetings every Friday in someone's flat, mine or Roy Battersby's [a television director] or Tony Garnett's to begin with. They went on every Friday for four or five years – aimed at show business, actors, writers, producers, etc. I think Dennis rather reluctantly came to one or two of them in the early days, but then so did Ken Tynan, Christopher Logue, David Mercer – it's a long list.

In 1993, Graham Fuller asked Potter if he had identified with the New Left in the late Sixties:

To a degree. They were interesting in the sense that they rejected Stalinism and all that aspect of left-wing politics. They were opening new jars, finding new lids, but they were very ideologically driven as well, and . . . that became oppressive, emotionally and intellectually. I always kept one foot outside the circle.

Paul Foot, who saw Potter at Goodwin's flat, confirms the accuracy of this:

There was a fantastically fraught meeting, with Roger Smith and Ken Trodd and a lot of other people. I have a feeling Daniel Cohn-Bendit [the German student who had led the Paris student riots] had been invited. There was some proposition about what the Left should do now – which way forward? – and I remember Dennis was very, very sceptical, very reluctant to engage in this, but nevertheless wanted to be there. I don't think he really engaged with the Left by this time.

Potter reported this meeting in his *Sun* column on 17 June:

Hush, hush, little bourgeois baby. No need to wet the bed or shake your rattle in a fury. Sleep tight. Naughty Danny the Red has flown back to Germany. Mummy and Daddy are quite safe now here in this Land of Nod.

Mind you, Tariq Ali is still hanging around, threatening to abolish money and arguing with the BBC about his fee. But don't fret about him, little one. He used to be all done up in white tie and tails as President of the Oxford Union and is so cuddly that he might end up on *Jackanory* before the red revolution comes . . .

Tell Mummy and Daddy to put your name down for Eton, there's a good little chap. It will still be there. It will still flourish. Our home-grown revolutionaries are making only too sure of that. The impotent squawking, posturing, finger-jabbing nincompoops.

Angry? You bet your next prescription charges I'm angry. For I understand only too well why Danny beat it back to Frankfurt. Boredom, comrades, boredom . . .

I was at the hectic party in a Cromwell Road flat last Tuesday to greet him and other rebellious student leaders. There they all were. A boiling bubbling collection of the militant British Left, draping themselves on the expensive furniture, the light of battle glinting through their fringes.

I have been to many comic gatherings in my time. A BBC script conference. A magistrates' court. The Proctors' office at Oxford. A strip club. The Coronation. This one outdid them all for sustained hilarity. It was a bit like a benefit concert for clapped-out seaside monkeys . . . Except it was not worth a tanner. Or even a copper – with or without a helmet.

John McGrath, another regular at the political meetings at Goodwin's flat, explains this joke: 'There was a Special Branch guy stationed permanently outside, clocking people in – we used to offer him cups of tea!'

Potter's report continues:

Oh, I shall always remember the night I met Danny.

Daniel Cohn-Bendit was an impressive figure, so much in touch with hard reality that he could keep his marvellous sense of irony. I listened to him talk, a stocky, voluble, undogmatic, amusing and optimistic individual. A bringer of hope, a dismantler of prisons.

Danny and the Paris students had shown that it is possible to begin shovelling away some of the filth called capitalism. They had taken the role of detonators. And the explosion still reverberates. Man shall not live by sliced and homogenized bread alone. Man can still stand up and dare to be free, really free.

But each nation, each people, must reach out for the future by standing on the bent back of its own past and its own traditions. Which means we have to do our own thinking for ourselves. London is not Paris. [Harold] Wilson is not De Gaulle. And you do not create a revolution out of tea-bags and coffee spoons and well-heeled ex-Presidents of the Oxford Union gibbering about the abolition of money.

Small wonder that when Cohn-Bendit submitted to questions a look of incredulity slowly spread up to meet his dyed locks. Public-school voices talked about the need to give arms to your actual workers, and other such horsehair. The discussion soon degenerated into utter farce, with competing vanities, meaningless jargon, ideological confusion, grandiose threats and boutique chatter filling the air like water trickling into a cistern. A classic and bitterly comic demonstration of why the Left in this country is more impotent at the moment than it has ever been.

Even the booze ran out a couple of hours too soon. After all the capitalist alcohol had been swallowed I found myself wandering around the room with a punctured can of imperialist Coke, saying that I wanted to be shot. A few of those present would no doubt be more than willing to oblige. Especially now. But I'm not worried. They'll never get the chance. Half of them couldn't strike a match let alone detonate a huge change in our smug and class-ridden society . . . The only real challenge to the established order was the ejection of the man from *The Times* . . . What on earth he could have been writing, goodness knows. Unless he was trying his hand at an epitaph.

John McGrath agrees that a lot of Goodwin's circle were 'naïve' in their behaviour, and points out that Trevor Griffiths, who also attended these gatherings, 'did a travesty on it in his play *The Party*. Clive was very cross with Trevor about that, though he never had it out with him.' Malcolm Sloman, the TV playwright of working-class origins who sneers at his revolutionary friends in Griffiths's play, seems very like Potter, but Griffiths says that the character was drawn from David Mercer. 'I think I met Dennis no more than twice or three times,' adds Griffiths, 'and never, so far as I'm aware, at the Friday night meetings at Clive's.'

Roger Smith says that there was nothing new in Potter's behaviour to the *Black Dwarf* crowd: 'He'd done that at Oxford – he couldn't stand competition.'

*

In August 1968, Potter's illness worsened again. 'In some weird and wonderful way, it seemed, I had suddenly been given back my health and strength,' he reminded his *Sun* readers on 26 August. 'But now I am, just as suddenly, back with a walking stick, tip-tapping out a tiny route for my swollen toes. And waiting with an ill temper to go into hospital again.' On the night that Soviet tanks had rumbled into Prague, 'I could feel the hot fluid pumping into my fingers again. Pessimism sits on my mind like an old black crow on a shrivelled tree . . . I am writing this in the middle of the night, under pressure. The walls of the room seem to have moved in towards me.'

He considered reproving himself for selfishness:

Oh, stop feeling sorry for yourself, you smug cripple. And start feeling sorry for the world. But I can think of no better way of writing about the events of last week. Images of sickness exactly fit the situation . . . 'Try not to be too depressed,' said my doctor, doling out capsules as prettily coloured as the squares in a child's paintbox. And perhaps the advice holds good in my wider analogy too. Now is not the time for political despair or Cold War rant. Try not to be too depressed.

The Russians in Czechoslovakia and the Americans in Vietnam are finding that freedom is too powerful an antibiotic even for their huge plagues . . . And that means, surely, that we dare not subside into despair or pessimism . . . Despair is, I understand, listed as a grievous sin in the literature of the Church. That is one theological position I can fully support . . .

He was readmitted to Birmingham Skin Hospital, so that Dr Fairburn could try Methotrexate again. For three weeks he was unable to write for the *Sun*, but on 30 September he told his readers:

Tomorrow I begin my fourth week in this huge, trolley-clanking hospital. But now there is a light at the end of the tunnel as I sing the praises of a biliously yellow little tablet called Methotrexate.

Until the last few days the most burning issue in my mind has undoubtedly been whether to turn over in bed or not . . . An hour ago . . . a formidable nurse descended upon me like Joshua upon Jericho and began massaging some foul slop into my scalp. 'What is it?' I gasped. 'Basically,' she replied, pummelling away, 'it's coconut oil.' . . .

Tonight in the small hours, when all the lights are out, I am very carefully, very deliberately, going to burn a small black hole in the sheets with my cigarette . . . hitting back at the huge white figures towering over my bed . . .

His illness was, however, responding to the drug, and when he left hospital after six weeks, in mid-October, Fairburn noted that 'approximately 75 per cent control had been achieved. Regular monitoring of marrow, kidney and liver function had revealed no abnormality.' Methotrexate was potentially harmful to these parts of the body.

On 21 October, Potter told *Sun* readers that his freedom was conditional on good behaviour:

I was to stay in bed for a while. I was to stay indoors for much, much longer. No working trips. No social jaunts. No unnecessary stress or tension. A weekly blood count. And assorted bottles of biliously coloured tablets . . .

All this was supposed to browbeat me into submission. Instead, I responded with an eagerness which probably tempted the poor man to call in an outside opinion, preferably psychiatric . . . How was he to know that one of my secret ambitions has been to be placed under house arrest? That he was giving sanction . . . to my perverse desire to be like the hermits of childhood fairy tales?

Travel nauseates me. Hotels are a damn sight worse than hospitals. The conversation of strangers is, for me, a mixture of boredom and foreboding, triviality and terror. I am almost certainly the only Oxford graduate of my generation who has never been abroad. April in the Forest of Dean is, for me, an infinitely sweeter prospect than the same month in smelly Paris . . .

O, hustling, bustling, chattering, chanting world, I withdraw gratefully from your buses and trains and headlong imbecilities. It is enough, surely, to tip-tap on a stick from one room to another – especially with winter about to flex its muscles . . .

So here I am, back home again, the great drama of family life once more encasing me like a huge protective shell. This column can pick up where I dropped it, a mixture of self-revelation and opinionated comment delivered from the same armchair as before . . . Normal service will be resumed next week . . .

But it was not. The Methotrexate began to cause gastro-intestinal side-effects, and was now failing to control the psoriasis. He was taken back to hospital – never to resume the *Sun* column – and was probably still there on the night of 13 November, when his second play for ITV, *Shaggy Dog*, was transmitted.

Back in May, Potter had described it in the *Sun* as 'an anguished sort of comedy which was in large part written with my ballpen strapped on to my right hand', and said that, like *The Bonegrinder*, it was 'not a masterpiece either. I suspect that the stress will spill out on the page, insufficiently controlled.'

Written for a London Weekend series featuring five actors ('The Company of Five'), *Shaggy Dog* is a *jeu d'esprit* rather than one of Potter's angst-ridden examinations of sexuality, though it has a disturbing undercurrent. It opens with the main character, Wilkie, walking along a city pavement, 'suitably uniformed in bowler hat and sober dark suit', though like George King in *The Bonegrinder* he is sexually repressed. Riding up in the lift to the offices of RestAwhile, where he is to be interviewed for a job, he drools helplessly at secretaries. Meanwhile the RestAwhile executives who will interview him are just as tense, through the stress of their jobs. In a vain attempt to break out, one of them dons a clown's bulbous nose and a long blond wig. Wilkie, ushered in for his job interview, goggles in amazement at this, but behaves even more insanely himself. Pulling a gun, he begins to tell them about an extinct animal called the Rary – 'It was gentle. With soft rubbery paws' – and then breaks off to shoot them. Amid the carnage, he delivers the punchline to his shaggy-dog story – 'It's a long way to tip a Rary' – and jumps fourteen floors to his death.

No recording of Gareth Davies's production of *Shaggy Dog* has survived. The cast included John Neville as Wilkie and Cyril Luckham as one of the executives. The majority of critics were unimpressed.

Michael Billington in *The Times* judged it 'amusing and enjoyable but it seemed to utilize only a small section of its author's considerable talent.' However, Peter Black in the *Daily Mail* thought it 'his best play for some time'.

*

A Beast with Two Backs, written more than a year earlier, followed hard on the heels of *Shaggy Dog*, being shown as the *Wednesday Play* on 20 November 1968. It was filmed in the Forest, but the director, Lionel Harris, failed to get across most of the nuances of Potter's script. Nancy Banks-Smith wrote that the death of Joe's bear left her 'thinking he ought to get a monkey. It was a flip, defensive giggle. And, for me, the play had failed.' Maurice Wiggin in *The Sunday Times* wrote approvingly of Potter's '*saeva indignatio*, a terrible anger . . . Swiftian in its ferocity', but Stanley Reynolds wondered why Potter had 'bothered to write the play at all'.

The National Theatre project had come to nothing, but Potter's own stage adaptation of the Nigel Barton plays (under the title *Vote, Vote, Vote for Nigel Barton*) ran for four weeks at the Bristol Old Vic in November and December 1968, with a cast including Janet Henfrey, repeating her screen performance as the schoolmistress. Potter, out of hospital, managed to get there. 'I saw him walking with a stick,' says Keith Barron, the original Nigel, who came to the first night. 'It went down incredibly well with the audience. There was laughter in all the right places, and I thought Dennis would be absolutely delighted, but he told me he'd rather have his work seen by millions – on the television.' The production earned cool reviews. Michael Billington in *The Times* found its multiple flashbacks 'structurally rather confusing'. Jeremy Brien in the *Bristol Evening Post* thought it 'sadly disappointing . . . a bastardized version of two plays written wholly for the . . . screen'.

A few weeks later Potter told Philip Purser, 'I'm quite happy for any of my plays to be done in the theatre, as *Nigel Barton* was done at Bristol, as long as it's *afterwards*, and subsidiary to TV.' In 1970 he said in an interview, 'The theatre is a kind of middle-class privilege, a dying, sort of minority thing . . . Only television is classless, multiple . . .' Elsewhere that year he remarked, 'Television is the biggest platform and you should kick and fight and bite your way on to it.'

Though his *Sun* column had ceased (presumably because of his absences through illness), his commitment to *The Times* had now increased to a book review each week, and he was given the lead position on the page. Philippa Toomey, who was the deputy literary editor, describes the difficulty this entailed:

The great problem was physical. He had to write his review in that strange, cramped handwriting, with those awful hands, and sometimes he simply couldn't do it. He couldn't dictate it, and Margaret bought him an electric typewriter at one point, but he couldn't manage to use that either. So we did have problems, when copy didn't arrive on time, and there were a number of anxious calls between Margaret and me. I thought she was great – she was the mediator between him and the hard realities of life.

He said in 1986, 'I can't use a typewriter because my trailing fingers would hit more than one key at once.'

His spirits were very low, and he used one of his December reviews for more self-exposure: 'I often need a stick to walk. Arthritis twists at my joints. I have chronic psoriasis: a manic-depressive getting through the day on steroids and librium, the night on sodium amytal.' Librium is a tranquillizer, sodium amytal a sleeping tablet. In *The Singing Detective*, Marlow refuses to take tranquillizers: 'I'm not taking those things! I've got work to do.' But Gibbon, the hospital psychotherapist, tells him, 'Most chronic dermatological patients are on tranquillizers or antidepressants, you know. Almost as a routine. The skin, after all, is extremely *personal*, is it not?'

Potter's *Times* book review continues:

Five times in hospital and they want me back in again. 'Classic stress illness,' says a specialist, the tips of his fingers together, making me want to apologize.

But I have gone through and beyond the despair and even the hatred which has so often powered me in the past. After a particularly harrowing year of physical illness and mental self-exploration I clutch at the realization – call it intolerable arrogance if you like – that I might one day write something which will 'survive'. A vocation rather than just a perpetual therapy to exorcize personal hobgoblins: a writer alive and alert rather than a cripple squirming on the end of a pin that grows out of guilts too dark and obscure to explore here.

CHAPTER 5

The rhythm of an obsessive

Around this time, Philip Purser witnessed both the manic and the depressive sides of Potter:

I first met Dennis Potter after I had attacked his worst play, *The Bonegrinder*, in the *Sunday Telegraph*. Potter replied in a column he had in the . . . *Sun*, partly in rage, partly in mock-humility. I guessed I would be his enemy for life. When a few months later I was invited by the *Daily Telegraph* magazine to write a profile of Potter, I told them that he would never see me . . . They rang back to say he would be delighted.

We met in a Kensington restaurant, his bright carrot hair a beacon in the gloom. His hands were already deformed by his illness, so that he held a glass with difficulty and smoked a cigarette as if wearing boxing gloves. Because of the steroid drugs he was on, he had to choose between wine or meat. He chose wine. But this was a good day; he was feeling fine, he was optimistic, he talked and talked in the non-stop, lucid torrent that became familiar from his television appearances.

The published interview begins:

Dennis Potter might be the survivor of some grim Inquisition, his painful limp a legacy of The Boot, his fingers twisted and the nails blunted an opaque yellow by screwed instruments . . . He suffers from arthritis and also psoriasis . . . Potter says it's the biblical leprosy and that both troubles are classic stress illnesses. Sometimes he blames the Bomb, the wrongness of the world; at other times he dates it all back to the onset of guilt he felt when as a Forest of Dean miner's son who'd been to Oxford he returned with a TV unit to make a patronizing documentary . . .

When the illness is at its worst he cannot even eat, for his jaw muscles seize; he cannot read, for the psoriasis gums up his eyelids. In periods of remission he is gay and fiercely hopeful. 'This time I feel it might be over for good, this time it's different.'

He told Purser that he had been having 'a fight that morning – as usual – with the producer of a new play', and that, after the meal, he would 'walk slowly through the pale Kensington sunshine to Paddington, where his wife is arriving to spend an evening in town with him'. Purser was charmed by him:

I find him enormously likeable and entertaining: instant good company . . . I think it must be some quality of . . . affirmation: a zest, an ardour for living. He is a lively talker, with the insistent lilt and wide vowels of the region and rarely any hesitation in finding the right word, though sometimes echoing himself three sentences later, as if he were quoting from a familiar argument.

Purser wrote the first draft of the article, but was asked by the editor to supply some more details, 'so a week or two later I drove to his home in Ross-on-Wye . . . This time it was a bad day. His skin was aflame, his joints rasping. He lay in bed sipping milk and whisky, and when he needed to go to the lavatory he made me go downstairs so that I wouldn't see him dragging himself across the landing on all fours.' Purser added this passage to the article:

The Potters have a three-storey Victorian house . . . warm and welcoming inside. Margaret Potter is fair, capable, brave. The kids have an unself-conscious directness about them – 'Is he staying to lunch? Is he staying the *night*?' The elder girl is helpful, always running errands; the younger hugs herself in a trance-like ecstasy before a Beatles LP on the radiogram; the little boy lumbers around giving the impersonation of a tiny King Kong that all little boys give. But Potter is back in bed with a regression of the illness. His face and arms are aflame. He winces as his joints scrape and click. He sips milk laced with whisky and chain-smokes Player's Gold Leaf.

Here, on the good days, he follows an anti-routine which consists usually of sleeping during the morning, attending to journalism and script rewrites during the afternoon – he dictates his newspaper articles, even his lengthy *Times* reviews, directly from rough notes, without ever writing them out, much less typing them – and watching hours of television, which he loves. Only at night, sometimes not until midnight, can he get down to writing the television plays . . .

Sarah Potter says that her father soon gave up dictation. 'It wasn't very successful as a method, and he hated having people around him, in that sort of situation. And he use to say, "There is nothing like the physical act of putting words on the page."' She confirms Purser's account of his working hours:

He was always an insomniac. He could survive on very little sleep, and he liked to work when the place was at its quietest, often through the night. I'm not sure that he had an office at this period, though there were plenty of rooms to spare in the house. I think he used to write on the table in what we called the breakfast room.

He wasn't the kind of person who set an alarm clock, got up, and did a certain predetermined number of hours – though later on in his life, when he was into a project, he was very disciplined, and would work at remarkable speed. But Mum said to me that, earlier on, she remembered large gaps between him doing things, when he would read a lot and generally was around the place, gathering himself for the next onslaught. It wasn't all frantic activity. But definitely he was happier when he was working. And that addiction to his work grew. And he became more of an insomniac as he got older – the combination of the drugs and the drink and the coffee; he drank enormous amounts of strong black coffee (we couldn't talk him out of it by saying, 'This might be contributing to your not sleeping.').

Gareth Davies says that not only would Potter write at night, he would telephone at all hours: 'Dennis was a great ringer-up at 3 a.m., on the assumption that everyone else was awake. I'm sure a lot of things he asked for or suggested got passed because if you said yes to him you could get back to sleep again!'

He gave up his weekly *Times* book column at the end of February 1969, telling his readers that he considered it a waste of time. In his final piece – a review of two critical volumes about modern poetry – he wrote: 'The combination of these two books – and of the increasing sense I have of the unalterable impermanence of weekly reviewing – finally persuades me that I . . . should pack it in.' But Philippa Toomey guesses that it was the physical strain and the demands on his limited energy that made him stop.

Later, he recalled of this period of his life: 'I was . . . becoming more and more reclusive. I would go up to London for the one day, and stay overnight, but then my skin was so bad it became as much a social problem as anything, like leaving layers of your skin in a hotel bedroom.' He described this as 'a stage when I wouldn't acknowledge it. Anyone with a serious skin illness is usually very loath to talk about it. They try to use every stratagem or device to hide it.'

*

Purser's article makes brief mention of Potter's latest play, *Moonlight on the Highway*, which ITV transmitted on 12 April 1969. The producer was once again Trodd, who had now left the BBC. 'Towards the end of 1967,' he says,

there was a round of ITV franchises, and the new London Weekend consortium was successful. And they approached me and Tony Garnett to go and work for them. And Garnett and I decided to say, 'We'll come, but we'd like to come not as individuals, but as a company.' To our amazement, they bought the idea, and so we became Kestrel Productions, recruited an accountant and a lawyer, and David Mercer for cosmetic purposes, went to them, and became the first independent production company working for a franchise-holder. And we were contracted to supply virtually all their drama for the first two years. And we did, and I produced virtually all of that, while Garnett – with the other bit of Kestrel, which was Kestrel Films – started making *Kes* and things like that.

During that period, among the things I did was a couple of Simon Grays, the first Colin Welland piece, and Dennis's *Moonlight on the Highway*.

Though *Moonlight on the Highway* is now remembered only by a few Potter enthusiasts, it is arguably the masterpiece that he had convinced himself he would write one day – at least, the original text is; unfortunately the production did not match up to it. At last, he had found a way of expressing his own sexual predicament in a form that was entertaining as well as horrifying. He would never write better than in this short, forgotten gem of a script.

The first page of the manuscript is written entirely in capital letters, as if with a kind of fury:

MOONLIGHT ON THE HIGHWAY

JUST AS NO ACTOR WORTH HIS SALT TAKES TOO MUCH NOTICE OF THE STUFF IN BRACKETS WHICH EMBROIDERS THE DIALOGUE, SO NOBODY IN HIS RIGHT MIND WOULD READ AN AUTHOR'S INTRODUCTION.

BUT

THIS IS A PLAY WHICH NEEDS TO BE READ AND, OF COURSE, PERFORMED WITH THE MUSIC ALWAYS IN MIND.

THE MUSIC IS FOREGROUND, NOT BACKGROUND.

IDEALLY, THE DISCS SHOULD BE CUT UP INTO THE PAGES, AND THE PLAY READ WITH A STYLUS.

AND THE LEAD PLAYER, DAVID PETERS, MUST ALWAYS BE AWARE OF BEING A SOLOIST, SYMPATHETICALLY FRONTING THE ORCHESTRATED MENTAL LANDSCAPE – THE RHYTHM OF AN OBSESSIVE.

DENNIS POTTER

1 Dennis's father Walt Potter (right) with his cousin-by-marriage Harry Baglin, returning home from a shift at the pit in 1930.

2 Dennis's mother Margaret ('Mag'), née Wale, as a young woman in London before her marriage.

3 Mag Potter with Dennis in her arms at Brick House, Berry Hill, where he was born in 1935.

4 The young Dennis in the arms of Mag's brother Ernie, who afterwards did 'something foul and terrible' to him.

5 The Potter family: Walt, Mag, Dennis and his sister June.

6 Dennis at Christchurch School in 1944, aged nine: 'I was clever … It set me apart…'

7 Three years later, at Bell's Grammar School, Coleford.

8 Potter (right) playing Canon Chasuble in *The Importance of Being Earnest* at Clement Danes School, in 1951, aged sixteen.

9 Potter (right) talking to a fellow National Serviceman at the Joint Services School for Linguists at Bodmin in 1953.

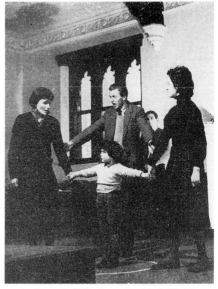

10 A rehearsal of *The Caucasian Chalk Circle* in 1959, Potter's final year as an Oxford undergraduate: Margaret Forster (left) as Grusha, Potter as Azdak, and Julia Gaitskell, daughter of the Labour leader, as the governor's wife.

11 The photograph which accompanied a profile of Potter in *Isis* during his final Oxford year.

12 Dennis Potter marries Margaret Morgan: the wedding reception at Berry Hill Club on 10 January 1959.

13 Margaret and Dennis Potter with their children Jane and Sarah at their home in Kingsbury, North London, around 1964, just as Potter was about to become known as a television playwright.

14 Potter photographed for his manifesto as Labour candidate.

15 Nigel Barton (Keith Barron) insults the Tory candidate in *Vote, Vote, Vote for Nigel Barton*, just as Potter had done in his constituency. (*BBC*)

16 The school scene in *Stand Up, Nigel Barton*: Janet Henfrey as the schoolmistress accuses Keith Barron as Nigel, with Johnny Wade as George Pringle looking on. (*BBC*)

17 Frank Finlay in the title role of Potter's *Casanova* (1970). *(BBC)*

18 Tom Bell as the 'angel' and Christine Hargreaves as Cynthia in Potter's 1970 play *Angels Are So Few*. *(BBC)*

19 Kenith Trodd. (*BBC*)

20 Caroline Seebohm. 'I know that you do not desire me,' Potter wrote to her. 'But I love you I love you.' (*Studio Edmark*)

21 Potter opening Berry Hill fête at the period when his psoriatic arthropathy made a walking stick necessary.

22 Kika Markham in Potter's 1976 play *Double Dare*, which grew out of an extraordinary evening she spent with him.

23 Mark Boxer's *Sunday Times* cartoon of Potter, which Harold Evans described as 'looking like a consumptive down and out'. (*By courtesy of Anna Ford*)

24 Dennis after being prescribed the miracle drug Razoxane in 1977. 'It's like living with a human whirlwind', said Margaret. (*Mark Ellidge*)

The second page consists of a 'running order of songs', specifying the LPs on which they will be found (most come from Ace of Clubs ACL 1178, *Al Bowlly with Lew Stone and his Band*). The first page of the play itself is headed: 'MOONLIGHT ON THE HIGHWAY – A Comedy with Music'.

The play opens in a hospital out-patients' department, where, like Ronnie in *The Rivers of Babylon*, David Peters is waiting to see a psychiatrist. Before the camera reaches him, it explores a series of 'mostly old faces' among the other patients, 'well-cratered, expressionless, dumpy, boiled-cabbage, dead faces'. Each face 'appears to *whisper* a tiny fragment of a personal memory', though there is no lip movement; the whispers overlap each other faintly, 'like a pile of leaves disturbed by the lightest wind'. An old lady recalls 'when my knickers fell down in the playground', an old man 'when our Tom's Elsie kissed me in the kitchen', another old man 'when that bleedin' bird's egg broke in me mouth', and so on. Meanwhile behind the whispers we hear the instrumental introduction to the Bowlly–Stone recording of 'Moonlight on the Highway'. At last the camera reaches Peters:

> (*Early thirties, by far the youngest, sitting almost impossibly tense and cruelly rigid on his chair. This whisper has no trace of the other whispers attached to it. If a whisper can be a scream, this is it.*)

PETERS: (*out of vision*) I do NOT remember being sexually assaulted by a man with spiky hair and eyes the colour of phlegm. When I was *ten*. I do NOT remember. NO.

> (*His memory-bit ends exactly as the Al Bowlly vocal begins.*)

AL BOWLLY: (*sings*)   Moonlight on the highway
Moonlight on the plain
Turn your light on my way
Through memory lane.

> (PETERS *has been m.c.u.* [medium close-up], *like the others, but very soon after the vocal begins, we move in closer and closer, seemingly more and more relentlessly, until the song is pouring out of his eyes, ears, nose, mouth. The face at 'memory lane' gives a momentary spasm, a definite physical twitch.*)

> Moonlight on the highway
> Guide me while I roam
> Shine upon each by-way
> That leads me to home

(*We have held him, poked at him, in b.c.u.* [big close-up], *beyond the point of normal visual tolerance. This is necessary.*)

PETERS: (*softly*) Mother?

(*Very difficult now: keeping the song and* PETERS *and a series of briefly, almost subliminally, superimposed images over, with and through* PETERS'S *face and, ultimately, perhaps, eyes.*)

BOWLLY: A place where roses remember
          And folks forget me not
          What else is worth dreaming of?

(*Superimpose, like a flash, but longer on coffin: Face of the spiky-haired, middle-aged man contorting with lust. Coffin. Brief, child-like shout 'No!' Mouth of man, teeth baring. Burial service at graveside. A mouse in a cage, treadwheeling. VJ mug, King George VI. Man with spiky hair. Coffin. 'No!' Scrap of burial service. Mouse in cage. Coffin lowering. Dead bird, feet in air. 'Please!' Coffin being lowered. Man with phlegm-coloured eyes. Mouse in cage, frantic. Coffin. Hand grabbing mouse. Coffin. VJ mug. The Al Bowlly vocal is continuing . . .*)

Potter's own experience of sexual assault had happened 'between VE Day and VJ Day'.

In one of his *Sun* TV reviews, he had written:

'Cheap music can be so potent,' purred Noël Coward a long time ago. And he's right, blast it, absolutely right. For there is no easier pathway through to the chaotic jumble of memories or moods, which lie coiled like blind old reptiles in the far corners of the mind, ready to spring at a signal from the tinkling piano or throbbing big bass drum.

The late Sixties saw the beginning of fashionable nostalgia for the Thirties.* Reviewing a book about the Spanish Civil War in 1968, Potter had written somewhat contemptuously about this trend:

Nostalgia . . . for a far-off decade which supposedly saw its issues in simpler terms . . . Young men with bright eyes went off to fight. Al Bowlly sang about aching hearts or breaking dawns, young girls wore bright curls . . . Extend the list, rummage about for bitter-sweet quotations . . . make a montage out of the stale scraps of a mind's celluloid. And then the passion can be powdered down, the politics neutered into a dated syncopation and the continuing relevance of protest or heroism safely bracketed with all These Foolish Things

* Though Ken Trodd emphasizes that this was very slight compared to the later craze for the Thirties, and in this respect *Moonlight on the Highway* was a pioneer work.

to which the ghost of God-knows-what clings . . . The Thirties are coming back *in*, man.

He was always careful to distinguish between mere nostalgia, such as he scoffs at here, and the power of the past to illuminate the present:

Nostalgia is a means of forgetting the past, of making it seem cosy, of saying, 'It's back; there – look how sweet it was.' But you can use the power of nostalgia to open the past up and make it stand up in front of you. This is why I use popular songs. Often the initial reaction is, 'Oh, how sweet to hear that thing again!' but then the very syncopations can bear in things that have been knocked away by the present and that are important, that tell you what you are . . .

As the song 'Moonlight on the Highway' ends, David Peters 'half says out loud' Bowlly's final words, 'Please lead me to love', and his neighbour in the hospital waiting area, a crotchety old man, grunts, 'You speaking to me, then?' Peters attempts to explain: 'Moonlight on the Highway . . . Recorded – Twenty – no, no Twenty-first March – nineteen thirty – thirty – *eight*. The great Al Bowlly. Bowlly.' The old man mishears the name: 'What – him as used to keep the eel and pie shop? . . . In the Broadway. Bowler. That's it. Al Bowler . . . Jew-boy, he was.' Peters becomes furious – 'You silly bloody old fool!' – but then starts to giggle hysterically. The camera moves in on his face, which suddenly goes blank.

The song starts again, carrying us to a prostitute's room, in the middle of the night, where Peters is waking in terror at the memory of the sexual assault. 'Al Bowlly,' he mutters like a prayer to calm himself. 'Al Bowlly with Lew Stone . . . Recorded 21st March 1938. Good old Al.' The prostitute in bed next to him wakes up, but Peters snaps angrily at her:

PETERS: Stop talking. Stop talking to me. I don't want you to talk to me . . . I hate you.

PROSTITUTE: Thanks.

PETERS: It'd be all the same to you if – if – I said I loved you, wouldn't it? . . . You disgust me. Bitch.

(*She laughs but a little uneasily.*)

PROSTITUTE: Anyway, you said it earlier on . . . Love. (*Cackle*) You said you *l-o-o-oved* me. Never heard a bloke with such a sweet tongue –

eh? What's the matter?

(*He has covered his face.*)

PETERS: You make love sound – sound –

(*His distress is too obvious so, defensively, she laughs.*)

Don't you laugh at me! Don't you dare laugh at me.

(*She laughs, head back.*)

Back in the hospital, Peters is called in to see the psychiatrist. Before he gets there, we see a frenzied montage of prostitutes' and striptease advertisements – 'French Model', 'Young Girl gives French lessons', and so on – while Bowlly sings a bouncy 1933 song:

> Oh, isn't it heavenly
> To share every scheme with you
> To be able to dine with you and dance with you and dream with you . . .

Arriving in front of the psychiatrist, Dr Chilton, Peters gabbles at him, 'Al Bowlly recorded that in August 1933. It is nonsense to say he ever kept an eel and pie shop.' Calming down, he explains that he cannot sleep, 'because I'm wicked'. Chilton asks him to explain, and, to a background of Lew Stone (without Bowlly), Peters describes the sexual assault:

PETERS: When I was ten years old . . . There was this alley, see. Side of the chocolate factory . . . And – and – this man. Spiky hair. Eyes like phlegm. And – and – he – I – big walls. Narrow. He – (*He covers his face . . .*) I am wicked, I know that, just listen to the songs. Come here, he said. Chocolate Roses . . . Oh, isn't it heavenly, to share every – Mum? Come here! No! I said. I shouted. Mum! MUM! The walls were too high. Nobody. Mum? Nobody came . . . Al Bowlly has such sincerity, that's what counts in the end . . . Al Bowlly makes sense of it . . . He pulled my arm up behind my back. He pulled my. He pulled. Mum! Mum! The *hurt.* Oh. Oh! . . .

(CHILTON *lets him cry, which he does, hard.*)

The scene ends with Chilton asking Peters, 'Who is Al Bowlly?', and a glimpse of the 'madly treadwheeling mouse'.

We now go back to the day before the hospital visit. In his bedsitter in 'the seedy part of Fulham', Peters is editing the magazine of the Al Bowlly Appreciation Society. He puts Bowlly's version of 'Lover Come

Back to Me' on the record-player, and mimes to it in the mirror, though the words ('No wonder I'm so lonely') carry too much meaning, and he stares, anguished, at his reflection. The music is interrupted by an impatient knocking, and he goes to the door, expecting complaints about the noise from his landlord. But (according to the direction) 'in the doorway is – this is a musical, folks – a stunningly beautiful young girl, a real swinger'.

She introduces herself as Marie Holdsworth, a researcher from Severn TV, which is making a programme on Bowlly, and needs Peters's help. He is delighted, but 'is extraordinarily awkward with her. She is too much, too blatantly, the dream girl they sing about.' Indeed he begins to talk to her in the words of Bowlly songs:

PETERS: Just Let Me Look at You.

MARIE: (*laughingly sharp*) What?

PETERS: You know it? The Al Bowlly song. 'Just Let Me Look at You' –

MARIE: No –

PETERS: It suddenly *bounced* into my mind. No, not bounced. Too – um – vulgar a word for such a sweet, sweet sound. Looking at you, sitting there, on my chair, and the words of the song – 'Darling, stand there for a while, just let me look at –' (*Swallow.*) Beg pardon, miss.

MARIE: What for?

PETERS: For, for – (*He clenches his eyelids.*) – you're the girl He sings about.

She tries to leave, but he insists on playing her Bowlly singing Jerome Kern's 'Just Let Me Look at You' ('the very peak of romantic Thirties stuff', comments the direction). As the record spins, he moves slowly in on her, making her feel 'like something caught in a trap'. The vocal ends, but he is still quoting from the song:

PETERS: You're so sweet, so terribly sweet –

MARIE: That's all corn.

PETERS: Oh, listen. List-en. Somebody. To talk to. Not pay for –

MARIE: Get off!

(*He is clambering all over her, not with lust, but with a kind of despair.*)

She hits him in the face and runs off, leaving him with blood spurting from his nose, as the music plays on and Bowlly reprises the saccharine lyric.

We return to Dr Chilton asking 'Who is Al Bowlly?' Peters reveals that his mother has just died, and shouts out, 'I didn't love her!' (We learn that his father was killed and his mother maimed in a 1945 air raid.) Chilton is already writing out a prescription; Peters hints that he still has something wicked to confess, but the doctor, ignoring this, warns him not to drink alcohol or eat cheese while taking the pills – cheese will make his head ache, alcohol will make his 'tongue flap'. Peters is hustled out to get his drugs, to the ironic accompaniment of the Bowlly song 'What a Little Moonlight Can Do!'

The date on which all this is happening, 17 April, is the anniversary of Bowlly's death (he was killed in the Blitz), and the Al Bowlly Appreciation Society is meeting in a hotel. 'All the throng . . . are middle-aged or elderly,' explains Potter. 'The same people, in fact, whom we saw in the out-patient department. But this time they have smiles on their cratered faces, and a sparkle in their eyes.' The elderly couples dance to the Bowlly records put on by the committee, and the President assures them that their idol 'will go on through the years when the sickening Sixties and the grubby long-haired dirty-mouthed so-called pop singers of today are happily gone and forgotten!' (Ken Trodd says, 'There was never a specifically Al Bowlly society, but there was a magazine called *The Golden Years*, run by a chap in Cardiff, and I supplied Dennis with copies of it.') From the Bowlly gathering, we flashback to the hospital, where Chilton is discussing Peters's condition with two medical students who sat in on the consultation. Speaking of the childhood sexual assault, Chilton says:

The victims are always the ones who feel guilt. That is a horrible fact. The eaten rather than the eater. You know that? Do you know that the incidence of mental illness is higher in Hiroshima than elsewhere in Japan? . . . The survivors think they should not have survived. They feel more guilty, *more* sick, *less* human than those great big wholesome white men with blueberry pie between their teeth who *dropped* the blasted bomb.

Potter said the same when talking about his own experience of sexual abuse to an interviewer in 1992: 'It's the child that assumes guilt.'

One of the students asks if it would not have been better to let Peters confess his 'wickedness', but Chilton says he hopes he will 'tell somebody else *first*. A friend. A relation . . . Somebody.' However, it is the members of the Al Bowlly Appreciation Society who hear the confession, for Peters has ignored the warning about alcohol. 'I have to tell you', he announces, swaying drunkenly at the microphone, 'that I have slept with one hunder– hundred and thirty-shix – thirty-six, one hundred and thirty-six women . . . Prostitutes!' The mike is cut off, and the Appreciation Society, 'shocked to the marrow of their bones', ignores Peters and dances to Bowlly singing 'Moonlight on the Highway'. But Peters, having made the confession, gurgles with delight as the final credits roll.

*

By organizing the story of *Moonlight on the Highway* in this fashion, Potter avoids the need for the psychiatrist to explain Peters's obsessive need for prostitutes (their number has risen by thirty-nine in the two years since *The Rivers of Babylon*). The play's premise, that Peters is a compulsive user of prostitutes because he was sexually abused as a child, and has had an unhappy relationship with his mother, is never explored. But Potter does allow Chilton to surmise that Peters is obsessed with Thirties pop songs because they are the music he heard 'from the wireless downstairs as he was drifting off to sleep' in the guilt-free years before he experienced the abuse.

It is clear that Peters has two personalities where love and sex are concerned: the compulsively 'wicked' user of prostitutes, and the idolizer of unreal sexless dream-girls. The Thirties music – substituted for the psalm-imagery of *The Rivers of Babylon* – summons up the 'good' Peters rather than his 'evil' *alter ego*. ('You know that cheap songs so-called actually do have something of the Psalms of David about them,' Potter remarked to Bragg.) Peters is happy because the public confession has, for the first time, allowed each of his identities to admit the existence of the other. But once this is achieved the play ends abruptly, and he still seems a terribly crippled individual, with little prospect of normal human relationships.

In 1993, Graham Fuller asked Potter about the dream-girl/whore dichotomy which Peters and many of his other male characters make in their imaginations:

FULLER: Your films and plays often present this tormenting, quasi-religious, and ultimately misogynistic notion of women as both angels and whores. Do you think that male dichotomy is something that can be resolved – are the two things reconcilable?

POTTER: No. The two images are ludicrously far apart and they should both be destroyed . . . But . . . it's a fact . . . of human relationships, which have to contend with both our animality and our grace.

Moonlight on the Highway was transmitted on ITV's *Saturday Night Theatre* on 12 April 1969. James MacTaggart, who had also left the BBC to co-found Kestrel, was the director, and Ian Holm as Peters achieved everything that Potter's script called for. However, the script was drastically cut (Potter wrote it at ninety minutes, but the transmission time was only fifty-two), and the scene in the prostitute's room and the montage of prostitutes' advertisements were dropped, so that Peters's confession in front of the Al Bowlly fanatics came out of the blue. Trodd also added some archive footage of Bowlly himself singing.

In consequence, reviewers were mostly puzzled. Richard Last wrote in the *Sun*, 'This was an almost copybook piece about mental disturbance . . . Well scripted, atmospheric, beautifully acted by Ian Holm: and at the end the only decipherable note on my pad was, "Why?"' Sean Day-Lewis in the *Daily Telegraph* thought it 'lurid', and Stanley Reynolds in the *Guardian* described it as

a new play by the irritating Dennis Potter . . . What comment was it making? . . . David . . . goes to prostitutes . . . he's been to 137 [*sic*] of them. This I reckon is £685 at the normal rate of £5 a time. Being out of a job, David has problems . . . Potter overloaded this black comedy and made it sink into a sea of make-believe without a bubble. Only real life can get away with that sort of loaded dice.

The play contained Potter's first public allusion to sexual abuse in childhood, and it was probably watched by his Uncle Ernie, the abuser, who was still living with Potter's parents in Berry Hill. Mag Potter, who at the time still knew nothing about the assaults, does not recall that her brother reacted in any noticeable way to the play, but six weeks later, while playing cards, he suddenly died.

CHAPTER 6

A kind of illness towards me

'I know that you do not desire me . . . But I love you I love you. And I hope that you will sometimes allow me to say it.' This could be David Peters quoting an Al Bowlly song in *Moonlight on the Highway*. In fact it is Potter writing, around the time of composition of the play, to someone with whom he had become obsessed.

Caroline Seebohm heard of Potter at Oxford when they were both undergraduates. 'I don't think I did meet him then,' she says. 'I went up in 1958, so he was still there, but I was a convent girl without any knowledge of politics, so I glimpsed him as a distant figure, this sort of legendary, fiery revolutionary, with his flaming red hair. He had a tremendous gift of the gab, a great confidence and anger – such a tense, coiled anger. He was like a fury.'

Seebohm was the daughter of a banker, youngest of three children (her elder sister Victoria became the writer Victoria Glendinning). She describes herself as

a very spoiled jolly creature with curly blond hair and few signs of intellect. I went through boarding school (St Mary's, Wantage) thinking I was a pony a lot of the time. I came up to Somerville to discover that at Oxford the ratio was five males to one female. There weren't very many girls who could cope with that, but I spent my whole time making eye contact in the Bodleian and going to champagne-laden parties in glorious surroundings.

Margaret Forster, also at Somerville, describes Seebohm as 'extremely attractive – in an era of horrible clothes she always looked graceful – longish cotton skirts, unusual in the 1950s, and a wicker basket over her arm in which she carried her books like flowers – very chic'.

In her second year at Oxford, Seebohm fell 'madly in love' with

Roger Smith. 'And I totally turned my back on my Christ Church social life, and became a Labour Party leftie, because you couldn't go out with Roger and not be that. And Dennis was their hero. This was 1959, and he'd gone down. And they regarded him with a mixture of awe and jealousy.' Leaving Oxford in 1961, she became the first woman trainee at Granada Television; but gave it up to marry Smith during 1962.

It was now that she came to know Potter:

Roger and I used to go to Dennis's flat in Hammersmith, which was very cramped and claustrophobic, and hot – I think because he was quite sick with the psoriasis. Nobody really knew what would happen with the illness, and I remember wondering if he was going to die. It was the first time I'd really met him, and I was petrified, though I suppose it must have been then that Dennis got fixated on me. I didn't know it at the time, though he was quite kind to me.

Margaret was like a kind of servant – she'd come in and out with the tea, and never really join in the conversation. And one night Dennis got us outside, on the street (I think Roger was there too), and poured out this absolutely agonizing confession, about his addiction to prostitutes. He said Margaret didn't know, and he was mortified by it, but he just couldn't stop. I remember some figure, the number of prostitutes he'd been with – at least a hundred. I found it very sad and haunting, and imagined this lonely man standing in doorways. He pictured it like that.

Seebohm's marriage to Smith soon came to an end, though they remained friends. She spent some time in California, then returned to London in 1967 and drifted into the Clive Goodwin circle. 'Clive seemed to me very sad, a hollow man,' she says. 'He'd married a pop artist called Pauline Boty, but she died of cancer. He had parties for them all, and was a bit of a father figure, but I always got the feeling that he was living off them.' She decided to write a television play, and was helped by another Goodwin client, Tom Clarke. 'Tom was about twenty-five years older than us, and he'd started out as some kind of businessman, with a very conventional marriage, and in the Sixties he threw it all over, did the hippy thing, and became a successful television writer.' Her own play was televised by ATV. 'Meanwhile I'd got a job as an advertising copywriter, and found a flat of my own in Westbourne Terrace. I was twenty-seven, so I wasn't a spring chicken.' (Potter was now almost thirty-three.) But she admits that men constantly pursued her, and she sometimes yielded. 'People often fell in love with me – it was par for the course. But Dennis was different.'

On 30 April 1968 she wrote in her diary, 'Dinner with Clive and Dennis Potter – joined by Christopher Logue . . . Dennis is a rare man: he plays no games, has none but the most tangible barriers about communication. It showed Clive's extraordinary inability to cope with *himself*, his escape routes into "conversation".' Potter, who as usual had come up to London from Ross-on-Wye without Margaret, invited her out, and told her that he had long been obsessed with her.

On 6 May, back at home, he sent her this long letter:

Caroline,

I want to write to you. It is very tempting to compose a lyrical and passionately declamatory letter – and I am certainly capable of doing so; indeed would like to do so. But there wouldn't be much point and it would also be impertinent. Let me say, though, that I was so very happy to be with you, for however brief and tense a time it was. And I am moved by a deep gratitude that you did not brush my feelings aside as intrinsically ridiculous or (even worse) as simply dishonest. Inevitably, I expressed myself badly and couldn't get out all that I wanted, needed, to say, if only for the fear that you would think that I just wanted to get into bed with you. I do, of course. But there is so much more, so very much more, than that, and I hope you can believe that I would rather we never got even remotely near such a situation if it meant that I would lose contact with you. I want to know you decades from now. I want you to feel a trust and a reliance for whenever or wherever you might need it, however remote such a prospect might now seem to be. I cannot now withdraw in confusion and bewilderment and fear as I did before after having half revealed what I felt about you, felt *for* you. Please, please Caroline, let me be your friend, in the full and honourable meaning of that precious word.

That last sentence – I have just looked at it, for I am writing this very carefully, even to the point of ponderousness – would in itself be enough to provoke hoots of derisive laughter from some people. But not from you. Please not from you.

You are entitled to say that I am drawing on or building upon some deeply rooted but essentially adolescent fantasy, that I do not and cannot 'know' you. You may say that you are most decidedly not the sort of person I think you are.

But I do not accept this. Sometimes, no matter how rare it is, one human being can be suddenly lit by an awesome illumination, a kind of God-given lightning which is so powerful that it strikes open all sorts of perceptions which continue to reverberate for ever. I remember things you have said and the way you said them, from years back. I have thought deeply about you from behind an iron-clad assumption that I would never, ever reveal any of it to you. So when I blurt out the fact that 'I love you' there is no easy, short-term, rule-book way in which I can at the same time communicate the dimensions or the relevance or the essential *serenity* of that love. You have only seen me awkward and stumbling with words you must have heard so many times and so painfully before. One day, if you will permit me, I will be able to show you what I mean.

There is no threat to you in this, Caroline. You cannot know this now, but I would rather be a complete cripple than hurt or humiliate or degrade you in any way at all. If I can simply sit with you from time to time I will have gained more than I ever expected. I should want to touch you, and touch you with my life as well as my hands, but not feverishly or lustfully. Can you see this, or any bit of it? Can you dare to believe that you will not always be afflicted with predators?

I have known a great deal of physical pain as well as mental anguish in my life, and for years I have been scarred by feelings of guilt about sex. Margaret has preserved what is good in me and kept me somewhere near whole through the blackest period. She has known for a long time and once greatly feared what I felt about you – but (and this, I believe, is no betrayal) she cannot 'know' in that final sovereign, irreducibly [*sic*] lonely sense the full meaning of those feelings because the only person on earth to whom they could be communicated is, of course, *you*. And for once I do not feel guilt or shame about it. All relationships which mean anything at all are tinged with anguish and so is mine with Margaret, but we have created something enduring and beautiful together: and, after you had so innocently and inadvertently moved me beyond endurance into revealing some of my love for you when we met for the first time after your return from America, I had to retreat in shock back into that relationship. I feared my own emotion. I doubted whether I could face the consequences of that emotion without inflicting hurt and betrayal on my wife, for never could I leer that classic lie 'she doesn't understand me'. She did, and does, even while still in some degree fearing. She is a remarkable woman who now grasps, however apprehensively, some of the power or enormity of what I feel towards you. And right there at the centre, in the fundamental sense, she too is serene about it.

So, rightly or wrongly, there is no guilt or deceit. I can tell you now what you mean to me, even should you scorn and reject or undervalue it. I cannot tell you easily. I cannot make you see it all at once. But, please God, don't let it be totally barren, take it as a gift. I do not believe you would deliberately hurt me and I do not want to frighten you with any strident or rhetorical intensity. I *think* about you a great deal and have done so for very long. The day you came to the football match at Tottenham with Roger and me was, quite literally, the most pain-ridden and poignant day of my life. I longed so desperately to offer you some comfort or solace, but couldn't. I have prayed for you to be protected, Caroline, and longed for someone to cherish you.

I am too moved now and the words must be coming out wrong, wrong. Oh don't let me frighten you away!

No I must stop because I am in tears and I wanted this to be all controlled, this letter.

Please let me see you, that's all. Please. And write to me, Caroline, if you will, as soon as you can, as briefly as you like. Be kind, with words just for me – I would treasure them.

Dennis

Don't worry about it. I am alert. I *am* in control. And *pardon* me if I have said too much. I am coming up soon. Is it possible that I can see you for a while on Tuesday evening, the 14th? Could I spend some time with you? It would make me very happy.

They met on the evening he suggested, and afterwards Seebohm wrote in her diary:

May 14. Dennis.
A letter of physical intensity. It glowed. I trembled at his depths. And tonight? I feel we travelled 100 countries, talked 100 years. But it's only midnight, and again I tremble. The unwearying attack, a dog worrying a bone, tenderly, lovingly, protectively – but I still feel threatened. Why? The responsibility – he has chucked his steroids, he feels fit & full of energy (Caroline the Catalyst).

The day before, he had jubilantly reported to readers of his *Sun* column that he had just stopped taking his 'heavy daily dose of steroids'. Seebohm recalls, 'He got terribly excited because he was managing to do without the steroids. And he said to me, "It's you that's making me feel better, I'm a new person."'

Her diary entry for that evening continues, 'He overwhelms me with a love I feel unable to return. He asks for nothing. But he asks for every-thing.' She felt that he had been 'in love for years with a fantasy . . . He has a bright shining light in him which I cherish. But it blinds me. I don't love him. Tonight I even found him too heavy. On too many occasions I found things humorous which he could not see. Surely humour is a part of happiness.'

He told her repeatedly that evening that Margaret would like to meet her. 'So what must I do?' she asked herself. 'Be his monthly mistress? Would I mind that? Goodbye Margaret, it's Caroline night.'

The next day: 'Margaret phoned [me] in an explosion of hurt &
bitterness – so Dennis promises her he'll never see me again. But Tom
[Clarke] phones me – I must see him.' Seebohm explains that, though
Margaret Potter had telephoned her in a fury, 'Tom (who wanted to
sleep with me himself, and tried several times) said, "Look, Caroline,
you *must* sleep with Dennis, because it's the only way he's going to go
on getting well." I thought this was a horribly unfair thing to say, a
kind of sexual blackmail. And I couldn't imagine sleeping with Dennis,
I just couldn't – I was terrified by the thought of seeing him without
his clothes. I thought I would be physically repelled, and not just
because of the illness.' She does not recall that he made any further
mention of prostitutes. 'But it may have had a bearing on my feelings
about him, my refusal to be physically available.'

She spent another evening with him: 'I talk to Dennis about our non-
future,' she wrote in her diary. 'I don't *love* him. Maybe I would never
love him . . . And yet he is *better* – health-wise.' Looking back nearly
thirty years later, Seebohm recalls this and other dinners with him:

It would always be very, very painful. His eagerness was very offputting. I can
see his face now, a mixture of pleading (which was humiliating for him) and
yet sometimes very harsh, because he had a terrific turn of phrase – he could
suddenly say something very cruel, which made me feel it was all a pack of
cards. He smoked a lot, though it was very difficult for him to hold a cigarette –
his hands were very gnarled. His carrot hair was thinning, and he sweated a
lot, so that his face was very shiny, with patchy red skin. He was such a
powerful, verbal, *desperate* man. And I felt sucked into this frightening
vortex.

They did not talk about his writing. 'I wasn't really aware of his
public persona, or his success as a writer – he hadn't yet had that much
success. I just saw him as a man with an illness, and a kind of illness
towards me.' She adds, 'He was never self-pitying about the psoriasis,
never.'

He wrote her another letter after their second evening together. 'Let
me *do* things with you,' he pleaded, 'take you to the theatre, the
cinema, for a walk or even on a Battersea roundabout. I have rented
Tom's flat from next Tuesday for the six months (at least) that he is in
Cornwall. Two days or sometimes three days a week I am going to be
in town . . . Car-o-line. I love to say your name.'

She was willing to go on seeing him, but allowed him no more than a kiss on the cheek. 'I felt that if I gave him even the slightest encouragement, I would be somehow engulfed. I felt violence, sensed that he was a violent person. I was alarmed that I might unleash that. I had never met anyone with such intensity. I felt inadequate. (It was also flattering, of course.) It seemed vital that I be completely honest and truthful with him. I wanted to defuse this intensity.' He seems to have realized this. 'No – I am not destructive, my love,' he wrote in another letter. 'OK, so I feel strongly for and about you but that doesn't give me the right to suffocate you with words and tears and tension and timidity.' He persisted in telling Caroline that Margaret – despite her angry telephone call to her – understood and accepted his feelings. 'He had this fantasy that we were going to be a team, Margaret and I, helping Dennis on his way. But he never mentioned his children. It was as though they didn't exist, and he wasn't a father.'

Sarah Potter, who was six at this time, says, 'He definitely had crushes on people, which didn't make it easy for Mum. But I don't think it was ever so difficult that there was a question of their breaking up. There were strains, but they were handled and talked about. They talked about what drove Dad to that kind of behaviour. And I think Mum understood him sufficiently to be able to cope with those things.'

Roger Smith, who ironically describes his ex-wife's effect on Potter's health as 'the raising of Lazarus', alleges that 'there was a time – about the Caroline period – when Dennis went out of his way to set up an affair for Margaret. I think Clive told us. But none of us would oblige!'

Caroline Seebohm speculates that her own relationship with Smith may have been a key part of the story: 'Roger and Dennis had a very, very complex relationship. I now wonder whether that had something to do with it – that I'd belonged to Roger, which may have inflamed Dennis's interest a bit. They loved each other, really. Roger's a very passionate and emotional person, and Dennis was too at that time. You don't get interested in your best friend's woman without there being implications.' Ken Trodd makes a similar point: 'One of my girl-friends, though she never had much to do directly with Dennis, certainly had a feeling of rivalry with him in her relationship with me (this was in the mid- to late Eighties). Somebody remarked that we men, in our group of friends, were all desperately and incompetently trying to re-create, with the women in our lives, the relationships that we couldn't have with each other.'

Potter went on seeing Caroline in the summer of 1968. In another letter to her, he describes a July evening 'when I cried in the street' and people had stepped sideways to avoid him. 'I am well aware of the sort of fool I must have appeared last summer,' he told her, 'particularly at the end when I had to listen to all sorts of "advice" from people who will use any synonym or dredge up any half-understood bit of psychiatric claptrap rather than simply acknowledge the simple strength of a simple but overwhelmingly strong emotion.'

When his illness worsened severely in the late summer, it brought a temporary end to the meetings and correspondence; but Caroline received another letter from him in January 1969. 'I have written at least ten times in the last month,' he told her then.

I haven't been through the front door for the last four weeks. I am yet again engaged in a seemingly endless, almost hour-by-hour struggle against the gross indignity of physical pain. This is not a statement squeezed out by self-pity, the most ignoble of all the emotions, but just as a matter of accuracy. I work hard and well, no matter how my hand throbs. I love my family and I am blessed with Margaret: in short, I have a very great deal for which to be grateful.

He assured Caroline that all he wanted was 'a sort of communication' with her. But he had 'nearly choked with shame' when he discovered that 'you had had to ring someone up to say, "What shall I do about Dennis?"' She explains that this was Tom Clarke: 'And Tom was a *provocateur*, and it got back to Dennis, and I was mortified.' So was Potter, who told her 'at this present time my own pride and self-respect are more vital to me than ever before. So, if you feel like it, simply tear up this letter, but I beg you not to scatter the pieces where they hurt.'

He wrote that he had bought her a Christmas present, but, as there was no time to give it to her, he had 'left it in the taxi on the way to Clive's rather than devalue it by using it for any other purpose'. He would be coming up to London soon. 'I will telephone you then, after nervously staring at the phone for an hour. Try to see me. It will be one hell of a lift for me at a time when I need it.' Meanwhile he had some news about his work: 'At last, I have written a good play, and it came out of the episodic, inconclusive, ultimately humiliating events of a few months ago – I hope you will see it, it was for you.' This was *Son of Man*.

*

In 1972 Potter remarked that while the BBC 'drew a very firm line at any blasphemous attempt to interfere with dear little Cinderella', they 'did not mind me mucking about with Jesus Christ'. Indeed there seemed to be a vague hope at Television Centre that *Son of Man*, Potter's eighth *Wednesday Play*, would be seriously controversial.

'Controversy has stalked every play by Dennis Potter and *Son of Man* will be no exception,' promised Russell Twisk in the *Radio Times*:

I met Dennis Potter at a hotel above Paddington Station; he rather dislikes coming to London and stays as close to getaway point, the railways, as he can . . . He suffers greatly with arthritis and finds it painful even to walk. We sat in the hotel and he talked in his rather high Gloucestershire voice about *Son of Man*.

'I wanted to write a play about a man deluded with the thought that he might be Christ. At the start of my play we see Jesus in the wilderness, with cracked lips, emaciated, his mind high on thoughts, perhaps delusions. In such a state he would not be saying, "I am the Messiah" but "Am I the Messiah?"'

'We think of Jesus as being meek, gentle and mild. We have forgotten what the *man* might have been like. I wanted to strip away the dogma to go direct to the sources.'

During 1967 he had envisaged a play about 'a religious revolutionary', to be called *Take this Water*. Trodd had hoped it would be ready for Easter 1968. In 1976 Potter told Joan Bakewell,

Initially I thought of it being about a retired chapel preacher in the Forest of Dean fencing with his lifelong images of Christ. Then I thought, that's too indirect. Why don't I address myself to my images of Christ, which are Christ in the Forest of Dean: the valley of the shadow of death, say, or where Jacob wrestled, the pond near Cannop pit. Joseph and his coat of many colours I thought of as thrown into the quarry which I passed on my way to school. So I was able in *Son of Man* to get clear of the religiose Christ by using the Forest of Dean. Though that isn't directly apparent in the work.

John McGrath takes a cynical view of the play's origins: 'I always felt Dennis had a cunning awareness of what was newsworthy, like doing the life of Christ. He was very good at knowing what would make the hard news rather than just the review columns. I didn't trust that.'

Potter denied that this was his intention. Asked if he had been throwing down a gauntlet to the Church, he said,

No, I don't believe in throwing down gauntlets, despite appearances to the contrary. Other people have suggested that, including some critics . . . but I look at them with blank incomprehension because that's not what's in my mind. If I had something to say about the Church I'd write an essay or use a polemic. But I don't think it's a function of drama.

Nevertheless he felt 'a certain amount of anger at the milk-and-water Christ, the Holman Hunt *Light of the World* Christ, or the Catholic Christ, the supra-mystical, risen-from-the-dead Christ'; and his play certainly avoids this sort of portraiture. (Other recent screen portrayals of Christ had included Samuel Bronston's *King of Kings* (1961) and Pier Paulo Pasolini's *The Gospel According to St Matthew* (1965). Potter mocked Jeffrey Hunter as Jesus in Bronston's film – 'walking on eggshells and water' – but praised Enrique Irazoqui's 'severely pale and hypnotic' portrayal of him in the Pasolini.)

Potter told Philip Purser that most of *Son of Man* was written in the autumn of 1968, during six weeks in hospital in Birmingham:

Of course I'd been brooding on it for a long time and had about a third of it down already. Physically it was difficult. The pen had to be strapped to my hand because I couldn't hold it. The paper got sploshed with the steroid grease they were putting on my skin. In other ways it was easy. I wrote it more easily than any other play. I finished at two o'clock in the morning – the BBC had someone waiting to take it away to be typed.

Gareth Davies, who directed it, recalls, 'Some of the *Son of Man* script had literally got drops of blood and cortisone grease on it.'

In 1992 Potter talked of the hero of *Son of Man* in words he could have applied to himself:

There's this brave, witty, sometimes oddly petulant, man striding around in an occupied territory knowing and then not wanting to know that he's bound to die and to die painfully. And in the middle of it all, to say things that have never been said, and are still not said, about love. As a model of what human behaviour can be like, it still stands supreme.

The play is a truncated version of the Gospel story from the Temptations in the Wilderness to the Crucifixion, omitting the miracles and most of the parables and other teachings, and proceeding directly from the Sermon on the Mount to the episode of Jesus over-throwing the money-changers' table in the Temple. Potter took the play's title from one of the names by which Jesus is said to have referred to himself. The Potter Jesus is a man rather than the Son of God, alternating between fiery, short-tempered enthusiasm and a profound, almost self-destructive doubt about himself and his vocation ('Is it? Is it *me*?'), rather in the manner of a manic depressive.

Although at one moment he paraphrases W. H. Auden – 'We must love one another or we must die' – he usually speaks in the idiom of the late Sixties, telling the crowd, 'Never mind about money. You cannot love money and love God, so you cannot love money and love man.' Potter might have cued 'Can't Buy Me Love' to come up on the soundtrack here, as he did in *The Rivers of Babylon*. When Jesus withdraws to Gethsemane, it is 'to meditate', like a Flower Power pop singer. On the other hand his frequently irritable outbursts (he tends to snap 'shut up' at hecklers) make him more idiosyncratic than a classic peace-preaching Sixties hippy.

The Crucifixion happens almost wordlessly, though Potter's camera directions have much to say: 'Meticulously observe the hammering on to the cross. He screams in terrible agony . . . Hold camera rigid. No cutaways. No relief. Nothing. Hold for as long as we can tolerate an unendurable sight.' Jesus screams, 'My God! My God! Why have you forsaken me?' whereupon 'a spurt of blood chokes the words in his mouth', as the play ends.

Potter told Russell Twisk that he saw *Son of Man* as positive and affirmative compared with what he had recently been writing:

I had gone through a period of illness and depression before I wrote this play; in fact it was written while I was in hospital. In a way it got me out of my depression. Despair leads to destruction. I want to transform what I feel into something more positive and meaningful. In my last *Wednesday Play*, *A Beast with Two Backs*, I was expressing what I felt to be the beast in man. Usually I see the beast. This play shows the way we might behave to each other.

In the past I took the easy way out, coated everything with a black brush. Now I realize that there is light as well as shade.

To Philip Purser, he implied that he himself had religious feelings, even if he was not a full believer: 'We live amongst the litter of religion. It's part of our culture, part of our instincts . . . In illness I pray, even if I simultaneously disown the prayer. We cannot deny Christian feelings, or at any rate feelings inherited from Christianity.' In a discussion on BBC1 on the Sunday following the play's transmission, he described himself as having 'no faith' but 'a yearning for there to be something else'. Similarly in a letter to Caroline Seebohm, he used the phrase 'my christian-tinged agnosticism'. Yet *Son of Man* ends with no hint of the Resurrection, and seems to suggest that Jesus's philosophy of universal love is likely to lead to violence, death and failure. There is more optimism in the concluding moments of *Moonlight on the Highway*, and even *A Beast with Two Backs* suggests that humanity will continue to muddle on with its mixture of hypocrisy and sexual appetite.

Elsewhere in his conversation with Purser, Potter provided rather a different, and probably more honest, account of the origins and purpose of *Son of Man*:

I suppose the play represents a retreat from political positions I previously held. I was staying in a flat in London when Danny le Rouge came over that time. All the left-wingers met there one evening, Tariq Ali, everyone – debating away. I listened and felt very lonely and out of it. The same old hates, the same old dogma, the same belief that if only the systems of the world could be changed everyone would be happy. No concern for the sick and the bereft and the lonely and the suffering. Jesus was *their* man.

Potter had written of Cohn-Bendit in the *Sun* as 'a stocky, voluble, undogmatic, amusing and optimistic individual. A bringer of hope, a dismantler of prisons.' This exactly corresponds to the Jesus of the play, and his summary of Cohn-Bendit's message is much like Jesus's teachings in *Son of Man*: 'Man shall not live by sliced and homogenized bread alone. Man can still stand up and dare to be free, really free. But . . . we have to do our own thinking for ourselves.' Similarly, his sneering portrayal of the Clive Goodwin circle, as they listened and responded to Cohn-Bendit, with their 'competing vanities, meaningless jargon, ideological confusion, grandiose threats', closely resembles the behaviour of Caiaphas and the Jewish Establishment in the play.

Looked at in this light, *Son of Man* becomes a parable about the failure of the old-style Left during the Sixties. Potter's Jesus is indeed a contemporary figure – a 1968-style revolutionary who perceives that the traditional left wing (Judaism) has made a pact with the 'occupying powers' of capitalism and Admass (the Romans), and who tries to expose and disrupt this corrupt alliance by inciting his followers to public demonstrations. He fails (just as Cohn-Bendit eventually failed) because of the feeble-mindedness of his supporters – 'Half of them couldn't strike a match let alone detonate a huge change in our smug and class-ridden society', as Potter had written of the *Black Dwarf* crowd in the *Sun*. For all his admiration of Cohn-Bendit's/Jesus's personal qualities, Potter comes to the conclusion (not for the first time) that direct action of this sort will never succeed. We have, instead, to find a different language for understanding and tackling the mess that is human nature, the predicament of 'the sick and the bereft and the lonely and the suffering', just as Potter had already done with David Peters in *Moonlight on the Highway*.

In 1993 Graham Fuller observed to Potter, '*Son of Man*, your play about Jesus, is actually one of your most secular plays, I think.' Potter made no comment.

*

He saw Caroline Seebohm several times during the three months before *Son of Man* was televised. 'Oh Caroline I am so frightened of sex,' he wrote to her on 18 January 1969; yet he admitted,

I do, do want to make love to you, the physical expression and extension of my feelings for you. But I would be so scared, so helpless, that I once dreamed I could be allowed just to lie by you and whisper away the torrent of raw fear into that gentleness and awe which is at the very core of my emotion for you. Please, I must say it, just once, for the shyness will long linger.

They met in London. 'It was so very, very nice to spend an evening with you,' he wrote afterwards, 'and wonderful to feel the tension ebbing away until I began almost to be myself . . .' She was going away for a while. 'Hell – why should I bother to go abroad?' he asked her (he had still not done so). 'Unless, of course, you took me . . .'

He had persuaded the BBC to schedule *Son of Man* as a *Wednesday Play* rather than in a religious slot. 'I also asked for Colin Blakely to be Jesus,' he told Philip Purser, 'after seeing him in *Saint Joan* on *Play of the Month*. He was the Brother at the trial who is so hostile to Joan. He had a marvellous pent-up hatred and aggression. It was the pent-up quality that I wanted, not of hatred this time but of this other, unprecedented thing that was pent up.'

He said to Russell Twisk that he regarded *Son of Man* 'as the end of my apprenticeship as a dramatist, the first play I am pleased with'. But he was disappointed by the BBC's decision that Gareth Davies should direct it entirely in the studio, which had been kitted out with what Potter described as a 'plastic and polythene' landscape. In 1992 he recalled it as 'a set that looks as though it's trembling and about to fall down, a Galilee that's a sea of glass'.

Advance press coverage emphasized that the play was likely to offend ('Storm over TV Christ'), and the BBC decided to postpone it from Holy Week until the second week after Easter. On 17 April 1969, the morning after transmission, the *Daily Telegraph* duly reported that *Son of Man* had 'angered many viewers', one of whom had likened Colin Blakely's mildly Irish-accented Jesus to 'Brendan Behan holding court in a public house'. Potter himself alleged that 'one indignant lady complained . . . that Jesus "actually had *hair* on his chest"!' Talking in 1994, Potter recalled that 'Mrs Whitehouse wanted me prosecuted for blasphemy', and that there had been 'a row in the Australian Parliament about it'.

In fact public reaction was generally mild – 'Quiet Reception for new *Son of Man*', reported the *Guardian* – and critics were disappointed rather than shocked. Maurice Wiggin in *The Sunday Times* perceived 'a distinct advance, a maturing' in Potter's writing, but said he had known 'more eloquent and impressive figures' than Potter's Jesus. Stanley Reynolds in the *Guardian*, noting that the BBC had 'received no more telephone calls than usual for a *Wednesday Play*', judged the play 'important' and 'serious', but described the low-budget production as 'a bit of a crucifixion in itself'. Nancy Banks-Smith was doubtful about the play's real value – 'To tell God's truth – I don't know' – while Sylvia Clayton in the *Daily Telegraph* shrewdly observed that Jesus's manner of teaching was 'more like a party political broadcast than a divine revelation'. Ian Hamilton in the *Listener* was disappointed by Potter's Jesus – 'a crude, Identikit assemblage of . . . supposedly "human" characteristics' – and by the play's language: 'The soul-searching, apparently the nub of Potter's daring view of Christ, was enacted by two or three fractured soliloquies . . . The speeches . . . were always less than riveting.' Philip Purser, too, thought Jesus's big speeches weak: 'Slang just won't work, out of its own period. Adjectives like "flaming" stuck out like electric light bulbs.' Purser much preferred *Moonlight on the Highway*: 'I watched [it] twice, and it gets better and better; a little gem.' So did Ned Sherrin, reviewing for the *Observer*: 'This sad, clinical investigation of a mind obsessed by Al Bowlly was at times unbearably moving . . .'

Son of Man was immediately adapted by Potter for the stage, and was performed at the Phoenix Theatre, Leicester, in October 1969, with Frank Finlay as Jesus and Robin Midgley directing, transferring to the Roundhouse in London the following month. The stage version (which was revived by the Royal Shakespeare Company in 1995, with Bill Bryden directing and Joseph Fiennes as Jesus) has a more optimistic end: Jesus lifts his head triumphantly on the Cross, and cries out: 'It – is – ACCOMPLISHED!'

*

By June 1969, two months after the TV transmission of *Son of Man*, Caroline Seebohm was trying to persuade Potter to cease seeing her or writing to her. He accepted that this 'now seems the only meaningful act of love that is left to me. Yet still I pray that the time has not yet arrived and so I still evade that final grief. I long to see you . . .'

He had proposed two new *Wednesday Plays* to Graeme McDonald, the current series producer. One, with the working title *Condescension*, had as theme 'the attitudes of the middle age of condescension towards the very old and the very young'. The other, to be called *Prostitute Reformer*, would be a 'modern parallel, in the form probably of a Nonconformist minister, to Gladstone's attempts to reform prostitutes'. Meanwhile Mark Shivas, then a drama producer working for BBC2, commissioned *The Last Nazi*, which was to be about Rudolf Hess in Spandau. None of these reached script stage, and the first-half fees, which had been paid to Potter, were transferred to other projects, or written off altogether. Ken Trodd and Gareth Davies both emphasize that, for all its obtuseness and bureaucracy, the BBC at this period was always a generous patron towards its writers.

Meanwhile Trodd himself, at Kestrel, was making another Potter play for ITV, which was recorded in October 1969. Set in the mid-Fifties, *Lay Down Your Arms* is slight stuff, though Potter thought highly enough of it to plunder it more than twenty years later for *Lipstick on Your Collar*, and it has some intriguing autobiographical glimpses.

The hero is Private Robert Hawk, whose National Service number, 22920071, is Potter's own. Like Potter he is a Russian Language Clerk to MI3 in Whitehall, and is mocked by the middle-aged office blimps for his intellectual ambitions and emotional immaturity. He responds by taking refuge in the invention of personalities for himself – telling 'whopping great lies', as his Yorkshire miner father bluntly calls it – but is unmasked by the blimps as a lonely virgin: 'What do you do? Wank?' one of them enquires ('wank' was changed in production to 'play with yourself').

Retreating into Russian soulfulness, Hawk buys a gallery seat for *The Seagull*, and imagines himself as Chekhov's young Konstantin, crushed by unrequited passion – as of course Potter himself was when he wrote the play: 'It's not in my power to stop loving you, Nina . . . I call out your name. I kiss the ground where you've walked . . .' In his letter to Caroline Seebohm about her holiday plans, Potter had written, 'You are probably going away soon. Please don't go if the winter turns brutish again – rather the cherry orchard than the three sisters.'

Desperately lonely after the Chekhov performance, Hawk manages to lose his virginity to a Soho prostitute. (Though Potter had been writing scenes featuring prostitutes since *Cinderella* in 1966, this was the first to get on the screen.) Meanwhile the voice of Anne Shelton belts out the 1956 hit that gives the play its title:

> Lay down your arms
> And surrender to mine.

The play is set in the summer of Suez (a year later than Potter's own National Service had ended), and briefly looks like becoming a satire on the death throes of Britain's imperial ambitions, but Potter eventually decides that his theme is Hawk's mendacious role-playing. Assuaging his loneliness by posing, in a pub, as a Russian footballer, Yashin from the Moscow Dynamos, Hawk is accidentally unmasked by the arrival of Pete, an old schoolfriend from Yorkshire. 'I felt *alive*,' Hawk tells Pete in justification of the deception. *Lay Down Your Arms* ends with him stealing a classified document, in the hope of proving that he is not really a liar.

Directed by Christopher Morahan, with Nikolas Simmonds as Hawk, *Lay Down Your Arms* was shown on ITV on 23 May 1970. Peter Black in the *Daily Mail* described it as another instalment in Potter's 'revenge on persons who under-rated, ignored, disliked or patronized him on his way towards becoming one of the most complete television dramatists we have'. Philip Purser in the *Sunday Telegraph* said much the same, but was disappointed by *Lay Down Your Arms*: 'oddly self-indulgent . . . Right until the end you couldn't be sure which way it would fizz.'

Asked if she ever had the feeling that Potter was playing games in his declarations of passion for her, like Hawk in *Lay Down Your Arms*, Caroline Seebohm says, 'No, I thought he was honest. And the letters are painful to read because they seem so honest – describing himself weeping in the street after he'd been seeing me. He can't have been doing all that just as a game.'

By the end of 1969, she had at last persuaded him to leave her alone. He wrote to her that 'the disappointment is huge and my grief now is terrible', but 'there remains deep inside me that tiny little spark, unquenchable . . . I shall work now, work with a sort of held-down fury, and one day I will produce something that justifies my life and assuages all its pain and I shall dedicate it to Margaret and you . . . I love you, and you know that. Keep knowing it. Please.'

But she was nervous that it might all start again. 'The following year,' she says, 'I decided to go back to America – part of the reason was to get away from all this. I don't think I went until the end of 1970, and I must have seen him again, because before I went he gave me a book, a biography of Berlioz.' (Trodd says that Potter once proposed a play about Berlioz.) 'At the time, I didn't even read it, but now I suppose it was because Berlioz had an obsessive love for some-one too. I think I wrote to him twice from America, guilty about my flight from him and worried about him, but he didn't answer. He must have moved on.'

CHAPTER 7

Mother – sister – whore

▬

'Dennis Potter wasn't able to shake hands when we met because his fingers were still swollen from the latest attack of arthritis,' wrote Gordon Burn in the *Radio Times* in October 1970.

He had secretarial help for a time; it didn't work because he can't dictate. 'I must see the words coming out on the page, otherwise it doesn't seem real.'

His new play, *Angels Are So Few*, is about a man who has sublimated his fears and phobias and eased his sexual tensions by convincing himself that he is an angel. 'This isn't just some sort of ha-ha comedy illusion,' says Potter. 'The man sincerely believes he is an angel and this fantasy is the total justification for his behaviour and his being. We all entertain fantasies of one kind or another. In a sense the play is about the way we manipulate our fantasies to protect ourselves and what happens to us when they are ripped away. A lot of people do have their wings pulled off in life, after all.'

The BBC had not expected this play. Gareth Davies says, 'I can remember meetings when Dennis had handed in a play which was totally different from the one that had been commissioned, and people would go into a spin! But I would just say, "Is it a good play?"' On this occasion Ann Scott, who was now script editor for *The Wednesday Play*, noted, 'He has now delivered us a play which bears no resemblance to *Condescension* . . . but which we would like to accept in place of that commission. It is entitled *Angels Are So Few* and he delivered it on 15th December, 1969.'

Ann Scott was an Oxford graduate who had recently arrived at Television Centre from BBC overseas radio at Bush House. She describes Potter as 'an inheritance' to her and producer Graeme McDonald from the previous *Wednesday Play* team: 'He already had a well-established record, and there was always an excitement when another of his plays was said to be imminent. The fact that it wasn't necessarily what had been commissioned didn't, on the whole, cause problems. It would usually go straight into production, and we were only too pleased to have it.'

Angels Are So Few was shown as the BBC's *Play for Today* − successor series to *The Wednesday Play*. Ken Trodd says Potter told him it was a satire on the naïvety of Roger Smith's revolutionary politics: 'He said something like, "It's based on my perception of Roger joining causes." But did he just say that to get out of it? Because I don't think it's an analogy that really works.' Smith himself believes that the part of Michael Biddle, the 'angel', was written for him: 'I'd done a little bit of acting in television, and Dennis said he'd written it for me, though in the end Tom Bell played the part.' Possibly the play − a much more successful handling of the 'visitor' motif than *The Bonegrinder* − is also an oblique comment on the Caroline Seebohm affair, or non-affair, which was coming to an end while Potter was writing it.

Subtitled 'A Fable for Television', *Angels Are So Few* opens with the caption, 'Be not forgetful to entertain strangers: For thereby some have entertained strangers unawares − Hebrews 13:1.' It is a day of biting cold, and a muffled postman, blowing on his frozen hands as he empties a suburban pillar box, is astonished to see Biddle, a youngish man, prancing down the road in summer clothes and sockless sandals, singing 'We're Marching to Zion' (the hymn sung by children in *The Rivers of Babylon*). Seeming not to feel the cold, he offers the postman a fallen leaf: 'God made it, a tree dropped it, I found it.' The postman spurns the gift, and drives off, whereupon Biddle sighs, 'I feel *sorry* for you . . . The dog is turned to his own vomit again . . .' We cut abruptly to 'the climax of a terrible road accident' − the postman's van is being crushed by a lorry. 'We shall never know', directs Potter, 'whether the obviously fatal accident is merely out of [Biddle's] imagination or something which really happens; or whether it is coincidence or a direct result of the postman refusing Biddle's present.'

Meanwhile, inside a house in the same street, housewife Cynthia Nicholls, 'slim, blonde, thirtyish, bit untidy, bit on edge', is fretting at the bars of her suburban domestic prison, while her toddler watches the morning children's TV programme. Suddenly the doorbell chimes. It is, of course, Biddle. 'I have come to tell you of beautiful things,' he tells Cynthia. She assumes that he is a Jehovah's Witness or some other kind of itinerant evangelist; but he does not behave like one. 'You have beautiful eyes,' he coos at her. 'Fan-tas-tic . . . And your lips, your lovely lips . . . .were just made for . . . prayer.' Pitying his vulnerability, Cynthia invites him in for a hot drink. When he tells her, in all serious-ness, 'I am an angel', she bursts out laughing, and almost spurns his offer of the fallen leaf. He tells her, 'I feel sorry for you', and – as with the postman – we have a brief vision of Cynthia lying dead (stretched out on a bed, having taken an overdose). But this time the death happens only in Biddle's imagination, for the real Cynthia is now ejecting him from the house. 'I'll be back,' he tells her, blowing her a kiss. 'I am interested in your – salvation. By-ee.'

Cynthia is married to a very correct, repressed assistant bank manager, and we see the couple, that evening, watching a TV docu-mentary about Danish pornography. Richard, the husband, is scandal-ized, but Cynthia, revealing her own sexual frustration in this stale marriage, defends the programme: 'That whore, as you call her, seemed to be exceptionally – extraordinarily – well balanced and alive and – it's the sick people who are scared of sex, the miseries, the tremblers and shakers, the bored and the – the sick people.' To which Richard responds, 'Then I suggest you go to the nearest mental hospital and offer yourself to the first male patient you see.'

A few streets away, Biddle has picked on his next victims, an elderly couple, the Cawsers. He tells them that he is 'a celestial being', and that his wings are folded away beneath his shirt. When Mrs Cawser remembers the image of a female angel on a chapel banner in her childhood, Biddle's face contorts:

BIDDLE: Lady angels? You mean with tits? . . . (*Savagely*) Tits! An angel with tits! No no no no no. We don't have that sort of stuff. There is no sex in heaven. No no. None of that sort of – sort of (*shouts*) filth. We don't put up with it. There is far too much of it. Bodies on top of each other. Disgusting. No room to breathe. Flesh rubbing together. It hurts. It hurts. It bloody well flaming well hurts. Ach! How – how can people *touch* each other like that? (*He is breathing deeply, but then slowly gains control over himself . . .*) But it's all right. It's all right. I don't have to worry about that sort of thing any more. No. I don't have to worry. I'm protected you see. I am *safe*. I am an angel myself. A celestial being.

Mr Cawser protests – 'You're a madman' – and tries to eject him, but Biddle once again pronounces his curse ('I feel extremely sorry for you') and the old man suddenly collapses and dies. Biddle 'runs his tongue along his lips . . . contemplating what he takes to be evidence of his divine powers'. He then pays another visit to Cynthia. Mindful of her husband's sarcastic remark that she should sleep with a mad-man, she lures him to the bedroom, gets him into bed, and tricks him into having sex; but after he has had an orgasm (during which we see a montage of angel statues) he hisses, 'Filthy bitch of Babylon . . . Dirty whore!' Having used him, she now mocks him: 'Fly away, angel. Spread your sexy little wings – and *beat it*!'

Scrambling to the bedroom window and opening it, Biddle protests, 'I am an angel. I am. I am!' But, looking down and realizing what will happen if he jumps, he admits defeat, and runs from the house, 'a man stripped of all his magic, all his fantasy, all his charisma'. Cynthia feels a pang of sympathy – 'Poor angel' – though she is also triumphant at having cuckolded her husband like this. The camera follows Biddle down the street as, on the soundtrack, Al Bowlly sings the song which gives the play its title:

> You may not be an angel,
> For angels are so few,
> But until the day when one comes along,
> I'll string along with you.

Biddle is, of course, another version of David Peters in *Moonlight on the Highway* and Hawk in *Lay Down Your Arms*, a lonely, damaged individual who is (in Potter's own words to Seebohm) 'so frightened of sex' that he takes refuge in obsession and fantasy. Like Hawk, he draws others into his imagination so that they almost believe his lies about himself, while his fondness for despatching the un-deserving (the postman and Cawser) to their deaths suggests that he has a writer's power of life and death over his 'characters'. In other words, despite his apparent lunacy, he is simply a neurotic individual with a writer's imagination. The withered leaf he offers Cynthia, imploring that she recognize its true beauty, seems to carry a hint of Potter's anxiety about his own disfigurement by psoriasis. Instead of rejecting this strange suitor, as Caroline Seebohm had done, the madonna turns whore, but the sexual act arouses deep loathing in Biddle, as it did in Ronnie in *The Rivers of Babylon* and Peters in *Moonlight on the Highway*.

Angels Are So Few, transmitted (in colour, like *Lay Down Your*

Arms) on 5 November 1970, featured a splendidly tortured performance by Tom Bell as Biddle, opposite Christine Hargreaves as Cynthia. Mary Malone in the *Daily Mirror* said that Potter's angel had 'put the fear of the devil into me', and Nancy Banks-Smith, who had now moved to the *Guardian*, wrote, 'Intended, perhaps, to be painfully funny, it was more painful than funny. But then a thing with its wings torn off is only funny to the under-fives.'

This was the last of Potter's plays to be directed by Gareth Davies, who no longer felt enthusiastic and confident about the direction his work was taking: 'I think Dennis perceived that I wasn't particularly sympathetic to his psycho-sexual problems. I felt there was a self-indulgence, a sleazy, masturbatory tone that I didn't like very much. (He talked a lot about the masturbatory aspect of his writing – he'd say, "In my plays, I can create women who do what I want.") We didn't have a row, but it happened that we didn't work together again, and neither of us minded that.'

*

By the time the BBC transmitted *Angels Are So Few*, Ken Trodd had parted company with Kestrel. 'We did those two years at London Weekend, but the regime there fell apart because they didn't get the ratings, and there was an enormous crisis with David Frost and other key people leaving. Kestrel was asked to stay on with the new regime, but we decided not to. I was then poached to go to Granada, which I did for two years, where we made Dennis's *Paper Roses*.'

Trodd explains how this play – one of Potter's second-rankers, but with striking aspects – came into being:

Dennis talked enthusiastically about writing a piece which drew upon his days on the *Herald*. And I guess I was still hoping, even at that point, for him to write something more directly naturalistic and committed – because Kestrel had done Colin Welland's first piece, *Bangelstein's Boys* [1968], about an area of experience, working-class Rugby Union, which nobody knew existed. And it was a new kind of voice and feeling, and very, very un-arty, not the stylish voice of a writer. I also did a Jim Allen piece, with Kestrel for London Weekend, called *Talking Head*, which denounced the way writers were treated by television. And I was still working with Tony Garnett, and not yet quite accepting the separate identity Dennis had as a voice.

Jim Allen, from a working-class background in Manchester, had written for *Coronation Street* before Trodd accepted his play about the building trade, *The Hard Word*, for the BBC's *Thirty Minute Theatre*, beginning Allen's career as a left-wing realist TV playwright. Potter wrote of Allen in 1977, 'His Trotskyite convictions and passionate seriousness have given us some of the most unflinching drama on the box. He challenges and argues and fights every inch of the way.' This was the kind of play Trodd hoped that Potter would write about journalism – perhaps an exposé of the decline into gutter journalism of the *Sun*, which had just been taken over by Rupert Murdoch. 'But when Dennis delivered *Paper Roses* to me, it wasn't like that at all, and when I'd read it, we had one of those rows on the street, in which I denounced him for not writing more of an exposé.'

The play's original title was *Scissors and Paste* ('Paper Roses' is the title of a Fifties pop song, not heard in the production). It portrays the last day in the life of Clarence Hubbard, an ageing Fleet Street hack mocked and spurned by his office colleagues. On the screen we see montages of his headlines over the years, one of which, 'FAITHFUL DOG FACES EVICTION', highlights his own predicament. In deep depression, Clarence orders up all his old cuttings, tips them out of the window, and kills himself.

Trodd's row with Potter about it was 'very, very bitter. I said to Dennis, "You've written a sad piece about an old person." But Dennis, of course, insisted on being himself, despite abuse from me.' Indeed, in production the play moved even further from naturalism, with the addition of a 'frame' story – a television critic who is watching *Paper Roses* at home, and at the end phones in a scornful review of the play. Trodd explains that this 'frame' was added during post-production. The Granada executives had objected to a story, told by a character in the play, about Hubbard exposing his uncircumcised penis to the newsroom staff to prove that he was not Jewish. 'Dennis came up with the idea that we should cut away, at the height of the anecdote, to a critic who is watching while playing miniature golf in his sitting room – we see his reaction to this story rather than the story itself. And from that we built the whole concept of the critic seeing the whole play.'

Paper Roses ends with the critic writing a dismissive review of it – a clever trick on the real reviewers. 'Providing his own review was either an act of deep masochism or a shrewd wheeze to disarm criticism,' wrote Barry Norman in *The Times* after the play was transmitted on 13 June 1971. 'I suspect the latter. Either way, I insist on disagreeing with him: I liked the play.' So did Peter Black in the *Daily Mail*, though he thought that Hubbard (played by Bill Maynard) 'didn't hang together'. Peter Fiddick in the *Guardian* (whose former office building had been used as the play's principal location) judged *Paper Roses* 'the most accurate, detailed re-creation of a newspaper office and newspaper people that I have yet seen on the screen'.

Trodd and director Barry Davis had persuaded Potter to change Hubbard's death from a plunge into the Thames to throwing himself down the office liftshaft. But his defenestration of his cuttings – as he mutters 'Words, words, words' – is his true suicide. The play does not really deal with journalism at all* but, like *Lay Down Your Arms* and *Angels Are So Few*, examines story-telling as a way of constructing one's own identity. Throughout *Paper Roses*, we see Hubbard in flashbacks in his prime, dictating 'stories' down the telephone. Prevented by his age and his peers from continuing to story-tell, he ceases to exist.

*

Asked how much communication he would have with Potter when a play was in gestation, Trodd says,

It depends on the situation. There would have been some where there wouldn't have been very much communication. *Lay Down Your Arms* we talked about because of the common experience [National Service as Russian language clerks]. We would commission knowing roughly what we were going to get from him – but occasionally, with Dennis, knowing less of that than with other writers, and the organization [the BBC or ITV company] knowing even less than we did.

Only very rarely do I remember him putting down even the rudiments of an idea on paper.

From a play about story-telling as self-delusion (*Angels Are So Few*) and another which shows how we become our own stories (*Paper Roses*) it was a small step for Potter to write about someone whose whole professional life has been built round a lie. Adrian Harris in Potter's *Traitor*, televised as the BBC's *Play for Today* on 14 October 1971 (four months after ITV had transmitted *Paper Roses*), is a former Soviet double-agent who has defected to Moscow, as Kim Philby did in 1963. Like *Paper Roses*, *Traitor* does not come from Potter's

---

* Though Ken Trodd says that Granada *World in Action* journalists 'praised Dennis's documentary authenticity in his portrayal of the tabloid world'.

depths, but it is a competent excursion into John le Carré territory.

Potter denied that it was meant to be specifically about Philby: 'That would be a ready-made package . . . to make it directly Philby would be to enter a sphere of writing that I am just . . . not interested in.' So what attracted him to the subject of political treachery? Caroline Seebohm supplies a possible answer:

Roger [Smith] and his gang had become very anti-Dennis. They thought he'd sold out. He'd been their great hero, and there was endless talk of his betrayal of them – of his being a traitor to his class, who'd turned his back on it, and was becoming too successful. And there may have been a part of Dennis that felt this too. He seemed angry with himself, both at his success at making money, and that he couldn't still be a Forest of Dean person. He was a man in conflict about himself.

Potter hinted at this in a *Late Night Line-Up* interview discussing *Traitor*. Asked if betrayal was a theme that obsessed him, he answered,

I think . . . a feeling of betrayal . . . is almost part of our metabolism. I mean, we have at one stage . . . our ideals . . . and then you go into jobs, you compromise, you get sick because you can't think too personally about exactly what it is you are trampling underfoot, and you write, buy food, occupy a big house, take a big mortgage, all the things that I'm doing.

He did not admit that he had deserted the Left, but described himself as 'a kind of liberal social democrat, whatever that may mean'.

Traitor portrays the ex-spy Harris being confronted in his Moscow flat by a team of Western journalists, who are puzzled by his claim to love the England he has betrayed. Gulping whisky, Harris belligerently defines Englishness, mocking the 'so-called patriotism' of his Etonian upbringing. Potter emphasized that this was the centre of the play: 'Flags and drums and pomp and circumstance are all anathema to me, whereas there's that long, long, long beat of Englishness which can be very aggressive but on the whole is slightly melancholy, slightly rueful, and in many important ways extraordinarily gentle.'

Although Harris's silver-spoon childhood and upbringing appear to be outside Potter's experience, there are points of resemblance. Harris has had as tormented a relationship with his father as did Nigel Barton. The father has 'spent most of his life digging below the top-soil', as an archaeologist rather than a miner – he is in search of the remains of Camelot, and likes to quote from Tennyson's Arthurian poetry (as does Guy Burgess in Alan Bennett's *An Englishman Abroad*, shown eleven years later). Harris's schooldays, like Nigel's, are marked by his realization that he is different from the herd. Set in this context, the murder for which the adult Harris has been responsible – the killing of a Soviet defector who was about to unmask him as a spy – seems no more immoral than the violent slap administered to the young Harris by a sadistic teacher.

At the end of *Traitor* we are jolted into realizing that we too may have been deceived by Harris. In the final minutes of the play, a flashback shows him, just before the journalists arrive, discovering a KGB microphone planted in the flat. 'For God's sake remember the microphone,' he tells himself as he begins to entertain the visitors. Everything that has been said by him in *Traitor* may, therefore, be a lie.

Traitor was the first of three Potter plays to be directed by Alan Bridges, whose style was more sophisticated than Gareth Davies's. Potter wrote admiringly of him the following year, 'Bridges dips into scenes that you sense have already begun: he catches his characters in mid-activity, cuts in and out more swiftly, more dynamically than any other director now working in television, and even ensures that his extras do not look like wax dummies on the point of melting.'

Nancy Banks-Smith was more impressed by John le Mesurier's performance as Harris than by *Traitor* itself: 'Cursed with so Hamlet-like a face, he seems to have been coerced into comedy. This, his Hamlet, was worth waiting for.' Sylvia Clayton in the *Daily Telegraph* thought that 'Harris emerged as a less interesting and complex character than Philby', but Chris Dunkley in *The Times* judged it 'a superbly persuasive portrait'.

*

Graeme McDonald, who produced *Traitor*, sometimes visited Potter at Ross. 'He was very much easier to converse with on his home ground,' says McDonald, 'so one went and saw him there. Margaret was always very welcoming.' Gareth Davies says he 'stayed for the weekend once or twice. Margaret was a very considerable woman, who held that family together, and somehow coped with Dennis. There was the atmosphere of a perfectly happy home, and I don't think for a moment that he was a bad father – he always seemed concerned about the children.' Davies also recalls 'Dennis giving me a long lecture that I wasn't making enough provision for my pension. He'd read PPE at Oxford, so he had a fair knowledge of economics, and he gave me a long talking-to about it. He was very organized about his finances, very practical; not at all what you might expect.' Stanley Rosenthal, who became Potter's accountant in 1978, says, 'One didn't have to explain twice to Dennis anything to do with financial matters. He grasped everything immediately.' Frank Bloom, the lawyer who dealt with his film and TV contracts in later years, says the same and adds, 'Dennis was always very practical and realistic, not somebody to waste time by fighting over every last detail.'

Ann Scott paid a few visits to the Potters at home: 'On one occasion, Dennis was very ill, and it was like a visit to a sickroom. Another time, Margaret had laid on a formal tea, with sandwiches, and I was a bit startled by this. But you could see that he really loved the family, he was very wrapped up in them all and proud of them.'

Ken Trodd has no recollection of going to Morecambe Lodge: 'There was a lot of activity between us on the phone. A lot of telephoning. And of course he was always coming to London. But I don't think I ever set foot in the Ross house. He just didn't want it.' (Jane and Sarah Potter recall Trodd visiting once, when they were very young.)

As before, a few journalists were allowed to see Potter at home. Philip Oakes, writing a *Sunday Times* profile of him in the autumn of 1971, around the time of *Traitor*, reported:

Potter lives with his wife Margaret and their three children in a roomy Victorian house at Ross-on-Wye, only eight miles from the village where he was born. He has never been abroad. 'To me, travel spells travail.' Planes fill him with dread. No sane man, he says, would choose to step into one of those things. He measures distance by the time it takes to get there on foot: 'I belong to a walking culture, entirely pre-motor.'

But mostly interviewers were kept at bay, and seen in London.

'Dad wasn't a practical man,' says Sarah Potter, who was ten at the time of Oakes's visit (Jane was eleven and Robert six).

If there were any jobs to be done, and Mum couldn't do them herself, she had to get somebody in. Dad once had to wake her up in the middle of the night because the lights had fused.

He couldn't do the washing up because of his hands, but he was the most generous man you could come across with money – he just wanted Mum to have everything she ever wanted. As soon as they were well enough off to have a dishwasher or a domestic help, a gardener, she had it. He couldn't have been better in that respect.

One of his great pleasures was padding down in the middle of the night and making one of his favourite meals in the slow cooker. He'd have the contents of tins of tomatoes all over the wall! Great bits of something else on the knobs of the kitchen units. But it was a real pleasure to him. He mostly made stuff to go with pasta – he'd never follow a recipe, just make it up as he went along. Sometimes they were wonderful, sometimes not. But it gave him a lot of pleasure. Although he didn't want to go abroad at this stage of his life, he was very adventurous in his taste in food.

Sarah's elder sister Jane says that the children 'were all involved in Dad's work from early on – I clearly remember watching *Where the Buffalo Roam*, and Dad reading his scripts to me and Mum. Indeed we all went to the "shoot" [in the Forest of Dean] for *A Beast with Two Backs*.' However, Sarah emphasizes, 'We didn't get taken to the studios – the first time I went on a set was for *Dreamchild* [in 1984–5, when she was in her early twenties]. When we were still at school, Mum and Dad didn't want us to be involved in it all. I think that was a very conscious decision on their part. I think they'd seen what had happened to other people's children, and didn't want us to feel any pressure.' Potter himself said of this, 'We didn't want them to grow up in that media world I'd belonged to.' Sarah continues, 'Obviously we were aware of the fact that he was different, through the illness alone. And we knew that he was widely talked about. We were never picked on as such, at school, but there was some general teasing, particularly after *Casanova*.'

*

Oakes's *Sunday Times* profile was to mark the start of transmission of *Casanova*, which was to begin its six-part run on BBC2 on 16 November 1971, a month after the broadcast of *Traitor* on BBC1. 'The Corporation calls it a six-part series,' wrote Oakes. 'Potter, on the other hand, regards it as a single play divided into six episodes.' The subject-matter proved far more congenial to Potter than newspaper hacks or ageing spies, and *Casanova* contained some of his best writing to date, though its success was hampered by a stylistic mis-judgement – the over-use of flashbacks.

He explained that the project had originated several years earlier:

I had a weekly slot as a book critic on *The Times*, briefly, and one thing that came in was a new translation of [Casanova's] memoirs. I thought, 'Oh, that's interesting. That's something one might write about.' But of course as soon as I said that I had to stop reading them, and I never reviewed them because, as a writer, I didn't want to know too much.

This would have been one of the twelve volumes of Willard R. Trask's new translation of Casanova's *Mémoires*, published between 1966 and 1971. Potter admitted that he had soon stopped reading the enormously long text: 'The credits say [*Casanova*] was "based on" them but that's crap. I had a list of his dates, when he was in prison, when he escaped, how he ended, and the details of some of the women, but that was about it. Most memoirs are self-serving and adorned with lies and I thought his were probably the same.'

The posthumously published *Mémoires* may all be one enormous tall story ('I simply don't believe them,' Potter told Philip Oakes), but they do give a vivid picture of an era when, as one of Casanova's biographers writes, 'the sex act was in general no more to be hidden than the act of eating'. Besides detailing the narrator's numerous conquests of women (and occasionally men), they tell how the adventurer Giacomo Casanova, born in Venice in 1725, made a spectacular escape from a prison sentence in the Doge's Palace, and later worked as a spy for the Venetian Republic, before spending a respectable old age as librarian to a German duke.

Interviewing Potter about *Casanova*, Philip Oakes suggested that the BBC saw the serial as a successor to their Tudor period piece *The Six Wives of Henry VIII* (shown in 1970). Potter responded contemptuously:

To me, the term 'costume drama' means something totally pickled. It doesn't interest me in the slightest. What first seized my imagination was the myth of Casanova . . . he was concerned with religious and sexual freedom, and these are things we have to address ourselves to now . . . He lived in a time very much like our own. The same fear of sex as a liberating agent is abroad now: we even have our own Inquisition.

He probably meant Mary Whitehouse's campaign to 'clean up' television.

He also told Oakes that writing *Casanova* as 'a six-part play' was 'wildly ambitious', adding, 'I wanted to do an accumulative portrait, something that wasn't swallowed up as soon as the screen went dark.' He explained the appeal of the six-part format:

I wanted to do a portrait . . . that accumulated, that sifted through layers of various incidents, and how they changed perspective, like the things we think about. We're walking compendiums (in a way) of memory, and previous instincts embalmed by present states of mind, and we know that we change perspective as we mature or decay . . . And to do one's own thing over six hours suddenly seemed to be a valid and rather exciting thing to attempt . . .

He framed the highly episodic story with the most exciting thing in Casanova's life, his imprisonment and attempts to escape. In the first episode Casanova is caught *in flagrante* with one of his female conquests, is charged with atheism and fornication, and is thrust into a tiny cell beneath the eaves of the Doge's Palace. (Potter told Mark Shivas, who produced *Casanova*, that he had never been abroad, did not want to, and imagined Venice and the other settings much more vividly than he would ever have experienced them.) After a while Casanova's skin breaks out in 'weeping angry sores' and is treated with sulphur ('the stuff out of hell', comments Lorenzo the gaoler), and he describes himself in words that Potter could have used during the worst bouts of his illness: 'a degraded and humiliated lump of confused flesh'. When, after being denied pen and ink, he manages to use mulberry juice to scrawl a message about an escape route to a neighbouring prisoner, one recalls Potter's own remark, 'I was depressed and ill and in pain, and I found that my writing was a pass out of it.'

Casanova's recollections take striking visual form. In several previous plays, Potter had developed the device of subliminally swift and repeated flashbacks or cutaways to suggest what is passing through a character's mind – in *Traitor*, for example, we see the murder of a defecting Russian spy several times in brief glimpses – and *Casanova* makes extensive use of this technique (too extensive, as it turned out). This is one example of many, from episode 2:

ROSE: Do you love me?

CASANOVA: From the moment I set eyes on you.

(*She looks at him, a questioning sort of look, peculiarly vulnerable.*)

([*cut to*] *A bedroom doorway. Another girl, framed exactly as* ROSE, *gives him the same sort of look. Cut swiftly.*)

(*A bedroom doorway. Only the face changes. Cut swiftly.*)

(*A bedroom doorway. Another duplication, another girl. Cut swiftly.*)

(ROSE *looking at him.*)

I may not mean it the way other men mean it. But I mean it all the same. In my way.

This form of *déjà vu* – which Potter later described in his first novel, *Hide and Seek*, as 'hypnogogic images, the strangely potent montages which come at a mind already lapsed into a sort of sleep' – expresses Casanova's ambiguous feelings about his women much more effectively than words could do. At other moments, images of sexual abandon are juxtaposed with those of terrible violence (glimpses of the public execution of a would-be regicide), again suggesting doubts and confusions in Casanova's mind at the very moment of sexual conquest.

By the fifth episode, Potter has developed another startling visual trick. Lorenzo the loutish Venetian gaoler suddenly metamorphoses, in Casanova's mind, into a beautiful young nun with the laugh of a whore, who pulls off her habit to reveal her nakedness. Coming to his senses, Casanova endeavours to explain what he has seen and heard:

CASANOVA: Oh God – she undressed . . . The nun.

LORENZO: (*cackle*) A nun? Undressed?

CASANOVA: (*mutter*) Mother – sister – whore.

LORENZO: You are mad, signore.

CASANOVA: All the same. They are all the same.

(*Without any ceremony* LORENZO *kicks him.*)

LORENZO: Get back into your bed!

CASANOVA: (*scream*) I hate them! Hate them!

(*Pause. A matter-of-fact* LORENZO *looks down at* CASANOVA *with a mild interest.*)

LORENZO: Who do you hate, signore?

(CASANOVA *is crying like a child.*)

Who?

(*Pause.*)

CASANOVA: (*whisper*) Women. I – hate them, Lorenzo. I hate women.

The image of the naked nun, chanting 'Mother – sister – whore', haunts the last two episodes of *Casanova*.

Potter later said, 'I assumed Casanova must have had that thing they biologically refer to as *tristitia post coitum* – the sadness after fucking . . . Even if, like Georges Simenon, he had penetrated 10,000 women, or however many it was, that was a very obsessive and driven thing to have had to do . . . ' But he offered no psychological explanation for such a compulsion.

In the fifth episode, Casanova experiences a tormented relationship with an Englishwoman who does not sleep with him (she seems to be separated from her husband). 'It doesn't matter about – my loving you,' he tells her, in words that could have come from Potter's letters to Caroline Seebohm. 'It is. It exists. It won't change. It can't be altered. It belongs to me now. Just let me say it. That's all. Just let me hear myself saying it . . . Dear God, I mean it.' But does he? Could he be just another story-teller, like Hawk, Biddle, Hubbard and Harris? 'I always listen to myself,' he tells her, just as Nigel Barton had said to Jill.

Casanova ends cheerfully, with an ingenious double climax (in both senses of the word). The young Casanova makes his escape through the roof of his Venetian prison, just as we see his older self dying, in a German castle, at the very moment that a girl with curly blond hair has allowed him a final sexual encounter. Her name is Caroline.

CHAPTER 8

I went through everything
Marlow does

———

'People hated it,' Potter recalled of *Casanova* nearly twenty years later. 'It was voted the worst series of the year by the critics.' This is untrue. Reviewers' response to the first episode, shown on 16 November 1971, was warm. 'The entwining of past and present was elegantly done,' judged Peter Black. 'It was fascinating to watch Frank Finlay [in the title role], with his peculiar ability to project opposite qualities at once, clothing Potter's intentions so faithfully.' Nancy Banks-Smith admired 'the shapely swing of the thing, the night–day, waking–dreaming swing between his imprisoned despair and the liquid idyll of a love remembered in flashback'.

However, Richard Last in the *Daily Telegraph* thought that, even in the first episode, the 'constant use of flashback' had got 'rather out of hand'. One episode and many flashbacks later, Last was feeling 'as disorientated as Casanova in his prison cell'. By the fifth episode, Alan Brien in *The Sunday Times* was mocking it as 'a six-part serial by Dennis Repeater in which each successive episode repeats all the most boring sequences of its predecessors so that the final episode will be nothing but a trailer for the first'. Mary Whitehouse was now complaining of the serial's 'lewdness'; Brien pointed out that, in Italian, her surname would be Casablanca.

When *Casanova* was repeated in 1974, as two long episodes shown on two consecutive nights, Potter allowed it to be re-edited so that the story was all told from the perspective of Casanova in old age – thereby destroying much of the *raison d'être* of the original.

With *Casanova* finished, ideas for plays were tumbling out of him. Roderick Graham, producer of a BBC repertory series called *Company of Eight*, commissioned a Potter script to be called *Mustang Has*

Already Been Used, in which 'a major British car firm employs a famous poet (of the Auden generation) to think of a name for their latest car'. Potter also signed up to write a *Thirty Minute Theatre* script, *Instant Mammon*, in which 'a clergyman agrees to advertise an ethical product for an advertising agency'. Mark Shivas, who had produced *Casanova*, commissioned a play about Stalin: 'His last days, surrounded by his confederates in Moscow. His memories and reflections on the past.' This was to last two hours, and Clive Goodwin noted that 'Dennis very much regards it as a peak in his TV writing career.'

Meanwhile he had already delivered another play to the BBC. 'It's my first really religious play,' he explained to Philip Oakes, 'about the experience of knowing that there is a God, and then losing it.' Oakes gathered that

the man it happens to is an actor, and the loss of faith occurs when he's filming a dog-food commercial on Barnes Common – a filthy place, says Potter, spectacularly littered with contraceptives.

He saw his script on its journey round the BBC's Television Centre and noted a memo pinned to the first page. 'It read: "Does this play have to be so contraceptively explicit?" Well, it does. And for the first time ever I added my own note. It said: "Don't alter a word."'

Of all the battles he's fought, says Potter, this promises to be the bloodiest.

However, there was no battle. The BBC were delighted with the play, *Follow the Yellow Brick Road* – as they should have been, for it was his best (and most personal) script since *Moonlight on the Highway*.

It opens almost identically to *Moonlight*. Jack Black has an appointment to see a psychiatrist at 'an old London hospital', and he is irritating an elderly patient in the waiting area. Instead of Al Bowlly songs, Jack's head is full of the conviction that he is in a television play. 'Not much action, is there?' he complains. 'Hardly any dialogue at all. Just background noises . . . People will switch over. Or switch off.' He turns to the camera:

JACK: (*soft hiss*) Stop looking at me.

  (*Camera moves in, steadily.*)

  (*Louder*) Stay still!

  (*Camera stops. He stares out at us belligerently. Then, the camera not moving, he visibly relaxes. Fast zoom into big close-up. He flaps at it as though beating away a venomous wasp buzzing at his head.*)

(*Panic*) Get off! Off!

(*Camera retreats, fast. He stares out at us. Pause. Then bullet-fast zoom right into his eyes.*)

(*Shout*) Get away! Get away!

Potter had framed *Paper Roses* with a jokey reminder (the watching critic) that it was just a television play. Now the joke has turned into nightmare, and invaded the play itself.

'I don't want to be in this play,' says Jack pathetically; but we quickly learn that being on television, trapped in other people's scripts, is his job – he is a TV actor. The old lady in the hospital waiting area recognizes him from the Krispy Krunch biscuit commercial, in which he tiptoes downstairs for a midnight snack and finds his wife already eating the biscuits. 'I caught her all right,' Jack agrees with the old woman; but in real life he has caught his wife *in flagrante* with another man. 'Had her mouth full, didn't she?' remarks the old lady, still thinking of Krispy Krunch. 'Really enjoying it and all.'

Dr Whitman, the psychiatrist, recognizes Jack from the commercial, too, and suggests that he must prefer acting in plays. Jack denies this: 'The commercials are *clean* . . . Husbands and wives who love each other . . . There's laughter and . . . sunshine and kids playing in meadows. Nobody mocks the finest human aspirations . . . It's the *plays* that do all the damage . . . They are dirty and corrupt! . . . Despair. Violence. Filth. Sadism. Adultery . . . They turn gold into hay . . . Angels into whores. Love into a s-s-sticky slime . . . ' His sexual disgust is mixed up with hatred of the New Left politics of the television people: 'They go to Trotskyite meetings. They sleep with the same women . . . The whole world can be reduced to a hairy lump between a woman's legs . . . That stinking hole!'

Whitman tries to reassure Jack that his conviction of being in a play is not abnormal: 'A lot of people think God writes the script.' Jack agrees that he once had this feeling:

JACK: When I was little, I thought God was watching me all the time . . . I remember once . . . I was riding this tricycle down a hill near where we used to live . . . The clouds massed up in great banks over the valley down below took on this – this (*searches for the word*) radiance . . . I got off my trike as quickly as I could . . . Trembling like a leaf . . . Because God was *too near*.

WHITMAN: So – all your life you've felt – watched. Observed.

(JACK *nods, dumbly.*)

And do you still believe in God?

(*Silence. The word is, as it were, dragged out of him. It sounds strangled, or peculiarly reluctant.*)

JACK: No.

WHITMAN: I think perhaps you do. I think you want to –

JACK: (*shout*) He isn't there! . . . For years and years I hadn't thought about it, hadn't considered it. I just – assumed – somehow – that he – it – was there, still there, still watching, still *present.* Then . . . one morning – daybreak – I – well, I'd been up all night. Couldn't think. Couldn't sleep. Couldn't sit. Couldn't stand . . . I was alone. I could see light in a chink through the curtains. First light . . . New day starting. What for? What *for*? So . . . for the first time in years and years . . . I got down on my knees and I closed my eyes and I put my hands together and I said to myself I won't ask for anything . . . I'll just let *you* come. I'll just see if you are there . . . I'll wait for . . . *the word* . . . I waited and waited. I just wanted the word to drop into my mind. I was open for it. *Ready* for it. In my mind I got off my tricycle again and ran to the side, ran to the grass bank – (*He stops.*)

WHITMAN: (*quietly*) You mustn't expect childhood exp–

(JACK *interrupts with a near shout.*)

JACK: Slime!

WHITMAN: (*blink*) What?

JACK: That was the word! Slime! That was the message I got. No God. On my knees with my eyes shut I got this one word or feeling or impression or – I don't know – but there it was, long slippery strands of it – slime – nothing else but slime. (*Chokes.*) And dirt and – stinking slime contaminating everything. All over my hands. All over my face. In my mouth. In my eyes.

Jack lurches out of the consulting room, about to vomit, and Whitman sighs, 'Dear God. Why do we suffer so?'

Stumbling into the car park, Jack finds his wife, Judy, waiting in her sports car. 'The car stinks,' he mutters at her. 'A bitch on heat. You can't mistake it. Follows you round, that particular stench.' When she asks where he is living, and why he doesn't come home, he answers, 'Because I don't like coming in and finding my wife being screwed in my own bed.' He allows her to drive them both to Barnes Common, where he has taken part in a dog-food commercial for Waggytail Din-Din, with a Great Dane: 'A nice dog . . . They put down plastic butter-cups on the grass.' Judy now admits that, while the commercial was being shot, she went to bed with yet another man, Jack's agent. Jack hits her, knocking her down, and then kicks her. 'You cheap sex-sodden little slut,' he says coldly. 'You've got to tell me all about it. Otherwise . . . I'll walk down the road to Hammersmith Bridge. And I'll wait for the camera. And then I'll jump in the stinking, garbage polluted river.' (This is the first of many allusions to that bridge in Potter's work.)

We flashback to the seduction of Judy by the agent, Colin Sands, whose surname hints at Clive Goodwin, and whose flat is 'as trendy as a new boutique'. Judy tells Sands about her husband's sexual problems: 'Jack can't do it. Or *won't* . . . He – starts all right. Like it used to be. But then . . . It's as though he's *transfigured* with . . . disgust . . . He says that love is more than just *a sticky slime*.'

Jack's response to Judy's account of this is to jump into her car and drive it straight at her. Before we know whether he has hit her, we cut (via the Waggytail Din-Din commercial) to Jack in Sands's flat. He seems to have come to kill Sands, but the agent is out, and Jack is being entertained by Sands's nymphet wife Veronica. To her astonishment, he admits that he has long been infatuated with her:

JACK: I remember when I first met you . . . Two years ago, almost . . . And then I didn't see you for months and months . . . Pure. You are *pure* . . . Pure and clean and honest! . . . I wrote to you. Lots of times . . . But I ripped them up. The letters. You wouldn't have understood them . . . Every time your name came out on the page it danced and danced on the end of my pen. Things I had no right to say . . . Ver-on-ic-a . . . I was writing to God . . . Look at you – clean – pure – so, so – so *divine* . . . I love you. I love, love, love, you.

Not over-endowed with intelligence, Veronica has been gawping at Jack, but she understands these last words, and responds briskly: 'OK. We've got an hour . . . Unzip me, Jack.'

The Waggytail commercial cuts in as an ironic commentary ('Dogs can't wait for it – Dogs can't live without it') and takes us back to the psychiatrist's room, where Jack has arrived once more. This time the sensitive Whitman is absent, and a younger, tougher doctor, Bilson, who sat in on the previous consultation, has taken his place. Jack keeps muttering Veronica's words in horror: '*Unzip me . . .*' Bilson asks what he has been up to since they last met. 'Went to Barnes Common,' answers Jack. 'Plastic buttercups . . . And dogshit on the grass . . . And French letters hanging on the bushes. Like punctured balloons.' There is no mention of Judy or what may have happened to her.

Bilson briskly dishes out tranquillizers to Jack: 'They are very new. Very good. Mogabrium . . . We are making considerable advances in biochemistry these days . . . The crucial thing to realize is that there is absolutely no need to walk around burdened with a sense of disgust. No man should carry *that* sort of cross nowadays . . . If Mogabrium had been available two thousand years ago – well, I can think of at least one wild man who would have stuck to carpentry' (an echo of Dr Childs's remark about Bunyan in *Moonlight on the Highway*). As Jack leaves, we see Bilson himself downing a handful of his own tranquillizers.

Once again, Judy is waiting for Jack in her car – but we are no longer in reality. This is a commercial for Mogabrium, backed with 'Somewhere Over the Rainbow' – Potter specifies 'the original Judy Garland vocal if possible'. Back projection 'totally encapsulates the seemingly speeding car with glorious cornflake-packet colours', as we see Jack and Judy, 'heads back, hair blowing', laughing and laughing 'like the happy cretins in a TV commercial'. The car grows smaller and smaller, disappearing into a 'glorious blue'; then the commercial cuts to a laboratory, where Jack, in white coat, quotes from St Paul as he holds up his phial of Mogabrium: 'Whatsoever things are true, whatsoever things are honest . . . whatsoever things are of good report, if there be any virtue –' Then he dries, and mutters, 'Oh shit! Sorry everybody!' The camera pulls out and we are, of course, in a television studio. 'Never mind, Jack,' instructs the voice of the director. 'Try it again. Keep it punchy!' Jack begins again, and the camera pulls even further back, leaving us with a final glimpse of 'all the disconcerting electronic mess'.

Potter has lifted his hero's name from Jack Black, the sex-hating cobbler in Dylan Thomas's *Under Milk Wood*. 'Follow the Yellow Brick Road', as Judy reminds Sands in Potter's play, is the song that 'all the little dwarfs' sing to her namesake Judy Garland in Oz (dwarf references abound in *Follow the Yellow Brick Road*: Sands is trying to book 'a dwarf with a German accent' for a TV play, and Veronica's poodle is called Dwarfie). But Sands remarks, 'The Wizard of Oz was a *fraud* . . . a sad, watery-eyed old impostor', and the play contains no hint that Jack's childhood belief in God was more valid than his overwhelming sense of slime, or his ludicrous conviction that Veronica is pure.

The Yellow Brick Road also stands, of course, for glitzy commercialism (*The Wizard of Oz* is a satire on the American Dream), indeed for television itself. Potter wrote in the introduction to the published text of *Follow the Yellow Brick Road*:

The single play is one of the last areas of television where the irritating cadences of the individual voice can still be heard. While this is so I am (perhaps perversely) honour bound to submit scripts for the mauling. But I cannot help at times grieving for work that has been swallowed and perhaps even for a talent which is being exhausted. I follow a yellow brick road.

In Jack Black, Potter finally finds the perfect expression of his sexual and religious turmoil. Yet he himself, writing twelve years later, referred to *Follow the Yellow Brick Road* as a 'low point' in his career, remarking that

the manuscript . . . might well have been delivered up to the BBC Television Centre in Wood Lane with tell-tale stains of old vomit on its wide, white margins (coals to Newcastle, so to speak) . . . [It] reads now, to me, like the memory of a thumb being pressed too hard down upon a tender ganglion of protesting nerves . . . What is certain is that if I had continued in the Jack Black vein, I would long ago have ceased to write anything worthwhile at all.

Nevertheless, while he was waiting for *Follow the Yellow Brick Road* to be produced, he wrote another (and a far less successful) play in the same vein, a *Thirty Minute Theatre* script for the BBC called *Mushrooms on Toast*. It opens with the 'very, very English' Janet Poole coping with a surprise visit to her home by 'two menacing young Americans', Jim and Clyde. Their Connecticut company has just taken over a British pharmaceutical firm, for which Janet's husband Dick, a research chemist, is developing a new strain of mushroom. At first, the Americans manipulate her mercilessly, insinuating that her sex life is 'unstable' and implying that Dick is having an affair with his secretary.

Then Dick phones from the office, and tells Janet that the Americans are 'hatchet men' who are vetting her suitability as a Company Wife. We see him putting the phone down, grumbling at Janet's apparent inattention to what he has been saying ('Bloody stupid thick vicious selfish spoilt *snake*!') and leering at his secretary – the Americans have obviously sniffed out the truth. But Janet isn't stupid, and she now does her best to ruin Dick's prospects with the company. She insults the visitors: 'Americans. You look the same, think the same, talk the same. Like billiard balls.' She insinuates that they are homosexuals, shocks them by saying she is known in the neighbourhood as 'an easy lay', and throws them out of the house with the words 'Go screw a mushroom!' However, when the rector pays her a visit, she reveals the depth of her own loneliness, begging him to embrace her. He leaves, embarrassed, and – in the last few moments of the play – Janet phones Dick at the office:

JANET: I'm just ringing to say you'll find your meal in the oven. No. That's all. Bye. (*Fractional pause. She comes back into room, shuts door, leans against it for a moment. Then sits down. Lights cigarette. Giggle*) Mushrooms and something. Or something with mushrooms. (*She stops smiling. Move in to big close-up. Whisper*) In the oven. With – with – (*Pause. Hold. Pull back. Brightly*) With my head.

Mushrooms on Toast was rejected by the producer of *Thirty Minute Theatre* in January 1972 – no reason for this is recorded in the BBC files – and Potter was paid only the first-half fee. Typically, he eventually reused most of the ideas in it.

In April 1972 Graeme McDonald commissioned a *Play for Today* from him with the working title *The Angrier Brigade* (the Angry Brigade was a terrorist group that had recently carried out several bombings in Britain): 'A group of people have kidnapped someone for political ransom and have to decide whether or not to kill him when their demands are refused.' But Potter was soon in no position to write anything.

*

Since his last spell in hospital, three years earlier, the doctors had tried to control his psoriasis with steroid ointment and pills, and with polythene dressings; after the initial trial, Methotrexate was not used. Philip Oakes, interviewing him in the autumn of 1971, noted that he required 'eight hours' medication a day'. The children nicknamed him 'The Ghost of Morecambe Lodge' because they would hear the polythene rustling in the night. For long periods he was unable even to touch them. 'Obviously he couldn't play with us,' says Sarah, 'especially after his hands gave way. But Mum was very tactile, so we didn't feel insecure about it. Dad used to tell the story of Rob playing with his friends in the garden and seeing him appear at a window. Rob shouted to his friends, "Look, quick, see his hands." It was just a point of interest.' Jane says, 'Mum was the one who did all the touching and kissing and cuddling. Dad found it difficult, quite apart from the state of his hands, but he addressed that, and he got better at it later.'

Sarah emphasizes that he bore it patiently. 'He had to learn how to do everything again, simple things like filling a kettle or opening a tin. It was like losing a sense. But I don't ever remember him whingeing or complaining. He would just strap a pen to his hand so he could carry on writing.' He told Oakes:

I believe that we choose our illnesses. I was always angry, and I have the feeling that the anger in me was turned inwards. Either it turns into your mind, or you're fortunate enough for it to turn into your limbs. I was in hospital five times, and finally came to terms with what was happening. I had to acknowledge that it was incurable; but at the same time it was controllable.

However, soon after this interview, at the end of February 1972, the situation changed dramatically.

The steroids were now failing to control the psoriasis, which had spread over most of his body – indeed, the medication seemed to be making his skin worse. One day later that month, he was visited by his general practitioner, Dr Smith of Ross-on-Wye, who brought with him a dermatologist from Cheltenham. They found that the palms of his hands were so severely fissured from the psoriasis that he could not flex his fingers, 'a movement already difficult,' they noted, 'on account of the arthropathy of the small joints of the hand'.

They decided to take him off the steroids at once, and considered putting him on Methotrexate once more; but there was a likelihood that this would cause liver damage, unless he gave up alcohol. 'He drinks quite a lot of alcohol and smokes heavily,' the specialist noted. 'I cannot see this patient becoming a teetotaller.'

A few days later he developed a dangerously high temperature of over 104 degrees, apparently in reaction to steroid withdrawal, and his psoriasis became so bad that he could not open his eyes. 'The skin closed around my fist. I could only move my left arm. I was clad in clothes which continually itched. I had gone into a fever and was suffering from a steroid reaction. I was under the illusion that there was a cat in the bed and that it was eating my ankles. I thought, it can't be, you silly bugger, but I still believed it. I was in such hellish pain that I couldn't tell which limb was which.'

Haydn Lloyd, dentist to the Potter family and one of the few close friends that they had made in the Ross area, came to see him, and recalls finding his arm 'incredibly hot' when touching him. 'It was as though he was balancing Lux flakes on the arm – the skin was flaking so fast and falling off, on to the ground, as you watched.'

An ambulance took Potter to Cheltenham Hospital. 'People say they've got psoriasis,' he remarked years later, 'and they mean they've got some really uncomfortable itches, which don't hurt and don't make the skin flake off. With the extreme psoriatic arthropathy that I have you can't find a point of normal skin. Your pores, your whole face, your eyelids, everything is caked and bleeding, to such a degree that without drugs you could not possibly survive.' Jane Potter says, 'We all thought he was going to die.'

He was put back on steroids. As soon as his temperature had dropped and he could see again, he insisted on going home, though he was scarcely able to walk or even stand up for long. His hands were now almost useless: Dr Smith noted that each middle finger was 'acutely painful and swollen and fixed now with flexion deformity', so that writing was out of the question.

'He has borne his illness with great fortitude,' observed Smith, 'but now feels no longer able to carry on as things are.' He had cut down his drinking severely, and was prepared to try Methotrexate again, though he was well aware of the risk to his liver. It was decided to send him to a London teaching hospital, and on 13 May 1972 he was admitted to the London Hospital in Whitechapel.

'I think the hospital didn't allow children to visit,' says Sarah Potter.

An exception was made, but we only went once or twice, and the experience was harrowing. It was our first experience of loads of sick people in one place, and Jane and I were a bit spooked by the whole thing – and also, obviously, by seeing Dad in that condition (Robert was too young to understand).

When it was time to go, I remember Jane crying, and I think it was even worse for Dad. So after that, we were farmed out to relatives – Dad's parents, or Mum's brother and sister-in-law, who lived in the Forest – and Mum would travel up to see him two or three times a week.

Margaret recalled her feelings in an interview six years later: 'I saw his poor hands going . . . For three months he lay on his back. Then month after month I watched him struggling to form letters with a thick black crayon wedged in the crook of his bent forefinger. I used to look at him struggling and think, "Oh my God, what next?"'

Ann Scott, who had been script editor for *Angels Are So Few* and *Traitor*, invited Margaret to stay with her in Notting Hill when she was visiting Dennis. 'I remember her being almost surprised when a friend of mine called in,' says Scott. 'She hardly seemed to know that there were other people in London besides Roger Smith, Ken Trodd and Clive Goodwin, Dennis's little group of friends, who were the only people she ever saw there.'

Ann Scott learned quite a lot about Margaret during these visits:

I realized she was Dennis's shield, his reality; she was where he was grounded. She was very domestic, and she saw me as belonging at the other end of that spectrum. She had three children and looked after a house, and I was doing anything but that, at that time, so she would talk to me as though I was missing out on real life, which always rather puzzled me, because it felt quite real where I was, too. But I think she was a bit defensive in London.

Scott herself visited Potter in the London Hospital:

I went several times, and he was struggling with the awful things that were happening around him in the ward – people dying in the next bed, and so on. I remember asking him, why he didn't go into analysis, since clearly stress was the trigger for psoriasis. And he gave the reply that he gave everybody who asked him that: that it might stop him writing.

In Potter's 1973 play *Only Make Believe* the disturbed writer who is the central character says, 'I can't go spilling out all that valuable material to . . . a quack on the far side of a walnut desk. No fear. I should never write another word if my dim shapes and shadows and gibbering hobgoblins were cleaned up and swept up and disinfected and castrated . . .'

Ann Scott continues, 'Also, he wouldn't take responsibility for the illness, but handed it over to the doctors – it was not something that he was going to deal with from the inside out. Not giving up cigarettes and coffee, when clearly they're both involved in arthritis – it was as if he was saying, "This is me, and I smoke and drink coffee, and they can look after the illness."'

The London Hospital consultants initially gave Potter the drug Azothiaprine, to treat his arthritis. This was administered by suppositories, which caused diarrhoea. His hands were put in splints and he was smeared all over with Vaseline. 'I couldn't sit up. I could just about move my left arm.' The medical notes confirm this: 'Most of his joints were affected by this stage, particularly the hands, spine, neck, knees, feet and right elbow.'

He usually played down the autobiographical element in his writing, but did not dispute that *The Singing Detective*, written thirteen years later, was an accurate portrait of his illness in 1972: 'I went through everything Marlow does, the pain, the bitterness, the "why me?" anger, the degradation.' He also displayed Marlow's wry humour: 'When I was desperately trying to get to sleep I used to say the words "Ludovic Kennedy" over and over again. It always worked.' As to his neighbours on the ward:

I spent the whole dreary summer on my back in a sprawling East End hospital where every other bed in the ward (including mine) seemed to be occupied by one or other sickly manifestation of Alf Garnett . . . I now sit through *Till Death Us Do Part* with much the same tight smile of discomfort, embarrassment and relief which I used to feel upon being lifted on to the bedside commode. Johnny Speight's not altogether comic dialogue is at times so devastatingly authentic that I hear again the rodent squeak of the drug trolley coming down the passage, full of pills and poisons momentarily interrupting the overlapping monologue of assembled Alfs addressing themselves to the unpalatable fact that three subdued Pakistanis had somehow managed to infiltrate into the ward under the pretence of chronic sickness. We all knew as a matter of course that these cunning brown bastards were only there to draw Social Security payments, an argument which temporarily wavered when one of them so miscalculated his ruse that he actually went so far as to die. 'There's yer bleed'n curry for you,' observed my nearest Alf, not entirely without compassion.

Hoping to be able to put Potter back on Methotrexate, the doctors quizzed him about his drinking and smoking – cigarettes had been linked with severe psoriasis: 'He gave a history of considerable tobacco intake,' they noted, 'forty to sixty French cigarettes daily, and a moderately excessive alcohol intake – two thirds of a bottle of wine, two pints of Guinness and a quantity of spirits daily.' Not until he had spent six alcohol-free weeks in the hospital was it decided to risk Methotrexate. After a few days, the drug caused some improvement in the psoriasis, but less than had been hoped.

Follow the Yellow Brick Road was shown on the night of 4 July. 'I didn't actually see its first transmission,' recalled Potter, 'because I was in a bed at the London Hospital, unable to move much else besides my left arm and maybe my penis, in an occasional erection which imperiously seemed to take no account of my collapsed hands, caked and cracked skin and feverishly swollen joints.' Perhaps it was as well that Potter was not watching the play, for both Denholm Elliott as Jack Black and director Alan Bridges treated it as a light comedy, skating over its psychological agonies, and reviewers were disappointed. Peter Fiddick in the *Guardian* was dazzled by the 'Pirandello effect of a real camera watching an actor desperate at being watched by an imaginary camera', but wondered exactly what was being satirized. Peter Black in the *Daily Mail* described the play as 'a disappointing yell of rage', and even the usually perceptive Philip Purser in the *Sunday Telegraph* did not perceive that Potter had reached a peak.

*

In mid-July 1972, after Potter had been in the London Hospital for two months, the registrar in the Skin Department noted his state of mind:

During his long stay he has quite naturally been through some rather despondent periods, and he was rather distressed at the delay in using Methotrexate. However, in general he has been very philosophical and co-operative. His main anxiety is his skin, whereas his crippling arthropathy is almost of second importance.

Among the medical students at the London Hospital when Potter was admitted was Patrick Rahilly (now a doctor working in Australia). 'We weren't aware of Dennis Potter as a famous person at all,' he recalls.

He was in his own room off the main ward – not a private room (they were elsewhere), but one that the hospital could provide for cases which needed privacy. The first time I saw him, I was in a group of other students, to whom he was being demonstrated as an unusually severe case of psoriasis. He was quite crippled; his hands were folded in on themselves, and his fingers were stiff.

I was allocated to him, and went back to see him by myself, and he was very grumpy and fed up – yet, at the same time, almost laughing at himself for being so grumpy. They had given him painting-by-numbers to do, to get his hands working, and when I looked at what he'd done, and said (as one does) 'That looks nice', he snorted: 'It's a bloody platitude of a picture. And I can tell you another platitude: it's bloody awful being stuck inside this body.' In fact his behaviour was very like Marlow's in *The Singing Detective*, which I got to know well when it came out years later.

What I remember so well is that he wanted to make me more sensitive to him. He said something to the effect of 'I'm an individual, a person, as well as a case'; and honestly it was the first time I had really had that brought home to me by a patient – it was an important stage in my medical education. I became fascinated by him; he was clearly a very strong character, and had something important to say. He played down his profession; I think he just said something like 'I write a bit', but he didn't seem to want to be taken up on that. In fact his whole message to me was, 'Don't put labels on people.'

After a while, the medication brought him out of the worst of it, and I think he became a bit euphoric, and started to chat up the nurses, and maybe got a bit loose with those clenched-up hands.

By the beginning of August he was getting very restless, and the hospital let him go home. 'His arthritis has gone on improving steadily,' they noted, 'so that now only the hands are disabling. From being bedridden on admission he is mobile and active and can do some writing despite the severe flexion deformities of his fingers.' Meanwhile he had come up with another *Play for Today* idea, this time for Ken Trodd, who was back at the BBC. It was to be called *Ghost Righter*, and the plot echoed *Message for Posterity*: 'A writer is hired to produce an "autobiography" for an image-conscious industrialist. Their lives and histories become unpredictably entwined.'

The hospital had decided that he should take Methotrexate once a week, though they warned that it would cause nausea. This was an understatement. 'It was so toxic that I used to vomit two days of the week,' Potter said. 'I suffered total nausea, diarrhoea and headaches.' There was some talk of a surgical operation on his hands, but in the meanwhile physiotherapy and the splints kept them just about useable. 'His energy and muscle power are gradually returning,' noted a doctor, 'and he is able to write.' Indeed, he was at work on a novel.

CHAPTER 9

The Mountains of Tasgi

In 1990 Potter told John Cook, who was writing a book about him, that his first novel, *Hide and Seek*, had been completed in January 1972, shortly before he went into hospital. He said he had begun the novel

by pretending that it was my hobby, and that my real work was writing whatever television play I was involved in. Therefore the first part of the novel came extremely slowly, like any hobby – I was pretending not to take it seriously in order to free myself to take it seriously. And then it came in a rush. And I just got enormous pleasure out of playing with it and being hurt by it and being in control of it – and then losing control of it, and knowing exactly when you did lose control of it. It's a feeling I haven't got in writing a play.

Follow the Yellow Brick Road proposed the alarming idea that an individual's life might really be a television play. *Hide and Seek* played a similar game with the novel. 'It's a stripping away,' Potter said of it. 'Not only am I writing a novel, I am also saying, "How ridiculous to write a novel." It's one of the ways of keeping the novel form alive, because it's really embalmed.' The book is in one sense very bare compared to his plays, less colourful and quirky, and clearly intended for dons rather than coalminers. But by eliminating any element of condescension to a mass audience, Potter is able to take his own ideas more seriously, and to further what Philip Purser had called his 'intermittent . . . autobiography'. The novel is less memorable than the plays in its overall story, but is a much more candid 'exercise in self-exposure' than Potter ever attempted on screen, and is full of vivid, shocking detail.

The book opens with yet another confrontation between an

obsessive, possibly deluded individual and a psychiatrist in an old London hospital. This time the sufferer's name is Daniel Miller, and his supposed delusion is that he is a character in a novel. 'He knows I am trying to escape,' Daniel tells the doctor. 'The Author of this Book . . . The Book I am in.' Yet he realizes that 'the most disconcerting thing a character in a novel can do is to announce that he is indeed a character in a novel'.

Daniel, a lecturer in liberal studies, 'a hard-working Oxford scholarship boy who did very well in later endeavours', is recollecting this scene while driving down a tree-lined track in the darkness. He is looking for a remote woodman's cottage which he has impulsively rented in the Forest of Dean, his childhood home, in the hope of finishing the writing of a critical biography of Coleridge, and of escaping his 'malignant and sex-obsessed' Author. But it had been useless trying to convince the psychiatrist that

it was *the Author* who had made him do and say what he had said. The Author who had stretched out all those women under his joylessly heaving limbs. The Author who made his joints burn, his skin itch . . . Who else could have put the dirty pictures of six variously copulating couples in the inside pocket of his wallet? The Author The Author The Author it was who stiffened his penis as he walked by darkened doorways, who wasted his seed . . .

Daniel's strategy for weakening his Author's grip is to quote from other authors, such as Hazlitt or Thomas Hardy; but he has to concede that 'it was impossible for a modern character to infiltrate himself successfully into the landscapes, relationships and serenities of earlier works'.

His awareness of the Author is, of course, very close to some people's consciousness of God, but though Daniel quotes fragments of the Bible fluently, he has lost faith in the Nonconformist Christianity of his childhood. He has also split with his wife Lucy, who has walked out of their Shepherd's Bush flat ('suspended above traffic snarl, pavement noises, an eel-and-pie shop') because he is abusing her physically and verbally, shouting 'Bitch! . . . Dirty fucking whore!' and knocking her down. In his 'thirty-five years' (Potter was now thirty-seven), Daniel has 'achieved little more than . . . one hundred and fifty-six prostitutes [twenty more than Peters in *Moonlight on the Highway*] and a wife with lucid green eyes sobbing on a settee with a stinging red weal on half her once gentle face'. His life seems to him 'a dirty book, peopled with foul creatures, stained flesh, dirty pictures, faithless women with rotting cunts, sucking mouths'. Or so it seems; yet if the Author is writing Daniel's life, then 'those memories . . . were *not* his memories at all . . . Any author was duty bound to give his characters a past . . . '

The psychiatrist has sneered at Daniel's delusion – 'I would like to see this – ah – book of yours' – but in Part Two of *Hide and Seek*, with the narration switching to the first person, we find that there is indeed an author of Daniel's story. Moreover he seems to be as 'malignant and sex-obsessed' as Daniel asserts. He, too, lives in the Shepherd's Bush flat over the eel-and-pie shop, and he insists that (unlike Daniel) he is totally in command of the narrative:

These paragraphs . . . are in no sense a victory for the sick and guilt-ridden creature I had decided several months ago to call 'Daniel Miller'. He is stuck where I left him, and if I want to abandon him there, uncertainly oscillating between stripped woods and consulting room, then that will be his permanent state, his eternal dislocation. Too bad!

I will concede that characters in books do upon occasion get out of control . . . But . . . Miller . . . remains an aggregation of words. I am, in short, totally in control of my material . . .

Yet this nameless Author is in a state of panic. There is, he says, a growing tendency in the literary world to confuse a writer with his characters, to suggest that 'what one writes in fiction or drama is . . . what one *is*'. He himself has emerged from behind his fiction because he fears that 'my erstwhile friends' will allege that there are 'disgusting similarities' between himself and his creation, 'Daniel Miller'. They are already circulating some 'ridiculous love letters' supposedly written by him to 'a syphilitic television actress', in truth forged by a 'lank-haired lout with smelly feet'. Indeed, he now detects a conspiracy by an 'envy-ridden and sex-obsessed faction' which even includes his agent, to whom the Daniel Miller story (as far as it goes) has already been delivered. This conspiracy is attempting to humiliate him to the point where 'I will no longer be able to function as a talented and highly original writer, perhaps the most gifted of my generation'.

He therefore deems it necessary to list the similarities and differences between himself and Miller. They were both born and bred in the Forest of Dean (though, to be accurate, 'Miller was born only in my head'), both intend to write lives of Coleridge, are 'almost exactly the same age', and both went to Oxford. Miller suffers from psoriatic arthropathy, and the author admits that 'there is a misunderstanding abroad that I also suffer from this unpleasant ailment', but he denies it:

I visited this nasty ailment – the one I have not got – upon Daniel Miller in order to show how the guilt or evil in his mind finds physical expression in and on his body. If I had done the things he has done, if I had copulated with whores so indiscriminately and shamelessly, then I too would expect to find some signs of evil upon my frame . . .

The relationship between sin and sickness is uncompromisingly acknowledged in the Book of Common Prayer . . . 'It wasn't me,' a man can say after some foul abomination such as hitting his wife or putting his penis in a prostitute's dribbling mouth. 'It wasn't really me, I am not responsible.' . . . But what the flapping tongue denies the pain-scorched limbs confirm. The illness of Miller is directly attributable to his conduct . . . sin made manifest in bone, guilt outcropping in itchy red layers on the skin, shame bubbling in hot pain in the ligaments.

Although he claims not to suffer from the illness, and therefore not from the guilt, the Author admits that 'some very nasty gossip' about him has been going round – he has even noticed a young couple giggling at him on Hammersmith Bridge. On the telephone, his agent lets out that a mutual friend, Robert, has been indiscreet about some 'trouble or guilt' that the Author confided in him. When he has got over his paranoid rage at this betrayal, the Author admits to us that there was indeed some such conversation with Robert, 'my closest friend and ally' since Oxford days, who owns a 'pile of old Al Bowlly records'. It was in Robert's room in London that

I *appeared* to confess to him . . . that during the past six or seven years I had gone to bed with more than one hundred and fifty prostitutes. I may even have said in the spirit of the joke that it had been one hundred and fifty-six whores, for all the world as though it was of an obsessive importance for the actual number to be known with absolute accuracy! This is the way one over-embroiders invention when playing complicated verbal games or intellectual hide-and-seek with one's closest friends.

Determined to 'communicate the true nature of my attitude or (more important) my actual behaviour towards women', the Author admits that the reader may choose to believe Robert:

If Robert came to you and said in his gentle, somehow caressingly placid voice that I had admitted or confessed to him in 'obvious distress' that I had pushed my penis up between the hired legs of more than one hundred and fifty tarts . . . then you would probably believe him. Prurience is universal . . . People have minds like sewers.

The Author now abandons his comfortless flat (where the electricity has been cut off) for a coffee bar, where he cannot take his eyes off a girl sitting with a fat woman and two noisy West Indians, 'an entrancing creature, pale and dark-haired and naturally elegant'. Returning to the flat, he admits that his response to her is typical of his attitude to women:

This person, I thought, is what a woman *should* look like . . . the very essence of femininity, the quality bestowed in at least some measure upon mother, sister, wife, daughter . . . Who would want to soil such a figure? Who could be so abominable and foul and so devoid of proper awe that he might heave and push and grunt and pant above her parted legs? Surely not even Casanova himself?

I am disgusted by the thought of spoiled human flesh. Mouth upon mouth, tongue against tongue, limb upon limb, skin rubbing at skin. Faces contort and organs spurt out a smelly stain, a sticky betrayal. The crudest joke against the human race lies in that sweaty farce by which we are first formed and given life. No wonder we carry about with us a sense of inescapable loss, a burden of original sin, and a propensity to wild, anguished violence . . . We are spat out of fevered loins, or punctured rubber, or drunken grapplings in creaking beds.

But none of this disturbed my mind or body as I looked across at the girl in the coffee bar. She was not the whore who lurks under the demure exterior of even the most respectable wife and mother. She was not an angel capable of mutating into a writing, biting snake on a soft mattress. To me, at that moment, she was instead the Snow Queen, the Snow White in the glass case, the Princess at the Ball.

He admits that women like this have inspired him to write 'letters glowing with warmth and tenderness'. Indeed, 'Some of my best writing has been lost in this way, for I have reason to suppose that the letters were not kept . . . ' And he asks how could 'a man who feels as I do' have behaved in the way he appeared to have confessed to Robert – how could he 'have fornicated with one single prostitute', let alone repeated it so often and obsessively?

Imagine exactly what this would involve . . . the sordid exchanges in doorways or park benches . . . the anxieties about disease, the fears of recognition and the intolerable pressure of guilt . . . When you have thought about all these things . . . you will realize . . . that I could not by the very nature of my being be so implicated in such a maze of lust and filth . . . I do not leer at the advertisements along the underground escalators. I do not possess any pornographic publications or pictures of couples in lubricious postures, though . . . I have seen these things in Robert's room and in my agent's office. The two people, in fact, who lead the campaign against me!

Obviously, they are by doing this attempting to discharge their own guilts . . .

He feels obliged to reciprocate with 'an almost incredible tale about my former friend Robert'; but by now he is cold and exhausted, having written for hours, and is becoming aware of 'something greater than or beyond myself and my body, something sustaining me, feeding me, encouraging me'. He suddenly remembers Daniel Miller, who must be 'stuck on the page where I left him', and decides to show some mercy: 'I will let him go into the cottage . . . He can sleep.'

Sure enough, the narrative about Daniel now resumes: 'When he woke up, chilled and stiff, he could not at first understand where on earth he was . . . ' Daniel now feels liberated from his malevolent creator: 'The Author was gone . . . He was free.' But the Author himself is now trapped: 'When he woke up, chilled and stiff, he could not at first understand where on earth he was . . . ' He has fallen asleep while writing, and has become a character in a story written by somebody else.

Trying to resume writing, he finds his mind drifting back to the girl in the coffee bar. The invisible narrator now reveals that she is a prostitute, named Sandra, who is sizing him up as a potential customer. He, meanwhile, oscillates in his mind 'between the image of the pure lady . . . and the idea of her calling out in a thrashing orgasm of female pleasure as he spurted and spurted in ecstatic triumph on top of her. Romantic dreams and sexual callisthenics, chivalry and rape, roses and semen, chocolate boxes and contraceptives . . . '

We learn that Sandra, too, is from the Forest of Dean, a victim of sexual abuse by her stepfather, and her mind is full of the same landscape as the Author's. He, meanwhile, is recalling his own abuse during childhood in the Forest, by an Italian prisoner of war with eyes 'the colour of phlegm'. The invisible narrator now reveals that the Author has an appointment with a psychiatrist, and intends to rent a cottage in the Forest; he is, in other words, indistinguishable from Daniel.

Back at his desk, the Author is still trying to tell his 'incredible tale' about Robert – is trying (in fact) to make out that it is Robert and not himself or Daniel who visits prostitutes. But the invisible narrator relentlessly describes one afternoon when the Author was 'wrestling with the ways in which it appeared to him that Coleridge had made use of a now little-known book, Ridley's *Tales of the Genii*'. This conjectural source for Xanadu* describes how the merchant Abudah is shown a gorgeous vista by the Genius of Riches, a golden dome which rises to the clouds. As he meditates devoting 'a whole chapter' to this in his biography of Coleridge, the Author, walking through a district of down-at-heel houses, encounters a Guyanese prostitute: '"Ten pounds for a nice long time," she said, anxiously, invitingly. "You can take an hour if you like, honey. Ten pounds for that, eh? And another five so that you can spunk in my mouth."'

He agrees, his mind still filled with Ridley's tale:

He looked up at the stairs. Abudah had to make his way through that cavern, that dungeon of lust . . . 'It's OK,' he said, voice quavering. 'I – well, I've never paid for it before.'

He always said that in the vain hope that the girl would respond to him differently from all the others who had so casually used her body . . .

When Abudah had made his way through this slimy cavern he emerged upon a mountain top in the clean air. Ten thousand voices called out in praise 'Long live our sultan, whom the mountains of Tasgi have brought forth!' §

The Author now understands the symbolism of these mountains; after the 'dungeon of lust' they should offer 'healing release' in their 'pellucidly clear air', as well as 'triumphant ejaculation'; but for him

the mountains of Tasgi were dank with decomposing vegetation, malodorous genitalia, fleshly betrayal, fathomless melancholy . . . The voices did not acclaim his deeds with a loud rapture, but became whispering voices, conspiratorially accusing, viciously sniggering. Murderous ejaculation and deeper entombment.

He tries, once more, to pass off his own story as Daniel Miller's – it is Daniel (he asserts) who comes up the stairs to the prostitute's room, and who is alarmed when he sees that her child is sleeping in the corner, and when the light fails and she burns paper (an incident repeated from *The Rivers of Babylon*). But then he reverts to the first

* James Ridley, *Tales of the Genii* (1764).
§ Potter's original title for the novel, on the typescript (no manuscript survives), was *The Mountains of Tasgi*.

person, explaining, 'The "I" is not I, nor yet quite Miller, nor you. Just I, the writer, the God, the one who sees, who understands.' Having issued that caveat, he describes undressing in front of the prostitute:

As I removed my clothes I was glad that the light was so poor. My skin was undoubtedly near to normal in appearance, but a bright light might have exaggerated the slight roughness or the diminishing pinky-red cartography of certain areas on my body. When this happened I used to make up elaborate and probably unconvincing stories about car crashes, burns, skin grafts, incompetent surgeons and so on, anything rather than use the word 'disease'.

As he recounts how the prostitute fingered his penis – 'My pleasure-dome' – he inadvertently lets his wife into the narrative. We gather that she does not know about his obsession with prostitutes, though on one occasion he was 'on the edge of confession'. He used to read Coleridge to her in bed rather than make love, because of his conviction of the dirtiness of sex:

There had been long periods when I could only enter you and come in you by secretly pretending to myself that I did not know you, that you were a tart I had picked up in a bar or on the street corner . . . But when you were My Princess I could not bear to imagine you stained by me. I did not and could not touch you where you wanted to be touched. It made me feel sick.

Oh, the moments after we had made love. The gloom that fell upon me was deep enough to make me want to die. I cannot, cannot, cannot explain it, cannot understand it.

He recalls that the encounter with the Guyanese prostitute was on the day that he nearly confessed to his wife:

I . . . tried to read to you that night . . . Three hours earlier a lilting voice had told me that I had a nice big cock. She had enough honour in her to be mindful of the considerable fee. She put her mouth over it, licking, sucking, dribbling, both of us unaware by now of the child sleeping three or four paces across the half-dark room . . .

'Dirty rotten fucker, dirty cunt!' I say, not yet exploding with pleasure . . . 'Slimy bitch. Filthy whore. Slippery cunt.' . . .

I must have shouted out at that precise moment where exultation turns to disgust, the moment of spilling, of defilement.

A shout loud enough to wake the child . . .

Did you expect me to tell you *that*?

And now the Author, his hands 'lustrous with silvery scales flaking off ugly patches of red . . . scarcely capable of holding the pen', impetuously tears up everything he has written, contemptuously rejecting 'all that fiction' in favour of his Coleridge biography, which is 'real'. But as he does so, we are back in the first scene of the novel, with the Author himself telling the psychiatrist that he is trapped in a novel. 'Where did it start and where did it end?' he asks himself. 'Or does it go on and on and on and on?' Mercifully not, for he – and we – are now about to reach 'the open air on the far side of the back cover', where voices greet him with a shout of 'Long live our hero, whom the mountains of Tasgi have brought forth!'

But since I am not real and they are not real you might as well stop reading at this point. Go back to Part Three [Daniel waking up in the cottage], which was supposed to provide the original ending. My hand aches. My real hand does, too. I am, in the mid-course of my life, looking for the straight path through the trees.

And with this allusion to Dante, *Hide and Seek* ends.

The book is dedicated: 'For Margaret, my wife.'

*

Hide and Seek seems to have been devised as a trap for Potter's biographer, whose research was bound to reveal that he had had an appointment with a psychiatrist at an old London hospital, made confessions that he had been with a certain number of prostitutes, and at the same time idealized women sexlessly. The novel lies in wait for the discovery of these facts, which seem to disclose the 'real' Dennis Potter. Its message seems to be: I have been playing hide-and-seek with you. You think you are writing my life, but I am leaning over your shoulder, writing it for you. You, even you, are a character in my story. I can manipulate you too.

But this, of course, is itself a manipulation: to take the most private facts in one's life – knowing that one day they will certainly be dis-covered – and present them as if they were a series of deceptions. Similarly, to give Margaret the present of a novel describing a psoriatic writer's sexual anguish and degradation may have been a way of disguising confession as fiction. (Sarah Potter says that, at this stage of her life, her mother 'read everything, and saw everything that he wrote, and he talked his work through with her'.)

By the end of the book, Daniel Miller, the Author and the invisible narrator have all been revealed as the same person, with the same history and memories and the same sexual angst. The final 'message' of *Hide and Seek* seems to be that, despite all their claims to the contrary, writers write the truth about themselves. The ultimate cleverness of Potter's first novel may be that it is not a novel at all, but the plain facts.

Potter himself hinted at this in an interview to mark the publication of the book:

What I did was very consciously use an autobiographical convention – not autobiographical facts as such; if I wanted to write autobiography, I would, as it were. But there's something very powerful about a man fencing with himself. Now, this isn't a fictional fencing; what contains the book is a fencing with *me*, with me myself in my own memories, my own experience, some of my own shames. And fencing with my invented character is a way also of fencing with my real character.

Certainly by the time he wrote the novel his real character had begun to resemble the Author in it. Gareth Davies and his wife recall a strange evening in a West End club. 'It was an extraordinary night,' says Davies. 'Dennis mentioned an uncle abusing him, and made some sort of crack to us both on the lines of, "Well, *you're* happily married", and then he started to tell us stories about being on to his thousandth tart, or what have you – some enormous number – and saying that he used to shout Old Testament texts at them, Whore of Babylon, dogs returning to their vomit, and so on, while he and they were banging away. This, I must say, was totally outside our experience!'

Davies's wife, the actress Christine Pollon, continues the story: 'He then accused me of not being shocked – I was listening to this, and he said, "You don't even seem interested." I said, "I'm sorry, Dennis, everyone to his own thing. If you want prostitutes, you go off with prostitutes." But what did shock me was that he said he used to go home and tell Margaret – that was part of the kick. And that I did *not* like.' Davies adds, 'Mind you, that's what he *said* he did. It could have been just a further attempt to shock us. And we certainly had the sense that we were being told this stuff in order to be shocked.'

CHAPTER 10

I gave him half his lines

David Williams in *The Times* called *Hide and Seek* 'exciting, honest and strongly imagined . . . a powerful and deeply felt book . . . which gives you plenty to think about', but Rivers Scott in the *Sunday Telegraph* thought it 'less than convincing' and found the ending 'obscure', while the anonymous reviewer in *The Times Literary Supplement* said it had been 'carefully and complexly done', but wondered if the intricacy was in the end 'really only trickiness'.

Potter resumed weekly television reviewing for the *New Statesman* shortly after leaving hospital, in September 1972, and continued for a few months. His articles were as dyspeptic as ever. 'Pictures, crabbed pictures, ever on tap, every night of the week every week of the year,' he grumbled. 'Inevitably, television is in perpetual danger of being turned into a mere domestic appliance for passing the time, painless and undemanding.' Reviewing a disappointing BBC2 *War and Peace*, he observed, 'It is now only in the rare, fiercely independent documentary or in the so-called one-shot play not written to a series format that we can still pick up the no doubt irritating cadences of the individual voice.'

Two months after Potter had finished this *New Statesman* stint, in February 1973, the *Guardian* carried a profile of him by Stanley Reynolds, who noted that he was 'terribly crippled. His fingers are bent over with the tips pressing into his palms. He can straighten his index fingers but they are not strong enough to work a typewriter. He has to write with a felt pen which doesn't take a lot of pressure to mark a page. He turns his plays into the BBC in longhand.' Reynolds remarked that Potter stood apart from those television playwrights who dealt dutifully (and trendily) with social issues: '[He] reacts to some sort of crazy music inside his own head. He is inner directed.'

Reynolds reported that Mary Whitehouse had complained about the latest Potter play, though Potter himself was puzzled by this: 'I can see why she didn't like *Casanova*, but I cannot see what she found objectionable in this last play which, if anything, is a religious play.' This was *Only Make Believe*, subtitled 'Companion piece to *Angels Are So Few*', which had been written about three years earlier, immediately after *Angels*. When she had read the first draft, Ann Scott had asked for some major rewrites, and the second version – less autobiographical and more tightly scripted – had then waited some while for production.

Later, Potter recalled that *Angels Are So Few* and *Only Make Believe*

were meant to be part of a trilogy, conceived under the generic title of *Visitors*. God knows what happened to the third one. It probably didn't get written, or was abandoned, or was interfered with. It was just contingency that the script the writer was dictating in *Only Make Believe* was *Angels Are So Few*. Of course I'm always suspicious when people say that – as the Marxists say, there's no such thing as coincidence. But I wouldn't have thought there was much of a relationship between those plays, except they're both about damage: sexual inhibition and deep sexual anxiety.

Asked in this interview if he was using the figure of a writer as a window into universal experience, he replied 'I hope not. It's very dangerous if I am. I use writers probably because I've run out of knowledge about what other people do for a living . . . Writing, the reclusiveness that goes with it, in my case health problems, is what I most vividly and practically and most intensely know. It's that that's my work, and that's what I have sometimes used.

Only Make Believe continues Potter's relentless self-exposing, this time with a degree of wish-fulfilment. It opens with Christopher, a television playwright, dictating his latest script, Potter's own *Angels Are So Few*, to an agency typist named Sandra George, 'a golden girl,' writes Potter, 'but she seems oddly remote, locked away, wary. A Snow White in a glass case.' Christopher – Potter's second name (George was his third) – has to dictate because his right hand is bandaged, and we soon learn that he has deliberately burnt it on the electric ring of the cooker, in a melodramatic gesture after his wife Sarah left him.

'I've never dictated my work before,' he tells Sandra. 'Don't know whether I can do it . . . It's rather like asking you to share my fantasies . . . Like inviting you to clump up and down inside my head.' But she remains icily uninvolved, and fends off his florid but clumsy passes. When she leaves abruptly at the end of her first day's work, Christopher mutters, 'Cold little bitch. She'd make a great story editor.' This seems to be a gibe at Ann Scott, whom Potter had now cast in Caroline Seebohm's former role in his life. 'He was angry with me for inviting Margaret to come and stay when he was in hospital,' Scott recalls.

I didn't understand this till afterwards, but it broke some image he had of me, which wasn't actually *me*. He'd written me a couple of very maudlin letters, but I hadn't been able to answer them, couldn't deal with them at all, and hadn't wanted to keep them. I remember Dennis once asking if I still had them, and he seemed really startled when I said no.

I don't think we were ever alone together except when I was visiting him in the hospital. 'Maudlin' isn't quite right, but they didn't feel real. I was carrying out a function for him, filling a slot, as some kind of unattainable person, and it just happened to be me who was available to fill it. And then as soon as reality intruded, in the form of Margaret and me actually spending evenings together, he was angry, and the spell was broken.

Christopher in *Only Make Believe* has exactly this tendency. 'I can *make up* characters,' he tells Sandra,

All sorts of people . . . But I can't manage real flesh-and-blood characters. The ones you bump into in the street. The people at the bus stop. At a party. Or girls. Or even my wife. *Ex*-wife. Or – or you. I can put a stream of lovely words into your head, entrancing and enchanting words, but you will never say them. Not to *me*, anyway. Probably never even think them. I'll have to make do with videotape . . . I can't even put the words in my own head. I rehearse things to say to people, but they never come right . . .

Consequently his initial attempts to win Sandra come to grief: 'Your hair is lovely,' he tells her. 'I like the way it almost touches your shoulders but then turns back into your neck. As though it is as nervous of touching you as I am . . . There, that's the bit I rehearsed.' To which Sandra responds, 'Yes, it sounded like it.' When he complains, 'The permissive society – would somebody please stand up and tell me where the hell it is', she replies, 'In your plays, perhaps.'

In the first version of *Only Make Believe*, Christopher's emotional history includes both childhood sexual abuse and prostitutes. For the first (and only) time in Potter's writing, the abuse is identified as the cause of the obsession:

CHRISTOPHER: Between VE Day and VJ Day. (*Shout*) I was ten! I was only ten! And he said, this man with grey bristles on his chin, he said, let's go down this lane . . . He twisted my arm up behind my back. I screamed . . . I thought he had a big snake between his legs . . . When they dropped the bomb on Hiroshima I already knew what it was all about. There are no angels. There is no God . . .

(*He puts his hands over his face and sobs like a child. She just sits looking at him. But he cannot stop. This is the first time he has been able to say that he was sexually assaulted as a child. The release is too much . . .*)

All my life I have wanted someone to *take away* that pain. By listening. Sarah – she – I could never tell her, never get it out . . . So I always tried to *buy* that peace. I talked to – to – prostitutes. They *had* to listen. Perhaps they are the only angels left.

Christopher uses this revelation manipulatively, to arouse Sandra's pity and make her succumb to him sexually; whereas in the second draft of the play, which lacks the abuse-and-prostitutes confession, he simply 'grabs her as though she is a lifebelt'. She protests, then 'responds, fiercely', and 'they coil together', whereupon we cut away to the closing moments of *Angels Are So Few*.

A few days after this, Sandra, back at the flat to finish the script, has retreated once again into self-protecting iciness, ignoring the fact that they have made love, and telling Christopher, 'I'm not an angel. Not your angel . . . I'm not make-believe . . . You can't put words into *my* head.' Nevertheless in the first draft Potter propels her back into Christopher's arms as the play ends. The second version ends in-conclusively, with the two of them staring at each other, and Potter observing, 'It could go either way.' The play as transmitted has Sandra walking out on Christopher, who nevertheless tries to assure himself that this rejection is 'only a dream', and that everything will turn out fine.

Ann Scott may have made the suggestion that, in real life, Sandra would not have stayed. She does not recall saying this, but emphasizes that Potter was always happy to take criticisms of his first drafts: 'He loved arguing, so if there was something in the plays which was good for an argument, he was happy to have it. And then he would either change the script or not, as he chose.'

Keith Barron, cast as Christopher, brought an echo of Nigel Barton to *Only Make Believe*, which was directed by Robert Knights and transmitted as the *Play for Today* on 12 February 1973, while Georgina Hale's buttoned-up Sandra earned praise from all reviewers. In the play, Christopher observes to Sandra, 'I've never really written a convincing woman's part before', and Nancy Banks-Smith commented of Potter, 'Nor has he now'; but she called it 'a play which not only left you more awake than you were at the beginning but more alive'. Clive James in the *Observer* wished Potter had explored 'the possibility that his hero might have been faking a certain amount of suffering in order to get the girl', and said he preferred less introspective Potter plays in which the questioning was 'all directed outwards' (he did not specify which). Potter himself, watching *Only Make Believe* again a year later, judged it 'studio-bound and wordy', but he made no major changes when adapting it for a stage production by Richard Wilson at the Oxford Playhouse in December 1974. Frank Dibb in the *Oxford Times* complained that the 'divided stage, with revolve', required for the excerpts from *Angels Are So Few*, 'still smacks . . . of the television screen'.

Keith Barron recalls that, when he and Potter had a drink during the making of *Only Make Believe*, 'Dennis was having to hold a glass like a squirrel'. One of his doctors noted that in April 1973, two months after the play was shown, he had 'foolishly stopped Methotrexate abruptly', presumably because of the nausea and vomiting, with the consequence of 'a severe relapse'. He retired to bed and resumed the drug again. 'On examination,' wrote the doctor,

he looked well and there has been complete regrowth of his hair, which he lost because of the severe illness last summer. There is moderate, shallow discoid psoriasis on the trunk and limbs, but it is sparse. The hands remain fixed and clenched . . . I have advised Mr Potter that he must remain on Methotrexate for the time being . . . taken every ten days or so . . . He does not want any hand surgery . . .

He had developed a method of writing despite the condition of his hands. 'He writes with a pen clamped in the center of his bent fist,' noted an American journalist some years later, 'the same grip he uses for all his manual tasks including smoking the pack or two of cigarettes he gets through in a day.'

In the first version of *Only Make Believe*, Potter describes Christopher as someone whose 'tension or barely held-down distress' can 'so easily spill over into verbal aggression or even overt violence'. Roger Smith had a painfully aggressive encounter with Potter himself, around the time the play was transmitted:

We had this terrible row, in about 1973. By then I was very involved with the Workers' Revolutionary Party, which changed my relationship with most of my friends. I'd written a play called *The Operation*, which Roy Battersby had directed and Trodd produced [in 1972]. There was a sequence when a town planner is sexually compromised by a girl. [Trodd describes this scene as 'the first blow-job on television'.] And there was a row about the scene in the House of Lords. And Battersby and I wrote to *The Times*, and said there was a lot at stake here, about liberties, freedom, the right to self-expression.

I went to a party, at Clive Goodwin's, and I was talking to Dennis and Margaret Potter, and I said that what astounded me was that not a single other writer in the country had supported us during this row. And Dennis said, 'That's nothing to do with it, it was your own incompetence.' And I had a glass of whisky in my hand, and I'm afraid I just chucked it straight in his face, and said, 'You bastard.' And he got up and was going to fight me, and I said, 'Don't be ridiculous.' And Colin Welland was there, and said, 'Come on, lads', and broke it up. And I left in tears, and never spoke to Dennis again, until Tom Clarke's funeral.

*

An untitled *Play for Today* was commissioned from Potter by Trodd in July 1973: 'A hack writer discovers that the subject he is required to cover is gradually falling into his power.' The following month, Trodd commissioned Potter to adapt Edmund Gosse's *Father and Son* for the BBC series *Playhouse*, and in September Potter agreed to script Angus Wilson's novel *Late Call* as a four-episode BBC serial. 'Sometimes people approach you to do something and it can be as much a stimulus as what generally holds your interest,' he said of this commission. 'The BBC asked me to do *Late Call*, and told me they only had five cents to make it. Reading it, I thought it could lead one either to cynicism or adventurousness.' Meanwhile he had dramatized a Thomas Hardy short story for a BBC2 Hardy series, *Wessex Tales*.

Potter later emphasized the differences between Hardy and himself: 'Hardy's world picture is not even remotely close to mine. He was an atheist and a pessimist who was driven by other beasts, if you want to call them that, than the beasts that drive me.' Yet he admired Hardy's way of 'constantly winding the wheel to make fate conspire against human emotions. You know Hardy's characters are in danger the moment they fall in love or struggle to express something really deep and moving; that something is going to happen to swat them down. He also liked Hardy's lack of 'English condescension' in portraying the rural working-class life from which he (like Potter) had emerged.

A Tragedy of Two Ambitions, the Hardy story allocated to Potter by the BBC, is a cynical, anti-clerical tale about class. Two brothers, Joshua and Cornelius Halborough, have raised themselves above their lowly origins by training for the priesthood. 'I tell you', Joshua observes in Potter's adaptation, 'that the Church confers material advancement and social prestige at a cheaper price than any other pursuit or profession . . . Besides, we are in for Christianity as a career, we two.' They scheme to get their sister Rosa married to a squire, and when their drunken millwright father threatens to frustrate these well-made social plans, they allow him to drown in an accident.

In the original story, old Halborough, the father, is seen exclusively from the sons' viewpoint, as the flaw in their ambitious lives. Potter rightly allows us to understand that the old man is not just a drunken monster, and gives him a touch of Nigel Barton's father's confused feelings about his son. 'Scraped my fingers to the bone for all dree [three] on um,' he complains.

And for what? For what thanks? Not even a penny piece for a twist of baccy for their old dad! That chunt right, be it? . . . (*Proudly*) Got two boys, I have, as is going to be *pa'sons*! . . . Good lads. Aye. Clever lads. (*And he bursts into tears.*)

The sons' destruction of such a father undermines all their ambitions, just as Nigel's feelings of betrayal haunt his achievements. 'I would rather have stayed on our old level,' says Joshua Halborough at the end of Potter's script, 'with my crust of bread and my liberty!'

A Tragedy of Two Ambitions, screened on 21 November 1973 with a cast including John Hurt and Edward Petherbridge, was directed by Michael Tuchner and produced by Irene Shubik. Two months later, Shubik commissioned a science-fiction play from Potter, for the series *Playhouse*, with the working title *Futuristic Medicine*. 'As yet the idea is not concrete,' she noted. 'The play will probably deal with a future development in medicine relating mind and body.' Potter backed out of this project two months later. Meanwhile his own medical condition had worsened again; his local doctor noted that he was 'going through something of a flare-up of the psoriasis, which he has come to expect at this time of year. I am particularly worried about his hands which are becoming increasingly disabled.'

Resuming television reviewing for the *New Statesman* in January 1974, he mentioned his 'present depression and sickness' in one of his columns, adding that he was 'functioning at the moment by the bio-chemical courtesy of Methotrexate, and anxiously awaiting another liver biopsy'. He went back to the London Hospital for this during April; the test showed no evidence of damage from the drug, and he refused to see the hospital's rheumatologists about his hands. 'My own feeling is that only major hand surgery could improve the con-tractures,' wrote a consultant, 'but the patient has no appetite for this at present.'

His next original play, *Joe's Ark*, had been commissioned by Ann Scott in January 1971, with the theme 'a suburban Noah prepares for the end of the world' (it was then untitled). Once again, a very different play eventually landed on her desk, one of Potter's most powerful and least self-exposing pieces. It begins with rain falling ceaselessly on a small Welsh town, where Joe, a widower, presides over an Ark stuffed with animals – the local pet shop. But unlike the biblical Noah he rejects God, because his beloved daughter Lucy is dying of cancer upstairs:

JOE: (*almost a cry*) There's no sense in it, Dan. No sense in it.

PREACHER: No sense *we* can see, perhaps . . . It's almost too hard to bear, I know. But God – He calls the good to himself –

(*Almost before he can get it out,* JOE *thrusts his face into the* PREACHER's *face.*)

JOE: (*hiss*) What – did – you – say? . . . It's words like that which stick in my craw! I don't want to hear it! I don't want it! *Do you understand*?

PREACHER: (*dully*) Yes . . . When she was at the Sunday School she knew words, long words, which even Miss Thomas couldn't quite pick up –

JOE: Osteogenic-carcinoma.

PREACHER: Pardon?

(JOE *spits out each syllable.*)

JOE: Ost-e-o-gen-ic-car-cin-o-ma!

(*Pause.*)

PREACHER: (*uncomfortable*) Is that what it's called, Joe? This – ah – (*almost whispers the word*) – cancer?

JOE: That's it! That's your love of God for you!

Anger against God is a running theme in Hardy's fiction, but Potter denied that Hardy had influenced *Joe's Ark*:

It's not like Thomas Hardy shaking his fist against what he called 'the President of the Immortals'. It's simply that ordinary human feeling of being abandoned and betrayed and left to endure. Even if a tree struck by lightning falls across a car, killing a little girl in the back seat, you can't say, 'God is working His purpose out.' You can't bellow one of those hymns and understand why a cat tortures a mouse.

Potter does not omit sexual disgust from *Joe's Ark*, but relegates it to a secondary role. When Lucy's brother Bobby, estranged from the family and working as a dirty-joke comedian partnered by a stripper, hears that his sister is dying, his suppressed revulsion at his job surfaces in an outburst to a waiter who is sweeping up rubbish: 'You shouldn't sweep all that shit in front of anybody when they're eating! . . . I came here to *eat* not be sick . . . Put bluebottle maggots on the menu, you dirty sods! Tinned maggots!' By the end of the play, Lucy's death has not only reunited Bobby with his father, but has prompted him to propose marriage to his stripper partner – that is, to turn his back on 'dirty' sexuality.

Potter felt that this degree of hope at the end of the play marked a change of direction in his work: 'The resolution makes more than a wry nod at possibilities which can comprehend pain, or disgust, or the implacable presence of death itself . . . I won't dare to say that I wanted to send people to bed feeling *happy* . . . but the discerning critics (all three and a half of them) perhaps noticed . . . a momentary but descending modulation in what had otherwise been one long scream.' Among them were Peter Black, who thought *Joe's Ark* 'the strongest, simplest, most accessible Potter play so far', Richard Last in the *Daily Telegraph*, who called it 'an honest attempt to articulate the unspeakable, human reaction to death', and Peter Fiddick in the *Guardian*, who judged it 'gripping and human'.

Freddie Jones and Angharad Rees gave powerful performances as father and daughter, and Denis Waterman was the comedian brother.

Attending a rehearsal, Potter realized that director Alan Bridges was 'excavating the solemnity rather than the intrinsic comedy of the piece', but 'I was at that time either too ill or too diffident to do anything much about it'. His regular doses of Methotrexate were now giving him headaches and diarrhoea, as well as nausea and vomiting, and the search for some other drug that might control the psoriasis had so far been fruitless. In June 1974, four months after the transmission of *Joe's Ark*, he wrote to Elizabeth Thomas, the assistant editor of the *New Statesman,* that the Methotrexate side-effects made it impossible for him to continue a weekly column:

We would get the irritating & increasingly ludicrous situation of one week on – two weeks off, or worse. No doubt the Methotrexate will pull me back into functioning order yet again but I have fallen so far behind with my own work, and feel so anxious about my own long-term prospects, that it seems sensible to make this decision now . . . Perhaps I will be able to contribute the occasional one-off piece . . . and maybe when my successor on that back column has done his/her stint you might want to see if I am still alive and well and viewing here in Ross-on-Wye.

I regret not giving you more time, but I seem to be in a bit of a pickle at the moment. The demands of a weekly column are too inexorable in my present state, which is that of a sort of biochemical siege.

By the end of the summer he was in much better shape, and resumed the *New Statesman* column in September. Two months later he reviewed Colin Welland's play about a clothing workers' strike, *Leeds – United!* – which had been produced by Trodd. He said of Welland, 'There is no one writing in any medium today who can so successfully use simplicity as the mask for complex truths or who demonstrates such instantly recognizable warmth and affection for his characters without squelching haplessly into those ever waiting bogs of sentimentality.'

His own next play had been transmitted on 20 June as a BBC *Play for Today*, with Trodd producing and Barry Davis directing. Completed the previous autumn, *Schmoedipus* returns to the 'visitors' motif, and is both more disturbing and more muddled than previous Potter plays of this type.

It begins like a re-run of *Angels Are So Few*. A suburban housewife, Elizabeth, is apparently trapped in a listless marriage to an older husband, Tom, who lives only for recapturing his boyhood with the aid of his model railway. One morning a neighbour, Dorothy, warns her that a young man is lurking outside her house. Reluctantly, Elizabeth lets him in. His name is Glen, and he claims to be her son, the child of her teenage pregnancy, who was taken from her and sent to Canada. Shocked, she accepts the truth of this, but Glen's behaviour – and the play – soon become increasingly strange.

For a little while, Glen seems to have Oedipal designs on Elizabeth, chanting 'I spy with my little eye something beginning with B', as he looks pointedly at her breasts. Telling her he is 'fed up with being a grown-up', he demands to play with Tom's trains, then sits down at the piano and croons her the schmaltzy old song about Mother –

> M is for the mercy she possesses,
> O means that I owe her all I own . . .

– with organ and vocal backing ('as in a musical', instructs Potter). When Glen returns to the model railway, threatening to smash it to bits, Elizabeth phones desperately for Dorothy. There is now no sign of Glen, but the railway is smashed, and amid the wreckage we hear the sound of a baby crying.

Dorothy arrives just as Tom returns from work (he works for a food company and is trying to grow a perfect mushroom – the first recycling of the rejected *Mushrooms on Toast*), and, as he and Dorothy listen, Elizabeth pours out the story of how she became pregnant as a school-girl – and smothered the baby as soon as it was born. Dorothy is horrified, but Tom, observing Elizabeth's psychological state, is concerned about only one thing: 'You haven't done anything to my trains . . . have you?' In fact the railway layout is unharmed, and Tom and Elizabeth are soon carrying on as if everything were normal. Dorothy cannot take this:

DOROTHY: (*hysterical*) This is too much! I can't stand it. Are you both mad or what? . . . It gives me the creeps. I can't even begin to – to –

ELIZABETH: Stay and have some tea.

DOROTHY: What?

TOM: Yes. Do stay. We're both grateful to you, really we are.

DOROTHY: (*shrill*) I'm not staying here!

TOM: There's no need to be like that, Dorothy. It was only – a sort of –

ELIZABETH: Game.

TOM: Yes. A game. Nothing to get het up about.

(DOROTHY *stares at them both then turns and, with a little choked cry, runs away. They wait. Slam! goes the front door. Silence.*)

Elizabeth.

ELIZABETH: I know.

TOM: (*severely*) You must *not* involve other people. You simply must – not – do – it . . .

ELIZABETH: I know. I know . . . (*Smirk*) He'll be back, though . . . I know he'll come back . . . He's *bound* to come back!

TOM: Just so long as he doesn't break the trains, Elizabeth. Is that clear? Is that once and for all clear . . . *Is that clear, child?*

ELIZABETH: Yes, Daddy.

TOM: Good girl.

(*Smiling, he goes out to the kitchen. She chews her nails. Swell up music . . . End.*)

Potter said little about *Schmoedipus*; he described it as one of 'that group of plays in the early Seventies [that] had the same kind of obsession: basically, that there's somebody outside the house who's going to knock, and you draw him in, but really he's inside your head. I probably return to that theme again and again.'

Peter Fiddick, reviewing *Schmoedipus* in the *Guardian*, remarked that Potter's 'astonishing first novel' *Hide and Seek*, 'which grows more layers than Peer Gynt's onion', was proving to be a useful primer to his plays. Three out of the four most recent had, like the novel, revealed 'worlds within worlds within worlds' – the exception was *Joe's Ark* – and Fiddick felt Potter was now pushing this too far:

There is no point in waiting until virtually the end of a play to reveal that what you are talking about is not the 'plot' of 'frightened wife and intruder' but the inner life that causes the marriage to be 'oedipus–schmoedipus' – the husband finished up with head buried in wife's lap exactly mirroring the fantasy son's (but what if you never heard that 'what does it matter so long as he's a good boy and loves his mother' joke in the first place?) (And that's only three parentheses, Dennis.)

Other reviewers felt equally duped by the play's ending, though all admired the performances of Anna Cropper as Elizabeth and Tim

Curry as Glen, who delivered a fine impersonation of Al Jolson in the 'Mother' song.

Near the end of 1974 Potter delivered to the BBC yet another play about a mysterious visitor to a suburban household – one that would cause a furore and help to change the direction of his work. Ann Scott saw the new script. 'There came a point,' she says,

where I just didn't like what he was beginning to write. I suppose that happened with *Brimstone and Treacle*. I just really hated that script, when it arrived, though in any case I wasn't available to be story editor for it. And from there on, it seemed to me that his obsessive picking-over of what he didn't like about sexuality was so unlike anything that I could connect to that I stopped being interested in it as art, and didn't want to follow those trails. Also, soon afterwards, I got married and then rapidly had three children. And there wasn't a single word from Dennis from that day.

I had thought we were friends at some level, but my marriage and children wrote me out of his script, as it were. I didn't understand that till later, and was quite hurt at the time by the abrupt and total silence.

*

Brimstone and Treacle was accepted by the BBC, and the second-half fee (£712) was paid. The next month, December 1974, Trodd commissioned a *Play for Today* from Potter to be called *Memory Man*, about 'a man who decides that planned amnesia is the best way out of his problems and ennui'. The BBC Copyright Department occasionally commented on the number of plays for which Potter had been paid a first-half fee, but which remained unwritten: 'Potter has obviously got a lot on his plate and you may wish to discuss priority . . .'

He had now completed his four-part dramatization of Angus Wilson's *Late Call*, which was shown on BBC2 during March 1975. Twelve years earlier he had written in the *Daily Herald* on an Angus Wilson TV play, *The Invasion*: 'Wilson does not use a bludgeon on English idiocies. He stands back, sardonic but involved, allowing his serious observations to trickle through almost slapstick humour.' *Late Call*, published in 1964, is a claustrophobic novel about Sylvia Calvert, manageress of a seaside hotel for the elderly, who retires, with her old reprobate of a husband, to live with their son Harold, a self-important headmaster in a new town. The book is a study of the loneliness of the elderly in the Admass-and-television-dominated society; also an essay on the failure of liberalism, as personified by the bossy, insensitive

Harold, who has the right ideas but no understanding of people – not even his own children, let alone his ageing parents.

Potter's adaptation was hampered by a tiny budget, which restricted the number of sets, so that most of the action – which in the book ranges over an entire community – had to take place in the Calvert family house. He had decided to use his favourite device of repeated flashbacks to give psychological depth to Sylvia; but there was no money to provide an Edwardian farmhouse interior for these scenes (taken from the prologue to the novel), in which Sylvia as a child is cruelly knocked about by her parents for supposedly tempting another little girl into naughtiness, an experience that has conditioned her into sheep-like acceptance of her fate. 'So I set all [this] among the modern furniture in the living room of this new-town house,' Potter recalled. 'Not one critic, not one letter, not one telephone call to the BBC – nothing. Nobody noticed . . .'

In fact *Late Call* attracted almost no attention from the critics, an exception being Stanley Reynolds, then reviewing for *The Times*, who praised the three main performances by Dandy Nichols (Sylvia), Leslie Dwyer (her husband Arthur) and Michael Bryant (Harold), and added, 'Angus Wilson could find himself in no better hands than those of Dennis Potter.' Yet, apart from the flashbacks and a brief burst of Al Bowlly on the soundtrack in the second episode, there was almost nothing in the script that bore Potter's stamp. 'An adaptation . . . must be an act of loving criticism as well as vandalizing bravado', Potter had written in the *New Statesman* two months before *Late Call* began transmission; yet he had neither vandalized Wilson's story nor criticized it lovingly, but had simply transferred it accurately to the screen.

He was back at the London Hospital for two weeks shortly before the series began, during January 1975, for liver tests and a review of his treatment. 'When asked in hospital if I wanted to watch any television,' he told *New Statesman* readers,

I pulled the sheet up over my head and made growling noises, thus risking both the incredulity of my sickly neighbours and an unwanted tranquillizer at the next drug round . . . The television set along the next corridor was almost permanently clamped to the commercial channel, the switch presided over by an amiably bronchitic master of ceremonies who between rattling coughs pronounced at suitable intervals that it was all shit.

In his reviews, Potter was inclined to agree with this amateur critic.

From the hotchpotch of indifferent programmes, he singled out an appearance by Enoch Powell,

stiff white triangle at his top pocket, stiff white rhombus above his Adam's apple, a tight knot on his tie, tighter muscles on his cheeks, three microphones in front of him, the devil not quite behind him. A curious dazzle of lightning flickered suddenly across his deeply etched visage. I thought at first it was a press photographer's flash, but it might well have had its source inside and not outside the bones of his head. Next booking: *Doctor Who*.

As usual in his reviews, he had a dig at BBC executives. Praising a *Play for Today*, Roy Minton's *Funny Farm*, set in a psychiatric hospital, he observed, 'The patients didn't seem to watch much television, another disturbing similarity to the inmates whose doors open on to a long corridor that goes round and round the Television Centre and never quite makes it out into the real world.' He mocked Ludovic Kennedy putting portentous questions 'to a mute camera lens', and recalled that 'my mother used to do the same sort of thing to the family dog. "One day he'll bloody well answer," my father said.' He cooed over *Come Dancing*: 'Watching it is like chewing poppy seeds while massaging the eyes with mashed bananas . . . Compère Terry Wogan puts his tongue so far into his cheek that it almost tickles the lobe of his ear. Everything is as smooth and indigestible as a dollop of Brylcreem.' And he was moved to switch off by Colin Welland asking 'How many of us really believe in eternal life?' in an ITV Easter programme. 'All I can tell him', wrote Potter, 'is that ten seconds later there was still a faintly luminous afterglow at the centre of the mysteriously emptied screen, scarcely bigger than the mote in a clergyman's eye . . . The room was quiet except for the sound of children resolutely munching chocolate eggs and the dog licking its genitals.'

He now displayed an underlying pessimism about television. In an October 1975 article he suggested that the medium was part of 'the amiable conspiracy that keeps our heads full of soft and pale marrow', and the following month he deplored the loss of Reithian idealism at the BBC, observing that its programmes were now designed merely to 'hold as many viewers as possible until the next programme thumps out its noisy signature tune'.

Shortly after he had written this, his father died suddenly of a heart attack at the age of sixty-nine. Jane Potter says, 'I never saw Dad cry until I gave him the news that Grandad was dead.' Sarah says their mother had warned Dennis that this might happen, 'and that Dad ought to make more of an effort to go over and see him. But of course he didn't.' In *The Singing Detective*, Marlow finds it hard to believe his father has died – 'There's so much I want to say – I need to talk to him, very badly' – but an old man from the Forest remarks, 'Thou's never did give the poor bugger credit when him was alive! Got too big for thee boots, disn't?'

Eighteen years later, Potter could be moved to tears when talking of his 'lovely, gentle father'. Yet he told Melvyn Bragg he had 'had a better relationship' with Walt after his death, 'in the sense that I see more and I feel that I understand more of his gentleness and of his desire to reach me, and I feel that I am being reached . . . I can feel him genetically in me . . . I plug into that now more, more easily, that's all I can say.'

In an interview only a year after Walt's death, he said that since the bereavement he had written no original work: 'The grief has been so pitiless. I didn't want to turn myself to anything but that.' Strikingly, the next play he wrote at this period, *Double Dare*, begins with a 'blocked' writer, but since it was televised immediately after *Late Call* had finished, in April 1976, it must have been written some while before Walt's death. Indeed, in 1993 Potter denied to Graham Fuller that he had ever experienced writer's block:

POTTER: I guess at those writers' struggles. I don't – maybe alas! – have many of those blocks or difficulties. I just get on with it. But it does occur to me, as I facilely cover the pages, what it would be like not to be able to write – which is probably the source of some of those alleged 'sufferings' the writers have in my plays.

FULLER: Have you ever suffered from writer's block?

POTTER: Once or twice maybe, and then I melodramatized it into something else. In other words, even while it was a so-called block I knew it wasn't really.

FULLER: It was a means to an end perhaps?

POTTER: It was a means to draw something else out of myself, yes.

Double Dare continues the enigmatic what-is-truth game of hide-and-seek. Tom in *Schmoedipus* warns the game-playing Elizabeth, 'You must *not* involve other people', and now, for the first time, Potter did just this, drawing a living person into the make-believe web of a play.

The result was his most accomplished script since *Follow the Yellow Brick Road*, both highly autobiographical and immensely entertaining.

*

It all began with a phone call to Trodd. 'I was pressuring Dennis for a script,' says Trodd, 'and he had a block, or said he did, and he suddenly rang me and said, "I think I've found a way of breaking the block. Will you arrange a meeting with Kika Markham?"'

Then in her late twenties, Kika Markham's most recent television appearance had been in Harold Pinter's *The Basement* alongside Pinter himself; she had also starred in François Truffaut's *Les deux anglaises et le continent*. Off screen she had lived for several years with David Mercer (she says that Mercer's *Let's Murder Vivaldi* is partly about the break-up of their relationship) and was active in the Workers' Revolutionary Party. 'I don't know where Dennis first saw me,' she says,

or where this thing about wanting to meet me came from. I was known as quite a militant campaigner within Equity – but I think that would have been the last thing Dennis would have been drawn by! Anyway a phone call came from Ken – I don't remember an agent being involved: 'Dennis Potter has got a block, and he wondered if he could have a meal with you, maybe talk over some ideas.' I suppose he might have said, 'There could be a part in it for you', but I don't think he did.

They met one evening at a central London hotel where Potter often stayed at this stage in his life, the Regent in Carburton Street, in the garment district north of Oxford Street and a few hundred yards from the BBC's Broadcasting House. Kika Markham describes it as 'an anonymous glass and concrete block near the BBC, with awful Muzak, no atmosphere at all. I had some bags or parcels with me, and Dennis said, "We'll take them upstairs to my room." I was thinking, "What does he expect?" and I imagine *he* was thinking, "I wonder what she thinks I'm expecting."'

Double Dare opens in exactly the same way, with the actress Helen walking towards a contemporary-style London hotel; we also see her in mirror image, so that she is constantly hurrying towards her own reflection; meanwhile Al Bowlly sings 'I Double Dare You' on the soundtrack. At the hotel, the writer Martin Ellis is waiting fretfully in his twin-bedded room. Potter describes him as 'a not quite standard man approaching forty' (his own fortieth birthday had fallen in May

1975). In Martin's imagination, seductive female voices tempt him to phone an escort agency, but instead he rings home, speaks to his young son, and then reassures his wife, 'I haven't taken a single tranquillizer.'

He goes downstairs to meet Helen, and finds that she is laden with shopping bags:

HELEN: I've been buying a few clothes.

MARTIN: Would you like to leave them in my room?

(*But something about the way he says this puts her on her guard.*)

HELEN: (*looking round*) Isn't there a cloakroom or something down here?

MARTIN: Let's just dump them in my room. And then go and have a drink.

[*They get into the lift.*]

I'm not used to meeting people any more . . .

HELEN: Ben told me you'd been (*hesitates*) unwell.

MARTIN: And I can't use the telephone. It's a hateful instrument. That's why I had to arrange all this through Ben. I've known him since Oxford so (*slight shrug*) I can just about talk on the phone with him . . .

[*They leave the lift and reach the room.*]

HELEN: Oh. This is a *nice* room.

MARTIN: (*glint*) Do you think so?

HELEN: Well, as hotel rooms go.

MARTIN: Are you going to agree with everything I say?

HELEN: (*blink*) What?

MARTIN: I mean, is this a nice room, or is it not a nice room?

(*Slight pause.*)

HELEN: (*measured*) I have no very strong opinion one way or the other. Should I?

MARTIN: No. Not unless you say (*mimics*) 'Oh. This is a *nice* room.'

(*Silence. Then he makes a helpless little gesture in the air.*)

Jesus Christ! I'm so sorry.

HELEN: It's a sort of *middling* room.

MARTIN: I've forgotten the way people talk to each other. I've forgotten how utterly unimportant the literal meanings of the words are that they say to each other . . . I had also forgotten how lovely you are.

HELEN: Thank you.

(*Silence.*)

MARTIN: My throat has gone completely dry. (*Pause. Gabble*) I've got to get a drink of water.

(*And he rushes into the adjoining bathroom. She stands still a moment, with a slight frown. Then, with an almost imperceptible shrug, sits on one of the beds, her hands clasped on one knee.*)

HELEN: (*softly*) Cor. Blimey.

Kika Markham says that this – and indeed all the dialogue between Martin and Helen – exactly captures what happened that evening: 'It wasn't a chat-up in the ordinary sense, though he'd summoned me to a hotel rather than a restaurant, and I suppose his fantasy might have been that after dinner we'd go upstairs. But the whole evening was another kind of challenge, when we went downstairs for drinks.'

In the play, Helen and Martin settle down in the hotel bar:

MARTIN: I have set up this meeting between you and me because it is exactly – no, nearly – reproducing or rather anticipating the kind of tension between a man and a girl that I see in this new play. But if I am too explicit, I shall destroy that tension.

HELEN: A man and a girl.

MARTIN: Yes. But they don't know each other.

HELEN: And you're thinking of me for the part of the girl.

MARTIN: More.

HELEN: (*wary*) How do you mean?

MARTIN: How real are invented things?

HELEN: I don't think I understand.

MARTIN: (*half contemptuous*) No. You wouldn't . . . Because you are an *actress* . . . You use your body, your face, your eyes, your voice to play invented people. Your *own* body. Your *own* face. Your *own* eyes. Your *own* voice. And – who knows? – even your own *mind* . . . Could you play a prostitute?

HELEN: Of course.

(*They look at each other. He is the first to lower his eyes.*)

Is – is that what your play is going to be about? . . . Or is it all still too vague?

MARTIN: Very vague . . . Of course, you have the sovereign right to refuse the part. If it ever gets written . . . On the other hand you will still be on the page. Even if played by someone else's body, face, eyes and voice.

HELEN: (*edge*) And do you rest on the seventh day?

MARTIN: (*surprised*) Pardon?

HELEN: You haven't invented a single whole person. Not even yourself. Nobody can do that . . . And you haven't the *faintest* idea of what sort of person I am. Nor of what moves me, frightens me, excites me, bores me, *anything*.

MARTIN: No? (*Slight pause. He works his mouth, distressed. Whisper*) Are we *alone*, then? . . . Are we *separate*? . . . Everybody. Every single soul.

HELEN: (*gives a brittle little laugh.*) We shouldn't talk like this in a *bar*.

MARTIN: (*jeer*) Where else? A church?

'I gave him half his lines in that play,' says Markham, 'because I really did argue back. And he kept that in, though I think my answers didn't always please him – and even that is incorporated!' She confirms that the conversation was mainly about 'what it meant to *act* a part – he was confused as to whether you *were* what you were acting. I'm sure that was very central in him – he had trouble with the boundaries of reality.

'In effect he kept asking, "Are you really a whore?" It was true that I'd had to take off my clothes in quite a few things. And I suppose I had been victimized and exploited, prostituted, by some of it.' In *Double Dare*, Martin soon brings up Helen's participation in a chocolate commercial:

MARTIN: (*intense hiss*) *Why did you do it?* . . . That chocolate thing. That biting the bar thing . . .

(*And crash into the 'chocolate thing' he means: a simulation of a familiar ad.*)

COMMERCIAL: HELEN AND THE 'FRAGGIE BAR'

A pastel haze. A sultry HELEN *lifts a long ridged bar of chocolate to her mouth. And, as it were, sucks a bit of it off. A chocolate penis.*

INTERIOR. HOTEL BAR . . .

MARTIN: (*sweating*) I mean – I mean – all I want to know is . . . The director of that commercial . . . did he explicitly say that you were to – to – simulate – ah –

HELEN: Oh, Martin! We were all falling about – it's so *funny*!

MARTIN: (*dogged*) In so many words, did he *say* – look, this bar, this chocolate, is a – a penis?

HELEN: That wasn't the word he used.

(*She is close to out-loud laughter.*)

MARTIN: Does it matter what you act in? . . . That's what I intend to find out . . .

HELEN: (*stiffening*) And how are you going to find that out?

MARTIN: (*painfully slow*) I have – peculiar – delusions . . . That I – well – that I am some sort of *puppet master.*

HELEN: (*crisply*) Occupational hazard . . . You're a writer . . . You push people around on a nice clean white page. Do this, do that, you say. Speak. Be quiet. Cry.

MARTIN: And when I look up from the page?

HELEN: You see real people.

MARTIN: (*echoes the familiar phrase ruminatively*) Real People.

HELEN: (*she speaks with an edge; a sort of warning*) And we don't all do what you want or what you expect, Martin . . .

MARTIN: (*very quietly*) We'll see. Won't we?

'Curiously,' says Markham, 'a few years after *Double Dare*, I took part in just that sort of commercial – for Cornetto ice-creams. But it was funny rather than sexy – I had to lick a lot of shaving cream!

'Dennis was interested in seeing if he could root out what disillusionment I had – asking just how much would I sell my principles for when it came down to it, if I wanted a part that badly. It was, "Uh huh, Kika's left wing, so we'll get her in this commercial, really prostituting herself with a chocolate bar, selling her soul." And when he talked about the actress having to play the whore as well, I said, "Why must she be there as well?" And he just answered, "Don't you want two parts in it?"'

Potter called the play *Double Dare* because, alongside the edgy exchanges between Martin and Helen, a more overtly sexual duel is taking place a few yards away, between a businessman and a girl he has booked from an escort agency. The script specifies that the call-girl is to be played by the actress who is playing Helen – and when *Double Dare* was made, both parts were taken by Kika Markham.

'I think there really may have been another couple in the hotel that evening,' says Markham, 'and Dennis may have fantasized about them being a whore and her client, and told me I could play that part too, and she would be my double. But by this time I think it was getting rather difficult and intense, and maybe we didn't know (as in the play) quite where it was going to end. And so – I don't know what excuse I made to go to the phone – but I rang Ken, and he turned up, and it got really embarrassing.'

Trodd recalls: 'Kika phoned me, saying, "I don't know what he's up to – will you come over?" And I did, and what happened next was more or less as in the script.' In *Double Dare*, Ben's arrival makes things even more tense. 'Is he giving you a bad time? . . . Gives you the creeps, does he?' he asks Helen, while Martin fetches more drinks. When Ben discloses that Martin is in love with her, she says she feels sick. 'You'll get a good part out of it,' Ben reassures her, but she snaps, 'You filthy stinking *pimp*.' Ben then leaves for the theatre ('I was going to the theatre,' confirms Trodd; 'also, I didn't want to get drawn into Dennis's crypto-sexual game'); and Helen now considers the implications of the double rôle Martin intends to write for her, 'one being me and the other being a whore, who is *also* me'.

Martin tries to express his feelings to her, but is rebutted – Helen has had enough, declines his dinner invitation, and asks to collect her things from his room. They ascend in the lift, just after the client has taken the call-girl to his room, which is next door to Martin's. We see the second couple in bed together, and, when the girl taunts the client for failing to perform sexually, he begins to strangle her. Next door, Martin becomes transfixed by the noises coming through the wall, though Helen can hear nothing:

MARTIN: 'You stinking whore,' he's saying. I can hear it. He hates her. Hates
her! She's biting and kicking and – that's it! That's it! I *knew* it would
happen! I knew! Hands round her throat! . . . Squeezing the life out of
her, the sex out of her, the *pretence* out of her. (*He stops. Cruelty and
excitement die on his face.*) It's all over. I knew how it would end . . .
(*Comes from wall, faces into room . . . His breath sucks in, in a long
shudder of horror.*) No!

The camera whip-pans to the bed, where *Helen* lies strangled; and we
discover that the next-door room is occupied by an ordinary, respectable couple. The play ends with Martin looking at Helen's lifeless
body, 'cracking his fingers, tut-tutting, twitching', and telephoning – to
the escort agency.

John Mackenzie, who was to direct *Double Dare* (with Trodd
producing), did not initially want Markham in the part that she had
helped to create. 'He thought she wasn't sufficiently in the forefront of
the young and pretty actresses,' explains Trodd. 'But I don't think
there was any other name put forward.' She got the part – or parts, for
she played the call-girl as well – and Alan Dobie was cast as Martin
(he played him as a slightly solemn Welshman). Joe Melia, who had
known Potter and Trodd since National Service, was chosen for Ben.
'I didn't know there was anything truthful behind the play,' Melia says,

though Kika was a very beautiful woman shrouded in a kind of mystery, with
a gentle, madonna-like sweetness, and you might imagine there were raging
fires underneath. I was only on the shoot, at Ealing, for a couple of days. The
old ways of the BBC were starting to get a bit more fluid, and *Double Dare*
was all on film, so we only sort of rehearsed. I remember Dennis at the read-
through, clutching his pencil with those terrible hands, and spilling his coffee,
and laughing at himself.

Markham found that she not only had to do the 'Fraggie Bar'
commercial, but was required by the script to take part in a sex scene
featuring Helen and a young male actor, recalled in Martin's mind. 'It
was quite a mortifying process,' Markham says, 'much more explicit
than I'd ever done before – it meant stripping off and making love with
a total stranger, which was very cold-hearted and distressing. So
Dennis got his way there, I suppose.' (The stage direction specifies 'a
fury of flesh', and Martin describes this scene as 'as near to actual
screwing as anybody has ever seen on television'.)

'I didn't actually see much of Dennis during the production,'

Markham continues. 'And he kept rather at arm's length after *Double Dare*, sadly, because I would have loved to have talked to him more about it all. In a way, he won, in the play – he killed me, killed Helen. But I always wanted it to end with me getting up from the bed, and saying, "Wait a minute – you can't do that to me!" Even so, I think it's the best play ever written about acting and writing, full stop. Thereafter he wrote a lot of plays about the dubiousness of exploiting women, but he never again gave them a mouthpiece with which to answer back.'

*

Potter described *Double Dare* as 'very menacing and dangerous and *very* sexually disturbing'. It was reviewed in the *New Statesman* by Martin Amis:

Potter is one of our funniest and most wayward TV playwrights – just as he is the best equipped of its critics . . . *Double Dare*, ominously, was about a mad TV playwright . . . All the parts were slightly overwritten, of course, and as always the relationship that was less intimate to Potter – escort agent and lout – was observed with far more poise than the writerly agonies of the mad TV dramatist, whose tranced, twitching disorientation had me reaching for my electrodes every time he appeared on screen. For all its alienations, however, *Double Dare* worked well enough naturalistically to double my nicotine intake during its screening, and there were the usual three or four scenes with Potter at perfect pitch, where each line of dialogue made you either wince or gloat.

Potter has recently been putting it about that the present trilogy [*Brimstone and Treacle, Double Dare* and *Where Adam Stood*, his adaptation of Gosse's *Father and Son*, which the BBC was to show in quick succession] is a study of religious aspiration, or at least a secular displacement of it. Well, the religious aspiration that interests him most seems to be simply the act of writing: he is intensely aware of being able to do things to people on a page. Potter sees this as a Promethean gesture – a raid on God's fire – and it worries him. (His novel, *Hide and Seek*, was about little else.) Accordingly, his author figures are updated versions of the Romantic loon, spluttering, apoplectic, touched; and his minor characters are only stylized projections of the author figure's drives and fears. This is why his plots are obliged to fold in on themselves, and why his themes tend to equate creativity with infatuated rant. It is also, no doubt, why his plays have audacity and nerve.

Potter later said about Martin Amis's own fiction, 'Amis is very tight, supremely skilled, very funny, and sometimes disturbing. But he's trapped as a novelist. He's like that bit in T. S. Eliot – he does a piece in all these different voices, a complicated perpetual parody. It's funny but it's not real, and you're always aware of that.'

Double Dare also earned praise from Peter Knight in the *Daily Telegraph* – 'This was Potter at his tantalizing best' – and Shaun Usher in the *Daily Mail*: 'At times, in the presence of a play-within-a-play – squared to infinity – one felt giddy. "If you were an actor – but you're not," the girl remarked to the writer. Who was, among other things, Alan Dobie – who *is* an actor.' Kika Markham did not divulge to the press that there was yet another layer to the onion.

CHAPTER II

Outrage

Double Dare was shown as the Play for Today on 6 April 1976 –
against Potter's wishes. The slot was supposed to have been occupied
by Brimstone and Treacle, with Double Dare following a week later
and Where Adam Stood being shown on BBC2 a week after that. On
20 March the news broke that Brimstone had been banned by the BBC.

In his New Statesman column a few weeks later, Potter gave his
version of events:

Brimstone and Treacle was delivered to the BBC in early December 1974,
discussed, praised, accepted and paid for in January 1975, assigned to a
producer (Kenith Trodd, thank goodness), discussed again in long and
involved meetings, given the crucial nod by the Head of Plays [now
Christopher Morahan], handed over to director Barry Davis, discussed yet
again, then cast, rehearsed, brought into the studio, videotaped, dubbed,
scheduled for transmission . . . Everyone along the labyrinthine chain of
command which makes the BBC so delicately elephantine had a chance to
throw in his or her two pennyworth of unhelpful comment. Actors, designers,
wardrobe, lighting, cameramen and sound engineers – and about £70,000 –
were deployed . . .

In fact there had been some anxiety about the project at Television
Centre from the outset. 'They have sat on the play for two years,'
Potter told the People newspaper in October 1975 (it was actually less
than a year), 'but now they have suddenly taken courage.' In the same
article, Trodd was quoted: 'It's true that the play's subject was a
problem in the minds of some people in the Drama Department at first.
But . . . I think it's great.'

Brimstone and Treacle was recorded at Television Centre on 2–4 March

1976, a month before the date scheduled for transmission, with Barry Davis directing. The next week, the Controller of BBC1, Bryan Cowgill, had his attention drawn to the play by an aide who had read the synopsis, and he asked to view the tape. He felt that 'a few minor changes', and a warning to viewers before the play began, should take care of any problems, but he decided to refer the matter upwards to Alasdair Milne, who was now Director of Programmes, Television. Milne watched the recording and found it 'repugnant'. He writes in his memoirs, 'It has always seemed to me that it was the broadcaster's duty at times to shock, but that he must take care not to outrage his audience; otherwise the dialogue between them would become wholly one-sided. But outrage was, it seemed to me, what Dennis had achieved . . .'

The play opens with two epigraphs, seen as captions: '"There resides infinitely more good in the demonic than in the trivial man" – Kierkegaard', and '"A spoonful of sugar helps the medicine go down" – Andrews', meaning Julie Andrews, who sang the line in *Mary Poppins*. In a London street, Martin Taylor, 'a young, pale man with soulful eyes, neat and intense, the sort of person who might be found taking his Bible tracts for a walk', is trying to trap a passing businessman by pretending that he knows him. But the man isn't fooled:

BUSINESSMAN: What's my name?

MARTIN: *(alarmed)* What?

BUSINESSMAN: *(cold)* My name. What, then, is my name?

MARTIN: *(brazen)* Sam. Sam Coleridge.

BUSINESSMAN: No it isn't! *(And he moves on, with a brisk snort.)*

MARTIN: Oh dear. I'm *so* sorry – not Samuel Taylor Coleridge – I could have sworn . . . Do you read poetry then? Shall we talk about poetry? . . . Or any other subject. We can talk about music or sport or demons . . . *(Calls after him)* I know a lot about demons, sir! Didn't you smell the *sulphur*?

Martin, then, is clearly a counterpart to Michael Biddle in *Angels Are So Few*, a damaged individual who believes he is a supernatural being – this time, a (or maybe the) devil.

He now collides accidentally with another middle-aged man, Mr Bates, and manages to convince him that he is a friend of his daughter. But Martin nearly reveals the deception by failing to know that two years ago, the girl was knocked down by a car and is seriously brain-damaged, unable to speak. Bates manages to disentangle himself, but Martin has stolen his wallet, and has found his address. 'Sick, sick people in metal boxes,' Martin mutters, gazing at the passing cars. 'They do not know the taste of blood in their mouths. They do not know the glory of the hunt as *I* know it, as *demons* know it . . . I must buy some mints to hide the smell of sulphur. I've *got* him, *got* him.'

That evening, Bates and his wife are bickering in their suburban home about their daughter, Pattie, who lies burbling to herself in a bed in the sitting room. Bates prefers to think of her as 'only a vegetable', but his wife is convinced that 'something in her is trying to come back to us'. The doorbell rings ('an elaborate St Clement Danes', Potter specifies of the chime), and Martin arrives with the wallet – having removed forty pounds. Claiming that he was once in love with Pattie, he learns that she was the victim of a hit-and-run. 'They never did find the driver,' says Bates. 'All I hope is that whoever did it dies full of cancer, screaming his head off.'

Martin spins a tale about having proposed to Pattie – 'she will always, always be for me the girl all the songs sing about' – and begs to move in with the Bates family for a few days, and relieve Pattie's mother of some of the burden of nursing. Bates remains suspicious ('I mean, you might be a – a pickpocket or the devil himself for all *we* know'), but Martin gets his way, chiefly through his camp flirtation with Mrs Bates ('Mumsy . . . That's how I think of you now'). He is given Pattie's old bedroom to sleep in, which has been left untouched since the accident. Prowling round it, Martin 'strokes' her under-clothes, then takes a bra and lies down on the bed with it, 'like a "B" movie strangler with a bit of rope', specifies Potter. The direction continues:

He seems to go into a catatonic trance, clenching his teeth, marbling his face muscles, hissing his breath . . . His eyes . . . horribly turn milky white, losing the iris altogether. And then, worse still, even more slowly, his eyeballs go deepest crimson. As the light fades, a laugh. A cackle. Pull back. The curtains are streaming out into the room . . . He screws the bra up . . . and squeezes a jet of blood out of it. Then collapses back on the bed with a long hiss.

Next morning, while Bates is at work, Martin persuades Mrs Bates to go to the hairdresser and leave him in charge of Pattie. He addresses her in sing-song verse –

> Now the time has come to see
> What will happen 'twixt you and me.
> You'll find the Devil is hard to beat,
> You're at his mercy my little sweet!

– then turns directly to the camera, and tells the viewer:

> If you are a nervous type out there,
> Switch over or off to get some calmer air.
> But you have to be very smug or very frail
> To believe that *no man* has a horn or tail.

He unbuttons the top of her nightdress, murmuring 'Now let Daddy see dem ickle boo-boos'. We cut away briefly to a flashback of Pattie's accident, and when we return to Martin he is 'on top of the girl . . . panting'. He gasps out yet another rhyme:

> Oh, cinnamon and spice
> Ain't half so nice
> As giving a girlee
> The right sort of whirlee.

Pattie 'starts to make loud, gibbering noises', and Martin 'puts his hand over her mouth, blocking out the sound'.

When Mrs Bates returns, Pattie seems calmer than usual. Her mother explains that, after the accident, one of the doctors suspected that 'she might be suffering as much from the *shock* as the injuries', and 'might – *come back*, sort of'. Martin tells her 'We've got to have faith', and suggests that they pray together. Kneeling with Mrs Bates at Pattie's bedside, he begins by quoting the Witches from *Macbeth* ('When shall we three meet again . . . ?'), but then comes out with a conventional prayer: 'Almighty God . . . Dear gentle Father in heaven . . . Reach out, O Lord, in thy holy mercy and touch this innocent young girl . . . '

That evening, Bates wants to eject the intruder from the house, but Martin discovers and panders to Bates's Enoch Powell–Alf Garnett racism ('Send them back to their own countries'). Meanwhile we learn that, just before Pattie's accident, Bates was paying a visit to Pattie's tarty friend Susan: 'She was in the amateur dramatics with Pattie,' explains Mrs Bates. 'She played a prostitute . . . ' Later that night, Martin tiptoes downstairs and again clambers into Pattie's bed, muttering, 'I reckon you enjoy this as much as I do. You greedy little girl.' But this time Pattie screams, and Martin pulls on his clothes and rushes away from the house. A flashback now shows us that Pattie ran into the path of the car because she was in shock after finding her father in bed with Susan. Moreover Martin's second attempt at sex with Pattie has awoken her from her catatonic state, and her first lucid words are: 'What happened? Daddy?' – referring as much to her father's adultery as to Martin and the rape. Meanwhile Martin has bounded off down the suburban street and picked on yet another middle-aged man as his next victim.

Discussing *Brimstone and Treacle* with Melvyn Bragg in 1994, Potter spoke of the play's iconography in religious terms, with Martin as devil:

It's a simple flip-over of an orthodox, of an ordinary sentimental religiose, rather than religious, parable, in that there is an afflicted house – variously afflicted, but in particular with a crippled, seemingly mindless, struck girl, young girl. And there is a visitor, and the visitor brings her to life and makes her speak. Now, if that visitor were an angel, then all you would have is sanctimoniousness, you would learn nothing about anything . . . What if it were the devil? . . . So instead of the angel coming and rescuing the cripple and the dumb and the afflicted, I had the devil do it. The evil act can lead to good consequences; a good act can lead to evil consequences. This is often the case, and . . . it is incomprehensible. It is as though, you know, the rain falls on the just and upon the unjust.

Yet in April 1976, the month in which the play was to have been transmitted, Potter told Sean Day-Lewis that if the message of *Brimstone and Treacle* had to be put into one sentence, it would be 'forms of good can arise out of evil', and he made no mention of the diabolical.

Arguably, *Brimstone* is a rewriting not so much of a religious parable as a fairy story, *The Sleeping Beauty*, in which a young man cuts his way through a bramble hedge – in this case, the suburban *mores* of the Bates family – to bring a sleeper back to life by awakening her sexuality. (In the earliest recorded form of this tale, the fourteenth-century French romance *Perceforest*, the prince Troylus awakes the princess Zellandine by raping her.) The story's relevance to Potter is not hard to perceive: by this stage of his life he might have felt that Uncle Ernie's sexual interference with his own childhood had been a kind of emotional and intellectual 'awakening', which – for all its horror – had motivated him to become a writer. Discussing the play, he emphasized that Pattie's first words on awakening are 'an accusation against her father' – and the abused child's natural reaction is indeed to turn to the parent, who has failed to protect against it, and ask, 'What happened?'

Nowhere in the script of *Brimstone and Treacle* does Potter specify that Martin (who has the same first name as the writer in *Double Dare*) is the, or even a, devil. The nearest he comes is to describe Martin's toenails as 'very long, curling and claw-like' – but since Martin *thinks* he is a devil, he may have let them grow in order to resemble one. In the production, Martin was given the power to cause lighting changes with a flick of his fingers (in the scene when he prays with Mrs Bates), but this is not specified in the script. The devil would not pray to God, as Martin does, and Martin has no advance knowledge of the Bates family, as a supernatural being surely would. In some respects he is not even immoral – he weans Bates away from the extremes of racism by parodying his opinions (urging Bates that blacks should be put in Hitler-style death camps), so that Bates eventually says, 'I shan't renew my [National Front] subscription.' The scene in Pattie's bedroom, in which Martin acts out sexual fantasies with her underwear, seems designed to emphasize his extreme sexuality (in preparation for his violation of Pattie, which would otherwise come out of the blue) rather than to make him seem satanic.

Potter denied that *Brimstone and Treacle* was meant from the outset to create a mould-breaking *cause célèbre*: 'I have never felt the need to do that. It has come, the mould, if broken on any one point, has come out of the need to do what I was doing.' Trodd, however, is certain that Potter intended the play to shock and cause a stir.

Alasdair Milne writes that, when he watched it, 'such was the brilliance of the acting, particularly by the girl with her swollen tongue and slobbering grunts, that the act of rape made me almost physically sick'. In fact, as others who were shown the tape pointed out, the rapes (there are two) are not shown, whereas *Double Dare* had included an explicit sex scene; yet Milne, single-handedly it seems, 'decided that we would not transmit *Brimstone and Treacle*, most reluctantly, because Dennis's work had brought great distinction to the BBC'.

Milne seems to have communicated this decision to Cowgill and others on Friday, 19 March 1976, two and half weeks before transmission. Potter was not called to Television Centre to discuss the play; Milne says this was because the *Radio Times* was about to go to press with a feature on *Double Dare*, *Brimstone and Treacle* and *Where Adam Stood*, so a decision had to be taken at once if one of these was to be dropped.

'SATAN PLAY BANNED BY BBC,' announced the *Daily Mail* next morning, reporting that *Brimstone* had been 'withdrawn from the programme schedule . . . after an extraordinary scene at the Television Centre . . . during which it is understood BBC1 Controller Bryan Cowgill stormed out of a room in anger'. Potter told the *Guardian* that he found the banning 'depressing'.

'I wrote to Dennis,' says Milne, 'and explained my reactions . . . There was, of course, a great row.' The BBC issued a press handout explaining that the 'rape by the devil . . . of a girl physically and mentally crippled' was 'likely to outrage viewers to a degree that its importance as a play does not support'; but meanwhile Trodd had managed to show the play clandestinely to selected television critics, and they disagreed.

Peter Fiddick wrote in the *Guardian* on 22 March, 'The play which, last Friday, senior BBC executives decided could not be screened . . . [is] disturbing on the level Potter wants, not shocking as Alasdair Milne and Bryan Cowgill fear people will be shocked . . . I hope the BBC will look at *Brimstone and Treacle* again, in calmer mood than was possible last week.' Sean Day-Lewis told *Daily Telegraph* readers that the play ranked 'with Potter's finest work' and was 'worrying but not, I think, outrageous'. There was praise from other critics for Barry Davis's direction and Denholm Elliott's performance as Mr Bates (a part that suited him much better than Jack Black), and *Time Out* told its readers, 'We had seen the tape . . . and our first reaction to the news that Cowgill had fulminated against the rape scene was "what rape scene?" . . . Potter's play is tight, fierce, black, honest and outrageous.' A week after the banning, the *Daily Mail* alleged that Milne was 'facing an open revolt by some of his top producers who accuse him of introducing a new wave of censorship' – Jack Gold's film of Quentin Crisp's *The Naked Civil Servant* had also been banned.

Day-Lewis reported that Potter had considered applying for a court injunction preventing the BBC from showing the other two plays in the 'trilogy' if they would not show *Brimstone*, but 'this move has now been abandoned in favour of a submission to the Annan Committee asking it to propose appeal machinery for cases of this kind'. Potter was quoted in the *Daily Mail* – 'What is sad is that a generation of second-rate bureaucrats is leading the BBC down from the heights' – and he allowed reporters to see two sentences from the letter to him in which Milne explained the banning: 'I found the play brilliantly written and made, but nauseating. I believe that it is right in certain instances to outrage the viewers in order to get over a point of serious importance, but I am afraid that in this case real outrage would be widely felt and that no such point would get across.'

Devoting his own *New Statesman* column to the row, Potter called Milne's letter 'brief and insolent', and described the banning as

a decision which in more than my not entirely disinterested opinion reveals a lot about the changing nature of the BBC and the sort of television we're going to get in the future . . .

Milne and his immediate subordinates are, of course, entitled to exercise editorial control over what is to be transmitted by the BBC. I have had scripts . . . rejected before now, and not even the most rabid paranoia, nor the worst excesses of arrogance, can allow me to argue that the BBC should be compelled to screen my work . . . [But] Milne is wrong. Television critics . . . say [*Brimstone*] is at the very least an interesting play that should be shown . . . The Drama Department, the Arts Department, many directors and writers, and all those concerned in making the play are of similar mind. They are not so much angry on my behalf as on their own: the programme-makers detect signs of a loss of nerve in those set above them . . .

Brimstone and Treacle is near my heart (or liver anyway) because I think it may be the best play I have written. The fast-diminishing residue of what was once an almost evangelical passion about the place of drama on the television screen, rather than simpering self-love, makes me demand that you should be *allowed* to see the play. Unlike Alasdair Milne, I am assuming, of course, that you are grown up and know how to work the off switch. You can reach him if you wish to object to his censorship by telephoning the BBC on 01-743 8000 and asking for the Ghost of Lord Reith.

In a *Radio Times* interview previewing *Double Dare*, Potter had said he expected that he would soon give up writing for television, because of the decline of the medium; and he had written in 1974 that 'the feeling that your work so totally disappears into the endless electronic flux reduces you to a near-paralysis in which you can see the videotape being wiped at the very moment the dialogue forms at the end of the pen'. But after the banning of *Brimstone*, in May 1976, he told the *Daily Express*, 'Strangely enough, the argument has made me realize afresh the importance of television . . . If I can get that kind of reaction to a play, maybe it is saying something important.'

*

Where Adam Stood was shown on BBC2 as scheduled, on 21 April 1976. A far better play than *Brimstone*, it resumes Potter's theme of the inability of formal Christianity to explain the contradiction between a supposedly benevolent deity and a world full of pain. 'I only took a few pages of it,' Potter said of his dramatization of Edmund Gosse's celebrated book about his naturalist, fundamentalist parent, *Father and Son* (1907). 'The play is in no sense an adaptation.' He selects a few episodes (and invents another) to convey his message that a doctrinaire upbringing – such as he himself had experienced at Salem Chapel – leaves a child utterly unprepared for a crazy, sex-obsessed world.

The invention is of a character and incident not in Gosse's book. The village madwoman, Mary Teague, singing, shouting and farting, represents total animality. She is the opposite pole to Philip Henry Gosse (Edmund's father), whose purely intellectual religion calmly accepts the fact of his wife's death; he is willing to see his only child – who suffers from a persistent cough – go to the grave as well if it be God's will. This, of course, is the precise opposite of Joe in the earlier play, whose pet shop, where fish can devour each other in the tanks, and Joe himself can choose to starve them all, is a microcosm of the godless cruelties of the world.

Gosse is so determined to reconcile the evidence of the Darwinian biologists with the teachings of Genesis that he blinds himself (godlike) to his son's emotional needs, and gives him no warning about the 'slime' (to use Jack Black's word) of the real world. Consequently the child runs off innocently with Mary Teague to the woods, where she lies on her back and tells him 'You'm *nice* boy . . . Come here – come on . . .' Potter said of this episode, 'It was just one of those things that would happen in a village at that time, one of the realizations that the world is different and more complicated than the simple vision God is giving you.' (This was in his interview with Graham Fuller, and he added, 'I am feeling uncomfortable. Please move on.' Even in 1993, his childhood sexual abuse was not a subject he found it easy to talk about.)

The play's title comes from Gosse-the-father's attempt to persuade himself that, from 'where Adam stood' in the Garden of Eden, everything would have looked the same as it does now – that the supposed evidence of evolution had in fact been planted deceptively by the Almighty. But Potter emphasized that the title has a double meaning: 'The shape of the little drama is exactly like the Garden of Eden, and the boy's final self-knowledge is like Adam and Eve's self-knowledge. It's the boy who draws the line . . .' By the end of the play, young Edmund – more worldly wise after his encounter with Mary ('liberated' like Pattie after the rape by Martin) – has indeed realized that he, as well as his father, can play God, or at least can claim the authority of the deity to sanction his own will.

Throughout the play, he has been pining for a toy ship in the window of the village shop, and Gosse senior tells the boy to pray for guidance – he will leave it to the Lord to say whether 'a mere plaything' should 'intrude into his communion with Thee'. After the boy has duly prayed, his father asks him what answer he has received:

EDMUND: The good Lord God says I am to have the ship, father.

(GOSSE *is astounded. At first, he cannot get the words out.*)

GOSSE: (*struggling*) Are you – are you sure that is God's answer?

EDMUND: Yes, father. Quite sure.

GOSSE: I –

(*The father looks at his son, decides he is in an impossible situation, and also gets up. They stare at each other. But the boy does not wilt. Without more ado, face dark,* GOSSE *strides from the room. Pause. The boy starts to laugh, softly, victoriously, vaguely aware that he has crossed some crucial frontier.* EDMUND *gets back into bed, nestles down. Then leaps out again, and puts a chair against the door, enough to stop anyone coming in. Turns back to window, looks out, smiling, confident. Freeze picture . . . Final credits.*)

In the production, at this final moment, we hear in voice-over Darwin's words about the survival of the fittest – which now, of course, apply to Edmund himself, who has learned to contend with a hostile world.

Potter was particularly pleased with *Where Adam Stood*: 'It's probably the most complicated and probably the best of all the things, in that sense, that I've tried to do,' he told Fuller. 'It's the most complete statement of all those difficulties that yet remain very simple.'

Nancy Banks-Smith in the *Guardian* objected that the play was 'not the book', but called it 'witty, lovely and easy'. There was praise from all the critics for actors Alan Badel and Max Harris as father and son (the boy gave an outstandingly sensitive performance), and for the work of the play's young director, Brian Gibson, who had recently been studying *The Origin of Species* while reading medicine at Cambridge.

'Dennis and I were due to meet, for the first time, for *Where Adam Stood*,' recalls Gibson, 'and Ken prepared me, somewhat surprisingly, by telling me a lot of intimacies about Dennis, including how he'd visited prostitutes in the past. And I never had any conversations with Dennis about it. Personally, I would say it's a pretty tough thing to dissect out whether it was his fantasy, or whether it was true, or whether it was partly true and exaggerated. If I were a real betting man, I'd probably go for the third.'

*

Trodd writes that the banning of *Brimstone and Treacle* 'more or less coincided (probably not by chance) with the BBC lapsing into one of its fits of paranoid confusion and trying to get rid of me as a contract producer because a brainstormer in Intelligence Liaison told them I was part of an international Trotskyist threat'.

Although the BBC had carried out political vetting of employees (in co-operation with MI5) since the Thirties, this had rarely been noticed by the staff themselves. However, the growing allegiance to the New Left among young British intellectuals during the late Sixties and early Seventies led to accusations in the right-wing press that the BBC was run by 'Workers' Revolutionary Party [WRP] people', and MI5 set up a special desk to investigate 'subversives in the media'. The Plays Department of BBC Television, much of whose output was openly left wing in sympathy, was especially monitored, and Alasdair Milne recalls that there was an 'anxiety' among senior BBC management about the department's political bias.

Trodd agrees that several members of the department were indeed 'flirting' with the WRP, and that there was 'quite a lot of penetration by members of that party' into television and the theatre, but emphasizes that he himself was only a fellow-traveller. Since his return to the BBC, he had been employed on a series of one-year contracts, but he was now told that this would cease:

They said, 'We're not making a judgement about *you* – we just need to change things from time to time, and we're sure you'll be coming back.' And I got a tip-off that this was not just some ordinary professional thing, this was a purge of lefties. And that became a buzz in the business. And I got two pieces of apparently incompatible advice. One from Dennis, who said, 'Probably true, but do nothing. Just lie low, we'll get back in there, don't make waves.' And Clive Goodwin, who wanted to organize petitions in *Time Out*, making me a real martyr to the left cause.

And I steered a kind of middle course, which was actually quite effective. Everyone who'd worked with me spontaneously signed a petition. I didn't go along with the *Time Out* campaign. What I did was to use the available mechanism inside the BBC to pester and pester and pester. And the two key figures at that time, in television, were Milne and Ian Trethowan [then Managing Director, Television]. I kept exercising my right to discuss this matter, but they wouldn't give, and I remember one session with Trethowan when he said, 'I really would advise you against leaning on the conspiracy view of history.'

I went back one more time to Milne, and we talked in a civilized way, in a fifteen-minute appointment, and finished the meeting, and on the way to the lifts he said, 'Anyway, I don't understand why you're concerned – your beliefs are very well known, and you stand by them, and you ran for Parliament', and he said goodbye, and I went back to my office – and suddenly thought, they're confusing me with Roy Battersby, my director friend and colleague, who *had* of course absolutely declared his politics, had left the business, or more or less been blackballed out, and had run for Parliament twice, for the WRP.

The misunderstanding took some time to clear up, so Trodd 'finished the film I was making in Ireland and took a temporary job at the National Film School'. No recantation or apology was ever offered by the BBC, 'but they came to me in a very short time and said, "We'd like you to go back to Dennis Potter and see if there's something else he'd like to write for us." And that became *Pennies from Heaven*.'

PART THREE: 1976–1986

Now that I've got the power

———

CHAPTER I

Washed clean

On 14 July 1976, four months after the decision to ban *Brimstone and Treacle*, James Cellan Jones, Christopher Morahan's successor as Head of Plays for BBC Television, signed a note commissioning Potter to write 'six related plays' under the overall title *Ghost Writer*. They would have 'a linking character, who is a ghost writer for the famous'. This revived the *Ghost Righter* idea from 1972 ('A writer is hired to produce an "autobiography" for an image-conscious industrialist. Their lives and histories become unpredictably entwined') and would obviously be another of Potter's layers-of-the-onion games.

Trodd – who says that by this date he was 'moonlighting' between the National Film School and the BBC – guesses that when the BBC suggested that Potter and he might come up with a new idea,

they were probably thinking in terms of an olive branch commission for a seventy-five-minute play, but Dennis, never one to believe that forgiveness should come cheap, asked for the space to write a 'novel for television', about eight or nine hours' worth. In one of those institutional ironies that aren't very funny at the time, the BBC pushed the decision back at me. Just reinstated as producer of *Play for Today*, I was told that Dennis could have his big spread only if I agreed to give up six productions by other writers. I agonized for them but not for long.

Potter assumed that the serial 'was only commissioned because a few people at the BBC felt just a little guilty about the banning . . . That's the way things used to work – a smack and then a kiss.'

'Dennis didn't know what he would write about,' continues Trodd,

but the big crazed risk was obviously the one to take and his was the talent in the ascendant. So we were suddenly committed to delivering quite quickly the biggest instalment of dramatic television ever to come from one writer, and were off into a wonderful period of freedom with everything to lose. The BBC didn't want to hear from us at all until we had something to budget . . .

Trodd emphasizes that he and Potter were on their own: 'In those blissful days, "development" was only for dark rooms and "executive" went with suites; "treatment" belonged to doctors and "committees" were kept in town halls . . . We were left to our own creative devices . . .' Yet at first, Potter was bereft of ideas for the project.

At this point he changed agents. He seems to have felt that Clive Goodwin had not supported him sufficiently during the *Brimstone and Treacle* row, and Trodd decided to introduce him to a young agent named Judy Daish. Ten years younger than Potter, Daish (the daughter of an aeronautics engineer) had trained as a secretary and worked for the Royal Shakespeare Company before joining Granada Television as a production assistant. After a few years she switched careers, and joined the writers' agent Emmanuel (Jimmy) Wax as an assistant. At the Wax agency she soon built up her own list of clients, including Simon Gray and Ronald Harwood.

One day in the spring of 1976 she received a phone call from Trodd, who had known her at Granada, asking if she would like to see *Brimstone*. 'Of course,' she says,

everybody wanted to see it! So I went to Television Centre, and was surprised to find that I was the only person in the viewing room. At the end, Ken arrived and we talked about it, and he said, 'Dennis is looking for an agent. Would you be interested in meeting him?' I was bowled over, and I wrote to him – and heard nothing at all for a while. But some weeks later, when he was in London, he phoned me and asked if he could come round and see me. I was nervous, but we talked, and a few weeks later we met and had dinner.

I remember him telling me that he had a commission from the BBC to write a six-episode original serial, and that he was thinking of handing the money back, because of the way they had behaved over *Brimstone*. I remember saying, 'Why don't you just sit on it for the moment? Don't pull out.'

Potter asked Judy Daish to take him on, and wrote to Clive Goodwin, who was upset, but agreed to agent the new commission jointly, after which Daish would take over. (The following year, Goodwin died tragically in Hollywood; he had a sudden brain haemorrhage in a hotel, was thought by the staff to be drunk, and was locked up by the police – and then found to be dead.) But as late as the autumn of 1976 Potter evidently still felt very uncertain about the commission, since he made no mention of it to Joan Bakewell when she came to Morecambe Lodge to interview him for *The Sunday Times Magazine* (the profile was published in November).

'I enter a friendly house,' Bakewell wrote.

His wife Margaret leads the welcome. Jane, aged sixteen, Sarah, fifteen, and Robert, eleven, are introduced; their dog barks a greeting. Dennis holds back: I go to meet him, holding out my hand to renew a friendship. And I meet the illness. 'No, I can't do that any more. When you last met me I still could.' The fingers of both hands, crippled by arthritis, are closed in on the palms . . . He reaches for another cigarette, smokes more than he approves of, frowning as they heap the ashtray. 'I'm very jumpy this morning. Sorry.' . . . Is it my questioning? 'Well – er – yes!'

He explained to Bakewell that at present he was taking Methotrexate once a week, over a period of twenty-four hours, which frequently made him vomit for up to two days. 'But it keeps the arthritis at bay,' noted Bakewell;

the left knee is no longer stiff, he moves easily, even lithely. Only the hands have gone too far. 'These went in 1972, but I can still get quite a good hold.' He demonstrates for me how he holds the pen. 'When the thumb goes, that's when my column doesn't appear. I tried dictating. It didn't work . . . I like to make a distinct mark.' . . .

He works in 'any room that takes me. I don't like having to be pinned down. Sometimes I work on this table, sometimes on my lap in the other room. There's an office at the very top. If it's going well I can work anywhere. I seem to get by on four or five hours of sleep. So if I'm working I go on to the point of physical exhaustion . . .'

He showed me eighteen pages of a new play – *Don't Sit Under the Apple Tree* . . . with few corrections, lines fastidiously placed on the page – 'that's because I know how to time the length. I had a hydrocortisone injection a couple of weeks ago. I only hope the thumb holds.' But now the play has been set aside uncompleted. He has been adapting *The Mayor of Casterbridge* into seven episodes. The BBC will film it next summer.

Don't Sit Under the Apple Tree has disappeared. The script editor who commissioned *The Mayor of Casterbridge*, Betty Willingale, recalls that 'we were doing an episode of one or other dramatization [of a classic novel] *every week*' (on BBC2). She met Potter to discuss his undertaking Hardy's novel. 'We didn't need a long conversation, because he so clearly understood about the book . . . I usually kept in close touch with the writers and knew their thoughts. But Dennis . . . announced he wasn't going to send it in episode by episode.' When he delivered the seven handwritten scripts exactly on time, six or seven months later, Willingale was amazed: 'His writing was somehow clearer than any typewriter and . . . it was all perfectly to length . . . He was diligence itself.'

Potter later wrote a brief introduction to a paperback edition of the novel itself, in which he admitted the limitations of televising such a work:

No matter how skilled the acting and the direction however, nor how competent or diligent the dramatization, what eventually reaches the screen cannot in the end be other than a pale glimmer of the book. Marvellous vignettes get lost, patterns of sombre depth are brutally chopped or tidied, and although the drive and the settings of the novel can be heightened by the urgent rhythms of a different medium, the especial cadences of Hardy's novel resist transposition.

Elsewhere, he described the novel as 'the long, unravelled consequences of a drunken, shameful, one-act play . . . the long, long reverberation which nothing one does can prevent. Sooner or later it's going to rise up and smack you down.' This 'one-act play' consists of the young itinerant hay-trusser Michael Henchard getting drunk at a country fair and selling his wife Susan to a sailor for five guineas. In the first episode of Potter's version, this is seen as a series of flashbacks, recalled by Susan many years later, as she and her grown-up daughter Elizabeth-Jane return in search of Henchard, who is now a rich corn-dealer and Mayor of Casterbridge.

Michael Ratcliffe, reviewing the first episode of *The Mayor of Casterbridge* in *The Times* in January 1978, thought that this device was a 'miscalculation' by Potter, diminishing the impact of the wife-selling 'by placing it, as it were, between parentheses'. Potter made few other departures from Hardy's story-line, presumably finding the novel so filmic that he could mostly confine his work to judicious selection – for which he was praised by Christopher Ricks in *The Sunday Times*: 'Mr Potter knows what are the great lines . . . the crucial deep sayings are present and potent . . . Mr Potter doesn't plod in the novelist's footsteps: he seizes the novel's lines of force, converging on the heart of the book . . . '

According to Ricks, this heart was Henchard's relationship with his supposed daughter, Elizabeth-Jane. Strikingly, Potter chose to expand the scene of her reunion with her real father, the sailor Newson who bought her mother, which of course makes her realize that Henchard has been fooling her:

ELIZABETH-JANE: But he kept you from me, Father, all these months, when you might have been here?

NEWSON: Yes. 'Tis true. But –

FARFRAE: (*sternly*) No buts. He ought not to have done it.

(*The realization is sinking deeper into* ELIZABETH-JANE.)

ELIZABETH-JANE: He – (*she puts her hand to her mouth as though to be sick*) – he's not – we're not the same flesh and blood at all – he *knew* that every time he kissed me and – oh, it's *horrible!* . . .

(*She is crying in an obscure anguish, which has darker things at its root . . .*)

The 'darker things' are of course sexual. While Hardy has Henchard setting off on his suicidal trek, towards the story's end, with a miscellaneous handful of her belongings, Potter makes him take just one glove, which we see him holding caressingly against his cheek, like a lover.

The serial, produced by Jonathan Powell and directed by David Giles, was made on location in Dorset, with Alan Bates, who had co-starred in John Schlesinger's film of Hardy's *Far from the Madding Crowd* eleven years earlier, playing Henchard – 'looking for all the world', wrote Michael Ratcliffe, 'like the quick spirit of that other man of the west, Isambard Kingdom Brunel'. *The Mayor of Casterbridge* reached American audiences via *Masterpiece Theater* the following September, the first of Potter's work to be seen in the United States; indeed, advance publicity and reviews made almost no mention of his name, putting the emphasis on Alan Bates.

After finishing the Hardy scripts, Potter began to manoeuvre to get *Brimstone and Treacle* seen publicly despite the BBC ban. As a first move, he made a stage adaptation, which was performed at the Crucible Theatre, Sheffield, in September 1977. 'I have rewritten it considerably,' he claimed to the *Yorkshire Post*. 'Not the content but the whole flow of the play. I added to it and expanded it but I think I have narrowed the focus and the theatre will concentrate it more on the claustrophobic family relationship at the centre.' For the first time he admitted that the banning had affected his self-confidence: 'I keep wondering will [the] next one be banned. It acts as a kind of self-censorship which leads you on dangerous ground.' A few months later he told an interviewer, 'After *Brimstone* was banned, it took me a year to get functioning again.'

In fact, as with his stage versions of the Nigel Barton plays and *Only Make Believe*, he made no major changes from the television original. The play ends with Pattie saying, 'I remember now . . . Daddy! No, Daddy! No-o-o-o!', but this left the *Daily Telegraph* reviewer at Sheffield, Eric Shorter, rather puzzled: '. . . the father is . . . possibly guilty of something. Running his daughter over? Seducing one of her friends?' David Leland, who directed the play in the studio theatre at Sheffield, says that Potter did not attend rehearsals: 'He came and saw it and that was all he did.' The stage *Brimstone* had several other productions, including one at the Open Space in London in February 1979, with George Cole as Mr Bates.

The banning of *Brimstone* had led, in April 1976, to Potter being interviewed about his religious position by Mary Craig, on Radio 4's religious programmes *Sunday* and *Thought for the Day*. He said he believed in 'a loving Creation [which] is in continual battle with, and tension with, and obvious opposition to, the misery, cruelty, crudity and pain of an imperfect world', and admitted that he was now some-what more of a believer:

I have changed, but even within what people I suppose would call faith I have maintained doubt . . . Whatever faith I may have, or hope to have, it would be . . . walled in by doubt. And doubt is the necessary response of man at this period of time to such awesome claims by religion. But yes, I've changed . . . I cannot now live without . . . some idea of a loving God.

Asked about churchgoing, he replied, 'I'm not at that stage – I'm almost tempted to say I'm not *yet* at that stage, but I would be unhappy if it wasn't there.'

Perhaps on account of these remarks, a few months later he received a 'surprising invitation' from the BBC Religious Department to give a talk on the meaning of Christmas, which was broadcast on Radio 3 on 27 December 1976. In the talk, he said that to approach the question of religious belief head on made him feel 'evasive and uncomfortable', and went on:

A fretful scepticism grates at my mind with the noisy insistence of rooks at dusk, and although I often settle upon the thought of 'God' in the silence of my own head, and although I yearn for 'God' in the speechless ligaments of my being, I find the word 'God', and the words 'Jesus Christ', in my mouth, a genuine embarrassment. My tongue, already dipped and coated with the acid of hypocrisy, feels no more than a sliver away from cant and sanctimoniousness.

Again, I do not yet know how to pray, except perhaps for a monosyllable squeezed out between clenched teeth . . . Even when brought by something quick and compelling inside myself, which can be identified peculiarly enough as both anguished and light-hearted, I find that the door does not in fact swing open as promised – no more than the length of a chain, anyway. If there is such a door, and if it's the right door, then my knock is not firm enough.

But I do know that doubt, even doubt malignant enough to drain life of colour and purpose, is part of the provenance if not the language of faith. Its shifts and stirrings take their stubborn power from that way of seeing existence which is called 'religious'; and therefore are against not only the grain but the whole weight of the utterly secular comprehension which has become the dominant mode of perception . . .

He said that he felt himself to be 'on what feels like a voyage . . . Even when grief and pain and despair are carried in the hold, there is still this glimmer of light, or thread of grace, pointing away to an alternative, the only possible alternative . . .' And he concluded: 'The cradle song of Christmas celebrates the birth of God in the hungering soul, and at this time, even that which is properly cautious and evasive and sceptical in me will not hold back the imagination; I cannot, thank God, do other than strive and hope.'

By the time he wrote this, he had become the television critic of *The Sunday Times*. Godfrey Smith, then the editor of the paper's Review section, recalls that 'we got him entirely due to a letter Harry [Harold] Evans [the editor] wrote him when he was at a very low ebb and which he found it impossible to refuse'. He was paid £100 per review. His first, published on 10 October 1976, described Margaret Thatcher (not yet prime minister) as seen on TV from the Tory Party Conference: 'She kept her glossy head tilted at a rather too carefully alert angle, and occasionally made small pawing gestures with her hands in a manner which . . . reminded me . . . of everyone's favourite celluloid bitch Lassie. "Oh, look – she wants us to follow her," as some observant bystander seems to say in every Lassie film . . .' After reading this, Harold Evans sent Potter a telegram: 'PERFECT POTTER PROSE. MANY THANKS.'

Godfrey Smith recalls Potter as 'prickly but professional. From the day his first copy arrived, it was clear we were listening to a remarkable new voice. On a rare visit to the office, he sat down and gave each of us in the room (some half dozen) a very long, lingering, and intense stare. I remember thinking we were clearly being stored in his remarkable computer for possible use in some future play. It was a memorably unsettling moment.'

A week after comparing Thatcher to Lassie, he described a BBC reporter's eyes glazing over because the autocue had broken down – and the following Sunday had to apologize to the makers of the machine, since the fault had lain elsewhere: 'I was very wrong to blame the autocue, and far from wishing to cast doubt on the reputation of this useful device, I look forward to the day when everybody has one of his own.'

The cartoonist Mark Boxer supplied *The Sunday Times* with a drawing of Potter which was used at the head of his column – until Harold Evans wrote to Boxer, 'Do you absolutely insist on Dennis Potter looking like a consumptive down and out, with drooping cigarette? [It] lends an air of debris, rather than hubris.'

On 9 January 1977, Potter told readers that he had been viewing his screen 'from a horizontal position', and this would have to be 'my last TV column . . . It's just that I cannot *quite* take the particular strain of a weekly column any longer – valedictory words which already permit me, in returning to the less hectic world of writing plays for the little screen, to look once again at television critics as sadistic monsters beyond all possible redemption.' Evans, however, did not accept that this was the end. After the words 'last TV column', he added 'for the time being'. He told Potter he wanted to give him 'the option to come back – and we would very much like you to do that. You have been enormously successful and, though it may not give you anything like as much satisfaction as a play, it has certainly given great pleasure and stimulation to the readers.' Three weeks later, Potter managed to reply at length:

I was compelled to abandon the column for no other reason than my health, but this does not stop me from feeling that I have let you down: the euphoria of a very fine spell as regards my health back in the summer made me far too confident in my assurances that I would be able to cope.

Alas, I did not (and do not) expect to be able to 'come and go' as I did on the *New Statesman*, which is why I did not discuss my problems with anyone at *The Sunday Times* at the beginning of this month. The fact that you wanted to add 'for the time being' into my final column, and the exceptionally generous tone of your letter to me, makes me think that I have been needlessly hasty in some, at least, of my assumptions.

I *would* like to return to the column, but at the same time I have to say that when I am under severe attack with my particular combination of ailments I find writing a great strain – not so much the actual column as the note-taking while watching the television set. It would be stupid as well as dishonest for me to say otherwise.

But just as I am weathering this present storm, so I will others. It was the fear that once I said I was 'sick' I would have to relinquish the column for good which added a new psychological strain to the physical one. Have I been silly?

If it were possible to come back with the understanding that I *might* have to 'let go' for a few weeks when in physical difficulty (and, of course, that might not happen for months and months nor even, pray God, at all) then one element of stress would be lifted & I could function as I used to on the *New Statesman*. You see, I was so ashamed of the emphatic assurances I gave before taking up the job that I could think of nothing else but total resignation.

I have thought a great deal about this letter. I would be very happy if I could take up the column again in about four weeks – say, the first or second Sunday in March. Naturally, I shall understand if this is not felt to be possible.

Evans, of course, agreed; and the next month Potter's health suddenly and dramatically improved.

*

Among those who had read Joan Bakewell's interview with him in *The Sunday Times Magazine* in November 1976, in which she mentioned the side-effects of Methotrexate, was Professor Kurt Hellmann of the Imperial Cancer Research Laboratory in London. He wrote to tell Potter about another drug, Razoxane, which the laboratory had developed. Hellmann believed it might control his illness without causing nausea and vomiting, and suggested that Potter might like to take part in clinical trials. He at once decided that he would.

Razoxane had been developed some years earlier for cancer chemotherapy, and since 1969 had also been given experimentally, with excellent results, to a number of patients with psoriasis. However, no sooner had Potter expressed willingness to try it than the Committee on Safety of Medicines requested that Professor Hellmann's team should not treat any further humans with Razoxane, until they had done a two-year toxicity study with mice and rats. Hellmann explained this to Potter, who said he would take full responsibility himself for any side-effects, and on this basis he was admitted in February 1977 to the cancer ward of Guy's Hospital in London, where Razoxane was administered to him.

On 24 February he wrote to his children:

Dear Jane, Sarah and Robert,

I am writing a letter in common to the three of you not simply because I am lazy and graceless but also because the three of you, Potter kids, have the same kind of voice, the same kind of faces (beautiful), the same eyes (open and honest), the same wonderful qualities and (oh, indeed yes) the same trouble-some, noisy, indolent, stubborn and untidy natures. I nevertheless think of you three, and your dear mother, a great deal of the time that I stare at the pale green walls, the sick old men and the bandy legs of the ugly nurses in this place. Your letters, from each of you, have been a delight to me, mis-spellings and bad jokes notwithstanding.

Oh, oh, I see the chair at the desk at the end of the ward that has surely come to take me to X-ray. It has an Irish porter who whistles Irish jigs under his breath. Thank God Sarah is not here to tell me, him, us, anybody one of her atrocious 'Irish' jokes.

I have high hopes of more effective treatment with the new drug. My temper might even improve, though I cannot guarantee it. Fulham might stay up, though I cannot guarantee it. But whatever the future holds I thank God I have three such *splendid* children and such a truly lovely wife. Look after her, be good, WORK and READ. All my love and thanks

Daddy

Soon afterwards, the Razoxane began to have a dramatic effect. 'I experienced a state of total euphoria,' he recalled. 'There is damage done. My knees, hands and toes will never return to normal. But I felt as if the whole world had been washed clean.'

He used these words in *Desert Island Discs* a few months after being put on Razoxane:

The new cytotoxic drug that I'm taking in a clinical trial has brought me considerable, huge, tremendous, emancipating relief. In fact, when I came out of hospital in March, I thought the whole world was washed clean, new, shining. It's a marvellous experience to have – you know, to see as though sort of things had been removed from in front of your eyes, so that you could actually see what a joyous and gorgeous world that we actually do live in.

He was discharged on 3 March. 'My hands are a bit too far gone with previous arthritic damage to open properly, so I could not clap them,' he recalled of that day. 'Instead, one of the first and most bizarre things I did when I got out of the hospital on an appropriately sunlit morning last March was to lie down on the pavement and bang my feet together in the most exuberant applause possible.' He told his daughter Sarah that another thing he did was to go into a church, though he did not say whether he had given thanks for his recovery.

The hospital reported, 'He has really made very satisfactory progress since starting on Razoxane treatment, although when his initial euphoria subsided he became aware of some relatively minor side-effects which are common with high-dosage treatment with this drug.' Potter himself told a journalist, 'There was one side-effect. They [sic] make me infertile. At first I thought I was going to be impotent. I said, oh no, I would rather be sick. I also bruise very easily. But the relief is marvellous.'

Word began to spread about his almost miraculous improvement. On 20 March, Oliver Gillie, the medical correspondent of *The Sunday Times*, told readers that Potter would resume television reviews at the beginning of April, and explained that it was an article in the paper that had led to his switch to Razoxane:

Potter says he now feels normal for the first time since his illness began . . . The drug is not a cure. But it has eased the constant itching and stopped the diarrhoea and nausea. He can move his joints without feeling the old, intolerable pain.

He can do all the ordinary things that other people take for granted. He can go to a football match one day and not feel too exhausted to go to a dinner party the next day.

The article was accompanied by a photograph of Dennis and Margaret dancing together in the garden at Ross.

Two weeks later the *Daily Mail* sent a reporter, Anne Batt, to Ross-on-Wye:

It's three years since I last visited the Potters at home . . . The change in them is so startling half the time you can't look them in the eyes in case you cry . . . Jane, seventeen-year-old daughter of Dennis Potter . . . told me yesterday, 'All the time when we were children we couldn't even *touch* Daddy: it would have hurt him too much. Now, suddenly, for the first time in our lives, Sarah and

Robert and I can wrap our arms around Daddy and hug him and it's – oh, just incredible.' . . .

Mrs Margaret Potter, forty-three, said, 'It's a mini-miracle. We're all in a state of shocked euphoria here. Quite dazed. It's as though after sixteen terrible years our family life has turned overnight from a slow, sad waltz into the most marvellous quickstep . . .

'For sixteen years his illness has been the pivot of our family life. It's meant no holidays. No day trips to the seaside. No family walks. It's meant me bringing up the children almost single-handed. It's meant Robert never having a daddy to kick a football with him. No piggy-backs. No family romps. It's meant Dennis not being able to drive. It's meant no social life at all because I could never tell when the side-effects of the drugs would flare up. It's meant me not being able to arrange even to see a film with a friend without worrying if he'd be fit enough to leave . . . Mind you, I've never known him self-pitying. I've only seen him put his head down and weep once . . .

'I was highly sceptical [of the Razoxane]. We've been through this so many times before . . . [But] the moment I arrived with his clothes at the hospital I noticed the difference. He wasn't just walking normally – he was pacing furiously up and down like a caged animal. I saw years and years of pent-up energy in that pacing . . .

'He came back home to us in such a state of euphoria that we're all still reeling from the onslaught. He showered us with presents. He bought lashings of champagne . . . He took me out to dinner three times in one week. He romped with the children. Last Sunday, he piled us all in the car and drove us all fifty miles . . .

'Dennis is planning a first trip to the barber – I used to cut his hair before because even that was so painful. He's getting new specs, just going to see an optician would have been too much of an ordeal before. There's been such a change I still feel I am suffering from the after-effects of a huge emotional shock. I think the children feel the same. It's like living with a human whirlwind.'

Understandably, the miraculous-seeming recovery seems to have strengthened his inclination towards religious belief. A month after leaving hospital he wrote in the Easter edition of *The Sunday Times* about Zeffirelli's *Jesus of Nazareth*, which ITV was screening. He was scathing about actor Robert Powell – 'a Christ nourished on the disinfectant bottle . . . made to look as though he has a bad case of piles' – but went on:

I gladly assert (even with the rancid taste of hypocrisy clinging to the roof of my mouth) that there is, literally, nothing better I can do with my time on this

Easter Day than read about and think about and yearn for the Jesus of the
Gospels . . .

This is not a justification, by the way, for my own studio-bound television
play *Son of Man* . . . It was (forgive me) more interesting than *Jesus of
Nazareth* because it had traces of energy and wit and violence at its core, but
I never really came to terms with the Gospel narratives as a drama because I
had not then dared face up to the Christ who haunts me now.

The play was mostly written in hospital in Birmingham, at a time when
anger and distress were at my throat: precious emotions, these, which
gradually brought me to a richer sense of religion which I shall not and must
not lose now that I have, so to speak, picked up my bed and walked. But I can
only dimly recognize *Son of Man* now, realizing that the rough, tough, central
character was the Jesus of the agnostics, wildly signalling me on into a
stranger and often stonier landscape.

Potter also had news for *Sunday Times* readers about his current
work. In his article on the Razoxane treatment, Oliver Gillie reported,
'After two weeks [in hospital], he began to feel so much better that he
wrote a play, *Pennies from Heaven*, which previously he could do no
more than think about. It will be shown on television next February or
March.' Potter later recalled that it was 'as they were administering
Razoxane and I was at Guy's [that] I started *Pennies*'.

On 14 March 1977 Trodd told BBC Copyright, 'Dennis Potter has
now delivered the first play of the six plays in the series *Ghost Writer*,
which I would like to accept. The title is *Down Sunnyside Lane*, and
the series is now called *Pennies from Heaven*.' The script of the first
episode was written in a hardback A4 notebook, with scarcely a word
crossed out, and there is no evidence that any rough drafts had
preceded it. But it had not been achieved without difficulties.

'During that whole period when we were playing around with what
Pennies would be,' recalls Trodd, 'the only givens were that it was
going to be a six-parter, it was going to be Thirties, it was going to be
music.' Potter himself told a journalist that originally he had 'wanted
to do something about Al Bowlly', and Trodd confirms this:

Al Bowlly himself, or a fictional version, was for a time the model, but the
trainspotting possessors of the Al Bowlly ark and archive would have noisily
distracted too much attention (they loathed *Moonlight on the Highway*), and
to write nine hours set in Thirties show business would have meant taking
on bio-pic conventions and defining the fictional world too heavily in terms
of posh night-club London. Also, as producer, I certainly didn't want our

characters to be musicians because I'd just done Colin Welland's *The Wild West Show* about Rugby Union where the task of finding actors who could handle a ball next to prop forwards who could speak a line or two was pretty terminal.

At this point Potter came up with two completely different ideas. 'I remember one morning he rang me very early,' says Trodd, 'when I was still in bed, and said, "How do you react to this? Forget the Thirties: we'll do a six-parter about childhood, with all the children played by adults." And I said instantly, without even waking up properly, "That sounds like a single film, not a six-parter."' Next (Trodd recalls),

we talked about doing a story around a perfect murder, and it was here that something very essential . . . began to emerge. I came across a not very famous, not very perfect Thirties murder in which a commercial traveller – with a prissy wife he didn't get on with . . . tried to incinerate a lookalike and assume his identity. Suddenly the ingredients . . . were all there. And . . . the idea of the double, the person who may be mistaken for you . . . So the *Pennies* universe was forming, but for every cutting or trial transcript I was sending him I would probably send ten songs.

Trodd observes that, up to now, he had been little more than 'a professional enabler' for Potter's plays. 'But *Pennies from Heaven* was genuinely collaborative. And also there was a sense in which, with its use of the Thirties music, it was an act of love to me.'

A little while after they had agreed on a murder story, Trodd received another early-morning telephone call from Potter:

He rang me again and said, 'Listen to this: the first scene – suburban husband and wife waking up, a bleary, dreary Monday morning, he wants to make love, she doesn't, he's got to go to work, she's very repressed and uptight, it's a dingy room, suddenly we hear music. And maybe the lighting changes, and suddenly the husband is singing "The Clouds Will Soon Roll By" in the voice of Elsie Carlisle.' And I said, 'Right on, but I can get you a male vocal version of that same arrangement.' And he said, 'No, I want as much dislocation from the conventional as possible in this first scene.' I thought afterwards that, even when he called me, he might have written most of the first episode, and was pretending – he might have, he might not; maybe it had even been finished a week earlier. But I suspect that he was excited by that essential crystallization, and wanted to have it endorsed.

Trodd did initially endorse it – and was then 'seized by a panic that didn't recede fully for months'. This was caused by Potter's extra-ordinary use of the music that Trodd had been feeding him. The first script was headed:

PENNIES FROM HEAVEN
Six Plays
by
Dennis Potter
with 50 great songs!
which enlivened 'a low, dishonest decade'
I: Down Sunnyside Lane

'Low, dishonest decade' is W. H. Auden's judgement on the Thirties. Fifty songs was a rough guess. In the event there were to be more than sixty.

In this first script, Potter explains his new-found device at some length:

(*Move across to the double bed, where a husband and wife are asleep . . . Moving into close-up of the husband . . .* ARTHUR PARKER, *mid-thirties . . . a 'commercial traveller' in sheet music . . . He turns to look at* JOAN, *his wife . . .*)

ARTHUR: (*urgent*) C'mon Joanie – sugar – wake up, my pigeon.

(*She tries to wriggle from his grasp, pushing his hands from her breasts.*)

JOAN: No – Arthur – don't . . .

ARTHUR: (*sullen*) You never want to nowadays . . .

(*He looks down at her with a steady, baleful expression . . . At which point, start music: 'The Clouds Will Soon Roll By', recorded by Ambrose & his Orchestra, July 1932. The intro by the band – before the vocal begins – oozes quietly under dialogue . . . Then, suddenly* [ARTHUR] *appears to sing – he mimes to the voice of Elsie Carlisle . . . He does it wholly in the conventions of a musical – totally in earnest. For a moment,* ARTHUR *and* JOAN *are in a film musical.*)

ARTHUR: (*mime-sings, Elsie Carlisle's voice*)
Somewhere the sun is shining,
So honey don't you cry
We'll find a silver lining
The clouds will soon roll by . . .

In everything he said or wrote about *Pennies from Heaven*, Potter emphasized that the songs were the heart of it. 'It was the nature of the songs which interested me,' he told an *Evening Standard* reporter while the serial was being shown.

Their sweetness, their banality, their sugariness – you can almost lick them they are so sweet, and yet they have this tremendous evocative power – a power which is much more than nostalgia.

Those songs stood together as a package in that they seemed to represent the same kinds of things that the psalms and fairy-tales represented: that is, the most generalized human dreams, that the world should be perfect, beautiful and loving and all of those things. A lot of the music is drivel, in that it's commercial and never too difficult, but it does possess an almost religious image of the world as a perfect place.

He had already created a character who saw the world in terms of Thirties songs – David Peters in *Moonlight on the Highway* (who at one moment actually mimes to a Bowlly disc). Graham Fuller asked Potter if, since writing that play nine years before *Pennies from Heaven*, he had been thinking of a more extensive use of the device. 'I was probably half thinking of it,' Potter answered.

I often used song titles as *my* titles, for example. Noël Coward has talked about the potency of cheap music – it was that kind of thing. I knew there was energy in that sort of music, and I knew there must be a way of being able to use it in the way that I perceived people used it themselves, for example the way that they would say, 'Oh, listen, they're playing our song.'

By making his characters mime to old records ('I tried it with myself in a mirror,' he told Bragg) he was renewing his struggle against naturalism in television. In the summer of 1977, after he had written *Pennies from Heaven* but before it was transmitted, he gave a paper at the Edinburgh Television Festival, during which he argued the case for 'non-naturalism', not just as a gimmick, but as a vitally important act of subversion:

Most television ends up offering its viewers a means of orientating themselves towards the generally received notions of 'reality'. The best naturalist or realist drama, of the Garnett–Loach–Allen school for instance, breaks out of this cosy habit by the vigour, clarity, originality and depth of its perceptions of a more comprehensive reality. The best non-naturalist drama, in its very structure, *dis*orientates the viewer smack in the middle of the orientation process which television perpetually uses. It disrupts the patterns that are endemic to television, and upsets or exposes the narrative styles of so many of the other allegedly non-fiction programmes. It shows the frame in the picture when most television is busy showing the picture in the frame. I think it is *potentially* the more valuable, therefore, of the two approaches.

He took immense trouble in choosing the recordings from the enormous number Trodd had given him: 'It was a very difficult thing to do, trying to find the right songs from the hundreds I played.' On each occasion he needed to find something that felt 'as though it had just been written for that occasion . . . as though I *had* written the song', even though it might be 'an extraordinarily banal tune and nonsensical lyric'. So, in the first episode of *Pennies from Heaven*, when Arthur leaves Joan and drives off to Gloucestershire to sell his sheet music, he 'sings' the 1935 hit 'Roll Along, Prairie Moon', imagining himself as a cowboy heading along the trail (much as Willy might have done in *Where the Buffalo Roam*); while Joan, left in the land of privet hedges, romanticizes her loneliness with 'Blue Moon', and performs 'Smoke Gets In Your Eyes' as a duet with a seductive door-to-door salesman. Potter explained that his frequent use of male voices for female characters and vice versa was because 'I wanted to make quite clear that it wasn't *them*, and that we're in another realm when this goes on.'

One of the characters in *Pennies from Heaven* is constructed almost entirely out of music. On his way westwards, Arthur gives a lift to 'a peculiarly jerky, rather odd individual' with a piano accordion. The Accordion Man is a religious busker, who trudges round the country playing 'sacred songs and solos' to indifferent passers-by. Almost incapable of speech, he is moved to 'song' when Arthur buys him a meal – the song being 'Pennies from Heaven' itself, with its clear message that we should accept heaven's blessings even if they come in the disguise of misfortune:

> If you want the things you love
> You must have showers . . .

Potter made no secret of the fact that the serial was written on the crest of his own recovery of health and religious enthusiasm. 'I find it very difficult to say exactly what the plays are about,' he said a few months after writing *Pennies from Heaven* (which he evidently still regarded as linked plays rather than a serial).

I think because of my change of mood when I was in hospital . . . I wanted to write something about the resilience of human dreams . . . I believe that there is a sort of religious yearning that the world shall be whole, and what I want people to recognize by the end of the plays is that the songs are only diminished versions of the oldest myth of all in the Garden of Eden.

He told another interviewer in the spring of 1978, 'I picked the Thirties . . . because the popular music was, perhaps, at its most banal and its most sugary, least challenging – and yet it also encapsulates, somehow, some diminished image of the human desire for there to be a perfect and beautiful and just world . . . dreams of a longing for Eden and for peace and for joy . . . '

The BBC press handout for the serial stated that its message was that 'in the last resort . . . no matter what, life is all right', and Potter repeated these words in interviews, for example telling Michael Church of *The Times* that he had 'tried to find a mode of religious drama which says that, in the last resort, everything really is all right'. He said to W. Stephen Gilbert of the *Observer*,

There is some sense in which you can actually assume the ultimate optimism, no matter the degradation, the miseries that the world inflicts on you. The final claim is that it doesn't matter – it matters in your ligaments, your emotions, your betrayals – but that there is some sense of order, a rationality that is sheer optimism.

Though any character in *Pennies from Heaven* is likely to burst into optimistic 'song', most of the dreaming of a better world is done by Arthur – despite the fact that he is a liar and an adulterer, who eventually lives off immoral earnings and connives at a murder. Indeed, he goes to the bad very largely because he believes too literally in the songs; Potter remarked that Arthur, 'lacking any sense of God or faith, literally believes in those cheap songs to the depths of his tawdry, adulterous little lying soul'. Yet his own frailty does not undermine his passionate conviction that there is a better world. 'Months and months I been carrying this stuff around – these songs – all these lovely songs – I've always believed in 'em,' he tells a group of fellow commercial travellers, waving his briefcase.

ARTHUR: But I didn't *really* know how it was or why it was that I believe in (*slaps case*) what's in here. There's things that is too big and too important and too bleed'n simple to put in all that lah-di-dah, toffee-nosed poetry and stuff, books and that – but everybody feels 'em . . . I'm not what you call a clever man, and I've had a bit of Jerry shell in my bonce since

I was sixteen years old in the effing trenches – cor, that was a bloody lark! – but we had something, we stuck it out, and it was what we sang – oh, yes, worth more than a dry blanket, they was – them songs. But that's not the half of it. It's not just packing up your troubles in your mucking kit-bag, no sir . . . (*He gropes for words like one groping for air.*) Blimey, I can almost taste it! It's looking for the blue, ennit, and the gold. The patch of blue sky. The gold of the, of the bleed'n' dawn, or – the light in somebody's eyes – Pennies from Heaven, that's what it is. And we can't see 'em, clinking and clinking, all around, all over the place – just bend down and pick 'em up!

At another moment in this scene, Arthur's words are undoubtedly those of the Razoxane-cured Potter: 'You walk around with grit and gravel in your eyes. You can't see what a beautiful world it is we live in . . . It's shining, the whole place, *shining*. Can't you see?'

Potter's past failure to see this had been caused by sexual tension as well as ill-health, and the most startling thing in episode 1 of *Pennies from Heaven* (apart from the miming) is the apparent casting off of all uneasiness about sex. Actually the old angst is still there, but it is passed on to two subsidiary characters. The physical disgust that previously afflicted Potter's heroes is now the attribute of Arthur's wife Joan ('You filthy beast' is her usual way of addressing the lecherous Arthur), while the Accordion Man takes on the religious guilt about sex. The latter seems to be the harder for Potter to be rid of, since all through *Pennies* it is made clear that the accordionist is, in some inexplicable way, the *doppelgänger* of Arthur (a leftover from Trodd's and Potter's 'perfect murder' plot), and he eventually commits a sex-motivated crime (abusing and strangling a blind girl) which seems really to have been Arthur's – and maybe even Arthur's creator's, since the date of the crime is given as 17 May 1935, the day on which Potter himself was born.

Indeed Arthur protests too much about his lack of sexual hang-ups. 'I sometimes think', he tells Joan, 'that if I had the chance and it was a dark night, I'd fuck my own grandmother!' (The word 'fuck' was blanked out on the soundtrack.) And when Joan protests at his obsession with sex – 'Does it really matter *quite* so much?' she asks him – he answers, 'Of course it does! It's the main thing, ennit?' He claims to have 'sniffed around the ladies'; yet one glimpse of the young Forest of Dean schoolmistress Eileen in a music shop in Gloucester (towards the end of episode 1) is enough to send him spinning into fantasies about her angelic purity, just as Jack Black did over his agent's wife in *Follow the Yellow Brick Road*. 'Never thought I'd see an angel,' Arthur 'sings' to an unnoticing Eileen across the shop. Later that evening, Arthur picks up a local tart in a pub, has sex with her in the back of his car, and after orgasm begins to cry, just as one of Potter's earlier and more obviously self-torturing heroes might have done. We are on familiar territory after all.

*

A month after Potter had left Guy's Hospital, at the beginning of April 1977, Margaret told Ann Batt of the *Daily Mail*:

It was almost a relief when he stopped dashing madly around and picked up his pen and skipped upstairs to his study. He wrote a new play in hospital – *Pennies from Heaven*. Today [4 April], he fastened his jacket buttons himself – something he couldn't have done before – and set off gaily to London on his own with a second play he's just whizzed through in the past eleven days.

Episode 2, *The Sweetest Thing*, opens at 'Joyfill Junior School, Berry Slope' in the Forest. Asked by the headmaster to read Psalm 35 at morning assembly, Eileen instead 'sings' an Elsie Carlisle vocal, 'You've Got Me Crying Again' – a comment on the head's fierce behaviour to the children. Potter alleged that the song was 'a straight translation of that particular psalm'. Although in this instance there is almost no resemblance – the psalm is one in which David pleads for God's help against his enemies – he often made such a comparison, describing the songs in *Pennies* as 'like the Psalms of David' because of their expressions of hope and yearning.

In fact as the serial progresses he uses the musical numbers more and more ironically. While Eileen is taking her class for a nature walk and telling them the story of Rapunzel – one of Potter's favourite pure-princess narratives – Arthur is pleading for an overdraft with his bank manager by means of song ('Life can't go on/Without that certain thing'). Ejected by the manager for impertinence, he is also refused cash by Joan, who has a legacy from her father; whereupon he tries to get round her by putting his hands gently on her breasts. We then see the 'might-have-been' of Arthur and Joan making love on the song-sheet cover of the saccharine ballad 'Isn't It Heavenly', while Bowlly sings it; whereas in real life Joan is removing his hands and slapping his face. When Arthur, back in the Forest, tracks down Eileen and declares his love to her, her father and brothers, in their miners' clothes, provide an improbable backing group as he sings 'You Couldn't Be Cuter'. Best of all in this episode, sardonically pointing the contrast between the pure dream of love and the steamy reality of sex, as Arthur pulls off Eileen's knickers we see and hear them both merging into another Bowlly hit, 'Love Is The Sweetest Thing'.

Trodd paid for this second script (Potter was to receive £2000 per episode), but became anxious about the way the project was going. 'Nostalgia' was acceptable to viewers, but despite the Thirties setting Potter was spurning it. ('I dislike nostalgia,' he often said. 'Nostalgia is a very second-order emotion.') As Trodd recalls it,

after seeing the first two scripts, I summoned Dennis to London, and we had a drink or a meal in the Kensington Hilton, and I said, 'Look, there are far too many songs. The fact that you and I have a penchant for this music is not enough excuse to inflict it on a large television audience. What was that D. H. Lawrence novel you wanted to adapt? Why don't we convert the commission here and now?' And Dennis listened to this, and then said, 'I'm going to get a train home and start writing the next episode.'

Daish recalls that Potter telephoned her after this conversation with Trodd: 'He was absolutely furious with Ken.' But Trodd points out that 'in a way, Dennis responded to my criticisms, because it's quite a long time in episode 3 before you have a song; but what you do have is a woman putting lipstick on her tits!' It is true that episode 3, called *Easy Come, Easy Go*,* begins with Joan, desperate to regain her husband, revealing to him that she has rouged her nipples ('You said you wanted me to'). But the comparatively restrained use of songs in this episode seems to reflect the darkening of mood, as Eileen, pregnant and abandoned by Arthur, leaves her Forest home for London and prostitution, rather than any loss of confidence by Potter in his newly invented genre.

Realizing that he would not be deflected, Trodd sent the script of the first episode to a director, Piers Haggard, a great-nephew of Rider Haggard, the Victorian adventure novelist. Haggard had moved to television after working at the Royal Court and the National Theatre,

---

* The Faber edition of *Pennies from Heaven* wrongly gives the title of this episode as *Hand in Hand* (it was changed during production). Similarly the fifth episode, *Painting the Clouds*, is wrongly given as *Tiptoe Through the Tulips*.

and had directed several TV musicals, including an adaptation of Alun Owen's *No Trams to Lime Street*. He had also made a TV version of the Chester Mystery Plays, which had caught Potter's attention. 'Piers . . . had tremendous stamina,' writes Trodd, 'which I knew this enterprise would die without an excess of. And he was an optimist . . .' Haggard says he had first heard of the new Potter project before a word of it had been written:

I was working on a drama at Thames Television, and I got this phone call, in the winter of 1976–7, from Ken Trodd, whom I knew from the BBC. He said, 'I wanted to ask you if you'd be interested in maybe doing the next Dennis Potter.' Dennis was fairly famous, and it was exactly the sort of thing that someone at my stage would be very pleased to be offered. And I said, 'What's it about?' And Ken said, 'I don't know, really', and did one of his secretive, shy, self-deprecating half-giggles – which is particularly his charm. I suppose we must have talked some more, because when I went on holiday to Australia a short time later, I left some addresses. One of them was on the way home – I was going to be at the Taj Mahal Hotel in Bombay. Sure enough, on checking in with a screaming baby, I found a buff manilla envelope with a BBC sticker on it. And this was the first episode. And it became clear that there was going to be music, which had never been mentioned. And it was very astonishing, with depth and menace about it, and a dark sexual obsessiveness – all of which I adore, it's absolutely me. And then those songs.

Haggard decided that it was essential to treat the project as a musical, giving the songs maximum production values. 'And there never was a musical with so rigorous and sombre a text,' he remarked in a newspaper interview a few months later.

At the centre of this sandwich is religion – when you get down to it, Dennis is saying that this cheat and liar has a spiritual life, that he's precious because he's a lily of the field. And it has that vintage Potter pain. I have to hold the balance, a sort of classical poise: the result has to show all that, not resort to cheap laughs, but still give a lot of light-hearted pleasure.

Haggard recalls that 'Dennis was writing incredibly fast, but I had to start work with only two or three episodes.' Episode 4, written at the same speed as its predecessors, completes Eileen's metamorphosis from Madonna to Whore. Since Potter is determined that his hero should have a purely animal attitude to sex, Arthur's reaction to her downfall is generally enthusiastic. He is aroused by her admission that she scarcely minds being paid by other men for sex – 'By God, you *are* a gel!' – though he does occasionally raise objections to 'you selling yourself'. In fact his response scarcely matters, since he has now become a passenger in the drama while, freed from his fantasies about her, Eileen is able to take over as protagonist. 'I was already dead there,' she says of the Forest. 'This way [prostitution] feels like dying – but I'm still alive, in a way. I can see everything, feel everything . . .' She asks him if he has 'the guts' to run away with her, and he admits, 'I ain't got no guts at all.' She says, 'Don't worry. I've got enough for both of us.' Their partnership is celebrated in the gutsy song 'Okay Toots'.

Trodd believes that Potter was now writing about himself in the guise of Eileen,

the *ingénue* from the Forest of Dean. First she is seduced by someone who represents a glamorous London. Then once she is 'up there' herself it isn't long before she's showing wisdom and insight well beyond those of her mentor. The trajectory is that of Dennis's own early career – from being a virgin in the pastoral sticks to becoming a desirable and successful metropolitan icon almost overnight.

Yet what precisely were Eileen and Arthur to do in the remaining episodes, now that this transformation had been wrought? Potter presumably had no answer waiting at his elbow, since (as he told Melvyn Bragg in an interview the following spring) 'I never write a synopsis, my main concern is to know, "What is going to happen?"' He said the same thing in another interview about *Pennies from Heaven*: 'When I'm writing, I don't have a synopsis or a plot.'

Potter occupies as much time as he dares, in the second half of the serial, with the police pursuit of Arthur for the murder of the blind girl, which is presented as an Agatha Christie parody ('Something's jolly well got to be done, Inspector'). The script dallies with – but quickly abandons – political satire, when Eileen briefly attempts to blackmail her most lucrative customer, a Tory MP; then metamorphoses into a *Bonnie and Clyde* road movie, with Eileen telling Arthur, 'We've got to get out of London. That's what we're going to do.' Once they are in the countryside, Potter has Eileen shoot a voyeuristic farmer with his own rifle. Arthur asks her why she did it (as well he might), and receives the reply, 'Because I felt like it.' Indeed the killing is not only motiveless but has no function in the plot, since the body is never discovered. Much of the final episode is taken up with a court scene in which Potter breaks his own rule, allowing the judge and prosecuting counsel to allude to the fact that they have just performed a musical number: 'Did you like my whistle . . . ?' 'It was a very nice whistle, m'lud.' Arthur is duly hanged – and is immediately resurrected to rejoin Eileen for a final musical number on Hammersmith Bridge.*

Potter's assertion that the message of *Pennies from Heaven* is 'no matter what happens, life is all right' has, of course, been flagrantly contradicted by Arthur's fate – it requires the supernatural intervention of the author to set things right at the end. The implication seems to be that God must similarly work miracles to set the mess of the world in order; which of course does not happen. By the end, the serial is conveying exactly the opposite message from the one that Potter alleged that he intended.

In *Moonlight on the Highway*, he had used the Bowlly songs to expose and dramatize the damage to David Peters's personality. We would expect this from a writer whose early mission had been to criticize the exploitative and harmful effects of popular culture (Admass, women's magazines, and so on) upon a vulnerable working class. In *Pennies*, Arthur, whose lower-class status ('common') is constantly being emphasized by his *petit-bourgeois* wife, is not psychologically vulnerable like Peters – he has no history of abuse. Yet he uses the songs exactly as Willy employs his cowboy fantasies in *Where the Buffalo Roam* – as a retreat from a hostile and uncomprehending world. Eventually he half realizes that he is being destroyed by this escapism, and by the Admass-style lies concealed in the music and lyrics. 'I'd like to smash up every record in the shop,' he tells Eileen in episode 4, and a little later he and Eileen do just that – go on the rampage and destroy the contents of the record shop he has just opened. But by then it is too late. 'Life is all right' is the message of the songs, and by accepting it uncritically Arthur has put himself at the mercy of the blind Fate which lurks behind the song-sheets.

The message of *Pennies* itself is quite different. It is first hinted at in episode 3 when a distraught woman emerging from the doctor's surgery (where Eileen has gone for a pregnancy test) cries out, 'What's the point? Where's the sense in it all?' There is no reply – the direction

---

* According to Jane Potter, 'Pennies originally ended with the hangman's hood over Arthur's head, but after reading the final episode I was totally distraught. So Dad changed the ending so that Arthur and Eileen could be reunited.' Sarah Potter recalls this too.

states 'Everyone looks away' – but Arthur has his own purely animal answer. 'It's all between the legs. Ennit? . . . Or in the belly,' he tells another commercial traveller, in a rare moment of coming down to earth, after achieving his objective of seducing Eileen; to which the other man – who had previously heard Arthur rapturously explaining that the songs revealed the true beauty of the world – comments gloomily, 'So that's it, then. That's all there is.'

Before *Pennies from Heaven*, Potter's writing had been powered by a furious anger against an unjust world – a world of abuse, illness, frustration and betrayal. 'That's it!' Joe had shouted against his daughter's cancer in *Joe's Ark*, 'That's your love of God for you!' Most other Potter heroes – Nigel Barton, Willy Turner, David Peters, Jack Black and the rest of them – would have said the same. Now, in his own life, Potter was trying another tack: persuading himself that the world was, after all, the creation of a benevolent God – and no sooner had he begun this experiment than, sure enough, he had been 'washed clean' by Razoxane, like a New Testament miracle. Understandably, he immediately set out to write a drama encapsulating this new-found optimism. But he was too honest a writer to manage this. While apparently fooling himself that he had written an optimistic work, he had in fact created as black and pessimistic a narrative as ever. 'Where did it all go wrong, Arthur?' asks Joan when she visits him in the condemned cell, and she receives the truthful reply: 'The day I was bleed'n' born.' Arthur is no villain, nor even a tragically flawed hero; he is simply one more damaged Potter protagonist, battling futilely against a world full of Thomas Hardy-style booby traps. He keeps trying to convince himself that he has revealed the world's true beauty – 'The gold of the, of the bleed'n' dawn' – but in the moments before his execution, talking to the warders, he realizes that the only gold to be found is mundane, indeed obscene:

ARTHUR: When I was a kid at school, and you put your hand up to ask to go out to the whatsname, the teacher would bring this bleed'n' great long pointer down across your knuckles. You had to sit there and hold it, and that was that. Or do it in your trousers.

ARNOLD: We used to see who could pee the highest up against the wall.

ARTHUR: That's funny. And we did! . . .

HORACE: I could pee the highest.

(*Pause.*)

ARNOLD: Not as high as me, I'll bet.

(*Pause.*)

ARTHUR: A great big golden arc.

By the end of *Pennies from Heaven*, even Arthur has learned that the only gold that will pour down from the God-less, song-less sky is a stream of urine.

On one occasion, in an interview after the Hollywood remake of *Pennies from Heaven*, Potter let slip the real meaning of the work: 'I wanted to use the musical convention that . . . everything is fine, even when I'm saying everything is *not* all right.'

CHAPTER 2

Best friend

───

The remaining three *Pennies from Heaven* scripts were in Trodd's hands by the end of June 1977. His doubts about the project had not dispelled. Piers Haggard recalls, 'Ken was very nervous of it. And even Dennis wasn't quite sure that it would work.'

Potter recalled talking about the project to a BBC drama executive, who 'looked at the scripts, listened to me talk, shuffled a bit in his sockless sandals and then asked with the faintest tinge of alarm or incredulity, "What? You mean they pretend to sing in every episode?"' Nevertheless casting began, and Trodd writes that Potter, 'at least 60 per cent seriously', suggested Roy Hudd for Arthur and Spike Milligan for the Accordion Man – suggestions that were not followed up.

Piers Haggard's first choice for Arthur was Michael Elphick, 'but Ken said to me, "There's this cockney guy called Bob Hoskins, I think we should see him."' Trodd says he had 'a hunch which first seemed cranky' to try Hoskins, who had played a small part (in a middle-class accent) in Potter's *Schmoedipus*, and had achieved some celebrity as a lorry driver in a BBC adult-literacy series, *On the Move*, which had been reviewed enthusiastically in the *New Statesman* by Potter. Hoskins recalls that Trodd and Haggard sent him

about nine hours of script. I said, 'You've got to be kidding, that's a month's reading.' I just took it home, put it in the middle of the room, and kind of kicked it. Then . . . Piers Haggard told me to read three scenes. When I read them, I realized how good it was. I stayed up all night reading. The next day I gave the audition of my life. If they had turned me down, I would have jumped out of the window. It was a great part. It had humour, humiliation, weakness, strength. Everything. Arthur Parker is everybody.

At the audition, Haggard decided there was 'something about [Hoskins] that might be extra special'. In fact Hoskins, whose own marriage was breaking up, identified closely with Arthur: 'I played a lot of myself in *Pennies* . . . I knew what a man in that state is like. It wasn't an easy part to play, but I knew where I was coming from. Because most of Arthur Parker is *pain*.' For Eileen, Haggard auditioned Cheryl Campbell, whom he had seen in Ibsen. 'She read wonderfully for us. But she wasn't well known, and I saw a lot of other people before I called her back. What got her the part was this virginal quality, with a concealed, passionate sexuality.'

Cheryl Campbell recalls that Potter was initially dismayed by this casting. 'Ken and Piers had auditioned me, in an office in Television Centre,' she says,

and I gathered afterwards that I had got the part because of the way I said goodbye to them and walked away, in a horribly self-conscious, blushing way, down that long curving corridor – I suppose it looked appropriately virginal! Dennis saw me for the first time at the read-through, and he said afterwards he had found it very hard to swallow his disappointment, because I was the antithesis of what he'd imagined, which was some dark-haired, large-eyed, palpably erotic creature, and I was sitting there with my long blond hair that you could sit on, looking like something that had fallen off the top of the Christmas tree. But he said that as soon as I started to speak the thing fell into shape, so that was OK.

Trodd confirms that 'initially Dennis wasn't very keen on the casting. I don't remember him coming to *Pennies* very often. He was certainly at the read-through, and I think when we filmed in the Forest he was around.' Piers Haggard remembers him watching the first scene being 'blocked' on a marked-out floor in the rehearsal room, and at the end, after Hoskins had 'sung' for the first time, 'he gripped my arm with a fierce glint in his eye and said, "It's going to work."' Haggard says that only minimal rewriting was required during rehearsal: 'I remember disliking some of the musical numbers, and asking if we could have something else, and Ken would go to a massive cupboard in his office, which was full of discs he'd got from the BBC Gramophone Library, jumbled up with dirty socks and coffee cups, and he'd pull stuff out, and make me up a tape with another ten beautiful numbers. Ken's contribution on that side was gigantic.'

Asked about the Potter–Trodd relationship, Haggard comments:

They were the Odd Couple! They'd fight and bicker and be rude and bitchy, and Dennis, who was more lethal and wicked and had the ultimate power, would tease Ken inexhaustibly, calling him a Trotskyite and so on. I'm very, very fond of Ken. His gift of insight into writing, and his courage in pursuing moral and political concerns – despite his occasional illogicality or irrascibility, and the fact that he never picks up the tab, and silly things like that – made him a very great producer, one of the heroic figures of the golden age. And he's a very warm, passionate man – he's got deep, dark, warm, Celtic eyes – an enormous emotional response. And he's fearsomely intelligent, too.

Trodd writes that the making of the serial 'was the sunniest and most gratifying of all the works by Dennis that I've been associated with', and Spencer Banks, who played Eileen's younger brother, says there was an unusual optimism among the cast: 'When we were doing *Pennies* we all kept thinking, maybe it's going to be something special . . . There was a different feeling in the cast that was like electricity.' However, Judy Daish, who went to some of the read-through and some of the studio recordings with Potter, says that 'even Ken was still looking very unconvinced, and Bob Hoskins said to me, "I feel like a bloody 'ippo sitting behind the wheel of that car, singing me 'ead off – I don't know what's going on."'

Just as production was getting under way, Potter presented his paper on non-naturalism at the 1977 Edinburgh Television Festival (which included a screening of the BBC recording of *Brimstone and Treacle*). The paper opened with a familiar Potter theme, the passivity of the TV audience:

'What's on the telly tonight?'
  'Oh. Nothing very much.'
  Switch on for one thing, though, and it's very likely that you will be pulled into the stream. One programme trickles into another, quite painlessly. It takes something like the sight of, say, Humphrey Burton to make most of us switch off.

He asserted that programmes were now scarcely distinguishable from dog-food commercials, and continued:

I have been writing for television for almost thirteen years, and my experiences lead me to suggest that if one were pressed to define the purpose of the great bulk of television, and television drama, then one would be forced to answer: its purpose is to pass the time, and in doing so to make sure that the viewer . . . is not sufficiently bored or offended or puzzled to opt for the alternative yet strictly similar way of passing the time offered by each of the other channels.

He concluded by arguing that non-naturalism, among its many other merits, 'reminds the viewer . . . that he is at least watching a play. A Play. A *Play*.'

The paper was discussed by a panel that included the playwright David Hare, who says he 'had a row with Potter' when the session ended.

Dennis had made a speech saying that the audience couldn't discriminate between the dog-food ads and the plays. TV, he said, was received by a passive audience sitting there with no special discernment, but just receiving everything as one unending stream, to all of which they attached equal significance. This seemed to be such a perverse and untrue position for a noted writer of TV plays to take up that we had a very lively discussion in a bar afterwards in which I apparently used the words, 'I used to admire you.' He certainly wrote a column later in *The Sunday Times* describing the incident and attributing the words (bitterly) to me.

In fact Potter, in his column on 6 November 1977, said that Hare had attacked not the lecture but his *Sunday Times* reviews:

I was swallowing whisky, and shuddering, in a crowded pub in Edinburgh after delivering a paper on television drama when a youngish sort of fellow with a cropped head and cold eyes suddenly came at me like a kamikaze pilot or, worse, a football supporter. It was the playwright David Hare, the muscles of his face marbling with tension and anger.

'I think you should give up your column,' he snapped, straight to the point of my already quivering jaw.

'Oh? Why?'

'Because you are doing damage – to yourself and to others. Your reviews are mean-minded and malicious. You take your own pain seriously, but not that of others.'

Drinking my cigarette and smoking my drink, and wondering in my confusion if I had been mistaken for B[ernard] Levin [then the theatre critic of *The Sunday Times*], I asked him to give me e-e-examples of the m-malice. Hare quoted my review here [in June] of Barrie Keefe's *Gotcha!* and of the *Arena: Theatre* edition which featured interviews with playwrights Trevor Griffiths, Howard Brenton, Keeffe and others. 'They read as though they were motivated by personal dislike. Writers shouldn't be critics,' and so on, until I felt like the Burke to his Hare.

In this review, Potter had written of the 'loathing' he felt when watching these interviews, and went on:

These New Reactionaries cannot see change unless everything changes. They glimpse fascism round the corner because they refuse to look at what is capable of repair in the road directly in front of them. Violence and corruption take the centre of the stage, and there is nothing else in the wings. Their wilful pessimism and occasionally overblown rant is shameful to contemplate when placed alongside the Czech writers shown in last week's *Panorama*, struggling so bravely against real tyranny.

Potter was clearly shaken by Hare's outburst, and had no real reply when he reported it in *The Sunday Times*. 'David Hare is not alone in his hostility,' he wrote.

I have been told that Jim Allen wants to break my jaw, and several whining letters from other dramatists have all said 'addressing you as a playwright, not a critic –' (a fellow prisoner, not a warder) in terms which insist that I am 'letting the side down'. And all of them, of course, share the curious assumption that criticism is meant to be for the programme-makers rather than mere viewers and readers.

He returned to the attack two weeks later, describing another Barrie Keeffe play, *Nipper*, as 'the sort of plot which the *Monty Python* team might have dreamed up in one of their more blackly manic spasms', though he did praise 'the sizzling immediacy of Keefe's brilliant dialogue'. However, a few months later he gave Hare's own *Play for Today*, *Licking Hitler*, an almost ingratiating review, calling it 'dangerous, and subversive, as is all good writing . . . How often does a television programme leave one so alert and so wary?'

The following spring, on Radio 4's *Start the Week*, he admitted to a certain schizophrenia as a playwright–reviewer:

I think you use different parts of your imagination when you're a critic and when you're a writer . . . and when I'm reviewing a programme, I don't think of the effect it would have on the writer . . . but simply, does it represent what I felt about the programme . . . ? But when I've written a programme, then that usual typical writer's paranoia about critics . . . comes bobbing up to the surface . . .

He responded to the suggestion that he sometimes wrote abuse by describing it as 'polemic, not abuse . . . it's abuse if you disagree with it, or are on the receiving end of it. But you've got to be very careful not to abuse – just to set out to pick someone to pieces . . . it's got to be triggered by something you really genuinely felt.'

Invited to lecture at the Cheltenham Festival of Literature, a few weeks after giving his Edinburgh paper, he went on the attack again. This time his target was the 'the prevailing tone of contemporary high culture' – by which he meant a pretentious disdain for the audience:

We are reaching towards the stage in so many of the arts when only 'non-students, outsiders, and uncultured people whose interests are commonplace' [a dictionary definition of Philistines] seem to have the necessary gumption to ask the simple, direct and even hostile questions which no legitimate artist or writer should ever fear . . . I am here to argue that the derided Philistine should not be quite such an easy object of contempt . . . Let us, for once, bow with due humility and praise the middle-aged, middle-class, middle-minded married man with a mortgage . . .

The modernists and their heirs, in a series of dazzling innovations, have succeeded in turning literature back into itself, with the result that even literary criticism has precious little truck with anything so arcane as (chuckle) human values . . . Literary festivals can go some little way towards making amends by flushing out visiting scribes and bards and showing that far from being a special priesthood guarding esoteric knowledge or holy mysteries they can be, at times, much closer to the sourly Philistine view of them as pretentious layabouts. Hallelujah.

*

In the Cheltenham lecture he mentioned seeing a fire-hose on an art-gallery wall, and realizing that some passers-by were wondering if it was an exhibit. This was at the Museum of Modern Art in New York. During September 1977, he and Margaret spent a two-week holiday in that city. As *The Sunday Times Magazine* put it, at the top of the article ('An Innocent Abroad') which he wrote about the trip, 'Last summer Dennis Potter went abroad for the first time in his life. It was also his first holiday anywhere for fifteen years and his first-ever trip in an aeroplane'.

'Until last summer,' Potter told readers of the magazine,

there seemed little prospect of ever going abroad. A long and irritating illness which needed a lot of attention meant that it would have been rather uncomfortable to spend more than, say, three nights away from home, and the temperamental affinity I had necessarily found to fit these circumstances persuaded me that I was in any case reluctant to squander money disturbing the relatively peaceful equilibrium of my English prejudices.

Why take in new sights and sounds when I had not used up anything like enough of the old ones? Work is the standard (or most socially acceptable) means of blanking out anxiety, and I imagined that Holidays were an even more potent means of releasing it . . . Holidays? Thank you, no . . .

And then – POW! ZAPP-P-P! – everything changed . . . A new drug . . . suddenly and marvellously transformed every prospect . . . Alluring shapes began to form themselves in my mind. The Manhattan silhouette. Rearing skyscrapers. New York. *New York* . . . A thousand celluloid images had always been waiting to dance back into my imagination . . . If we could afford it, Margaret and I were going to go. I think the phrase, announced in nervous belligerence, was, 'We'll damn well do it!'

Sarah confirms that illness had been his principal reason for not travelling: 'Just going up to London was difficult – Dad and I used to go up regularly to watch Fulham play, and if we had to stay over, Mum would pack Dad's long johns, and dressings and stuff, so that he wouldn't drop skin all over the carpet. He was a very private man – you'd think, oh, it's just a hotel room, it doesn't matter, but to him it did, enormously. So that would certainly have curtailed travel. The difference caused by the Razoxane was so different, so enormous.'

David Hare says Potter told him that, until Razoxane, 'he always had to choose a hotel according to the colour of the carpet. He tucked his trousers into his socks, and when he took the trousers off, so much skin fell on to the floor that if the carpet was dark it was immediately visible. He favoured beige or white carpets for that reason.' Hare asked him if he had read a John Updike article in the *New Yorker* about suffering from psoriasis as a child. 'Dennis just looked at me darkly and said, "I thought Updike had never really suffered from psoriasis." His own diseases had been so much worse that he couldn't take Updike's literary agonizing about mere rashes very seriously.'

The Potters decided to take an airline package holiday which would give them two weeks at the New York Hilton. Dennis had to get his first-ever passport; and then came the flight: 'I was quietly debating with myself whether I rated a single paragraph obituary in *The Times* or merely a full down-page column in both the *Ross Gazette* and the *Dean Forest Guardian*. That was before we actually saw the plane. When the gigantic 747 loomed into view . . . there was just a deplorable lump of fear.' The United States Immigration officer was the next hurdle: '"Whatdyado to your hands?" he said, looking hard at me . . . We struggled on through, my face as red as a tomayto [*sic*].' Hustled into a taxi, they were appalled by the 'filth and rubbish' to be seen on the drive into Manhattan. 'Images of decay and poverty sped past.'

There were the usual communication difficulties – a waitress 'couldn't understand my accent, rather as though I had a Dutch cap in my mouth' – and a sense of *déjà vu*: 'The fear of being mugged that I suddenly felt when stupidly walking at night in one of the many wrong parts of New York was almost exactly the same fear that I had felt four decades earlier about being waylaid by one particular bully in the high-hedged lanes which led away from my Forest of Dean primary school.'

They took 'cautious walks in the Park', went on boat trips around Manhattan and down the Hudson, and watched 'incredibly bad television'. Potter was 'fascinated and appalled and totally disorientated' by the city. 'New Yorkers have hard, snapping eyes,' he wrote.

And yet, too, an electric sense of personal freedom, a cordite smell of endeavour and enjoyment which both tightened the throat and relaxed the emotions . . . It was impossible not to believe that this was an alluring, earthly version of Paradise – a mock semblance of heaven . . . You felt both exhilarated and ashamed, free to be anything and yet trapped for ever in a cornucopia of tinsel. A swanky, vulgar city of endless display and cruelty . . . Certainly I – we – were changed by the experience. Travel may broaden the mind, but it shakes you up.

Returning home in late September, he resumed his *Sunday Times* column in a new frame of mind towards his medium, and indeed his country:

Coming back to British television after an unwise and vertiginous 'holiday' in horrendous New York (where the police sirens on the juddery screen in the corner of my double-locked and chained hotel room were taken up and amplified on the murderous streets way down below) is a bit like sipping Malvern Water after lying face down for a couple of weeks in a polluted ditch . . . Never having been outside Britain before, I had not realized how like a convalescent hospital the dear old place really is.

Sarah says that, now her father's 'no holiday, no abroad' rule had been broken, there were occasional foreign trips with the family. 'But to be perfectly honest, some of them were difficult, because Dad wasn't somebody who could relax easily. If he wasn't working, he was unhappy.'

*

Although *Pennies from Heaven* had not yet been completed, Trodd was already commissioning another original six-part serial for the BBC from Potter, with the working title *Me and Some Others* – 'Six related plays using an autobiographical form and convention . . . individual titles as yet unknown.' A few months later they discussed a *Play for Today* to be called *The Merchant's House*, about 'an Imperial family on its last legs and its last days'. Yet at the end of 1977, Potter said on *Desert Island Discs* that he was doubtful about the direction his work should now take:

I'm forty-two, and going through the usual mid-life crisis about the importance or otherwise of what one is doing. Maybe I'm just more disillusioned than I should be with television. Although I still want to write for television, I think it gets a bit more difficult, and people are just that little bit more timid. I've been commissioned by the Oxford Playhouse and by the National Theatre, and I'm responding to that.'

Judy Daish says she thinks that this National Theatre play was going to be about a writer in a hospital bed. However, Margaret Potter told the *Daily Mail* in April 1977: 'He's preparing to adapt his banned play *Brimstone and Treacle* for the National Theatre and he's preparing a play for the Oxford Playhouse.' Sir Peter Hall, who was head of the National Theatre from 1973 to 1988, writes:

I knew Dennis slightly, but to the best of my belief no play was commissioned by the National Theatre during my time, and I had no dealings whatsoever with him until just before his death, when I was in conversations about possibly directing that early play about an eminent politician being painted [*Message for Posterity*]. The dates, as they say, didn't work out. So I have no recollections – only admiration.

The National Theatre does hold a contract for a Potter play dated 19 January 1978, but there is nothing to indicate the subject-matter, and the play was not written.

Once again, during 1977, the BBC asked him to give a radio broadcast on the subject of Christmas. This time he looked back to childhood, in a programme called *A Christmas Forest*, broadcast on Boxing Day. The Potters' youngest child Robert (then twelve) took part as a reader, and the Berry Hill Band and schoolchildren were heard too. In his script, Potter described himself as 'a hesitant Christian'.

Pennies from Heaven was due to be transmitted on BBC1 in March and April 1978 (preceded by *The Mayor of Casterbridge* on BBC2 from January to early March). Judy Daish says that 'it wasn't really until they'd assembled episode 1 of *Pennies* that the BBC realized they had something special. I remember getting a call from Jimmy Cellan Jones, who said in incredibly excited tones, "For God's sake, get yourself over here *now* and *see* it."' Among those given a preview of the first episode was Michael Church of *The Times*: 'The videotape version I saw was in black and white,' he reported on 3 February, 'punctuated by a burst of colour each time a Bowlly or an Elsie Carlisle number came up. This framework is, however, now going to be discarded in favour of colour throughout; Potter and producer Ken Trodd both felt that the repeated use of such a heavy device would crudely over-simplify their intention.'

On 14 February Potter appeared on London Weekend Television's *The South Bank Show*, where he told Melvyn Bragg that, while his 'evangelical notions about the importance of television drama' had 'slightly diminished over the years, been buffeted a bit', he still felt that it was '*the* arena for a writer to address his fellow citizens'. He talked about his search for religious belief: 'There is a very important human appeal in an order which says justice and mercy and pity and peace are actually there . . . Those are just other names, to me, for what I think of as God.'

On the day that this was broadcast, Potter was interviewed for *Time Out* by the paper's television editor, John Wyver, a young Oxford graduate who was a huge admirer of his work, and had been shown the first two episodes of *Pennies from Heaven*:

I'd seen him speak the previous summer at Edinburgh, and was electrified by that – it was more startling and interesting than the later MacTaggart Lecture, very passionate, very deeply felt.

We did the interview in his hotel room at the Kensington Hilton. He stayed there a lot when he came up to work, and I can remember meeting him there in the coffee shop, and realizing how close the situation was to *Double Dare* – I was quite shocked by it. His look, his manner, the setting, the room were all uncannily the same. I took a very good photographer with me, whom Dennis was unbelievably twitchy about – he found it very, very difficult to be photographed. And he wasn't in any sense as confident at that point in his life as he became later, in talking about his work.

The transcript of the interview (in its unedited form) begins with a cold-ridden Potter, in his hotel bedroom, offering his guests a drink:

'I'm swamping it with alcohol today . . . Could I ask you to take that top off for me? Ta.' Removing bottle-tops with his own hands was, of course, almost impossible. (On the video recording of the *South Bank Show* interview his ubiquitous cigarette is clenched between fingers that look totally immobile, so that one wonders how he had managed the perfect handwriting in which *Pennies from Heaven* is written.) 'It's tough,' he told Wyver of the bottle-opening challenge. 'I just crush it in the door. I mean, they make them for – I don't know what. King Kong's hands.'

In his introductory remarks to the published interview, Wyver wrote, '*Pennies from Heaven* are brilliant plays with writing of a quality unlikely to be bettered on television until Potter's next drama.' A *Daily Express* preview by James Murray called the serial 'a magical welding together of popular music, trenchant humour, high drama and all the tricks of television technology. It's all so refreshing, I think it will galvanize the whole country.' A preview in *The Times* on the day of the first episode, Tuesday, 7 March 1978, said, 'Dennis Potter's *Pennies from Heaven* is superb. Just that. Not to be missed.'

Michael Ratcliffe reviewed it in the same paper next morning: 'Mr Potter has hit on a kind of televisual equivalent of the serialized Victorian novel . . . There seems no reason why the impetus should not be sustained.' Ratcliffe praised its 'delicious lightness and perfect pace' and 'the unsentimental generosity of the whole enterprise', adding that it was 'performed with immense charm'. Nancy Banks-Smith called it 'an enchanting musical . . . delicious, delightful and delovely with a dark undertow and runs for six weeks, so aren't you lucky? . . . Extraordinary. Quite extraordinary.' The following weekend, David Coward, standing in for Potter in *The Sunday Times*, judged the first episode 'smashing'. However, Martin Amis in the *Observer* wrote that episode 1 'left me only half engaged'. He called the story-line 'typical if slightly below-par Potter – i.e. it was pretty good', and said that the miming 'just doesn't work . . . Men mime to women's voices, women to men's; conventions are juggled with affection, but somehow without particularity or point.'

Potter laughed this review off the next morning on Radio 4's *Start the Week*, calling Amis 'a little dot-dot-dot-dot' (that is, shit). But Philip Purser in the *Sunday Telegraph* had expressed doubts too:

If advance plaudits for the show had been less extravagant I think I might have been more irresistibly delighted by the opening episode . . . Are the sunny, sentimental, unreal lyrics meant to be taken as coded expressions of sexual longing (Arthur) or as nice, wholesome alternatives to the beastly business (Joan)? Knowing Potter, probably both, plus extra interpolations to come. We shall see.

A week later, Sean Day-Lewis reviewed episode 2 in the *Daily Telegraph*: 'At the core is [Potter's] new-found religious optimism, his belief that despite all the evidence to the contrary "everything is all right" . . . The performance of Bob Hoskins as the hero is extraordinarily clever.' But Clive James in the *Observer* was no keener than Amis had been: 'The show ought to work, but on the evidence of its second episode the light touch is fatally absent. Potter shows welcome signs, for once, of wanting to lift our spirits, but there is so much social analysis going on that there is hardly any room for people . . .' Three days later, after episode 3, even Nancy Banks-Smith began to feel doubtful: 'When Sammy Cahn was writing songs in the Thirties, he was told: "We don't want 'em good. We want 'em by Tuesday." Some of these episodes read as if they were wanted by Tuesday. I'd say six is probably too many. Like a Thirties murderer Dennis Potter might well ask himself if, in retrospect, he has divided his beloved into too many pieces.'

Philip Purser still had his doubts, but, after episode 4, these were overwhelmed by sheer enjoyment. 'Is it a hit or a miss?' he asked.

It started so-so, declined dangerously the second week, only picked up the third . . . In many ways *Moonlight on the Highway* was a more subtle and more perceptive product of Potter's fascination with the popular music of his childhood. But how often can you return to a show each week . . . in the expectation of entertainment so beguiling, so inventive, so enjoyable without being soft, and so wholly belonging to television? . . . It presses its Thirties songs into service rather as Benjamin Britten pressed Victorian hymns into his operas . . . I wouldn't miss the rest for anything.

Whatever individual critics felt, *Pennies from Heaven* quickly became an undoubted hit with the public. After only two episodes the *Evening Standard* described it as 'the series that has become compulsive viewing on Tuesdays . . . The consensus of opinion is that it is the most creatively innovative and ambitious attempt at changing the conventions of TV drama ever attempted.' By this time it was being watched by around 12 million viewers, Potter's largest television audience so far.

The third episode prompted a complaint to the BBC from Mary Whitehouse's National Viewers' and Listeners' Association:

Dennis Potter is a brilliant playwright with perceptive things to say. It is all the more to be regretted therefore that he was served by a production team whose approach can only be described as 'kinky' . . . The close-up shots of the woman sitting up in bed having painted round the nipples of her breasts with lipstick, and the ones in which the man took her breasts into his hands, with the accompanying dialogue, amounted to a gross intrusion into the privacy of the viewer . . . If individuals wish to behave like the couple in the play that is their affair. The rest of us should not be turned into voyeurs of kinky sexual practices.

There were also complaints about the Berry Hill Primary School children appearing in episodes which 'included sex scenes', but the mother of one of them described the filming as 'the experience of a lifetime'.

At the conclusion of *Pennies*, Sean Day-Lewis wrote:

There cannot have been a richer television serial . . . The richness has become evident through the polarity of enthusiasm and hostility the work has aroused, and through the persistence of us *aficionados* in finding different images, messages and meanings within its generous, paradoxical texture.

The quality has been uneven, but each of the six plays has included at least one scene written, directed and played with such memorable sensitivity as to make the occasional corner-cutting crudities and evasions disappear to the back of the mind.

The BBC repeated the serial at the end of 1978, and the following spring it won two BAFTA awards (Best Writer and Most Original TV Production).

Writing fifteen years later, Philip Purser still had reservations: 'Potter's evocation of the Thirties struck me as having been whistled up from Great Western Railway posters and mouldering copies of the *News of the World*.' But John Wyver voices many people's feelings when he says, 'I was simply knocked out by it. I still think it was Potter's supreme achievement.'

*

Two months after the last episode of *Pennies* had been shown, the BBC commissioned Potter to adapt Anthony Powell's sequence of novels *A Dance to the Music of Time* as twelve ninety-minute episodes. Trodd says of this project, 'I think it was probably my idea. Dennis and Judy and I went down to Frome to see Powell, and my abiding memory is of being sick on the journey – I was so guilty about not having done my homework on the books that I was sitting in the back of Judy's rather small car, nervously mugging up, and it made me car-sick.' They had a rather tense meeting with Powell – the largely aristocratic milieu of his novels can scarcely have been to Potter's taste – and it was agreed that the script of the first episode would not be delivered for a year; Potter would then have a further eighteen months in which to finish the job. By October 1978 the project had been assigned to a company called Pennies From Heaven Ltd, to whom the BBC paid £3000 as a 'development fee'.

Potter explained to the *Daily Mail* that the purpose of this new company – of which the directors were himself, Trodd, and Judy Daish – was to realize 'a writer's dream of being in total control of his work'. There were now (he said) 'several small production companies trying to make tiny dents in the monolithic structure of British television'; the BBC was 'sniffily affronted' by these newcomers, and ITV was 'nervously wary', but 'round the next corner . . . is the Fourth Channel'.

Trodd says of 'PFH Ltd', as the company came to be known: 'The idea was that we should have a production company which would give us more control over what we were doing – it came out of a combination of the banning of *Brimstone*, the success of *Pennies*, and a sense that the way the business was organized was even then beginning to change.' Another of its purposes was to exploit the success of *Pennies from Heaven*, and as early as March 1978, just before transmission of the serial, the *Guardian* had reported that 'Potter . . . Haggard, and Ken Trodd are . . . trying to set up an idea for a feature film.' Haggard says this was an exaggeration: 'I said to Ken, "We should make a film of this." But I was so busy that I didn't push it.'

Potter told an interviewer at the time of *Pennies* that he had already 'tried his hand at film writing twice', so far without success. The first of these projects was *The Sins of the Fathers*, an original screenplay written while he was still a client of Clive Goodwin – probably a commission, since the script is in a binder labelled 'World Film Services Ltd' (a company run by the British film financier John Hayman). Set in the mid-eighteenth century, its hero is John Newton, an opinionated young English mariner who is drawn into slave-trading after he has survived a near-drowning at the hands of his fellow sailors. The screenplay abounds with bare-breasted slave girls, and there are scenes of rape and torture. Potter seems to be aiming at a Joseph Conrad-style tragedy, but after a brisk start the narrative becomes repetitive and shapeless.

In 1975 he was asked by Fred Zinnemann, the veteran Hollywood director domiciled in London, to make a cinema adaptation of John Fowles's 1969 novel *The French Lieutenant's Woman*. Sarah Potter recalls 'meeting Zinnemann with Dad in a hotel lobby somewhere. Dad was slightly in awe of him, and I hadn't really seen that before.'

Fowles's text, with its theme of Madonna versus Whore, and its startling authorial interventions, has considerable affinities with Potter's own preoccupations; yet his film adaptation of the novel, which went through several drafts, is a disappointingly tame affair, probably because Zinnemann, not the most imaginative of film-makers, wanted it that way. Potter renders the story of Charles Smithson, his engagement to the virginal Ernestina, and his love for the supposedly 'fallen' Sarah, as a Victorian costume drama without modern interpolations. The book had become famous for its alternative endings (the reader can choose which woman Charles ends up with), but Potter supplies only one – Charles's rejection by the emancipated Sarah – though the final page of the script describes it as 'An Ending' rather than 'The End'. Zinnemann never made the movie, and the book eventually passed into the hands of the director Karel Reisz, whose 1981 version, scripted by Harold Pinter, interleaves the Charles–Sarah narrative with a parallel love affair between a contemporary actor and actress who are playing them in a film of the novel – a cinematic equivalent of Fowles's then-and-now game which was judged very successful by audiences and critics.

By the end of 1978, Potter had been approached about a film of *Pennies* by Greg Smith, a British film producer who had made money out of *Confessions of a Window Cleaner* and other titles in the *Confessions* series. Potter's first attempt at the screenplay (which seems not to have survived) apparently made few changes in the story. After Smith had read it, he asked Potter to try resetting the story in Chicago, and said he would pay for him to visit the city and look for a Midwest equivalent of the Forest of Dean. Potter agreed; he had more time on his hands, since his *Sunday Times* television reviewing had ended abruptly a few weeks earlier.

The proprietors of the paper, Times Newspapers Ltd, had threatened to suspend publication of *The Sunday Times*, *The Times* and other publications in the group at the end of November 1978, if the print unions continued to refuse to sign agreements about reduced manning and new technology. In his *Sunday Times* column on 26 November, Potter went into battle against his paymasters:

I gloomily turned to Monday's *Panorama* (BBC1) to find out what is happening to this paper . . . It is surely characteristic of the sniffily inept management revealed in such tawdry light on the programme not to have informed its contributors about their futures. But as I was about to teeth-grind my way through this review I was told that two other people would be writing here about last week's *Panorama*, so I cannot take up the kind of space which would permit apoplexy its due momentum.

Two points, please, guv'nor: first, and public, how cruel of *Panorama* to demonstrate so conclusively that a pair of newspapers by no means free of the usual canting humbug about the plight of Britain or the woodrot of her industries should all the time have been pathetically worm-ridden examples of the very malaise they so ponderously curse in others. Secondly, and more personal, this will in the event of 'suspension' or closure (lock-out is the proper term) be my last column for this sadly embattled journal.

'Unless you have a date (for closure) you don't get anywhere,' piped 'Duke' Hussey, the obviously catastrophic Managing Director of Times Newspapers on *Panorama*. Quite so, old boy – and I am giving him slightly more notice than his team of seemingly devious nincompoops have even yet given to me.

But those who are most grievously affected by the astonishingly sordid manoeuvrings depicted in the programme cannot always afford such spittle-flecked bombast. They needs must comport themselves a little like the cautious Head Maltster in Vaclav Havel's *Audience*, the second of two plays by the Czech dissident in last Tuesday's fascinating *Play for Today* spot on BBC1 . . .

He ended the review: 'Turn on, tune in, drop out – and farewell.'

Assuming that *Sunday Times* editor Harold Evans would reject or censor this piece, Potter passed it to the *Guardian*, which telephoned Evans for comments, then reported as follows on Saturday, 25 November:

The Sunday Times goes to press tonight for what might be the last night for some time leaving behind a row over how the paper's temporary obituary should be written.

Among those involved is Dennis Potter, the paper's television critic, who says he has been accused of a 'betrayal of the journalists' by the editor,

Mr Harold Evans, for remarks he makes in a column he wrote for tomorrow's paper.

Mr Potter says he has told Mr Evans that if *The Sunday Times* suspends publication in what he describes as 'a good old-fashioned lockout', he for one does not wish to work for the paper any more.

And he said that if Mr Evans refused to publish it, he would make sure it was printed elsewhere . . . Mr Evans said last night that he did not know whether he could use the Potter review of the *Panorama* programme . . . Last night Mr Potter said that he had had 'intense discussions with Harold Evans' late yesterday afternoon over his review. 'I have put down what I think I am entitled to say and he has said he is entitled to print what he edits.'

In fact Evans cut very little of the Potter piece, but he wrote to Potter the same day:

Dear Dennis,
I am sorry you are resigning . . . I find it discourteous and unprofessional to find that the *Guardian* has a copy of your column while it is still being discussed here and that parts of the conversation between you and me are in print before your own review appears in *The Sunday Times* . . . You have chosen to believe the worst of some of your associates here and add a particularly wounding incident at a time of deep distress and anxiety . . .

Potter did not reply. The lock-out went ahead, and lasted for a year, ending Potter's final stint as a reviewer.

He set off for Chicago early in January 1979, taking Judy Daish with him. 'He needed to be able to drive around the place,' she explains, 'and I'd driven in America before.' Afterwards, Potter said that, compared to New York, he 'quite (yes, *quite*)' enjoyed his research. 'We were there for only a few days,' says Daish, 'and we drove down through South Chicago (which was pretty rough) on Route 1, to Paris, Illinois, which actually has a very small Eiffel Tower in it! And Dennis was fascinated by the area.

'He wasn't exactly ill while we were there, but on some days he didn't want to travel or do anything, despite the Razoxane.' (He had missed some weeks' reviewing on *The Sunday Times* the previous autumn, because of bad headaches apparently caused by the drug.) 'Yet it was still a wonder to him that he could make that kind of trip at all,' remarks Daish. She says she 'knew him pretty well by that stage, and the family too – in fact, it was as if I was becoming part of the family.'

She had arrived in Potter's life when his marriage was under new strains. Margaret had told the *Daily Mail*, soon after his discharge from hospital in 1977, that his new energy had 'exhausted us all' to the extent that 'I feel a bit like an old woman', and Sarah emphasizes that, ironically, life now became far more difficult for her mother: 'After Razoxane, Dad had this enormous sense of freedom, and I think it was a traumatic time for Mum and him. Mum felt insecure, because she'd had a life caring for him, and then suddenly he didn't need it. I remember Mum saying, "You don't need me any more", and Dad being absolutely horrified.'

Ken Trodd says that, around this time, Potter made another confession to him:

While *Pennies* was in pre-production, Dennis told me quite clearly that he was having an affair with Judy. It seemed to be part of this whole rejuvenation thing. And then I never kept up, or was kept up, with whether it stopped – I assumed it stopped, didn't think about it, but now I'm inclined to think that something probably carried on, though Judy was virtually integrated into the family – it was again Dennis fashioning conventional tropes in a way that made them very purpose-built for his own needs – absolutely not the mistress back in London.

Eleven years later, in 1988, Potter told the actress Gina Bellman that (in Bellman's words) 'Judy had been his mistress for years'.

Asked if she had an affair with Potter, Judy Daish herself says, 'Not physically. I absolutely deny that. It simply isn't true. But obviously Dennis was very fond of me, and I of him, and we had a very close friendship, and a very, very good working relationship. And I suppose that what Ken says Dennis told him may have been Dennis's way of interpreting that.' Does she think Potter was in love with her? 'I think he loved me, but I don't think he was "in love" with me.'

She continues:

I *was* very close to him, and obviously I was aware that people thought it was a physical relationship. But people have very prurient minds, I think. I had various romances in my life, but I was very ambitious, and it doesn't always fit in. I remember making the decision when I was with Jimmy Wax. Somebody rang me up, who was just about to leave the National Theatre to go and work with Clive Goodwin, and she asked me, 'What's it like, working in an agency?' And I remember saying to her, 'My advice to you is, if you really want to make it work, don't have any personal life.'

Brian Gibson, who had directed *Where Adam Stood*, describes Daish, then in her early thirties: 'She was absolutely beautiful – everyone was always saying she looked like Jacqueline Bisset. A beautiful face.' However, Jane Potter says, 'She didn't dress at all glamorously in those days – jeans, raggedy hair, she looked like she'd just come from a rock festival.'

Daish says that Margaret Potter seemed happy to let her accompany Dennis to Chicago: 'She didn't want to come, because she'd hated New York, and felt the whole country was dangerous. She didn't seem worried by Dennis going off with me.' Yet there is evidence that Margaret was anxious. 'I know she wondered about Judy,' says Margaret's sister, Mavis Wood. Clive Lindley, who joined PFH Ltd some while after its formation, and knew the Potters socially at Ross-on-Wye, agrees that 'Margaret wasn't too happy about it', and adds, 'I never quite knew what the relationship was with Judy, but I thought it was none of my business. There were assumptions being made, but nobody ever talked about it, and Dennis wasn't the kind of person who would discuss that sort of thing – he and I didn't have a bar-room, nudge-nudge, wink-wink sort of friendship.'

Sarah Potter believes that physical affairs were impossible for her father after he had switched to Razoxane: 'I know for a fact that sex would not have been involved, because from the late Seventies Dad wasn't able to – and that was as a result of Razoxane and other drugs.' Does she believe that this remained the case for him thereafter? 'Yes, it did. Which is one of the reasons, I think, for some of that flirting, some of that longing.' Judy Daish agrees: 'I remember Dennis telling me that – that it was one of the side-effects. And that must have been pretty devastating.' Potter himself said to a journalist in 1980 that he had been impotent only 'at first' after taking Razoxane, but in a 1981 proposal for what eventually became *The Singing Detective* he wrote that the 'new drug' being taken by the principal character, a psoriatic television playwright, had among its side-effects the 'decimation of the fast-dividing reproductive cells', which made him 'all but impotent'.

Sarah says she 'did once talk to Dad directly about his relationship with Judy, and he said, "I'm just amazed that people think it's an affair – what sort of physical condition do they think I'm in?"' Sarah continues:

It's easy to assume affairs, and to imagine that relationships which were obviously close went that extra step, but with Dad it was rather a different set of circumstances. I think he was quite repulsed by the whole idea of it, really, and he was very disappointed that certain people always made that assumption about him.

Of course it was a close working relationship, and I think he did love Judy, because he loved a lot of people. And she almost became an extension of our family unit. At times that did make Mum feel uncomfortable. But it was always made all right by Dad talking to Mum about it, with whatever his explanation was. And if Mum had been really fearful she would have put her foot down and said, 'Judy's not coming at Christmas', or 'Judy's not coming on holiday with us.' And Dad would have withdrawn the invitation to her – there was no way that would have gone ahead if Mum hadn't wanted her in the house. And Judy wouldn't have come if Mum hadn't made her comfortable. Meanwhile Dad never tired of trying to drag Mum along with him to everything he was doing.

In March 1978, the month that *Pennies* began transmission, Daish left the Wax agency and set up on her own, as Judy Daish Associates, in a room in the Globe Theatre, Shaftesbury Avenue. She explains that 'Dennis and Ken put some money on the table' to make this possible, and Trodd says that Potter insisted he matched the amount of cash he himself was putting into the agency – and that Trodd should become Daish's client: 'The reason I joined Judy's agency was that Dennis said, "If you don't, and put money into it, I won't form PFH Ltd." We both financed her.' Daish says that Potter was 'enormously generous, incredibly kind. And loyal.' Did she feel much closer to him than to the other writers she represented? 'As a friend, I think I did, yes. In a curious way, he was my best friend. It was as simple as that.'

She also emphasizes the strength of the Potter marriage: 'Margaret was an incredibly warm person, who understood Dennis astonishingly well, and was immensely supportive. She was very close to the children, and wonderful with them. She had a grounded strength, from which she never seemed to depart.' But she accepts that Margaret was worried about her: 'Yes, I think she was.'

CHAPTER 3

Working in the bank

▬

Shortly after he had got back from Chicago, in January 1979, Potter met John Wyver, who was to interview him for the *Guardian*, in a small rented flat in Queensway, West London, which he said had been 'leased for the scripting' of the *Pennies from Heaven* film. He told Wyver he was wary of discussing work in progress – 'You know, it's amazing how much it changes things' – but he did reveal a certain amount:

On second draft I'm setting it in Chicago, which brings it closer, in a sense, to Arthur's dream, because . . . there are no substitutes in the European sense for that culture. You know it is an *American* dream.

I'm up to here in it. And the time scale is very different, because I have to do in two hours what I did in eight hours, and to be that much closer to the movie musical conventions . . . I'm sweating a bit over it at the moment . . . I've had to reshape it altogether, and think of it as a new piece . . . On the first [draft] I just had the six [television] scripts in front of me all the time . . . and they kept getting in the way . . . Whether it comes off – I just hope it does, because I think it would be the kind of film I would like to see. But never assume anything.

The interview was chiefly about his new television play, written the previous summer and due to be transmitted by the BBC at the end of January. Wyver asked him if it had been hard to follow *Pennies from Heaven*, and Potter answered, 'Not consciously . . . But . . . I always find it hard to start something after I've finished anything. There's always a break when I feel I'm not going to write anything again – for about a fortnight.' Asked if the new script marked a change of direction, Potter said, 'I see it as going over the same old ploughed field again and again. I think you're trapped in one small acre and that's it. I think if I try and look too far over the hedge, I won't have toured my own little patch properly. I think it's very much a continuation of existing themes and images [though] the end product may not look like it.'

Wyver supplied a plot summary of the new play for his readers:

Four boys are playing in an English wood in 1943. War games, the killing of a squirrel, bickering and the teasing of two girls occupy their morning. The girls in turn torment Donald 'Duck', a shy, uncertain boy hiding in a barn. At one point they are all scared by the siren from a nearby prisoner-of-war camp; later they witness and are all involved in a tragic accident.

Simple, certainly, but not quite *that* simple. For the seven children are all played unselfconsiously by a well-known adult cast . . .

The manuscript of *Blue Remembered Hills* – which bears the words 'FURTHER ADVENTURES OF THE SECRET SEVEN' over the play's title – opens with this direction:

EXTERIOR. DAY. (MORNING.)

The long summer holiday, 1943. West Country. A seven-year-old boy, played by a mature adult, is walking along a path that meanders from some distant houses into a stretch of gorse and scrub 'common' . . . He is eating a large cooking apple. At first sight, no doubt, he will appear to be a cretinous adult rather than a normal child – his walk, his fidgets, his expressions and, above all, his mannerisms being modelled on the non-stop near-gymnastics of a seven-year-old, brought into compelling focus by the adult body rather than simply parodied or caricatured.

Wyver asked Potter if *Blue Remembered Hills* was explicitly autobiographical. 'No,' said Potter. 'I wanted it to look as though it was . . . When Colin Welland [cast as Willie, the boy described in the opening direction] first got the script he said, "Did that happen to you?" No, it didn't happen, but it could have done.' In fact Potter's sister June thinks there was some drawing from life:

He said there was a spiteful one [Audrey] and that was me . . . I was never very pushy anyway. Helen Mirren [playing Angela] had my doll . . . Dinah. I've still got Dinah . . . but the other one [Audrey] was the bossy one. So Helen Mirren must have been Doreen Dart. But it was based on his children's experiences as well. He mixed it all up.

Blue Remembered Hills starts exactly where *Pennies from Heaven* left off, with two boys discussing who can 'pee the highest'. *Pennies* set out to prove that everything was all right, and discovered that the opposite was true. In the new play, Potter tries to find out why – where did we go wrong? Was it, as Arthur in *Pennies* suggested, simply by being born?

The play's title is sarcastic; Housman's 'blue remembered hills' of childhood, overlooking a 'land of lost content', are a sentimental mirage. As Potter himself put it,

Our culture has long since acknowledged that childhood is not transparent with innocence, and that its apparent simplicities are but the opacities of the very anxieties and aggressions which we occasionally seek to evade by means of a misplaced nostalgia for those 'blue remembered hills' of Housman's aching little verse.

In the play, Willie and his friends may seem to inhabit a sinless, untroubled Eden, but (as John Cook has pointed out in his book on Potter) from the outset Willie, playing at wartime fighter planes, imagines violent death by burning – 'At-a-tat-tat-tat-tat-tat-tat! . . . Them be all dead . . . Burnt to nothing' – and death by fire will actually happen at the end of the play. In between, a squirrel is murdered, and the child protagonists miss no opportunity to taunt and bully each other, only holding back from violence and verbal abuse when they are uncertain of winning. Lying and thieving are accepted as the *status quo*, and the sole innocent aspect of their lives is the absence of sex – Potter carefully places the play in 1943, shortly before he himself was shocked into awareness of it. Yet the cruelties are mitigated by earthy humour and an abundance of physical energy and inventiveness, which allow them to forget disappointments almost at once and plunge into the next game or activity. Potter described this as 'continual twitchy action . . . the constant present-tense preoccupations of childhood'.

If *Blue Remembered Hills* had been written for child actors, it would have come out as a watered-down *Lord of the Flies* (Golding's boys indulge in more sophisticated cruelties). With adults playing the parts, sentimentality is eliminated ('I was trying to avoid twee and coy responses,' said Potter) and child behaviour is physically magnified. Potter always emphasized this when talking about the play – 'I used adult actors to play children in order to make them like a magnifying glass' – but he only once mentioned its real secret, when talking to John Wyver: 'For adults to play children . . . would remind us more, because they are the same size and shape roughly as we are.' Watching

Blue Remembered Hills, we the audience are deprived of our usual 'adult' condescension to 'childish' goings-on, and are projected back into the agonies and hilarities we ourselves experienced in childhood, simply because the actors are the same size as us. 'If you are seven and the bully is seven,' Potter said to Graham Fuller, 'then it's as bad, as terrifying, as being mugged on the street as an adult.'

Ken Trodd chose Brian Gibson, who had made such a success of *Where Adam Stood*, to direct *Blue Remembered Hills* – though Gibson recalls that he was originally signed up for a different project:

The idea was that Dennis would write a piece about the Tsar's daughters, the Romanovs. I was quite excited about that, because I like the idea of historical drama, so I made myself available for the summer of 1978. I would check in with Ken about it – I didn't call Dennis directly – and he'd say, 'Oh yes, Dennis is writing.' And then suddenly Ken revealed that he hadn't been writing that piece, he'd been writing something totally different. And we were sent *Blue Remembered Hills*.

And Ken called me and said, 'What do you think of it? I'm really not sure.' I said, 'It's very strange.' There was some very interesting writing in it, but it took two or three readings for me to appreciate its true quality.

Fourteen years later, Potter explained how the subject-matter had changed:

I just had this one image of the Russian royal family under arrest by the Bolsheviks, in this village, and a peasant soldier pushing aside the fronds of the leaves . . . A few months before, he would have thought of them not only as the royal family, but as demi-gods . . . And maybe it was that that led to the prisoner-of-war camp that I remember in the Forest of Dean . . . the Italian prisoners of war [the children in *Blue Remembered Hills* fear that one of them has escaped and will attack them] . . . That may have been the connection. Something must have been.

It was arranged that Gibson and Trodd should discuss the script with Potter at a Greek restaurant in London. Judy Daish was there:

Dennis and Brian and I were waiting for Ken, who was delayed, and there were carafes of red wine on the table. Ken comes in through the door and sits down, and starts saying to Dennis that he wonders whether it's advisable to have adults playing the children. And it became quite a heated conversation, and suddenly a stream of red wine went right across from Dennis's mouth on to Ken's face! And Ken got up furiously and left.

Brian Gibson remembers it the same way – 'Ken arrived late and Dennis spat retsina at him' – emphasizing that this 'seven-year-old' behaviour showed that Potter was still living in the play. Daish thinks he was trying to show Trodd how well adults playing children would work. Potter himself recalled that 'Ken Trodd wanted to cast children in *Blue Remembered Hills*'.

Trodd admits to having felt 'the usual nervousness' about the adults-as-children device, but does not believe he was raising that point in the restaurant. In a programme note when *Blue Remembered Hills* was staged at the National Theatre in 1996, he writes,

Dennis wanted to deliver the script rather formally at dinner and it might well have been Easter Sunday because as I drove, late and guilty, to the restaurant, *Sunday Half-Hour* was doing 'Low in the Grave He Lay', and I thought that'll be me before the night's out. To be late for Dennis Potter was peril enough but late because rushing from the Cork Film Festival (Abroad *and* Ireland *and* other people's movies!) was excommunicable.

As I came in, Brian Gibson, who was to direct the film and who'd also been in Cork but had the sense to catch an earlier plane back, was telling the table how much fun I'd been having there.

Trodd explains that he thinks Potter was jealous because Gibson had been describing him (Trodd) having an affair at Cork (Trodd has never married, but has had a string of girlfriends). Gibson says, 'I don't remember telling Dennis anything about Ken's conquests of women at Cork, though he has always been surprisingly successful in that respect for a man who – well, he's not Kevin Costner, is he?'

Trodd's programme note continues:

I sat down and before my apologies could even begin, Dennis leaned across somebody (our agent Judy Daish I think) and deposited the masticating contents of his mouth skilfully into mine. Like many other pieces of inventive aggression that passed between us over the years, it was probably an act of thwarted love and probably the only time in the strange cycle of our relationship when I didn't attempt some pathetic retaliation on the spot. Instead I left swiftly, without dinner or dignity, to catch on the car radio the last of the Resurrection hymns – the one about the strife being past, the battle done, and the victor's triumph won.

Like most of our little skirmishes, this one rendered grownupness infantile rather as *Blue Remembered Hills* (the script, by the way, eventually reached me, with a bread roll attached, during the small hours) uses the adult to redefine the child in a landmark way . . .

Judy Daish says she was already used to Potter and Trodd quarrelling like small children: 'While Dennis was in Guy's Hospital, they had a furious row about something, and Ken stormed out, and came back later.' Sarah Potter says,

I can't remember a time in their relationship when they weren't battling. Some of it was quite shocking to listen to. The phone at Morecambe was in the front hall, and I remember once when I was quite young I came out of the living room with a tray of coffee cups just as Dad was on the phone to Ken, and he was saying, 'Fucking hell! Don't you ever fucking this and that', and I was so alarmed that the tray shook! But afterwards Dad said, 'Oh, that's nothing, Ken and I always talk to each other like that. Don't take any notice.'

Brian Gibson believes that the aggression between Potter and Trodd was at the heart of the creative relationship between them:

Ken was always a great doubter – his strength was to come from a position of scepticism about a lot of things. Dennis seems to have thrived on a certain sort of empowering negativity that he got from Ken. Some writers need to be adored, and told, 'You're a genius.' That was not what Ken gave to Dennis, nor was it presumably what Dennis required.

Gibson himself suggested one major change to *Blue Remembered Hills*. In the first draft, after the semi-outcast Donald 'Duck' has trapped himself inside the blazing barn, he 'comes hurtling out through the door, a ball of fire'. The other children try to help but can do nothing. We then see their adult faces dissolving into those of actual children: 'They are looking down in dumb horror at the charred body of a dead child. One of the boys is quietly sobbing. In the distance, some soldiers are running towards them with rifles and fixed bayonets.' Gibson suggested to Potter that they should 'keep the adults' in these final moments, and that the play should end with lines from Housman's poem, spoken in voice-over by Potter himself. 'Otherwise,' says Gibson, 'as so often with Dennis's writing, very little was changed compared with other writers.' He adds, 'A Potter work is so clearly defined, so eccentric in its perspective, that it's very difficult for a director to usurp it, to obliterate that vision.'

Gibson says he 'agonized' over casting *Blue Remembered Hills*,

but Dennis was helpfully philistine, and said, 'Don't make such a big fuss about it.' The read-through was pretty depressing. Some people played their parts as children, others did different things, and I remember at the end of it

I turned to Dennis, and said, 'Do you have any comments?' And he said, 'I want to be sick!' And this was in front of the actors!

I realized what I had to do was to work backwards – to get the actors to create these characters *as adults*, and then work backwards. And I asked Dennis to give me some one-liners to feed to the actors; I remember he said that the Michael Elphick character [Peter] was going to grow up into a lorry driver who would never let anybody pass him. Other than that, he was surprisingly uninvolved. After the read-through, he never sat in on rehearsals, and only came to the shoot for a couple of days.

Colin Welland says that, as the first 'child' to appear on screen, 'my task was to take the audience through the laughter barrier'. Potter recalled that, in the first five minutes, he felt 'panic' at the sight of 'Colin Welland's great fat arse' in giant shorts, 'sploshing through mud making aeroplane noises', fearing that 'it ain't gonna work'. Welland describes the filming as the 'most satisfying' experience of his acting career, and Janine Duvitski, who played Audrey, agrees:

Blue Remembered Hills was the job I have most enjoyed; I think actors are in their element playing children and it was difficult to stop. At the end of the day's filming the hotel was noisy with drunken seven-year-old behaviour. Any hangovers and bags under the eyes next morning helped, as the director had decided I looked too young for the part and made me have ageing make-up applied every morning, which is a bit disconcerting when you're playing a seven-year-old. I think we were all self-conscious at the start, especially when at the read-through Dennis said, 'Well, it can only get better!'

It did, to the extent that, when it was transmitted on 30 January 1979, Philip Purser judged it 'perfect, unflawed'. Similarly Peter Knight in the *Daily Telegraph* could not recall 'one jarring line or a word out of place'. Both Purser and Nancy Banks-Smith responded to the play's theological implications, Purser judging its message to be 'childhood is not a state of grace, it's a state of unspoiled original sin', and Banks-Smith writing, 'Fear and flight and fire ran through the play like a lighted fuse . . . Eden, I suppose, ended like that with fear and shame and a sword flaming like the burning barn.'

Although Potter never made a theatre adaptation of *Blue Remembered Hills*, the original script is easy to stage, and (since its publication in 1984) has proved hugely popular with amateur dramatic societies as well as professional companies. In the programme of the

1996 National Theatre production by Patrick Marber, Trodd writes that 'It begins to feel like Dennis's most durable piece.'

*

'PFH WILL NOW PRODUCE SIX POTTER PLAYS WITH LWT' announced the *Stage* on 24 May 1979, four months after the BBC had screened *Blue Remembered Hills*. It explained that 'Dennis Potter is to write six plays for London Weekend [Television]', and that PFH Ltd would make them 'within the LWT Drama Department'. They would also supply LWT with three plays from other writers, two by Jim Allen, to be directed by Roland Joffe, and one other 'not yet confirmed' (the actor–writer Ken Campbell was later named as its author). *Time Out* reported that London Weekend's Director of Programmes, Michael Grade, said at a 'euphoric' press conference announcing the project, 'We believe that this arrangement . . . will be a model for co-operation between existing drama departments and independent producers.' Peter Fiddick noted in the *Guardian* that the project should provide a matrix for 'the sort of new independent producer who is intended to get a guaranteed presence on Channel 4 when it comes, and who might also give the British film industry a filip'.

Potter saw the project in more personal terms, telling Sean Day-Lewis that it was 'cocking a snook at the BBC'. Trodd describes it as 'Dennis making an attempt to get at the *power* in the business – breaking out from being solely a writer'. Potter himself said much the same to the *Evening News* at the time of the LWT announcement: 'I decided that I shouldn't be so reclusive . . . And now that I've got the power – because people respect my work – and the opportunity, I can do something.'

The Anthony Powell *Dance to the Music of Time* scheme was now put on ice – 'Neither Dennis nor I really had our hearts in it,' says Trodd – and Potter began to face the challenge of writing six single plays in quick succession. Trodd admits that, in this and other respects, the LWT–PFH deal had an unrealistic feel from the outset: 'Dennis and Michael Grade formed some airy fantasies over lunches together, and we then had to bring it down to earth.' The three plays that actually got written and made were, as Trodd observes, 'all derived from Dennis's previous work'.

The first to be filmed, *Rain on the Roof* (which takes its title from a 1932 Lew Stone–Al Bowlly disc), presents us with the familiar Potter situation of a bored young wife, whose marriage has become loveless and sexless, involving herself with an intruding young male. Like Willy in *Where the Buffalo Roam*, Billy is illiterate, and comes to the house for tuition – hence Potter's choice of 'Janet and John', names from the reading primer, for the husband and wife. As the sexual tension mounts between Billy and Janet, the lad passes out; later, we learn that he has eaten cheese while taking tranquillizers, something that two earlier Potter characters were warned not to do.

Uncharacteristically, Potter made two full-length attempts at this play, and did not throw away the first one. After Billy's collapse, the first draft takes us to John's workplace, which is none other than the newspaper office from *Paper Roses*, where again we witness the friction between the elderly reporter Clarence and his younger colleagues, complete with jokey headlines. Potter changes the old hack's surname from Hubbard to Stubbard, but otherwise makes few alterations in this borrowed chunk of his 1969 script.

In the third act of the first draft of *Rain on the Roof*, John brings the dejected Stubbard home for dinner, and they arrive just as Janet has got herself under a duvet with the naked Billy ('as in a farce', observes Potter's stage direction). But Billy has failed to respond to Janet's sexual advances; he is disoriented by his father's recent death, and has got religion. Potter here seems to be mocking his own recent near-conversion. 'I've met Jesus, enn I?', grunts Billy. 'You don't know how low I was, how down. Everything was like it was raining all the time . . . the way the rain sort of glints all dull like on the slates. On the roof.' Now, he explains, 'It's all noo. Like I been washed clean.'

Extricating herself from the duvet, Janet makes supper. Everyone drinks too much, and Billy runs off into the night. Janet goes after him, while John on an impulse – and without any obvious motive – smothers the sleeping Stubbard with a cushion. Returning, Janet fails to notice that the old man is dead, and she and John go upstairs to bed. John comes down again, covers Stubbard's body with newspapers, and in the last moments of the play suddenly addresses the camera: 'Read all about it. It'll help to pass the time.'

Trodd, who did not see this draft, guesses that Potter had recycled *Paper Roses* because of tight deadlines:

I think there was quite a lot of pressure for Dennis to get those scripts in, because the relationship with London Weekend was new, and we were nervous about costing. Incidentally things got off to a bad start on this project between me and Dennis because, for me, it was an absolutely crucial part of the deal with LWT that we would make all six plays on film, on location. You still couldn't call plays 'films' at the BBC, but film was the way things were going in TV drama, and you could see the difference in those of Dennis's plays which had been done entirely on film, *Double Dare*, *Where Adam Stood* and *Blue Remembered Hills*. But most of *Rain on the Roof* was interiors, so of course it could have been made on tape in the studio, so that was what LWT asked us to do – and Dennis was pressuring me to agree to it.

Eventually Trodd was allowed to make *Rain on the Roof* on film. Meanwhile Potter had rewritten it, revamping Billy into a sex-hating prowler who spies on Janet and John as they make love. He removed the *Paper Roses* material, expanded the scene of Janet teaching Billy, gave John a job in advertising and an adulterous affair with a neighbour's wife, and brought her and her husband to the house as the dinner guests instead of Stubbard. Billy now became the killer, returning to the house late at night to stab John, the somewhat perfunctory motive being his fear and disgust of sex.

When Potter discussed his work at the National Film Theatre immediately after the first showing of *Rain on the Roof*, a member of the audience questioned him about the conclusion of the play:

QUESTIONER: I felt that the husband's death came rather abruptly . . . If I'd been the producer of that play . . . my inclination would have been to say to you, 'This text is incomplete, there ought to be more work on it, I ought to know more about this character, the husband.' What would have been your reaction as a writer if I'd presented it back to you and asked you to do more work on it?

POTTER: I think I would have told you to fuck off.

(*Laughter*.)

Trodd chose Alan Bridges (whose last Potter play had been *Joe's Ark*) to direct *Rain on the Roof*, and Cheryl Campbell was cast as Janet. Potter denied that this implied any connection or resemblance between the characters of Janet and Eileen in *Pennies from Heaven*, and said he never had particular actors in mind: 'If you did, it would be very dangerous because you would start writing for that actor.'

Campbell says she asked for one change in the script of *Rain on the Roof*: 'Janet was supposed to get out of the bath, admire herself in this full-length mirror and, expecting him to knock at the door, utter the immortal line, "Have I got a surprise for you, Billy boy?" I said, "I'm sorry – no way!"' The line was cut, but Campbell adds, 'I think people had begun to regard [Potter's] work as too sacred to tackle and they weren't tough enough with him.'

With *Rain on the Roof* written, Potter turned immediately to his second LWT script. *Blade on the Feather* recycles much of *Traitor*, in this case improving immensely on the original. Once again an elderly upper-class spy, this time a retired Cambridge don, Jason Cavendish, has the precarious calm of his old age shattered by a visitor, Daniel Cartwright, son of a British diplomat whose murder Cavendish seems to have engineered (as in *Traitor*, we see the murder in repeated flashbacks). But Daniel is not what he seems. He deprives Cavendish's daughter of her virginity, strangles the old man's trophy wife in the shower, and persuades Cavendish to commit suicide. Jack Hill, Cavendish's butler, crony, and KGB minder, attempts to kill Daniel, but finally realizes that they are both on the same side; Daniel has been sent by Moscow to eliminate Cavendish and his wife before the old man confesses everything in his memoirs.

Taking its title from the Eton Boating Song (crooned almost homo-erotically by Cavendish and Hill), *Blade on the Feather* is littered with images from earlier Potter plays, such as young Daniel giving the ancient Cavendish the kiss of life when he has collapsed (like young Clara and ancient Browning in *Message for Posterity*), and Daniel obsessively describing an attack of nausea in a hamburger joint, a repeat of Bobby's outburst in *Joe's Ark*. In his National Film Theatre interview Potter admitted to repeating this last image:

In 1970 I saw that happen in the Wimpy Bar in Hammersmith Broadway . . . a man who was obviously in the grip of some total disgust . . . and he tipped up his plate and shouted . . . about 'the filth I'm eating' . . . and he said to the man in the chef's hat, 'I'll have you know I'm a shareholder in this organization!' And so it stayed as a scene. You know, I'd like to use it in about ten plays.

Blade on the Feather is untypical for Potter with its sustained portrayal of a rich upper-class country-house milieu (there is also a nudge at the recent electoral victory of Margaret Thatcher when Cavendish's daughter drawls complacently, 'Our lot are in'). Potter told Peter Fiddick of the *Guardian* that he hoped the play would 'convey something about my sense of the decay of English life, of it being an over-ripe plum ready to fall – if not already rotting on the ground'. Trodd asked the distinguished American director Joseph Losey to direct it for LWT, it being (as he felt) a Losey-like subject and setting.

Losey accepted, and David Niven and James Mason were offered the roles of Cavendish and Hill. 'But it emerged quite quickly,' says Trodd,

that those two didn't get on at all – something to do with what they'd done or hadn't done in the war. So Joe called me to say he was off to do an opera in Vienna instead. I protested to him that it wasn't like a movie – you couldn't call it off just because we couldn't get the leads we wanted – but that was that. So I got Richard Loncraine to direct instead. Meanwhile I asked Dennis if he had any ideas for the two lead parts, and he rang me back and said, 'I've got it – Jimmy Jewel and Max Wall.' And he was serious!

The parts were eventually taken not by these elderly comedians, but by Donald Pleasence and Denholm Elliott, with Tom Conti playing Daniel.

Trodd explains that Richard Loncraine 'was already very big in commercials – and had a toy factory as a sideline, so he was quite a strange figure, not like your average British director at all, a weird guy, insecure but very rich. He was quite a handful.' Loncraine responds, 'Well, I'm not very rich – I wish I was! But insecure, certainly. I think most directors are. Incidentally I'm very fond of Troddy – he's one of the few really good producers we have in this country.'

Like Cheryl Campbell, Loncraine felt that Potter's work should not be treated with automatic respect:

In my opinion he'd write a scene of genius and then one of absolute rubbish, almost as if he was trying to catch you out, to see if you'd spot it. He was always testing people to see if they would take the bullshit. I think he did with his audience as well. But he also got lazy and recycled the same ideas too many times. I think he looked down on his audience, he thought the world was full of arseholes and he patronized them.

Potter seems to have taken no interest in Loncraine. 'Dennis didn't have a clue about directors,' says Trodd, 'and over the years he gradually built up a completely unjustified suspicion of them as a breed: that they didn't contribute anything, they sold him short, and so on. In fact he had some of the very best.' Loncraine was surprised by how little concern Potter seemed to have over the production: 'I saw sod all of Dennis. He hardly showed his face. I did quite a bit of rewriting, and he didn't seem to mind.'

Kika Markham, who had helped to inspire *Double Dare*, was cast in *Blade on the Feather* as Linda, Cavendish's wife. 'I saw very little of Dennis during it,' she says. 'I got murdered in the nude, right at the end, and I always remember that when I saw it, Richard Loncraine had shot really close up to my nipples, and I felt terribly abused, almost raped – I'd had no say in it at all. It wasn't in the script, so I don't think Dennis had anything to do with it.' Loncraine says she is exaggerating the intimacy of the shot.

Potter found inspiration for the third LWT script in a short family holiday he took with Margaret and the two younger children at Eastbourne in the summer of 1979. Jane, the eldest, had now left Ross Grammar School to study art at Newport in South Wales. She says that her father had always encouraged her to draw and paint:

When I was only about six, I remember I wanted to paint one night, and Dad took a picture down off the breakfast room wall, and said, 'Paint on top of that.' And Mum said, 'Don't be so absurd!' And he said, 'She'll do a much better job.' So I painted over it! And he put it back on the wall, and said, 'That's much better' – though of course it was absolute crap!

Sarah, still at school, was making a name nationally in junior women's cricket. She explains:

I was a tomboy, and always playing football, and at Ross there were two boys of about my age next door, and we all used to go off and play. And in the summer they'd play cricket, so I picked it up from that, and played in the boys' team at school. And one year, just by chance, there was a women's cricket team playing at the sports centre in Ross, and I saw them one day, and thought, this is amazing. So I joined the club, and was sent off to various county things. I was seventeen when I had my first trial for Junior England (under-nineteens), and I was selected for that. I was a fast bowler at that stage, and later became an all-rounder, and I think I finished up a better batsman than a bowler.

Her love of sport created a special bond with her father: 'We used to go to most of the Fulham home games together, though it was a big effort for Dad – I often thought he wasn't going to make it to the end of Fulham Palace Road. But we loved it. It was something special to share that passion with him. Of course what I really wanted to do was play for Fulham!'

Potter was delighted to talk to journalists about Sarah's prowess. 'Fast bowler,' he told one of them. 'I saw her play the West Indies at the Oval, pounding 'em in. The Oval! I've wanted to play there all my life and there was my *daughter* – !' In another interview he described her as 'the fastest woman bowler in the world'.

Eastbourne was chosen for the July 1979 family holiday because he wanted to stay in the Grand Hotel, where in his childhood the BBC had broadcast music from the Palm Court. In 1966 he had written, 'I do not think I can ever remember a time when the bathroom-echoing Palm Court orchestra did not lurk as a distant threat, helping to make the British Sunday what it is.' His choice of holiday resort amazed everyone:

My media-numbed acquaintances expressed an almost scornful amusement, and my family a forehead-puckering consternation . . . In the event, the holiday was just about the best one I have ever had . . . The trouble was, I did not know at the time that I was enjoying myself, being too busily occupied in finding fault with everything in sight, and everything not there, with such a hungry diligence that I even complained about the click-click of the wooden toggles against the window frames.

I was looking for the past, of course, and would more readily have accepted the cream cakes at tea time if they had been drenched in formaldehyde. Early evening drinks in a splendidly vaulted salon were curdled for me by a piano afflicted with the succubus of an electronic attachment. Well aware by now that the soapy ghost of lost Sunday evenings could not be assuaged, I fell to thinking . . . about how some peppery old sod of the kind I eventually hope to become would feel if he ever returned to such subverted munificence.

Out of this came *Cream in My Coffee*, in which an elderly couple, the dyspeptic Bernard and his long-suffering wife Jean, revisit the sea-side hotel where, four decades earlier, they had stayed for a premarital fling. The play intercuts between past and present. Their Thirties idyll is spoiled when the young Bernard is called away by his father's death, and the return visit by the elderly couple is equally marred by Bernard's ceaseless bullying of Jean. While young Bernard is away at the funeral, Jean has a one-night stand with the singer in the hotel band, who croons the song that gives the play its title. Similarly the elderly Jean is released from Bernard by his sudden death – in the final scene, he collapses during yet another burst of rage with her.

Like *Rain on the Roof* and *Blade on the Feather*, *Cream in My Coffee* has a nihilistic message. In *Rain*, even sex and death seem to be handed out arbitrarily by a malevolent universe, while in *Blade* Cavendish tells Daniel, 'Nothing makes sense, you see. At bottom,

human affairs are all compounded of absurdity. Once you acknowledge that, the only real enemy is *boredom*.' In *Cream*, Bernard's only
pleasure lies in looking forward to annihilation. 'We can pretend we're
waiting for a boat,' he tells Jean, as they watch a speedboat leave for
a trip round the harbour; and when she misunderstands this allusion
to death, he snaps, 'We are . . . We are! You stupid old woman.'

When Potter published the text of *Cream in My Coffee* with *Blue
Remembered Hills* and *Joe's Ark*, he gave the volume the overall title
Waiting for the Boat, as if to emphasize that Bernard's defeatist image
applied to all three plays. Yet when discussing the three LWT plays at
the National Film Theatre in October 1980, he repeated, more
strongly than ever, his claim that he was propagating an essentially
Christian message:

I believe absolutely and without qualification in a loving creation, in a loving
God . . . I think of myself as a religious writer. I know people don't pick that
up, they don't see it, they don't understand the two poles, they don't understand either the disgust for a soiled, brutalized and diminished world, or the
hope in it that we have a duty and an obligation to make that world – to make
the Kingdom, if you like – to make that world more just, more beautiful, more
perfect, and fill it with more mercy and more light than we bother to do.

Reporting this NFT interview in the *Guardian*, Peter Fiddick remarked
on Potter's religious claims and commented drily, 'Forget that the last
several [Potter] plays have all ended in violent death.' The figure was
actually five: *Pennies from Heaven, Blue Remembered Hills, Rain on
the Roof, Blade on the Feather* and *Cream in My Coffee*.

*

Though star casting had proved impossible for *Blade on the Feather*,
Trodd managed it with *Cream in My Coffee*. Dame Peggy Ashcroft
(who had just appeared in another film produced by Trodd, Stephen
Poliakoff's *Caught on a Train*) accepted the role of the elderly Jean,
alongside Lionel Jeffries as old Bernard. Gavin Millar, who directed,
was given a big enough budget to evoke hotel life in the Thirties on a
lavish scale (using as location the hotel that had inspired the play, the
Grand at Eastbourne), and Trodd hired musical director Max Harris
to re-create a large period dance band for Jean's crooner–seducer Jack
Butcher to front. Interviewed for *The Times* at the end of filming in
mid-April 1980, Potter declared himself contented with LWT, even

though they were driven by commercial motives. BBC management, he said, were 'creating a malaise right down. You can feel it when you go into the place. At least with London Weekend we know their value system.'

This interview, by Nicholas Wapshott, begins: 'On first meeting Potter, he holds out his hand to shake. "Don't squeeze too hard," he says. The hand is a bunch of crooked fingers and swollen knuckles, like a dead chicken's foot . . .' The previous year Potter had told another reporter:

Recently I was buying a pen in a shop and I asked the cashier to put the change down on the counter so that I could scoop it up. And she said, 'No, I'll put it in your pocket for you', and moved forward as though she was going to drop it in the top pocket of my jacket, which would have been hopeless, because I wouldn't have been able to get it out again. So I said, 'No, please put it on the counter,' which she finally did. And as I was leaving I heard her turn to someone and say, 'Ah, they do like to help themselves, don't they.' I left the shop red with fury.

Three months after the interview with Wapshott, the PFH–LWT relationship was suddenly over. 'LWT DROPS POTTER FILMS,' reported the *Daily Telegraph* on 29 July 1980. London Weekend had 'suddenly announced' that, after the completion of the three Potter plays that had already been filmed, no further PFH scripts, by him or other writers, would be put into production:

An angry Mr Potter . . . said last night that he would contest the decision . . . He said he was 'appalled' at the way the agreement had been broken and in particular at the 'bad faith' of Mr Michael Grade . . . He had been discussing with Mr Grade last Friday the need to 'talk through our problems'. Yesterday he discovered that he had gone on holiday after authorizing a letter to be hand-delivered to him and a statement to the press.

In the statement, Grade said that the cost of making *Rain on the Roof*, *Blade on the Feather* and *Cream in My Coffee* had 'escalated from production to production with generous budgets being heavily overspent'. He added, 'PFH have found it very difficult to work within our normal budgeting constraints and production disciplines.' The three Potter scripts had cost more than a million pounds to make, some £130,000 over budget, and Jim Allen's *Commune*, two ninety-minute plays about the effects of the Thatcher government's public-spending cuts on the people of an Oldham council estate, would have exceeded budget by more than 50 per cent if they went ahead.

Speaking today, Grade is inclined to blame the collapse of the LWT–PFH partnership on 'the lack of budgetary control by Ken Trodd, who thought he had a blank cheque'. However, Gavin Millar, director of *Cream in My Coffee*, defends Trodd and blames LWT: 'They didn't let Ken control the whole budget – all their departmental heads, design and so on, were allowed to charge PFH what they liked.'

Judy Daish recalls a crisis meeting with Grade at which Potter, coming up by train from Ross, arrived later than her and Trodd. 'I knew what Dennis was going to do, and sure enough he did. He came in carrying his briefcase, dumped it on the table, and said, "Michael, there's cash in here to make up the difference." Actually it was full of old newspapers or something – it was sheer *chutzpah*!'

At the time of the crisis, Potter suggested to the *Daily Telegraph* that the political content of Allen's *Commune* might have been 'one of the things LWT were uncomfortable about'. Grade, however, says he greatly regretted not filming it. *Commune* was eventually made at the BBC, with Trodd producing, under the new title *United Kingdom*. As to the three other Potter plays envisaged under the LWT–PFH deal, none had been written, though Potter and Trodd had discussed ideas. 'There was to be something about Dickens,' says Trodd, 'and there was one I put to Dennis, which he didn't take to, that was dreamt up by an actress I was then living with. It was about a working-class woman poet from Bristol in the late eighteenth century, called Ann Yearsley.' Potter himself later recalled contemplating a play about Hitler in the bunker in 1945, especially

the fact that there were children there, Goebbels's children . . . They were little blond kids, about five of them, and their great joy, apparently, was to sing to Uncle Adolf. They all knew the game was up and yet fantasy had also taken over. Also, there was this whole thing about Hitler being a vegetarian. It seemed to me that in such a nightmarish scenario there must be something to say about all of us.

The day after LWT's statement had been released to the press, the *Daily Mail* carried a full-page article by Potter, headed 'WHY BRITISH TV IS GOING TO THE DOGS AND I'M GOING TO CALIFORNIA'. He declared that LWT's decision was symptomatic of

the stodgily inflexible nature of British TV, and the ever-growing difficulties of making decent home-grown films for the little screen . . . I shudder to think of the future of our native TV drama. All the doors are closing against it. The single play or film is expensive, awkward, difficult to schedule – but is the sole remaining area where the individual voice and the personal vision are still allowed their little space between soap opera imports, old movies, spangled varieties, and duff talk shows.

He exhorted his readers to ask themselves if they were getting the kind of television they wanted. 'I'm afraid I cannot wait around for the answer. I have to go to Hollywood next week to work on a big MGM movie that everyone over here turned down flat.'

*

During 1979 Greg Smith, who had bought the film rights of *Pennies from Heaven*, had been trying to raise British money to make it. According to Potter, Smith had been 'instantly turned down by, apparently, everyone of consequence in the remaining segments of the British film industry'. Meanwhile the American film director Herbert Ross, who was in Britain to make *Nijinsky* at Pinewood, had become very interested in the project.

Ross, who was eight years older than Potter, came from a dance background, and was married to a former ballerina, Nora Kaye. His first work in films had been as a choreographer of musicals, before he turned director with Woody Allen's *Play It Again, Sam* (1972). 'It was Nora who saw the BBC *Pennies from Heaven*,' Ross explains, 'and she said to me that it was the most wonderful thing she'd ever seen, and I had to do it.'

She would have seen it on an American public broadcasting channel – Potter noted that it had been 'shown twice in Los Angeles, for example, and twice in New York'. It was achieving minor cult status there; Trodd remembers meeting people in New York who were 'obsessive' about it.

As Ross recalls it, he was able to set up a *Pennies from Heaven* movie himself at Metro-Goldwyn-Mayer:

I believe they thought they were going to have a big old-fashioned musical comedy. I don't think they knew what we were doing – we were so crazy about it we sort of blackmailed and faked our way through it. But we got the deal on it, and then brought Dennis to New York [where Ross lives] to work on it. I was trying to elevate the quality of movies that I was doing, and I thought he was the best writer that I had ever had the good fortune to meet.

Potter himself, writing not long after the event, claimed that he himself had played a crucial part in the deal:

I coaxed myself on to the Los Angeles plane, chain-smoked my way into whatever gilded sanctum I could get into, and eventually managed to sell the film rights to MGM. This is shorthand, of course, for a series of not always dignified adventures which, with suitable adjustments for gender, might rival those of Alice in Wonderland. But I *did* emerge clutching something like a quarter of a million dollars and the outline of a contract – or, rather, my agent Judy Daish did, with an aplomb that did not fail to match my own, shall we say, hitherto innocent bravado.

Daish corroborates this: 'I went with Dennis to Los Angeles on several occasions. I was also selling the film rights in Brian Clark's *Whose Life Is It Anyway?* to David Begelman at MGM.' Potter said that, arriving in Hollywood for the first time, he felt 'almost like somebody from Mars'.

On 22 February 1980 he sent a picture postcard to his daughter Jane from the Beverly Wilshire Hotel:

Dear Jane,
This is A Small Corner of our hotel, where they slice up footballs and call them tomaytos. Rain drips off palm trees. I've dripped cigar ash all over a 32-ft sofa in Bogart's old house . . . MGM wanna make *Pennies from Heaven*. It rains dollars for me (*not* you). You're poor here if you have a last year's Rolls-Royce. I'm in Demand (!), so must finish now to go tap-dancing down Sunset Blvd. Yet miss you. Home next Friday.

John Cook, in his book on Potter, explains why Metro-Goldwyn-Mayer was interested in taking on *Pennies*:

By 1980, the erstwhile home of the Hollywood musical was a studio in decline, its last major film having been *Straw Dogs* nearly ten years before. MGM, however, was under new management. David Begelman, a former executive at Columbia, had taken over the reins with a brief to turn the studio around in one year and restore it to somewhere near the pre-eminence it had once enjoyed. Hence, just as *Pennies* was being offered, he needed to get ten or twelve major projects quickly into production in order to signal a decisive break with the previous decade of decline. What better way to announce MGM was back from the grave than with the production of a big-budget 'musical', the genre with which the studio had once been so successfully associated?

As well as doing a deal on *Pennies*, Begelman signed Potter up to write another script. 'MGM have hired Potter for *Midnight Movies*, a very American story, set in New York,' reported Peter Fiddick in the *Guardian* on 29 July 1980. '"I wanted to see if I could write American," Potter says wryly. "Not just the language, but the ways of thought and life. And touch wood – sorry, knock on wood – I have managed so far to do it."' He said he had been reading Studs Terkel and watching old American movies to get the feel of 'the American syntax, crude and lively'. Meanwhile Herbert Ross had commissioned him to write an original screenplay about ballet dancers.

Suddenly, therefore, he was working on three Hollywood projects at once. Fiddick noted that he was about to make 'his fourth trip to the USA this year'. He was off there again a few weeks later, in the autumn of 1980, when he told another journalist, Graham Wade of *TV & Home Video*, that 'in three months I've earned close on $900,000 (about £380,000)'.

Most of this enormous sum was being ploughed into PFH. 'I've put myself on a salary,' he told Wade, 'which is only a very small proportion of what I earn.' (He would not give figures.) In the trade journal *Broadcast* he wrote, 'The money gained [from the film deals] is not going into my own pocket. I have ceased to be self-employed so that these sums go to PFH Ltd, which pays me a monthly salary.' The aim was to use the money to 'make the banned *Brimstone and Treacle* into a movie here in England in the spring'. He told John Wyver, interviewing him again for *Time Out*, 'PFH is going to make *Brimstone and Treacle* as a film . . . I'm going to do the script for nothing, Ken is going to work for nothing, our executive producer is raising the money for nothing. And we are going to shoot with facilities that are cut to the bone.' In *Broadcast*, he made the bravura declaration that *Brimstone* was 'the first of what will be an annual [PFH] British movie'; he and Trodd were 'set upon changing what now happens within the British film and television industries'. To Fiddick, he said, 'The ultimate aim, obviously, is to make decent British films – not in a trumpeting, giant corporation way, but with enough to do them the way we want to.' He realized that this was a huge challenge. 'But . . . I have been around long enough to know something of what is possible and what isn't.'

He had already been working hard at the Hollywood scripts. *Midnight Movies* had reached its 'revised first draft' at the beginning of July 1980. Based on a novel of the same title by David A. Kaufelt, it is the story of James, an uptight New York stockbroker who drops out into an underworld of sex and drugs presided over by a queeny gay dressmaker, Dutch Cohen; and of the beautiful Jean, damaged daughter of film-star parents who both came to violent ends. Jean is relentlessly pursued and sexually humiliated by a corrupt aide of the New York mayor, and Dutch meets a violent end – castrated and thrown from a rooftop – which would probably never have passed the film censor had the picture been made. Potter tried to put his stamp on this lurid material by making James into a talented jazz pianist, and having Jean and Dutch sing at various moments.

By the time that he had finished writing *Midnight Movies*, the *Pennies* screenplay had been through three more versions, the third optimistically headed 'Final draft 27 June 1980'. Another 'final draft' was written in August, and in October came a 'revised final draft'. Later, Potter commented:

That's average on an American script. You respond continually to Demand A, Demand B, Demand C, without quite knowing where they're coming from. It could be from an actor, a director, a production designer, it could be the studio – you just don't know. I never actually wrote while I was there. I'd go, I'd talk, I'd recede before it became a problem, and then understand or pretend to understand what they wanted.

He also complained that he was never allowed to get on with a Hollywood script without interference: 'The Americans . . . continually say, "Can we see some pages, sir?"'

Trodd guesses that 'of the dozen or so drafts he wrote of *Pennies*, draft 5 or 6 was probably optimum, but if he'd refused to do any more rewriting, they'd have replaced him'. In retrospect Potter agreed that 'the endless drafts of *Pennies*' had eventually 'compromised what I started out with, but that was the system, and that's what I received the cheques for'.

He described trips to Hollywood as 'going on safari among the bloody savages', a 'learning curve' out of hell: 'You're either sliding down it so fast you don't know what's hit you, or you're crawling up it by your fingernails.' Yet in several respects he valued the experience: 'I needed four or five years out of British television. I was digging a hole for myself. How long can a writer write without any external stimulation?' He certainly felt that it had improved his screen-writing technique:

It did me good, and it affected my subsequent work . . . It just made me more alert about the whole process of . . . communicating with an audience. They [Hollywood] go too far, and deal in manipulation of feelings, and drain meaning out of it, far too often. But there's that discipline, and the grammar of making the point effectively, swiftly, moving on, gathering up your forces for the next scene, and so on.

He was also glad to work in Hollywood because of its cultural resonance:

I've always had an ambivalent relationship with popular culture, which is partly expressed in *Pennies* and a few other things. There is some sense in which I have been Arthur Parker myself, attempting to escape some of those rigidities of the English class system through demotic, popular drama . . . It was important for me to do that [work in Hollywood] partly because it was American culture, and therefore I was tapping some part of my own mind.

But primarily he saw it as a business venture:

I . . . sensed things were changing in England, and I needed to get some American dosh into my hands, to make sure I had more manoeuvrability than I otherwise would . . . Whatever else happens you do get your hands on more money in Hollywood if you tend not to say, 'No, I won't do this; no, I won't do that.' Poor T. S. Eliot had to go and work in the bank. I regarded going to America as working in the bank – but I was on the right side of the counter.

Judy Daish agrees: 'Dennis was an exquisite businessman, and this was business.'

He felt no affection for Los Angeles – 'It's alien, and you feel alien, or at least I do, and you're walking along those streets where no one walks!' He kept his visits as short as possible.

The longest I was ever there was ten days. I would go over for five days, seven days, whatever. It wasn't possible to stay longer because of my health – I have my ointments, dressings, drugs and so on – and also I didn't want to. I would stay in the Beverly Hills Hotel or the Beverly Wilshire, and I thought, 'If I turn up Rodeo Drive once more, I'm going to be ill.' So I travelled back and forth.

Yet he did find some pleasures there. Herbert Ross says, 'He was very sexual, constantly making passes at waitresses, chatting up pretty girls. I think it was a sort of mind-fuck – I think he just got off on flirting.'

Judy Daish accompanied him on most of these trips. Potter would insist that two first-class round-trip tickets should be part of any script deal; producers were told that, because of his hands, he could not carry luggage, and needed someone with him. 'Judy was wonderfully solicitous about him,' says Herbert Ross. Daish recalls that the spectacle of Potter in Hollywood was 'extraordinarily entertaining, and terrifying at the same time. There was a great deal of respect for him and his work, but his irony was never understood.' Asked if he remained in command of the situation, she replies, 'I don't think I've ever seen Dennis *not* in command of a situation! He was always able to knock spots off them.' Did she have the sense that he was grovelling for work? 'Absolutely *not*!'

Trodd was not involved with any of Potter's Hollywood projects, not even *Pennies from Heaven*, though he says, 'Dennis fought (more than I knew at the time) for me to be involved with that film, and Herbert Ross – whom I never met at the time – told me recently he wished I had been.' Ross himself confirms this: 'I only met Ken after Dennis's death, but I now wish we had had him on *Pennies*.'

Soon after the film had gone into production, Potter met the man who would eventually displace Trodd for a time. Judy Daish recalls the occasion:

Ken Adam, the production designer on the MGM *Pennies*, invited Dennis and me to Malibu one weekend, and we drove out there. I suppose there were about a dozen people having lunch on the beach, and there was a young American who seemed to be in awe of Dennis, very charming and funny, who subsequently wrote a note to Dennis at his hotel. There was a line producer on *Pennies* who (I think) had become ill, and this young man told Dennis how much he admired the film and wanted to work on it, and hoped that he would become line producer. Actually he's billed as executive producer – it was Rick McCallum. And that's when they first met.

Rick was immensely attentive to Dennis, and became a point of reference, a contact for him in Los Angeles. They were really fond of each other, and a lot of projects came out of that.

Rick McCallum, then aged twenty-five, had an English mother and an American father. 'I spent most of my childhood in Missouri,' he says, 'and then I went to a French school outside Geneva when I was thirteen, and stayed in Europe, but went to New York to finish college.' He got his first toehold in the film industry with ABC News in Europe, before working with Merchant–Ivory and Joseph Losey. 'Rick was streetwise, energetic,' says Sarah Potter. 'Dad liked his language and was drawn to his personality. He was a bit of a rough diamond, but refreshing to have around.'

'I'd already seen *Pennies from Heaven* while I was on a trip to

England,' McCallum explains, 'and also *Double Dare* – an incredible little film, which I thought would make a fantastic American movie.' He began to try to set up film deals for Potter, who (he says) made quite an impression on the American movie-makers: 'He began to realize that he had a real personality, that he had impact with people. He'd been shut out of the process of making his work at the BBC.'

McCallum's mother was married to the actor Michael York, who met Potter several times in California. 'There was a great mystique about him in Hollywood,' says York,

thanks to the original *Pennies from Heaven*, which had filtered through on public broadcasting. He was here when Rick decided to get married. Dennis was in town, and came to the feast, which was arranged very quickly, at Michael's Restaurant in Santa Monica. It was all very cheerful, and suddenly Dennis turned on me in the middle of it all, and said, 'Listen, you're always so bloody *nice*. Tell me what you really think about me!' So I said, 'Frankly, Dennis, I think you're a poor, pathetic gimp!' And from then on we were firm friends.

McCallum says this was typical: 'Dennis would read you very quickly. He'd strip off one layer of skin after another from you, and you were left bleeding. He'd say, "You're weak, you're this, you're that" – his little repertoire of slicing you to bits.'

McCallum explains that he got married because of Potter. 'My partner and I had been together since we were about seventeen. And Dennis could not understand why I hadn't made a commitment to her. And he and I had a very drunken evening together, when he kept asking, "Do you love her, do you honour her? You *have* to make a commitment to her, that's what life really is." So I asked him to be best man.'

*

Herbert Ross had recently won much admiration for *The Turning Point* (1978), a film about the private lives of ballet dancers, starring Anne Bancroft and Shirley Maclaine; hence his commission for Potter to write another screenplay with this setting. 'I remember introducing him to a lot of ballet dancers at New York City Ballet,' Ross says. Seven drafts of this screenplay, *Unexpected Valleys* (which had the alternative working title *The Next Step*) survive among Potter's papers, the earliest dating from January 1980. 'I thought *Unexpected Valleys* was going to go ahead with Sherry Lansing [as producer] at Twentieth

Century-Fox,' Potter said ruefully some years later. 'Like many of these things, it seemed to be on the brink of getting made.'

He described the film to Peter Fiddick as 'about a ballet dancer torn between her career and motherhood'. Fiddick made no comment, but if a competition had been set to devise an unsuitable subject for Dennis Potter this would surely have been the winner. He did his best, but it remained intractable. The dancer, Zina Gant, the young star of a New York ballet company, is a man-eater who becomes pregnant by one of her many lovers. They include Andrew Blake, an English writer who travels to New York in the hope of resuming his affair with her. Zina finally decides against motherhood, while in contrast Andrew is drawn home by his small son's sudden illness, and becomes reconciled with his estranged family. The phrase 'unexpected valleys' comes from Tolkien's *The Hobbit*, which is being read aloud to the sick child; Potter uses it as a metaphor for the surprising turns that life can take. (Jason Cavendish in *Blade on the Feather* has written a Tolkien-like children's book, but Potter said he did not admire Tolkien. 'You could lay hold of a good ten-minute cartoon from any of the fictions of the late Professor Tolkien,' he wrote in 1983, 'whereas the *Pilgrim's Progress* would surely need at least six episodes.')

Giving a press interview in London to promote the imminent showing of his LWT plays in mid-October 1980, Potter referred briefly to *Unexpected Valleys* – the reporter understandably misheard it as 'Unexpected Ballets'. The transmission of the LWT plays was to overlap with a two-week retrospective of all his work that survived on videotape and film (including *Brimstone and Treacle*, still under the BBC ban) at the National Film Theatre, from 13 to 30 October. It was the first time that a television playwright had been so honoured, but, thanks to his Hollywood dealings, it seemed that the Potter NFT season might lack a crucial work.

'WHAT PRICE PENNIES FROM HOLLYWOOD?' asked the magazine *Broadcast*, reporting 'doubts about the availability of *Pennies from Heaven*'. The article alleged that, 'in line with his contract with MGM', Potter had 'bought back the copyright' of the original six-part *Pennies* from the BBC, 'in order to minimize competition'. This led to 'the disturbing possibility' that 'there will be even less chance of ever seeing that production again than of seeing *Brimstone and Treacle*'. The article continued:

Hollywood's practice of suppressing an original classic in order to boost the chances of what is usually an inferior remake is one of the most shameful examples of the industry doing the dirty on its artistic heritage, and Herbert Ross's track record as a director doesn't inspire confidence that any Hollywood remake . . . can match the original BBC production . . . What is even more perplexing is that an artist of such passionate and hitherto unquestionable integrity [as Potter] should appear to be conniving at such a practice.

Potter defended himself against this charge in a letter to *Broadcast*:

It is a possible argument to say that the author of something that has been shown on television should not then be allowed to sell the work to a film studio, whether here or in Hollywood. But as a professional writer with legitimate ambitions, inevitable anxieties, and a fair measure of what used to be called avarice, I'm afraid I do not find that line of reasoning particularly appealing.

He explained that MGM would proceed with the film only if the BBC did not license the serial to any more TV stations or public venues. The BBC had eventually agreed to this for a payment of $100,000 and half of any further profits that Potter and PFH might make from the film. Potter described this as 'extortionate'. He added that the MGM deal and his other Hollywood commissions were 'part of what is turning out to be an exhausting strategy' to fund PFH's British projects. 'You can question my integrity if you like . . . But no one who stands on the sideline is entitled to doubt the commitment of myself or my colleagues towards the British television or, now, film industries.'

He said that *Pennies* could be shown at the NFT if MGM agreed. They did not, and it was also absent from a BBC retrospective of his work seven years later, not being seen again on British television until 1990. Bob Hoskins says that he and everyone else involved with the original production was 'really pissed off' by this: 'It's like eight months of my life down the pan.'

The October 1980 Potter season at the NFT included the new LWT plays, and concluded with him being interviewed on stage by Philip Purser. The BBC turned down the invitation to film the occasion, so PFH Ltd provided their own cameramen and sound recordist, since Potter believed the interview should be preserved for possible future use. He opened the conversation with Purser by criticizing the standard of television reviewing: 'There was an item in . . . the *Evening Standard* . . . which said that Miles Kington had been appointed television critic on *The Times*, but . . . he had not got a television set . . . That is utterly characteristic . . . ' (Kington says, 'I never claimed to be a TV critic without a TV set. All I said was that when *The Times* asked me to do some TV reviewing, I asked, "Oh. Will this mean my having to get a TV set?" And the arts editor answered, "I rather think it will." So I did.') Potter also revealed that he did not want to see his old plays again himself ('I do not wish to revisit them'); admitted to being a workaholic ('if I'm not working I feel extremely troubled and unhappy'); and said he believed that it might be possible to make a play 'for the cinema and television at the same time – that what is called "theatrical distribution" might be possible abroad, in order to make the single play still live on British television'. This soon came to pass with the arrival of Channel 4.

Purser asked how much he liked to be involved with the production of his plays. Potter answered:

I like . . . in real terms to be involved as little as possible. When I've handed over the script, a series of other sovereignties come into play, and drama is a very collective enterprise, which is one of its charms . . . In the past, I've been extremely dissatisfied with the way a thing was done, either directed or acted or shot or lit, or whatever, and then I used to try and get involved (as you put it) more and more. But I think that becomes a mistake.

The only thing I would resist is the cinema tradition, where the writer is a sort of appendage, and the film belongs solely and wholly . . . to the director. I think that has cut away certain possible traditions of literacy and imagination from the cinema. One of the things I like about television is, because of its bastard roots . . . from theatre on one side and cinema on the other . . . the creative imagination, if you like, comes initially from the writer.

For *Cream in My Coffee*, for example, I did not go on location at all . . . When I first saw it assembled I turned to Gavin [Millar] and said, 'It's the best interpretation of my work that I've ever seen.' . . . The ideal relationship . . . is where the director has so impregnated himself with the script . . . that he is able to take it, pick it up, put it somewhere else, and I wouldn't dream of interfering with that sovereignty.

He also explained his current political position:

I'm . . . a socialist, I hope not in that canting, banner-waving, thick obnoxious way in which the claims of your political belief exclude any comprehension of the values and the poetry (in a way) of what they call right-wing beliefs. Because sometimes I get out of bed on the wrong side in the morning and think of myself as extremely right wing. And I've no doubt that some of my writing is extremely right wing, because I value things like order, like self-discipline, like tradition, in the sense of being able to locate and root and care for and water and tend those things in your life which you know that you've inherited from the past, and that you know you will pass on to the future.

Purser ended the evening by describing Potter as 'the most consummate television playwright of our age'. Writing in the *New Statesman*, Julian Barnes agreed – 'Compared with other TV playwrights Potter is a giant' – but felt that the three LWT plays, shown on the ITV network on consecutive Sunday nights (*Blade* on 19 October, *Rain* on 26 October and *Cream* on 2 November), were not quite up to scratch: 'Potter's 1980 vintage is not for laying down.' *Cream*, however, won the Prix Italia.

The *Daily Telegraph* previewed the three plays by sending Sean Day-Lewis to interview their author. He found Potter enjoying 'new affluence' in a Kensington hotel, thanks to the 'large sums of money' he and PFH were earning from Hollywood, but Day-Lewis gathered that Razoxane was 'now producing its own toxic side-effects and he was apologetically in the shadows when I met him'. Another interviewer, Graham Wade, found him in a flat near Paddington (rented by PFH as offices), looking 'very tired'. Wade learned that *Midnight Movies* was about to go into production in Hollywood, but the MGM *Pennies* would not begin shooting until early next year. Meanwhile Potter was 'about to fly out to Los Angeles' yet again.

Having finished the Americanized version of *Pennies* for MGM, he turned the script into a novel, to be published by Quartet Books. Though this was primarily a money-making exercise, with no pretence at serious literature, he seems to have enjoyed himself, judging by the exuberance with which he met the challenge of telling the story without the song lyrics:

'Good day, Parker,' said the banker. Show this bum out into the real world. The one which doesn't fool around. The one which sets aside a nice little space for your dreams: like, say, a square foot or two, rented out by the minute at the highest rate the market will bear.

Go on, Parker. Get out. You are on *this* side of the rainbow, mister. And you had better not forget it.

Trouble was, Arthur wanted to rewrite the script. The suffocating, so-called Real World was getting him down. The place could certainly do with a few better lyrics, and the horrible, dead materiality of things needed a bit more rhythm. Something to tap your toes and click your fingers to.

And even now, even here, in his anger and disappointment, a movie musical unwound a few frames into his heart. A sweeter version of the bank and the bankers was lodging itself in some small corner of his mind or in some small space out of the corner of his roving eye.

A song. A song. Please cue in a song!

Though the 'revised final draft' of the *Pennies* screenplay is dated October 1980, further revisions were requested by Herbert Ross and the studio right up to the film's completion late in 1981. Meanwhile Potter was becoming dismayed by Ross's interpretation:

When I went to visit the studio, I was shown the schoolroom set for the 'Love is Good for Anything That Ails You' number – a simulation of a genuine rural Illinois schoolroom of the Thirties – and I thought it was great. Then they said, 'Now we'll show you the fantasy schoolroom,' which was this much bigger, all-white duplication of it. That was the moment I realized they were never going to make it work . . .

In the BBC original, this song is mimed in an ordinary classroom by the children of Berry Hill Primary School, with toy trumpets and saxophones – one of the most exhilarating moments in the serial. MGM not only constructed the duplicate all-white set, but dressed and choreographed their team of highly trained child performers as for a Busby Berkeley spectacular, complete with white grand pianos. 'You had these huge production numbers and some of them were terrific,' said Potter. 'But they failed to understand that it was supposed to be a *home-made* musical.'

Unfortunately he felt unable to convey his doubts to Ross and the production team: 'When you go out very late in the shoot and they show you what they've been working on all that time, one doesn't have the brutality to say, "No, I don't like it." So I only told them about the things I did like, and left the rest unsaid.' With hindsight, he felt there had been a 'cultural gap in understanding – the English use of ironies in speech and so on. I should have been more explicit, more forthright, when I talked to Herb Ross and the MGM people. I should have made sure that they understood the original series better than they appeared to. But being explicit is the very thing I hate doing before I begin writing. So there was this dilemma.'

Ross says he was not at all aware of Potter's doubts while the film was being made: 'Dennis was the most enthusiastic supporter of everything he'd seen – he was on the set and everything else. And we were very, very good friends, so I was sort of bewildered when I read in interviews, later on, that he didn't like the production of *Pennies* – I was really genuinely surprised.' Ross defends the film passionately: '*Pennies* came out exactly the way I expected it would. I knew that it was never going to be a popular movie, but in my view it's the only movie I've ever made that is exactly how I envisioned it.'

Potter, however, described it as 'a stripped-down, soulless précis' of the original. This was partly due to substantial cuts made after a disastrous sneak preview in Denver, Colorado: 'The audience couldn't understand why the hero did dislikeable things,' said Potter, so 'a lot of cuts were [made] in relation to Arthur being nasty.' Part of the fault also lay in the casting. Steve Martin was relentlessly jolly, and Bernadette Peters curiously wooden, as Arthur and Eileen. Yet Potter's script was as much to blame as anything Ross had done. For all the redrafting, he had merely edited *Pennies* down from eight hours (the final duration of the BBC serial) to one and three-quarters, so that many of the best passages had simply vanished.

Ross contributed some good visual ideas for the musical numbers, such as the Accordion Man singing and dancing the title song amid a shower of copper coins, and Arthur and Eileen, watching Fred Astaire and Ginger Rogers in a cinema, going up to the screen and taking over their performance of 'Let's Face the Music and Dance'. (Many of the songs were different from those in the BBC serial; once again, the actors mimed to original pre-war recordings, but many of these were lengthened with interpolations recorded by a studio band, and, just before Arthur is hanged, Steve Martin actually sang 'Pennies from Heaven'.) Yet, as Potter said, the lavish staging missed the whole point of the venture: 'The very brilliance of the musical numbers destroyed the reason for their being there.'

The film was released in the USA just before Christmas 1981, and in Britain in May 1982. American reviews were mixed. The anonymous *New Yorker* critic loved it – 'the most emotional movie musical I've ever seen' – but 'R.C.' in *Time* magazine had seen the original, and was disappointed: 'The BBC show was an enchanted cottage; this is the Las Vegas Grand Hotel.' The trade journal *Variety* hated it, giving its review the memorable headline 'Makes no cents'. The *Variety* reviewer called it 'one of the most hopelessly esoteric big-budget Hollywood pictures ever made . . . It's anybody's guess what commercial potential the studio saw in such despairing, obscure material.'

Box-office receipts in the USA were appallingly low – only about 7 million dollars were taken, about one-third of the production costs – and, far from improving MGM's fortunes, the film merely accelerated the studio's decline. In retrospect, Potter was amused by this: 'I like to play with the American studios. You both gamble and they end up losing a hell of a lot of money. I've built up record-making losses for MGM.' However, his screenplay was nominated for an Academy Award (the only nomination *Pennies* received), and this ensured that producers would continue to seek him out with further commissions to write films; though by now his Hollywood reputation was for strange, bleak or savage writing, and, as he said himself, 'The first response to my scripts is frequently one of misunderstanding, if not incomprehension.'

In Britain, reviewers of the MGM *Pennies* admired the staging of the musical numbers but were disappointed by the Americanization of the story. 'It was the very Englishness of the original,' wrote Tim Pulleine in the *Guardian*, 'opening up a gap between claustrophobic Anglo-Saxon gentility and the extrovert expansiveness of the Tin Pan Alley ditties, that provided its distinctive flavour.'

Potter recalled that, during post-production of *Pennies*, Herbert Ross, still confident of its success, 'started trawling through all my old work. They must have thought, "Oh God, we've got this guy who's written all these plays." "This is the wave of the future," is what Herb Ross said. You're not immune to that kind of flattery and you're also not immune to the large sums being discussed.'

Double Dare, championed by Rick McCallum, who had seen the BBC production while in England, made a favourable impression, and Potter was commissioned by MGM to rewrite it as a movie; he was paid $100,000 for the first draft and revisions, with a further $200,000 to follow if the film was made ('That was a five-minute deal I did with MGM,' says McCallum). The result was a script called *Love Me, True*, finished in the spring of 1982, shortly after the American release of *Pennies*, into which Potter tried to get some of his feelings about the American film industry. It was, he said,

about an English writer who arrives in Hollywood and has 'double' experiences, the same as the character in the BBC play but transplanted, transposed, and even more distant from his roots, his feelings. Hence the alienation in it is much stronger. There is greater sexual fear, banked up with cultural fear, as well as the sense of selling out. The dislocation of place and time in his mind in the nowhere city of Los Angeles is very much part of it.

In fact *Love Me, True*, like the MGM *Pennies*, is a sadly anaemic version of its original, with obvious concessions to Hollywood taste. Helen May, as the actress is now named, is glimpsed in a real porn movie rather than a Fraggie Bar commercial, and her verbal exchanges with the playwright, now called Peter Ellis, scarcely trouble to explore the question of a writer's power over a performer. The anonymous businessman with his tart has become Al Velati, a time-share shark, and Ben the producer has metamorphosed into Sam Hofman, a typical Hollywood over-the-top mogul ('Your novel, Peter, your novel! What can I say! . . . I tell you – I hyperventilated!'). At the same time the story has grown more complex, with the addition of the writer's wife, back in England (a third part to be taken by the actress who plays Helen and the call-girl).

Herbert Ross recalls that he held a reading of the script, 'with Al Pacino and Bob de Niro'. In the screenplay, Peter Ellis the writer comments that the film he is planning will be too complicated for American taste. So it proved, and *Love Me, True* was eventually filed away in one of Potter's boxes of unmade scripts – alongside, as it turned out, *Midnight Movies* and *Unexpected Valleys*. Herbert Ross still treasures the original manuscript of the latter that Potter gave him, in an ornate binding. 'It was written in longhand,' he says wonderingly.

CHAPTER 4

Out there in the film business

▬

Potter took his entire family to Los Angeles for the première of the MGM *Pennies*. Sarah, now aged twenty, had begun to work as his secretary and book-keeper, when her cricketing commitments permitted. (Jane had done it for a little while, 'but I just didn't enjoy it. And I'm hopeless with figures.') 'When I left school,' Sarah explains,

I went to college in Cheltenham, to do business studies and sports management. And in 1981 I had nearly eight weeks touring India with Young England (under twenty-fives). Meanwhile Dad was wanting someone to help him, and when I got back to college I found it really difficult to settle, so I started to work for him.

He'd never allow the work to get in the way of cricket. He was very supportive; if I had a game, a midweek match or something, there was never any doubt that I'd be allowed to go off. I began by doing the book-keeping and filing for Pennies From Heaven (Overseas) [another company formed to process his earnings], and answering letters for him.

Sarah had been 'appalled' that, until she took over the work, he very rarely answered letters:

He did have some guilt about it. I remember, before I had started to work for him, he might sometimes pack piles of letters into a case to haul off to London on the train, saying, 'I might have a couple of hours – I'll do them up there.' Lo and behold, three or four days later they'd come back, unopened. But it did weigh heavily on him. And later, the things he really did have to reply to would be passed on to me.

On *Any Questions* in 1970 he spoke of 'the letters that one doesn't write, that you say "must have got lost in the post"; the letters that you simply, for one reason or another, have postponed . . . I'm always appalled by this, in myself.' Even Judy Daish's files are bare of letters from him. 'He'd answer by phone,' she explains, 'or when we met.'

Sarah says that her working relationship with her father was quite stormy: 'He sacked me twelve times and I resigned on ten occasions. Usually, he was quite justified: I was wanting to go off and play cricket. He always said he employed me because no one else would. But in later years, particularly, we were very much a working partnership. I was given responsibilities, and he'd ask my opinion.' Did she feel she was the closest to him of his children? 'Our family wasn't like that; I don't think any one of us would have been allowed to feel that.' In 1983 she told a *Sunday Times* interviewer, 'I enjoy being part of what he's doing, and I feel I'm developing as a person because of his presence . . . He's very loving, very very kind, utterly charming. His greatest attribute is he will never compromise himself. And he's always so calm.'

Robert Potter had left school at sixteen without going into the sixth form. 'Rob probably had the most difficult relationship with Dad of the three of us,' says Sarah, 'and he can be quite difficult at times – you're not sure whether you're getting through to him. He would just shrug about things and walk away, whereas Jane would fight back, in your face, and I would listen to something and then come back at Dad about it. We're all very different, and we were allowed to be.' Potter himself said much the same in a 1983 interview: 'They have different sets of emotions and they touch me in different ways. Jane . . . is very explicit . . . Sarah watches . . . We're a very emotional family . . . Except for Robert, he'll just shrug and walk away.'

Sarah adds, 'Mum and Dad were determined not to push us academically, or make us do things we were timid about. The idea of any of us going to university wasn't talked about.' Robert says of his decision to leave school early:

Looking back, I think it was probably a mistake, but it was just the way I was. Either to his credit, or otherwise, Dad allowed me to leave. I think with hindsight there probably should have been pressure for me to carry on. I lived at home till I was about nineteen, then I moved out and rented a house with a few friends. Then we had a bad winter, it snowed and our electricity meter ran out, and I moved back home again shortly after! I finally moved out permanently three or four years later.

Even then, he did not move far – to a flat only a few streets away in Ross.

Asked if he took any interest in his father's work, Robert smiles and says, 'Not a great deal. It was just what Dad did. That was as far as it went. It was never a big thing.' Did he feel that his sisters were closer to his father than he was? 'No. We were all treated pretty much evenly by Dad.'

Sarah and her father largely kept different working hours. 'Generally, he would write at night, though not always. He had become such an insomniac, barely sleeping, that he would often be completely exhausted, but he'd get an enormous amount done at night. He could take sleeping tablets and they wouldn't have any effect.' Potter said of this, 'I've suffered from insomnia since I was a child, so the idea that you can work at night is emancipating. There is nothing else you can reasonably do at 3 a.m. . . . I like the concentration that you can build up. It's like going into a tunnel and not letting anything in or out until you are finished.' In 1988 he told the *New York Times Magazine*:

'When I'm writing, I don't like there to be daylight at the window.' He usually starts at about 11 p.m., when the rest of the house is asleep, and keeps at it 'as long as the thread is coming'. When exhaustion sets in, at noon or so the next day, he'll stop, pour a Scotch, open his fourth pack of cigarettes, slip a disc into the compact-disc player, perhaps 'Creole Love Call', and lie on the settee until sleep comes. When he wakes, it's back to the desk again. His daughter or his wife will carry food up on a tray – quietly, so as not to have their heads snapped off.

Arriving at her typewriter in the morning, Sarah would find 'little notes for me, asking me to do this or that – they'd have been gobbledegook to anyone else, but there was a code between the two of us.' She never saw rough drafts of his scripts: 'I always found that a bit surprising. By the time I got a script to type, usually in an A4 pad, it all seemed so perfectly laid out. He must have spent hours thinking about it before he put it down – thinking in images, as he put it. Obviously there were crumpled up bits of paper, but not to the extent that you'd expect.' The *New York Times Magazine* interviewer noted, 'He is obsessive about getting things just right. If he wants to make a small change, he'll do the entire page over.'

Sarah says that despite the condition of his hands, 'he wasn't any slower with a pen than anyone else – he went at normal speed. And he always used to say that the blank page in front of him wasn't a daunting prospect. It was like going to a bookshop and buying a book, that journey when you open the pages and start to enjoy it. It was a thrill for him.'

She describes him, without hesitation, as a strong father: 'He was so central to our lives, always sorting out our problems, that for years I thought he was invincible. He was the voice of reason and the only one who could make everything all right.'

Asked if he thinks Potter had any close friends apart from himself and Judy Daish, Trodd says 'No' – and then adds that there were some at Ross-on-Wye. Sarah confirms that her father had a 'very small circle of meaningful friendships' at home. 'It was mostly just Mervyn James and the Lloyds that Dad was willing to see. They were Mum and Dad's closest friends.'

Mervyn James, a Welshman brought up in Hammersmith, was already running a gentlemen's outfitters in Ross when the Potters came to live there. 'I think the friendship began purely on a business level,' he says.

Margaret came to the shop, wanting some clothes for Dennis, and we arranged to have one or two items sent up to Morecambe Lodge, as was done in those days. And Dennis came to the shop soon afterwards, and I got to know him. We had Hammersmith in common, where my roots were – and Fulham where football was concerned – though of course he would pull my leg and say, 'Mervyn, don't be so fucking Welsh!'

Haydn Lloyd, with a dental practice in Hereford, was a Welshman too. 'Dennis used to say, "I bloody hate the Welsh!"' he laughs. 'But it's the same Nonconformist tabernacle, mining sort of background.' He and his wife Anne met the Potters in 1970 at a party to watch the General Election results.

Edward Heath and the Conservatives were getting in, much to Dennis's annoyance, particularly when the daily help kept coming upstairs and saying, 'We're winning!' Soon after that, Dennis and Margaret came to dinner with us, and I admitted not only that I'd voted for Heath – who seems like a Liberal Democrat compared to what came afterwards – but occasionally shot pheasants (we were having a brace that evening). Dennis said, 'My God, I'd never have guessed that I'd be eating with a pheasant-shooting Tory.'

Compared to most of the 'county set' in the Ross-on-Wye area, Mervyn James and the Lloyds were thoroughly liberal. Even so, they were sometimes shocked by Potter's behaviour. 'You'd be at a dinner party with him,' says Haydn, 'and out would come a four-letter word – and this was at the period before it was OK to do that. Everybody would draw in their breath, and I once said to Dennis, "Why did you do that?" And he answered, "The conversation was so bloody banal before. And did you notice how much more sensible it became afterwards?" And I must say it did.' Anne Lloyd agrees: 'It freed them to be much more interesting.' Mervyn James says that Margaret would give Dennis 'a look' on such occasions, trying to restrain him. 'But those social occasions almost deserved it at times, begged it – I wish I could do it myself, but Dennis had more guts than me.'

The Lloyds eventually received a dinner invitation to Morecambe Lodge, where they saw another side of Potter. 'We were a little bit late,' says Haydn, 'and there was Dennis standing in the corner, looking very wound up, and I said, "How are you?" And he said, "I shall be all right now that the tension of waiting is over." He relaxed after that, and we had a marvellous time.' The Lloyds and Mervyn James realized that he was fundamentally a shy man who had to gear himself up for social or public appearances. Yet when he did, outrageous things would happen. 'We used to go to an Indian restaurant,' recalls Haydn Lloyd, 'and one evening the waiters kept coming up to me and saying things like, "Mr Lloyd, I have a grandmother in India, and I would be so grateful if you could arrange things so that . . ." I discovered afterwards that Dennis had told the staff I was the head of the British Immigration Service!' Anne Lloyd adds of this, 'He loved to set a scene – he wrote his plays as he went along.'

Sarah Potter recalls that her father became involved in a personal crisis among these friends: 'Mervyn's wife left him when we were still at school – she ran off with the husband of somebody who was also in Mum and Dad's circle of friends, and Dad went with Mervyn to Bristol to see her and talk it all through, and he had to tell him, "Mervyn, she's not coming back."' Mervyn James confirms that Potter helped enormously: 'He did – he was good, very good. He was a very great chum, an ally. He was the one who articulated a number of things. I remember he said to me, when I was going through the trauma, "Let things settle down. If you want sex, go out and buy it." In other words, don't jump into some other relationship right away, just be practical about it.'

Asked about Potter's own marriage, Mervyn James says, 'Dennis truly loved Margaret, absolutely loved her. She was consistent, and she'd never lose her cool, even when he had a go at her, which he did sometimes when he was drinking. But she'd tell me that he'd be full of remorse afterwards – he'd almost weep when asking for forgiveness. And I always had this hunch that when it came to Dennis and anything extra-marital, it was purely a flirt – though I think if he wanted sex, he might have bought it.' Anne Lloyd says, 'I think he spoke to Margaret very honestly about things – he needed to tell her like a baby tells a mother.' Haydn agrees: 'If he was having an affair, he would have told her.'

Apart from these three friends, Potter avoided Herefordshire social life. 'It wasn't exactly a contentious point between Dad and Mum,' says Sarah, 'but she would bring it up from time to time – "When are we going to see some *other* people?" – though neither of them was really a social animal.'

*

When the writer and poet P. J. Kavanagh came to Morecambe Lodge to interview Potter for the *Sunday Telegraph Magazine* in the summer of 1982, he noted, 'He and his wife Margaret appear to be friends, as well as married.' But he was slightly disconcerted by Potter's fluency:

He leans back on the sofa in his neat Victorian house outside Ross-on-Wye (pink Herefordshire stone, with daffodils spick as guardsmen in the clean-edged beds) and the sentences come out of him sculptured, quotable, an interviewer's dream. Let the tape-recorder roll and you have him: his past, his present practice, his plans. You have, that is to say, the tidied version of a deeply private, daemonically driven man.

Kavanagh also noted, 'Behind the slightly tinted glasses the friendly, surprisingly mild eyes have stains of fatigue round them. He has been up all night, and for several nights, finishing two film scripts.' These were probably *Cradle Song*, begun in January 1982 and rewritten in the summer, under the title *Orphan Star*, and *The Man Who Would Not Die*, finished in July.

The first was intended, says Judy Daish, for 'a new kind of cinema', and Herbert Ross, who commissioned the script with the support of Twentieth Century-Fox, confirms this: 'It was what we called the Special Project, to create an environment in the movie theatre which amplified and extended the two-dimensional plane of film. It was to be a pre-theatre and after-theatre experience.' Jane Potter recalls her father talking about 'specially designed cinemas that would emit various smells from concealed units into the audience, also temperature changes in the cinema and live actors coming into the audience from walls'.

Potter's script for this early attempt at virtual reality was loosely based on a 1978 science-fiction novel, *The Night of Kadar*, by a British author, Garry Kilworth. Earth has been made uninhabitable by nuclear and chemical warfare. The survivors dispatch a giant spaceship – a vast 'cradle' containing hundreds of frozen human embryos (which provides a spectacular opening to the script). After a thousand years of travel through space, it finds a planet that can harbour human life. As it prepares to land, the embryos come to life, and swiftly mature into adults, learning the whole of human history and culture from microcomputers implanted in their brains. Meanwhile we see (in flashback) how, back on Earth, the initiator of this vast project, a scientist called Gornik, has had to battle against sceptical colleagues to make it all happen. In the process, he discovers that Earth itself was originally populated by human beings in just this fashion – through the arrival of an identical spaceship in Mesopotamia (the Garden of Eden) thousands of years ago.

Cradle Song/Orphan Star is another of Potter's Chinese-boxes screenplays, for at the end he reveals that the whole story is a dream experienced by the 'real' Gornik, a nuclear scientist in the Eighties who has suffered a nervous breakdown and fears the imminent destruction of human life. The Special Project was considered by Twentieth Century-Fox, but neither it nor the script came to anything.

The Man Who Would Not Die, another Herbert Ross commission with Fox backing, earned Potter $175,000 for the first draft, completed in July 1982. Based on a science-fiction thriller of the same title by an American author, Thomas Page, it concerns one Daniel Forrester (the name is Page's invention, but it sounds like a typical Potter *alter ego*) who dies in an air crash, but is brought back to life again and again by an experimental medical machine. Unable to pass into the next world, his restless ghost pursues his friends and enemies, and his lover, Kate. Potter stuck closely to Page's story-line, except at the end, when he allowed Daniel to find peace as the machine is suddenly shut off. *The Man Who Would Not Die* was never filmed, but the theme of a man's brain experiencing an anguished consciousness after the death of his body resurfaced more than ten years later in Potter's own *Cold Lazarus*.

During 1980 and 1981 he had made several drafts of a screenplay for the feature film of *Brimstone and Treacle*, and PFH had issued a prospectus for potential investors, which he wrote himself. It optimistically described the project as 'the first crucial stages of the profitable resurrection of . . . the British film business'. The BBC ban on the original play was presented as a selling point:

Let there be no doubt that the film *will* be controversial. The media will discuss and argue over it at length. It will be an urgent topic of conversation. Those who have not gone to their local cinema to see it will be quickly made aware that they are missing something. Even the label 'the film the BBC would not let you see!' is one to queue behind.

The film was to have a 'relatively small budget' of £550,000. Richard Loncraine (who had made *Blade on the Feather*) was to direct, and 'the international star David Bowie has signalled his eager desire to play the part of Martin'. In the last paragraph of the prospectus, Potter let rip: 'The door is opening on to a vista that, for all concerned, is perhaps wider and more spectacular than any of us yet dare to see.'

In the early stages of the project, Potter enlisted the help, as fund-raiser, of a Gloucestershire-based businessman, Clive Lindley, who had become a director of PFH. In the late Seventies Lindley, who lived near Ross-on-Wye, was putting together a franchise application for a commercial radio station to serve Gloucestershire, to be called Severn Sound, and he had written to Potter to ask if he would participate. Potter was initially hostile – 'I thought, "How can I stop it?" Then I decided to join . . . Gloucestershire has been ill-served by the medium.'

Lindley says that they quickly became friends:

We were similar in age, had both been Labour candidates, and had then both become disillusioned with the Labour Party – I eventually stood for Monmouth as the Liberal Democrat candidate in the European elections. Dennis used to tease me about that, and I used to tease him about his champagne socialism. Well, he decided he would join in on this radio thing, and he had lots of theories about how commercial radio should run, and actually wrote the whole programme content of the franchise application for us. And he was terrifically sparkling when our group was interviewed at the IBA.

We got the franchise, but Dennis resigned discreetly after a while – he had serious ideas about what radio could be, but I had to run a business that worked, based on a lot of advertising, and commercial radio doesn't attract intellectual audiences. But he and I remained friends, as my wife Maureen had become with Margaret, and the four of us used to go and eat together when he was down at Ross. Dennis was always outrageous in restaurants, and Margaret would tell him off – but he was always very nice to us.

He asked me to come into PFH Ltd as a commercially minded director – he said he had lots of good contacts, but none of them was very businesslike. So I thought it sounded like fun, and I got involved. I took no salary or expenses, it was just an old pals thing, on the understanding that if it ever started to make lots of money perhaps I'd take some. When it came to the film of *Brimstone and Treacle*, he asked me to do what I'd done with the radio station, which was to find small investors. He wanted £600,000, and I said I probably could raise that. I had an apartment in Belgravia in those days, and we had a reception there for about thirty people, who were addressed by me and then by Dennis, and several of them agreed to come in for ten thousand, twenty thousand. I knew I could manage £600,000 on that basis.

But then I went to a PFH meeting, and I was told that the budget had doubled to £1.2 million. I was appalled. Ken Trodd said, 'That's the way it is, we've just got to put up with it, got to raise the money.' I said to Dennis, 'I don't believe we can raise that much money by this small-investor approach – do you mind if I back off?' And he didn't mind – he said he could raise the money in a traditional way, in Hollywood.

In fact Potter turned next to a London publisher, Naim Attallah of Quartet Books, who had published his novelization of *Pennies*, and who had a small film-financing company. Attallah admired Potter but found him tricky: 'If you caught Dennis in a bad mood he was totally impossible. And he was very suspicious. He would misinterpret people's motives, see things that weren't there.' Attallah raised money from an investor, and the remainder of the finance for *Brimstone* came from American producers, even though David Bowie was no longer available to play Martin. The part finally went to Sting, the thirty-year-old singer–songwriter–bassist from the band Police, who had appeared in the 1979 film *Quadrophenia*. 'Sting wanted to do it just as an actor,' says Trodd, 'but the American half of the finance wanted a Police album out of it. So Dennis came with the idea that he should sing, but Loncraine vetoed that as just another *Pennies*.' Eventually it was agreed that Sting should sing a pre-war song behind the closing credits, and Trodd made up a cassette of about two dozen possibilities, out of which Sting chose 'Spread a Little Happiness'. Released as a single, the song made more impact than *Brimstone* itself. (Potter himself remarked, on the Terry Wogan chat show a few years later, 'I think I was sent into this world to spread a little misery.')

Loncraine says he found Potter strangely detached from the project:

Dennis wasn't interested in being around. His attitude tended to be, 'If you don't like anything, fix it.' I don't think he liked me very much . . . He wasn't good at dealing with intelligent barrow-boys which is what people take me for though I'm really a cheap public-school boy . . . He showed bursts of interest and then absolutely none and he never came on the set. A strange man.

When Loncraine watched the original BBC production of *Brimstone*, he thought it 'bloody awful'. Potter, on the other hand, judged Loncraine's film, when it was finished, to be 'definitely less successful' than the BBC version. Actually there is little difference between the two versions. Denholm Elliott, again cast as Mr Bates (after Trodd and Loncraine had failed to attract a bigger name), gives a rather more confident, ironic performance than before, and Joan Plowright manages to make Mrs Bates's infatuation with Martin a little more plausible than Patricia Lawrence had in the television version; but Sting's performance is anodyne rather than diabolical, lacking the witty camp of Michael Kitchen, the original Martin.

The film, released in September 1982, earned lukewarm reviews and little money. 'We made naïve assumptions that it was possible to make the film at a certain price,' said Potter some years afterwards. Having agreed that payments to him should be deferred while costs were recouped, he eventually realized he would earn nothing from it, even when it was released on video. 'It led to a realization of exactly what it is like out there in the film business,' he said ruefully.

Naim Attallah commissioned Potter to write a novelization of the film. He agreed, but then passed the task on to Sarah. 'Dad wants me to start writing short stories,' she told an interviewer who asked about this. 'He makes suggestions and warns me against over-writing, nothing more.' Attallah was struck by the strength of his relationship with Sarah: 'He was utterly devoted to her, and she was the closest person to him.'

*

While *Brimstone* was going on release in late 1982, Potter adapted *Schmoedipus* into a screenplay with an American setting, first called *Tears Before Bedtime* and then renamed *Track 29* – words from the song 'Chattanooga Choo-Choo'. He had added this musical number to the script, to be mimed by a convention of model-railway enthusiasts, led by the husband whose marriage takes second place to toy trains.

Once again it was hoped that Joseph Losey would direct, though *Schmoedipus* was far less in his style than *Blade on the Feather*. Nevertheless Losey, now in his early seventies, was keen to do it, largely because it would give him a chance to work once more in America, from which he had exiled himself during the McCarthy era. Trodd persuaded the BBC to co-produce, even though the film was to be made initially for cinema release before being shown on television; Channel 4, which came on the air in November 1982, had now set a precedent for this with its Film on Four scheme. Rick McCallum was involved too; he explains that 'Dennis put me on a salary – and for a writer to be giving a producer money is unheard of, especially if you're American! It was such an amazing gesture.'

Filming was to take place in the Dallas area of Texas, in July and August 1983, with Vanessa Redgrave as the frustrated suburban housewife and Lee Marvin as the train-mad husband; but the co-production deal failed to come off. It was another lesson in the unreliability of films compared to television. But Potter was determined to make a success in the cinema. He now had a Hollywood commission to adapt a thriller set in Russia, *Gorky Park*. He was also expanding his 1964 television play *Alice* into a feature film.

In June 1983, soon after he had finished the first draft of this, he was asked to take part in the Radio 4 series *In the Psychiatrist's Chair*. He declined, fearing once again that to expose himself to psychological interrogation (by Anthony Clare) might expose and thereby damage the roots of his writing. 'It is not for me to get too close to why I do it,' he said some years later. 'I don't want to threaten the source of what I do . . .' Yet for years he had been on the edge of talking openly about one crucial experience, the sexual abuse. For example, in a 1977 *Sunday Times* review he wrote, 'I cannot specify – except in fictional or dramatic form – the kind of assault which I endured in the summer between VE Day and VJ Day, when I was ten years old.' In the summer of 1983, perhaps prompted by the Radio 4 suggestion, he managed to approach it more closely. It was now that, while writing an introduction to the texts of *Blue Remembered Hills*, *Joe's Ark* and *Cream in My Coffee*, which were to be published by Faber and Faber, he referred briefly to 'something foul and terrible that happened to me when I was ten years old, caught by an adult's appetite and abused out of innocence' – the most explicit statement he had yet made.

This introduction was partly based on a lecture he had given in Dublin the previous summer. A number of writers had been invited by the Irish government to take part in a centenary celebration of the birth of James Joyce, to be held on Bloomsday, 16 June 1982. These guests were told they could do what they wanted: lecture, or read, or just attend. Potter chose to speak, in the Round Room of the Mansion House. He did not enjoy the visit, disliking Dublin ('the most depressing place I have ever been this side of Los Angeles') and feeling out of place among the novelists and poets, who included Jorge Luis Borges, Anthony Burgess and Hans Magnus Enzensberger – 'I was the only one whose work had been almost wholly within television'. Moreover 'the microphones did not work properly', and the audience contained 'a high proportion of academics', which added to his discomfort. However, the Irish writer Colm Tóibín, who was in the audience, recalls Potter's lecture as 'electric, like an old-fashioned sermon. He may have been working from a script but it didn't seem so.'

The lecture seems to have steered clear of direct reference to his own work, but in the preface to the plays he voiced some unease and uncertainty as to its future, saying that it was 'possible . . . that I have once again reached the point where my apparent fecundity (or, at least, diligence) has been stemmed or diverted'. He revealed that he felt 'anger and frustration' at the thought that 'I may well have written my last 'original' or (as they call it) one-shot, one-slot play for television. It is now nearly four years since I last handed one in, by far and away the longest such interval for nineteen years.' Elsewhere in the collection of plays – in the separate introduction to *Cream in My Coffee* – he was more self-searching, suggesting that 'buried somewhere in myself is a better and more wholesome writer than I have yet found out to be. I do not know how to coax him out into the open, and the stubborn recluse may never agree to emerge at all. But it is the thought of his presence, however illusory, which makes holding a pen the most challenging, the most exhilarating, thing I could ever do.'

*

Adapting Martin Cruz Smith's novel *Gorky Park* for the Hollywood production company Orion was not a task that was likely to coax out that better writer; Potter afterwards admitted that it was 'a disappointment which never looked or sounded right'.

At the time that the film was released, he wrote an article for *The*

Sunday Times Magazine chronicling his own involvement with it. In the summer of 1981 he had been in Hollywood, 'seeing what was happening to *Pennies from Heaven* at MGM', when he was invited to lunch by two independent producers, Howard Koch Jr and Gene Kirkwood, who had 'apparently put down a huge amount of their money' to acquire the screen rights to Smith's best-selling thriller (Herbert Ross says he had recommended Potter to them). 'The fact that they *said* they had mortgaged their own substantial homes to make possible the purchase did not necessarily mean this was not true,' continues Potter sardonically.

He read the book, whose hero immediately struck him as being 'Philip Marlowe in Moscow' – a laconic Russian militia detective, Arkady Renko, who is trying to discover the identity of three faceless bodies which have been discovered beneath the ice of the eponymous park, and is obstructed at every turn by the KGB. Potter felt that Smith's 'fat book' had 'something much sleeker and faster locked inside it', so that 'the scalpel which has to be used in any movie adaptation of a prose original could for once be employed to get down to real bone and healthy marrow'. He was 'very anxious to get the job', but made it a condition that Koch and Kirkwood would let him omit the part of the story set in New York, and concentrate on 'a mythic Moscow . . . with lethal mysteries eddying down long grey streets', the right background for 'a Soviet Marlowe'. He got his way: 'I was hired. And delivered a script within a month.'

He wrote it in France. 'Mum and Dad spent six weeks in Provence,' recalls Sarah Potter, 'where Dad worked on *Gorky Park*.' Initially they stayed in Monaco, where Rick McCallum's mother and her husband Michael York had an apartment, then in a villa. York remembers Potter being delighted by 'a beach I loved to go to, where all these secretaries came for a lunchtime swim, topless. It was very much in Dennis's milieu!' York says that he and his wife were devotees of homeopathic medicine,

and we tried to get Dennis interested – a homeopathic doctor in London said he thought he could help Dennis in his condition. We arranged for him to go there, but at the last moment he chickened out, because he thought maybe it might affect his writing, his creativity.

What I really remember was him talking to me and Pat about sharing a bedroom with an uncle, who obviously molested him. What was so interesting was to see the crooked hands go straight down to the genitals, already cupped as if for protection. I'm not a psychiatrist, but I wonder if there's some strange connection between the molesting and the crippling.

As soon as the Potters had settled into the French villa, they telephoned Mervyn James and Haydn and Anne Lloyd and invited them to join the party. Mervyn flew out first, and was enlisted to do the driving. 'One day we decided to go over to Italy,' he recalls,

and we went as far as San Remo. We found a restaurant, and Dennis got absolutely pissed (Margaret would always get distressed when that happened). And I remember vividly he went into a Cockney vernacular – 'fuckin' this' and 'fuckin' that', like a football supporter. And on the way back I was petrified as we went through the frontier at Menton, because the French gendarmes were armed, and there'd been some punch up between France and Germany at football, and Dennis kept braying the German centre-forward's name aggressively at them. I really thought something very unpleasant was going to happen.

The Lloyds came a week later. 'Dennis and I would drink outrageously each night,' says Haydn Lloyd. 'He could now afford wines that I could only dream of, and I remember one evening we had three bottles of Krug champagne, quite apart from the wines with the meal. Eventually I would collapse into bed and oblivion – but Dennis would retire to his room and write *Gorky Park*!'

He delivered the script on time, but there followed a year's wait while Koch and Kirkwood offered the project to studio after studio. Finally a company called Orion took it on, and a director was chosen, Michael Apted, an Englishman who had only recently moved into feature films from television. Now (continues Potter's chronicle) came the demands for rewrites:

Second Draft. Third Draft. Revised Third Draft. Revised Revised Third Draft. Final Draft. Revised Final. The Americans, who are bloody ignorant in matters of spelling, use the same letters for this giddy process as (perhaps appropriately) they do for a wayward eddy of air coming through the cracks in the walls. I felt I was in the middle of more of these so-called 'draughts' than there are in an abandoned cowshed in a blustery March. Naturally, I was sufficiently churlish to think degeneration rather than improvement was taking place.

Elsewhere he said, 'Although each change might be justified in itself, the cumulative effect was to shift the axis of the reason for doing it in the first place. It's very characteristic of Hollywood that they buy what they want and then change it into its very opposite.

There were the usual problems over casting: 'Dustin Hoffman . . . held out for too much money: probably about enough to keep the National Health Service afloat for another month or so.' The part of Arkady finally went to William Hurt, with Lee Marvin co-starring as the American villain, and the cast and crew set off for Helsinki, which was to stand in for Moscow. So did Potter, accompanied by Margaret. 'By the time I arrived for the rehearsals,' he writes,

every vista was a Christmas card . . . When a film unit is on location for a long time in foreign parts it tends to resemble too many of one's memories of National Service. In wintering Finland there were shoeleather reindeer steaks on the menu, live bears in the rehearsal rooms pretending to be human beings, and (most intolerable of all) every other person in the frozen streets looked exactly like David Hare [who has fair-haired Nordic looks] . . .

It is easier to suppress incredulity and amusement when your cheeks have just been flayed by a bitter wind: but no power on earth will stop my eyes taking on a Wedgwood glaze when I am forced to listen to the anxious monologues of the New York school of acting, which are mostly about 'motivation' and 'space' and what the character's grandfather's second cousin is likely to have eaten for breakfast.

This was a backhander at William Hurt, a Method actor. Potter said elsewhere that his style was 'almost diametrically opposed' to that of the 'very able British character actors' in the cast, who included Michael Elphick, Richard Griffiths, and Alexei Sayle – '"Is this what you want? Or this? Or *this*?" they say, without once talking about "the space around me".' The third co-star was 'the beautiful Polish actress Joanna Pacula', and Potter 'cast a gleaming eye across the dinner table' at her and tried the joke about the actress who was so naïve about the film business that she tried to further her career by sleeping with the writer. 'But no, she'd heard the joke too.'

His *Sunday Times Magazine* article ended with an injunction to his readers to see the film, which was released in Britain at the end of 1983; but ten years later he was dismissive about it, saying that it had been 'severely cut, which only added to the apparent complications of it', and adding that it 'didn't really have any political footing'. He also said, 'I saw a script gradually decline and decay', and admitted that he had 'hated' the result.

The film starts briskly, with Potter's characteristic use of flashbacks (in this case of the killings) nicely building up the atmosphere; but the complexities of Smith's storyline eventually weigh it all down. There are some good chase-and-fight scenes, but since Osborne, played by Lee Marvin, is self-evidently the killer from the moment we first see him, there is little suspense. (Potter said he was delighted that in the novel the 'unscrupulous and appallingly sadistic villain is graced with the name of John Osborne'; in the film this is changed to Jack.) At the time of release of *Gorky Park*, Derek Malcolm wrote in the *Guardian* that it 'never builds up a full head of steam'; he too was scathing about Hurt's acting style – 'it amounts to draining his face of all expression and behaving like a suspicious suet pudding'. He felt that Potter had done 'a consistent job, and I doubt if it is his fault that the picture suffers from international filmitis'.

*

In October 1983, nine months after his Helsinki trip, Potter was told by the doctors to give up taking Razoxane, which was still being prescribed only experimentally. 'The drug seems to be giving some of the control people cancer,' he explained to John Cunningham of the *Guardian* a few weeks later. 'My cells seem to be dividing in an odd sort of way,' he added. 'I had two lumps cut off right in the middle of my penis.' He said he had had to go to America soon after the operation. 'Hollywood is the right place to go with stitches in your cock.' Elsewhere he said that Razoxane had caused 'little warty growths to break out everywhere which had to be removed and then broke out again'.

Cunningham met him in a London *pied-à-terre* which he had now bought, Flat 2, Collingwood House, a modern apartment block on the corner of New Cavendish Street and Great Titchfield Street, very near the hotel where he had met Kika Markham. He installed himself there in April 1981. Sarah Potter says, 'I don't think Dad was ever that fond of it, but because of its position it was perfect. And it was comfortable.'

Cunningham's interview was to promote Potter's first original stage play, *Sufficient Carbohydrate*, which was about to open at the Hampstead Theatre. He told another reporter that his earnings from *Gorky Park* had bought him some space, and he 'thought it was time he attempted live theatre', because 'after twenty years of writing for television the form and technique had ceased to bother him and he wanted a challenge'.

Typically of his output at this period of his life, the play reuses

material from three old television scripts. *Mushrooms on Toast*, the
1972 rejected *Thirty Minute Theatre*, supplies the transatlantic food
corporation which has taken over a British company – a metaphor
for Potter 'selling out' to Hollywood. 'He's not very crazy about
Americans, is he?' one of the characters observes of Jack Barker, the
middle-aged Englishman who has done the deal. 'Although he was
happy enough to sign the take-over deal and pocket the cash.' From
Follow the Yellow Brick Road comes Barker's attempt throughout the
play to regain the sense that 'God look[s] after the world', and his
discovery that instead there is nothing but 'rotting, slimy stench'. And
from *Cream in My Coffee* Potter takes the image of 'waiting for the
boat', in this case a mysterious black freighter which (or so Barker
alleges) sails along the horizon early each morning, viewed from the
Greek island where he, his wife, and his new American boss and family
are all staying.

What is new to Potter's writing is Barker's alcohol-fuelled, middle-
aged, impotent despair – 'Insomniac, because I've nothing whatsoever
to dream about.' Sex is out of the question: 'My vital equipment is well
and truly pickled. I'm as limp as a piece of airline celery.' One of the
few emotions that still moves him is hatred of Americans: 'I'm
helplessly, compromisingly bloody well damned well English.' With
hindsight, he looks like an early sketch for Marlow in *The Singing
Detective*.

The play was to be directed by Nancy Meckler. 'I thought it was
incredibly well written,' she says, 'but probably my overriding reason
for wanting to do it was that it would mean getting to meet Dennis
Potter.' When they did meet, in Judy Daish's office, the conversation
started disastrously. 'Every time I made a suggestion about something
I thought I would want to have changed,' says Meckler,

Dennis would get incredibly contentious and argue fiercely. After about forty-
five minutes, I thought, oh dear, this isn't going to work out. And I said, 'I
really don't mind if I'm not the right person to direct it. If we can't get on and
agree, maybe we should just call it a day.' And Dennis said, 'No, no, we're just
testing each other out.' And after that, I was amazed – he was one of the most
positive people I've ever met.

Though he had come to London to attend rehearsals of *Sufficient
Carbohydrate*, withdrawal from Razoxane was causing another
psoriatic crisis. 'He said he was going to try taking no drugs at all,'

recalls Nancy Meckler. 'He wanted to see if he could come out of the end, burn it all out.' Judy Daish says he became 'really ill', and John Cunningham of the *Guardian*, meeting him in early December, found him 'slewed on a couch, at anything but his ease. His clean shirt is blotched.' Bryan Appleyard of *The Times* who interviewed him in January, reported:

By Christmas Eve he was immobilized, his body temperature was out of control, he was hallucinating – he remembers clearly believing a folded blanket was an animal. On New Year's Day [1984] he took his first dose of another drug – Etretinate. By 9 January his condition had stabilized . . . [But] Etretinate has side-effects too – it raises the level of fat in the bloodstream dangerously. He has had to cut out dairy foods and make serious inroads into his eighty-a-day consumption of cigarettes: he was continually counting out his ration when we met.

Etretinate was a recently developed 'retinoid', a vitamin-A-based treatment for psoriasis (marketed as Tigason) which reduced the production of keratin, the protein that forms on, and thickens, the outer layer of the skin. After Potter had been on the new drug for some while, Steve Grant of *Time Out* noted, 'His disease . . . now hits him in periodic bursts which can leave him utterly ravaged and weak, unable to venture beyond the bedroom or beyond mental revisions of work already in progress.' He told Grant he had switched from Marlboro cigarettes to the milder Silk Cut, but had no intention of giving up, despite the doctors' advice: 'What a way to go . . . with a cigarette in your hand.'

Sufficient Carbohydrate had opened at Hampstead in early December. 'The chief pleasure of the evening resides in the superb dialogue,' wrote Francis King in the *Sunday Telegraph*.

In contrast, Mr Potter's way with his plot is often embarrassingly cack-handed . . . In the first half of the play, the Englishman is constantly attacking the American for the squalor of his business ethics; in the second, for the squalor of his marital ones . . . The halves never truly cohere . . . The play concludes with the Englishman . . . gazing out to sea, at a freighter . . . which the American insists is not there . . . Unlike Chekhov's seagull or Ibsen's wild duck, the symbol lacks roots in the subsoil of the play and remains merely a piece of cerebral ornamentation.

James Fenton in *The Sunday Times* was even more scathing about Potter's ghostly ship: 'I find surreptitious Christianity of this kind particularly tiresome . . . The idea of a modern creed reduced to "I believe there is Something Out There, which if I can hold on to it will give my life Meaning. Amen" – what's that supposed to be? It's not religion. It's an evasion.'

Potter himself became doubtful about this aspect of *Sufficient Carbohydrate*. Bryan Appleyard reported, 'After watching a few performances at Hampstead he began to perceive the ending of the play as "preachy" and not entirely dramatically justified. The West End version will have been significantly modified. It is a luxury the production momentum of films and television has always denied him.' *Sufficient Carbohydrate* transferred to the Albery Theatre in the spring of 1984, for a run of several months.

Potter helped to publicize it by appearing on Radio 4's *Midweek*, whose presenter, Libby Purves, recalls:

He was giving out the usual line about how putting the word 'TV' in front of 'play' was like putting the word 'processed' in front of 'cheese'. The point being he did not get the respect he would have had if he had been a full-time 'serious' theatre playwright. I thought he was being unnecessarily chippy about this, and was greatly enjoying having him on the programme as he always threw off such an electrical charge, so I said that I didn't think he needed to worry as he had virtually become the elder statesman: the honourable part of the British Cultural Establishment. He replied that if I said that again he might very well bite me in the leg. There was something about Dennis Potter which made me never entirely sure that a threat like that was a joke.

In his interview with Potter, Bryan Appleyard shrewdly noted that he seemed 'perpetually on the verge of making . . . a religious commitment', and quoted him saying, 'I feel sort of vaguely Christian without taking the title.' Potter also remarked, in this interview, 'Cardinal Hume said, let us find God in the cancer. It caused a lot of offence among so-called Christians. But that is the sort of voice I am willing to attend to.' He himself had begun to worry if he might be 'brewing up some kind of cancer related to the Razoxane', noted Dr Rendall the dermatologist in the summer of 1984; but it was a false alarm.

*

He told Bryan Appleyard about his next project, the Lewis Carroll film. 'With *Dreamchild* about to go into pre-production under Verity Lambert at EMI,' wrote Appleyard, 'he is in high spirits – particularly since the first clause in his EMI contract says his script will not be tampered with. "I think it's the best thing I've ever done – it's the most complex and yet the most accessible."' Elsewhere he described the film's genesis:

I read a paragraph somewhere – I don't know where – which said that Alice Liddell went to New York when she was in her eighties. I said, 'Jesus Christ.' A couple of days later I was writing it . . . I wrote [it] in four and a half days, probably because I'd occupied that territory before with *Alice*, in 1965 . . . The idea of that tied-in, repressed, strange, playful, tormented, yet joyously inventive man [Dodgson/Carroll], and an old woman thinking back because of the culture shock of arriving in New York at that time – that was the engine that started running.

Dreamchild was therefore yet another recycling of old material, and, like *Sufficient Carbohydrate*, a chance to portray the Anglo-American culture clash. He now framed his original *Alice* play within the story of Alice Hargreaves, née Liddell, travelling to New York in 1932, at the age of eighty, to receive an honorary degree from Columbia University in the centenary year of Dodgson's birth. In reality, she was accompanied by her son, but Potter substitutes Lucy, a pretty but naïve paid companion to the old lady. The girl is alarmed to find herself pursued by Charles, a New York journalist – Potter seems to see this as a parallel to the child Alice's confused response to Dodgson's ambiguous attentions. Like Potter, Mrs Hargreaves begins by being thoroughly hostile to America, but soon discovers the attraction of being paid large amounts of dollars. Forced by people's questions to confront her suppressed memories of Dodgson, she makes a speech at the centenary celebration which comes to terms at last with his feelings for her: 'At the time, I was too young to see the gift whole, to see it for what it was, and to acknowledge the love that had given it birth. I see it now. At long, long last. Thank you, Mr Dodgson. Thank you.'

Rick McCallum had offered *Dreamchild* to MGM, who turned it down, and then to Thorn EMI Films in Britain, whose head of productions, Verity Lambert, thought it might be that elusive creature, a British film that would appeal to international audiences. She agreed to co-produce with PFH; the budget was to be nearly 3 million pounds, to include the cost of Jim Henson's Creature Shop making and operating several Muppet-style *Alice in Wonderland* characters. Shooting was planned to begin in the summer of 1984, and Gavin Millar, whose handling of *Cream in My Coffee* had pleased Potter so much, was chosen to direct.

Meanwhile there were two television projects in the offing for Potter. The first was a BBC2 *Classic Serial* adaptation of Scott Fitzgerald's *Tender is the Night*, commissioned in August 1983, with Potter to be paid £8,750 per episode. Jonathan Powell, then BBC head of drama series and serials, recalls: 'I'd always wanted to do *Tender is the Night*, and it took ten years to get the rights to the bloody thing. I remember ringing up Judy, and saying, "I know Dennis must be busy, booked up, but I'm just trying this one on you, because I have a feeling –" And it took him about a minute – she called back and said, "Absolutely, he'll write it now." And he did it incredibly quickly.'

The second was rather more vague. Powell recalls that, by early 1984, the BBC Drama Department was in a state of crisis. Granada Television had trumped the Corporation with two immensely popular series, made lavishly on film, *Brideshead Revisited* and *The Jewel in the Crown*. 'The perception was that the heartland of BBC drama was being colonized by ITV,' says Powell. 'The management was in a flap.' Judy Daish hinted that Potter might be willing to write a serial for them, and he and Powell met for lunch in Potter's then favourite Italian restaurant, the San Marino in Sussex Place, near Paddington.

'As he unfolded the story he wished to tell,' continues Powell, 'my excitement mounted to the point of salivation. An American service-man meets a girl at the VE Day celebrations. Some time later he returns to find her. The serial was to be the story of this search. There was no need to say more. It was what we needed: a thumping great story by television's premier dramatist.' Powell left the restaurant and 'rushed to Michael Grade [who was now Director of Programmes, BBC TV], and said, "Dennis is going to write a fantastic wartime thriller – let's give it a Sunday night on BBC1." And Michael said, "Fine, off you go."'

The commissioning note in the BBC files was signed by Powell in February 1984. Potter was to write a six-part serial called *Smoke Rings*: 'Set in London at the end of the Second World War, the story of a private investigator tracing a missing girl who is believed to have disappeared with a deserter from the American Services.' The fee was £14,000 per episode. It was the beginning of *The Singing Detective*.

CHAPTER 5

Not autobiographical at all

———

Potter was credited as joint executive producer for *Dreamchild*. 'The more control you have,' he told the *New York Times* of this, 'the more likely something will come out somewhat as you hoped.' Trodd says sardonically, 'This was in the heyday of Dennis fancying himself as an entrepreneur', and in fact the project was little happier than Potter's Hollywood experiences.

Potter had employed Rick McCallum to co-produce, which Trodd regarded as a personal snub; meanwhile Potter decided that Trodd was not pulling his weight. 'There were two producers on *Dreamchild*,' he said a few years later, 'Rick doing all the work.' Trodd admits that he was involved with other projects at the time, but responds, 'If there are two producers, then for one of them to work effectively, the other one shouldn't always be in his hair. And I was taking the opportunity to make other things at the BBC, including Mike Leigh's *Four Days in July*, which was shooting in Northern Ireland.'

Gavin Millar, who was directing *Dreamchild*, describes the Potter–Trodd relationship as 'a tragi-comedy':

They loved each other and they hated each other in equal measure, and you could never know which mood would prevail at any moment. Although Dennis obviously felt affection for Ken a lot of the time, he was so fiercely unsentimental that he suppressed any display of it, while Ken was shy and wary of emotions, because of his Plymouth Brethren upbringing. So it was a very uneasy relationship – though they obviously respected each other's talent immensely, otherwise they wouldn't have lasted that long together.

When *Dreamchild* was finally released in the USA in October 1985 and in Britain the following January, the performances by Coral

Browne as the elderly Alice and Ian Holm as Dodgson helped to earn excellent reviews – 'a small sentimental gem of a movie . . . marvellously acted . . . a lovely, wistful little fairy-tale for grown-ups . . . The theme of repressed paedophilia . . . is handled with unerring good taste', wrote Stephen Holden in the *New York Times*. But there were problems with distribution. 'EMI had to sell their rights to Universal,' says McCallum, 'who had never released a movie so small, and they didn't know how to market it.' Consequently it came and went before most people had had time to become aware of it.

Potter vented his current feelings about Trodd when a *Sunday Times* interviewer, Sue Summers, met him in September 1985. '[He] is good humoured and almost mellow,' she wrote. 'But he can still put in the knife. At present his target is Kenith Trodd . . . The origins of the dispute are unclear, but Potter will not even speak to his erstwhile collaborator. He has even asked Trodd to resign from his new series, though he will in fact be a joint executive producer. Trodd says he hopes and believes the rift will be healed in time.'

Summers learned much from Potter about this new series. 'He has written a new six-part drama for BBC1,' she reported,

which will be his first major original work for the corporation since *Pennies from Heaven* in 1978 . . . *The Singing Detective*, seven-and-a-half hours of drama due to start shooting in January, which, says Potter, will make *Pennies from Heaven* look like a rehearsal. It is about a writer of cheap detective fiction (Michael Gambon is likely to play the role) in hospital with 100 per cent psoriasis. He loses control of his body temperature and starts to fantasize. This is something which happened to Potter himself, although he claims the series is not autobiographical.

'I'm playing with the conventions – the musical convention, the situation-comedy convention, the detective-story convention – in order to try to see what TV drama can do,' he says. 'Once I'd got my skates on I felt I could just fly with it.

'I think the days of the single play are more or less over, unfortunately. The series is the one thing left now which can do what the cinema and stage can't – take seven or eight hours to develop characters and situations. *Tender is the Night* is an example of what can be done with an existing piece of work.'

His Fitzgerald adaptation was about to begin its six-part run on BBC2 (from 23 September to 28 October 1985). 'I haven't put [the novel] in embalming fluid, like the film of *The Great Gatsby*,' he told

Summers, 'because the more faithful you are to Fitzgerald, the more unsuccessful you become . . . Of course, there is a lot of American money in *Tender is the Night*, from the cable TV network Showtime. But . . . the BBC, not the Americans, had the creative control.' Some years later he admitted that this was not entirely true: 'Of course Showtime did exert an influence and it wasn't what it should have been.' Twentieth Century-Fox and an Australian company were involved financially as well, providing enough money for Fitzgerald's story to be filmed in its true locations (chiefly the Alps, the Riviera and Paris), and for a glossily international cast to be booked, headed by Peter Strauss and Mary Steenburgen as Dick and Nicole Diver. After watching two episodes, *Daily Telegraph* critic Richard Last feared that 'the packaging, lush, loving, and reeking of lucre, could outrun the content. Beautiful people . . . can become tedious company.' Philip Purser wrote, 'I just can't help wishing that a tenth of the millions spent here . . . could have gone into a new original television work by Dennis Potter.'

*

Trodd says that, as soon as the BBC *Pennies from Heaven* had been made, 'I did nurture the hope that there might be some kind of sequel to it. And I remember making the suggestion to Dennis of World War II and ENSA [the services' entertainment organization, which sent performers around the war zones]. But that was probably too crude and obvious for him.' In fact Potter had pursued this idea. In February 1979 Judy Daish wrote to Charles Denton of Black Lion, the film wing of Associated Television:

We understand that you are willing to advance £3000 as 'development' money in order that the quite demanding research for six plays about ENSA should go ahead. As you know, Dennis does not like working to a synopsis, and indeed always positively refuses to do so. So, the procedure for this would be the same as for *Pennies from Heaven* . . . Ken bombarding him with material, cassettes, recordings, clippings, etc., which Dennis then uses and weaves into his scripts . . . Both the BBC and Thames are eager to get their hands on such a project . . .

By August 1979, as many as thirteen one-hour scripts were envisaged – though when a contract was drafted this was reduced to six.

This project languished, but the following year, after the LWT–PFH deal had collapsed, Potter drafted a 'proposal for new association between LWT & PFH', which included 'a new television series of twelve episodes, of one hour each', which he was to write himself. In June 1981 a budget for this 'Dennis Potter series' was being worked out by LWT, and a letter from the company on 8 July refers to it as *Under My Skin*. A typed proposal (not in Potter's papers, but preserved by John Wyver, who thinks that Trodd gave it to him) outlines this project:

Under My Skin
A series by Dennis Potter

This is a thirteen-part series in the studio, with the barest minimum of film, that, quite apart from its story, attempts to celebrate the styles, techniques and virtues of electronic drama. *Under My Skin* deliberately uses an allegedly 'autobiographical', or first-person, narrative mode. It begins in the public ward of a large London teaching hospital, where Jack Black, the hero, is virtually unable to move with an exceptionally severe psoriatic arthrosis: his joints are immovable with arthritis, and his skin hideously on fire with psoriasis, so that he is also running a dangerously high temperature. Pain, humiliation, a hilariously abrasive anger, and the occasional hallucinatory consequences of an out-of-control temperature sometimes cause Jack to think that he is the victim of a particularly malevolent writer in a particularly odious TV drama. Jack himself is a television playwright, who imagines that his working life is horribly threatened. He may not be able to turn over in the bed properly, but he has full, and comic use of his tongue. Half paranoid, and half sardonic, he tries to convince the world around him of his dire circumstances.

Jack is given the chance to take part in the early clinical trials of a dangerous new drug which puts him in a Catch-22 situation. It works very well, allowing him to zoom back into the world, but one of the as yet uncharted side-effects is that its decimation of the fast-dividing reproductive cells makes him all but impotent. To compensate, he accepts a commission to write a series of plays about Casanova or Don Juan, and falls foul of the Clean-Up TV brigade. His private life becomes a hectic and comical denial of his new drug-induced troubles, and the conviction grows upon him that he has to hunt down and eliminate the abundantly malevolent author who has kept him in such wretched circumstances. A search, of course, for himself.

The style cannot be divulged here, or the content. Sometimes there is a studio audience for the sit-com-like dilemmas of Jack. Occasionally, clips from an already filmed lecture of one Dennis Potter at the NFT help Jack to identify his odiously smug and falsely acclaimed 'enemy'. Jack's most prized possession, particularly in hospital, is a little black box with buttons for

435

'LAUGHTER, APPLAUSE, GASPS'. Even at his worst he is just about able to press one of these buttons and so trigger the right response.

Similarly the series uses sequences of song and dance, whether in hospital ward, private office, or domestic environment. *Under My Skin*, in short, will use any device already familiar to TV viewers to unfold its comedy, its allegory, its metaphors and – perhaps most movingly – its new, electronic *Pilgrim's Progress* of a narrative. Thus, any description at this stage will sound odiously pretentious: in purpose, *Under My Skin* will be an uninhibitedly bold attempt by Dennis Potter to use all that he has learned in nearly two decades of TV writing to tell a story that, while remaining inventive fiction, is nevertheless not *too* distant from his own.

Attached to the proposal is a note from LWT that the serial would be 'made in the studio and recorded on tape', and that the company 'would like to offer [it] to Channel 4'. But PFH and LWT could not agree terms, and it was called off in August 1981.

Trodd says that the proposal was 'an attempt not just to restore the relationship between PFH and London Weekend, but to reinstate Dennis as a writer who worked primarily in the studio rather than on film'. He remarks on the proposed use of Potter's National Film Theatre interview, 'Typical of Dennis to want to use something that might otherwise have been wasted. We filmed that interview in the hope that it would become part of a documentary on his work, but nothing had happened.'

Potter later recalled that *The Singing Detective* had 'started as an idea for a sitcom', intended for the electronic studio rather than film:

The whole thing began to take shape several years ago when I was feeling rather sad about the death of the studio TV play. It seemed to have gone for ever, but I wrote down some ideas I had, a series of scenes in a hospital ward which I thought were quite promising. I just wanted to make use of some of the comedy that takes place in a hospital. I had no idea what story they fitted into, but the ideas stayed with me and much later they fell into place.

The *Smoke Rings* idea – 'the story of a private investigator tracing a missing girl who is believed to have disappeared with a deserter from the American Services' – seems to have arisen as a separate project (Trodd says he does not think Potter ever wrote any of it). *Gorky Park* had helped him rediscover his predilection for Raymond Chandler's archetypal detective Philip Marlowe. He had included a passage from

ARTHUR: (MIME CONT.) No, sir, Not without that certain thing.

Life would be such a very lonesome thing

Be no wedding bells, no wedding ring

No, sir, not without that certain thing."

THE MANAGER HAS MORE OR LESS USHERED HIM
TO THE DOOR. ARTHUR SHAKES HIS ARM
FREE, ON THE VERGE OF VIOLENCE. THE
MANAGER RAISES A WARNING FINGER.

MANAGER: ('SINGS' – MIMES) "Love is the king

I'm talking about

Love is a king overall

Love is a theme

Life can't be without

Humble rich and poor, an all fall

Life can't go on without that certain thing

Be no happy song of love to sing

No, sir, not without that certain thing."

ARTHUR: All right, King Kong. All right. I know my own
way out. No need to push!

THE PICTURE 'TURNS OVER' TO–

5. EXTERIOR. DAY. PATH IN WOODS. FOREST OF DEAN.

EMERGING OUT OF WHAT SEEMS A THICKET – BECAUSE OF A
SPIRAL IN THE NARROW PATH – COME THREE BLACK-FACED,
BOOTED, WEARY-TREAD COALMINERS, CARRYING 'BREAD' SATCHELS
AND (UNLIT) CARBIDE LAMPS.

THEY TRAMP ON TOGETHER, NOT TALKING : A FATHER AND
TWO SONS — EILEEN'S FATHER AND BROTHERS. EVENTUALLY ONE
OF THEM – MAURICE, THE YOUNGEST – SPEAKS.

MAURICE: Dist thou see thik butterfly?

THE OTHER TWO CANNOT BE
BOTHERED TO ANSWER

IN A MOMENT, UP AHEAD, THE CHATTER OF APPROACHING CHILDREN.

25 A page from one of the notebooks in which Potter wrote *Pennies from Heaven*. He described his handwriting as 'appallingly neat, clear and orderly'.

26 Bob Hoskins as Arthur and Cheryl Campbell as Eileen on Hammersmith Bridge at the end of *Pennies from Heaven*. (*BBC*)

27 The 'children' in *Blue Remembered Hills* (1979): left to right, Colin Jeavons, Michael Elphick, Janine Duvitski, Colin Welland, Robin Ellis, John Bird, Helen Mirren. (*BBC*)

28 The Potter family in 1976: Margaret and Dennis with (left to right) Jane, Robert and Sarah. (*Sunday Times*)

29 Dennis and Margaret in New York, 1977. 'Holidays? Thank you, no … And then – POW! ZAPP-P-P! – everything changed.' (*Sunday Times*)

30 Judy Daish (left) with Margaret and Dennis Potter on holiday in France.

31 Hammersmith Bridge again: Michael Gambon as *The Singing Detective*. (*BBC*)

32 The writer and his masterpiece. (*BBC*)

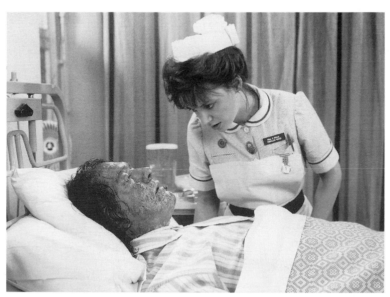

33 'I shall have to lift your penis now to grease around it.' Joanne Whalley as Nurse Mills with Michael Gambon in *The Singing Detective*. (*BBC*)

34 Gina Bellman: a publicity shot for *Blackeyes*. (*BBC*)

35 Gina Bellman and Potter. 'I loved Dennis so much,' she says. 'I really loved him and cared about him.' (*Sun*)

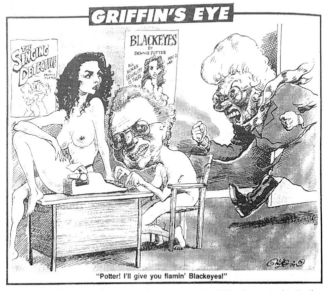

36 'Potter! I'll give you flamin' Blackeyes!' cries Mary Whitehouse in this *Daily Mirror* cartoon, printed the morning after the first episode.

37 Louise Germaine as Sylvia in *Lipstick on Your Collar*. 'Dennis corrected all my grammar,' she says. 'He gave me books ...' (*Stephen Morley*)

38 Potter clowns with actor Clive Francis (playing a War Office major) in *Lipstick on Your Collar*. (*Stephen Morley*)

39 Potter photographed at London Weekend Television, after recording his interview with Melvyn Bragg on 15 March 1994, a few weeks before his death.

40 Kenith Trodd (left) with Renny Rye during the making of *Karaoke* in 1996. (*BBC*)

the first Marlowe novel, *The Big Sleep* (1939), in the BBC Radio 4 anthology programme *With Great Pleasure* in September 1976, explaining that it was 'one of my riper fantasies' to imagine himself as Marlowe. 'Sometimes, yes, I *am* everything the well-dressed private detective ought to be.' (He read the passage in what he called 'my ludicrous Gloucestershire American'.)

By calling the hero of *The Singing Detective* 'Philip Marlow', Potter was almost over-stating the obvious – and he managed to get in another literary allusion: 'You'd think my mother would have had more sense than to call me Philip,' Marlow remarks. 'What else could I have done except write detective stories? She should have called me Christopher.' From which – in the published script – we cut to the basement night-club, Skinscape's, an overheated underworld, with Marlow voicing-over lines about Hell from Christopher Marlowe's *Dr Faustus*.

Sarah Potter believes her father wrote the first draft of the serial in the spring of 1985. 'I don't think he really knew where it was going to take him,' she says, 'and where it took him was quite close to the bone.' Potter himself remembered experiencing 'that sense of dread when you know you're digging out something'. While the serial was being televised in 1986, he recalled:

When I sat down to write *The Singing Detective*, I was uneasy about the project. I continually tried to hold it away, thinking it would be nauseous for the viewer. Then I thought, write it. Get it out of the system.

I couldn't write a horror story, which is what it would have become, so I used all the conventions I like – detective stories, musicals, situation comedy.

In a *Radio Times* interview to promote the serial, he said, 'When I was working at MGM . . . they would ask . . . was it a detective story? Was it a musical? Was it a romance? . . . That sort of thinking throws a terrible carapace over the writer and one of the things I wanted to do in *The Singing Detective* is break up the narrative tyranny.'

Gareth Davies had once teased Potter about his lack of sub-plots, and Potter had replied that they bored him. But *The Singing Detective* is a bravura demonstration of plotting and sub-plotting. Its multiple narrative strands constantly cross-refer and cue to each other but come conclusively together, revealing the fullness of their meanings and inter-relationships, only in the sixth and final episode, called *Who Done It*.

The first of these strands is, in effect, the sitcom sketched in the proposal for *Under My Skin*. It portrays the immobile psoriatic thriller-writer, Philip Marlow, agonizingly confined to his hospital bed, whose view of the world is indeed – in the words of the proposal – 'half paranoid, and half sardonic'. Like most of Potter's original work since *Pennies from Heaven*, *The Singing Detective* is largely a reconsideration of old material, which Potter handles with more sophistication and detachment the second time around; and for the sitcom element he looks back to, and improves on, his 1966 hospital comedy *Emergency – Ward 9*. Once again, liberal anxiety about racism is mocked, this time by the writer–hero himself, in collusion with the cheerful Asian in the next bed, when they are confronted by the sanctimonious Dr Finlay (whose name is from the old BBC *Casebook*):

DR FINLAY: Are you having trouble with this fellow?

ALI: (*beam*) Oh yes, my God yes.

DR FINLAY: Has he been making offensive remarks about your origins?

ALI: (*puzzled*) Origins?

DR FINLAY: Your – ah – race, or – ?

ALI: Race?

DR FINLAY: (*irritated*) Yes. Your race!

MARLOW: Go on. Tell him. You brown bugger.

> (ALI *gives a huge whoop of laughter.* DR FINLAY, *taken aback, goes to say something but – bleep-bleep-bleep! goes his bleeper, and he turns on his heel to stride away, angrily flustered.*)

Potter even harks back to his *TW3* caricature style with a running joke involving two other patients in adjoining beds. Mr Hall, a small-minded shopkeeper, bullies the semi-literate Reginald, but is ingratiating to the nurses, thereby allowing Reginald to get his revenge. But the sitcom strand of *The Singing Detective* is chiefly the blackest, most painful kind of farce, as Marlow's dignity and privacy are assaulted in every possible way. He is regularly anointed (as Potter had often been) with medicinal grease. This is done by the beautiful Nurse Mills, so that it becomes a denial of Marlow's sexuality:

NURSE MILLS: (*matter of fact*) I shall have to lift your penis now to grease around it.

(MARLOW's *face is suddenly a cinema poster, so to speak, for* The Agony and the Ecstasy . . .)

MARLOW: [*who is experiencing an erection*] I'm very sorry. It – that's the one part of me that still sort of functions. I do beg your pardon . . . It seems to have a will of its own.

NURSE MILLS: We don't need to talk about it, do we?

Nurse Mills speaks to him as a nanny might address a pre-sexual child, and when the consultant in charge of his case arrives for a brisk inspection, Marlow is once again treated as a helpless infant. He fights back. 'The last time I experienced anything like this was in my bloody pram!' he rages at the doctors, and makes them into figures of fun in his imagination by fantasizing that they are lip-synching 'Dem Bones, Dem Bones, Dem Dry Bones'. This is the first fully choreographed musical number to erupt into the serial, which uses songs much more sparingly than *Pennies* did. ('I first used the device [of lip-synching] in *Pennies from Heaven*, but I now think that we overdid it,' Potter said just before *The Singing Detective* was transmitted. 'This time we've been more selective.')

The hospital makes yet another assault on Marlow's adulthood when Dr Finlay appears, out of uniform on a Sunday afternoon, at the head of a tambourine-waving bunch of born-again Christians, demanding that the ward sing a Sunday School hymn out of Marlow's childhood. Marlow responds furiously: 'We don't want this crap! Leave us alone!' Yet he is far from irreligious; when the hospital psychotherapist, whom he reluctantly agrees to see, accuses him of writing mere pulp fiction (surely a reference to Potter's belief that people treated writing for television as trash), Marlow responds, 'I would have liked to have used my pen to praise a loving God and all his loving creation.'

The hospital-sitcom strand of *The Singing Detective* takes place in 'real time'. Over six weeks (the period taken for the serial to be transmitted) we see Marlow's gradual physical recovery until, like Potter leaving the London Hospital in 1972, he is able to resume something like normal life. This is not the result of a wonder drug; Marlow has already been given Razoxane and all the other treatments Potter had been prescribed, and it is implied that his recovery is the result of the psychological self-knowledge he gradually acquires in the hospital.

In contrast, the Forties thriller which Marlow is 'writing' (or rewriting) in his mind, to combat his boredom and misery, has no such orderly progression, intruding into the hospital narrative in fragments and flashbacks. It opens with the arrival at Skinscape's night-club of the sinister, debonair Mark Binney, who finds himself obliged to buy over-priced champagne for the 'hostesses'. Potter told Clive Lindley that he had done some research for this scene:

There was a place in Mayfair, a real sort of come-on night-club, and Dennis told me he went to do some research there – he needed to go into a night-club and buy champagne for hookers and all that sort of thing. And he told the story as a joke – he said he had far too much to drink, paid through the nose (something like a hundred pounds for booze), and stayed far too long, and came up to the street and threw up in the gutter! And that was the end of that.

Binney brings one of the hostesses back to his flat, a Russian girl, Sonia, who is afterwards found murdered. In the hope of proving his innocence, Binney hires the Singing Detective – Marlow himself, dressed and speaking like his Chandler namesake – who is so called because, when not solving crime, he croons with a dance band. This device allows Potter the double irony of overlaying the self-parodying *film-noir* thriller with Forties hit songs, almost as banal and saccharine as their Thirties counterparts in *Pennies*. But the question of who killed Sonia (her death has something to do with Nazi scientists and Soviet agents) recedes in importance as *The Singing Detective* progresses, and the murder is finally left unsolved – if, indeed, there was a murder, for by this time the thriller has merged with Marlow's paranoid fantasies about his ex-wife, Nicola.

By the sixth episode, the only survivors from the original whodunnit are two Mysterious Men, classic gangster movie 'hoods', who play a bewildered Rosencrantz and Guildenstern to Marlow's Hamlet, and are disconcerted to realize their total ignorance of what is really going on: 'We don't know a bloody thing about our – who or what or why or – I mean, it's all blank, ennit? . . . We're padding. Like a couple of bleed'n' sofas.' In Marlow's imagination, they invade the hospital ward for the classic shoot-out which must end all such films. Yet it is not they but Marlow the Singing Detective who shoots dead his real-life *alter ego*, Marlow the writer – a *coup de théâtre* which the Detective then explains: 'I suppose you could say we'd been partners, him and me . . . But hell, this was one sick fellow, from way back when. And I reckon I'm man enough to tie my own shoelaces now.' So the thriller strand, too, ends with the healing of the sick man – the destruction of his 'ill' persona by his strong, reinvented self.

The strand of *The Singing Detective* most likely to confuse the first-time viewer or reader of the serial is Marlow's relationship with his ex-wife Nicola, which slips from reality to fantasy without any visual clues. Potter endows Marlow with an experience of prostitutes and a disgust at sex. In the fifth episode we briefly see him in flashback, hiding his psoriatic skin as he apologizes to a prostitute ('Sonia' from the thriller strand) for 'calling you names' while having sex with her. His first reaction when Nicola visits him in hospital is to call her names too: 'The plain fact is that you are a filthy, predatory and totally wanton bitch who is always on heat.' Later, though seeming to desire a reunion with her, he lapses again into the language of disgust: 'I want to sleep with you again . . . With a big mirror alongside . . . So I can turn my head while I'm doing it and leer at myself. And so that when it starts shooting up in me and spurting out I can twist to one side coming off your hot and sticky loins and *spit* straight at my own face.' Gibbon, the psychotherapist, reminds Marlow of a self-revealing passage from his novel *The Singing Detective* which is lifted almost verbatim from Potter's own *Hide and Seek*: 'Mouth sucking wet and slack at mouth, tongue chafing against tongue, limb thrusting upon limb, skin rubbing at skin . . . Faces contort and stretch into a helpless leer, organs spurt out smelly stains and sticky betrayals. This is the sweaty farce out of which we are brought into being.' Gibbon observes, 'You don't like women . . . Let me rephrase that . . . You . . . think they are – well – capable of being idolized . . . You don't like sex.'

It is implied that Marlow, like many pre-*Pennies* Potter heroes, has failed in his relationships with women because he cannot resolve the Madonna–Whore dichotomy. Yet the cause of this angst is not explored in *The Singing Detective*. Instead, Marlow fantasizes that Nicola (a middle-aged actress) is plotting with a non-existent person from his own imagination, Binney from the thriller strand, to steal the screenplay of his novel and sell it to Hollywood. Taken autobiographically, this suggests that by 1985 Potter was more anxious about professional betrayal than sexual infidelity (one recalls Naim Attallah's description of him: 'He would misinterpret people's motives, see things that weren't there'). It means that Nicola's role in the healing of Marlow is never clearly established, and that once again, Potter has failed to incorporate a strong, right-minded woman into his scheme of things.

He does, however, allow Nicola a crucial taunt at Marlow: 'You . . . use your illness as a weapon against other people and as an excuse for not being properly human . . .' Gibbon the psychotherapist has already said much the same: 'Chronic illness is an extremely good shelter . . . A cave in the rocks into which one can safely crawl . . .' In the final moments of *The Singing Detective*, Marlow emerges from the cave; the direction describes him, as he leaves hospital, struggling 'along the corridor to freedom' which is 'resonant with . . . birdsong and the sound of the wind in the leaves'. And he is 'leaning on Nicola'.

'In *The Singing Detective*,' Potter told Melvyn Bragg, 'I used the Forest of Dean, I used the physical circumstances of psoriatic arthropathy . . . and it seemed so personal . . . but . . . it isn't.' And to Alan Yentob he added, 'People say to me, you know, that must be autobiographical. I feel greatly offended when they do, because it's one of the least autobiographical pieces of work that I've ever attempted.' Just before the serial was broadcast in 1986, he remarked, 'Although associations abound, the facts are not autobiographical at all.'

Certainly the adult Marlow, a little-known hack author divorced from an actress wife, is not Dennis Potter. Even the portrayal of his illness differs markedly from Potter's: Marlow's psoriasis is cured by self-knowledge, whereas Potter's remained incurable, and such relief as he experienced was brought by drugs. Yet when he began the strand dealing with Marlow's childhood – which scarcely features in the first episode, and may not have been part of his original scheme for *The Singing Detective* – he dug into an area of his own early life that he had not explored since his abandoned novel *The Country Boy*, the move from the Forest to London.

The clever son of a Forest miner, the young Marlow, who has already learned at school the power of telling lies and manipulating others, is removed to the metropolis by his London-born mother – transported from a cramped cottage uncomfortably shared with grandparents to an equally claustrophobic urban working-class home. Pining for his absent father and the Forest landscape, the boy soon returns there, alone, just as Potter had done. But the reason for young Philip Marlow's return is very different. Potter came back to escape from his abusing uncle. Philip makes the journey because he has revealed to his mother that he has witnessed her adultery, deep among the Forest trees, with a family friend, Raymond Binney (hence the recurrence of Binney as a dubious character in the adult Marlow's imagination). Philip's mother's response to this accusation is to throw herself into the Thames from Hammersmith Bridge.

Or this, at least, is the story that Marlow tells Gibbon. But the psychotherapist questions its truth. A young woman is fished out of the river in Marlow's pulp thriller, and Gibbon asks, 'Is it very likely that you would so exactly duplicate such a traumatic event in your life in the pages of a – ?' Marlow sidesteps this; in any case, Potter seems to be directing Gibbon's hint at himself – no, he seems to be saying, this is not what happened to *me*.

'That's all wrong!' says Potter's real-life mother about this part of *The Singing Detective*. Asked if she minded when her screen counterpart was portrayed as adulterous, she laughs, but adds, 'I do mind inside me because I'm not that kind of a woman.' Legal action was taken when Mary Whitehouse alleged that the young Potter really had witnessed such a scene.

The real trauma in Potter's childhood is very faintly hinted at in *The Singing Detective*. There is a comic 'rape' in the first episode, when a senile patient on Marlow's ward, known as 'Noddy' because all he can do is nod his head and stutter, climbs into Marlow's bed in the middle of the night, muttering, 'Mabel . . . Where you been . . . Mabel?' As the ward explodes in laughter, the night nurse calls out, 'You can't do that in here! Stay in your own beds! Oh, you naughty boys.' When young Philip Marlow is taken in by his mother's London family, his uncle, a returned soldier, 'ruffles Philip's hair. But his manner is more menacing than jovial.' And Philip's reaction to the death of his mother – to hide from everyone, even his father, by climbing a tall forest tree – undoubtedly reflects Potter's response, at the same age, to the sexual abuse. 'Doosn't trust anybody again!' the boy tells himself in the last episode. 'Hide in theeself. Or else . . . they'll hurt you! Hide! Hide!'

But this is only sketched lightly, and *The Singing Detective*, as Potter emphasized, carefully avoids crude autobiographical revelation. He had exposed himself more personally and painfully in such early plays as *Stand Up, Nigel Barton* and *Moonlight on the Highway*. Marlow is a careful construction rather than a self-portrait; Potter observed that, at the beginning of the serial, he has 'no faith in himself, no belief in any political, religious or social system. He [is] full of a witty despair and cynicism. Now I have never been like that . . .'

Oddly, those of his own characteristics which Potter does hand on to Marlow – guilt about some childhood trauma, and the Madonna–

Whore sexual dichotomy – do not sit comfortably on Marlow's shoulders. He is something quite new in Potter's writing, a man in command of his own life. During *The Singing Detective*, he scans his past in search of an explanation for the mess he has made of himself. But he rejects glib answers: 'All solutions, and no clues. That's what the dumb-heads want . . . I'd rather it was the other way around. All clues. No solutions. That's the way things are.'

Marlow also despises the easy, vaguely Christian optimism that Potter had tried to adopt for a while. At the end of the fifth episode he quotes St Julian of Norwich's dictum 'All shall be well, and all shall be well, and all manner of thing shall be well', and turns ironically to Noddy, saying, 'You do agree, don't you?' Noddy, of course, 'blank-eyed, slack-mouthed', nods – but then he always does. 'Life is all right' is not Marlow's philosophy. He believes that, in a world where there are no answers to the riddles of existence – all clues and no solutions – the only thing we can depend on is our own, individual judgement. We have got to have faith in ourselves, otherwise there is nothing. As Marlow keeps asking himself throughout the serial, in his Singing Detective persona, 'Am I right? Or am I right?' In other words, we cannot risk self-doubt.

Just before *The Singing Detective* was transmitted, Steve Grant of *Time Out* asked Potter if he was still an optimist. 'In a way,' he answered. 'Keep going. That in itself is an optimistic phrase. Mine is an optimism that is veined with the sardonic. Optimism is acceptable provided one accepts that there's no justification for it.' Here, certainly, Marlow and Dennis Potter are one and the same.

*

Jonathan Powell recalls the arrival of Potter's new serial at the BBC in the summer of 1985:

Dennis would never let you read scripts before he'd finished the whole thing. And of course, when they arrived, they were absolutely nothing to do with what he'd described to me. I read it – I'm not entirely sure I absolutely understood it, but it was heart-stopping material, especially the childhood stuff. And I went and told Michael Grade that it wasn't a thriller, but was about somebody with a terrible skin disease, and he said, 'Is it any good?' And I said, 'I'm not quite sure, but it's got some fantastic stuff in it.' And he said, 'OK, off you go and make it.' Which we did.

Trodd had already begun to look for a director. 'Various people turned it down,' he says. 'Stephen Frears, Richard Eyre, the crop of what was the British film industry at the time. It wasn't the scripts, but they couldn't waste time on a television project for eighteen months and hold up their film careers! And in the event almost none of them managed to make a film while we were doing it!'

Frears says he 'wasn't offered *The Singing Detective* – to my regret', though Potter later invited him to direct a movie version of it. Eyre, who had done a stint as producer of *Play for Today* and shared an office with Trodd, recalls that he

was asked to direct several of Dennis's scripts, including *The Singing Detective*. Unfortunately, when this came up, Alan Bennett had already offered me his play about Kafka, *The Insurance Man*. But Dennis was a hard man to say no to. We met at our mutual agent's and I explained that I had this other script that I was committed to doing. Dennis said, 'You're making a terrible mistake. I'm offering you the chance to make television history.' No irony. Wonderful.

While the search continued, Potter began work on a novel. In her September 1985 interview with him, Sue Summers reported that he had written 'the first fifty thousand words'. She added,

Thanks to a new Swiss drug, Etretinate, which gives him massive doses of vitamin A, Potter is still free of pain from the psoriasis which for years caused him crippling arthritis. His last drug had potentially carcinogenic side-effects which threatened to overwhelm him. 'I'm still at risk for a while,' he says, 'which is partly why I'm working my arse off.'

At the time of *Sufficient Carbohydrate*, he had told Bryan Appleyard that he had 'tried one novel but is now unable to believe in the medium: "I feel the form hasn't the mileage, the guts, the bravado to be of its time. Nabokov's *Pale Fire* is magnificent of course but each time something like that happens it seems like one more cul-de-sac, one more door closed."' This roused the novelist Paul Theroux to send Potter an indignant postcard, accusing him of being ignorant of contemporary fiction. 'I wouldn't have bothered with anyone else,' Theroux said later. 'I thought he was worth saving.' Then – as Potter told Steve Grant of *Time Out* – there came into his mind the image of a man breaking down in tears on a train. 'It could have made a play,' noted Grant, 'but he thought about Theroux's postcard and started work on his second novel . . . a ferocious burst of sixty thousand words over a sixty-day period in between drafts of *The Singing Detective*.' He called it *Ticket to Ride* – his only borrowing of a title from a contemporary (rather than antique) pop song.

In the restaurant car of a London-bound train, a man realizes he is suffering from total amnesia. Arriving at Paddington, he takes a room in the station hotel, but can find nothing in his clothes to identify himself. The narrative switches to his home, a little earlier, where we learn – from the viewpoint of his wife, Helen – that he is John Buck, a recently sacked advertising executive who has retreated into a reclusive life, making miniature paintings of wild flowers, and can talk to Helen only in an oddly pre-arranged fashion. 'There it was again,' she notes after he has been speaking. 'The odd formality and stiffness of his sentences. From the first day she had known him, his speech had always sounded to her as though he had written it down in advance, or was quoting, with a slight satiric edge, from some more self-important predecessor.' One recalls Philip Purser's description of Potter 'echoing himself . . . as if he were quoting from a familiar argument'.

Ticket to Ride is full of echoes. It seems that Helen – the same name as the Kika Markham character in *Double Dare* – is a former agency call-girl whom John first met in a hotel. John is disgusted by sex, yet picks up prostitutes (or fantasizes that he does), kidnapping a helpless young hooker and ordering a taxi driver to drive them to 'New Cavendish Street . . . At the corner of Great Titchfield Street' – the exact location of Potter's London flat. Left alone at home, Helen has an unexpected male visitor (named Martin, like another Potter intruder) whom she seduces, as so many bored Potter housewives have done before her. Martin ends up with a kitchen knife buried in him, like John in *Rain on the Roof*. There is a hospital scene where the hero finds himself in a ward of mad old men. At the end, once again, it seems that the whole thing may merely have been a fantasy in the minds of the protagonists.

Since *Ticket to Ride* was not reviewed by television critics, when it was published in September 1986, it was not recognized as a reworking of old ideas. 'This is one of those novels which it would be easy to dismiss on grounds of "unreadability",' wrote Robert Nye in the *Guardian*. 'But if the reader persists he will find that it generates its own spell upon his attention . . .' Miranda Seymour in the *Evening Standard* called it 'an electrifyingly readable book, with a baffling conclusion', and Anthony Clare of *In the Psychiatrist's Chair* was enthusiastic in *The Sunday Times*: 'The portrayal of psychological decay . . . is . . . uncannily plausible.'

Trodd had now found a director for *The Singing Detective*, thirty-eight-year-old Jon Amiel. 'I never had a burning ambition to direct films,' says Amiel.

I went from university to a job as a literary manager at the Hampstead Theatre Club, and I directed in theatre, working my way through to the Royal Shakespeare Company. When I was fired by Trevor Nunn, who didn't like my production of *Twelfth Night*, I decided to produce in television, went to the BBC, and got a job as a script editor for a year and a half. Then I got offered a directors' training course, and after it I directed studio drama for about five or six years, before I did *The Silent Twins*, which was the first thing I had done on film. It was a true story about the celebrated black girl identical twins, who had refused to talk to anyone in the outside world.

Trodd says that he and Amiel 'sort of knew each other, and had discussed ideas together, and I, having been rejected by the aristocracy, was looking around'.

Amiel recalls that Trodd

came into my office in that sidelong way that he specializes in and put these six scripts on my desk. So I started reading and I realized halfway through the first one that my hands were actually shaking. I felt absolutely convinced that I was in the presence of a masterpiece and I was terrified both that I might not be asked to do it and that I *would* be asked to do it. In fact I was only asked after five or six more eminent and obvious choices had turned it down for various reasons.

Trodd arranged for Amiel to meet Potter, and then left for Italy to work on another screen project, a thriller called *The MacGuffin*. Potter seems to have seen this as yet more evidence of Trodd's declining interest in his work; this was the point at which he told Sue Summers that he was trying to have him removed from *The Singing Detective*. 'But I had done everything that Dennis needed at this juncture – found a director,' says Trodd. The BBC agreed that Trodd and Rick McCallum would be taken on as joint executive producers of the serial, with a BBC staff man, John Harris, as producer.

When Jon Amiel met Potter for the first time, over lunch at the San Marino, he realized that 'Ken and Dennis were in the midst of a full-scale marital split, and Dennis was turning to Rick McCallum as his new producing partner'. Amiel told Potter that 'I thought it was very important Ken stay on the project. It needed his in-fighting skills to protect it inside the BBC.'

Amiel was also determined to prove that he 'wasn't just scared' of Potter, 'which I was, completely'. At lunch, he told Potter that 'I felt strongly that the script wasn't quite there'. Potter 'grabbed his favourite tipple of the time, Gévrey-Chambertin, with his buckled hands, and he looked at me rather as Sebastian must have looked at the Roman soldiers as one arrow after another entered his body'. The lunch 'ended fairly neutrally and we agreed to meet again a couple of days later'.

When Amiel arrived for this second meal, in the evening, 'Dennis was already drunk'. McCallum was there too, 'grinning with anxiety'. Amiel continues:

Dennis greeted me with 'Jon, you're looking a lot older than when I last saw you,' and he proceeded to be vile for two hours in a way which only those who've had detailed dealings with him can quite appreciate. He was always at his most cutting when he had one person as his audience and another as the butt. He was very good at it and being pissed only made him better at it. After all, he was a man whose brain and tongue were his only weapons in an effectively useless body.

Finally, by about eleven o'clock, Amiel 'realized I could not and would not work with this man. And, more out of despair than courage, I finally turned to Dennis, and I said, "God, you're a patronizing cunt." He then did what he often did when you got angry with him, which was look at you with a surprised and aggrieved look, and say, "Jon, have I said something to *offend* you? Why so *aggressive*, Jon?" He was utterly maddening in any kind of argument of that sort.' Eventually the encounter 'just petered out', leaving Amiel with 'a savage headache'. Next morning he telephoned McCallum to say he could not work with Potter.

McCallum was conciliatory, telling Amiel that Potter 'felt a bit guilty' and would like to have one more meeting. A week later, 'very gingerly', Amiel returned to the same restaurant:

Dennis was always obsessively on time and furious if you were late, which I tended to be, so I deliberately arrived early. He came in and put a Pepys *Diary* on the table and humphed a bit and said, 'I was buying a new copy of this so I thought I'd get you one as well.' As it happened, I'd bought him a book too.

He said, 'Christ, Amiel, can't I ever get one up on you?' I couldn't know it at the time but that was the last moment of conflict we ever had.

Amiel began to outline the changes he wanted. 'Firstly,' he recalls,

Dennis had lost interest in the thriller strand after the first episode. By the second it was fading, and by the third it had completely disappeared. Secondly, Marlow's relationship with his wife, Nicola, was hopelessly under-developed, so that when the happy ending involved Marlow walking out of the hospital with this woman, you felt nothing about it, because she was a cipher. We had to make her a much more real character. And thirdly, the last episode did not work – it was not the sum of the component parts.

Every time he made a point, Potter would interrupt him – in agree-ment: 'Yes, yes, I get it, shut up, shut up, what else?' Again and again, Amiel would get halfway through a thought, and Potter would say he understood and agreed. 'I had to learn to trust he would get it, which he always did,' says Amiel. 'The thing he hated more than anything was being told what to do.'

After the meal, they went back to Potter's flat 'and talked for another hour or two about structure and plotting until he got tired. Then I called Ken, who was getting anxious, and I said, "We went back to Dennis's flat", and he said, "You did *what*? You went to his *flat*? I've never been to his flat!" I hadn't realized that this was an immense gesture of trust and inclusion, taking me into the *sanctum sanctorum*.' (Trodd says that, by the end of Potter's life, he had been to the flat 'once or twice'. Amiel recalls it as 'a little austere, but quite well cared for. It had pictures on the walls and lots of bookshelves.')

Meeting Amiel for a fourth meal, Potter told him the full history of his illness and treatments, to give him more understanding of what Marlow has been through. Amiel says he did this

completely dispassionately and without any self-pity. It was so appalling that the tears rolled down my cheeks. When we left the restaurant, I offered him a lift and he said he'd rather walk. I watched him go, this very thin man, six foot but stooped and with a very stiff walk. And I found myself intensely moved by him. I did really grow to love him in a way that quite astonished me . . . Much later, in a radio interview, he said we were like brothers on the script.

On one occasion Amiel went to Ross-on-Wye: 'Margaret answered the door – this wholesome, hearty, attractive woman. I was completely unprepared that someone like her should be Dennis's wife. I'd expected some haggard, haunted-looking woman, and Margaret exuded a natural, wholesome, feet-on-the-ground-ness. The moment I met her I understood something else about Dennis – how he'd survived for as long as he did.'

Pre-production time was now running short. Amiel had begun detailed planning when 'Dennis rang me and said, "Jon, you'll be very pleased to know I've decided to rewrite the whole thing." At which point I panicked – I think my voice went up an octave: "But Dennis, we only need to work on a few specific things." "No, no, I can't do that, I'm going to rewrite the whole thing." Having worked as a literary manager, I knew how often writers could throw the baby out with the bathwater, and I was enormously anxious.' But Potter knew what he was doing: 'He rewrote one episode a week,' says Amiel, 'completely from beginning to end, all in longhand. And there wasn't a weak line or a bad scene that he didn't strengthen, there wasn't a strong line or a good scene that he threw away. I have never known any writer edit their own work with such astounding surefootedness.'

Potter said of this drastic rewrite:

I became aware that I was holding back on something, some sharpness – it needed to be more honest – and Jon's very good at pushing stuff at you or pulling stuff from you, perhaps a bit of both. But I knew if I started changing Scene A and Scene G, say, then it wouldn't be A and G that would change, it would be A to Z, so I decided I would redo them all . . .

I made Marlow suffer more. I made him more bitter at the beginning, and I made his relationship with his wife stronger, but I also allowed her to attack his evasion in using his illness both as a defence and as a form of attack rather than addressing what was really going on. Small changes in scenes here, there and everywhere would gradually become more dominant, so I would have to rewrite what was around them as well and rethink the emotional trajectory of it.

Most of the first draft of *The Singing Detective* has disappeared, though Potter incorporated some typed pages from it into his revision. Only the typescript of episode 2 survives complete, and this confirms Amiel's feeling that the original draft 'wasn't quite there'. The plot and characters are the same, but the writing often lacks the tautness of the revision. The second draft, handwritten by Potter on loose-leaf sheets and dated 'October 1985', corresponds almost exactly to the published text of *The Singing Detective* – with the exception of the sixth and final episode. 'The last episode,' says Amiel, 'though greatly improved, still wasn't quite right so he sat down and did it again. I had location managers tearing out their hair because they didn't know what to book for episode 6.'

This final draft of the episode, made in December 1985, removed a characteristic Potter end device. John Cook, who interviewed Potter in 1990, was told by him that the serial was originally to have concluded with the revelation that the arch-manipulator of all the narrative strands had been not Marlow, but Noddy, the old man who clambers into bed with him. Moreover Noddy was to have been revealed as none other than Potter himself – a throwback to *Under My Skin*, where Jack Black's 'enemy' was to be revealed as Potter. The pen-ultimate draft of episode 6 has a hint of this: the patient Reginald, who is reading Marlow's novel, discovers that he and Mr Hall appear as characters in it, saying lines that they have indeed said in real life (out of Marlow's earshot). Marlow denies any knowledge of this – he says there is no hospital in his book – and it appears that even he is the creation of an all-controlling author. Meanwhile we see Noddy cackling maliciously at this conversation between Reginald and Marlow.

Potter told Cook that this was 'a joke Jon [Amiel] couldn't live with', and Amiel says it was too much 'like a solution to a crossword puzzle'. Potter removed it, though the serial as produced does retain traces of a mysteriously close relationship between Noddy and Marlow.

While Potter and Amiel were slogging it out, Rick McCallum departed abruptly for Hollywood. As Amiel puts it, 'Rick jumped ship in favour of Nic Roeg's *Castaway* which Dennis felt as an acute betrayal.' McCallum denies this: 'Absolute bullshit. He used to say to me, "Why do you keep sticking with me? Why don't you make your own movies?"' Trodd says that the BBC staff producer, John Harris, was 'just an in-house official, so I graduated to being the effective producer'.

Jonathan Powell watched the ups and downs of the Potter–Trodd partnership with some amusement:

You never knew what was really going on between them – whether all the rows were for real, or a kind of manufactured hothouse that was necessary to them both, in order to produce work – that they had to be in this kind of tortured relationship. It drove me barking! But I am curiously fond of Ken, and admire him a lot. He's a very warm character, and he can genuinely articulate his reasons for doing things much better than most people I know.

Jon Amiel describes the partnership as having a sado-masochistic tinge – 'forged in pain and conflict' – with 'Dennis willing to dish the abuse, and Ken willing to absorb it. Dennis afterwards said that Ken's main contribution [to *The Singing Detective*] had been panic and despair. The one thing that had really occupied him was the music.'

Potter still hoped that the hospital scenes in *The Singing Detective* (like the proposed *Under My Skin*) would be made chiefly in the studio, on videotape, as true television rather than film ('Dennis felt that film downgraded the power of the writer, compared to the electronic studio,' says Trodd). 'But in the end everybody wants to use film,' Potter said a few years later. 'Jon obviously did, and that decision was made very early on, and without any struggle from me . . . The money [for filming] was there if we agreed to do it all on 16 mm., which we did.'

The part of Marlow had been earmarked for Nicol Williamson, who had also been considered for Arthur in the BBC *Pennies*. But Amiel 'felt passionately that he was the wrong choice – he had the rage, cynicism, irony, eloquence, but he would never make you cry'. When Williamson turned it down, Trodd and Amiel turned to Michael Gambon, with whom Trodd had worked on Beryl Bainbridge's television play *Tiptoe Through the Tulips*. 'Michael was acting's best-kept secret,' says Amiel. 'Every actor listed him among their ten best actors, and yet virtually no one in the public knew who he was.'

Like Marlow and Potter, Gambon came from a working-class background. Brought up in Camden Town, he had failed the Eleven Plus and left school at fifteen to become an apprentice toolmaker. He never trained as an actor, and moved straight from the Communist-run amateur Unity Theatre in London to the professional Gate Theatre in Dublin (where he had been born) and thence, as a spear-carrier, to Olivier's founding company at the National Theatre. In 1985, having just appeared as Oscar Wilde in a three-part TV drama, he was playing Lear at Stratford.

Gambon, like Amiel, was in awe of Potter's scripts – and of Potter himself. 'I remember he attended the very first read-through,' says Gambon, 'in a church hall in Kensington, and sat opposite me, and we read through all six plays. And I just shook all the time. I was frightened to look at him, because it was such a brilliant piece of writing I couldn't possibly match it, couldn't come up to it.' Amiel recalls that 'at the end of the read-through – where Dennis himself had read the part of the schoolteacher, wickedly well – he was white in the face. I went up to him, and he said, "I never realized this thing was so fucking near the bone." '

The first assistant director on *The Singing Detective*, Rosemarie Whitman, who was later to work closely with Potter, recalls him at the read-through:

Ken Trodd had said he was very difficult, and consequently no one spoke to him, and he was sitting there all by himself. And the read-through broke for lunch, and I needed to ask him some questions. And he was very friendly, and I was quite shocked, because I'd been told he'd bite my head off. He was fiddling with his hands, and I asked if there was a problem, and he said his skin was causing him great distress, and he'd have to go soon. He just hid his hands under the table and sat very quietly. I just felt very sorry for him.

As usual, he mostly kept away from the filming. 'I think he came to the shoot twice,' says Amiel. 'He sat around looking very listless and rather bored, and I teased him that I knew why he wasn't coming more often – he hated not being the centre of attention. He grinned ruefully, by way of acknowledging the truth of this.' Gambon recalls that 'Dennis came to the hospital [an abandoned hospital in Tottenham] once or twice, to watch us shooting these scenes'. Gambon found his presence both helpful and disarming: 'My discussions with him were about things like what it's like to have your hands locked with arthritis, his skin problems and things. He showed me how he held a cup. And I got a bit shy lying in this hospital bed . . . pretending to be a man suffering from what he actually had.' Yet Gambon did experience a little of what Potter had been through: 'The make-up I wore to make me look like I had psoriasis had a huge effect on people. Nobody ever wanted to have lunch with me. It was an odd feeling when people got embarrassed and shied away from me. I spent most of my time on my own.'

Amiel made further alterations in the script while shooting. 'I cut large chunks,' he recalls,

and made considerable changes without warning [Dennis], and he never commented once. One of the traps of his work is that he writes with such specificity and authority that the temptation is to treat the text as some golden treasure map that must be adhered to. If you want to change it, you damn well better replace it with something as specific and intensely felt . . . That he never intervened in that was another of the many surprises of working with him.

However, he joined Amiel for the editing, where they agreed on yet more changes, increasing the number of 'associative' cross-cuts between the various strands. Potter described this as the 'last and most important rewrite of all'.

During the editing, Amiel witnessed a classic row between Potter and Trodd. 'We'd all been watching episode 2,' says Amiel,

and when it was over, Ken began one of his enormously periphrastic commentaries, full of qualifications and subordinate clauses. Dennis cut him off with: 'Ken, you've got a bogey on your nose.' Ken, deeply offended, brushed his nose, and started again. But Dennis wasn't going to have any of this: 'Ken, you've *still* got a bogey on your nose.' That was it. 'Don't be so *fucking* silly, Dennis,' yelled Ken, threw a chair across the room, and went out, slamming the door. And all this under the absolutely appalled eyes of the editor, who thought he would be sitting in on a conference of the greats. Actually it was the only 'creative discussion' I ever heard between Dennis and Ken!

*

On Monday 17 November 1986, the morning after the first episode of *The Singing Detective* had been shown on BBC1, the *Evening Standard* diary column reported Potter as saying, 'I feel as if I've scraped out my bone marrow to offer viewers.' A little later, he recalled 'the tensions and difficulties of sitting down [to watch] the first episode, and wondering what the hell people are going to make of it – and then finding that they actually do follow me, they *can*, and they're not to be underestimated, people.'

Hugh Hebert wrote in the *Guardian* that morning, 'It was worth the cost of a pair of opera stalls just to see Michael Gambon . . . A lot of this film . . . directed with enormous panache by Jon Amiel . . . is about the anaesthetic power of the imagination to quell the body's suffering, a subject on which Potter has a fat file of painful personal research . . . He uses and abuses the conventions of the Chandleresque pulp thriller brilliantly.' Mark Lawson wrote in the *Independent*, 'So extensive and intemperate had been the advance publicity . . . that, sitting down to watch it, you thought: this had better be a masterpiece. On the evidence of episode 1 alone, it is.'

The same Monday morning, Potter appeared again on Radio 4's *Start the Week*. 'It was a startling performance,' wrote the author of an anonymous profile of him in the next weekend's *Sunday Times*.

Disregarding the customary politeness which prevails on such occasions, Potter irascibly bore down on his fellow guests, Ian Hislop and Frederic Raphael, in a way which embarrassed not only them, but many who heard it. All over Britain, an opinion was being formed. Dennis Potter is a prickly, misanthropic man with a grudge against the world.

What was not generally known is that Potter is currently in the midst of one of his periodic attacks of psoriatic arthropathy . . . Potter, in acute discomfort, had spent a sleepless night steeling himself for the radio ordeal . . .

Ian Hislop, editor of *Private Eye*, recalls that Potter

began by laying into me, describing something I had written as the lamest and most depressing thing he had ever heard. He said I had made him feel even iller than he usually did. Potter then began talking about his critics and Raphael decided to get stuck into Potter. He asked him why on earth he was so grumpy since everyone told him he was a genius the whole time and offered him more commissions than he could possibly write. 'What more do you want?' asked Raphael . . . Potter smoked and fumed and it all became extremely aggressive.

The day before the second episode of *The Singing Detective* was to be shown, the *Daily Mail* printed an interview with him by Steve Absalom, who wrote, 'You will never hear a word of self-pity pass his lips, and he will turn the conversation with a shaft of wit to head off any attempt to sympathize . . . "I haven't conquered [the psoriasis] yet. I know for example that I will probably be out of action between February and April next year . . . But after twenty years I am prepared for it. That is the glimmer of hope which I want to come out of *The Singing Detective*."'

The third episode included the scene of Mrs Marlow having sex with Binney among the Forest trees. *Today* newspaper reported that 'some BBC officials' had been demanding that Michael Grade should 'order cuts' in this, fearing 'yet another political and moral attack on the BBC. (Trodd says that Potter had leaked this to the press, realizing that the coverage would attract more viewers.) After an 'emergency meeting', Grade had 'accepted the programme-makers' case that the scene was vital to the plot'. Potter himself confirmed this: 'Michael Grade called a meeting which I could not attend because of illness and they impressed upon him that he would be in much hotter water if he made the cut than if he left the scene in.'

Grade himself says:

I quizzed Ken and Jon about the scene's context in the piece. We looked at it frame by frame – I wanted to be sure we could defend the angles from which it had been shot, and that it wasn't lingering. And I told Jonathan [Powell], 'I haven't got this far in television to start cutting Dennis Potter's work.' I didn't refer it to Alasdair Milne [Director-General] – we didn't cut a frame of it.

The day after the episode was shown, *The Times* quoted Grade as saying it was 'not an easy decision . . . There are very few people in television drama you are prepared to trust with scenes like this. Dennis Potter is one of them.' Mary Whitehouse said that the episode reinforced the conviction of her Association that 'broadcasting must be brought under the Obscene Publications Act, and I shall write . . . to both the Prime Minister and the Home Secretary.' Potter told Steve Grant of *Time Out* that he put four-letter words into his scripts to distract the television bosses from larger issues: 'It's always good to sprinkle a few "fucks" around just to keep the dogs off the scent. I only care if they start telling me what the theme should be and tell me what I should be saying.' The fuss about the scene in the woods did indeed bring more viewers to *The Singing Detective*; having started out with about 8 million viewers for the first three episodes, it acquired around 10 million for the second half of the serial.

Nicholas Shakespeare, reviewing the third episode in *The Times*, described it as 'the most compelling television drama I have ever seen', and judged that the BBC 'must be fundamentally healthy at its core' to have 'the courage, imagination and production values to make something like this'. He added, 'A man who can create such a dramatization of his own life, illness and fantasies . . . is quite simply a genius.'

Radio 3's *Critics' Forum* discussed *The Singing Detective* the day before the showing of the fifth episode. A. S. Byatt called it 'an extraordinary work of art . . . most beautifully put together', but had 'slight doubts about the narrative structure of the actual detective story . . . I feel that there's something a little weak . . . about the series of motiveless murders and spy plots, which I don't see becoming completely resolved'.

The series won thirteen BAFTA nominations but only two awards – to Michael Gambon for Best Actor, and to the graphics artist. Jon Amiel describes the award ceremony as 'a sick joke. That Dennis could be sitting there getting progressively drunker and not hear his name mentioned once was simply a crime . . . The Writer's Award . . . went to the guy who wrote *Only Fools and Horses*.'

Sarah Potter says that her father did not realize what he was achieving in *The Singing Detective* until it was finished. 'It was when he tried to turn to the next project that he realized how much of himself he had emptied into it.' He had said as much to Jon Amiel after the read-through – 'I hadn't realized it was so close to the bloody bone' – and to an *Observer* journalist while the serial was being shown. 'Although he has two projects already written,' reported this anonymous profile-writer, 'he has not been able to work since *The Singing Detective* started shooting and he blames this on causing Marlow to be too similar to himself . . . "Without planning it, I have got too close to something."' He admitted he thought it possible that watching the final episode, in which the Singing Detective shoots his sick *alter ego*, might galvanize his writing self into life again. He added, 'In finally exorcising Marlow, I hope that somehow I may leave my illness behind.'

PART FOUR: 1986–1994

The ending is sooner than I thought

———

CHAPTER I

Dirty old man

—

It was untrue that he had not been able to work since *The Singing Detective* started shooting. He had written the first draft of episode 1 of a new television serial, *Blackeyes*, in October 1986, the month before the start of transmission of *The Singing Detective*. Sarah had made a typed fair copy for him.

Blackeyes takes its title from a Russian folksong which had become a Thirties hit, and was recorded by Al Bowlly. This first draft opens in 'a nightmare laboratory', with the severed head of an elderly writer, Maurice Hay, trapped but alive inside a glass dome. The lab is full of 'beautiful near-naked women', who taunt the head as if they were posing it for fashion photographs: 'All we want you to do is move your eyes . . . Down! Up! Left! No, left! Up! Down! You asshole!' It is literally a nightmare (which Potter would repeat in *Cold Lazarus*), and Hay wakes in his seedy Fitzrovia loft apartment. 'The Sisterhood strikes again,' he mutters to himself, lighting his first cigarette of the day. 'Bloody women. Can't trust them . . . Where've you got to this time, you selfish little trollop?' He is addressing a battered fashion dummy, which is buried beneath his blankets – 'In sheets that need washing,' grumbles the dummy in a sexy movie-actress voice, for in Hay's mind he conducts conversations with it.

Looking down into the street, still in his grubby underwear, Hay sees (according to the direction) 'a strikingly beautiful young woman – known as Blackeyes – who is tip-tapping on high heels along the far pavement. She has long, jet-black hair . . .' Hay mutters, 'I don't know whether to kill her today, or . . . to wait a bit.' Blackeyes goes through the entrance to the Underground, and (while an offscreen barber-shop quartet sings 'Ain't She Sweet') descends the escalator past a lingerie advertisement in which she herself is the erotically posing model. Reaching the platform, she stands in front of a huge body-lotion poster, again featuring herself, on which someone has scrawled 'THIS ADVERT IS OFFENSIVE TO WOMEN'. We then hear in voice-over Detective Inspector Blake, speaking in the Marlow manner: 'Tell you what, old son, a tube train can make a right old plate of scrambled eggs . . . Question is – did she jump, or was she pushed? Who broke the bleed'n' eggs?'

We see that Hay is standing just behind Blackeyes, and as the train roars into the station he lurches forward as if about to push. We cut to the dummy in the loft apartment, purring sexily, 'Oh me. Oh my. You naughty, naughty boy.' Cutting back to the Underground, we see Blake and a young policeman examining a covered body which is presumably Blackeyes. The camera moves in on the big poster with its lotion bottle, and we dissolve to the bottle itself, on a table in an advertising agency. In the next room, bikini-clad models are lining up to audition. Blackeyes is among them, and Rosie, a busty model, makes overtures of friendship to her:

ROSIE: You've got pretty little tits, love.

(BLACKEYES *is a little offended, but tries not to show it.*)

BLACKEYES: Yes, I know. Too little.

ROSIE: Oh, no! Look at *these*, willya? You'd think I'd had silicone stuffed in, wouldn't you? (*Laughs.*) Like bleed'n' great melons, ent they?

(BLACKEYES *laughs, relieved by the obvious lack of enmity.*)

BLACKEYES: I shouldn't complain if I were you.

ROSIE: Oh, no? My fella says they bruise his bleed'n' ears.

Back in the loft apartment, old Hay is urinating in the sink ('Auden did it,' he says when the dummy complains), and protesting that his latest novel has not been shortlisted for the Booker Prize (Potter's *Ticket to Ride* had just been called in by the 1986 Booker judges but was not on the shortlist). 'It's your attitude to women,' the dummy tells him. 'That's why they ignored you.' We dissolve to the audition room at the agency, where Andrew Stilk, who will direct the body-lotion commercial, is about to turn down Blackeyes because they only want blondes. However, Jamieson, chairman of the lotion company, insists that she be auditioned (he clearly lusts after her). Stilk tells her that when the music starts, 'You can do anything you like . . .' Blackeyes reacts to the roomful of men with a 'strange near-blankness . . . a formidable indifference'.

In the loft, Hay hears the radio news announce the death of one the Booker judges, a woman critic who has always attacked his work. As he is exulting, the entryphone buzzes. A spiky-haired young journalist, Mark Wilshir of *Kritz* magazine, has arrived to interview him, and a photographer soon follows. Hay protests that he did not agree to a photograph – 'Is this the way you would treat Henry James?' – but Mark tells him, 'Listen – they're going to put you on the cover . . . You're on your way to being a *cult* with our lot.' This was based on Potter's memory of being interviewed, a few weeks earlier, for *Blitz* magazine. The journalist, Jonh (*sic*) Wilde, described him 'ducking from the camera' and treating it as an 'intrusion' into his flat. Potter told him, 'I hate the young, passionately. I wish them *all* ill.'

We revert to the scene of Blackeyes with the other models at the agency, and this time we hear Hay's niece Jessica (in voice-over), herself a former model, telling him he has imagined the scene with Blackeyes and the other models all wrong – they do not behave like that. She is in a taxi with her uncle, taking him to an expensive lunch. As they reach the restaurant, we cut to Blackeyes in the studio of Tony, a photographer, who is giving her the same posing instructions as in Hay's opening nightmare: 'Down! Up! Left! No, left! Up!' Her eyes fill the screen – and become the tunnel in a Ghost Train at a funfair, where a little girl, Jessica back in childhood, is riding with her uncle. 'It was *lovely* and nasty, Uncle Maurice!' she tells Hay.

In his studio, Tony pretends that Blackeyes' blouse is reflecting unwanted light. She agrees to take it off. We cut to the adult Jessica giving her uncle lunch, and it now appears that Blackeyes' experiences at the lotion audition were actually Jessica's. Her uncle is going to use them in a novel, his first for twenty-seven years – presumably the one that will fail to make the Booker shortlist. Jessica protests at this exploitation of her memories: 'Can't we talk about something else?' Hay tells her, 'But this is my *research*.'

We cut back to Hay being photographed for *Kritz* – 'Look straight at the lens . . . That's it! You got it!' – and then to the funfair, where Uncle Maurice gives the young Jessica a doll he has won at a shooting gallery, hinting that her family does not approve of him: 'Don't tell your mother *I* won it, will you? . . . She'd stab it to pieces with a pair of scissors!'

Her audition complete, Blackeyes is taken out to lunch by Jamieson, the body-lotion chairman, who is a wine snob. 'I know nothing about wine,' Blackeyes tells him, and later, in the same impassive tone, 'I don't have orgasms' – a remark that causes Jamieson to choke on his wine. We follow Blackeyes to the beach at the Cannes Film Festival, where she poses with other leggy models, while dispassionate voices discuss her statistics as if recording the details of a corpse. And this is what Detective Inspector Blake is doing with the body of Blackeyes, after her death in the Underground. The pathologist has found a note on her body, wrapped in plastic. 'It was in her vagina,' he tells Blake. 'It's a list of names . . . Men.'

At night in her London mews house, the adult Jessica has a disturbing dream in which the body-lotion audition, in front of a roomful of lustful businessmen, is overlaid with her fairground visit with her uncle long ago. Without explanation, the fairground music distorts into the 'heavy and fast' panting of male breath. The script ends with the child Jessica riding up and down on the fairground's gaudily painted wooden horses.

Potter immediately made a second draft of this opening episode, dated November 1986 (the month in which *The Singing Detective* began on BBC1). Again, Sarah typed it, and this version was sent to Judy Daish. This time the old writer is called Maurice Kingsley (Potter may have been thinking of Kingsley Amis as a type of the sybaritic elderly writer). Kingsley's flat, like Potter's, is in Great Titchfield Street, his bedmate is not a dummy but a teddy bear he once gave Jessica, and his opening nightmare is of Blackeyes drowning herself in the Round Pond in Kensington Gardens. Events proceed much as before, but the reporter from *Kritz*, who has been reading Kingsley's novel about Blackeyes, now suggests to him that the girl has a 'sort of zombie' manner 'because of what happened to her when she was a little –'. Kingsley hastily interrupts him; but the young man presses the point: 'I mean, where did this material come from? Did you use anything from your own childhood – Did something pretty bad happ–?' Kingsley, enraged, ejects him and the photographer from the flat.

The third version of *Blackeyes* was a novel. 'I wrote it,' Potter recalled a year later, between Boxing Day [1986] and St Valentine's Day [1987] . . . Because *The Singing Detective* had just finished, and I felt genuinely threatened by [it]. I went closer [in *The Singing Detective*] than I intended to some of my own, if not actual experiences, but feelings and emotions, and that's very dangerous. And I thought, I can't write. I can't put, 'ONE: EXTERIOR: KENSINGTON GARDENS, DAY.' I will start describing – that's the opening of the novel, the body in the Round Pond. I'll start putting it into prose, really to make sure I can still write, you know. And then it became like a dream, and I just kept at it, and there it was. But it was really to escape *The Singing Detective* more than anything else.

The novel *Blackeyes* – which is even shorter than *Hide and Seek* and *Ticket to Ride* – is dedicated 'To my daughters'. It opens with the adult Jessica, with 'murder in her heart', sitting down to write the truth about her uncle. After years of literary idleness, he has produced a bestseller which is tipped for the Booker. Louchely titled *Sugar Bush*, it has been plagiarized by Kingsley from Jessica's recollections of her modelling career, with her 'docility or sometimes astonishing passivity' as its central theme.

The novel uses all the events from the draft television scripts, with the additional strand of Jessica's sardonic comments on Uncle Maurice and *Sugar Bush*. Then comes a new scene in which Uncle Maurice is driving the child Jessica back to her home in the country from a day in Kensington Gardens, having bought her a doll, Clementine. She falls asleep, and he gets out to urinate, returning to the car 'without doing up his flies'. We cut away from this to the *Sugar Bush* narrative. Blackeyes goes on location to Africa to film a fizzy-drink commercial. She is also picked up in a British seaside hotel (complete with vintage-style dance band) by Jeff, a copywriter and would-be novelist, and she has a motorbike accident which leaves her with cut hands. Meanwhile the adult Jessica invites her uncle to supper at home. He gets drunk and falls asleep on the carpet:

She stared down at him, and noticed that his flies were undone . . .

'Why don't you cut it off?'

The voice came from the corner of the room . . . She had waited a long time for Clementine [the doll] to speak, for the little one was her only witness, and Jessica had never been able to tell her mother what had happened because she knew that she would be punished, or that some worse calamity would come leaping out at her at the turn of the stairs . . .

'My scissors are nowhere sharp enough anyway,' she said to the doll . . .

She begins to kick Uncle Maurice, gently at first, then furiously, breaking his ribs. As she attacks him he croaks 'Sweet Jessie', and she remembers those words from many years ago, in the car on the drive home from London:

'Sweet Jessie,' he had said, leaning across on his knees and kissing the top of her head. He had a snake with him which, mysteriously, became a sticky part of his body, and he made her stroke it, pulling at her hand when she tried to stop. She both knew and did not know what was happening. In the end, the snake frothed at its single eye, or mouth, and she cried out in alarm. He put his hand over her mouth and wept himself until they were both silent. She could smell the tobacco on his fingers and then the sweat on his body, and the arm or the leg of the doll dug into the top of her leg.

Now, contemplating her uncle as he lies helpless on her carpet, she stamps violently on his throat with her stiletto heels. 'It was a snake that did not want to be crushed.' After he has bled to death, she buries him in her backyard, then goes to Kensington Gardens and drowns herself in the Round Pond.

Though Potter said that *Blackeyes* was written to escape *The Singing Detective*, it is in the same multi-strand style, with the reader taking over the role of detective, and its denouement puts into place the piece of Potter's personal jigsaw that was missing from Marlow's story: sexual abuse in childhood.

*

Although it was now two years since Potter had stated in print that 'something foul and terrible . . . happened to me when I was ten years old, caught by an adult's appetite and abused out of innocence', Alan Yentob did not ask about this when interviewing him for BBC2's arts programme *Arena* (30 January 1987) while he was writing the *Blackeyes* novel.

Yentob remarked on the 'startling number of themes' in Potter's work 'which are either revisited or redrawn'. Potter replied:

I think any writer who keeps going over a couple of decades or so is going to be ploughing the same stretch of land, whether he knows it or not. In fact, you don't know it until much later on, and then you not only know it, you welcome it, because you don't ever plough the land properly and . . . there's always the possibility that some coin, or some richness that you didn't know that you knew, is there, waiting to be turned up the next plough round.

This became one of Potter's most frequently reused images, turning up (for example) in a profile of him by Graham Fuller in the March 1989 issue of *American Film* – 'I think any writer has a small field to keep plowing, and eventually you turn up the coins you want' – and in his 1993 interview with Fuller for *Potter on Potter*: 'I think any writer really has a very small field to keep ploughing, and eventually you turn up the coins or the treasure or whatever it is you want.'

Quite apart from reworking the same themes, he was still recycling entire scripts. Three weeks after the *Arena* interview, on 22 February 1987, his adaptation of his stage play *Sufficient Carbohydrate* was shown as a *Screen Two* film on BBC2 under the title *Visitors*. The screenplay, which had been through several drafts during the previous two years, moves the action from Greece to Tuscany, omits the mysterious boat which Jack Barker claims to see on the horizon, and ends with all the adults in the house-party being gunned down by Italian Red Brigade terrorists (the visitors of the title) – but only in the imagination of Clayton, the frustrated teenage son of the American food magnate.

In 1982 the film critic Robert Brown had written, 'Now that Potter is working more and more in the cinema, the time has surely come for this undoubted *auteur* to turn his hand to directing his own screenplays.' W. Stephen Gilbert had said the same in a *Listener* review of *Ticket to Ride*: 'You can feel Potter's movie experience, sense him "seeing the shots" . . . He *must* direct a movie.' In the autumn of 1985 Potter decided that the time had come for this; he would direct *Visitors*, then called *All of You*. Trodd was happy to let him have a go, feeling that it could do little harm to this production – 'small cast, virtually one location, BBC2, if it died it wouldn't matter that much. It would allow Dennis, under protected and benign conditions, to make a move which he and I had been discussing on and off ever since *Pennies*.' However, co-production money failed to materialize, the project was postponed, and when it eventually went ahead Piers Haggard was asked to direct it. Trodd says that Potter was unavailable because he was 'ill again or writing – or both', but Potter regarded it as an insult.

Haggard found that Potter had changed since they had worked together on *Pennies*: 'Dennis was really foul to me when we had dinner – slurping his wine, and saying, "What happened to your career, Piers? It hasn't gone very well." Before, he'd been much more balanced, much more generous.' (Resentment of Haggard taking what he saw as his place as director was probably the cause.) Haggard could also see that the Potter–Trodd relationship had deteriorated on both sides. Potter had given Trodd the first draft script of *Visitors* just before Trodd set off for Italy to work on a project by another writer. Almost as soon as Trodd arrived, he had a telephone call from Potter, wanting an instant response to the draft, which Trodd had not had time to read properly. 'We had the most blazing row,' says Trodd, 'on my side about my sense of being invaded too soon . . . and on his side . . . fury at not being given the right response . . . At the end of the long and bloody call, I tore up the script and deposited it in the bin.' His girlfriend Sellotaped it together again.

By the time that *Visitors* was shown, Rick McCallum had managed to raise finance for *Track 29*, the movie adaptation of *Schmoedipus* that Joseph Losey was to have directed, from George Harrison's company HandMade Films. McCallum had been working on *Castaway*, directed by Nicholas Roeg, best known for *Performance* (Mick Jagger) and *The Man Who Fell to Earth* (David Bowie), and Roeg now agreed to take on the Potter script. The *Track 29* screenplay had already been through a number of drafts at the Losey stage, and Roeg asked for more rewrites, which Potter carried out.

The original *Schmoedipus* had ended with the married couple revealing to the shocked neighbour that it was just all a game, but *Track 29*, as finally made, concludes with the wife (played by Roeg's own wife, Theresa Russell) murdering the model-train-obsessed husband (Christopher Lloyd) – though probably only in her imagination, like the mass killing in *Visitors*. Also, unlike *Schmoedipus*, *Track 29* gradually makes it clear that the 'son' who invades the wife's life (Gary Oldman) is totally imaginary, an invention of her frustrated psyche. An already uncertain story-line is fatally weakened by these changes.

The film was completed during 1988 and opened in Britain that summer, to some good reviews but poor box office. McCallum admits that this was characteristic of all Potter's work for the cinema, saying ruefully that he and Potter together managed to lose the film industry close on '$100 million'.

Potter was to have travelled to America during the spring of 1987 to attend filming of *Track 29*, but Sarah recalls that his health suddenly became 'as bad as in *The Singing Detective*', and Potter himself described it as a 'Gambon-like' attack. He had started to believe that writing *The Singing Detective* had exorcized the illness – 'And then, bang, out of the sky!' During the summer he reluctantly resumed taking Methotrexate, which as usual caused frequent vomiting, but by the autumn it had brought the psoriasis sufficiently under control for him to go to Los Angeles to discuss a new Hollywood project.

Warner Brothers were paying him $162,500 for the first draft and rewrites of a screenplay about the life of Alexander Pushkin, *The Bronze Horseman*. Judy Daish explains how she got the job for him: 'Quincy Jones had a production deal within Warner Brothers, and he was developing a film based on the life of Pushkin. I told them that Dennis spoke Russian, and I came back and got all the books out of the London Library for him.' She says there was a 'hilarious' air about the project – 'some of Quincy Jones's people seemed to be ex-boxers, and they'd say things about Pushkin like "This is a rock'n'roll guy!" which of course Dennis found quite extraordinary.'

An unsigned memo to Jones from one of his team suggests that the script should include 'the burning of Moscow by Napoleon', court scenes that would make *Amadeus* 'pale by comparison', and 'sex, songs, champagne'. What Jones got from Potter was an accomplished portrait of a writer who abandons his revolutionary politics when the Tsar offers an amnesty, but is destroyed by his wife's infidelity and the machinations of the chief of secret police. The screenplay's central motif, unfolded in flashbacks, is the story of Pushkin's great-grandfather, an African prince who was stolen as a present for the Tsar as a small boy. Pushkin realizes that his own angst, which has driven him to become a poet, is an inherited memory of his ancestor's longing for the vanished landscape of his boyhood – an emotion, of course, not unknown to Potter himself.

The Pushkin script was Potter's best-ever work for Hollywood, but was never filmed. Other producers suggested other screenplays – including bio-pics about Albert Schweitzer and Michael Collins. Judy Daish recalls that there was also an approach from a distinguished director:

Martin Scorsese wanted to work with Dennis, and I think had the germ of an idea. We went to Rome to talk to him and a producer, Irwin Winkler, but it was quite a tricky meeting, because Scorsese suffers from asthma, and can't be in a room with anyone who smokes. So all the windows had to be wide open. They seemed to get on, though, and Dennis wrote a sort of treatment called

The Way to Somewhere – and though that project didn't happen, nothing was ever wasted by Dennis, because I think some of the ideas from it were used in *Blackeyes*.

The Way to Somewhere, which Potter scripted in full, is indeed very close to *Blackeyes,* with the heroine's name changed to Melody.

By April 1987, *Blackeyes* had been commissioned by the BBC as a six-part serial, for a fee of almost £100,000. Meanwhile Michael Grade had determined to get *Brimstone and Treacle* on to the television screen at last. 'When Michael Checkland became Director-General,' he says,

he had no programme credentials, and I thought, 'Here's the opportunity.' So I wrote him a long memo, saying that he would endear himself to the creative community by dusting off *Brimstone* and transmitting it. I felt it was a great embarrassment to the BBC that it was sitting on the shelf. I got the BBC's Head of Religious Broadcasting, Colin Morris, to look at it, and he said there was no reason why it shouldn't go out. Armed with that, I managed to persuade Mike Checkland. We did a Potter retrospective, and it was shown at the end of that.

Potter was keen on the retrospective, writing to Grade that such a season would give him the opportunity to 'check on some of them to make sure that changes in fashion and technique [have] not cruelly disadvantaged the writing'. The retrospective (which included the Nigel Barton plays) ran on BBC1 during July and August 1987 and concluded with *Brimstone*. This was followed by an edition of Ludovic Kennedy's *Did You See?* in which *Brimstone* was discussed. Peter Fiddick, who had been one of its defenders in 1976, said, 'It's a curiously wordy piece in places . . . I'm not sure that it would be commissioned now.' The former BBC religious affairs correspondent Gerald Priestland was disturbed by the implication of 'the therapeutic value of rape', and W. Stephen Gilbert agreed: 'I find it less easy to defend now than eleven years ago . . . I don't think the use of rape is . . . clear in [Potter's] mind.'

Julian Symons, reviewing the *Blackeyes* novel in the *Listener* a month later, in September 1987, had similar reservations:

The basic theme is the humiliation of women by men. Blackeyes/Jessica is drooled over by almost every male who looks at her, sexually abused in childhood, rebuked when she resists rape, in general treated simply as an object to be penetrated . . . This would-be moral tale . . . surely finds its resonance in the very material it deplores, lingering over Blackeyes/Jessica's caressing gestures with the body lotion, the attempted rape, the sticky snake that Kingsley makes Jessica stroke.

Similarly, Graham Fuller, reviewing the American edition, remarked that the book 'both indulges and guys the soft-porn luster'.

These reactions did not deter Potter from resuming work on the screen version of *Blackeyes*. During the following year he wrote new drafts of it both as a television serial (in four rather than six parts) and a single screenplay. In these versions, Jeff the copywriter is revealed as yet another 'author' of Blackeyes' story, while Jessica is trying to record the details her uncle's abuse: 'In large letters and a slow and careful script, she begins, "THE OLD MAN WHO". She looks at the words, bites her lip, crosses them out, then writes, "THE DIRTY OLD MAN WHO" . . .'

By February 1988, when he made a second appearance on *Desert Island Discs*, Potter was able to tell the programme's presenter, Michael Parkinson, that, thanks to Methotrexate, his illness was now coming and going in fairly predictable cycles of six months' good health followed by three months' flare-up. 'I'm just about to plunge into a Hollywood movie,' he said, 'though I don't know whether it'll ever get made, so I'd better not talk too much about it. But it does involve the opera.' For his next record, he chose 'a bit from *Der Freischütz*, "The Wolf's Glen", which is grand opera at its most crazy'.

This music opens his film script *The Phantom of the Opera*, written in October 1987 and commissioned by Lorimar Motion Pictures. Potter's version of the Gaston Leroux story is set in June 1940, as the Nazi troops are occupying Paris. Erik, the so-called Phantom, is a former member of the opera company who has suffered appalling burns as a fighter pilot in the First World War; Potter describes his face as 'monstrous, ghastly . . . cruelly ravaged by old burns and the aftermath of terrible injuries'. Obsessed with Christine, the company's young diva, Erik watches over her from nooks and crannies, and is enraged by her love for Peter, a German officer with whom she had a romance before the war – Potter of course manages to sneak in some Thirties songs in the flashbacks portraying their affairs.

'It was a brilliant idea to move the story to the Occupation,' says Jon Amiel, who at one point was asked to direct Potter's *Phantom*, 'but somehow, having made that inspired leap, he never managed to get the synapses firing properly. And none of his movie scripts really had the personal signature of his television work. He would never expose the more raw and tender parts of himself to movies. They were more intellectual than passionate in their energy.'

Nevertheless Potter recalled that the producers were 'ecstatic' over the first and second drafts of *Phantom*. By this time, Amiel was off the project, replaced by a German director, Wolfgang Petersen, who sat down with Potter in Claridge's and told him he 'found the Germans in it unsympathetic and the writing too melodramatic and clichéd'. Potter continues:

I remember it was 1 March [1988], and there were a few flurries of snow in the air as I left Claridge's. Suddenly, as I crossed the road through the traffic, I realized I was nearly in tears. And I thought, 'Fuck it, that's it. Let them play. I'm not going to play with them.'

At that time all these things combined to make me say, 'Right, if the producers think a script is a sort of neat, useful accessory for their director to shit upon and scrawl on, without actually sitting down and thinking it through, then there is, indeed, only one place I can go. I will have to start directing them myself.'

The choice of the German Occupation as a background to the film may have come into Potter's mind because he was now working on a screen adaptation of Christabel Bielenberg's autobiography *The Past is Myself*, about her marriage (as a young Englishwoman) to a German, which meant that she had to endure the horrors of Nazi rule and Allied bombing. 'I had read a review of the book in *The Economist* several years before,' Potter recalled,

and there was something about the review that made me want to get hold of the book. It was out of print, but I got a copy published in Ireland, and then I decided to try and get the rights, for a couple of reasons. It was a story about married love in a way that was unselfconscious. It was the kind of writing that people who haven't written write, an unadorned, straightforward narrative, with a simplicity that left a great deal unsaid. It also felt like the Second World War in a matchbox, in that the great events surged around and beyond the story, and the domestic and the personal became paramount.

Potter arranged to meet Mrs Bielenberg in a London hotel, and she agreed to letting him have an option providing she and her husband had rights of consultation on the script. He bought the option, adapted *The Past is Myself* (in 1984–5) into a single screenplay called *All*

Through the Night, and offered it initially to Thorn EMI, who were then making *Dreamchild*. Eventually it was signed up as a four-part serial for BBC2, with American co-production money and Trodd as producer. Potter's fee was £16,400 per episode.

Potter said that writing *Christabel* – as it was now called – had been a welcome change from the narrative convolutions of *The Singing Detective* and *Blackeyes*. 'There was probably a . . . need for me – as an act of writerly hygiene, if I can put it that way – just to do a piece of naturalistic, straightforward, unadorned, chronological narrative. It was like washing my brain under the tap, a feeling that I needed to do that sort of thing now and again.' But he admitted that the Bielenbergs' right of veto had constrained him: 'I found it hard to write because there was somebody real out there.' Also, he had 'started with two strong prejudices – one against that class of English person, and one against the Germans'. Trodd agrees: 'Dennis's heart wasn't really in *Christabel*. He saw it as a good story, but hated the central character – an overpowering upper-class Englishwoman.'

The Bielenbergs were close friends of Adam von Trott, a leader of the underground resistance to Hitler within Germany, and most of the dramatic tension in *Christabel* is provided by von Trott's arrest and execution after the failure of the plot against Hitler's life, and by Peter Bielenberg's consequent imprisonment in Ravensbrück concentration camp. By this stage in the story, Potter endows Christabel with all the *hauteur* and self-confidence of her class, as she cuts through Gestapo red tape in order to find and save Peter, and uses her family connections in England to persuade his captors that she is a person of influence. But earlier in his script, she is presented as little more than a butterfly. 'I *hate* politics,' she laughs ignorantly as Hitler comes to power. 'What has it to do with me? With us?' This misrepresents the real Christabel, whose book shows that she had a full and sophisti-cated understanding of the political situation in pre-war Germany. Perhaps Potter was rewriting her story so that it was a mirror image of his own, in reverse order. 'She's at first apolitical,' he told an inter-viewer; 'then unpolitical; then sort of regarding politics as dirty but as something that is affecting one's life; and then finally seeing that . . . politics is actually the *totality* of one's life.'

He hinted that *Christabel* had a relevance to the contemporary political situation in Britain:

One of the things I hope people will brood upon when watching *Christabel* is the ease with which, despite people's dismissal of them, outside political events can gradually strip you of everything you took for granted. Without drawing too close a parallel, I wanted to show that some things are changing here which ought to alert us.

Yet, when asked directly what he felt about the Thatcher government, which had now been in power for nine years, his response was surprisingly sympathetic towards the Conservatives and critical of Labour:

You don't have to buy the whole Left/Right package. Some of the best opposition to the dangerous aspects of Thatcherism is certainly coming from within the Conservative Party and that paternalistic element I value. I may not agree with them but the Labour Party in its current spiritual crisis is using old words which aren't attached to the same meaning any more – an emotional rather than a descriptive rhetoric.

Asked about the portrayal in *Christabel* of a happy marriage, he said: 'Have I shown unhappy marriages? Yes, I suppose I have, from time to time. Well, it was a departure, and I didn't want to get trapped in my own little box of tricks. As I say, it was sort of an act of hygiene.'

Jon Amiel was asked to direct *Christabel*, but declined. 'I didn't connect emotionally with it – and I felt that Dennis didn't, either. He even went as far as to offer me a large sum of money, from his own pocket, to supplement what the BBC would have paid me. And it was very hard for him that I said no.'

There is a faint echo of *The Singing Detective* in the scenes in the Black Forest village to which Christabel flees with her children, emphasized by the casting as Bausch the village milkman of Jim Carter, who had played Mr Marlow. Potter also created a musical motif – the repeated use of a haunting pre-war song, Annette Hanshaw singing 'I'm Following You' – 'wistful and yet somehow oddly threatening', said Potter. But it was a single-strand, totally realistic script, offering little directorial challenge other than the re-creation of the bombing of Berlin on a BBC budget. Adrian Shergold, the eventual choice as director, managed this competently, but Potter felt that the pace was too slow.

The title role went to the twenty-two-year-old Elizabeth Hurley, who lacked acting experience. 'You can grasp the basics [of film acting] in a couple of minutes,' she told a reporter. Potter had auditioned her, but was unable to pay regular visits to the shoot – 'He was very sick,' recalls Hurley.

When *Christabel* was screened in November and December 1988, it attracted a large audience by the standard of BBC2 (an average of 7.5 million), but the critics were mostly disappointed that, as Elizabeth Hurley puts it, 'it wasn't singing and dancing and sexy, Dennis Pottery things'. James Saynor in the *Listener* called it 'disappointingly transparent', and even the Potter devotee Graham Fuller wrote in *Voice*, when *Christabel* reached Public Broadcasting channels in America, that the serial had 'only a faint echo of Potter's authorial stamp'. A year after the BBC2 screening, Potter himself described *Christabel* as 'a mistake'.

*

While it was being filmed, in March 1988, he made a rare public appearance in his home town, reading aloud a short story he had recently written at the opening of the new Ross-on-Wye Public Library. Called *Excalibur*, it begins with an elderly man of letters, Sir Ronald Morston (who resembles Maurice Kingsley in *Blackeyes*), listening in the garden of his manor house to his 'plump daughter' Clarissa reading aloud Tennyson's Arthurian poetry:

Poor Clarissa was as grounded a creature as any he had ever come across in all his long years of private living and public service. How in heaven's name did she get like this? Look at her! A middle-aged woman made of suet. Dear Lord, she's even sprouting some sort of moustache on the flap of her upper lip. Why did she let herself go? Whose fault is it? . . .

How peculiar, he thought, that such a big, such a *fat* face should have quite so narrow an aperture. A little nick in a pumpkin. Her mother's mouth was not like that. It used to look rather mean now and again, that's for sure: but it had also been, once upon a time, a shining red bow, stretching in slippery pleasure across the greedy promise of her slight overbite.

For her part, Clarissa is 'almost suffocating in boredom', longing to be released from the claustrophobic ménage with her father.

Sir Ronald is expecting a visitor, and is speculating privately about her:

Some nosy bitch . . . wanted to come and ask questions . . . Wonder what she looks like? Say what you like, a chap still judges a woman first of all by what she looks like. How she's upholstered. The titties, eh?

His brain went *heh! heh!*, but mostly in the back of that part of it responsible for maintaining memory. The sniggering ghost of an old and well-hidden salaciousness . . . She's probably one of those dried-up academics . . . A little monkey face and little monkey habits, turning and turning some paltry scrap of detail pulled down from one of the lower branches of the old Out-of-Context tree: a bloody forest, that. Getting hold of some scrap of so-called information, some alleged insight, and turning and turning it in her paws like a nut with a soft shell, which she'd chew up and splatter out from her busy mandible. Except it would be skin and bone. My skin. My bone . . .

And once they got hold of something, they never let it go. Biography or quasi-biography has become a whole new industry, and most of it posited on scandal. They don't hesitate to lift up a stained bedsheet, or plunder a private letter. Knock, knock, who's there? Seamus. Seamus who? Seamus All.

Sir Ronald has never allowed corporal punishment of his children, but has 'deployed sarcasm as though it were an artillery gun'. Now, he taunts Clarissa about her poor reading of Tennyson's verse: 'Are you pretending to be a fish on a slab? Well, it's a damned good imitation.' She tries not to capitulate to this abuse, but 'years of belittlement had shrivelled her spirit'. Then, suddenly, she flings the book at him, with a shout of 'Bastard!', and it hits him on the nose, causing a gush of blood. Swearing at her, he staggers into the house. The bleeding staunched, he peers out of the window – and sees Clarissa still reading aloud. She has reached the finding of the sword Excalibur, with its inscription 'Take thou and strike!' and is reading, at last, with feeling.

Potter got his eldest daughter Jane to read the Tennyson extracts during his public library performance of the story. She denies that there is anything autobiographical in the story: 'It was just something Dad thought up at the last minute, for the occasion.'

Angela Lambert of the *Independent*, interviewing him a few months later (not long after he had declined her offer to write his biography), noted that he was now providing employment for all his children: 'His elder daughter Jane, an artist, does story boards and picture research for him. His second daughter, Sarah, is his secretary, book-keeper and general assistant, while his son, Robert, works as a builder but is employed by his father's company.' Robert was (and is today) a director of Wyesquash, a company originally set up by Potter to build a squash court and sports centre in Ross-on-Wye, which Sarah would manage; this proved too expensive, and Wyesquash became a small company buying semi-derelict houses and restoring and selling them.

Angela Lambert noted that Potter saw 'nothing wrong' with setting up his children in this fashion: 'I'm putting an umbrella over them until they can do it for themselves. They do nothing shoddy. They're learning how hard work is, and how satisfying when they do it properly, and our society in general doesn't give people a chance to learn this.'

When Jane married for the first time, he provided her with a business as well as a home. 'We bought a shop and garage in a village in the hills above Monmouth,' says her sister Sarah, 'because Jane's first husband was a mechanic, and that was a way of setting them up – though it proved to be a bit of a hopeless farce in the end. And when the marriage ended, Rob took over the shop to keep it going. Dad wanted to set everyone up.'

Sarah gave up cricket in 1987. 'I realized that I was never going to achieve as much as I should have done,' she says. 'If there was anything written in the press about women's cricket, I would always be mentioned, on account of Dad, and that caused a lot of resentment among the others. Eventually I had enough of it all.' Thereafter she worked full-time as her father's assistant, commuting to Ross-on-Wye from a small house she had bought in Cheltenham.

*

A week after the transmission of the last episode of *Christabel*, Michael Grade, who had left the BBC to become Chief Executive of Channel 4, announced that he had brought off 'a real scoop' by signing Potter to write for it. Potter's contribution would be a six-part series called *Lipstick on Your Collar*, 'a semi-autobiographical portrait of post-war Britain'. It later transpired that no such deal had yet been signed (though Grade and Potter had discussed the project), but Trodd felt that, yet again, Potter was conspiring behind his back with Rick McCallum.

Trodd says that he now resigned from his role as joint producer (with McCallum) of *Blackeyes*, but that over Christmas 1988 he and Potter made up the quarrel, and he believed he had been reinstated. Yet, when (in early January 1989) he returned from a trip to Los Angeles to promote *Christabel*, he found that McCallum had been made sole producer by Mark Shivas, the current Head of BBC TV Drama. Shivas says that Trodd resigned a second time, 'and I let him go – I think he was rather shocked, but the two-producer set-up wasn't working'; but Trodd denies that he resigned again, and suspects McCallum of having manoeuvred against him.

News of the Trodd–Potter split took some months to reach the press; eventually it was reported in the *Mail on Sunday*, where Potter was quoted as saying of Trodd, 'I'd had enough of his over-played petulance and inflated ego. He'd resigned and apologized so many times before and I was sick of it . . . We just won't work together again. The leaves of the calendar have blown away and that's that.'

Trodd says he had an 'exceedingly unpleasant and exceedingly brief' telephone conversation with Potter at the time of the split – he recalls Potter telling him 'Never phone me again' – but Potter, speaking to John Cook a year after the row, said that Trodd 'didn't talk to me *at all*' but resigned impetuously – 'I mean, he's a resigner, is Ken.' He told Cook that Trodd had lacked the expertise needed to set up deals outside the BBC: 'Ken doesn't know anything about film, movies, money-structures, all those things a producer is – I mean, he wouldn't exist outside the BBC.' Trodd's retort to this is: 'I *have* existed outside the BBC, often and successfully.' He emphasizes that McCallum's role was that of a line producer, expert in budgets and logistics, 'which I am not particularly interested in, and which, if you've worked in institutional television, you haven't had to be'.

A few months after the split, Trodd told a reporter, 'I think if any move [towards reconciliation] came, it would have to come from Dennis. He may now feel that, for the foreseeable future, he has a producer he's perfectly happy with. It's a great shame. But I suppose I am more likely to be the loser than Dennis.' In the *Mail on Sunday*, he said, 'I will miss it very much. Of the writers I've worked with he was quite the best. We shared a love for the work; the hate tended to be at a personal level.' Though he regretted the loss of Potter, Trodd was not short of other projects. 'During 1989, I was producing, for the BBC, Simon Gray's *Old Flames*, with Stephen Fry and Simon Callow, and Peggy Ashcroft's last film, *She's Been Away*, directed by Peter Hall, which won a major prize at the Venice Film Festival.'

Before his departure from *Blackeyes*, Trodd had agreed that Potter could now realize a cherished ambition. The serial had been offered to Jon Amiel, but he felt it was 'a significant step backwards from *The Singing Detective*'. Nicholas Roeg, who was shown the scripts next, said it was not the way he looked at women. (As Potter remembered it, 'Roeg was on the brink of doing it, and then said no he wouldn't.') Shooting was due to begin on 6 February 1989, and time was running out. 'I decided I couldn't bear to hand it over to anybody,' Potter said.

He announced that he would direct it himself: 'I just feel that there's no place else for me to go. I feel compelled, and all I can say is that I think I'll do it properly.'

Trodd says, 'I didn't disapprove, but I was daunted by the scale of what Dennis was going to undertake.' Mark Shivas admits that 'probably only the BBC' would have agreed to a writer with no directing experience taking on an expensive four-part series, which was to be shot on 35 mm. in the hope that it would be re-edited as a feature film. Moreover Potter's health would not permit him to work at the usual director's speed. Shivas agreed that rehearsals and shooting could be spread over six months, an exceptional amount of time for four fifty-minute episodes, so that Potter could set aside weekends for taking Methotrexate and vomiting.

One of his first directorial tasks was to cast the title role. 'Initially, I went through hundreds and hundreds of photographs of girls,' he recalled. 'There were some women who were just models and some who were models/actresses . . . I made them read and talk to me, and discovered that models hide behind their bodies and don't show feelings; it would be bad for them if they did.' He told several interviewers that some of the girls who came to audition had 'a flick on some of their faces' which he thought hinted at 'casting couch and all that'. One journalist suggested that he was 'fantasizing, maybe?'

The part went to a twenty-two-year-old actress called Gina Bellman.

CHAPTER 2

I had to fall in love with Blackeyes

'I was born in New Zealand,' says Gina Bellman.

My parents emigrated there from Britain in the Fifties – taking the family car on the boat – and I had a wonderful, tomboyish, wood-nymph childhood, climbing trees and running round barefoot. Then, when I was nine, they decided to bring us all home, and we settled in the London suburbs, and it was traumatic. I felt caged.

I was sent to a very religious Jewish primary school, and though I never decided to be an actress as such, I started acting when I was very young, to get rid of my New Zealand accent, because I was being bullied about it. I spent the latter part of my schooldays going to auditions, and I was about to do my A levels when I got offered a part in a film called *King David* with Richard Gere. I was whisked off to Italy for six weeks, where we lived in luxury, and I thought, 'I like this!'

Then I did a big mini-series called *Mussolini* with George C. Scott, and after that I fell in love with an American boy, and went with him to Los Angeles for a year and a half. Around that time I wasn't pursuing an acting career – I was just enjoying being a teenager in love. Eventually I came home to London, got an agent, worked in a restaurant, went for auditions, and within a year, when I was twenty-two, I met Dennis.

Recalling his first sight of her at the audition, Potter said, 'Gina, technically speaking, was not the ultimate "beauty", but was nevertheless more beautiful in a real sense than those almost plastic kinds of models.' Rick McCallum says, 'When Gina came in, I didn't think she was physically the most beautiful, but there was something damaged and troubled about her, and that was the quality Dennis latched on to immediately.'

Gina Bellman describes the audition as unconventional: 'Dennis said to me: "What does it feel like to be an attractive woman in the Eighties?" Nobody had ever asked me a question like that in an audition before – it was always just "What have you been in lately?" – and I felt a joy, a euphoria, that someone had assumed I had a brain.' Did she not feel it was at least a faintly loaded question? 'At the time, I didn't think so. Now, looking back, I think I never really saw Dennis speak to a woman – no matter who it was – without there being an element of flirting.'

She says that, answering the question,

I talked like mad, because I was at an age when you want to be recognized as a woman. I'd been sexually active for a couple of years, with my first boy-friend, and I felt I had deep thoughts – the arrogance of youth! And my meeting Dennis was perfectly timed, because it was exactly at the moment that I wanted to express myself as an adult. Looking back, I don't think I *was* quite an adult, but I was on that cusp, that turning from adolescence into adult-hood, when there's this deep desire to be validated, to be taken seriously. And we just had this banter straight away – such a good banter between us.

Then he asked me to read aloud from the book of *Blackeyes*, and after that I left, and I got a phone call from my agent a few weeks later saying, 'Dennis and Rick would like to meet you for a drink in a bar.' I was so young and eager that I didn't think to say, 'This isn't very professional – can't we meet in their office?' So I went to this bar. And Rick – well, he just oozes testosterone! He thinks he's a real man's man, just Mister L.A. – 'You're a gorgeous chick, whaddya drinkin'?' I think Dennis really loved being around Rick at that stage. I don't think he respected Rick on an intellectual level, but there was a James Bond slickness in him that Dennis seriously wanted to have too.

The two of them just flirted with me, like children, for a couple of hours. And they talked about the nudity in the script, and asked how I felt about it. And I remember the hairs on my neck stood up a little – it was a really inappropriate time and place for that. I realized they should have sat me down in an office, with my agent, to discuss it.

Potter had, in other words, created a re-run of *Double Dare*, with a writer meeting an actress over drinks (with his producer) to ask how she felt about doing nude scenes. He was even fantasizing about other people in the bar, just as Martin the writer does in that play. 'Dennis, with his wine and his cigarette,' says Bellman, 'kept looking around at women and listening to other people's conversations – later I realized he was a terrible eavesdropper.'

She found the conversation about nudity 'quite manipulative. He seemed incredibly direct and thoughtful and caring. But as I've grown up and got older I've realized that's very manipulative, because when people are like that they get your trust and draw you in.' She says he told her, 'There's a lot of nudity in this piece, but it's a very important piece of work. It's about the exploitation of a woman. It's going to be very controversial, but it's going to have a profound impact on British drama.' Also,

he talked a lot about how he could have had a film-writing career, and he'd had this and that offer from Hollywood, but he wanted his work to get through to the *Sun* and *Mirror* readers, to get to coalminers – he always said 'coalminers' as his image for the common man. He was working to get my trust, to make me believe I was going to be involved in something incredibly important on an intellectual level. And it was all incredibly seductive. By the end of that meeting, I thought, this is really important – he's a pioneer, and I want coalminers to switch on and see how women are exploited!

After this session in the bar, Bellman 'read the novel of *Blackeyes*, and really loved it. And I really believed in the piece, and in his dream of it. I felt it was a once-in-a-lifetime opportunity.' Potter and McCallum now set up a screen test for her, not just the usual few minutes in front of a video camera in a production company's office, but an elaborate event on a full-scale set at the BBC's Ealing film studios, where *Blackeyes* was to be made. 'Normally you're given a scene to do,' says Gina Bellman.

But this was Dennis giving orders while the camera rolled – 'Walk over to the bed, sit on the bed, stand up, go to the window, look out of the window, walk across the room, pick up a glass, put it down, pick up a book, put it down.' And I didn't register at the time, but this was a very sexual thing to do – to give orders to a young woman who's feeling very vulnerable. And then we had to do the topless scene – the one when I meet the advertising executives, and stroke the bottle.

Potter himself said of the screen test, 'I just took "Tea for Two" – played the track of it – and made a little mini-drama, the length of three minutes, in which she had to do all these feelings while the music was going on. And she got them – virtually all of them, just like that, so I knew that she was the girl.' This replicates the audition scene in *Blackeyes* itself, when Stilk the commercials director tells Blackeyes to move to the music: 'There will be music. And . . . there is you!'

In a 1988 draft of the script, Potter described Blackeyes' manner as that of 'an alien trying to imitate human behaviour from an instruction manual and not getting it quite right'; and in another direction he writes, 'She has gone back into her mysterious shell.' Finding herself in real-life situations which corresponded to Blackeyes' experiences – the edgy conversation about nudity, the screen test – Bellman was coming more and more to identify with Blackeyes. Talking about the role eight years later, she still tends to use the first person – 'the . . . scene . . . when I meet the advertising executives, and stroke the bottle'.

She goes on, 'I had strong ideas about how I wanted to look, but Dennis wasn't having it at all. He had this one idea of a sexy woman, and it was so Seventies: "She's got to have long dark curly hair, red nails, bright red lips, she's got to be wearing mini-skirts and stilettos."' Bellman developed a breathy, little-girl voice for the comparatively few occasions on which the script allows Blackeyes to speak. Her own eyes are a very dark brown, so there was no need to use tinted contact lenses.

Potter now had to make the transition from writer to director. 'I don't think he was particularly interested in the cinema,' speculates Bellman. 'I don't recall him going to films with an eye on the director's style, or anything like that.' He himself said that, during pre-production of *Blackeyes*, he was not worried about 'where to put the camera, or any of that stuff'. His anxieties were whether his health would hold out, and that he would have 'to deal with lots of people, which is a habit you get out of'. He was about to meet 'more people . . . than I have in the last thirty years'. Gina Bellman remarks on this, 'He'd been a recluse for a long time, and suddenly he was God. Because a director is that – everybody hangs on your every word. And it was as if the only way Dennis was able to emerge from being a recluse was to be the absolute centre of attention.'

Being totally inexperienced, he would have to depend heavily on his first assistant director. Rosemarie Whitman, who had done this job on *The Singing Detective*, had been picked by Trodd (before he left *Blackeyes*) as the ideal person to stand at Potter's elbow. 'I'd left BBC Drama by then,' she says, 'and gone to work in Documentaries, but Ken phoned me up – he always had a stable of people, of which I was one – and said, "I really think you should come and do this – Dennis is going to direct." Dennis had remembered me from *The Singing Detective*, and needed someone he could ask silly questions to, because he didn't know how the whole thing worked.'

Arriving at Ealing, she found a very different Potter from the quiet recluse who had visited *The Singing Detective*:

During pre-production, he kept buying huge lunches for everyone. I began to get worried about the amount he was spending, and I said to him, 'There's no need, Dennis – they can claim the cost back.' I'm sure it was a way of dealing with his shyness. He used to talk about how he was sure people wouldn't like him. But they did, they warmed to him.

Gina Bellman says that later, when *Blackeyes* was on location, 'he'd always hold court at the hotel bar with the crew and the actors, ordering masses of drinks, and being the life and soul of the party (and getting fairly drunk)'.

Rosemarie Whitman discovered that, under all this manic *bonhomie*,

he was so embarrassed about his hands. He was convinced that people were recoiling from them, and that they could see how nasty the skin was inside where they were clenched. When we started shooting, I used to get the make-up artist to rub some make-up into his knuckles, to make them look a bit better. But Dennis was convinced that he was physically unattractive to people.

Whitman began to experience his outbursts of temper – and to learn that fighting back was the way to gain his confidence and affection: 'If you had the courage to stand up to that extraordinary tongue, which expressed no matter what emotion he was feeling at that moment, he was yours for ever. He was remarkably in touch with his own emotions, more than anybody else I've ever met. I think that's why he liked women so much.' Gina Bellman says the same: 'His emotions were so on the surface – he was so unguarded about them. He'd tell you something and burst into tears. That was incredibly moving, and the sense of privilege you felt that this person was confiding in you.'

When shooting began, McCallum suggested to Potter that he should start with a scene that should be easy to direct: that from episode 1 in which old Kingsley (a superbly goatish Michael Gough) wakes in the loft apartment from his nightmare about Blackeyes drowning herself, finds his teddy bear beneath the crumpled sheets, and peers from his window at Blackeyes in the street. 'I wanted him to start off in a room with one person,' says McCallum, 'not to have to worry about reverses and cut-aways and have to . . . overlap dialogue, deal with movements that are based on total continuity.' But McCallum quickly found that Potter did not intend to film it that way at all.

Potter said that, on that first morning, 'I thought, what the fuck am I doing here shouting "Action" – not shouting, really, actually croaking it.' He was so tense that several weeks passed before he could say it 'without sounding as though I was needing an oxygen tent'. But despite nerves, he started 'with a six-and-a-half-minute shot, just to put my mark down'. This immensely long take had the camera prowling around Michael Gough, as if it were another person, a character in the drama, without any of the conventional cuts to close-up or reverse angles.

McCallum put up with this enormously long take, but then realized that Potter intended to continue in this fashion. He told him it was 'wrong, it's a mistake, you're not connecting, you're afraid' – afraid, that is, of the usual directorial techniques. Potter was furious. 'We didn't speak for a couple of days,' says McCallum. 'There was . . . major tension . . . '

Potter refused to abandon his idiosyncratic method of shooting *Blackeyes*, and was still using it when a journalist, James Saynor, visited the set for the *Listener*:

Ten a.m. on Sound Stage 2 at the BBC's Ealing film studios. It's an important scene [in episode 3] – Jeff's ice-breaking encounter with Blackeyes in her minimalist flat, with its reject-shop furniture and window shaped like a cinema screen, all the better for peering through from the mews apartment opposite. Potter feels a little drugged up today. He's on a new course of medication that makes him feel frequently nauseous; so he has to carry around some other pills to stop him throwing up on the set.

During the course of a single take lasting several minutes, Jeff exchanges tea-drinking small-talk with Blackeyes; hears a potted history of her sex life; verbally abuses her; lurches into a close encounter of an arousing kind; pulls away; curses his own crude opportunism and priapism; then, after moments of some tension, hits the right platonic note by telling Blackeyes about his stifled literary ambitions. All in one take. If anything, though, this is a slightly more concise shot than usual; things are relatively broken up today, says Potter . . .

The sequence has already been four days in rehearsal, and the actors have the playing of the scene paced and inflected to perfection. But Potter is still endlessly fine-tuning. When [Nigel] Planer [as Jeff] embraces Bellman, Potter tells him, 'Go on the clinch a little bit more. Make it more Hollywoody.' When Bellman darts up with too much alacrity from her chair, he says, 'You're a very abrupt young woman in your rising. Give me a little less of a spring. It helps *them* [gesturing to the technicians]. But it might also help *you*, irrespective of them.'

Some months later, while *Blackeyes* was being transmitted, Nigel Planer appeared in his one-man show, *I, an Actor*, featuring the archetypal luvvie 'Nicholas Craig'. 'You have to keep everything *small*,' Craig told the audience, 'everything has to *come down*: the hands, the voice – the underpants if it's a Dennis Potter.'

During camera rehearsals Potter would prowl round the actors, making notes in his script. Then he would ask the cameraman, Andrew Dunn, to repeat his movements, with the grips pushing the camera around. The film journalist Nigel Andrew, visiting Ealing for the *Radio Times*, described Potter 'setting up one of these lengthy camera ballets, devoting a whole morning to getting it exactly right. It was fantastically complicated, involving a sort of miniature railway track for the crew and camera to ride about on. In the end this effort failed, and there was a lengthy adjournment while it was rethought and another approach decided on.' Peter Edwards, sound recordist on *Blackeyes*, says that the long takes with the moving camera made it the most difficult film project he had ever worked on – 'a bit like a live show. It was very, very nerve-racking.' The technicians were also worried about how Potter would be able to control and vary the pace of these lengthy one-shot scenes when editing. Edwards recalls: 'We said [to Potter] "How are you going to cut it?" "Don't worry about that," he would say.'

The actors found his technique just as demanding, since they often had to memorize several pages at a time, and had to negotiate a constantly moving camera. Also, Potter spoke his own language when directing them. 'He does ask you to do some weird things,' Nigel Planer told James Saynor. 'Normally . . . the writer wouldn't have such a complex way of putting what he wanted to say. You'd get the gist of what he was trying to do, and then *interpret* that. But with this it's quite difficult, because Dennis is actually specific about the *means* of interpretation as well. So you just have to go with it, and trust him.' Gina Bellman puts this more bluntly: 'Dennis was always incredibly specific about shots and the costume and the look, very involved in every visual detail. But he didn't know how to get a performance out of an actor. We talked for hours about the content of the piece, but creatively you were out on a limb, really.'

Talking to journalists, Rick McCallum kept to himself his reservations about Potter's style of direction: 'Most directors are such wankers – they're craftsmen, but they actually have nothing to say.' Cameraman Andrew Dunn spoke out in favour of Potter as director: 'The exciting thing is that it's a naïve, uncluttered approach. He doesn't know what's possible and what isn't, so he goes for the impossible.' But in private, McCallum was still scathing, dismissing Potter's claim that he was rewriting 'the grammar . . . of current film procedures' as 'bullshit' concocted for the media. Today, McCallum says of *Blackeyes*, 'In terms of direction, it's like a student film.'

Rosemarie Whitman, however, is convinced that Potter was not simply being naïve:

It wasn't that he couldn't cope. Dennis did know what he was doing. But he was at the height of his arrogance – he'd had this massive success with *The Singing Detective*, and everyone was very sycophantic to him. Consequently he believed he could do anything, and everyone was nervous of him. No one dared to criticize him, to tell him he shouldn't do it that way – though afterwards, when *Blackeyes* was being branded a failure, they were the first to blame him.

He was eager to explain his technique to journalists visiting the set. He told James Saynor, 'Film is totally unaware of what has been going on for most of this century in fiction and literary terminology.' By this, he probably meant that, whereas in modern novels there is much self-consciousness in the narration (what Potter called 'that classic question "Who is writing it?"'), film has generally remained unaware of this. 'There's probably nothing wrong with conventional film grammar,' he said,

except that nobody pays any attention to it. Therefore you get little sort of fibrillations within yourself, little danger signals, that if most people most of the time pay no attention to it, there's something wrong. And, all right, the risk of not paying attention, of not accepting that grammar, is enormous. But when did you last get really agitated and worried in the cinema about grammar?

Elsewhere he said that 'the usual, unthinking wire-fence patterns of film-making (establishing shot, midshot, close shot, reverse shot: all that sort of thing)' were so familiar as to turn every kind of filming into 'the same oatmeal of sticky "naturalism"'.

His technique with the camera made it into an extra character in

Blackeyes. This is most apparent in the opening scene of episode 1, which does not appear in the script and was devised and filmed at the end of the whole project. With the song 'I'm Getting Sentimental Over You' playing in the background, the camera prowls around a roomful of mannequins and finds just one living figure, Blackeyes herself. She backs into a crevice in the wall, holding her hands in front of her face to fend the camera off, as if it were a voyeur or worse. 'People said that the camera was moving voyeuristically,' commented Potter. 'But, in fact, it was supposed to be moving in an uneasy, sniggering, lecherous, male way.' Elsewhere he said he was 'trying to use the camera as the force of alienation itself. It was at one and the same time prurient and dispassionate. It was trying to get into the subject *and* prowl round it. It was trying to be objective at the same time as it was being contaminated.'

The technique worked particularly well for his characteristically long dialogue scenes between two characters. Filmed or recorded conventionally, these had always tended to slow down his plays since *Where the Buffalo Roam*. But the prowling camera in *Blackeyes* brings them alive; for example in the mortuary confrontation when Blake, the detective (played by John Shrapnel), confronts the guilty-seeming Jamieson, head of the body-lotion company (Colin Jeavons), with the corpse of Blackeyes. The camera, never still, examines both men and the girl's body with a mesmerizing restlessness.

Gina Bellman picks on this: 'The one scene I remember thinking was incredibly effective was the morgue shot.' But she emphasizes that Potter was not a perfectionist as a director: 'I've never met anyone with a shorter concentration span than Dennis. By the time he became a director he was bored with himself as writer, and then later, when he edited *Blackeyes*, he became bored with himself as director.' Sound recordist Peter Edwards agrees: 'With Dennis, you did it until Dennis was fed up, and then you moved on, and if Dennis was fed up on take 1, that was it, you never got any more.' Rosemarie Whitman allows that 'he didn't have a lot of patience, and filming is very slow – though he managed to keep the whole project on schedule'.

Potter admitted to being impatient, but saw it as a virtue – he said he had been able to 'forget the writer' and react to the script as if he were 'another person'. He also felt 'the joy . . . of the emancipation . . . [of] not having . . . any mediator between it and me'. He told John Wyver, who interviewed him at the end of production, 'I think the best part of directing was finding that it is exactly like writing. I abandoned my screenplays, really. I changed it as I went along.' To another journalist he said that directing soon came to feel 'remarkably like writing. When it's going well it really feels as though it's coming out of *you*.'

The crew found him unwilling to listen to suggestions. 'Obviously the more experienced you are,' says Peter Edwards, 'the less worried you are about people saying "Well, let me do this".' Potter refused any such offers. 'It has to be a single vision at the end,' he said, 'the sort of basic fascism of art . . . Otherwise it doesn't work, it's nothing.' And he told John Wyver, 'The odd thing [about directing] is that ultimately you are isolated anyway.'

Gina Bellman says that he would change a scene depending on his mood that day: 'Most of the rewrites weren't thought out – they'd be spontaneous. Like one day he'd be angry with me, and the scene would get really nasty. And the next day he'd love me, and it would all be flowers.' One striking change came in episode 2. In the script, Blackeyes and Jamieson are seen in a hotel bedroom just after they have had sex. Potter decided to film their actual copulation, during which Jamieson gasps, 'Spit on me!' Later, in post-production, he added these words and their orgasmic cries to the soundtrack of the opening of episode 1 (as the camera is pursuing Blackeyes in the roomful of mannequins).

Bellman realized that his mood was largely the result of his state of health that day: 'He was in a lot of pain. Some days, his lips would be white as a sheet, and he'd have no colour in his face at all.' On other days, 'you'd never see anyone drink so much, or smoke so much, or eat such rich food'. By this stage of his life, he was avoiding red meat. Rhoda Koenig of the *Independent* described a meal with him a few months after the shooting of *Blackeyes*: 'Salmon or chicken are all right for lunch, he says, at one point, but not red meat. "There's something about mammals – their nervous system is so similar to mine. But I don't give a tuppenny fuck about a fish, to be honest."' Sarah Potter says, 'He didn't like the thought of eating his fellow mammals.'

He said he had 'paid an enormous price physically' for directing *Blackeyes*, 'keeping going with a mixture of sleeping tablets and alcohol and sometimes vomiting on the set. Each weekend, when you're supposed to rest, I didn't have any rest, simply because of the demands of having to take Methotrexate.'

Rick McCallum recalls:

He was unbelievably ill on *Blackeyes*. Every single day, three thirty or four o'clock, he'd be retching for an hour, an hour and a half. On location, sometimes we'd get him an ambulance or a station wagon, and I remember looking through the tinted glass and see him curled up, with his hands cupped around his genitals. God knows the psychological factor behind the way those hands became like that – the business with his uncle. They looked as if they were bent to protect his genitals.

*

Gina Bellman says that, from the start of *Blackeyes*, she and Potter would spend time together. 'When we were rehearsing in Kensington, we'd have dinner in a little bistro on Church Street. Right from the beginning we were spending lots of time together. Straight away we just sparked off each other.' Rick McCallum comments, 'I think he was mesmerized by her, and she by him. They were incredibly close. They would spend weekends together, they'd talk, they'd walk.' Rosemarie Whitman puts it more bluntly: 'Dennis was a bit gobsmacked by her, and she was absolutely gorgeous. He did get silly and gooey about her, but that was part of his shyness.'

Bellman says that, in 'this first chapter of our working life together, I felt so honoured and privileged by his friendship, and there was an incredible exchange between us of secrets and dreams'. She explains:

We both had a sense of being foundlings in our own families. Without putting my family down, they're a very conventional, stereotypical, suburban Jewish family, and their dreams for me were never my dreams for myself. And Dennis used to talk for hours about his own childhood – he'd get tearful, and talk about how in a way he'd wished he *hadn't* been as bright and vivid and brilliant as he was. He'd had this incredible conflict about wanting to be his parents' child, but also celebrating his own discoveries and gifts. And though I'm not putting myself on a par with him intellectually, I think that on an emotional level we had that in common – that feeling of not belonging to our families – and he recognized that in me, and I recognized that in him.

He gave her the sense that she was the only recipient of his personal secrets: 'He'd say, "Gina, you don't know what it's like – every time I'm going to stay in a hotel, I have to get my wife or someone to phone up and check they can give me a room with a beige carpet, because of my flaking skin." And he'd get really tearful and upset about it. It made me feel I was his special friend, and I knew all these things about him that nobody else knew.' Asked if he spoke to her about Uncle Ernie and the abuse, she says, 'Yes. He told me about that. One of the gifts he had was to make you feel that you were the only person who knew a particular thing about him.' Today, she is slightly shocked to learn that he had already said these things to others.

He talked to her about the circumstances in which he had married Margaret:

He used to speak about being at Oxford and feeling ugly, having low self-esteem, being conscious of being ginger-haired. In his university days, he'd felt so unattractive and undesirable, and there were all these incredibly charismatic guys there getting laid. I had a sense that he'd run back home and married his childhood sweetheart as a sort of compromise. But also Dennis was a liar. And that could just have been something he was telling to a twenty-two-year-old attractive woman.

When I say he was a liar, I mean he was mercurial – one day he'd present himself as one thing, and then another time he'd contradict himself completely. But when he was sitting there saying to me, 'You're so lovely, you're just so lovely, you've brought such light into my life', that was all that existed for him. And to me, he'd obviously want to present himself as this incredibly frustrated sensual person, who could have had anyone, and deserved to have had anyone, but went for the safety and security of the sweetheart back home.

The flipside was that he loved Margaret deeply, and was completely committed and devoted to her. I never heard from him that his marriage was unhappy. He spoke so lovingly about her, and their home, and their life together.

I only ever met Margaret fleetingly. We never got beyond hellos and goodbyes and so on. But my impression was that she was incredibly supportive, and had a lovely dignity. She had a wonderful quality of being strong – she knew Dennis could be loud and obnoxious, but she wasn't judgemental, just very open. I think she emitted a lot of love.

Potter did not repeat his prostitutes confession to Bellman, but made fleeting mention of the subject:

He told me one story that I don't remember clearly about a hooker in New York. He used to call them 'courtesans'. And he told me other things that I never believed. He told me that Judy [Daish] had been his mistress for years, and I just laughed. I never believed it – though Judy has always been incredibly suspicious of me, and aloof and cold, and I don't know whether that's based on her thinking that I was too close to Dennis, or what kind of yarns he was spinning about me to her, or whether I knew something about her that she didn't want me to know.

He'd say things like, 'Elizabeth Hurley really fancied me', and I'd go, 'Oh yeah?' And he'd say, 'Yup, I went to visit the set of *Christabel*, and I had lunch with her, and she was playing footsie with me under the table, and then she put her hand on my knee and started stroking my thigh.' And you just knew it was absurd.

He'd say, 'Will you touch my hand? I can't remember the last time a woman stroked my hand.' And so I would – I would stroke his fingers, that were all blistered and pink and horrible, and the skin would be peeling off. And he'd say, 'Can I stroke your arm?' and his hands were horrible, they were hideous, but I'd let him gently stroke my arm. And he was a very sensual person.

He told me about his hands closing up at a very important time in his life as a man – his discovery of his own sexuality. It became a huge metaphor of his not being able to be a sexual being.

Today, Bellman is surprised to learn that his hands had closed up as late as 1972, when he was thirty-seven and had been married for thirteen years.

'He was always going on about being a puritan, but a true puritan couldn't have come up with the stories he did,' she says. 'He was such a contradiction, because there was a part of him that really was a dirty old man, and another part that was so honourable and so gentlemanly.' She gives another example of this contradiction:

He used to get real pleasure out of swearing – he'd say the word 'fuck' very intensely. On the other hand he once said, 'I'm going to give you a present of my two favourite words, and that's my present to you for the rest of my life.' He said, 'One is the word "euphemism", and the other is the word "elbow", and they're my two favourite words, and I give them to you.' He had funny little lips that were really cracked and dry and peeling, so ugly in a way. But he got so much pleasure out of words, and speaking them, that he became incredibly beautiful, magical, when he did.

Yet another contradiction was between his gentleness towards her, and what she perceived as a deep-rooted, sadistic competitiveness, based on sexual jealousy of other men who did not have his physical disability:

He was incredibly competitive, sexually competitive. Sex wasn't finite to him. It was a huge thing, that encompassed his intellect and his ambitions and his dreams.

For example, he'd say, 'Come to lunch tomorrow, I'm being interviewed by this young cub from the *Independent*.' And this young thing, fresh out of Cambridge, would arrive, and Dennis would just destroy him. It was excruciating, and you just hated him. His eyes would be twinkling, and his saliva would be spouting all over the place, and his white lips would be turning red from the wine, and it was like watching a monster. And you'd just see the reporter buckle. And it didn't happen once or twice, it happened repeatedly.

He loved to build people up and then knock them down. He did it to me all the time. He'd say things like, 'You're going to be a great actress, Gina. You've got your soul, you've got your spirit, you're one of the most intelligent people I've ever met.' And he'd give me these lovely images of myself I'll carry with me for ever. He'd always say, 'Gina doesn't walk, she glides on roller skates.' And he used to just watch me walking across the room. But then he'd shoot me down.

When some girls who had done Page Three modelling were coming to do the rape scene with me in *Blackeyes*, Rick and Dennis became so excited and salacious about it, and Dennis was really cold with me, and put me down by saying, 'That could be you – don't you fancy being a Page Three girl?' And I'd say, 'Dennis, yesterday you were telling me how intelligent I was, and how I had such deep feelings.' It was a horrible quality he had, to build up and then knock down.

Yet this painful awareness of his complexities did not disillusion her. 'I loved Dennis so much – I really loved him and cared about him. It was the most joyous time, a fantastic summer, with Dennis on location, in his panama hat, telling wonderful stories – an incredibly wonderful, magical time.'

Then the relationship moved into a second stage. 'Dennis started to have feelings for me,' says Bellman,

and we both indulged in it, verbally. The question of it being physically sexual was unthinkable, really. He was very very ill – he was going to his room on Friday afternoons and vomiting until Monday morning (he could barely stand up all day Monday). He had enormous demands on him during the working day, and he was going to rushes every night. But it did become sort of a romance.

It wasn't a sexual relationship, it wasn't a physical relationship, but he would profess his feelings for me, and we would have these dinners, and I would say, 'It makes me so happy that someone like you loves me – and I'm so in awe of you', and it was this incredibly innocent romance. But even that romanticizes it – 'romance' isn't an appropriate word, either, because it was feisty and fiery as well, and he'd pick on me and bully me as well. And we did indulge in quite loaded, sparky, fantasist-type talk. He'd ask me about my sexual experiences, and I'd tell him.

I didn't fall in love with him, but I had complex feelings – I loved being around him, it was like a crush in a way. And we used to get drunk together, drink oodles of champagne, and it was glamorous, and he gave me so much attention.

Asked if he would allude to the fact that the physical side of their relationship was not happening, Bellman says, 'Yes, he would. And he was crude. I don't know whether I ought to say this, because of its effect on his family, but he would say things like "I'd give such-and-such to fuck you", and I'd say, "Well, you can't, and we won't, and it's not going to happen", and that sort of stuff. And I think because he knew it wasn't going to happen, that's why he could say it.'

He made no mention to her of the impotence which Sarah believes afflicted him. 'He didn't talk about whether he was sexually active or not,' says Bellman,

but he spoke with the manner of someone who was – he didn't say things like 'I haven't made love to a woman in years.'

It wasn't going to be physical between us because I had no interest in sleeping with him whatsoever. Frankly, what good-looking raven-haired twenty-two-year-old was going to sleep with a fifty-five-year-old ginger, decrepit, decaying man whose skin was falling off and had to wear pyjamas under his trousers, tucked into his socks? That sounds cruel, and it's not how I mean it.

According to one source, Bellman privately told another actress that the relationship with Potter had become physical. However, Rick McCallum thinks that this is very unlikely to be true: 'On the basis of what I saw, there was never any manifestation of a physical relationship between Dennis and Gina throughout *Blackeyes*. But he yearned for her, all the time. The key word to Dennis's life is yearning.'

Told of the allegation, Gina Bellman says, 'In a way I don't blame people for saying there was a relationship, because in a way there was – it's just that he wasn't physically unfaithful to his wife, and I didn't sleep with him. We were engaged in this lovely romance of the mind, and it was all perfect.'

*

By August 1989, Potter was cutting *Blackeyes* with film editor Clare Douglas, who had worked on *Christabel*. Once again, he began rewriting it. 'Now, editing, I can forget the director,' he said during an appearance on BBC2's *The Late Show* in November. The script included numerous voice-overs by Kingsley, Jessica (Carol Royle) and Jeff, as each laid claim to authorship of Blackeyes' story. These voice-overs would have been recorded during post-production. But Potter now scrapped many of them, and substituted his own voice. Indeed, he began to make himself a character in the drama.

The first striking instance of this comes in episode 2, when the photographer has asked Blackeyes to take off her bra. As she exposes her breasts, Potter's voice breaks in urgently, 'No, I'm looking at her *eyes*. I know I'm losing myself in their luminous glitter. Steady! My foolish heart needs some other kind of comedy.' And we cut abruptly to the hotel dance band playing a novelty number. Later in the episode, as the camera moves in tightly on Blackeyes while she lingers in the hotel corridor, Potter again intrudes verbally:

Closer, closer! The closest I dare – near enough to kiss her eyelids. Oh my God, I'm making love to her – is that what I'm doing? I – stop! Stop it, *please*. (*Dissolve to the dance band.*) Let this music bear away what I must, must not say. That's what it's for.

Gina Bellman had no idea that he had added this narration until she saw a preview of *Blackeyes*. 'Suddenly there was his voice, talking about *me*, and about my rejection of him physically.'

Later, Potter explained the decision to write himself into the script:

There is a line in *Blackeyes*, said by Jessica, in which she says, 'There's no way that you, nor any other man, could ever understand what it is that you men make us women think of our bodies.' Now, the trouble is, it's written by a man – me. That was my dilemma. So I, I did several things at the same time: I made an ironic narrative with, as though it were me, myself as a character, in *Blackeyes*, which was saying, 'Yes, yes, I'm being seduced, I am seducing you, I am showing you – ', instead of, like, the old *News of the World* exposing a brothel, 'I then made my excuses and left', you know, I stayed and screwed, as it were, because I wanted to show it.'

And he told Graham Fuller:

Not only were you showing the manipulation within the story, you had this manipulator *narrating* it. I was hoping that out of that collision, that multiplicity of exploitation and manipulation being demonstrated in an almost explicitly Brechtian way, you would feel the alienation. The idea was to live within it instead of illustrating it. Instead of just moralizing and saying, 'Here is A, and A is bad, isn't it? and I am B, telling you that A is bad,' I wanted A and B to corrupt each other. That was the dramatic method.

Yet he also admitted to Fuller that the authorial voice-overs had been 'a last-minute, desperate attempt to pull all these strands together', while film editor Clare Douglas says that Rick McCallum thought 'the whole thing was totally incomprehensible and it needed someone to explain it'. However, the addition of yet another strand to the narration merely exacerbated the labyrinthine complications of *Blackeyes*.

Some of the commentary was detached and quizzical. For example, as Jamieson and Blackeyes reach their climax in the hotel bedroom, Potter's voice says, 'Fiction, how strange a thing it is. Was that a real orgasm, do you think? No, no, no, all fake, of course. But what happens to her, to me, if, made to pretend, we pretend too often? When do you collect the bill, and how pay it?' In general, though, as Bellman suggests, Potter's verbal intrusions establish him as yet another character who desires Blackeyes.

For example, a little later in the same scene, as Blackeyes spits on a photograph of herself sexily eating a chocolate bar ('Fraggie Bar' again, as in *Double Dare*), Potter says, 'Lips make the same shape for a kiss as they do for a spit. Blackeyes, my unattainable love, which is it I'm doing?' In episode 3 he remarks, 'My nerves still jump at the sight of her . . . *My* mind still plots and schemes to find a way into this narrative . . . ' And in the final episode he goes even further.

As Kingsley searches frantically for his teddy bear, which has been stolen by the reporter and photographer from *Kritz*, Potter's voice says,

No, the teddy bear is gone. And who would want to go down to the woods tonight? There's a dark secret buried in the glades. I know: it happened to me, in the long-ago forest of another's sick and terrifying desire. That's why I – but – ah, he's being tortured, made no more than a battered, moth-eaten old teddy himself, about to be thrown out of the push-chair, face down into a wet gutter, riveleting with old filth.

When the story finally reaches the sexual abuse of the child Jessica, all we see is Uncle Maurice leaning in through the car door, grinning slyly and saying 'Who's a little sleepy head?' But Potter's voice supplies the remainder:

No, you have to imagine the rest, if you must. The snake in his hand has become the worm in her soul. Recollections of abuse, my God, they're hard to deal with, even though I try. There are times when the pen in your hand becomes – becomes, yes, a knife in someone else's.

Potter gave several reasons for writing *Blackeyes*. One was 'to show . . . the way that people are turned into things, and the way . . . men . . . have so consistently used women in advertising, in fiction, in drama – in real life, most importantly of all, as sexual commodities'. Another was to demonstrate 'how men manipulate women, how women are obliged to counter-manipulate, and how that, in turn, damages men as well as women'; or, to put that another way, how 'men write the world and women are trying to rewrite men's writing'. But these purposes were displaced when he added his narration. He described the narrator's persona as 'this slightly creepy character within the plot, overwhelmed by desire and grappling with feminism . . . two impulses [that] sit very heavily inside the male head'. Yet the story his voice gradually unfolds has nothing to do with feminism. He tells us that he, like the women in *Blackeyes*, was once sexually abused; and also that he desperately desires, but cannot have, Blackeyes.

The script ends with Jeff getting the girl (he brings Blackeyes breakfast in bed, and indicates to us that he is just about to have her); but in the finished film she escapes not only from Jeff, but also from Potter's authorial voice, which – as she rejects everyone and walks away from the camera – pleads desperately, 'Hey, Blackeyes, come back!', before reluctantly accepting that she will not. Potter's final words are, 'Oh, Blackeyes, thank you for breaking my heart.' Gina Bellman has no doubt that this is Potter reflecting on his unconsummated relationship with her: 'And I remember sitting there during the screening feeling physically sick. It was as if he'd turned into the Kingsley character, because I began to have the sort of feelings about him that Jessica has about her uncle. And he *did* betray me in some ways – particularly when he made that stupid remark about having to fall in love with his Blackeyes.'

This happened while he was still editing the film. Appearing on a television show, *Saturday Matters with Sue Lawley*, he said he had had 'to fall in love with' Blackeyes if he was to make the production work on any emotional level. He made the same remark in an interview published in the *Observer*:

Potter fell in love with Blackeyes. In case anybody has any doubts, [he] says he can distinguish between falling in love with Blackeyes and Ms Bellman. Anyway, there is seems to be virtually no concern in the Potter household . . . 'If I say I'm in love with Blackeyes to Margaret, she'll just say "You silly man." She always brings me down to earth . . . Margaret is my touchstone. With her I know who I am and where I am.'

Bellman calls this public declaration 'incredibly irresponsible of him – I'll have to live with it for the rest of my life'.

Richard Brooks, conducting the *Observer* interview, met Potter in an editing room in Soho, which overlooked a strip joint with men queuing outside. Brooks asked Potter if he'd been tempted to join the queue. 'I'd rather go to a brothel than a strip show,' Potter answered. Brooks 'rather mumbled the follow-up question: had he ever been to a brothel? He heard it though. Silence followed.'

In his interview with John Wyver, published in the *New Statesman* on 24 November, Potter amplified the remark that had shocked Bellman:

Two things had to happen [for *Blackeyes* to succeed]. One, I had to fall in love with Blackeyes, and two, I had to behave with propriety . . . And of course I did fall in love with Blackeyes, and I found it a very painful experience, but utterly relevant. I mean, I know that now the shooting is over, she is no longer Blackeyes, it's different, thank heaven. But I was, in a proper sense of the word, proper use of the word, besotted.

He also told Wyver, 'It is very difficult to have . . . a true, enduring, honest and monogamous . . . sexual relationship . . . and always will [be].' Yet two years earlier he had told an interviewer, 'The only true passion is monogamy.'

He said to Wyver that directing his own work had made him feel an utterly different person: 'I made touch with my younger self, because I didn't used to be reclusive . . . So now it is emotionally impossible for me to hand ever again my work over to somebody else . . . It is my firm determination always to direct my work in future.' And to Nigel Andrew: 'I couldn't just hand over a script, now, for someone else to direct . . . It's like remembering how I used to be before I was ill. It's been a rediscovery – like the nerves prickling on a limb you thought was severed, then you look down and it's still there! I'm coming out of my shell – I feel it breaking around me – I'm spitting out the last bits of it.'

Wyver – who had not yet seen *Blackeyes* – referred to the confession of sexual abuse in *Waiting for the Boat*, hoping that Potter would talk more about this. But he refused: 'I am not going to describe it in any way, because I don't have the handle on it. It is not the kind of thing that you can solve . . . It's there in *Blackeyes* very palpably . . . the most horrible and vivid expression of hopelessness and dominance.' He told Wyver he thought *Blackeyes* was 'much better than *The Singing Detective* . . . *The Singing Detective* was understated.'

While editing of *Blackeyes* was still in progress, during September 1989, Potter and McCallum took some of it to the Telluride Film Festival in Colorado. Kathleen Tynan wrote in the *Observer*:

This was Potter's first film festival, and he does not care for Abroad. He told the Americans he didn't like the fact that they were consumers, not citizens; that they put ice in their drinks. He said he had only to be out of England for half an hour to feel unhappy, though he added that everything he hated most was English. As for the Scots, the Welsh and the dread Irish –

What movies would Potter be seeing? 'None,' he answered.

On being introduced to Daniel Day-Lewis he declared, 'Now we can indulge our mutual hostility.' Day-Lewis looked baffled . . .

Forced on to a seminar platform together, Potter, [Peter] Greenaway, and two black co-operative film-makers were united only in their reservations about Mrs Thatcher, David Puttnam, and the American deal . . .

That evening a social breakthrough was achieved when Stephen Frears and Dennis Potter sat down to drink and compared notes on cricket. Potter knocked back several bottles of red wine and . . . attacked Frears, told him he shouldn't be making commercials. What did he do it for? 'For the money,' Frears said crisply. 'You mean you're not selling out? You're doing it for the money?' Potter asked. Frears said he liked to practise his craft. There was a pause and Potter smiled broadly. 'Your craft?' he said. 'By that logic the hangman should be out in the street practising his craft.' Frears . . . took this calmly.

David Hare, who was there too, writes, 'Telluride is so politically correct that it's illegal to light a cigarette in a public place. The result was that I had to call the sheriff and say, look, there's this English writer who is suffering from a wasting disease, his only consolation is an occasional fag and he can't get through an hour's interview in the Town Hall without one. The law was waived.' Potter told Melvyn

Bragg in his last interview, 'In the remnant of the first-class train, InterCity, there is one bit for smokers, and . . . if I see people sitting there without a cigarette, I love to say, "You do know this is a smoking compartment, don't you?" Because I've [had] so many, you know – "You do know you're not allowed to smoke here."'

David Hare continues:

Dennis's interview [at Telluride] wasn't very good. He answered with those endless, curling long sentences he sometimes favoured, but also he seemed shrunken and parochial: talking about British television without any concession to the fact that it was an American audience, who might never have heard of Nigel Barton or Ken Trodd.

We adjourned to a restaurant where we had to sit outside on quite a chilly night, so that Dennis could smoke his cigarettes. He *was* confrontational that night – with everyone. But next morning, Rick, he and I all had breakfast together at Denver airport, and he couldn't have been sweeter – solicitous, funny, gentle, telling that awful thing about having to choose hotel rooms with light carpets, so that when he took his socks off the skin wouldn't show on the ground.

Frears recalls how Potter 'laughed at how much of MGM's money he had spent'.

On 22 November 1989, a week before transmission of the first episode of *Blackeyes*, there was a press preview of it in a West End cinema. Those attending included Deborah Orr of *City Limits*, who in her report of the occasion described the *Blackeyes* novel as 'turgid crap', and alleged that Potter's personality was as 'unpleasant' as his subject-matter. Maria Lexton of *Time Out* went even further: 'Potter is . . . a very sick man. He suffers from psoriatic arthropathy . . . It's not a disease that invites a lot of sexual activity and I dare say this may have contributed to the writer's twisted attitude to women and fucking . . . One thing you can't hide is when you're crippled inside.'

Potter was at the press screening, and answered questions after the episode had been shown. Deborah Orr reported that, 'when asked by a *Scotland on Sunday* journalist if he thought *Blackeyes* was indecent, [Potter] told the hack to "fuck off"'. The *Daily Star* made much of this on the morning after the preview. It carried a front-page picture of Gina Bellman, and ran a story headlined 'THIS FOUR-HOUR PEEP SHOW MAKES "THE SINGING DETECTIVE" LOOK LIKE ANDY PANDY':

Controversial playwright Dennis Potter went DOTTY yesterday when challenged about filthy scenes in his new telly series . . . he artfully told reporters to 'F*** Off'.

He searched for the most beautiful woman he could find for his title role. Stunning actress Gina Bellman fulfilled his dream. She's rarely seen with her clothes on . . . The series has little in it but sex . . .

Potter was involved in bizarre scenes yesterday with pressmen . . . who are the only people outside BBC executives to have seen the series. He lashed out at any suggestion the series was soft porn. 'You miss the point, you all miss the point,' he raged . . . And BBC2 boss Alan Yentob defended his decision to screen the series. 'I'm proud of the work,' he said . . . 'It is a major and important piece of drama.' . . .

Potter says Gina . . . is his and every man's 'ultimate fantasy girl'. 'She had to be stunning and I had to fall in love with her,' he said.

Bellman decided to get out of reach of the press: 'I had to run away. I went to the Mull of Kintyre with a friend, and when I went into the village they'd say, "There was someone who flew in on a private jet this morning with your photo, offering money for us to say if you were here." And they were digging out people like my grandmother and my ex-boyfriends.'

Meanwhile Sally Payne wrote in *The Sunday Times*:

The most disturbing scene in episode 1 involves the model stripping topless in front of a roomful of odious lechers. A continuous narration (by Potter himself) is contemptuous of the men, but there's no getting away from the lingering shots of the woman's body. Is this provocative drama or a simple turn-on for male viewers? My gut feeling was distinct unease which verged on outrage the more I thought about it. I became convinced that Potter was guilty of the crime he was condemning.

The next day's *Evening Standard* announced: 'Forget the collapse of Communism . . . One event dominates the week . . . There has already been a rowdy press conference involving the fifty-four-year-old author and scribes who wondered if [Potter] was a dirty old man . . . He gives his recreations [in *Who's Who*], I see, as "the usual personal pleasures, sought with immoderate fervour".'

By Wednesday, 29 November, the day that episode 1 was to be shown, Mary Whitehouse had been shown an advance clip, and commented, 'What I saw was soft porn.' Reporting this, the *Daily Mirror* gave its story a headline that punned on the name of a character in *EastEnders*: 'ALL CLEVER STUFF – OR JUST DIRTY, DEN?'

Reviewers who passed judgement on the first episode included Mark Lawson in the *Independent*:

Some of the single takes are as long as other people's plays. The camera creeps, stalks and stares . . . As elsewhere in Potter, you sometimes have the fear that the philosophical content extends no further than the thought that the child is father to the man, and/or it's funny how potent cheap music is. The message, however, is less important than his use of the medium; Potter . . . is the only small-screen dramatist who is a television writer rather than a writer who does television. His stories build in pictures . . . Too much contemporary writing covers its exits, regulating ideology and form against potential objections. Potter, like Martin Amis, is prepared to risk the funny looks.

Hugh Hebert in the *Guardian* implied that, whatever its faults, *Blackeyes* was required viewing: 'If you haven't seen it, you are by now as far adrift as you would be if you had seen it.' The *Sun* gave an entire page for its television critic, Garry Bushell, to deliver his verdict: 'There ought to be a public outcry about *Blackeyes*. Not because it is too sexy, but because it is a load of old COBBLERS! BBC Head of Drama Mark Shivas deserves TWO lovely black eyes for giving Dirty Dennis Potter the go-ahead . . . If this is art, Rolf Harris is Michelangelo.'

Christopher Tookey began his *Daily Telegraph* review:

Watching *Blackeyes* is about as jolly as being forced to pick through the contents of an exquisitely designed colostomy bag. However, much the same might reasonably be said of Strindberg and Swift. No writer other than Potter is daring to tell us so much about himself, or doing as much to challenge the conventional styles and structures of drama. It is too early to assess whether *Blackeyes* is a masterpiece. But, at the very least, it shows promise of being the most interesting, original and honest work he's done since *Pennies from Heaven*.

John Naughton said much the same in the *Observer* the following Sunday: 'What keeps one viewing . . . is not the profundity of his obsessive insights but his sheer creativity as a dramatist. He is the only writer I know who *writes television*. Others merely write *for* television.'

The *Sunday Times* critic, Patrick Stoddart, prophesied:

It will be an Eng. Lit. A-level question one day. Dennis Potter is (a) The greatest dramatist of the television age; (b) A flawed genius; (c) A dirty old man. Discuss.

On the evidence of episode 1 . . . the jury is still out, and frankly, I wish I had been too . . . Potter . . . has spent so much time and passion revealing something I would have thought most of us took for granted anyway . . . And I can't quite shake off this feeling that the only person involved in *Blackeyes* who is wearing less clothes than Gina Bellman is the Emperor Potter himself.

The *Sunday Express* asked, 'Is *Blackeyes* just blue nonsense?', and their critic John Russell wrote, 'If you or I had our names on the script . . . it would have finished up in the wastebin.' He judged it 'the world's most complicated porn film'.

Over 7 million people watched the first episode (very high for BBC2), but this dropped to just under 4 million for the second. After it, the *Daily Telegraph* headlined its review by Richard Last, 'TWO BORING BLACKEYES'. Last thought the serial 'immensely boring', and guessed that Potter's 'creepy, Peeping Tom voice-over seems to be telling us that the lustful fantasies of his disgusting old writer, Uncle Maurice, are at least in part his own'. Last called Gina Bellman 'a striking-looking actress who can't act', and suggested that soon Potter would be 'writing the music and appearing as the male lead, like Charlie Chaplin'. A week later, Jenni Diski in the *New Statesman* called *Blackeyes*

all very post-modern, but surely we've got to post-post-modern by now . . . Potter's self-satisfied narration is sleazy stuff. It distances the responsibility of the writer to truth, rather than making us look at the real complexity of character and relationship . . . What is lacking so far is any real analysis of male lust. There are endless descriptions of it, but the *why* is certainly not explored.

Among women critics, the harshest comment came from Julie Burchill, who described *Blackeyes* as designed 'to anchor itself to serious subjects such as misogyny and exploitation solely to provide a rationale for its own grubby wanking'.

John Russell's *Sunday Express* review of the final episode was headed 'POTTER PETERS OUT IN PORNO TWADDLE'. Noel Malcolm wrote in the *Sunday Telegraph*, 'In the end I couldn't care less about the exploitation of Blackeyes because her total passivity and lack of character made it impossible to identify or sympathize with her in any way.' Nancy Banks-Smith was loyal – 'It was painful, beautiful and obscure' – but Mark Lawson was now disappointed: 'The sadness of *Blackeyes* is that the latest piece by television's finest writer deserves to win awards for anything (acting, editing, photography, direction) except the script. The director was Dennis Potter, so he can still regard this drama as an advance.'

*

Gina Bellman says that only now, after the press furore, did she wake up to the full implications of what had happened:

Suddenly I became very conscious of the fact that I'd been used, exploited. But I couldn't admit it to anyone except Dennis. And we met a few times, and I said, 'I feel betrayed by you, exploited by you.' So things got tense between us, and we started to see less and less of each other, and Dennis behaved very childishly. He'd phone up, and if I told him I was busy, he'd say, 'You're so ungrateful – I've been called Dirty Den all because of you.'

Just before the last episode was shown, he let his feelings be known to Rhoda Koenig of the *Independent*:

'I'm in the pit of a real depression,' are Dennis Potter's first words. 'Which is why I grin like a fool.' . . . He is staggered by the criticism [*Blackeyes*] has received . . . 'The "Dirty Den" stuff in the tabloids has made me feel personally contaminated,' says Potter. He was greatly upset by the *Time Out* piece that portrayed him as an emotional cripple, by the *City Limits* one that, he says, concentrated on his supposedly 'unpleasant personality'. Not all the worst criticisms have been published. 'The letters I get are *filthy*.' . . .

'What affronts and appals me is that the criticism was personal. There has been a refusal to engage in the terms that have been laid down . . . I feel I've put my head over the transom, and the dumdum bullets have come whizzing at me.' . . . His confidence has been so shaken by the attacks, he says, that he is going to wait until after Christmas to decide whether to proceed with *Secret Friends*, a BBC film about a sexually obsessed couple.

To Radio 2's John Dunn he went even further, saying, 'For the first time in twenty-five years I have to honestly admit that this is probably the end of my television career.'

He told Koenig he was 'frightened' of the last episode:

If you listen to the voice-over, you'll see it's very clear why [what happened to] little Jessica – why that strikes my heart. I've never been able to speak directly about it – no one who's had such an experience has ever been able to speak about it except obliquely. It sits there and makes me sweat even now.

A *Sunday Telegraph* unsigned profile of him on 31 December dealt bluntly with this subject:

For Dennis Potter, loss of innocence came, brutally swiftly, at the age of ten, when he was a victim of child abuse. 'I don't speak directly of that,' he says. 'You lose childhood at one go. Maybe it's the source of the feeling I often have of disgust.' The abuser was a man, perhaps a relative? 'I don't think – I don't think I should say,' he replies.

Certainly this act was the source of the harrowing scene in the last episode of *Blackeyes* . . .

Blackeyes . . . was a failure, as even Potter now acknowledges. 'I messed it up,' he says. 'It was too complex, there were too many strands.' . . .

To *Private Eye* he is 'Den Plodder, the Whingeing Playwright.'

Some while later he told Mark Lawson, 'I knew from the beginning it was entirely about sexual alienation. And that the way to show that was to do it in an alienating way. In fact I seemed to alienate every fucking person in the country.' In fact some support came from the feminist lobby. 'Germaine Greer was very nice about it,' he told an interviewer. 'Well, she's never nice, exactly, but she said something like: "That uptight little shit saw what it was all about."' The interviewer repeated this to Greer, who laughed and said:

He's criticized because people always think that artists should write about what should be, rather than what is. I don't expect him to be politically correct or to write about liberated women because they don't exist.

What he's doing is writing in a bitter and tragic way about the female icon. Men are trying to pursue it and women are trying to be it, so they're both victims. If I see an outrageous female mask of tragic passivity and gross sensuality I don't think it's a reflection of me. But I can recognize the set-up. Fellini gets the same abuse when he gives shape to male fantasies of women. They are not saying this is how it is, they are saying this is how we see you.

Potter continued to argue that *Blackeyes* 'should have gone out as one piece; then it would have seemed much less complicated. It sank into its own complications like someone drowning in a bog!' Ken Trodd says, 'There was an edited-down movie version, which I've never seen – I don't think anyone's got it. It was shown at the Toronto Film Festival. There was a lot of money riding on it being a movie, but it didn't get taken up.' Four years later an interviewer noted, 'Potter . . . still feels *Blackeyes* was a failure. Yet, as he adds, "If you didn't fail, you'd never succeed. And who wants to plod along down the middle of the road? It's in the verges that all the interesting animals are."'

A few weeks after *Blackeyes* had finished, the *Observer Magazine*, in its regular feature 'The Expert's Expert', asked eleven television playwrights who they thought were the best practitioners in their field. Despite the reception of his latest work, Potter came out top with three votes. Alan Plater wrote, 'My expert would have to be Dennis Potter, for his daring and his audacity in taking risks and because of his enduring passion for the medium.' Anthony Minghella praised Potter's 'extraordinary body of work' and the fact that 'he challenges the boundaries of style and subject-matter of what constitutes television drama'. Andrew Davies agreed: 'The one I am picking is a bit bloody obvious, but it's got to be Dennis Potter. He's like the Starship *Enterprise*. He boldly goes where no one has been before and he makes it possible for the rest of us to write imaginatively. He is always an inspiration whether you think his drama works or not.'

CHAPTER 3

He couldn't control me

A month after the end of *Blackeyes* on BBC2 he gave another melodramatic interview about his reactions to the criticisms, this time to the *Daily Mail*:

Potter . . . plans to spend the next two weeks in bed reviewing his writing. 'I will stop taking the drugs and let my skin rage because I can think more clearly. I need to work out whether my writing is good and the critics wrong or not.'

Work was due to start at the BBC on an adaptation of his novel *Ticket to Ride*, but he said he could not work on it because of his emotional state. He may reintroduce it in November.

By taking up the pose of the writer temporarily broken by the critics, he was concealing the BBC's lack of enthusiasm for *Secret Friends*, the title he had chosen for a proposed screen adaptation of *Ticket to Ride*.

During the making of *Blackeyes*, he had given Gina Bellman another script to read. Called *Midnight Movie* – a title half stolen from his abortive MGM project *Midnight Movies* – it was his adaptation of a 1976 novel, *Moths*, by Rosalind Ashe, about a nymphomaniac film star who murders her lovers (Potter had bought the rights of the book). Bellman greatly disliked it: 'I told him I didn't think it was good. He was absolutely crushed. I thought by this time we were friends, I could be honest, I wasn't his protégée any more, I thought we were on a much more equal par. But he was livid – "You're so ungrateful, you think you know it all now." I laughed, rather than burst into tears.'

He continued to see her after *Blackeyes* was finished:

We'd meet for dinner in Needles Wine Bar in Clipstone Street, around the corner from his flat. And in a way the romance continued. He'd phone me up and say, 'Can you come and have dinner tonight?' and I'd say yes, and he'd say, 'Will you wear something sexy?' So I'd put on a little black number and a pair of high heels, and it all felt incredibly innocent.

I was sharing a flat with some other people, and I used to complain about the mess they made. Well, Dennis wanted to set me up on my own. He had this stupid fantasy that he could buy me a flat, and come and visit me whenever he wanted to. I remember laughing in his face. But he was an incredibly controlling person about people he loved. The most manipulative person. And I used to say, 'You're so manipulative', and he'd get upset and furious at being called that.

She was now in a stage production of *The Rocky Horror Show*, earning good reviews and shaking off the 'Blackeyes' label. But Potter would not leave her to pursue a career without him. 'He started phoning and saying, "I'm making *Secret Friends*, do you want to do it?" Well, of course I said, "I'd love to."' She had already read his novel on which it was based, *Ticket to Ride*. 'He'd given me a copy on location, and I loved it, and Helen [the wife–prostitute] was so different from Blackeyes, and I just wanted to be her, and I was so excited.'

Before transmission of *Blackeyes*, Potter told Richard Brooks of the *Observer* that *Secret Friends* was 'due to begin filming next spring', and that he hoped it would be the beginning of 'a lengthy feature film relationship' between himself and the BBC. The *News of the World* ran a story about it just after *Blackeyes* had finished:

TV'S DIRTY DENNIS NOW GETS EVEN MUCKIER!

Telly's 'Mr Dirty' – writer Dennis Potter – is set to shock viewers again with a new telly blockbuster packed with sordid sex scenes.

Insiders say the new multi-million pound show called *Secret Friend* [*sic*] will make his controversial drama *Blackeyes* look like *Bambi*!

While the BBC is doing its best to keep the plot of *Secret Friend* – due to be screened later in the New Year – under wraps, we can reveal:

A man will be shown BITING a woman's breast.

A woman is BEATEN unconscious while a man is seen LICKING her, and

A woman STABS a man to death as they make love.

The series, which follows the exploits of a woman-hater called John, who defiles women while listening to a voice in his head, is certain to outrage feminists . . .

Understandably after *Blackeyes*, the BBC was in no hurry to proceed with a project that was already attracting adverse publicity.

Potter realized he would have to look elsewhere. Meanwhile *Pennies from Heaven* was repeated on BBC2, between 7 February and 14 March. Potter said he was anxious that it might not 'stand up' after twelve years, but the public and critical response was as favourable as ever.

A Scottish graduate student, John Cook, who was writing a doctoral thesis on Potter, had approached him asking for an interview. Potter initially said no, but then learned that Cook was talking to Trodd, McCallum, and others of his circle, so he agreed to see Cook at Judy Daish's office in Eastbourne Mews in May 1990. (The thesis eventually became Cook's book *Dennis Potter: a life on screen*.) 'He was much taller than I expected,' says Cook.

He almost had a smell of sulphur about him, because of the skin lotions. He came in, and immediately ordered champagne, and Judy Daish brought a bottle down from upstairs. He started to chain-smoke and to drink the champagne, and he said, 'I suppose you want some of this too,' and poured it out for me.

He said he was still deeply upset by the reception of *Blackeyes* – 'the pain,' he told Cook, was 'still bumping within me'. He was keen that Cook should see his plays as part of a coherent 'body of work' which was 'consistent with itself' and had a larger purpose. For the first time, he talked about it in the past tense: 'I tried to do what other television writers had not tried to do . . .' Yet he also felt that his greatest play might still lie in the future: 'There is a sense in which I could abandon all my previous work as inadequate and incomplete versions of the work that one day I will write. Someday, somehow, all these threads will come together in one piece of work which will finally do what I'm at, maybe. And then I'll kill myself.' Two years later, he put this more succinctly: 'I'm writing one long play. If they don't get it, too bad.'

*

While waiting to make *Secret Friends*, he slipped back into his old reclusive ways. Sarah says that, at home in Ross-on-Wye, he rarely left the house:

We'd go out to restaurants – the few that there were – very regularly, and he'd know certain people; but he'd never dream of walking into town in the daytime – God forbid! I think he felt the town was too small – he'd be recognized, and he wouldn't have wanted that. Some people enjoy that aspect of fame, but it was something he wanted to distance himself from. Sometimes, though, when I'd picked him up from the train, he'd say, 'Let's drive through town.' And he'd comment on what had changed in it.

Sarah recalls one striking instance of his reclusiveness, a year before *Blackeyes*:

At Christmas 1988, we were all going to Moscow – just for something completely different – and we had to get photos for the visas. And there wasn't an automatic booth in Ross, so I had to phone a photographer we knew, who ran a shop, and make an appointment. And Dad got into quite a state about having to have his photo taken. He said to me, 'You'll come in with me, won't you?'

I said, 'Dad, I don't know why you get so agitated!' I drove him down into town, and the guy in the shop was really quite in awe of Dad, but they started chatting, and you would never have guessed that Dad had been at all ill at ease. We came out of the shop, and he took a deep breath, and I said, 'For God's sake, if I could perform as well as you've just done, I'd be out with people all the time.' And he said, 'I can't help it, Sarah – it's just the way I am.' That was the true man.

Jane agrees that he hated going into Ross: 'I had to go and pick his glasses for him, I had to cut his hair for him – he wouldn't go to a hairdresser.' Yet in Moscow, 'he had polished up his Russian, and he would speak it to strangers in the street, so that we were able to get off the beaten tourist track. And it was just when the Mafia were starting to get a grip, and I think Dad tried to intervene in some some sort of argument in a restaurant. That was typical: if he saw injustice, he would speak out, however shy he might really be.'

Robert Potter agrees with his sisters' estimate of their father's character – 'I think that's him, yes – the shy man was the real DP' – and does not remember him behaving aggressively as a father: 'It was the opposite. I remember pushing *him* to the limit, as you do when you're a teenager. And I can only recall two or three serious tellings-off, which were completely justified. I think when he did it to other people, it was a defence mechanism.'

Potter himself said, 'I think I am naturally a recluse, just am like that about people, and that in fact hides behind the illness, in a way.' Sarah agrees:

I think the illness had just heightened an 'I don't want people looking at me' feeling, which was there already. His London people will have very little sense of that in him, because it was like going into battle – he'd be so prepared that you'd see no chink in the armour in those working situations. Some people might have thought him a bully, but he'd almost have to create that state of mind, which was a mask for the true personality.

Whenever he assumed that mask, he tended to go too far. Sarah recalls his behaviour on a visit to Berry Hill in August 1990, for the christening of his great-niece Nicola (grand-daughter of his sister June):

Before the christening, Dad got himself in quite a state – it was going to be in the Forest, and there would be people there he didn't feel that comfortable with. And we went into the Globe at Berry Hill, and he was buying everybody a drink – it was his way of saying, 'I'm not stand-offish' – and of course then he got a bit drunk, and he didn't behave particularly well at the christening. Some people were perhaps a bit embarrassed by him, and Mum certainly wasn't pleased with his performance.

Next day, I came into work, and she was still upset. She asked me to talk to him – always, when there was something to smooth over, I'd have to do that. So I went up, into his office on the top floor, and I shut the door and sat down, and Dad's version of it later on was, 'I knew it was bad because Sarah came in and shut the door!'

And he said to me, 'I know – but do you understand any of it?' And I said, 'Dad, I think I understand perfectly why you behave like you do. But you've got to accept you can't do it with that kind of people – you can't embarrass your family.' So he was racked with guilt about it. That was the other side – the excessive behaviour he was prone to, when he'd had too much to drink.

June says that she and their mother 'didn't notice anything untoward' in his behaviour at the christening, but his cousin Graham Wale recalls: 'He was usually quite insulting at family gatherings. He always attacked Eddie, June's husband – I can remember, when I was about fourteen or fifteen, sitting next to Eddie, and being told by Dennis that we were just a pair of ignorant so-and-sos.'

*

Like *Pennies from Heaven*, *The Singing Detective* had been shown on certain Public Broadcasting channels in America. Marvin Kitman of New York *Newsday* called it 'the most fantastic program I've seen in my eighteen years as a TV critic . . . the kind of program that once in a generation comes along and permanently changes the parameters of what TV drama can do and reclaims TV as a creative medium'.

Saturday screenings at Joseph Papp's Public Theater in New York during 1988 were a sell-out. Potter was asked if he was surprised that Americans liked it. 'I am amazed,' he answered. 'I would have thought so many of the lines and jokes just could not travel, and they probably didn't.' Michael Gambon was asked by Marlon Brando, with whom he was appearing in the film *A Dry White Season*, if there was any chance of a *Singing Detective* film.

Potter himself must have thought there was, for in October 1990, while he was still trying to set up *Secret Friends*, he wrote a cinema screenplay of it. As with *Pennies from Heaven*, it moves the setting to Chicago; also, for no obvious reason, the period of the thriller strand is altered to the Fifties, with songs from that era. Marlow becomes 'Dan Dark'; the childhood strand is almost omitted (Dan's father runs a small-town garage in South Illinois, and his mother, caught in adultery, moves to Chicago with the boy and works as a prostitute); and almost everything which gave the original serial its appeal vanishes or is cut to the bone. As with *Pennies*, the American setting of the rewrite serves only to emphasize how very English is Potter's outlook – Marlow's 'witty despair and cynicism' does not sound right on American lips.

Nevertheless Potter himself believed in the project. 'The [American] *Singing Detective* script is written in such a way that it won't allow that kind of mistake to be made [the MGM version of *Pennies*], if the film gets made,' he told Graham Fuller. 'First of all, it's not in any sense like a précis of the original series, and secondly, it is totally rethought.'

Brian Gibson, who had directed *Where Adam Stood* and *Blue Remembered Hills*, was now working in Hollywood. 'I was asked if I was interested in doing the movie of *The Singing Detective*,' he recalls. 'At the time, I think Dustin Hoffman was attached to it.'* Jon Amiel was offered the chance to direct it, but says 'it felt to me as though all the passionate and personal element had been lost, and there was no way I could be involved in it'. Potter also approached Stephen Frears. But for once, Rick McCallum was not keen to help: 'I didn't think it

---

* Alison Barnett, who became assistant producer on *Secret Friends*, recalls, 'I had to do a budget for *The Singing Detective* movie when Dustin Hoffman was being considered for the part of Marlow. I asked Dennis who was going to be in it, and he said, "They're all arguing about it, but I can't have that funny little actor, because when he sits on the hospital bed his feet won't touch the ground."'

was a great idea, because I knew Dennis would get into the same problems we had with *Pennies*.'

By the end of 1990, Michael Grade and his drama executives at Channel 4 had agreed to part-finance *Secret Friends*. Potter had raised the remainder of the money from two New York producers, John Roberdeau and Robert Michael Geisler, whom he had met when they commissioned him to adapt D. M. Thomas's novel *The White Hotel* for the cinema. Alan Bates was signed to play the male lead in *Secret Friends*, and a new Potter company was formed to make the film, called Whistling Gypsy – the name of a song associated with Arthur Tracey, the Street Singer, the man who recorded 'Pennies from Heaven'. Rick McCallum was now disconcerted to find that Potter insisted on casting Gina Bellman opposite Alan Bates: 'Dennis was deeply committed to Gina, in a strange, bizarre way.'

Bellman herself found the situation embarrassing: 'Dennis would say, "Nobody wants you to do it, Rick doesn't want you, Channel 4 doesn't want you, the producers don't want you, they want a big name." And I'd say, "OK, well then, maybe I shouldn't do it." "But I'm a man of my word," he'd say, "and I gave you the book to read, and I said the part was yours, and we'll have to go through with it. I'm a man of honour."'

Consequently he decided to dispense with McCallum and find a new producer to run Whistling Gypsy. His first choice was Mark Shivas, whose contract as Head of Drama at the BBC was due to run out shortly. 'He asked me whether I would come and run his company,' says Shivas. 'I had a meeting with Judy and their accountant, and there were several jolly red-wine-filled evenings at Dennis's expense. But I was worried about producing one writer's work exclusively, and in the event I continued as BBC Head of Drama for another two years.'

Potter turned next to Rosemarie Whitman, who had now risen to the rank of producer within the BBC Documentaries Department. 'Dennis phoned me up and left a message on my machine. He sounded rather drunk, so I didn't reply. He said, "I'm going to form a company, will you come and join me?"'

She read the script of *Secret Friends*. 'Anyone could see that it wouldn't make money, and I told Dennis that to his face. But he was determined to give himself another opportunity to prove that he could direct. And I thought, "If you're that brave, you deserve a chance."'

Trodd is scathing about the formation of Whistling Gypsy: 'There was a time when Dennis was wobbling slightly at the top of his own tree, when he fell in with these pleasant guys who were never quite at the top of theirs, and therefore weren't much of a threat, and together they saw each other through.' In fact Potter treated Whitman as aggressively as he had Trodd and McCallum. 'There were moments when I felt I'd been punched in the stomach,' she says. 'But I'd think to myself, "Goodness, he expresses himself well, doesn't he!" And there was always an apology the next day.'

The journalist Ginny Dougary, writing about the making of *Secret Friends*, observed:

A high percentage of the key positions . . . are occupied by women. Potter lists them with a measure of pride: the producers [Rosemarie Whitman and the assistant producer Alison Barnett], the film editor [Clare Douglas] and director of photography [Sue Gibson] are all women. While this makes for a refreshing change, I cannot help wondering whether Potter's motivation is entirely altruistic. Are women, perhaps, more biddable? Are they likely to be more easily bamboozled by Potter's rhetoric? Gibson says, 'Dennis is probably less threatened by working with women than men. He doesn't want to compete with other men because of his disability.'

Clare Douglas, who had already edited *Blackeyes* with Potter, does not agree that he found women more biddable. 'Dennis was very, very insecure, especially with women,' she says.

He thought he was ugly, he thought he would repel people with his hands and everything, which of course he didn't. But he thought he did. And you had, not exactly to make friends with him if you hadn't seen him for a long time, but he wouldn't automatically assume that the friendship would continue, because he was too insecure to believe that it would.

I got on with him incredibly well. You could argue with him, and he'd listen to you. He did treat you as if you had a brain, which not all men in television do. And it was sheer, uncomplicated fun working with him. He made us all laugh so much.

Secret Friends also employed Jane Potter, who made the paintings of wild flowers which, in the film as in *Ticket to Ride*, are the obsessive hobby of the hero, John. At that time she was working as a set-painter for a firm in south London. 'I used to see Dad a lot. He was always very warm, giving me whatever I wanted emotionally, financially. In fact he was always one hundred per cent behind all of us, whatever we did, whatever mistakes we made.'

Potter described *Blackeyes* and *Secret Friends* as 'almost twins in a way, they went into deep, dangerous, personal territory'. He wrote a number of drafts of *Secret Friends*, one of which makes use of Al Bowlly songs – the disorientated John even lip-synchs to Bowlly and, when suffering from amnesia, registers himself at the hotel as 'Al Bowlly, 5 Memory Lane, Norwich'. By the time shooting started, Bowlly had been rejected in favour of a contemporary musical style (a specially written song, 'Secret Friends', is heard behind the opening titles and performed by the hotel band); but Potter reverted to another of his old techniques, the often-repeated flashback.

Indeed *Secret Friends*, made chiefly at Bray Studios, consists of almost nothing but flashbacks. In *Ticket to Ride* there was a fairly continuous main narrative – John losing his memory on the train, and his misadventures in London – but, when adapting the book into the film, Potter decided that this should be seen only in fragments, interleaved with scenes from John's childhood and marriage, and from his encounter with the call-girl who is also Helen, his wife. Further disorientation is caused by the intrusion of John's *doppelgänger* – his imaginary 'secret friend', who is sometimes seen as well as heard. 'The script was very confusing,' says Sue Gibson. 'Dennis was the only one who understood it. Alan Bates came up to me one day and said, "Sue, do you know what's going on in this scene?" I said, "No", and he said, "Oh, that's all right then, neither do I. I'll just watch Dennis and try to be like him."'

Potter was scarcely in a condition to give Bates a clear explanation. 'It was a short shoot,' he recalled, 'but by the end of it I was getting through on sleeping tablets and alcohol.' The sleeping pill was Halcion, later banned because of alleged mind-altering effects. Bates was sympathetic. 'Dennis was too ill to cope,' he says, 'but I admired him hugely and, despite the severe problems with *Secret Friends*, he was a good director.' Frances Barber, playing the role of Helen's and John's friend Angela, found him short-fused: 'He couldn't be bothered to wait for things like the lighting being got right – he was impatient, his mind was too fast.' Yet she, too, came to admire him greatly: 'We used to have long lunches during rehearsals, and Dennis was the most fascinating man I've ever listened to – sometimes cruel, always witty, always completely blunt and to the point. He would play games all the time, and always, always win!'

Barber had the impression that Potter's working relationship with

Gina Bellman was still warm and close – 'very fatherly' – but Bellman herself says otherwise:

He decided that he was going to punish me. I remember the first day on the set, when I didn't know anyone – they were all new people to me – and the first thing he said to me was, 'Gina, are you going to do the whole film in a New Zealand accent?' Now, I haven't spoken in a New Zealand accent since I was nine years old. And thereafter that was the tone on *Secret Friends* – he bullied me for the whole shoot. I felt horribly insecure, really intimidated by him.

He started adding bits to humiliate me. There was a scene when Helen stands there, and isn't supposed to say anything, and Dennis said, 'I want you to look into the camera and say 'Fuck me!' And I think I refused. It certainly wasn't used in the film.

He made no attempt to recapture the intensity of their relationship, and Bellman tended to keep apart from him when not on the set:

While we were on location, I was staying in a hotel with Alan [Bates], and Dennis was staying somewhere else, and I don't think we saw each other socially. But later, when we went on a publicity tour of *Secret Friends* in America, it got to the point where I said I'd only go if we were in different hotels, because he wanted all my time. He'd want to have a breakfast meeting, a lunch meeting, a dinner meeting, he wanted to know what I was doing.

Ginny Dougary found several of the Whistling Gypsy team expressing reservations about *Secret Friends*:

There is one particularly excruciating scene in which Bellman crawls around the floor in a leotard. I asked [Sue] Gibson how she felt when she was filming it: 'The male [camera] operator and I both felt it was unnecessary to shoot the scene in a way that is guaranteed to be titillating to certain members of the audience. To have someone's bottom stuck right in front of the camera is a bit demeaning. It's certainly neither nice nor beautiful. But Dennis is a very literal person. He is not a director who can divorce himself from the words on the page. And, in the end, it's very much about his own fantasy world, which I'm sure he'd admit.' . . .

Clare Douglas persuaded Potter to shorten Bellman's grovelling scene. 'You become so fond of Dennis that you understand his preoccupations,' she says. 'You may find them tiresome, but you see that they're valid for him. Once you start to understand the torments he puts himself through, his hang-up with young women and sex, the yearning for what he can't have, it makes a difference to the way you view his work. I just wish there was someone else making these films from a different perspective.'

Secret Friends contains none of the long tracking shots that had been Potter's hallmark in *Blackeyes*, and is stylistically very conventional. Nevertheless Dougary put it to Potter that perhaps he ought not to direct his own scripts. 'It is absolutely possible that I'm not a good director,' he answered calmly. 'It's particularly hard if you're trying to ally the style of the script with the style of direction. Let's put it this way: so far as *Blackeyes* and *Secret Friends* are concerned, I could shoot the fucking writer.'

Secret Friends was finished by Christmas 1991, but ten months passed before it managed to get distribution, and even then it was seen only in a limited number of 'art' cinemas. Reviewing it in October 1992, *Empire* magazine judged it a 'pile of psycho-twaddle', and *Sight and Sound* remarked that 'Potter's . . . recent work has suggested a psychological barrel scraped dry'. By this time, Potter himself was dismissive of the film. Asked by a journalist if he would be going to the cinema to see it, he replied, 'Oh, I might . . . for ten minutes. Until I see people walking out. Then I'll join them.' In 1993 he described it as 'an absolute disaster'.

Gina Bellman says:

I think we met twice more for drinks, after *Secret Friends* had wrapped, and Dennis apologized, and gave me a bracelet, and said, 'I know I've been a shit, and I love you, and we experienced something so special, and you escaped, you ran away, and I'm jealous that you've got your life ahead of you, and I was only a chapter in it.' And we sort of made up.

I don't think I hurt him by anything that I did, but I think it was something quite torturing for him. I was his fantasy woman, and I got away. He couldn't control me.

*

While *Secret Friends* was still waiting for distribution, in January 1992, the Museum of Television & Radio in New York held a retrospective – a series of public conversations and screenings – entitled *The Television of Dennis Potter*. Ken Trodd and John Wyver had helped to organize it. Potter and Trodd were now reconciled after a fashion. 'Dennis eventually broke the silence a few months before the New York retrospective,' says Trodd. 'He called me, and we had dinner. It was fine, but I had a slightly longer agenda – and by the time we got to the pudding, he was too pissed. And he wouldn't take the New York seminar seriously, or accept that it was an honour. He only wanted to promote and extol *Secret Friends* rather than discuss his earlier work. He was very, very aggressive about it.'

John Wyver's account of the retrospective confirms this:

The first evening, Alan Yentob threw Dennis softball questions about his life, and everybody loved Dennis. For the second, Ron Simon, television curator at the museum, had asked James Wolcott of *Vanity Fair*, a Potter enthusiast, to chair a discussion between Dennis and Steven Bochco, the very celebrated American producer of *Hill Street Blues* and *L.A. Law*, who had also done a show called *Cop Rock*, which (as far as Bochco was concerned) was an *hommage* to *The Singing Detective*, but as far as Dennis was concerned was a rip-off. And that evening, all of Dennis's anti-American, anti-popular-culture bile came to the surface, and it was a deeply unpleasant experience. He had obviously been drinking very heavily. Bochco in his field is a major figure, and Dennis was grossly rude to him.

In fact a video recording of the occasion shows that Potter's rudeness was confined to one remark, after the showing of a clip from *Cop Rock*: 'Was that *hommage* or plagiarism?' Despite slurring his words (and drinking more wine on stage), he got lots of laughs from the audience – for example, with his comment on the American dislike of smoking in public: 'I could pull a gun out and people would be less worried.' He was impatient with Wolcott's lengthy questions – 'Are you going to talk like a nut all the way through?' – and became bored towards the end, saying, 'I want to go.' When Wolcott told him, 'Just a few more questions', he snapped, 'Oh, for Christ's sake.' But even then he grew eloquent about his religious feelings ('I cannot pray; I've tried to pray – I cannot do it, but I know what it means to yearn to do it') and about his desire to go on directing his work. Here, he sounded curiously valedictory: 'It's something that I probably need in this last spiral of whatever stairway – whether it's up or down, I don't know, I don't care.'

Wyver continues:

I was meant to chair the third evening, which was to be Dennis and Ken Trodd talking about their working relationship, and the collaborative component of television drama. Most people thought Dennis wasn't going to turn up for it, but Judy Daish did get him there. By this point, he was just kind of tired and frustrated. I gave what I thought was a rather gracious introduction to him, and then we ran a montage of clips – he was sitting in the audience – which finished with the scene in *The Singing Detective* when Michael Gambon gets up and walks. And as people applauded, Dennis came up on to the stage with Ken.

The video shows Wyver asking an opening question to Potter, who is unable to speak because he is weeping. Trodd remembers this clearly: 'When Dennis had watched the clip from *The Singing Detective*, he couldn't speak – genuinely, not theatrically. He came up on stage and was just unable to speak at first.'

Eventually he managed to say, 'You shouldn't have ended with that clip.' Wiping his eyes, and swigging from a glass of red wine, he tried to explain:

That wasn't a good moment for me, to see that last bit, and then just come up and start. When I get tense and when I get anxious, I deflect it into aggression. Some of that seminar [with Bochco] last night – which to me was utterly and completely pointless – and I'm beginning to get – I don't actually want to do much more of this sort of stuff. And I will only say one thing, on behalf of all writers. [Turning to Wyver] You said in your introduction 'disinterested' when you meant 'uninterested'. Don't join in killing yet another English word.

Wyver says he was hurt by this put-down: 'It was extremely belittling – there were about three hundred people in the audience – and it was a very clear put-down to establish his power.'

With Trodd sitting alongside them, Wyver asked Potter what he expected a producer to contribute. Still sounding tearful, Potter answered, 'What do I expect of a producer? First of all, I expect him to *do* it. I expect some hostility, but I also expect to be left alone.' Trodd now spoke for the first time: 'Let me just try and cover that space, fatuously, probably. Because I'm inclined to say there are two things the producer doesn't do and doesn't have to do: and that is, endure that kind of pain, that kind of memory that the creator, the writer does. The producer's job . . . is altogether more trivial.' Potter chipped in, 'But to be fair to you – and I'm going to be fair once, and once only –' To which Trodd instantly rejoined, laughing, 'Surely not? Why break the habit of a lifetime?'

The discussion limped on, and Potter alluded again to his own aggression: 'Because I've shut that front door so consistently . . . because I've turned in . . . I forget certain social rules of behaviour. And I sometimes behave like a spoilt child, or . . . with enormous murderous impulse. Or I say the things that everyone in the room wants to say, and I find, "Oh my God, it's in *my* mouth."'

He described the BBC as 'still one of the prides and glories of the world', and got another dig at Trodd, who was describing his own growth of confidence over *Pennies from Heaven* in 1977:

TRODD: You gradually acquire confidence –

POTTER: Very gradually in your case!

TRODD: Well, I wanted to give you the opportunity to say that!

Yet at the end, just as he and Trodd were leaving the stage, Potter suddenly said, 'I'd like to thank Ken, who's had to put up with an awful lot of shit from me over the years.'

*

In February 1992, the month after the New York seminars, the *Daily Mail* reported that 'glamour model Louise Germaine', who had 'appeared in a commercial for Cadbury's Flake' (original of Potter's Fraggie Bar),* and had played a bit part in *Blackeyes*, would star in '*Lipstick on Your Collar*, a seven-and-a-half-hour drama . . . as a cinema usherette in Fifties Britain who becomes tragically involved with two men'. The serial would 'feature chart-topping Fifties songs'.

Whistling Gypsy was to make *Lipstick* for Channel 4, who had accepted that Potter would direct it himself. 'But I could feel that things weren't right,' says Rosemarie Whitman. 'And then one evening in November [1991], 'Peter Ansorge, the commissioning editor for Channel 4 Drama, asked Dennis to come and see him.' Ansorge describes what happened: 'He came into my office in Charlotte Street, and I asked him if he was really the right person to direct *Lipstick*. I was worried by what he had done in *Blackeyes*. And I was concerned that the musical numbers in *Lipstick*, the complexity of the show, the need to stick to a demanding schedule, all needed a director with more experience.' Why had Ansorge not raised this with Potter before he had begun pre-production? 'Cowardice,' says Ansorge candidly. 'But I didn't say to Dennis that he *couldn't* direct *Lipstick*. Indeed, if he had come back to us and said "I *am* the right person, for these reasons", we would have agreed to it.'

Potter afterwards described the confrontation melodramatically – 'One desk-light on. Gloomy. Two bottles of red wine on the table . . .' Ansorge continues:

---

* Germaine says it was not a commercial but a record sleeve in the style of the Flake advertisement.

Dennis became angry, and demanded to see Michael Grade. It was then about seven o'clock in the evening, but I went downstairs, and indeed there was Michael, and he agreed to come up. Dennis said he'd been insulted, he was outraged, but Michael said quite calmly that he supported his commissioning editors, and that all I wanted was to be reassured that he was the best possible director. But that made Dennis even more angry! However, he said he would think it over, and next afternoon he came to see me again, and said he was resigning as director.

Rosemarie Whitman says that Potter was 'devastated' by Ansorge's lack of faith in him – and so was she:

I'd been worried about Dennis directing it, simply because I didn't think his health would last. But I was determined that we would get him through it somehow. And then Channel 4 did this terrible thing to him. Quite apart from his feelings, it was so late – we were going to start shooting in a few weeks, the sets had been designed, the whole team was working together.

I just watched Dennis crumble. He said he was going to walk away from the production – and he thought it was my fault, that I was in league with Ansorge. He really turned against me. (Yet in the midst of all that, he paid for four of us to go to New York for the opening of *Secret Friends*, flights and accommodation for the weekend!)

Gary Williamson, who had designed *Secret Friends* and was now working on *Lipstick*, confirms that Potter felt let down by his own Whistling Gypsy team: 'He said he didn't give a shit who directed *Lipstick* now. He said, "Just make the fucking thing, and I hope you make a bad job of it."'

The pain of being sacked – as he saw it – from his own production led to a temporary reconciliation with Trodd: 'Dennis would phone me up at midnight, ask if I was alone, and then proceed to tell me how much he wanted me to return to the fold . . . He was so humiliated [by the sacking] he didn't know whether to sabotage [*Lipstick*]. I organized a putsch at the eleventh hour and tried to take the whole thing, with Dennis as director, to the BBC. They didn't say yes immediately, so the moment passed.' There is an echo of this in a *Daily Mail* news story dated 10 April 1992:

Television dramatist Dennis Potter is negotiating to return to the BBC . . . Potter and his old friend Ken Trodd . . . have met BBC2 controller Alan Yentob and are said to have discussed Potter adapting a novel into a major drama series, and writing an original TV script called *Femme Fatale*. Both would be filmed next year.

Meanwhile Rosemarie Whitman had drawn up a list of possible directors for *Lipstick*, from which Potter chose Renny Rye, an experienced television director who had worked in BBC children's programmes, and had earned a reputation as a reliable handler of such series as *Poirot*. 'Renny came in like a breath of fresh air,' recalls Whitman. 'He said he loved the scripts of *Lipstick*, and didn't mind that Dennis had planned it all already. I knew he didn't have a big ego.'

Rye himself says:

I think they thought they'd got a relatively easy-going guy, who would do what Dennis wanted. So I told him, 'I'm not just going to be a technical director – if you take me on, I'm really going to direct it.' He said, 'That's fine by me, because I'll have one lunch with you, and after that you're not going to see me again. I'm not going to have anything to do with the production, because I'm so hurt by being told that I can't direct it.' Then I got a phone call about a week later saying that Dennis was interested in casting Roy Hudd – he was meeting him, and did I want to come along well? So in effect I auditioned Roy, with Dennis sitting there auditioning me.

Even after this, he wouldn't talk to me. Yet I kept getting messages from him about what I should do. So I said to Rosie [Whitman], if he wants to have a creative input, tell him to come in and see me. And eventually he came and had lunch. This was about four weeks from the start of shooting, and I said, 'If you want to be involved, come and be the producer. You don't have to deal with the money – Rosemarie does all that.'

Potter accepted, and now styled himself 'creative producer' – though on the finished *Lipstick* his name appears alongside Rye's, on the final credits, simply as 'Producer'.

Potter still intended that Trodd should be involved with *Lipstick*. 'He said he'd ask Ken to be executive producer,' says Rye. But Trodd's involvement with the project was short-lived, thanks to Potter's behaviour to him. 'Dennis had summoned me to a meeting,' Rye recalls,

so he could complain to me about the lighting, which he thought was too dark for the brightness of the Fifties, and Ken was there too, and said to me, 'I think Dennis is right.' And Dennis turned on him and said, 'What the fuck are you doing here, Ken? I'm talking to Renny, we're going to resolve this, so just shut up.' So Ken told Rosie to get him a taxi, and went, and we never saw him again, though we credited him as 'Pre-production Adviser' on episode 1.

Trodd recalls it slightly differently, with Potter saying pointedly to him:

'How many producers have we got?' – implying that he himself was really the producer.

When he joined the production, Rye was dismayed to discover that Potter had already cast the completely inexperienced, twenty-one-year-old Louise Germaine in the crucial role of Sylvia, the cinema usherette. 'I was very worried about Louise, because she was completely raw,' says Rye. 'So I began the whole process of auditioning again, but I couldn't find anybody I was really convinced was right. And then I spent an afternoon really chatting to Louise, and I realized that if I could get her *own* personality on to screen, she'd be magical – because she'd had an extraordinary life.'

*

Louise Germaine had been one of the walk-ons in *Blackeyes*, at the age of nineteen. 'I had long blond hair and I was very chirpy, full of life,' she says,

and I'd go up and talk to anybody. One lunchtime I went and sat with this guy on the other side of the studio canteen. I thought he was a stagehand. I said, 'It's great this, isn't it?' He went sort of, 'Er – yeah.' I said, 'I've never enjoyed myself so much in my life.' He said, 'So what are you doing then?' I said, 'Oh, I'm just in the background, but I'm having a really good time.' I then went off and all the other girls said, 'Do you know who that was?' 'No, who?' 'Dennis Potter, the writer of *Blackeyes* – and he's directing us!'

Born in Margate in 1971, Louise Germaine had seen little of her father, and had a stormy relationship with her mother:

She ran a café, and a second-hand shop, and I never used to go to school – I used to work in the café all the time. The truancy people gave up in the end.

I came to London when I was fifteen, did some modelling, and got into glamour modelling, nude modelling. I didn't know anything different, and my mum wanted me to be a stripper.

The *Daily Star* stated that she had worked as a 'soft-porn model', and Germaine agrees that much of the 'glamour modelling' could be called this, but adds, 'I really didn't know what I was doing.'

She goes on:

When I got to about seventeen and a half, I had an Italian boyfriend and we travelled round Europe together, and he said to me, 'Louise, you really shouldn't be doing this [the glamour modelling].' After that, I started to do fashion modelling, and became quite successful. I came back to England, and an agent called Geoff took me on, and I didn't have anywhere to live, and he let me have a spare room in his house in Fulham in return for doing the cleaning. I was there for four years, and that gave me stability. Geoff was the one who got me the job on *Blackeyes*, as an extra.

She recalls that, during *Blackeyes*, 'Gina Bellman came up to me and said, "Dennis really likes you – he likes girls who wear flowery dresses", or something like that. And I just thought it was a weird comment. But I really liked him.' Afterwards she wrote to him: 'I sent him a letter, saying, "It was really nice to have met you." I didn't get a reply, but two years later he sent me the script of *Lipstick*. I'd never read a script before in my life. But when I read it, I thought, "Sylvia [the usherette] is *me* – I've really got to get that part." I knew it would change my life.'

When they met, she asked Potter how he had remembered her. 'He told me, "How could I ever forget?"' Rosemarie Whitman soon came to realize the shrewdness of Potter's choice: 'Lou had been a very gawky eighteen-year-old on *Blackeyes*, very awkward on film. But she was absolutely terrific when she did the screen test for *Lipstick*. She'd grown up, and she looked just like Diana Dors.'

Potter told John Cook that *Lipstick on Your Collar* had begun with 'this delicious idea of all the colonels that he remembered from the War Office miming to "Blue Suede Shoes" as his revenge on them'. Talking to Graham Fuller when the serial was in post-production, he denied that it was a conscious recycling of his 1969 play *Lay Down Your Arms*. He claimed it was a 'coincidence' that it had exactly the same setting (the War Office at the time of Suez) and several similar characters, and claimed that he did not remember the details of the earlier play. He asserted that there was 'more in the script [of *Lipstick*] than seems to be the case', even that 'in some ways, *Lipstick* outdoes *Pennies* and *The Singing Detective*', though he admitted, 'I don't like Fifties music very much.'

He made lavish use of songs of the period, padding out the tedium of War Office life with lip-synched Fifties hits, performed by the officers of the Russian Language section in the imagination of one of the National Service clerks, Private Mick Hopper (played by Ewan McGregor). Potter claimed that the use of these songs reflected a social change that was going on in Britain at the time of Suez: 'Underneath this stupid bravado of Suez the music is becoming proto-rock. Music is changing, language is changing, things are changing and there's nothing the people in charge can do about it.' There are moments when the script manages to convey this, most notably in a glimpse of Anthony Eden, the Tory Prime Minister, belting out 'Blue Suede Shoes' at the despatch box. However, most of the time the colonels get to their feet to perform a number by the Platters or Frankie Vaughan for little other reason than to pass the time.

Potter splits the hero of *Lay Down Your Arms* into two characters: the musically daydreaming Hopper, and a naïve young Welshman, Private Francis Francis (played by Giles Thomas). Lodging with an aunt and uncle in Fulham, Francis becomes obsessed with the girl upstairs, the cinema usherette Sylvia, who is married to the sadistic corporal from the Russian Language section. The couple's sexual antics keep Francis agonizingly awake at night, while outside, in his car, lurks Harold Atterbow, the middle-aged organist at Sylvia's cinema. Obsessed with Sylvia, Atterbow gives her a pound if she will masturbate him.

Potter's choice of the loveable Roy Hudd for the part of this dirty old man seems eccentric, but was very shrewd – only someone like Hudd could make this character even faintly sympathetic:

SYLVIA: I'm not interested in you.

(*He looks at her, wretchedly yearning.*)

HAROLD: I know you're not. How could you be? . . .

SYLVIA: Look, I rubbed you for a pound. That's because I was – because I was –

HAROLD: Short of a few bob. Yes.

SYLVIA: And I wish I hadn't done it. It made me feel – all sticky . . . If I tell my Pete he'll break your dirty little neck . . . And if I tell your wife. The poor bitch.

HAROLD: Please. Please don't.

(*Silence. She studies him.*)

SYLVIA: (*steadily*) It made me feel sick.

(*And she gets out of the car, her nose in the air.*)

For all his pathetic lust, Harold is an artist of sorts, a musician who can entertain a packed cinema at his multi-coloured organ console. He tries to distract himself from his sexual yearnings by thinking about his work – 'The notes! Think of the notes!' he exorts himself as he sits in his car, staring at Sylvia's window. In contrast, there is a glimpse in *Lipstick* of another kind of relationship between an artist – again, an older man – and a young girl. *Lay Down Your Arms* had included a passage from *The Seagull*, the scene where the young would-be writer Konstantin pines for Nina. Chekhov's play features again briefly in *Lipstick* (when the American colonel who occupies a War Office desk takes his niece Lisa to the theatre) but this time Potter picks a different excerpt, the beginning of the affair between Nina and the famous playwright Trigorin. 'What a wonderful world you live in!' Nina says breathlessly to him, and Trigorin answers, 'You talk about fame and happiness, and this radiant and interesting life, but . . . I'm obsessed day and night by one thought: I must write, I must write.' Nina is bewitched – just as Gina Bellman had been by Potter, and Louise Germaine was during the making of *Lipstick*.

*

'Dennis and I used to meet up quite a lot,' says Germaine,

and go through the script, and we talked about the character. And of course I'd never been to drama school, so he gave me a lot of help with how to do the part. We used to meet in a basement wine bar near his flat, and if the service was bad, he used to do really mad things like pinch an ashtray, or a salt and pepper pot, or a knife. And I went to his flat sometimes – we read through the script there. It was just a plain little flat, with loads of books everywhere.

He advised her about an acting career – 'My full name is Tina Louise, and Dennis said, "Drop Tina and just use your middle name, because it just sounds so much nicer"' – and he began to play Henry Higgins to her Eliza Doolittle:

Dennis corrected all my grammar. And if I was eating bread in a restaurant, I'd put the whole piece in my mouth, and bite off a chunk. He'd say, 'Don't do that, break it up into little bits.' And the way I used to hold a knife, or a pen, was all wrong. He showed me. It took me ages to get it all right, but one day it just clicked.

He gave me books – Rumer Godden's *Greengage Summer*, three of his own, and stuff by Ed McBain and Elmore Leonard. And he sent me to see *Pygmalion*, with Frances Barber as Eliza.

Did she feel patronized, the victim of manipulation, as Eliza eventually does in Shaw's play? 'Oh God, no, I needed it, I really needed it. He really changed my life.'

Potter became fascinated by Louise's personal history. 'I told him all about my life, and got so much out of my system – he was the first person I'd really felt able to tell everything to.' He recorded her reminiscences on tape, apparently intending to make use of them in some future play. She certainly supplied him with one idea he would pursue. 'Before *Lipstick*,' she says, 'I was working in a karaoke bar in Kingly Street in Soho, and I used to be the host, and you'd get all the City people in groups, coming to eat sushi. It was my job to create an atmosphere. But it wasn't a seedy place. Dennis came in there once, without me knowing, to see me perform.'

He did not confide in her as he had with Gina Bellman. 'He didn't talk much about himself,' she says. 'The game was all to do with me – he'd decided to make me into something. But he mentioned to me that he'd had a fixation for Gina – he did tell me that.' Comparing the two relationships, Bellman says, 'His creation of Louise was a repeat of what he'd done with me, but this time with an uncomplicated Page Three girl who wouldn't react in the complicated way that I did.'

Louise Germaine insists that the relationship had nothing to do with sex. 'If I gave him a hug, it was just a hug. It wasn't, "Ooh, is he going to – ?" Even from the beginning, it was never like that. I could put my head on his arm, and it never meant anything more than that.' Renny Rye says that 'Louise and Dennis both – on separate occasions – told me that there'd never been any physical thing between them. I once I made a lascivious remark to Dennis about her gorgeous tits, and he said, "If you ever lay a hand on her, I'll cut your balls off."'

She allowed him to buy her just one present, a Parker pen – 'It's my pride and joy' – but would accept nothing else. 'One day I said I was going to get a mobile phone, and Dennis said, "Let me pay some money towards that," but I said, "You must be joking" – no one's ever given me money in my life. He used to give me money for taxis, but I used to put it back while he was out of the room.' Summing up their friendship, she says, '*Lipstick* was the best experience of my life. When I look back to how I was before it, and how I am now, he did everything for me. He changed my life, and he never wanted anything from me for it.'

*

For about a month, Renny Rye continued to find Potter difficult to work with:

Dennis would give the actors notes after rehearsal, and I said, 'This isn't on – if you want to make comments, do it via me.' This sort of tussle went on for quite some time, and it was about four weeks into shooting *Lipstick* before I felt I was really running it. But once you'd stood up to him, and proved yourself, then he was like a puppy dog – he could be the sweetest, gentlest man, and intrinsically was that.

He always signed his messages to me and everyone else with a little heart, meaning 'love'. He said to me once, 'Margaret thinks I'm having a homosexual affair with you, because I've been on about you so much.' He did have this capacity of becoming completely enamoured of people. And I loved him, in a strange way – I've never felt as close to anyone else, quite like that.

Whistling Gypsy's designer, Gary Williamson, expresses it as strongly, saying that, soon after they had begun to work together, he 'fell in love' with Potter.

Rye also noticed how Potter would plan confrontations and other pieces of dramatic behaviour in advance, as if he were writing a script. 'I know he rehearsed situations – he would make virtually written speeches.'

*

Potter held a big round of interviews in February 1993 to promote *Lipstick*. A *Radio Times* journalist noted, 'He is not big on eye contact with people he doesn't know.' Mark Lawson, talking to him for the *Independent Magazine*, wrote, 'Potter smiles, and says that he is getting better with strangers. In the past, he could not even look them in the eye. He thought it might be slightly easier with me, because we had met on a radio programme.' Lawson noted that Potter was drinking Methotrexate with his coffee, and said he was wearing pyjamas under his suit. 'Beyond this, the condition is hinted at only in a startlingly albino complexion and crabbed hands, like big red boxing gloves.'

Steve Grant of *Time Out* was shocked by the hands. 'But meeting

Potter is never painful,' he wrote. 'You are always taken not just by his courtesy, humour and chain-smoking, but by the sometimes breathtaking power of the man's conversation. It is hypnotic, grammatically precise, aphoristic, gently phrased; as pulpit-powerful as the preachers he must have listened to back in the Forest of Dean.'

Ginny Dougary of *The Times* was taken aback when, after singing a few lines of 'Painting the Clouds with Sunshine', he suddenly made 'a hurried gesture which suggests he is about to burst into tears. His voice misses a beat and he talks about the sadness of losing his father . . .' Mark Lawson was the audience for more tears – and a highly personal disclosure: 'Towards the end of the interview, he called for a bottle of red wine and became weary, and teary. Margaret – "my tender and steadfast wife – she's the one that bore the brunt of everything" – was receiving radiotherapy treatment for cancer.'

Breast cancer had been diagnosed late in 1992, and Margaret had had a mastectomy at Christmas (Rosemarie Whitman recalls Potter breaking this news at the Whistling Gypsy Christmas lunch 'in floods of tears'). Potter told Steve Grant that the illness of his 'dear, darling, tender and steadfast' wife had filled him with 'sheer, fucking, blinding terror'. He went on, 'I know that I'm a bit unstable, emotional, difficult, writers often are. She's always been my rock, my centre, kept me together. Protected me.' As to her recovery, he said, 'You just have to hope.'

The first episode of *Lipstick* was shown on Channel 4 on 21 February 1993. '*Lipstick* lacks gloss,' declared the *Daily Star* next morning. 'There was a good twenty minutes of entertainment . . . Unfortunately the show lasted an hour . . . The characters are two-dimensional except lovely Louise Germaine as sexpot Sylvia, who had me groping for my enhanced 3D specs.' One of the lip-synch numbers in this episode, 'The Garden of Eden', included a bare-breasted blonde dancer wielding a penis-shaped snake – enough for the *Star* critic to brand the entire serial 'Dirty Den's Pervy Peep Show'. In contrast, Max Davidson in the *Daily Telegraph* thought the opening episode so bland that it must be 'an act of public expiation for the lurid excesses of *Blackeyes*'. Nancy Banks-Smith in the *Guardian* passed no judgement, but remarked that almost thirty years had gone by since she had taken over Potter's TV critic chair in Fleet Street. She reckoned that *Lipstick* was Potter's fortieth work for television.

The uncertain reaction of many critics to the first episode mostly turned to disappointment as *Lipstick* unreeled. Allison Pearson of the *Independent on Sunday* complained of the 'ennui' of the War Office scenes, and suggested that, though 'Potter is still our greatest writer for television', the lip-synching had become 'routine'. Hugh Hebert of the *Guardian* admitted, after the third episode, that 'it's no good pretending this show is in the same league as *Pennies from Heaven* or *The Singing Detective*', and Mark Steyn in the *Mail on Sunday* feared that 'Potter is tired and clapped out and trotting through the same old gimmicky formula'.

Gina Bellman says she was deeply disappointed by the new serial: 'I didn't like *Lipstick on Your Collar*. When I saw it, I felt betrayed again, because it was so safe, so formulaic, so much against everything Dennis had said to me that he wanted to do, all those yarns he'd spun me about the coalminers! I felt very let down by him as an artist.'

The critics' response was especially wounding to Potter, since he had told Graham Fuller he was sure *Lipstick* would restore his reputation. Sarah says, 'Dad was beginning to feel that perhaps his time had come and gone. It seemed that anything he did would be labelled "substandard" or "filth".' Yet he lost no time in getting his own back on reviewers.

Channel 4 was running a series called *Opinions*, in which speakers delivered a half-hour straight-to-camera script on 'the state of Britain today'. Previous participants had included Alan Clark and Sir James Goldsmith. Potter had been booked to appear on 21 March 1993, an hour before the screening of the fifth episode of *Lipstick*. 'What I'm about to do', he told viewers that night,

is to make a provenly vindictive and extremely powerful enemy, a sort of serial killer, metaphorically speaking . . . that drivel-merchant, global huckster, and, so-to-speak, media psychopath, Rupert Murdoch, a Hannibal-the-Cannibal who is in many important ways a deal more powerful in Britain than our own schoolboy parliament, its minority-elected government, and even its bumbling Mr Pooter of a prime minister [John Major]. A government, God help us, that the Murdoch press did so much, so dishonestly, to put into power.

He admitted that he was 'only taking this risk to my already apparently tattered reputation because I've been stung into it by some of the personal attacks on the alleged sensationalism and bad faith of my own writing'. He referred to the tabloid taunts of 'Dirty Den' and 'Television's Mr Filth', and said that there had also been an endearing reference to what must be my other, less priapic illness by that sub-literate, homophobic, sniggering rictus of a lout, Garry Bushell of Murdoch's the *Sun*, as 'Old Flakey'. 'Very lipstick-on-my-dipstick,' slurps Bushell, with the kind of saloon bar leer that presumably adds some kind of balance to what one might charitably call his talent – all of which you could just about press into that little space you get when you lift a plastic lavatory brush from its holder.

Bushell had not reviewed *Lipstick*; Potter seems to have been thinking of the article by another *Sun* journalist, Sally Brockway, after the first episode of *Lipstick*: 'Dennis seems to have lost his magic touch . . . The only thing that will get viewers tuning in for the second episode . . . is the prospect of lipstick appearing on parts a bit juicier than the collar.'

Next, Potter turned to the *Daily Star* headline, 'DIRTY DEN'S PERVY PEEP SHOW', and pointed out that, a few pages away, the same issue of the newspaper had printed advertisements for telephone sex, several of which he read out. 'The poor devil who's abusing me', he said, 'has his wages paid by employers who are, at least in my dictionary, by definition barely one remove (if that) from being –' He paused. 'Lawyers are reading this stuff, it's not live, I won't say the word, but you know what I mean. Let those dogs return to their own vomit; I ought to pick on someone my own size.'

This was Murdoch, 'the enormous toad who croaks at all our doorways and windows'. One writer had said there was enough evidence to hang him several times over. Potter did not advocate this: 'In my mercy I suggest that if Murdoch were to be strung up, he should be cut down while still alive and left to croak out expletives in something of the foul-mouthed style of Kelvin MacKenzie, the sharp little oaf who edits the *Sun*.' Murdoch had said he wanted to break 'the British broadcasting cartel'. In response, Potter defended British television as 'the least worst . . . in the world', and praised the BBC as 'the one British institution that really works'. The vital need was 'properly enforcing cross-ownership provisions so that a Murdoch or his clones either has his TV or his newspapers . . . No newspaper should own any part of any television company, and vice versa. Second, no person or group should own more than one daily, one evening and one Sunday paper. It's very simple . . . In short: Murdoch, go home. Wherever that is.'

Next morning the Murdoch-owned *Times* reported, 'Potter bites back to urge press reforms', but omitted to quote any of Potter's aspersions on its proprietor. The *Sun* and *Daily Star* remained silent, but the following weekend, in Murdoch's *Sunday Times*, Craig Brown alleged that Potter's performance had felt 'like being collared by a madman on the Tube', and continued:

Any viewer coming fresh to the programme would have thought that Murdoch's most dreadful sin was to employ journalists who were occasionally a little rude about Dennis Potter. Throughout the entire rant, the *only* examples Potter gave of the perfidy of the Murdoch press lay in their unfair treatment of the plays of Dennis Potter . . . This disastrously deflected this ostensible attack on Murdoch from its true target.

Potter's language was of a violence and paranoia more often to be found in anonymous letters . . . and he didn't worry himself or the viewer with any form of intellectual argument.

Graham Fuller's *Potter on Potter* was published a few weeks after this. Fuller had approached Fabers to propose an extended interview with Potter in book form. Potter had at first been reluctant, then co-operative, though Fuller says he was mercurial in his moods while the interview was being conducted (chiefly in the *Lipstick* production office during 1992). The book was launched at Riverside Studios in Hammersmith; Ken Trodd was there – 'it was almost the only time Dennis and I met during that period' – and recalls an 'aura of un-pleasantness and heightened assertions' in Potter's behaviour to him at lunch before the event. In the book, Potter described his current film projects: 'I've got four scripts out there [Hollywood], variously waiting for what may or may not be a green light – "forever amber" is probably a more accurate description of where they'll stay.' There were in fact five.

Mesmer, about the eighteenth-century hypnotist, had been contracted by an Australian producer in 1983, and was still being rewritten by Potter. 'I am currently having meetings about *Mesmer,* which I wrote nine years ago,' he told Fuller. 'Suddenly somebody is interested in making it. The same may well be true of *Double Dare* one day, and of the other scripts I wrote. You never quite know.' The central relationship in *Mesmer* is between the hypnotist and beautiful young girl patient, whose blindness seems to have been caused by her father sexually abusing her.

'*Mesmer*'s been at the starting gate four times,' Potter told Fuller, describing Mesmer himself as 'half charlatan, half genius'. Jon Amiel, who at one point was asked to direct it, remarks that the great problem is that Dennis's attitude to Mesmer is completely ambivalent – he never decided in his own mind whether Mesmer was a charlatan or not. And every time the film shows him as a charlatan, it sabotages any hold that character might have on our emotions. How can you care about his relationship with the girl when he's been so profoundly discredited?

Mesmer was filmed shortly before Potter's death, with Alan Rickman in the title role, Roger Spottiswoode directing, and music by Michael Nyman, but has not yet been released because of a legal dispute between the film's makers and its financiers.

The other four scripts were adaptations of novels. In the early Eighties, Potter had been approached by John Roberdeau and Robert Michael Geisler, who owned the screen rights of D. M. Thomas's Freudian fantasy, *The White Hotel*. Thomas, who had been at New College with Potter and was then living not far from Ross-on-Wye, wrote to say that he was delighted, and was surprised that their paths had not crossed. Potter replied, 'It *is* surprising . . . except I rarely venture out unless I can see in advance that there is no one up ahead! Most of the best meetings are accidental.' He assured Thomas that he would 'like very much to tackle such a difficult screenplay, and feel in my bones that I could properly respect and honour your truly remarkable novel'. Eventually he was paid to write a screenplay of the book. Potter's White Hotel has, of course, a dance band and crooner, who in the most spectacular scene perform the Ted Lewis recording of 'My Mamma's In Town' while Lisa, the heroine, feeds the hotel guests with her breast milk. At the time of writing, Roberdeau and Geisler say they still plan to film it.

Potter used old songs, too, in a screen version of Roald Dahl's *James and the Giant Peach*, commissioned by an independent producer. 'He was wonderfully enthusiastic about writing that,' says Renny Rye, 'and there was a cynical caterpillar he felt totally involved with. Disney didn't use his script when it was eventually made [in 1995], but he did get a credit somewhere or other – there were six writers listed!' Music also featured in his adaptation of an American comic novel, commissioned by Paramount, *The Woodrow Wilson Dime* by Jack Finney. This is an adult fairy story about a man who discovers he can live an alternative life, and find an alternative wife. Potter's screenplay, *Just One More Chance* (called *The Flipsider* in some drafts), reads like a pale echo of *Pennies from Heaven*.

There could be no lip-synching in Dickens's *The Mystery of Edwin Drood*, scripted by Potter in 1984 under the title *Opium Blue*, and revised in 1991. This was for a New York producer ('a hairdresser!' says Judy Daish) who had bought the rights to Leon Garfield's ending to the unfinished novel. Following Garfield, Potter has Edwin murdered by the opium-addicted cathedral choirmaster John Jasper, who lusts after his nephew's betrothed, the virginal schoolgirl Rosa. Renny Rye still hopes that this Potter script will be made one day – 'It's wonderfully Gothic.'

Some months after the Fuller interview, Potter wrote yet another film adaptation, *White Clouds*, based on the novel *Cara Massimina* by 'John MacDowell', a pseudonym of the writer Tim Parks. 'Dennis bought the rights,' says Daish, 'and I think he first of all thought of it as a series, but he then wrote it as a film script, and Mark Shivas at the BBC liked it.' It is a black comedy about an unscrupulous young Englishman in Italy, Morris Duckworth, who runs off with one of his English language pupils, Massimina Trevisan, and (unbeknown to her) demands a vast ransom for her return. Taking its title from a line of a Keats poem which Morris uses in his class ('So that we feel uplifted from the world/Walking upon the white clouds'), the screenplay – like the novel – moves from farce to violence, with Morris becoming a murderer in order to escape justice.

In the Fuller book, Potter also talked about the unlikelihood of directing more of his own work: 'I suspect nobody now would fund something that I was directing . . . If I had started with a straight linear narrative [in *Blackeyes* and *Secret Friends*] I could probably now pick and choose what I wanted to direct next, but I can't. That's the price you pay – that's the way of the world when you get so many chances. So that's it – I've had it!' Fuller asked him if he thought his future work would be based on the same concerns as before, or might shift. 'I don't know,' he answered, 'and I'm glad I don't know. Just in terms of work, I am going to roll on, I hope.'

A second book, a short account of his life and work by Peter Stead of Swansea University, was launched in May 1993 at the Hay-on-Wye literary festival, with Stead interviewing Potter, who behaved much as he had at the New York seminars. Alan Plater recalls that Potter 'requested, firmly but politely, that an ashtray be provided on stage in the marquee, in defiance of all known fire regulations. I spoke in the same tent a couple of days later and also asked for an ashtray, quoting

Potter as legal precedent. "He's been doing this for twenty-five years," I said. "Creating a right of way for the rest of us."'

Three weeks after his Hay appearance, on Channel 4's *Clive Anderson Talks Back*, Potter announced that he was trying to raise American money from his *Singing Detective* movie script to finance his next British project: 'We're finishing a film called *Midnight Movie*, which I had to invest in myself, so I needed money from over there – that's what I think America's for.'

Renny Rye believes that Potter was determined to make *Midnight Movie* because he had failed to persuade an American studio that Rye – who had now become 'his' director – should make the film of *The Singing Detective*. The Hollywood company Tristar was now hoping to make it, and Rye says:

I think the package had become Robin Williams in the lead, with Robert Altman directing. But Dennis wanted me to do it – which of course Tristar wouldn't accept, because I was just a TV director. And that was one of the reasons he pushed *Midnight Movie* so strongly. He wanted me to do a movie, then he could say I was a movie director, and studios would take me on to direct his work.

(Jon Amiel says, 'Robert Altman told me he'd been offered *The Singing Detective*, and had turned it down – he'd seen the television series, and said, how can anyone possibly do better than that?')

Another factor in *Midnight Movie* was probably Potter's wish to work again with Louise Germaine, even though *Midnight Movie* was far from suited to her. In the original script, written in 1987, the nymphomaniac is American, the wife of a Hollywood film producer who is in England to make a film called *Smoke Rings* (the original title of *The Singing Detective*). Potter anglicized the role for Germaine.

He offered *Midnight Movie* to Channel 4, but Peter Ansorge and the Head of Drama, David Aukin, turned it down. 'Dennis went berserk,' says Ansorge, 'and returned to the BBC who let him do the film. I think it's appalling that they allowed him to put a quarter of a million of his own money into it. I do, I'm sorry. The old BBC would never have done that. It was never a commercial movie.' Ansorge underestimates the sum involved. Potter himself wrote, 'I was able to put in more than half a million pounds of my "own" money into the ailing budget of a BBC film I had called *Midnight Movie* without any intention of ironic foreboding. By my becoming the Corporation's sole if minority partner, the movie was able to begin shooting.' Potter's accountant Stanley Rosenthal confirms that his investment in the film was about £530,000.

Mark Shivas, who was then Head of Films at the BBC, defends his decision to let Potter put this enormous sum into the project: 'My brief was to spend no more than £750,000 on each film. And Dennis and I tried to raise the rest from everyone else we could possibly think of. But no one was prepared to put any money in, and Dennis very much wanted it made.'

Potter talked about this when his old *TW3* writing partner David Nathan interviewed him about *Lipstick*:

Midnight Movie is being made with the BBC [wrote Nathan]. 'It's this new commercial world,' [Potter] says, 'and boy, have they learned the lesson: they're screwing me rotten. In the old days, you could screw them.' . . . He is putting a 'huge amount' of his own money into the film . . . 'Sometimes,' he says, 'you've got to go out on a wing. One of the things wrong with the British film industry is that people don't do that. You know what I get really angry about? I sent it to British Screen, set up by the Government to help the industry, in April. They returned it in August saying they were sorry it had taken so long. Of course, they said, the script works, but given their limited budget, they would rather put the money into something more experimental. If I had said the main character is a black lesbian who likes slashing Chinese men's balls off they would have said, "Yeah, how much do you want?"'

Renny Rye recalls that, when the BBC provided Whistling Gypsy with a production office for *Midnight Movie*,

Dennis made a big fuss that we were being forced to work in Television Centre. He said, 'I'll go into any office as long as it's not on the same floor as Trodd's.' And we *were* on the same floor, of course, and they saw each other in the corridor, and it was sticky. Yet when one of the top drama managers was rude about Ken, Dennis snapped, 'Don't be so *fucking* silly.' He was absolutely furious. He still believed in Ken.

Rewriting *Midnight Movie* to fit Louise Germaine, Potter had rendered the screenplay's already convoluted story-line almost incomprehensible through flashbacks, dream sequences, and excerpts from a film-within-a-film. He later asserted that '*Midnight Movie* . . . in my totally unbiased opinion was brilliantly directed by Renny Rye, who will one day be seen to be one of the great names in British cinema . . .' But Rye himself felt uncomfortable about the script, which he says 'fell between two stools' – a parody of the Hammer horror genre, and a sincerely tragic story. 'I eventually opted for taking it straight,' says Rye. But this put considerable weight on Louise Germaine, who says she 'hated' *Midnight Movie* after being obliged to act a sex scene. She also found that Potter was edgier with her than during *Lipstick* – 'We had a big row when I couldn't go to dinner to meet Brian Dennehy [playing Amber's husband], who had just arrived from America. Dennis was really foul, though we made it up afterwards.'

Whistling Gypsy had twelve months for theatrical release for *Midnight Movie* before the BBC screened it. 'We went from pillar to post, trying to get a distributor for it,' says Rye, 'but soon it was looking less and less likely.' It had a private screening in the Lumière Cinema in London, but otherwise was never seen on the big screen. Potter's £530,000 was not going to be earned back. Also, says Rye, 'Dennis was now having stomach pains, but we ignored that, because he was always ill. With hindsight, of course we shouldn't have.'

*

Since the inception of the Edinburgh Television Festival in the Seventies, there had been an annual lecture in memory of James MacTaggart, the original producer of *The Wednesday Play*. Speakers had ranged from John McGrath to Rupert Murdoch. The then Controller of BBC2, Michael Jackson, chair of the festival, invited Potter to give the 1993 lecture.

'Dennis kept ringing me up to try passages from it on the phone, and ask what I thought about the jokes,' says Renny Rye. 'And even on the day he was still asking me about bits.' The text was issued to the press in advance, and, despite a strict embargo, the papers hinted that Potter's targets would be Rupert Murdoch and the recently appointed BBC Director-General, John Birt. The latter was already under attack for his Thatcherite style of management, and had been pilloried in the press for allegedly avoiding income tax.

As with his 1980 appearance at the National Film Theatre, Potter wanted the lecture recorded for posterity. 'He said very explicitly that he didn't know how long he'd live, and he felt this would be his legacy to the industry,' recalls Rye. 'I think he tried to get *The South Bank Show* and other people to shoot it, and no one would, so he decided to have it shot himself.' Whistling Gypsy hired a camera crew.

Potter had announced that his lecture title would be 'Occupying

Powers'. In his 1982 Dublin lecture he had applied this phrase to the post-structuralist academics. Now, he adopted it for those he saw as his enemies among the media moguls.

The lecture was delivered to an audience of five hundred people – most of them television professionals, including Michael Grade – in an Edinburgh church, St Cuthbert's, a location that (as many people remarked) entirely fitted its pulpit style. 'I wondered if he was ever going to get through it,' says Sarah, 'because he'd been very ill the night before leaving for Edinburgh, and had barely made it to the train. And he had to wear gloves for the lecture. But he was great.' Sitting on a high stool behind a reading desk, with two autocue screens carrying his text, he began a sustained attack on what he called 'the strange new generations of broadcasting managements and their proprietors'.

He named one individual from ITV, Michael Green, head of Carlton Television, 'a big man in our business, a personable fellow who must nevertheless be held partly responsible for the predictable disappointment known as Carlton Television' – a line that raised a rather nervous laugh among the audience. Potter said he had 'recently and profitlessly' called on Green. 'Before going, I checked with a friend of his in red braces how best I could put Mr Green at immediate disadvantage.' (The recording shows Michael Grade, known for his red braces, smiling at this.) '"Ask him what he believes in," the friend said. But I could not bring myself to be quite so cruel.'

This was slight stuff compared to the venom that Potter now directed at the BBC, which only a few months earlier he had been calling 'the one British institution that really works' – though this was before it had accepted £530,000 from him for *Midnight Movie*. He told the audience:

The world has turned upside-down. The BBC is under governors who seem incapable of performing the public trust that is invested in them, under a Chairman [Marmaduke Hussey] who seems to believe he is heading a private fiefdom, and under a Chief Executive [Birt] who must somehow or other have swallowed whole and unsalted the kind of humbug-punctuated pre-privatization manual which is being forced on British Rail or British Coal.

Turning to the Birtist 'management culture', he asked:

Management of what? Management for what? Management. Management. Management. The word sticks in one's interface. Please excuse me if I dare to laugh, but I know that each age, even each decade, has its little cant word coiled up inside real discourse like a tiny grub in the middle of an apple. Each age, even each decade, is overly impressed for a little while by half-way bright youngish men on the make who adeptly manipulate the current terminology at precisely the right moment to make precisely the right impression on those who are a little older, a little less intelligent and considerably less alert. Ah, me! Which one of us here this evening has not fallen into one or other of these categories, and perhaps into the wrong one at the very moment we thought we were in the other? Life in the media business can be a hoot.

And, in a phrase that got more press coverage than anything else in the lecture, he observed of Birt and Hussey, 'You cannot make a pair of croak-voiced Daleks appear benevolent even if you dress one of them in an Armani suit and call the other Marmaduke.'

The desecration of the BBC (he went on) was a microcosm for the 'huckster' state of post-Thatcher Britain. And now he directed his venom once more at Rupert Murdoch, who had recently funded a Chair in Language and Communications at Oxford:

Murdoch did not turn up for the ceremonial meal to mark the largesse at Oxford, always a place where the gap between the cup and the lip can be measured by more than an inch of the sardonic. But Rupert has a touch of pure cruelty in his make-up. He sent Kelvin MacKenzie, the sharp little weasel that edits that daily stink they call the *Sun,* and the maladroit fellow had to sit and chew and probably even dribble a bit between two professors. Well, that was one set of cutlery not needed on the crisp linen, I suppose. But I hope for the sake of all concerned that both the professors were from the Anthropology faculty.

After a long digression about his own childhood and early days in television, Potter again called for a legal limit to the concentration of media ownership, and, more surprisingly, suggested that the BBC should be split up:

Why not separate radio from television? Why not let BBC2 be a separate public service broadcaster? Let us begin to consider afresh how the thousands of millions of pounds of licence money could be apportioned between two, three or four successors to the currently misled Corporation. One of the successors could certainly be a publishing or commissioning authority on the model of Channel 4.

Indeed, Channel 4, if freed from its advertisements, could continue to evolve out of its original, ever-precious remit into a passably good model of the kinds of television some of us seek. Michael Grade is becoming, by default, the new Director-General . . .

Calling for the nation to 'put Rupert Murdoch on public trial and televise every single second of it', he ended with a flourish: 'I . . . hereby formally apply in front of witnesses of substance, here at the Edinburgh International Television Festival, for the post of Chairman of the Governors of the British Broadcasting Corporation.'

After the lecture, Renny Rye went to look for Potter in the vestry – and found him smoking in the churchyard. 'Did they like it?' he asked anxiously. 'Did it go down well?' John Birt was not in the audience, but he came to the festival the next day and answered questions from a presenter on the BBC's own *Late Show*. 'It was powerfully argued,' he said of Potter's lecture, 'wonderfully lyrical, but it told a story about the BBC which was bleakly pessimistic and has no basis in reality.' The press tended to agree; Mark Lawson in the *Independent* called Potter's performance 'a flamboyant distraction from the battles rather than a contribution to resolving them'. However, Michael Grade describes the lecture as 'a beautifully crafted piece, and a very important text'.

Margaret and Sarah Potter had accompanied Dennis to Edinburgh. Sarah now 'had this aching feeling that things were not as they should be with Mum – she was complaining of a stiff back, and seemed very down. Already, I think, she was beginning to question whether she would be all right.'

The Potters had been invited by the festival organizers to a meal at a restaurant outside Edinburgh. 'Dennis insisted that all of us came,' says Renny Rye, 'though we hadn't been invited.' Sarah says this was typical of her father: 'He'd talk about "my people". If a meal was booked for us all at a restaurant, for example, and Renny or Rosie hadn't been invited, Dad would say, "I'm not going unless my people can be included." He was fiercely loyal.' Jon Amiel observes, 'Like all obsessively shy people, Dennis had a habit of clinging to people, once he'd traversed the membrane of intimacy. He would cling, sometimes defiantly, to his loyalties.'

At the meal, Rye found himself sitting next to Margaret Potter, whom he had not met before: 'I'd never been allowed to go down to the house at Ross. Now, I discovered that she was wonderfully strong, and very keen to talk directly and not to do the normal polite stuff. She said, "Den's always been so stupid about these girls. He likes to give the impression that he's had affairs, but I bet he's never done anything with anyone."'

*

The £530,000 needed to be recouped as soon as possible, since Potter had borrowed the money from his own pension fund. It was in this mood of financial anxiety that he found himself taking on 'two rich commissions' for a pair of six-part serials from the BBC and Channel 4.

The first of these, to be called *Karaoke*, had been signed up by the BBC some time before the MacTaggart Lecture, so that, at Edinburgh, Potter was biting a hand that was currently feeding him. It was after the lecture that he told Peter Ansorge at Channel 4 that he wanted to write a science-fiction serial about cryogenics and human memory. 'To be honest,' says Ansorge, 'my heart sank.' Potter explained that his interest had been aroused by speculation that 'virtual reality' techniques might allow human memory to be reprogrammed. 'They'll probably get a lot of it wrong,' he laughed. 'So England will be remembered as losing the World Cup in 1966.'

Ansorge goes on:

Dennis wanted to do twenty episodes which was completely mad of course. I told Michael [Grade], and he said, 'Maybe it should be eight', and John Willis [Director of Programmes] said, 'Maybe it should be six.' So we commissioned six hours. The creepy thing is that what came into my mind was *The Tempest*. Dennis said, 'Yes, I like that idea.' I didn't know then that it would be him breaking his staff; it *would* be his *Tempest*.

In late October 1993 he and Judy Daish were at a party in the Groucho Club given by Matthew Evans, Chairman of Faber and Faber, who recalls:

Dennis was very pissed. The first person he tore into was Tom Paulin, who'd just written a review of the Philip Larkin biography, and had said what a terrible person Larkin was. Dennis took great exception to this. He wouldn't talk to Paulin – all he wanted to do was insult him. And what emerged was a rather old-fashioned person, with old-fashioned values, objecting to the criticism of a national institution.

The high spot of the evening came when I spotted Maurice Saatchi with his wife Josephine Hart, and I took Dennis across and introduced them. Maurice put his hand out, and Dennis said, 'If you put your hand out, I will spit on it.' Saatchi didn't bat an eyelid. He just lowered his hand and cruised off.

By this time the stomach pain that Potter had begun to experience during the making of *Midnight Movie* was bad enough to send him to a doctor in London. After tests, he was told that it was caused either by an ulcer or a spastic colon. With hindsight, he wished he had also consulted one of the physicians in Ross.

Towards the end of 1993, Margaret's cancer was discovered to have returned, this time affecting her back and then her bone marrow. It was suggested that Dennis's supposed ulcer had been caused by worrying about her condition. But his own pain was getting much worse, and during December 1993 and January 1994 he was trying to control it with large doses of Panadol, while trying to write his new serial, *Karaoke*, for the BBC. He said afterwards that the pain had caused it to become a 'muddle'.

The script of this first attempt, which got no further than the first episode, is in uncharacteristically shaky handwriting. He said that the initial idea had come from seeing a florid Englishman singing 'Why Must I Be a Teenager In Love?' in a karaoke bar – presumably the one in Kingly Street where Louise Germaine had worked. 'Sums it all up, really, doesn't it?' he said to Steve Grant of *Time Out*. 'It's a useful metaphor, karaoke, the way in which you are allowed a few of your own little notes and flourishes as long as you keep to the tune, the job, the mortgage.'

The first draft of *Karaoke* opens with Jim Tuttle, an 'eccentric middle-aged A-list screenwriter turned so-called "Creative" Producer', dining in a London brasserie with his line producer Anna Crocket. Eavesdropping on the other diners in the usual Potter fashion, he becomes convinced that one couple – 'a beautiful if tartily dressed young blonde' and 'an older, palpably Essex Man' – are speaking lines from his latest script. In other words, we are back in *Double Dare* territory. The girl is called Amber, the name of Louise Germaine's character in *Midnight Movie*, and Potter later told Germaine that he had written the *Karaoke* role for her. Indeed the part is a portrait of the pre-*Lipstick* Germaine, with her 'estuary' English: 'Fanks very bleed'n' much . . . Whatchewmean? . . . Sod off, willya!'

The script of Tuttle's which is currently in post-production is called *Karaoke*, and we see scenes from it in the editing room. The director, Nick Balmoral, is arguing with the editor, who realizes that Nick's camera work has constantly favoured an actress called Linda, with whom he is obsessed – an obvious reference to Potter and Gina Bellman. Meanwhile Tuttle pursues Amber to the karaoke bar where she works; but by the final pages of this draft Potter seems less interested in pursuing a plot than in playing the sort of Chinese-boxes games with 'writing' and 'reality' that had occupied him in *Hide and Seek*, more than twenty years earlier.

By the time this draft was finished, his abdominal pain had become 'truly ravaging'. Later he recalled, 'I couldn't function. All I could do was walk up and down, up and down, up and down, wondering what the hell was going on, and thinking that if it were merely a spastic colon or a duodenal ulcer, then what a baby I was.' Sarah says he had also lost a great deal of weight. Eventually it was arranged that he would go into the London Clinic for an endoscopy ('You know, look inside you with a teeny-weeny camera', as Daniel Feeld explains in the later version of *Karaoke*).

Judy Daish drove him there on the morning of Monday, 14 February 1994 – he was later wryly amused that it had been St Valentine's Day. 'He was in terrible pain,' she recalls. 'He said it would probably take a couple of hours, and I arranged to come back and fetch him. I had lunch, and went straight back to the office, and one of my staff said, "Dennis has just rung, to say he's got bad news. Will you go over to the clinic?"'

Potter tells how the news was given to him in *Karaoke*:

DANIEL: What did you see down there in my personal pit? What sort of gold nuggets have I got?

(*Slight beat of tension. The* CONSULTANT *looks at him, choosing his words with skill until he knows what type of man he is dealing with.*)

CONSULTANT: A blockage. In the pancreas.

(*Tiny pause.* DANIEL's *expression does not change . . .*)

DANIEL: Blockage?

CONSULTANT: Blockage. Yes.

DANIEL: Is that a euphemism? Don't you mean *growth*?

CONSULTANT: Ah. But we don't yet know whether it's benign or malignant . . .

DANIEL: An obstruction . . . (*Smiling*) Well, that's what I've always wanted to be.

Potter stayed in the clinic overnight, and next day was given an ultrasound scan. This, in the words of one of the doctors, showed the presence of 'a sizeable pancreatic carcinoma which was infiltrating beyond the confines of the pancreas and several lesions in the liver which look like secondary deposits'. A biopsy was also taken. This confirmed that it was cancer, which had indeed spread to the liver. 'It is clearly distressing', wrote a doctor, 'to find such a sad result.'

He was told that neither chemotherapy nor surgery could offer any hope. All that the doctors could provide was pain control. They also made a rough guess as to how long he had to live. 'I remember him coming out to the car,' says Daish, who had driven to collect him, 'and he was looking very grave, and he came and sat in the passenger seat, and said, "I've got three months."'

CHAPTER 4

Back in charge

—

Renny Rye kept a diary covering the next few months:

Tuesday 15 February. I arrived home late from a titles test shoot. My wife, Ann, told me Dennis had phoned. He had cancer of the pancreas that had moved to the liver. He had been told he only had three months to live. He would phone me again later.

At about 11 pm he phoned. 'Can you believe the irony of the same family being struck twice within a year?' he said. And he did not stop. He talked constantly for about half an hour.

Rye says that his performance on the telephone was like a stand-up comic:

He didn't let me get a word in. I suppose he'd prepared it, because for twenty minutes he did this wonderful one-man show down the phone, delivering a series of black jokes – 'They say I'll be all right for the first couple of months, but in the end I'll become completely incontinent. What does it matter? I've been shitting on people for years.'

Towards the end, I said, 'What are you going to do?' And he said, 'I'm going to work, I'm going to write. I'm going to spend two weeks sorting out the lawyers and the family, and then I'm going to start, and I'll want to see you, because I want you to direct *Karaoke*.'

He phoned quite a few people that evening, including Rosie Whitman – and he told me afterwards that one of the reasons he agreed to keep seeing me is that I didn't sentimentally collapse. He said that Rosie and Alison [Barnett] had ended up in tears on the phone, and he couldn't cope with that.

Rosemarie Whitman says this is true:

When he phoned me to tell me, he wouldn't stop talking. He said, 'I'm dying, but I'm absolutely fine, and I don't want you worrying about me, Rosie, and

I'm going to write *Karaoke*, and you're going to produce it, and Renny's going to direct it, and it's going to be absolutely terrific.' By this time I'd sunk to the floor, crying my eyes out. He said, 'Do you know what I've discovered? I'd always thought that I was a coward, since I was a little boy, but I'm not a coward.'

Telephoning his own family was much harder. Margaret, in remission from her own cancer, was staying with her recently widowed sister Mavis Wood at Tetbury in Gloucestershire. 'Margaret was on her feet again, and looking very well,' recalls Mavis, 'when Dennis rang from London to say they'd diagnosed cancer. And she broke down, and said, "I just don't want to live if Den isn't going to be here."' He had already telephoned Sarah. 'Dad phoned me first,' she says, 'because he couldn't face ringing Mum and Mavis.'

The day after the diagnosis, he came home from London by train, and the whole family gathered at Morecambe Lodge. 'Dad tried to make it all right,' says Sarah, 'saying he was alive, feeling very serene, that he thought the world was lovely and thank God he wouldn't have to go through another Christmas. It was a quite amazing performance, from the very first.'

Sarah adds that it was never established whether Methotrexate or Razoxane had caused the cancer. 'But the pounding of those cytotoxic drugs over the years probably had something to do with it. Not that he would have done without them – they'd brought him a quality of life that he needed.'

A journalist interviewing him a few years earlier had discovered that he was terrified of dying: 'He's so worried about death he still secretly believes it isn't going to happen to him.' Now, he gave no indication to his family and friends that he felt any such terror. He admitted that there had been a 'moment of panic' when he realized that time, which usually seemed so plentiful, had suddenly run out on him. But he alleged that this panic had vanished in 'the time it takes to fall down a flight of stairs'.

He said that almost his first thought on hearing the news had been about the state of his finances. 'Obviously, I had to attend to my affairs . . . I remember reading that phrase when I was a kid, "He had time to tend to his affairs."' The £530,000 paid to the BBC had substantially reduced his pension fund, and if he could not finish writing *Karaoke* for the BBC and the science-fiction serial for Channel 4 before he died, his family would have to pay back £160,000 which he had received in advances.

He had also been lending money. John Roberdeau and Robert Michael Geisler, producers of *Secret Friends*, had asked him to bale them out when the withdrawal of investors from a theatre production threatened 'imminent financial calamity for both of us'. Potter and Judy Daish obliged with a joint loan of £75,000. When Potter learned that he was dying, he wrote to them asking for the return of the money, which was already overdue: 'The money *is* needed, *was* promised, and *must* be returned. You give me no indication of when you are going to repay . . .' Repayment did not take place; Roberdeau and Geisler say they hope to return the money from the proceeds of *The White Hotel* film, for which (in 1997) they signed Emir Kusterica to direct.

Potter's other loan was to Clive Lindley of Severn Sound radio, former director of PFH Ltd. 'Dennis lent me fifty thousand quid,' says Lindley,

with no security, no document, just on the old pals basis. I was in the most desperate trouble financially – I had a sizeable business, and had guaranteed a loan to a company in the group, and there was a fraud, and I knew nothing about it, but was the chairman of the group, and the company went down, and the guarantee nearly wiped me out. I had to go to court, and of course you don't get legal aid for that sort of thing, and I needed money very urgently in order to pay legal costs. I went to Dennis, and I knew very well that he'd lend it to me, I didn't have any doubts about that. He said it'd be a bit difficult, but he could give me so much a month for six months, and he'd always send me a little note with it – 'Keep smiling', all that sort of stuff. I think he probably got into trouble with Margaret for doing it! But I can never think of him without the warmest memories.

I won the case, and I think up to the time he died, I'd paid £24,000, and after he died I paid his estate the rest.

A few days after the diagnosis of cancer, Potter realized that he must 'concoct some sort of Family Trust to take care of all my works and their licences, and I had to make a will' – something he had never yet done. Despite his recent rashness with money, he would be leaving a substantial estate – almost £2 million, if Margaret's assets and the pension fund were included. Devising the trust with the lawyers and his accountant Stanley Rosenthal 'took me several long days of mind-crunching paperwork'. Sarah says:

Dad was absolutely brilliant in the way he set up the Family Trust. We thought Mum was going to be around for at least a couple of years, so she was included in it. But nobody else was, not even Grandma and Auntie June. A little later, one day in March, I had to fetch them over from the Forest, and it was really difficult. He said to them both, 'I'm not making any provision for you in the will, but this is what I'm doing.' He'd drawn them out cash, and he gave them both a sum of money – I truly can't remember how much. And there were no other legacies. He'd seen various people in London, and given them personal mementoes – a clock or a pen, that sort of thing.

Meanwhile another offer had come from Hollywood, inviting him to write 'a remake of an old but not very good movie' (Judy Daish cannot remember what film this was). He realized that the 'whacking great upfront fee the Americans guaranteed' would cover the repayments to the BBC and Channel 4 – presuming he could hide the news of his imminent death until the contract had been signed, and deliver some sort of first draft. However, he quickly decided that 'I didn't want to squander my last energies on work of this nature, where the better you make it the less chance there is of the film actually being shot. "No" went back down the transatlantic telephone line, and with it a few shards of saved dignity as well.'

But could the muddled *Karaoke* be made workable? Should he instead 'dive in, hell or glory' to the science-fiction serial, which had a title, *Cold Lazarus*, but was otherwise only a fragment of an idea? And, writing against the clock, and knowing he would not live to see these scripts produced, 'would I lose control of them, so that things yukky, maudlin and sanctimonious could come slinking and nudging across the ready-laid duckboards?'

After thinking hard for 'just one day and one night',

I decided that I would cast adrift all I had so far written of *Karaoke*, and start as from new, scene one, page one. And that then, oh, if there were time, that then I would plunge headlong into *Cold Lazarus*. Even if strength and spirit gave out during the progressive degradations of the growing tumours, and even if I ran smack into the most blank-eyed of writer's blocks, there would surely be enough pages of any kind of quality – gibberish, even – for my redoubtable literary executor, my agent Judy Daish, to resist any 'please pay back' affronts or solicitations.

He made some urgent calculations. If he could start on (say) 1 March – which would give him time to sort out the business affairs first – and could manage his usual ten pages a day, it would take him just over a month to write the six one-hour episodes of *Karaoke* the BBC had commissioned. Then, *Cold Lazarus* would require another thirty-six days – allowing no time to stop and think before beginning it. This meant 'seventy-two days without break from 1 March', which would take him to 11 May, a week before his fifty-ninth birthday (17 May), which 'I had somehow privately resolved to reach in the midst of all the prognoses'.

It seemed highly unlikely that he could complete this hugely demanding schedule without becoming too ill to work. 'But – *if* I tried *two four-parters* – ?' That would allow him to finish by mid-April.

The next task was to choose a doctor to look after him until he died. He had not consulted anybody at Ross-on-Wye for some while, but at Christmas 1993 he had met Dr Paul Downey, a thirty-three-year-old Liverpudlian who had recently been looking after Margaret on the National Health Service. 'I think I was the first to see Margaret when she was diagnosed as breast cancer,' says Downey.

I organized the treatment, and then other forces took over the care. Anyway, she came home from hospital pre-Christmas, and was very ill. Dennis came downstairs to tell me what was going on. That was the first time I met him. Over Christmas she got better. At that time, Margaret as a passing remark had mentioned, 'He's got a bit of tummy ache, but his doctors in London are sorting that out.' I thought no more of that.

Besides his conventional medical training, Downey had also studied homeopathy and acupuncture, which he sometimes offered to patients as an alternative treatment. Potter sneered at these as 'quack remedies', but seems to have realized that Downey was the kind of doctor who pays as much attention to the mind and the personality as to the body. Downey had seen *The Singing Detective*, and knew how Potter tended to view doctors. 'But when we met before Christmas to talk about Margaret, Dennis was quiet and charming to me, and very reserved,' Downey says. He found that Potter was extraordinarily protective towards Margaret: 'He didn't want her to know the diagnosis and outlook for her illness, if it turned out to be bad. He felt it would be detrimental to her to know. In fact at that time she was bright as a button, and remained so for the next three months.'

On 22 February 1994, a week after Potter's diagnosis in London, Downey had a telephone call from Sarah, to say her father had pancreatic cancer and would 'like to have a chat'. Feeling 'a little apprehensive', Downey went to Morecambe Lodge and climbed the three flights of stairs to Potter's office:

I saw that, unlike the traditional writer's garret, it was a very orderly room, painted white, with neat rows of bookshelves, filled with books and cassettes, and lots of pictures and posters of his plays and films. The desk was by the window, with a view of the Black Mountains and the plum blossom in the garden.

He was sitting (as always, I later found) at his desk, and my first contact was through a haze of Rothmans' smoke, for which he apologized. He seemed very serene. But he was testing me, I think, seeing what I was made of.

Although Potter had braved out the news with his family and friends, it was immediately evident to Downey that he was experiencing considerable anxiety, not so much of the fact of death as of the process of dying. 'We had multiple discussions about death and the mode of dying,' says Downey.

He wanted to know how it was going to end – pneumonia, jaundice, debility, coma, all those possibilities – and how I would deal with that. He wanted privacy; he was passionate that he wanted to remain private, with as few people fussing around as possible; and he didn't want to be in pain at the end, or to lose his dignity. I developed the strong impression of a very shy and private man, and I felt like an intruder into his world.

When the cancer had been diagnosed, the hospital had prescribed powerful analgesic tablets to ease his pain. Downey gathered that these were already proving inadequate. 'The maximum dose was three a day, but he was chewing one every two hours. He needed something stronger and more appropriate.' At the same time he explained his need to keep a clear head for writing, telling Downey that he did not want 'such side-effects that he could not work and think – he very much wanted to be in control of things'. Potter himself wrote that he wanted to find 'a path through all the opiates and analgesics . . . that would show up sufficient patches of calm or clear landscape where I could genuinely "write my all"'.

Downey, who describes himself as 'quite liberal with opiates' in the treatment of dying patients, said that morphine seemed to be required, and explained that there were three ways of taking it: slow-release tablets, a pump that provided a continuous infusion, or swigs of morphine from a flask whenever the patient wanted it. 'That's not really approved of by the experts, but Dennis opted for the flask.'

Downey recalls, 'He kept saying, "Can I trust you?" And I answered, "I'll care for you the way I'd care for my father if he had the same problem." Margaret later said to me, "I chose you for Dennis." She'd thought we would get on.'

*

Beginning the regime of morphine, Potter found that his mind was clearest in the early hours of the morning, after he had slept, so he abandoned his habit of starting work at midnight:

I made myself sit at my desk at five o'clock in the morning . . . and wrote the word KARAOKE in big bright capitals, and almost immediately ignited. As soon as I began to write I began to live again. Within hours I knew I was writing freely, within days I felt I was writing well, and I knew by the time the week was out that I was writing truthfully.

He had decided that the new *Karaoke* should abandon 'Jim Tuttle' for a central character far closer to himself – indeed, his hero should be under the same sentence of death:

I decided, as I have often in the past, to use the outward *forms* of auto-biography to give the engine-power *Karaoke* needed. My man had to walk alongside me in this adventure. He had to be ill, and in pain, and with an impending and intractable death sentence. He had to be more than a little withdrawn, a little sardonic and a little lost. And he had to be a proud writer. None of which, I hope it goes without further saying, means that he had to be *me*. Indeed, in many crucial ways (especially in terms of his isolation) precisely the opposite. No more like me, in fact, than the singing detective who had shared my natal patch and peeling skin. But like me enough . . .

This new hero was to be named Daniel Feeld. Maybe Potter was looking back at Daniel Miller in *Hide and Seek*, the writer who is convinced that he is being manipulated by another Author, while 'Feeld' recalls Potter's observation that his own writing ploughed the same field again and again (a Potter's Field, maybe). As usual,

I had no idea how the story was going to unfold, nor whom [Daniel] would meet along the way, except that I was sure the use of pictures in a cutting room was going to be something that both reverberated and explained, threatened and unravelled. I also had no idea how it would all end, except that he had to know that he was going to die and had to make appropriate arrangements with his affairs and himself.

Fairly soon after he had begun the new *Karaoke*, Potter realized that *Cold Lazarus* could be its sequel:

Getting to know Daniel Feeld made me wonder a lot about what kind of thing he was now writing, because he was obviously the sort to have something on the boil. And during this time, of course, in the physical effort and sheer joy of writing the eccentricities and styles of *Karaoke,* I too had lurking somewhere the original thoughts about *Cold Lazarus* which had made me put it up so eagerly to Channel 4 in the first place.

It came to me as strongly as the taste of the moistly raw shallot dipped in salt that Daniel was writing *Cold Lazarus . . .* The two works, so called, were actually *one.*

The rewritten *Karaoke* introduces a couple of new principal characters and splits another into two. Daniel Feeld has an agent, Ben Baglin, 'crumpled, rather pot-bellied, balding and . . . lapsing into unknowing spoonerisms when at all flustered'. The part was written for Roy Hudd, and this highly unlikely speech disorder introduces an element of music-hall or at least sitcom, with Baglin making such remarks as 'Surely it'd make a sot of lense', and irritably describing Daniel's TV serial, now in post-production, as 'kucking *Faraoke*'. The childish joke is part of a more serious game Potter is playing with language. He wanted *Karaoke* to show a writer losing control over his own material. Consequently words do strange things. A name appears back to front: Daniel reminds Ben that he spent his childhood in 'The Forest of Nead. N-e-a-d. Between the two rivers. And need, e-e-d, too!' The film director (now called Nick Balmer) and his editor run passages of dialogue backwards on their editing machine, so that Peter, the 'Essex Man', snaps: '?aylliw, ti tuoba esra elttil teews ruoy gniyrrow pots'. Meanwhile Ben spoonerizes.

The other new character is Arthur 'Pig' Mailion, underworld proprietor of a karaoke night-club, while Amber from the earlier script is divided into Linda, the actress in Daniel's *Karaoke*, and Sandra, the real-life version of the character she is playing – a hostess in Pig Mailion's club. His ironic name refers to his power over his girls – Linda (for whom he pimps) is completely under his control – but the true Pygmalion in *Karaoke* is Daniel himself, who builds a Higgins–Eliza relationship with Sandra, just as Potter had with Louise Germaine. 'I love the way you talk!' she tells him when visiting him in hospital. 'Not 'alf. I could listen to you for hours!'

At the beginning of *Karaoke*, Daniel is being given tests to determine the cause of his stomach pains. He is a man without personal commitments: 'No wife, no mistress. The occasional sleazy and all but commercial sneeze-like bonk, preferably with someone who has more to lose than I have. No children.' He has no psoriatic arthropathy, and no hang-ups about sex. Yet in some respects he is even more of a self-portrait by Potter than Marlow had been.

He has made enormous amounts of money from unfilmed Hollywood scripts. 'When are they going to catch on, those studios, paying for drafts they never actually make?' he asks Ben. He lives in a Fitzrovia flat to which even close colleagues are rarely invited: 'Look around as much as you like, Ben – or even open cupboards if you want,' he says when the agent brings him home from the hospital. 'It'll be your one and only chance.' Told that he is dying, he asks if there will be time to finish his next screenplay, 'about virtual reality and cryogenics'. And, looking around the neighbouring beds in the hospital, he observes wryly, 'I remember when I could make a whole ward sing.'

A more fundamental resemblance is Daniel's determination to control his own life, and the other people in it, as if it were a script he was writing. Told that he has a 'couple of months' to live, he realizes that this conviction that he is the author of his own story has been an illusion: 'There's been another story going on all the time. *This* one. The one I didn't know about. (*He half laughs.*) It's just that – well, the *ending* is sooner than I thought.'

Daniel quickly persuades himself that he has regained 'authorship', just as Potter was doing by putting his business affairs in order and writing against the clock. 'I'm back in charge of my own story,' he declares towards the end of *Karaoke*. 'I can take control of it now. I've got it back into my own hands and my own words. I know what to do now.'

Alongside the depth of feeling that Potter puts into Daniel, the other characters in *Karaoke* seem mere caricatures: the upper-class film director Nick, his wealthy wife Lady Ruth ('the only child of the eccentric peer Lord Collingwode'), the gangster Pig Mailion, and even the tart-with-a-heart Sandra, a character meant to carry emotional weight:

DANIEL: You woke a part of me that knew the words but didn't know the

song . . . Feelings that had been dormant for years! . . . Of *course* it's
physical, it's sexual, erotic . . .

SANDRA: (*pleased*) 'Ang about a minute –

DANIEL: (*sweeping on*) And of course I'd like to lie beside you and stroke
you and hold you and kiss you and – *rhapsodize* you . . .

SANDRA: Well. I could – um – I mean – (*Looks at closed door.*) Do you want
a hand job or something?

(DANIEL *bursts out laughing. She frowns, half rises, sits again, not sure
whether to be offended, or whether she has given offence.*)

DANIEL: (*gasping back laughter*) Oh, you dear girl . . .

Daniel kisses Sandra, and makes her a beneficiary of his will ('two
thousand five hundred pounds a month for the rest of your life'), but
makes no attempt to sleep with her. Yet *Karaoke* is not without a
disturbing sexual undercurrent.

Ben Baglin has a witch-like octogenarian mother, 'with chemically
vivid red hair, long false red fingernails and a kimono'. Ben's hobby is
building a model of Notre-Dame out of matchsticks, and, like Potter's
writing, this keeps him up all night. Bringing Ben his breakfast on a
tray, the old lady pauses in front of a mirror and, giving 'a tiny cackle',
pulls a hair from her armpit with a pair of tweezers, and places it
between Ben's poached egg and its slice of toast. 'Nice, is it? Is it nice,
Ben?' she asks him as he eats, 'with a glint of excitement flashing out
of her wizened and make-up-caked face', and Ben duly finds the hair
in his mouth and mutters 'Bunning old cugger!' (Potter probably got
this from a National Service joke about the army cooks putting pubic
hairs in the food.)

The other grotesque woman in *Karaoke* is Sandra's mother, whose
face, carved up many years earlier by Pig Mailion, 'is one-third scar
tissue, an unsightly mess, and the eye on that side of her face is pulled
down or askew, and is without doubt sightless'. She lives – lurks would
be a better word – in a small terraced house in Hammersmith,
occupying herself by doing jigsaws. Daniel, calling in search of Sandra,
finds her assembling one of Hammersmith Bridge, resonant in Potter's
work as an image of life-and-death (Arthur is resurrected on it in
Pennies, but Marlow's mother drowns herself from it in *The Singing
Detective*). The address where Daniel's encounter with the scar-faced
woman takes place is 56 Rednall Terrace: the house where Potter was

sexually abused. Is she a symbol of the mental scars that Uncle Ernie had inflicted there?

Asked if the morphine might have been affecting Potter's imagination while he wrote, Paul Downey says:

He would sometimes be scribbling away when I arrived to see him – he often had a little quarter-bottle of champagne that Sarah would bring him when he was writing, and his fags, and whisky – and I asked him just that: if he thought the morphine was affecting the way he was writing. He said the main effect was that it reduced his fear and anxiety while he was at work. And he joked about the effect of morphine on other writers – he mentioned Coleridge writing *Kubla Khan*, and said he was interrupted from an opiate trance by a character from Porlock. That's why he used the name 'Emma Porlock' in *Cold Lazarus*.

Much that is highly personal to Potter is packed into *Karaoke*. Yet these motifs are briefly uncovered rather than fully developed, and, not surprisingly given the haste of composition, the finished script reads like a first draft. The supposedly central theme of characters escaping from a writer's grasp becomes tangential, yet is still sufficiently present to cause confusion in the narrative. As in the first version, there are frequent jumps between 'real life' and Daniel Feeld's *Karaoke* screenplay. Potter briefly portrays the conflict between Nick the director and Daniel the writer, with Daniel punching Nick in the eye for changing his script; but this strand fades away. Potter wrote in the introduction to the published *Karaoke* that it contained some 'sly nods' at his earlier plays, but the arrival of two thugs hired by Pig Mailion to beat up Nick is an unsubtle reminder of the Mysterious Men. The conclusion, in which Daniel shoots Pig Mailion on behalf of Sandra, in revenge for the disfiguring of her mother, belongs to the self-mocking unrealities of *The Singing Detective* rather than the semi-autobiographical story of the dying writer.

The real end of *Karaoke* comes a few minutes earlier, when Daniel steps up to the microphone in the karaoke club and sings 'Pennies from Heaven' – except that, unlike the other karaoke customers, he lip-synchs; the voice we hear is that of Bing Crosby. Potter seems to be saying that, even in what amounts to a dying speech, his 'own song' is still part of 'the constant prewritten *Karaoke*'.

*

Potter wrote that he had begun *Karaoke* on 1 March, two weeks after the cancer was diagnosed, but it must have been earlier because on that day he met Renny Rye in London, and said that he had finished the first two episodes. Rye wrote in his diary:

I was dubbing *Chandler & Co.* in Dean Street. Dennis phoned during the morning session. He was up from the family home and wondered where we should meet. He suggested a wine bar . . . He knew Clare [Douglas], the film editor who had cut both *Lipstick* and *Midnight Movie*, was working with me, and suggested she join us . . .

At one thirty exactly he walked in, the same old Dennis (what had I expected?) wearing his distinctive short overcoat. Only when he took it off did I notice he had lost some weight. He was wearing a smart grey suit I did not recognize, not one of the green suits I had been accustomed to. 'I've had to dig out some old clothes, my usual trousers fall down.' . . .

'It's a bugger, isn't it,' he said, stealing the only opening line I had managed to come up with as a potential expression of sympathy . . . 'I've only got till the middle of May. Take my hand,' he said to Clare, offering his still arthritically clenched fist across the table. She did. 'It's catching, you know,' he said with a wicked twinkle . . .

He could no longer eat properly. In fact yesterday he had tried cooking himself a last fry-up but had been unable to swallow even a mouthful. He observed with the writer's detachment how the libido had died already and how this gradual stripping away of the old physical pleasures had enhanced his perception of the simplest of sensations left. At least there was now no need even to think about cutting down on his smoking or drinking! . . .

He had managed to smoke half-a-dozen cigarettes but to drink only two glasses of wine, a small ration by old standards. He felt hungry. At home he was surviving on soup and a branded vitamin-enhanced liquid sludge, with the occasional packet of crisps. The wine bar could only sulkily provide a bowl of peanuts, so I went to a local shop and bought two packets of plain crisps. I stupidly ran there and back, not wanting to miss a moment of the time we had.

He was talking about his funeral. He was planning the music and wanted to include 'Life Is But a Dream (Sh-Boom)' by the Crew-Cuts, as we had used it in a funeral scene in *Lipstick* . . . He had worked out a schedule which would allow him to finish both new scripts . . . He felt it was the best he had written since *Singing Detective* . . . Then he announced he was getting tired and needed to take his afternoon rest. He walked us back to the dubbing theatre, promised to make contact when he came up to town again and, after an awkward hug, disappeared into the crowded alley. It had been a *tour de force* as a performance. Witty, sad, controlled, inspiring – once again leaving little space for Clare or me to show any sentiment or even express our sorrow. We walked into the studio reception and I simply broke down and wept.

*

Two weeks later, he was at London Weekend Television for his last appearance on the screen.

Michael Grade explains how this happened:

Judy rang me, gave me the sad news about Dennis, and said, 'He wants to say goodbye to you.' So we fixed a time, I got some red wine in and some cigarettes – the usual props – and he came to my office in Charlotte Street. I was having difficulty hanging on to my feelings, because I adored the man. He sat down, and he was in wistful mood, and was incredibly generous, and said, 'I've enjoyed working with you – and I've especially loved the rows!' And we rambled over a whole range of topics.

Eventually he got tired, and said, 'I'm going home to the flat.' I said, 'Do you want a taxi?' And he said, 'No, I'm going to walk.' And we were going down in the lift, and I said, 'You know, Dennis, we've had a lovely conversation, and if you want to say any of this on screen, let me know.' And he gave me a very funny look, and we said goodbye and he went off. And I thought, 'Oh, shit, he thinks I'm after an obit.' So I rang Judy immediately and said, 'Please, please, tell him if he wants to do it I'll put it out the same night – let him have the pleasure of the audience reaction.' She rang me back and said, 'Yes, he'd like to do it.'

And I said, 'I think Melvyn [Bragg] should do it.' (I hadn't yet spoken to Melvyn about it.) And Judy said, 'I'll see what Dennis thinks of that.' And very quickly she rang back and said, 'Yes, he's happy for Melvyn to do it.'

So I rang Melvyn and explained.

'Mum didn't want him to do the interview,' says Sarah, 'because she felt he'd be deteriorating, wouldn't look good, and might not be able to cope with it. Whereas I strongly felt he should do it. I wanted the world to know what he was really like, and what it was like to be living through this. I felt it would be a comfort to us as well.'

Judy Daish asked for a large fee for Potter: 'I think it was twenty thousand quid or something,' recalls Grade. 'I said, "Fine, I'm not going to argue with it."' The money would of course go to Potter's estate, but on the unedited recording of the interview he pulls Melvyn Bragg's leg about it – 'Melvyn, I'm only doing it for the money.'

Daish told Bragg that the interview would have to be conducted early in the morning, Potter's best time, and he was uncertain how long he could manage in front of the cameras. Meanwhile Bragg decided not to illustrate the interview with clips from Potter's work; they would simply sit and talk in a bare television studio without a set. Grade calls this 'a brilliant decision'.

On 15 March, Daish collected Potter from his flat and drove him to London Weekend's studios very early – too early, says Bragg. 'They were supposed to be there at nine, but they arrived at a quarter to, and got lost in LWT. Consequently Dennis was in a foul temper when I met him. So I sat with him for a while and calmed him down.' Bragg himself was nervous as to what might happen:

We had been told that his body heat fluctuated out of his control, and so the lighting man and the producers had been there since six in the morning putting in special filters and pulling all the lights as far back as they could to keep the place cool. We were told that he would not mind a drink, and champagne was a good kick-start. So there it was on the table beside him with the black coffee and the ashtray for his wonderfully defiant smoking. A flask of liquid morphine which he knew he would need he handed to me, so that I could give it to him quickly and unscrew the rather stiff top.

'I can't keep food down any more,' Potter explained to Bragg. 'I can't have a meal, my digestive system's gone, but . . . the cigarette, well, I love stroking this lovely tube of delight.'

With the tape rolling, he told Bragg that he was not 'interested in reassuring people, bugger that'. He sneered at 'the kind of Christianity, or indeed any other religion, that is a religion because of fear of death, or hope that there is something beyond death' – that 'does not interest me'. But he spoke passionately of his newly acquired sense of the 'nowness' of life:

Below my window in Ross . . . the blossom is out in full now. It's a plum tree, it looks like apple blossom but it's white, and looking at it, instead of saying, 'Oh that's nice blossom' – last week looking at it through the window when I'm writing, I see it is the whitest, frothiest, blossomest blossom that there ever could be, and I can see it. Things are both more trivial than they ever were, and more important than they ever were, and the difference between the trivial and the important doesn't seem to matter. But the nowness of everything is absolutely wondrous, and if people could see that, you know. There's no way of telling you, you have to experience it, but the glory of it, if you like, the comfort of it, the reassurance . . . The fact is, if you see the present tense, boy do you see it! And boy can you celebrate it.

He said the same in the introduction to *Karaoke* and *Cold Lazarus*, written a few weeks later: '*Everything* feels different. Sometimes, too, in modes that are almost perversely serene or emancipating, thus making the whole experience far less dread-filled and ceiling-contemplative than I could ever have dared to imagine.'

He told Bragg that, when he was young, 'I thought, what kind of cruel old bugger is God . . . ?' Declaring that 'religion to me has always been the wound, not the bandage', he defined the state of religious belief that he had now reached:

I see God . . . as some shreds and particles and rumours, some knowledge that we have, some feeling why we sing and dance and act, why we paint, why we love, why we make art. All the things that separate us from the purely animal in us are palpably there, and you can call them what you like, and you can theologize about them and you can build great structures of belief about them.

He also explained that the root of his personality was profound shyness: 'I'm a really cripplingly shy person actually, I hate new situations, new people, with almost a dread . . . You try and compensate . . . so that can lead to aggression . . . the obverse, the reverse of shy . . . arrogance, if you like.'

A moment of high comedy came during the interview when he suggested that someone who has been told he has only three months wonders, '*Who would you kill?* . . . I . . . call my cancer, the main one, the pancreas one, I call it Rupert . . . because the man Murdoch is the one who, if I had the time – in fact I've got too much writing to do and I haven't got the energy – but I would shoot the bugger if I could.'

Bragg asked 'What are you writing?' and Potter told him about *Karaoke* and *Cold Lazarus*, adding, 'Whatever I'm doing now is my last work, and . . . I want it to . . . be fitting, I want it to be a memorial.' He then came up with an extraordinary proposal:

What I'd like to see, since it is my last work, and since I have spent my life in television, and since that life has not been insignificant in television, I would like the BBC's part [*Karaoke*] to be shown first by the BBC and repeated the same week on Channel 4, and then that inherited audience for the second part, *Cold Lazarus*, which would have some continuity in terms of character, but could still . . . stand separately, obviously, to be shown first by Channel 4 and repeated by BBC.

He was proposing this unprecedented collaboration between rival broadcasting organizations because there are two men in whom I place some hope . . . [for] British television, whom I place a great deal of hope in, and in a way I'd like their roles reversed. One of them is Michael Grade, of whom I've always been very, very fond, as it happens, and the other is Alan Yentob [then Controller of BBC1] . . . Yentob, in my opinion, should run Channel 4, and there is no question in my mind Michael Grade should be the Director-General of the BBC . . . Now . . . I haven't got space for meetings and things . . . [but] if I could get those two together . . .

Rick McCallum says of this extraordinary proposal: 'It was perfect Dennis! The final great fucking performance – and at the same time, "How am I going to make some money out of this?"' – for the immediate repeat of each serial on the other channel would greatly increase the earnings for Potter's Family Trust. Michael Grade had no idea Potter was going to say this – it had not been mentioned during the conversation in his office. 'It was a wonderful idea,' says Grade, 'though he stuck me with the expensive one!'

Potter also told Bragg, 'I've got a GP in Ross, Paul Downey, whose name should be celebrated if I do finish this, who has so gently and carefully led me to a balance between pain control and mental control where I can work, that he's . . . given me the liberty . . . to do ten pages a day.' He mentioned that his old illness was still haunting him – 'I've still got bloody psoriasis itching away at me, which is a bugger – you'd think that would lay off now, wouldn't you, but it won't!' – and said that his only worry was that he might 'die four pages too soon – if I can finish [*Karaoke* and *Cold Lazarus*], then I'm quite happy to go'. He added:

I haven't had a single moment of terror since they told me. I know I'm going to die, whether it's in four weeks' time, five weeks' time, six weeks' time, it might be longer. I might make eight, nine, ten, who knows? . . . The histology of it suggests that I should already be dead, but I know what's keeping me going, and . . . if those two organizations could do this . . . I could go out with a fitting memorial.

They concluded the interview here – Potter adding that it had been 'my chance to say my last words'. He took a further swig of the morphine, and left the studio to finish his champagne in the green room.

*

Nine days later, on 24 March, Paul Downey noted that he had finished *Karaoke*, and was making plans for *Cold Lazarus*. Five days after that he was in London again, to see Renny Rye, who wrote in his diary:

I had received the first two episodes of *Karaoke* the week before. Judy Daish phoned me at the weekend to arrange the time and place . . . She asked me to call at her office *en route* to collect episodes 3 and 4 which were now ready. When I saw her she was herself pale. 'It varies from day to day,' she said. Last week he had been in great form and had recorded an interview with Melvyn Bragg . . . Today he was exhausted by the train journey up from Ross but had shown some of the old sparkle at a meeting with Michael Grade that morning. 'You've got an hour,' Judy said. 'Ken Trodd and I will join you at four. Be prepared for a shock. He looks a lot worse.'

I arrived at the wine bar fifteen minutes early . . . At three precisely he came in and headed straight for the bar. I said I had some wine ready. 'I can't drink wine any more,' he said, 'can't keep it down.' He ordered whisky and black coffee . . . 'How is it?' I asked. 'Oh, you know, pretty awful. I get so tired.' But it was still Dennis . . .

I said I'd heard the interview with Melvyn Bragg had gone well. Yes, he was pleased with it. He told me that, later that day, Bragg had sent round a copy of a note a cameraman had silently passed to Melvyn when they had finished. It said the crew felt privileged to be there and hear him talk so courageously about his life and impending death. The simple gesture had touched him.

He started to talk about *Karaoke* and *Cold Lazarus*, insisting that Rye should direct them both:

'I've told Grade this morning and I'm going to tell Yentob tomorrow. They'll have to agree – it's one of my conditions . . . You'll do them well. And anyway, if you bugger them up, I'll come back and haunt you.' . . .

Louise Germaine had to play Sandra, and Roy Hudd had to play Ben Baglin . . . He had already spoken to Roy on the phone, but he said he had had to ring off when Roy broke into tears. 'Don't cry on me, I can't take that,' he ordered me. The week before he had seen Rosie Whitman and Alison Barnett. 'I shan't be able to see them again,' he said, 'they were too weepy . . .

'Oh yes, that's the last condition – Ken Trodd will produce [*Karaoke* and *Cold Lazarus*]. I know you don't get on very well but it'll be good for both of you. He's a bloody good producer and he'll be on your back all the time. He'll give you a kick up the arse when you need it just as I would if I could be there. And you'll make sure Ken doesn't run away and change it all.'

Trodd had been in Ireland when Potter's cancer was diagnosed:

Judy rang me saying he'd like to see me, and as soon as I was back in London, I was summoned to a wine bar. Dennis and Judy arrived. I already had a sick migraine, because of the tension of the occasion, and could only sip Perrier, but Dennis was urbane and in control, drinking champagne with liquid morphine chasers. He told me he was writing some new work, 'and I want you to produce it, though I have to say my family are going to be appalled when they hear that, because they believe you've treated me so badly over the years!' And I was never sure how much of that was irony and how much real bitching – a characteristic Dennis mixture. And he went on, 'I do have one very real fear of death' – a pause – 'that you might be asked to speak at my memorial service!'

At Rye's 24 March meeting with Potter, they were joined by Trodd and Daish. Rye notes that Potter asked Trodd what he thought of *Karaoke*:

'It's very good, brilliant [Trodd answered]. There are a couple of things –'

'There isn't time, Ken. Are you going to do it? Will you accept all the conditions? I want you and Renny to shake hands here and now and agree to go ahead on my terms.'

There was an awkward moment . . . Ken wanted to talk about the conditions. Dennis was appointing him as producer but stripping him of all the essential judgements a good producer should make.

'But you must realize,' said Dennis, 'I am the producer until I die. You are to take over only when I have gone.'

We solemnly shook hands and the tension eased.

Trodd does not recall it as a formal, binding handshake, but merely as 'a gesture of friendship in emotional circumstances, and professionally speaking highly ambiguous ones'.

Around this time, Potter also met Louise Germaine, in the same place, Needles Wine Bar. 'He came out with it,' she says,

about his dying – he said, 'Don't cry, don't cry.' And he told me about the part he was writing for me in *Karaoke*. I didn't want to talk about that. I said, 'I don't care, Dennis, just let me enjoy this moment with you.' Because I knew that was the last time I'd see him. He said, 'No, we've got to sort this out – you've got to do the part, and you'll do it brilliantly.' I think he wanted me to have the part so that I wouldn't worry about money, and it would really get my career going.

*

The Bragg interview was to be shown on 5 April. Word about it, and Potter's cancer, had begun to leak out, and on 25 March the *Independent* carried the headline 'Dennis Potter dying of cancer but still "full of life"'. *The Times* reported that he would be seen talking about his 'impending death'. A reporter rang Margaret, who said, 'There is a television programme which will tell all about it. We are not up to saying more at the moment.' A press preview of the interview was held the next day, and after watching it, Richard Brooks wrote in the *Observer* (on 27 March) that it was 'extraordinary . . . vintage Potter'.

The morning after the Channel 4 screening of the interview, the *Guardian* printed a full transcript. On 13 April *The Times* reported, 'Dennis Potter's wish to have his two final plays shown by both the BBC and Channel 4 came a step closer last night when the rival networks signalled that they would do all they could to fulfil his wish . . . Alan Yentob, Controller of BBC1 . . . said last night that he had been deeply moved by the interview. "I will do all I can to achieve Dennis's wishes and I believe it will be possible . . . Michael Grade, Chief Executive of Channel 4, also gave his support: "I think it is a very exciting idea and we would love to bring it off."'

Six years earlier, Potter had said on *Desert Island Discs*, 'The one thing about dying is, if only you could observe [people's] reactions!' Thanks to the Bragg interview he was now able to. 'Thousands of people reacted', writes Bragg, 'with phone calls and letters.' Jon Amiel sent Potter 'a long, loving letter. I cried when I wrote it. But he didn't reply – I don't think he wanted to deal with other people's feelings about his dying.' Amiel felt that the interview had shown people the 'real' Potter, gentle and thoughtful, rather than the aggressive figure he had usually presented on television. Renny Rye makes the same observation: 'Everyone said that in the final Bragg interview he'd changed so much. He hadn't – he just allowed that side of himself to be shown to everyone at last.' Michael Grade says, 'I've never known a reaction to a programme be like that, achieving such an intimacy with the audience. Of all the things I've enabled in television, it's the programme of which I'm proudest. Nothing stacks up against it in terms of impact.'

However, Gina Bellman hated the interview and the public reaction:

I felt bitter that he could be eulogized after the press had called him all sorts of names – and then suddenly the man's dying, and I thought the whole thing was so distasteful. He should have been eulogized throughout his life for being a pioneer and a maverick, not for dying! And the *slickness* of it – this syco-phantic man going, 'Tell us about what it's like to take morphine all day long?'

Bellman wrote to Potter some time after the interview, when she heard about Margaret being seriously ill too, 'but I never had a reply from him – not that I expected one'.

Thanks to the mention of him in the interview, Paul Downey now found himself deluged with requests (which he did not accept) from newspapers to write articles about the care of the dying. Also,

a drug company phoned up and said they were developing a new wonder drug for pancreatic cancer. They sent the literature to me, and I went to see Dennis and asked if he wanted to take part in the trials – they couldn't guarantee anything, but it might prolong his life by a little. And he just turned round, through the haze of smoke, and said, 'Tell them to fuck off.' We both felt that it was unlikely to help, and might well impair his writing, which was proceeding at a furious pace.

He had another meeting with Rye in Needles Wine Bar on 13 April:

Dennis walked in, straight to the bar, by now looking very frail. 'I'm having trouble with my ear, does my voice sound all right, am I shouting? . . . I've upped my writing to twelve pages a day . . . but each day the pain gets worse and the morphine dose has to be greater. One day soon I'll have a bad session and just won't come out the other side. I've written a sketch of the end just in case I die tonight and can't finish it tomorrow. Then you or someone else will have to put the end together . . .

'*Cold Lazarus* is my *Nineteen Eighty-Four*, my *Brave New World*, my projection of the world as it is today pushed to a soul-less conclusion.' It was, I said, a rather bleak vision. 'That's not so true as it goes on. Some of it is very funny . . .'

Cold Lazarus may have its genesis in Gordon Rattray's futuro-logical book *The Biological Time-Bomb*, which Potter had reviewed in *The Times* in 1968, summarizing its vision of the next millennium: 'Transplanted heads . . . Brains kept alive in a bottle . . . A greatly pro-longed extension of the human life-span, even up to immortality.' Potter's 1982 screenplay of Thomas Page's novel *The Man Who Would Not Die* had told the story of Daniel Forrester, whose consciousness survives after his death. The sequel to *Karaoke* combines these two ideas, so that Daniel Feeld, presumably having arranged for his head to be deep-frozen after his death, awakes 374 years later to find his consciousness and memory being reactivated by scientists living in a dystopic world that is totally owned by Rupert Murdoch-like media moguls.

Potter told a journalist that he had once had a science-fiction script rejected by Verity Lambert when she was the producer of *Dr Who* in the Sixties. As far as he could recall, it was 'about a schizophrenic who only thought he was a time-traveller'. He was concerned that *Cold Lazarus* should not 'look like *Dr Who*'; yet his last work for television, with its childlike delight in such sci-fi toys as voice-activated cars and virtual-reality helmets, has many affinities with the show that created the Daleks.

Not that he took the scientific element in *Cold Lazarus* light-heartedly. He would pass his sister-in-law Mavis, who had come to help look after him and Margaret, on the stairs at Morecambe Lodge, engrossed in background reading about memory and cryogenics. Mavis remembers 'Dennis saying, "I've got to digest all this" – showing me I don't know how many pages he had to read about the human brain'.

It is striking that a writer about to die should portray immortality as deeply undesirable. 'LET ME GO!' pleads Daniel to his scientific captors towards the end of *Cold Lazarus*. He desires to leave a world controlled by the Rupert Murdochs of the future, where the only kind of reality is virtual. David Siltz, President of Uniplanet Total Entertainment, has acquired 'the right to take over the memories of Daniel Feeld, edit them, and transmit them all over the world on his TV, his cable, his VRs, his videos, his whole crock of shit . . . He'll sweep the ratings when people out there see what it was *really* like to walk and talk and play and screw and eat and drink nearly four hundred years ago.' At the end of the serial, Siltz is shot dead, the fate that Potter playfully wished he could deliver to Murdoch.

Daniel's memories are of course Potter's own, among them the Forest children singing the hymn 'Will there be any stars in my crown?' (which he had quoted in the Bragg interview), and the nightmare of sexual abuse (a tramp assaults young Daniel in the woods); but there is one recollection never before used in his plays. 'I once knew a young woman whom all the songs were about,' says Daniel, 'a green-eyed dazzler I met in a Forest of Nead dance hall.' And for the first and last time, we see Potter's meeting with Margaret in Lydney Town Hall that

Saturday night in 1957. 'John says you're at *Oxford*,' the Forest girl asks in breathless admiration, 'is that right?'

While Potter was writing *Cold Lazarus*, Margaret's condition began to deteriorate again, and she started to experience severe pain for which no cause could be found. 'Nobody could ever describe what it was like, while Dennis was rattling through *Cold Lazarus*,' says Paul Downey, 'the pressures on everybody – Sarah, Jane, Robert, Mavis, Judy Daish and myself – trying to keep Margaret happy, Dennis happy. He didn't want her to know what was going on with her own illness (not that we did know yet), and he had his scripts to write. Everybody was being drained by it.'

None of this strain is apparent in *Cold Lazarus*, which is full of boyish energy, and tells a complicated story with considerable clarity, avoiding any of the narrative tricks that had obsessed Potter since *Blackeyes*. Yet, like *Karaoke*, it has an odd sexual undercurrent.

The laboratory in which Daniel's head is preserved is in the charge of Professor Emma Porlock (Potter's joke about his morphine), an 'acknowledged world authority on biotechnology at absolute zero temperatures'. Potter does not specify her age, but portrays her as a woman in her fifties or thereabouts. She personifies good sense and moderation throughout the serial; yet she is constantly abused verbally on account of being old. A computerized voice from the accounts department calls her a 'nasty old bitch', and a policeman addresses her as 'you dried-up old bag'. She is portrayed as having ridiculous sexual desires; when Siltz invites her to lunch she remarks that he 'will not rape me. Alas.' And Siltz himself expresses his contempt for her in strongly sexual terms: 'I'll squeeze that milk from your withered udders, you hoity old cow.'

These are incidental details, but several scenes of *Cold Lazarus* are devoted to the sexual rapacity of another ageing woman, Martina Matilda Masdon, Siltz's rival media-owner and Emma Porlock's employer. Here, Potter is specific about her age: she is a 'carefully preserved sixty-five-year-old witch'. Lounging by her pool in California, smoking a highly illegal cigarette (for smoking has been outlawed in this future world), she displays 'a lot of scraggy old flesh', and amuses herself sexually with a series of gigolos, berating one of them for failing to get an erection – 'If there's anything worse than a dickhead, it's a *limp* dickhead.' Ken Trodd has described this element of *Cold Lazarus* 'a comic reversal of sexual stereotyping with Martina

Matilda Masdon's whole retinue of male bimbos'; but it pervades the whole serial, and Renny Rye says he wishes he had been able to cut much of it.

There is also the curious figure of Dr Rawl, a cadaverous medic introduced by Potter towards the end of *Cold Lazarus*, who describes himself as 'especially interested in sexual arousal . . . And erectile tissue.' One of Siltz's henchmen, he intends to stimulate Daniel's brain into the recollection of sexual experiences. He alleges that the out-of-the-body sensation that Daniel has experienced when dying can also be caused by 'energetic copulation'. Potter ends *Cold Lazarus* with Daniel, released at last from terrestrial life, travelling down a swirling tunnel of memories towards a 'child's image of angel wings and cherubs, white on white', as he cries 'Ye-e-e-e-es!' But this conventional glimpse of the heavenly does not erase the characteristically disturbing role that sexuality plays in Potter's final work.

*

On 17 April the *Mail on Sunday* had carried an interview with Sarah, who said that her father was 'trying to be as normal as possible. We don't see any weak moments . . . He'll put words on the page until physically he no longer can . . . Sadly, however, he is deteriorating quite fast. He hopes to survive until 17 May, his birthday, but we think he only has about two weeks to live.' The paper reported:

He and Sarah have discussed his cremation, memorial service – and he has even dictated letters cancelling his credit cards. Margaret is contemplating widowhood. 'Mum feels frightened by the future,' says Sarah, 'but we will all pull together to help her through the dark patches . . . Thank God they can treat her. We are sure she'll get better.'

Paul Downey noted that Potter finished *Cold Lazarus* on 20 April: 'Now that his goal had been achieved, Dennis seemed a little deflated.' During the following week he wrote an introduction to *Karaoke* and *Cold Lazarus*, which were to be published by Fabers. In it, he expressed regret that work on the scripts had led him 'to neglect those in front of me who were suffering as well, particularly my own sick and struggling wife, Margaret, the steadfast green-eyed one ever'. But he believed that she and the family had understood that 'doing what I did in the way that I did meant that I was able to live by the means of this work – and to live with the dignity they too needed for me and from me'.

On 26 April, he set off for a final trip to London, driven by Sarah. Renny Rye wrote in his diary:

I got a phone call from Judy saying Dennis was still planning to see me on Wednesday but his doctor and family were trying to persuade him he was too ill to travel . . . On Tuesday I got a fax. He was travelling. I was to go to his flat the next day at four.

Dennis's London flat was a very private place. Judy was the only person I knew to have been allowed to enter. His driver of many years, Terry, had once been severely reprimanded for daring to come to the door when Dennis had been ill before.* It was a sign of how ill he had become that I was invited there. I had an hour and then Ken Trodd would join us at five . . .

When Dennis opened the door I was shocked at his appearance and probably let it show. 'I have trouble keeping my balance,' he croaked as he let me in. It was as though he had aged the lost thirty years of his life in the two weeks since I had seen him. His normally beady eyes seemed to stick out from a cadaverous face and his voice was husky. He had to steady himself against the furniture as he moved into the tiny living room.

'It's not much of a place but it's been a useful bolt-hole,' he said, ushering me to a sofa . . . He apologized for his voice, said we might have to stop if the pain got too bad . . . I said Judy had told me he was now on the 'Brompton Cocktail', a mixture of morphine and heroin. He said the doctors were doing all they could, but there was less and less relief from the unremitting pain. Next week he was having a drip fitted, so he would have a constant supply that he could turn on fully when he had decided enough was enough.

He asked Rye to read out his notes on *Cold Lazarus*, and began to talk about the scripts:

As he warmed to his theme, he started to pace the floor – the old Dennis again. And then, as suddenly, he sat down again, his hands clasped to his stomach. 'For the first couple of months, I used to wake in the morning just thankful there was another day, so much more time to appreciate the wonders of everything around me. Now when I wake, all I can think of is the pain ahead. If I wasn't working I would spend the whole day contemplating the terror of dying.'

---

* Terry Tapping, who was employed as a Whistling Gypsy driver, confirms that this is true, adding that he and Potter became great friends. However, Rosemarie Whitman says that she often visited Potter at the flat, and Jane Potter writes, 'People did go to Dad's flat. Judy and I had helped to decorate and furnish it. Mum stayed there, of course, but they preferred to go to hotels most of the time. I stayed there many times, and once took it over while between flats of my own. Dad complained – "It is supposed to be my inner sanctum" – but, bless him, he stocked up his little fridge with food and got some wine in for me, and came back three weeks later.'

I said he had painted such a beautiful picture of the end in his script, the classic idea of approaching the blinding light. Did he fear it might not be like that?

'I'm talking about the process of dying, not death itself. I'm sure when I die I'll come through the other side and, whatever the answer is, my response will be, 'But yes, of course, how obvious, I knew it all along.'

And that, I said, is why *Cold Lazarus* ends with Daniel's final 'Ye-e-e-e-e-es!'

'Right! It's the final, all-embracing affirmation, a completely satisfying fulfilment – a happy ending.'

The doorbell rang: Trodd had arrived. According to Rye's diary, Potter said abruptly to him, 'This isn't going to be a pleasant meeting, Ken, because I've heard what's going on.' Despite their handshake a few weeks earlier, Trodd had been publicly questioning whether Rye was sufficiently skilled to direct *Karaoke* and *Cold Lazarus*.

Trodd explains why he did this:

A dangerous closed circuit seemed to have been set up by Dennis arranging that, though we would make *Karaoke* and *Cold Lazarus* after he was gone, all the conditions had been set by him. I was convinced that we needed the fresh air of an outside director, who would bring some scepticism and courage, and thereby do more justice to the work – a director who would not be over-influenced by the sentimental aftermath of Dennis's death – the great man gone in his prime, the awesomeness of last wishes. I felt the needs of the tale were of more long-term importance than respect for the departed teller, however emotionally imperative that felt in the summer of 1994.

Rye write that Trodd was 'somewhat thrown' by Potter's attack:

After some embarrassed verbal shuffling he said, 'Well, as you want us to be direct –' And there followed about ten minutes' discussion of my talents, whether they were first-rate or just lightweight, as Ken thought . . . Eventually Ken conceded that I was Dennis's absolute choice and that was the end of it. The matter would not be raised again and he gracefully accepted the situation . . .

Again, Trodd's recollection of the occasion differs somewhat from Rye's:

I don't remember Dennis throwing down a gauntlet to me, but he told Renny that I thought he was the worst possible director for the job – typical Dennis! – and so made sure that Renny and I had to bond, then and there, in that room. Renny is by no means an indifferent director, but I couldn't persuade myself that he was absolutely the best person available. So while Dennis was still alive, I was attempting, not very effectively, to tackle this.

Rye's diary continues:

The main fray over, Dennis began to wilt. He started to clear up and told us we must go. 'Otherwise you'll see me go to pieces before your very eyes and I don't want that.'

I quickly collected my things and a book he had given me on virtual reality. 'That's what Daniel throws across the room [in *Karaoke*],' he said. 'I haven't read it but you might find it useful.'

At the front door neither Ken nor I knew what to say.

'You don't think you'll be up again?' [they asked Potter.]

'No, the journey takes too much out of me. But phone me if you want to talk about anything. Margaret or Sarah will know if I'm able to talk to you.'

I moved back and gave him a final hug. 'Not too hard,' he said, 'it's very painful.'

I said I hoped that when the end came it would be as he had described it in the script, and backed away. By now only his diminished face was visible round the side of the door. 'Goodbye.'

As we stepped into the lift I heard a big sob from Ken and turned to see his eyes filling. For an awful moment I thought he was going to break down as I had once before. But he just managed to contain himself. 'It was still Dennis, wasn't it?' he said.

'I need a drink,' I said, as we stepped into the evening air. And we went off to talk together for the first time.

Trodd says Potter offered to embrace him, saying 'Goodbye, thank you, love you', but Trodd held back – 'It was partly that I thought hugging him might hurt him.' He says it is true that he and Rye went off for a drink together, 'but next morning I woke up and realized I was still convinced that Renny wasn't the right person for the job. I was sure we could get somebody of really high calibre, such as Danny Boyle or Michael Winterbottom, and again I mooted the question of Renny not being the right director when I next spoke to Dennis on the phone, but he said, "If you persist in raising this subject, I will not be able to die happy."' They did not discuss the matter again, and had what Trodd describes as several 'unreal but comforting' phone calls to each other between then and Potter's death: 'Dennis was more aware of the need to comfort other people about his death than of the need to be comforted himself.'

*

Margaret's pain was still unabated, and it was now decided to move her to St Michael's Hospice between Ross and Hereford. 'St Michael's was crucial,' says Downey. 'We couldn't have managed without them. It's a very tranquil place on the road to Hereford, in the grounds of an old convent.' Sarah guesses that the separation from Margaret 'hurt Dad more than his own impending fate. It was agonizing for them to be apart at such a time. Luckily they could talk on the phone.' Mavis Wood, who went to stay with her sister in the hospice because Margaret was frightened of being left alone there, recalls, 'Dennis would come in to see her, looking terribly ill, and I would get a glass for his whisky, and put his chair by the bed, and then leave them together.' Paul Downey says there was no question of Potter himself moving to the hospice: 'It just wasn't for him.'

At the beginning of May, just as Margaret had been installed in St Michael's, Downey began to keep a diary of his visits to Potter: 'It was only when he mentioned that I might be plagued by his biographers that I felt some facts should be recorded,' he explains. When he asked Potter if he minded a diary being written, 'he said he did not as long as I told the truth'.

The diary begins:

3 May. Weaker. Many stresses as his wife is admitted [to the hospice] and I feel the final phase has begun. Suggest more 'outside help' from our nurses, and the use of the [morphine] pump. Aiming to celebrate his [fifty-ninth] birthday [on 17 May].

More discussions on dying and the 'point between consciousness and eternity'. I have tried to reassure him that we will keep him pain-free, and discussed examples of this. Obviously frightened, but now more reassured.

Downey says, 'When I watched the end of *Cold Lazarus* – that tunnel [the swirling tunnel of Daniel's memories as he passes from this world] – it reminded me of our discussions about how he would die. Like Judy and Sarah, I find it very hard to watch those last moments, because of the discussions we all had with him. Some of those things that were said almost seemed to have been lifted into the script.'

During early May, still determined to keep working, Potter turned back to *Cold Lazarus*, and began to adapt it into a single screenplay for the cinema. His handwriting was still clear and firm, and he sped through the task, reducing the number of characters and trimming the story to fit the reduced screen-time. Renny Rye says Potter meant it to be 'an investment – he hoped that the family would get some more money'.

On 10 May, Potter dictated a letter to the film producers Roberdeau and Geisler, asking for the return of the loan. He told them:

I linger on and on until I've started to read what seem like my own obituaries here in the British press: and heart-warmingly generous they have been about my work over the years. The doctor nearest to me gives me at least another three weeks, and I hope he's right. I'm on the 'pump' and in a sort of opiate haze for a lot of the time, supposedly high on huge amounts of heroin. I am calm and relatively at peace with what has to be accepted . . . and I have two brand-new series, completed against the clock and all the other odds, which have been received with great relish I'm glad to say.

Paul Downey's diary continues:

15 May. The tragedy for D[ennis] and M[argaret] continues. Margaret had been in the local hospice for pain relief for her secondaries, but felt that she should be with D at home. Sadly the effect of her return was to drain them, both emotionally and physically. D seemed to be weaker than ever before, and Margaret's suffering was distressing for him.

Sarah had asked if her mother could come home, so that the family could be together, and Margaret was brought back by ambulance, in great pain from the journey. Mavis came with her, to help with Dennis too: 'There I was, with two very ill patients. Every time I moved Margaret, she would cry out. I would make their breakfast, and say to Dennis, "Come and eat something", and he'd come downstairs, though I knew he didn't want anything. And I'd leave them together until he wanted to go back up to his office.'

Sarah says:

Sadly, it was impossible to keep her at home. She was in agony whenever we tried to move her. Dad had had thirty years of controlling a painful condition. He was such an amazing bloke about what he could suffer. The medical people drew in their breath over the dosage of morphine he was on. But, of course, it was all new to Mum.

They were both on morphine pumps, which whirred into action every minute and a half, pushing morphine into them. It was an extremely nightmarish situation, but when I was actually dealing with either one of them, it wasn't such a nightmare because I was too busy and time was too precious.

Paul Downey says, 'I think it was apparent to all of us that Margaret was dying, but there was still no clear reason for the severe pain.'

Margaret was taken back to the hospice, and on 16 May Downey wrote in his diary, 'The strain and anguish of Margaret's suffering had taken a toll, but now she has returned to the hospice D is much brighter, and went to the pub yesterday.' Sarah recalls this:

Two days before Dad's birthday, he was in terrific form, and looked really good. Mum was in the hospice, but she'd gone there for pain management, and they were preparing her so that she could come out and be with Dad at the end. We went to see her.

On the way back from the hospice, it was almost twelve o'clock, and Dad said, 'Do you know, I almost feel I could go in and have a drink and something to eat.' So we pulled in to the Traveller's Rest, and sat in the car till it opened at twelve.

The next day, 16 May, Whistling Gypsy was due to open a production office for *Karaoke* and *Cold Lazarus* at Twickenham Studios. Rosemarie Whitman says that 'at precisely ten o'clock that morning Dennis phoned to make sure I was at my desk! I said, "I've got the red wine here, where are you?" But that was putting my foot in it, because he said, "Rosie, I can't drink red wine any more."'

He told Whitman that, with all the scripts finished, he was bored. She had a solution to this:

During *Lipstick*, Dennis had said, 'Let's expand Whistling Gypsy, and do the work of other writers.' I gave him a novel by Nina Bawden, *Family Money*, which I loved, and he read it and took out an option on it, and suggested Ruth Carter to adapt it. And I sold it to Channel 4, and got the development money just before he died. Also, I developed a series of ghost stories, an anthology series to be scripted by different writers. Dennis loved the idea, but I couldn't interest anybody in taking it on. Now, with him saying he was bored, I sent him one of those stories, A. S. Byatt's *The July Ghost*, and he started to make some notes about adapting it.

Whitman adds, 'He'd call me periodically again after that, but his voice was gradually getting weaker and I found that very upsetting.'

Downey's diary for 16 May notes:

I discussed if he felt he needed any other mental support, but he says that he has always been self-reliant, and does not know loneliness, as he turns in on himself for support. Today he says he still feels 'serene' despite the knowledge that Margaret's prognosis is now much less good.

Will he write more?

Some days later, he decided that he would.

*

On 6 April, David Johnson, editor of the Arts and Books section of the *Daily Telegraph*, had written to Potter saying how moved he had been by the Bragg interview. 'As a fan since your television reviews in *The Sunday Times* inspired my formative years as a journalist . . . may I offer you *carte blanche* to write the piece of your own choosing?' He suggested 'a reflective piece' on the changes in television over the past thirty years.

Potter did not reply until 16 May:

Dear David Johnson

My candle flame is obviously guttering very low at the moment, but I seem to be lingering on long enough to glimpse the far edge of the kinder of my own obituaries!

I am pleased to tell you that I have completed *Karaoke* and *Cold Lazarus* – which I regard as essentially one eight-part piece. Now all that effort is of course evaporating into an overwhelming sense of loss, I itch to scribble *something* and yet I do not feel able to write you even the smallest piece about the changes in TV, etc., over the past decades, for I know nothing fresh on that subject would come from me. Sorry.

I apologize for my tardy reply, but was glad you asked me, and much heartened by your gracious and generous remarks.

Yours sincerely,

Dennis Potter

Johnson immediately wrote back, suggesting that Potter might write about 'the prospect of confronting imminent death', possibly as a piece of fiction – the Arts and Books section had been publishing new 1,700-word short stories by leading writers. Potter answered on 25 May, enclosing a typescript:

It seems I can still scrape out a word or two more, but I have no idea left of my critical judgement. What I do want to do, though, is to thank you for provoking me into making words on the page in some sort of consecutive order! There is, at least, something truthful in this, my first and last short story [he had evidently forgotten *Excalibur*] if only in the descriptions of how one has to cut a path through diamorphine swamps and the tenacity with which one unconsciously holds on to old creative ideas!

The story, published in the *Daily Telegraph* on 4 June, was called *Last Pearls*. Since it is Potter's final piece of writing, and his final exercise in self-exposure, it deserves to be printed in its entirety:

There came a day when Jack should have acknowledged that the writing had to stop. Perhaps it was the same day that the punctuation marks decided of their own will to mess about with their functions and their shapes. A comma that had been lying around ready for use started to wriggle at the edge of his vision like the worm it had so often threatened to be, and then tried to scoop up a subordinate clause he had had no intention of using.

'What is this? What is going on?' Jack asked out loud, although he was fairly sure there was for the moment no one else watching him in this odd-angled room at the top of the old house. But he could never be quite sure, so swiftly did the shapes come and go.

And now a slightly chipped full stop would not cease rolling loose along the top of the line, even when it bumped into another of its kind. The collision meant there was not enough space to complete the exposition. *Chink*! The sentence had to shorten had to shor had to *shh*.

'No, no,' he muttered, asserting his strength and reason for another few seconds.

He knew full well that these words and their accompanying marks had no volition. They could not be independent of his control. The writer was sovereign. It had always been up to Jack to make of these letters what he willed. Long slopes, smooth glides, shining cusps, abrupt halts, his pen weaving and willowing across the empty landscape.

But Jack had been on morphine for fifteen weeks now, at a steadily increasing rate. Hobgoblin images wafted or sculpted by the opiates contended with the sharper, cannibal bites of pain. His daily intake was now enough to stop a stampeding mastodon in its screaming tracks. Instantly, the beast formed itself with a savage undulation of trunk and threatening crash of feet, before spinning off into a grey whirl at the corner of the desk where something else cackled out of a wet mouth. Get off! Get away!

A syringe pump hung about Jack's now emaciated torso, regularly and inexorably jerking the colourless poison into his veins. Diamorphine was his dearest friend, and his most threatening foe, clearing space up ahead where he could fight these words in pain-free passages – but then closing it down again under amorphous blankets of suffocating numbness or lurid solicitation.

His task was to complete, and to burnish with gold, a story that he had scarcely started when the awful diagnosis had arrowed through the pain and the bewilderment. He saw three big billboard posters being pasted up at the crossroads just ahead: CANCER. INOPERABLE. THREE TO SIX MONTHS. Oh, God – would every thought, every emotion, now turn on its back and slither towards the one thought, death, and the one emotion, fear?

Jack found that it was not so. He was burning to right the wrongs he had inflicted on his own talent in the last piece of work he had had published, a tawdry narrative called *Black Pearls*. The pain he had already so stoically endured through a fatuous series of misdiagnoses had left him with too great a residue of waste. He sensed the rapidly growing tumour smack in the middle of his body (his soul?) as something that stood for all the sloth, the bile and the ill-will of the world. In a sudden incandescent flare of what must be joy, he determined to counter these common malignancies with the grace of – his face twisted for a second into the sardonic – with the grace of Art.

Black Pearls had been about a writer who had completed his novel and then found, at first to his whimsical amusement, that many of the events and some of the dialogue in the story were repeating themselves in front of him, even as he walked along the street. There – ! That black bin-liner bag blowing against the spiked rail. It had opened a paragraph on the last but one page of *Black Pearls*.

The coincidence of blown bag and spiked railing, shaped just thus, exactly on the beat of his old sentence, intrigued and challenged him, and he began to see many other such small juxtapositions as he settled with a lurch of pain at the continent of his desk. There were doorways back into the novel he had come to hate. The conviction was growing upon him that *Black Pearls* had somehow or other escaped into the world in the same way a virus might. How could it have been, he asked himself in a spurt of bitter agony, that in the wonder of good health and the serenity of his life as it had been, he had created a narrative that reeked with despair and evil, a negation of the human spirit?

The critics had loved it.

Jack now saw it as his moral duty to staunch the bilious leak between his last piece of fiction and the world out there in front of him. He could see now with all the clarity of a real sickness that the sour book he had published just six months before was not a worthy – no, not even a safe book to be wandering about the streets or slithering with reptilian glints into the various interstices of the day, someone else's day.

Now that he was so mortally ill, and all the barriers had crumpled, he could at last acknowledge how wicked it was to stain the sensibilities of his readers with arty filth. Genuinely nasty things had happened in that last novel: wanton cruelties and unnecessary little flicks of sadism made worse by being funny as well. And (he saw the bin-bag again) if any of these made-up events were by some necromancy coming true out there, then it was imperative that he divert them back on to other pages. He would cleanse them in the process. These would be the pages he was now writing, pristine at last. A tilt against the dragon.

Jack discovered that if he began to write at about half-past four in the morning, when a pale bruise of light edged nervously around the sides of the window, his mind was clear enough of the clogging dirt and his body sturdy enough to push away the rodentine pain for at least three and a half hours at a go, as freely as though the words had never been used before. He was turning black pearls into white ones.

Line by line, paragraph by paragraph, tugged free of morphine phantoms, Jack's resolve became an exultation as it fought across the pages. Much of the story came out in the dangerous present tense, for it was this which kept beckoning the most urgently at him. The pen bites into the smooth white, the thought pushes up on the crossbow of the way he carved his 't', and for minutes, no hours, at a time he was able to shove away the glowering imminence of his own demise in the everlasting glory of making words in the here, just here, and the now, just *now*.

Present tense called up first person. Jack makes his 'hero' walk with him in the arduous journey out of life. He revisits the places in the plot where the darkened thoughts of *Black Pearls* had found restless habitation. He is encountering once more the curdled beings who had in his new opinion sleazed and soiled the original story.

Each tough session is completed with a half-sigh, half-grunt of weary satisfaction: the sound of a wrong being put right. Then the diamorphine wheedles its way deeper, the eyelids cannot lift their own sudden weight, the face pinches in to defend itself against the mimicries of sleep as they insinuate through grotesqueries gnarled by the slightest change of position or the most minuscule shift of light. Objects float past, unanchored by consecutive thought.

And each night while he bubbled, murmured and sometimes cried out in the more fetid patches, two other pairs of eyes would briefly scan what had been written. His wife and his daughter looked at the words, looked at each other, sometimes smiled, sometimes cried and said little. They approved of his daily combat, which meant the prolongation of his own sense of self-hood and self-purpose, thus tempering much of their own grief.

'I have to work. Have to. Do you understand? There are serious wrongs to put right. So many things to correct,' he would say to the first of the two fair, green-eyed heads that poked almost tentatively around his door in the early morning.

Bzz-zup went his self-driven syringe. A scatter of spiky adjectives knelt at the edge of the line before deciding that one of them was a Prussian helmet about to be purred at and stroked by a slinky cat.

'Of course we understand. Of course you must work. It's wonderful to see that you can!'

The desk opened up into a big hole, but he was able to close it with a half-turn of his own head. The grains decided to dance in the wood, but kept clear of the white page.

'Black Pearls!' he said once, in a hiss of venom which startled the mild-mannered GP. The visiting doctor had not read the novel, but he had heard it spoken of as one of the best of its kind for years. Spare, truthful, bleak, a story about the last things that never strayed into the morbidly sanctimonious. Hadn't it won some prize or something? One of the very literary, prestigious ones?

The black bin-liner bag had blown against the spiked rail again, so Jack knew that he had reached the final pages of his new and, he believed, his greatest work. Just in time! The pen itself insisted upon changing its slender configuration, becoming stumpy in the clenched hand. The full stop continued to roll alternately an irritating piece of grit and a smoothly shiny billiard ball. And then the desk itself bounced upwards in rebellion to smack him hard under the chin.

'Just one more paragraph!'

That was the last thing he said before the great swamp of opiates sucked him under. But the injunction was easy enough for someone to execute. Jack had rewritten *Black Pearls* word for word. Everyone agreed that as an act of memory alone it was a formidable achievement.

He must have loved that book heart and soul, they said.

Renny Rye comments, 'How typical of Dennis to use even the last days of his dying as material for something.'

*

The day after *Last Pearls* was sent to the *Telegraph*, 26 May, Paul Downey 'had a phone call from the hospice to say they'd found the cause of Margaret's pain – micro-secondary cancers in the spine. I spoke to Jane, and asked whether we should tell Dennis, who was pretty weak by this time. And she said I must.' Downey wrote in his diary, 'Telling D was the most difficult thing yet. He finally broke down, not for himself, but for his "beloved M".' The diary continues:

After much interrogation on pain, cure, etc., I decided to see her for myself at the hospice. Despite all their help, she was obviously so ill. She was in such pain that she had to be sedated. She did respond briefly, to make a joke about D, and I told her that he was OK. 'He's behaving himself,' I said. 'I don't care if he is or not,' she replied.

Seeing D, I told him the results of my visit. I had been his ears and eyes. More tears, but at least he knew now exactly what was happening, and he said that helped. A cruel ending for them both not only to be apart, but to be dying at the same time. If anything, M looked more ill than D today, and I wondered who would die first.

That day, Thursday, 26 May, Sarah was in London, at the Royal Television Society awards ceremony at Grosvenor House Hotel, to collect a Best Dramatist award for her father. Mavis, who was once again staying at the hospice, reported that Margaret was now fading fast, and Potter telephoned Sarah the next morning to say that she should come home at once.

'I rushed back,' says Sarah, 'surprised at how calm I was. Dad – who being looked after by Jane – heroically insisted that we should all go and see Mum (Rob came on a little later in his own car). It was only just over ten miles to the hospice, but the drive on winding roads was extremely uncomfortable for Dad. He got hot sweats, and had to slug extra morphine, but we got him there. When he walked into Mum's room, she immediately became aware of him.'

Mavis remembers: 'They rang me and said they were coming in. I woke Margaret up when they arrived, and she opened her eyes and said, "Oh, Den, how nice."' Sarah recalls, 'The last thing I heard Mum saying to Dad was, "I love you, I always have and I always will." And it just made Dad crumble.'

Margaret died twenty-four hours later, with Sarah at her bedside: 'I didn't know whether or not I wanted to be there, but when the hospice phoned at midnight on Saturday to say that if I wanted to come I had to come now, I knew I had to be with her. I arrived just ten minutes before she went. I'm sure she knew I was there and that she was surrounded by love.'

Sarah went home to tell her father. 'He was devastated and said it was much more difficult to deal with than his own death.' Sarah, Jane and Robert agreed to suppress their grief in front of him. 'We wanted to be strong for Dad,' says Sarah. 'He didn't want weeping and wailing while he was still living.'

Paul Downey wrote in his diary, 'M died yesterday. D devastated, but feels he can say no more, as he is so close to her, and will be where she is soon. Mavis remembers, 'Dennis said, "I won't be long now, I'll give myself a week."'

His mother and his sister June came over from the Forest. 'When he was dying,' says June, 'he was the image of our dad. Never before had I ever seen he looked like either of them. But his last two weeks, it was shocking how much like our dad he got.'

Many people had written to Channel 4 asking for a transcript of the Bragg interview, and Fabers decided to publish it as soon as possible, along with the MacTaggart Lecture and the interview Potter had given to Alan Yentob on *Arena* in 1987, under the overall title *Seeing the Blossom*. Potter had decided on the dedication 'To my dear Margaret – Still the steadfast one.' But the advance copies did not arrive until after her death. He gave one to Mavis, with the inscription: 'To Mavis with the deepest love and gratitude for truly being our angel of mercy.'

Margaret was to be cremated in Gloucester on Friday, 3 June. 'Dad was determined to come,' says Sarah, 'so we ordered a wheelchair and got his suit ready, but on the day itself, it was obvious he just couldn't, he was very jaundiced and looked so ill that I ordered him not to, and I think it was a relief.' Paul Downey says that 'there was no way he could have made it downstairs'.

Only now did Potter agree that a bed should be moved into his office. 'It had been left as late as possible,' says Sarah. 'To begin with, he was sleeping on a sofa, because he didn't like a bed in his writing room – it was, I suppose, a symbol of giving in.' Paul Downey notes that 'the faithful glass of whisky was still always around, as were the cigarettes'.

Downey's diary continues:

3 June. D now so ill [that he was] unable to go to the cremation. Felt he was having schizophrenic thoughts. Discussed increasing sedation and analgesia. He chatted, through the usual haze of smoke, about the sadness of the situation being worse than any play he could conceive.

Dying. Two voices, the weak trying to overcome the strong. Unable to work, so no point carrying on. Talked about the afterlife, 'not thinking if there is one – if there is, there is'.

Downey explains this: 'I asked him if he believed in life after death. He said he didn't speculate whether there was one or not – "If there is, there is."' In a passage cut out of the Bragg interview, he had said, 'Maybe there is a present tense always. I don't know . . . I don't think about that. I don't know whether there is a present tense for ever or not. It always feels as though there is . . . I've ceased to speculate about this.'

Downey says Potter was now 'starting to go in and out of a sort of haze'. The diary notes:

Frightened of going over edge, but still being aware, and wanting to be able to come back. Reassured. Not time yet.

Unable to sleep, restless pain – wants to sleep well. Sedated and comfortable.

On Sunday, 5 June, Downey recorded that Potter was 'fighting the medication' – struggling against the opiate effect of the massive dose of morphine that was now being pumped into his body. He told Downey that he was 'OK-ish', asked what day of the week it was, and, on being told Sunday, replied, 'Sunday all day, as my mother used to say.' He added, 'My Forest accent is becoming more apparent', and when Downey described himself as 'a posh Scouser', he joked, 'There's no such thing!'

A few hours later, Downey wrote, 'This evening he seemed to fade, then come back. His resilience is astonishing. Restless, so sedated, but always seems to overcome it.' Downey was now giving him intra-muscular injections of morphine, in the hope of keeping his promise that the suffering would be controlled. On Monday, 6 June, he wrote, 'Still fighting – his years of illness must have instilled in him a tremendous resilience and determination. Visited late evening. Again, weak but not fading.'

Mavis Wood recalls that, on the Monday night, 'Judy and I sat with him. At about half-past six or seven o'clock in the morning, we decided that we'd call Paul. Judy went downstairs to wait for him, and let him in, and Paul came, and we left him alone with Dennis.' Sarah, Jane and Robert had been sitting up with him during the two previous days and nights, and were all sleeping when Downey arrived. 'Dad had been sinking much more slowly than Mum,' says Sarah, 'and we didn't quite know when he would go.'

'Asleep when I arrive,' notes Downey's diary. 'Further sedation.' And then: 'Died 8 a.m.' In Potter's medical notes, which went back to the onset of the psoriatic arthropathy thirty-two years earlier, Downey wrote, '08.00. RIP.'

*

That night, BBC2's *Late Show* ran an hour-long tribute to Potter; the Bragg interview was repeated on Channel 4 two days later.

The obituary in *The Times* judged that 'Potter was in many ways the Jonathan Swift of his time', and the *Financial Times* called him 'perhaps the best television writer that the world has yet seen'. Alan Plater wrote in the *Independent*, 'He was, by common consent, the leader of the pack.' Plater wondered what would happen if 'the next Dennis Potter' were to appear. 'Will the industry find time, space and resources to liberate the individual vision? Or will the broadcasters commission a couple of episodes of *The Bill* or *EastEnders*?'

Trodd contributed to obituaries in the *Guardian* and the *Daily Telegraph*. 'Dennis was his work,' he wrote. 'Our relationship was stormy, ludicrous and intermittent, like a misbegotten marriage which never quite fails.'

Potter was cremated in Gloucester. 'It was to be kept secret from the press,' says Paul Downey, 'and nobody was to go. In the end they did ask me, but by that time I was on call, and couldn't.' Mervyn James recalls that, when he knew he was dying, 'Dennis said, "Merv, the crematorium will definitely be my last smoke!"'

Dennis and Margaret Potter's ashes are buried side by side in Ross-on-Wye churchyard, overlooking the river. Margaret's tablet is inscribed 'All the way to heaven is heaven', and Dennis's has the words, 'All of it a kiss'. Sarah explains that this is a single quotation, from a novel called *Turtle Moon* by Alice Hoffman, which Margaret read and loved. 'Dad didn't actually care for [the epitaph] very much, but he said, "We'll do what your mother wants."'

Television continued to pay tribute in the weeks following his death. *The Singing Detective* was shown again on BBC1 in July and August, and an edited version of his MacTaggart Lecture was broadcast on Channel 4 on 23 August. There were two memorial services: in Ross Church, where Haydn Lloyd gave the address, and 'A Celebration of the Life of Dennis Potter' at St James's, Piccadilly, on 1 November. Music from his plays was performed by a dance band; Sarah read Housman's lines about the blue remembered hills; Alan Rickman read an extract from *Mesmer*; Cheryl Campbell and Freddie Jones performed the scene from *Pennies from Heaven* in which the head-master says farewell to Eileen; Melvyn Bragg read from *The Glittering Coffin* and Peter Jeffrey (who had appeared in *Lipstick*) from the writings of Hazlitt; Michael Grade, Alan Yentob and Ken Trodd acted the scene of Arthur and the salesmen from *Pennies*; Imelda Staunton (Nurse White in *The Singing Detective*) sang 'Roses of Picardy'; and the choir and congregation joined in 'Roll Along Prairie Moon'. Trodd raised a laugh when he told the congregation, 'Dennis . . . said, "I do have one very real fear of death. It is that you might get asked to speak at my memorial service."'

On 6 November the Everyman Theatre in Cheltenham held a tribute evening with readings from Potter's work by George Baker, Alan Bates, Frank Finlay, Kika Markham and many others who had appeared in his plays, and a debate about the future of television writing, with panelists including Michael Grade, Ken Trodd and Alan Yentob. During the evening, Yentob and Grade publicly confirmed their joint deal with Whistling Gypsy over *Karaoke* and *Cold Lazarus*. Yentob said, 'Michael Grade and I are delighted that both channels can fulfil Dennis's wishes that his final works would be broadcast jointly, as an appropriate initiative to celebrate a unique voice in television drama.' Grade added, 'It is fitting that this unique collaboration will elevate Dennis's final works into a national television event for viewers.'

Midnight Movie was finally shown on BBC2 the following Boxing Day. 'The whisper from Television Centre', reported the *Daily Express*, 'is that the picture is so dire it has plunged BBC executives into a gloom of despair. "It is absolutely unspeakable," says one. Potter . . . sank £500,000 of his own money into the project . . . '

Sarah eventually began to see a bereavement counsellor. 'That was not chiefly about Dad,' she says.

It was about the loss of Mum. I'm much more together about Dad, because I was expecting it. But we were such a close-knit family, and we had Mum, in particular, ripped away so quickly. We'd still been expecting that we'd have at least two years with her, and Dad had been telling us to look after her after he'd gone.

Jane, who in 1996 married for the third time, has said, 'I haven't felt safe since Dad died, and probably I never will again, because I always knew he would look after me.' Robert, now married as well, still runs the family building company, Wyesquash, with the help of Jane's second husband.

Karaoke was shot by Whistling Gypsy from January to April 1995, and *Cold Lazarus* from July to October. Despite his assurance to Potter and Renny Rye, Trodd continued, during pre-production, to express doubts about Rye's capability to direct them. 'Dennis had said to me, "I'm the producer till I die, then you take over." I believe he meant that I could then do the job I'd been hired for, which included choosing the director.' His doubts about Rye reached the press, and Sarah responded angrily, 'The deal was done when Dad was alive, and a deal is a deal. Ken voiced his reservations to Dad, who told him that Renny was the director and if he didn't want it, he should get off the project. He shook hands on it.' Trodd eventually gave up protesting when Channel 4 threatened to with-hold finance if Rye was not confirmed as sole director. 'After that,'

Trodd says, 'we all worked together to do our collective best for the scripts and for Dennis.' But by then relations between him and Rye, Rosemarie Whitman, Judy Daish and the Potter family were irreparably damaged.

Louise Germaine married around the time of Potter's death, and by the time that *Karaoke* went into production she was pregnant. Consequently the role of Sandra, designed for her by Potter, went to Saffron Burrows. In April 1996, just as *Karaoke* was about to be screened, *Time Out* alleged that, just as Sandra in *Karaoke* is left a legacy by Daniel, so in real life Potter had mentioned Louise Germaine in his will. This was entirely untrue: Potter's will leaves nothing to any individual outside his family, with the exception of four shares in one of Potter's companies bequeathed to Judy Daish in consideration of her role as one of his executors.

As to the role of Daniel Feeld in *Karaoke* and *Cold Lazarus*, Potter had decided against Michael Gambon as being too closely associated with *The Singing Detective*. He thought that Albert Finney would be ideal, but assumed he would be too expensive. After Potter's death, the part was offered to Nicol Williamson, who initially accepted, then turned it down, whereupon Finney was approached. In January 1995 the *Daily Mail* reported that Finney 'has secured a record payment for a television drama – £500,000 to play the lead in Dennis Potter's last major work'. Sarah was delighted by his performance: 'He constantly reminds me of Dad,' she told an interviewer, 'the littered office, the drinking, the corduroy jacket he wears . . . There is a scene in the first episode in which he is walking close to Dad's flat, near the BT Tower, when I thought I was watching Dad.'

Rumours about the large number of four-letter words in Potter's last scripts brought Mary Whitehouse out of semi-retirement at the age of eighty-five to make a formal complaint. Some embarrassment was felt at the BBC, which had recently laid down new, strict guidelines about language, but it was felt that these must be broken in the circumstances.

The first episode of *Karaoke* was scheduled for transmission almost exactly two years to the day after Potter had finished it, on BBC1 on Sunday, 28 April 1996 and on Channel 4 the next day. A fortnight before the screening, Ian Hislop sounded the first posthumous note of doubt about Potter, in the *Sunday Telegraph*:

His reputation as the greatest dramatist the medium has ever produced always struck me as inflated. What about Alan Bennett? Or Jack Rosenthal? Or any number of others? . . . He was used as a talisman for those who wanted to preserve a place in the drama schedules for something more than series about policemen and vets. While obviously sympathizing with this argument, I kept feeling that any critical view of Potter had been lost. The manner of his death confirmed his status as creative icon. Perhaps *Karaoke* and *Cold Lazarus* will prove me wrong. Potter says in the introduction to the published scripts that they are 'as fitting a summation as they are a testament, both to my character and my career, as I should ever want'. But what if critics do not agree? Will it be bad taste to say so? If they do they will at least have one consolation. Potter will no longer be able to play his old trick of being rude about them in his next play.

Mark Lawson, writing in the *Guardian* in advance of transmission, had seen some of *Karaoke* and *Cold Lazarus* and read the entire scripts. He prefaced his criticisms by saying, 'I do not really want to write this', and went on, 'Regrettably . . . they confirm the melancholy pattern of most artistic careers, which, represented as a graph, will almost always display a pyramid shape, in which talent accrues and then reduces . . . They are likely to be trounced in any ratings war.'

On the day of transmission of the first episode of *Karaoke*, A. A. Gill wrote in *The Sunday Times*: '*Karaoke* is simply dreadful.' Referring to the spoonerisms Potter had written for Roy Hudd, Gill suggested that Hudd's character 'would probably have called his creator Pennis Dotter. Now that really is funny; not just funny, but a deep comical truth. Without knowing it, I have always thought of him as a bit of a pennis and something of a dotter.' Next day in the *Evening Standard*, A. N. Wilson was equally damning: '*Karaoke* . . . must be one of the worst plays ever screened.' After the second episode, Jim Shelley wrote in the *Guardian*, 'Frankly, in terms of writing for TV, *The Bill* is in a different league.'

The *Daily Mail* reported that only 4.1 million had watched the first episode on BBC1: '*Karaoke* . . . was trounced by ITV's Customs drama *The Knock*, which pulled in 10.3 million viewers.' A month later, A. A. Gill wrote that *Karaoke* had 'lost a quarter of its audience for episode 2, and slipped to 2.7 million for the . . . finale. The repeats on Channel 4 were much as one would expect. Two million to start, slipping to 1.2 million for episode 4.'

Karaoke had its defenders. Sean Day-Lewis in the *Daily Telegraph* called it Potter's 'strongest drama' since *The Singing Detective*, and Richard Eyre wrote in the *New Statesman*, '*Karaoke* is not brilliant by Potter's own standards, but it's extremely entertaining stuff.' In the *Sunday Telegraph*, David Sexton allowed that it made 'better viewing second time around, when you have ceased to look for a story'. However, after all four episodes had been shown, Lucy Ellmann in the *Independent on Sunday* said she felt that '*Karaoke* bears all the hallmarks of a first draft and should never have reached the screen'. Lynne Truss in *The Times* felt the production's extravagant faithfulness to Potter's 'lacklustre scripts' had not 'done his memory any favours'. She guessed that 'without *Karaoke* and *Cold Lazarus* to contend with, there would surely have been a retrospective season by now, and we'd all be saying what a great playwright he was'.

Renny Rye remarks ruefully, 'Maybe the Bragg interview was his greatest last piece. It certainly hung over me while making those scripts.' Michael Grade says:

I was very pleased with what Renny did – despite Ken's attempt to railroad him out, which was classic Ken, bless him! But the circumstances had set up an expectation which nothing could have fulfilled. And to produce Dennis Potter scripts without Dennis being there through the production process, you were making a show with one hand behind your back. The results were fine, but not what they would have been if Dennis had been there rewriting, casting, having his input.

Previewing *Cold Lazarus*, which began its screenings on Channel 4 on 26 May, W. Stephen Gilbert (in the *Independent*) wondered whether 'anyone should have spent *any* money on this wandering, misshapen, strangely innocent (or perhaps *faux naïf*) script'. A. A. Gill warned, 'My dear, if you thought *Karaoke* was bad, are you in for a great roller-coaster of a surprise.'

The critics were dramatically divided over it. Stephen Pile in the *Daily Telegraph* described it as '*Planet of the Apes* with tubthumping', and Sean Day-Lewis (in the same paper, after the second episode) perceived 'flaws [Potter] would have corrected in revision'. '*Cold Lazarus* is a bewildering mess,' wrote Nigel Andrew in the *Daily Mail*, 'written by a man who was, I fear, succumbing to the effects of his medicinal morphine'. And Tom Lubbock in the *Sunday Telegraph* judged that 'it teeters on the verge of ridiculous. Yet,' he continued, 'there were moments . . . In the sequence . . . when Feeld's memory of his own death is played back on the screen – the out-of-body experience, the tunnel with the bright light at the end, the brief glimpse of angels – there was a touch of the old magic.'

Others were wholeheartedly enthusiastic. '*Cold Lazarus* stands up as one of the most powerful things he ever created . . . a work of extraordinary breadth, assurance, intricacy and entertainment,' wrote Chris Dunkley in the *Financial Times*. Barbara Ellen in the *Mail on Sunday* thought it 'great fun, a futuristic psychodrama laden with carefully camp performances and extremely tight bitchy dialogue'. Allison Pearson in the *Observer* felt that, while *Karaoke* had been 'a mess', *Cold Lazarus* was 'a more fitting memorial'.

Peter Ansorge, who commissioned *Cold Lazarus*, does not regard it and *Karaoke* as disappointments:

To end your life with a vision of the past, present and future, and the whole question, in *Cold Lazarus*, of where broadcasting is heading, was a brave thing to do. They may not stand as his greatest works, but you don't denounce the late plays of Shakespeare because they aren't *King Lear*. I think *Karaoke* and *Cold Lazarus* were appropriate works with which to end his career, and I believe they will be judged as such. And if you read the American reviews, you'll get a completely different response.

Certainly when both were shown on cable television in America in 1997, the reviews were the best so far. Tom Shales of the *Washington Post* wrote that they were 'worth their weight in plutonium'.

During the British screenings, the Royal National Theatre (headed by Richard Eyre) had been staging *Blue Remembered Hills*, directed by Patrick Marber, with a cast including Steve Coogan. Nicholas de Jongh in the *Evening Standard* called the play 'comic and highly disturbing. On stage the effect is even more intense.' Paul Taylor in the *Independent* said the production was 'a reminder of Potter at his best'.

Piers Haggard, who had directed *Pennies from Heaven*, says, 'I think *Blue Remembered Hills* is his masterpiece. It has what *Pennies from Heaven* lacks, which is concentration.' Charles Spencer, reviewing the National Theatre production in the *Daily Telegraph*, felt the same – that *Blue Remembered Hills* showed that 'at his best, few modern dramatists can touch Potter for originality and unsentimental depth of feeling'. John Peter wrote in *The Sunday Times*: 'Perhaps this beautiful 95-minute production is the true summation of Potter's talent. It suggests that his true home might have been the theatre.'

During the production at the National, Richard Eyre wrote in the *New Statesman*:

I find it difficult to say where you put a Dennis Potter piece alongside the great plays of the contemporary stage, but I'd rank him alongside Tom Stoppard or Harold Pinter: a singular voice who chose to write for this weird medium . . . A few of his plays will certainly live on in stage versions, like *Blue Remembered Hills* and possibly *Brimstone and Treacle*. But some of his finest work, such as *The Singing Detective*, could not work on the stage . . .

We must hope that, in these days of opportunistic culture, there are still enough people out there with the will to recognize and enfranchize another Potter, if a Potter were to come along.

Jonathan Powell, who commissioned *The Singing Detective* at the BBC, wonders about this: 'Whether anybody would make those scripts now, I don't know.'

The next Whistling Gypsy project, Ruth Carter's adaptation of Nina Bawden's *Family Money*, went into pre-production as soon as *Cold Lazarus* was finished, and was shown as a Channel 4 serial in the spring of 1997, with Claire Bloom starring. At the time of writing, Rosemarie Whitman is developing other scripts for Whistling Gypsy in hope of further productions.

It was Whitman's idea to set up an annual Dennis Potter Award for a new single television play by a writer who had not written one before, to be submitted in the form of a treatment backed by a BBC producer or an independent production company. The winning consortium receives £10,000 from the BBC towards the cost of production. The judges include Sarah Potter, Judy Daish, and a writer – Alan Plater filled this role for two years, and was succeeded by Paula Milne. The first award was given, in February 1995, to Richard Cameron for *Stone, Paper, Scissors*, which was shown the following year on BBC2. There have been two other awards since then, and both scripts are currently in production.

Peter Ansorge observes that, despite the Dennis Potter Award, the single television play is now the last place where a young writer would expect to make a name:

They'll usually start in the theatre, to get a reputation, and then work in the movies – though films are director-based rather than writer-based. Television is just bread and butter to writers now. Jimmy McGovern is the last one of Dennis's breed, and even he had to serve an apprenticeship writing eighty episodes of *Brookside*. And in some ways the soaps have taken over the issue-based drama.

Writing in the *Guardian* in December 1996, Linda Grant commented sadly on the takeover of television drama by the soap opera:

EastEnders is now probably the best-written drama produced on television . . . In the past year, soap opera has eclipsed everything that surrounds it – the internationally marketable costume adaptations of Jane Austen, the dramas funded by BBC and Channel 4 for cinema release, and the mini-series that by their nature rely on foreign locations. The decline of serious television drama has been so swift and so frightening that we have barely noticed that it's not there any more.

Grant noted that one of the *EastEnders* writers, Tony Hale, described Potter as 'the Chekhov of television writers'.

In 1982, Clive Hodgson had observed in *Films and Filming*, 'Dennis Potter writes television plays that stick in the mind like a chicken bone in the throat.' Potter himself was undoubtedly proud of his capacity to irritate, to cause an itch in the mind. In 1968 he wrote of his favourite literary figure, 'Hazlitt disturbed people – and can still do so, very effectively . . . A quirky, pungent, obsessive, honest and extremely forceful writer who alienated most of his friends, he exposed himself without mercy, and yet "never gave the lie to his own soul".' He would have hoped to read the same in his own obituaries.

*

Gareth Davies, who directed many of Potter's early plays, remarks on his capacity to handle his own life story: 'Now we're getting to the nub of Dennis. He rewrote it, or at least story-edited the whole thing.' Thanks to this, the dramas surrounding the making of his plays – the rows (especially the comic melodrama of his relationship with Trodd), the bannings, the personal atttacks, the obsessive relationships – were at least as gripping as anything he wrote, perhaps more so.

He himself said, laughing, at one of the New York Museum seminars in 1992, 'There's much more drama swilling *around* my work than there actually is *in* it.' Gina Bellman, contemplating the constant, disturbing overlap between what he wrote and what he was, asks, 'Where did life-imitating-art-imitating-life-imitating-art end?' As to the spectacular contradictions in his personality, Bellman adds, 'He was all these things: he was a pioneer and a shit and a genius and a sex-obsessed flirt and a great husband and father – all of these things – and every time he was one of them, he believed in it absolutely.'

Nancy Banks-Smith wrote in the *Guardian* the morning after the screening of Potter's final interview with Bragg, 'Potter's loyalty to television has been lifelong and absolute. I will always love him for making me feel it mattered.' Because he chose to write for an ephemeral medium, much – indeed most – of his work will probably slip out of sight as the years pass. Yet Brian Gibson, who directed *Blue Remembered Hills*, says, 'I do think Dennis is a lasting phenomenon – a kind of fallen angel. He's too unusual to be forgotten.'

Chronology of the works
of Dennis Potter

This list does not include Potter's journalism; the published texts of his play scripts; stage or radio adaptations of his television plays; television and film scripts which, at the time of writing, have not been made; his contributions to *Panorama*, *Bookstand*, or *That Was The Week That Was*; or his personal appearances on television and radio, or in public, with the exception of *Does Class Matter?*, *Desert Island Discs*, and his final interview with Melvyn Bragg.

I am indebted to the much more detailed list in *Fight & Kick & Bite* by W. Stephen Gilbert.

1958 25 August: appearance in *Does Class Matter?* (BBC Television)

1960 *The Glittering Coffin*, Victor Gollancz Ltd
Between Two Rivers (BBC Television, 3 June)

1962 *The Changing Forest: life in the Forest of Dean today*, Secker & Warburg

1965 *The Confidence Course* (*Wednesday Play*, BBC1, 25 February)
Alice (*Wednesday Play*, BBC1, 13 October)
Stand Up, Nigel Barton (*Wednesday Play*, BBC1, 8 December)
Vote, Vote, Vote for Nigel Barton (*Wednesday Play*, BBC1, 15 December)

1966 *Emergency – Ward 9* (*Thirty Minute Theatre*, BBC2, 11 April)
Where the Buffalo Roam (*Wednesday Play*, BBC1, 2 November)

1967 *Message for Posterity* (*Wednesday Play*, BBC1, 3 May)

1968 *The Bonegrinder* (*ITV Playhouse*, 13 May)
Shaggy Dog (*The Company of Five*, ITV, 10 November)
A Beast with Two Backs (*Wednesday Play*, BBC1, 20 November)

1969 *Moonlight on the Highway* (*Saturday Night Theatre*, ITV, 12 April)
Son of Man (*Wednesday Play*, BBC1, 16 April)

1970 *Lay Down Your Arms* (*Saturday Night Theatre*, ITV, 23 May)
Angels Are So Few (*Play for Today*, BBC1, 5 November)

1971 *Paper Roses* (ITV, 13 June)
Traitor (*Play for Today*, BBC1, 14 October)
Casanova (BBC2, in six parts, 16 November–21 December)

1972 *Follow the Yellow Brick Road* (*The Sextet*, BBC2, 4 July)

1973 *Only Make Believe* (*Play for Today*, BBC1, 12 February)
A Tragedy of Two Ambitions (*Wessex Tales*, BBC2, 21 November)
Hide and Seek, André Deutsch

1974 *Joe's Ark* (*Play for Today*, BBC1, 14 February)
Schmoedipus (*Play for Today*, BBC1, 20 June)

1975 *Late Call* (BBC2, in four parts, 1–22 March)

1976 *Double Dare* (*Play for Today*, BBC1, 6 April)
Where Adam Stood (BBC2, 21 April)
Brimstone and Treacle (made by the BBC but not shown until
25 August 1987)

1978 *The Mayor of Casterbridge* (BBC2, in seven parts,
22 January–5 March)
Pennies from Heaven (BBC1, in six parts, 7 March–11 April)

1979 *Blue Remembered Hills* (*Play for Today*, BBC1, 30 January)

1980 *Blade on the Feather* (ITV, 19 October)
Rain on the Roof (ITV, 26 October)
Cream in My Coffee (ITV, 2 November)

1981 *Pennies from Heaven* (cinema version)
Pennies from Heaven (novelization of cinema version), Quartet Books

1982 *Brimstone and Treacle* (cinema version)

1983 *Gorky Park* (cinema film)
Sufficient Carbohydrate (Hampstead Theatre from 7 December)

1985 *Tender is the Night* (BBC2, in six parts, 23 September–28 October)
Dreamchild (cinema film)

1986 *The Singing Detective* (BBC1, in six parts, 16 November–21 December)
Ticket to Ride, Faber and Faber

1987 *Visitors* (*Screen Two*, BBC2, 22 February)
     Track 29 (cinema film)
     Blackeyes, Faber and Faber

1988 *Christabel* (BBC2, in four parts, 16 November–7 December)

1989 *Blackeyes* (BBC2, in four parts, 29 November–20 December)

1991 *Secret Friends* (cinema film)

1993 *Lipstick on Your Collar* (Channel 4, in six parts, 21 February–
     28 March)

1994 *Without Walls Special* (Potter's interview with Melvyn Bragg),
     (Channel 4, 5 April)
     Last Pearls (short story), *Daily Telegraph*, 4 June
     Midnight Movie (Screen Two, BBC2, 26 December)
     Mesmer (cinema film, not yet released)
     Seeing the Blossom, Faber and Faber

1996 *Karaoke* (BBC1, in four parts, 28 April–19 May)
     Cold Lazarus (Channel 4, in four parts, 26 May–16 June)

Bibliography

___

Interviews, telephone conversations, letters for this book

Allen, Roger   Harrow, 18 March 1996
Amiel, Jon   London, 18 June 1997
Ansorge, Peter   London, 27 August 1997
Attallah, Naim   London, 25 April 1997
Baldwin, Tony   Exeter, 26 April 1996
Barber, Frances   London, 8 July 1997
Barnes, Kaye   Hatford, Oxfordshire, 20 December 1995
Barron, Keith   London, 29 November 1996
Bates, Alan   telephone, 24 September 1997
Bellman, Gina   London, 31 August 1997
Bragg, Melvyn   London, 8 September 1997
Brewer, Ron and Jean   Fareham, 19 September 1996
Campbell, Cheryl   Oxford, 4 June 1997
Cecil, Jonathan   London, 11 July 1996
Christopher, Bob   letter to HC, 14 September 1996
Cook, John R.   London, 8 May 1997
Daish, Judy   London, 5 March 1997, 9 April 1997, 18 September 1997
Davies, Gareth   Chippenham, 16 January 1997; telephone, 23 April 1997
Douglas, Clare   telephone, 21 September 1997
Downey, Dr Paul   Ross-on-Wye, 9 July 1997
Foot, Paul   London, 9 September 1996
Forster, Margaret   letters to HC, 11 and 17 June 1996
Germaine, Louise   London, 4 August 1997
Gibson, Brian   London, 17 April 1996
Grade, Michael   London, 8 October 1997

Gush, Philip — letter to HC, 3 May 1996
Haggard, Piers — London, 10 June 1997
Harvey, Jack — telephone, 12 May 1996
Hughes, Iris — Berry Hill, Gloucestershire, 13 March 1995
James, Mervyn — Ross-on-Wye, 18 April 1996
Lindley, Clive — telephone, 21 April 1997
Lloyd, Anne and Haydn — Hereford, 18 April 1996
Loncraine, Richard — London, 20 June 1997
McCallum, Rick — Leaversden Studios, 5 June 1997
McGrath, John — London, 25 October 1996
Markham, Kika — London, 11 February 1997
Mayhew, Lord — London, 17 July 1996
(Christopher Mayhew)

Meckler, Nancy — London, 25 April 1997
Melia, Joe — telephone, 27 January 1997
Ministry of Defence — letter from Miss L. F. Hearn, for Departmental Record Officer, Ministry of Defence, CS (RM) 2b, Bourne Avenue,

Hayes, Middlesex, — to HC, 23 August 1996
Nathan, David — London, 27 September 1996
Neal, Timothy — London, 25 April 1996
Newby, P. H. — Garsington, 24 May 1995
Potter, Jane (JP) — Lydbrook, 29 July 1997
Potter, Margaret, — Berry Hill, Gloucestershire, 13 March 1995,
June Thomas and — 21 February 1996, 7 May 1996
Ernest Thomas (MP)
Potter, Robert (RP) — Ross-on-Wye, 9 July 1997
Potter, Sarah (SP) — Cheltenham, 7 October 1996, 20 December 1996, 17 January 1997, 20 March 1997, 22 April 1997, 30 June 1997, 3 November 1997

Powell, Jonathan — London, 7 May 1997
Ross, Herbert — telephone, 20 April 1997
Rye, Renny — London, 23 June 1997
Scott, Ann — London, 20 January 1997
Seebohm, Caroline — London, 16 December 1996
Shivas, Mark — London, 7 October 1997
Smith, Roger — London, 24 September 1996
Taverne, Lord — telephone, 23 September 1996
(Dick Taverne)
Thomas, Sir Keith — telephone, 23 September 1996
Trodd, Kenith — London, 13 June 1996, 29 August 1996,

	22 November 1996, 23 December 1996,
	12 February 1997, 24 March 1997,
	30 September 1997, 23 January 1998
Tye, Noreen	Gloucester, 26 February 1996
Wale, Graham	London, 17 April 1997
Wale, Sidney	Croydon, 29 April 1997
Whitman, Rosemarie	London, 10 July 1997
Wilks, Horace and Coreene	Berry Hill, 7 May 1996
Williamson, Gary	London, 8 October 1997
Wood, Mavis	Tetbury, 21 November 1996
Wyver, John	Oxford, 25 October 1996
York, Michael	telephone, 16 May 1997

Works by Dennis Potter

All manuscripts, typescripts, drafts, rehearsal scripts, shooting scripts, camera scripts, transmission scripts, videotapes and letters, unless otherwise stated, are © Pennies From Heaven (Overseas) Ltd

Alice, manuscript; rehearsal script, BBC Written Archives

Angels Are So Few, original typescript, with manuscript additions

Beast with Two Backs, A, manuscript

Between Two Rivers, script, BBC Written Archives

Blackeyes, first draft; television serial, second draft; BBC TV version, manuscript; BBC TV version, draft (September 1988); BBC TV version, videotapes; novel, Faber and Faber, 1987

Blade on the Feather, rehearsal script

Blue Remembered Hills and Other Plays [*Joe's Ark, Cream in my Coffee*], Faber and Faber, 1996 (originally published in 1984 as *Waiting for the Boat: On Television*)

Bonegrinder, The, manuscript

Brimstone and Treacle, rehearsal script

Casanova, shooting scripts

Changing Forest: Life in the Forest of Dean Today, The, Secker & Warburg, 1962 (republished with revised pagination, Minerva, 1996)

Christabel (television adaptation from *The Past is Myself* by Christabel Bielenberg), Faber and Faber, 1988

Christmas Forest, A, BBC Radio 4, broadcast 26 December 1977

Cinderella, manuscript

Confidence Course, The, camera script, BBC Written Archives

Country Boy, The (unpublished novel), manuscript

Cream in my Coffee, see Blue Remembered Hills and Other Plays

Double Dare, shooting script

Dreamchild (film script), first draft

Emergency – Ward 9, manuscript; camera script, BBC Written Archives

Excalibur (short story), typescript

Follow the Yellow Brick Road, in Robert Muller (ed.), *The Television Dramatist*, Paul Elek, 1973

Glittering Coffin, The, Victor Gollancz, 2nd impression, 1960

Hide and Seek, Faber and Faber, 1990 (first publication, André Deutsch and Quartet Books, 1973)

Joe's Ark, see Blue Remembered Hills and Other Plays

Karaoke, first draft

Karaoke and *Cold Lazarus*, with an introduction by DP, Faber and Faber, 1996

Lay Down Your Arms, rehearsal script

Lipstick on Your Collar, Faber and Faber, 1993

Love Me, True (unmade film script), typescript

The Mayor of Casterbridge (Thomas Hardy TV adaptation), manuscript

Message for Posterity, rehearsal script

Moonlight on the Highway, manuscript

Mushrooms on Toast, manuscript

Nigel Barton Plays: Stand Up, Nigel Barton [and] *Vote, Vote, Vote for Nigel Barton, The*, Penguin Books, 1967

Only Make Believe, first draft and rehearsal script

Paper Roses, manuscript

Pennies from Heaven, rehearsal scripts; with an introduction by Kenith Trodd, Faber and Faber, 1996

Phantom of the Opera (film script), manuscript

Potter on Potter, edited by Graham Fuller, Faber and Faber, 1993

Purpose in Politics: Dennis Potter's Message to the Electors of East Herts, R. Brewer, Labour Hall, Hoddesdon, 1964 (copy kindly lent by Ron Brewer)

Rain on the Roof, first version manuscript

Rivers of Babylon, The, manuscript

Rumpelstiltskin, manuscript

Schmoedipus, manuscript

Secret Friends, draft script

Seeing the Blossom: Two Interviews and a Lecture, Faber and Faber, 1994

Shaggy Dog, rehearsal script

Singing Detective, The, Faber and Faber, 1986; (unmade) film script

Son of Man, 'rehearsal script' (*recte* camera script), BBC Written Archives; Samuel French, 1970

Sufficient Carbohydrate, Faber and Faber, 1983

Tender is the Night (Scott Fitzgerald television adaptation) transmission script

Ticket to Ride, Faber and Faber, 1986

Tragedy of Two Ambitions, A, rehearsal script

Traitor, rehearsal script

Waiting for the Boat, see Blue Remembered Hills and Other Plays

Wedding Night (unpublished novel), manuscript

Where Adam Stood, rehearsal script

Where the Buffalo Roam, rehearsal script; camera script, BBC Written Archives

Television review for *The Sunday Times*, 26 November 1978 (unpublished), manuscript

Letters to David Johnson, 16 and 25 May 1994

Letter to JP, SP and RP, 24 February 1977

Letter to MP, 4 December 1967

Letter to John Roberdeau and Robert Michael Geisler, 10 May 1994

Letters to Caroline Seebohm, courtesy of Caroline Seebohm

Other Sources

BOOKS

Bakewell, Joan, and Nicholas Garnham (eds.), *The New Priesthood: British television today*, Allen Lane The Penguin Press, 1970

Cook, John R., *Dennis Potter: A life on screen*, Manchester University Press, 1995

Gilbert, W. Stephen, *Fight & Kick & Bite: The Life and Work of Dennis Potter*, Hodder & Stoughton, 1995

Moline, Karen, *Bob Hoskins: an unlikely hero*, Sphere Books, 1989

Shubik, Irene, *Play for Today: the evolution of television drama*, Davis–Poynter, 1975

ARTICLES AND INTERVIEWS

Andrew, Nigel, 'Dark angel', *Radio Times*, 25 November–1 December 1989

Bakewell, Joan, 'Wrestling with a Vision', *The Sunday Times Magazine*, 14 November 1976

Batt, Anne, 'Man on the Moon', *Daily Mail*, 5 April 1977

Bragg, Melvyn, unedited video-recording of interview with DP, Channel 4, 5 April 1994, courtesy of London Weekend Television

Brooks, Richard, 'All in the dark eye of the beholder', *Observer*, 19 November 1989

Brooks, Richard, 'A matter of life and death', *Observer*, 4 June 1995
   (contains quotations from John R. Cook's 1990 interview with DP)
Brown, Robert, 'Dollars from Hollywood', British Film Institute *Monthly
   Film Bulletin*, July 1982
Connolly, Ray, 'When the penny dropped', *Evening Standard*, 21 March 1978
Cook, John R., extracts from transcript of interview with DP, recorded
   London, 10 May 1990, kindly provided by Dr Cook
Day-Lewis, Sean, 'Potter's last will of iron', *Daily Telegraph*, 24 April 1996
Dean, Michael, interview with DP, *Late Night Line-Up*, BBC2, 14 October
   1971 (BBC Written Archives, TV Registry Scripts, Films 35–6)
Dickson, E. Jane, 'Potter back on song', *Radio Times*, 20–26 February 1993
Desert Island Discs, DP interviewed by Roy Plomley, BBC Radio 4,
   17 December 1977, BBC Written Archives transcript
Desert Island Discs, DP interviewed by Michael Parkinson, BBC Radio 4,
   21 February 1988, BBC Written Archives transcript
Dougary, Ginny, 'Potter's Weal', *The Times Saturday Review*, 26 September
   1992
Grant, Steve, 'Potter's Art', *Time Out*, 8–15 February 1986
Grant, Steve, 'Potter Gold', *Time Out*, 10–17 February 1993
Jardine, Cassandra, interview with Sarah Potter, *Daily Telegraph*, 26 April 1996
Kavanagh, P. J., 'Potter to the Rescue', *Sunday Telegraph Magazine*, 4 June
   1982
Koenig, Rhoda, 'The pain of a black eye from the critics', *Independent*,
   18 December 1989
Lambert, Angela, 'The thin skin of democracy', *Independent*, 4 November
   1988
Late Show, transcript of interview with DP, BBC2, 9 November 1989
   (Wyver collection)
Lawson, Mark, 'Skin Flicks', *Independent Magazine*, 13 February 1993
Levin, Angela, 'I thought Dad was invincible . . .', interview with Sarah
   Potter, *Daily Mail*, 22 October 1994
Nathan, David, 'Private Pottah's post-war work', *Sunday Telegraph*,
   21 February 1993
National Film Theatre *Guardian* Lecture, DP interviewed by Philip Purser,
   30 October 1980, transcript kindly lent by Kenith Trodd
Oakes, Philip, 'Potter's Path', *The Sunday Times*, 8 November 1971
Oakes, Philip, 'A suitable sleuth for treatment', *Radio Times*, 15–21
   November 1986
Purser, Philip, 'A playwright comes of age', *Daily Telegraph Magazine*,
   2 April 1969
Raven, Susan, 'Relative Values' (interview with DP and Sarah Potter),
   The Sunday Times Magazine, 14 August 1983

Saynor, James, 'Black and Blue', *Listener*, 1 June 1989

Summers, Sue, 'Return of the prodigal Potter', *The Sunday Times*, 15 September 1985

Wade, Graham, 'Dennis Potter – rebel playwright', *TV & Home Video*, November 1980

Wapshott, Nicholas, 'Knowing what goes on inside people's heads', *The Times*, 21 April 1980

Ward, Alex, interview with DP, *New York Times Magazine*, 13 November 1988

Wright, Patrick, 'The last acre of truth', *Guardian*, 15 February 1993

Wyver, John, transcript of unedited interview with DP, recorded 14 February 1978; edited version published as 'Paradise, perhaps', *Time Out*, 3–9 March 1978, transcript kindly lent by John Wyver

Wyver, John, drafts of interview with DP, January 1979; edited version published in the *Guardian*, 26 January 1979, drafts kindly lent by John Wyver

Wyver, John, transcript of unedited interview with DP, recorded 1 October 1980; edited version published as 'The Long Non-Revolution of Dennis Potter', *Time Out*, 17–23 October 1980, transcript kindly lent by John Wyver

Wyver, John, drafts of interview with DP, autumn 1989; edited version published in the *New Statesman*, 24 November 1989, drafts kindly lent by John Wyver

MISCELLANEOUS

Blue Remembered Hills, Royal National Theatre programme, May 1996

Brimstone and Treacle prospectus, to raise funds for the film of *Brimstone and Treacle*, issued by Pennies From Heaven Ltd, n.d. [1981], © Pennies From Heaven (Overseas) Ltd

Karaoke and *Cold Lazarus* press pack, Channel 4/BBC1, April 1996

Dane, The, the magazine of St Clement Danes Grammar School (copies in the present school at Chorleywood)

Downey, Dr Paul, 'Dealing with DP': diary kept during DP's last weeks of life, courtesy of Dr Downey

DP's medical notes and doctors' correspondence, courtesy of Dr Paul Downey

Rye, Renny, diary of his last meetings with DP, courtesy of Renny Rye

Seebohm, Caroline, diary, courtesy of Caroline Seebohm

Harrison, Irving B., *Dennis Potter: his Doubles and Devices*, unpublished typescript (1996) kindly lent by Dr Harrison

Source notes

──

Quotations are identified by the first words cited. When two or more quotations from the same source follow each other with little intervening narrative, only the first quotation is used for identification. Members of the Potter family are indicated by initials: JP, Jane Potter; MP, Margaret Potter (DP's mother), June Thomas and Ernest Thomas, who were interviewed together; RP, Robert Potter, and SP, Sarah Potter. Frequently cited sources are identified in full in the Bibliography. Sources clearly and fully identified in the text are not cited again in the Notes.

Prologue

vii 'the last two words', *Karaoke*, 213; 'had a surprising number of things in common', Angela Lambert to HC, 19 June 1997; 'an instinctive recoil', DP to Angela Lambert, 18 July 1987, courtesy of Angela Lambert; 'complaining about the stairs', Angela Lambert to HC, 19 June 1997

viii 'I have thought and thought', DP to Angela Lambert, 24 August 1987, courtesy of Angela Lambert; 'Towards the end', SP interview; 'Biography is in some ways', *The Times*, 24 February 1968; 'the whorish clutches of incompetent biographers', *The Times*, 23 March 1968; 'How do you make that final, crucial leap', *The Times*, 16 August, 1969; 'I despise biographies', Brooks, 'A matter of life and death'

ix 'a glowing, generous, rewarding and extremely enjoyable exercise', *The Times*, 23 March 1968; 'played with the idea', *The Times*, 3 August 1968; '*The Singing Detective* played with', Brooks, 'A matter of life and death'; 'I'm a reclusive character', Cook, extracts from transcript of interview with DP; 'I do not believe what writers say', *Blue Remembered Hills*, 12; '*Telling stories* is a popular description', *New Society*, 15 May 1975; 'What I say about them', Cook, *Dennis Potter*, 321; 'That's what it's about', *The Singing Detective* (unmade film script)

x 'Several times publishers have written', Cook, extracts from transcript of interview with DP

xi 'You meet people sometimes', *Potter on Potter*, 84

PART ONE

Chapter 1

3 'I went to the Forest', Roger Smith interview; 'I'd heard scurrilous things', Gareth Davies interview; 'It was like a dream', Graham Wale interview

4 'The Forest of Dean is hilly', *The Glittering Coffin*, 41f.; 'a heart-shaped place', *Seeing the Blossom*, 6f.; 'enclosed, tight, backward', *The Times*, obituary, 8 June 1994; 'suffocatingly in-turned', *Seeing the Blossom*, 42; 'As a border person', ibid., 6; 'I . . . hated the Welsh', *Desert Island Discs*, 1977; '"Thee" and "thou"', *Potter on Potter*, 4

5 'How bist o' butty?', MP interview; 'those rather ugly villages', *Seeing the Blossom*, 6; 'The last place God made', *The Changing Forest*, 135; 'The first time he came here', MP interview; 'The Free Mining Rights were established', Humphrey Phelps, *The Forest of Dean*, Alan Sutton Publishing Ltd, 1995 edn, 10

6 'in an atmosphere of remoteness', Cyril E. Hart, *The Free Miners of the Royal Forest of Dean*, British Publishing Co. Ltd, 1953, 2

7 'all the villages were mining villages', *Seeing the Blossom*, 61

8 'Doesn't thee fret for I', Winifred Foley, *A Child in the Forest*, BBC, 1974, 14; 'My mother was a Forester', MP interview; 'went into service . . . [as] a skivvy', *Seeing the Blossom*, 10

9 'but Dennis wouldn't have wanted', Graham Wale interview; 'As kids we used to be able', MP interview; 'Fuller's used to make the best macaroons', *Blade on the Feather* rehearsal script; 'You had to pay your board', MP interview; 'my mother used to come down', *Seeing the Blossom*, 10 ; 'My mother came to the Forest of Dean', ibid., 42f.; 'eighteen or nineteen', MP interview

10 'duly impressed by my father's ever-shy little smile', *Seeing the Blossom*, 43; 'You didn't get near her', Horace and Coreene Wilks interview; 'Walt was a lovely man', Graham Wale interview; 'unless he'd had a bit too much cider', Sidney Wale interview; 'I once said, in a would-be casual aside', *Potter on Potter*, 5; 'My father . . . started work', *The Changing Forest*, 29

11 'I got engaged', MP interview; 'one up, one down', ibid.; 'an entirely male-dominated society', *The Changing Forest*, 32; 'Dad used to take a tin flask', MP interview; 'You could tell miners', ibid.

12 'squat on the backs of their heels', *The Changing Forest*, 45; 'chapel . . . like a warehouse', ibid., 11; 'has had a rugby side', *The Glittering Coffin*, 46; 'the place for the band', *The Changing Forest*, 72f.; 'And of course I was pregnant', MP interview

Chapter 2

13 'The District Nurse', MP interview; 'I have a sister', *Desert Islands Discs*, 1977

14 'We were poor', *Seeing the Blossom*, 8; 'We didn't have a flush lavatory', National Film Theatre *Guardian* Lecture; 'The lavatory had a long split wooden seat', *The Changing Forest*, 12–14; 'How can anybody eat', *The Singing Detective*, 67; 'The Front Room', *The Changing Forest*, 16; 'No. Sankey's *Sacred Songs and Solos*', *Desert Island Discs*, 1977; 'up the hill . . . twice', *Seeing the Blossom*, 7; 'one a Methodist outpost', *The Changing Forest*, 54

15 'they just, in their matter of fact way', *Potter on Potter*, 7; 'clean shoes, clean hanky', *Seeing the Blossom*, 59; 'The preacher at Salem', MP interview; 'At Salem, nearly all', *The Changing Forest*, 64f.; 'Dennis would latch on', Tony Baldwin interview; 'fundamentalist but not in that American', Dougary, 'Potter's Weal', and *Potter on Potter*, 4

16 'Sankey's *Sacred Songs and Solos*', *Potter on Potter*, 4; 'I am thinking today', *Sacred Songs and Solos: Twelve Hundred Hymns compiled under the direction of Ira D. Sankey*, Marshall Morgan & Scott, 1977 edn; 'makes me laugh', *Seeing the Blossom*, 8; 'in the red tin hut', *The Changing Forest*, 11 ; 'the sound of the village band', *A Christmas Forest*; 'the most endearing of expressions', ibid.

17 'My feeling is that words began', *Potter on Potter*, 4; 'As a child', ibid., 4–7; 'I remember', *Seeing the Blossom*, 60 ; 'writing things all the time', MP interview; 'difficulty in answering questions', *Seeing the Blossom*, 60; 'As a child I'd always thought of myself', Lambert, 'The thin skin of democracy'; 'It was an assumption', *Desert Island Discs*, 1988

18 'a place to collect birds' eggs', *The Changing Forest*, 21, 74, 31; 'a Londoner', *Blue Remembered Hills*, 33; 'I was four years old', *Seeing the Blossom*, 41; 'a few hybrid Foresters', *The Changing Forest*, 50; 'reserved occupation', *Seeing the Blossom*, 8; 'It took World War II', *Desert Island Discs*, 1977

19 'But there still wasn't much room', MP interview; 'shout "order, order"', *The Changing Forest*, 127; 'I said to myself', Tony Baldwin interview; 'lying in bed', *Start the Week*, Radio 4, 13 March 1978, BBC Sound Library, LP 38157; 'He'd shake its brim', MP interview; 'one-storeyed, ramshackle', *The Changing Forest*, 55; 'too high for a child', *A Christmas Forest;* 'had a bucket to catch the wet', Nathan, 'Private Pottah's post-war work'; 'but there was a separate Infant Department', Iris Hughes interview

20 'taught by teachers', *The Glittering Coffin*, 43; 'Miss Wakefield, one of the infant teachers', Tony Baldwin interview; 'always nicely dressed', Iris Hughes interview; 'There was a young woman', *With Great Pleasure*, Radio 4, 5 September 1976, BBC Sound Library, T 81877; 'I didn't really know', Cook, extracts from transcript of interview with DP; 'He was a very quiet boy', Iris Hughes interview; 'We didn't get to use many books', Tony Baldwin interview; 'Books weren't available', Iris Hughes interview

21 'big locked cupboard of books', *Seeing the Blossom*, 42; 'we always had books at home', MP interview; 'never looked robust', Iris Hughes interview; 'as a child, without question', *Seeing the Blossom*, 3f.; 'Potter says that he was', Dougary, 'Potter's Weal'; 'but only when I was alone', *Seeing the Blossom*, 62; 'Dennis would die rather than give in', Tony Baldwin interview; 'We used to be all one big gang', Horace and Coreene Wilks interview; 'a nervous boy', Olwen Birch, telephone conversation, 20 May 1996; 'He'd have a game of rugby', Horace and Coreene Wilks interview

22 'June was the boss', MP interview; 'At school, he was well above me', Horace and Coreene Wilks interview; 'awfully clever boy', Olwen Birch, telephone conversation, 20 May 1996; 'I was clever', *Daily Mail*, 27 January 1979; 'He was and he wasn't', Tony Baldwin interview; 'We never knew what he meant', Horace and Coreene Wilks interview; 'I love the sound of words', *Daily Mail*, 27 January 1979; 'It's a gift', Dougary, 'Potter's Weal'; 'the favourite of the headmaster', Olwen Birch, telephone conversation, 20 May 1996; 'the humiliating moment', *The Glittering Coffin*, 76f.

23 'she would say', *Blue Remembered Hills*, 33; 'knew he was very bright', MP interview; 'We used to get a football', Horace and Coreene Wilks interview; 'His mother drove him', Tony Baldwin interview; 'I had no trouble', MP interview; 'the times I had refused', *The Glittering Coffin*, 76; 'was very proud of the fact', *Potter on Potter*, 5; 'I used to tinkle on the piano', *Desert Island Discs*, 1977; 'reading is rather "soft"', *The Glittering Coffin*, 66

24 'I used to say', *Desert Island Discs*, 1977 ; 'all Dennis's early arguments', Tony

Baldwin interview; 'I was brought up to regard "tory"', *Isis*, 22 May 1957; 'always thought he was going to be an actor', Tony Baldwin interview; 'You used to dress up', Horace and Coreene Wilks interview; 'Anniversary Day', *The Changing Forest*, 67; 'the perpetual melodrama', *New Society*, 15 May 1975

26 'Out of every hundred working-class children', *The Glittering Coffin*, 67f.

Chapter 3

27 'He couldn't get out of the pit', MP interview; 'Most Forest miners', *The Changing Forest*, 94; 'We went up there', MP interview

28 'Why can't our Dad', *The Singing Detective*, 90; 'Dennis said to me', MP interview; 'I remember that the first time', *The Glittering Coffin*, 41; 'I couldn't believe that people', National Film Theatre *Guardian* Lecture; 'Although most of the kids', *Potter on Potter*, 7; '"Here, miss!"', *The Country Boy* manuscript; 'When we lived in London', *Potter on Potter*, 8

29 'a grim little boy', *Sun*, 8 February 1968; 'When I saw *The Count of Monte Cristo*', *Potter on Potter*, 8; 'I can remember once', MP interview

30 'I don't know whether it was too obvious', *Blue Remembered Hills*, 33; 'at the age of ten', *Seeing the Blossom*, 50; 'I remember something being talked about', SP interview; 'In the scale of things', Dougary, 'Potter's Weal'; 'attempted suicide in 1941', MP interview

31 'Ernie came to stay with us', Graham Wale interview; 'Oh God, I'd have killed my brother', MP interview; '*Why–Why–Why?*', *Seeing the Blossom*, 50; 'I knew instinctively', Dougary, 'Potter's Weal'; 'He said he found that impossible', Lawson, 'Skin Flicks'

32 'Certainly, with a kind of cunning shame', *Blue Remembered Hills*, 33f.; 'It did deeply affect me', Dougary, 'Potter's Weal'; 'If anyone cares to look', *Seeing the Blossom*, 50; 'I mean I was sexually assaulted', Cook, extracts from transcript of interview with DP; 'I wouldn't eat', *Potter on Potter*, 7; 'He must have done a bit more', MP interview

33 'it was . . . thought rather amusing', *The Changing Forest*, 78; 'one of the great governments', *Seeing the Blossom*, 8; 'things are going to be different', *The Changing Forest*, 49; 'He started off in the A-stream', Tony Baldwin interview

34 'I have this particularly strong image', *Desert Island Discs*, 1977; 'a person who knew what he wanted', Emlyn Richards, telephone conversation, 15 May 1997; 'We moved back to the Forest', MP interview; 'Dawn Wilson, one of our cousins', Gilbert, *Fight & Kick & Bite*, 39; 'impressed and bewildered', *The Changing Forest*, 91; 'there was a cinema in Coleford', *Potter on Potter*, 7f.

35 'You could hear a play', *Seeing the Blossom*, 45f.; 'It was already cold', *A Christmas Forest*

36 'No, I haven't', *Potter on Potter*, 10; 'Whenever I'm tempted to say', *Desert Island Discs*, 1988; 'We lived in a four-roomed cottage', Bakewell, 'Wrestling with a Vision'

37 'There was only a sort of curtain', *The Nigel Barton Plays*, 96; 'Even when I was fourteen', *Sun*, 8 April 1968; 'I still dream about it', interview with Michael Dean, *Late Night Line-Up*; 'About all sharing the same bedroom', June Thomas to the author, 23 October 1996; 'Here, most of the time', *Sun*, 8 April 1968; 'I could count the times', MP interview; 'sanctimonious, Guinness-swigging', *Wedding Night* manuscript; 'We took Dad as well', MP interview

38 'My father became a builder's labourer', Bakewell, 'Wrestling with a Vision'; 'Dad was almost literally shattered', *Wedding Night* manuscript; 'close-up acquaintance

with a football team', *New Statesman*, 9 May 1975; 'The only one Mum could get me in', MP interview

Chapter 4

39 'Grammar-school sixth forms', *The Glittering Coffin*, 65; 'Most of us', Bob Christopher letter; 'confident and a good mixer', Jack Harvey interview; 'a very pleasant, friendly sort of chap', Timothy Neal interview

40 'I never called him Dennis', Bob Christopher letter; 'None of the almost suffocatingly close', Bakewell, 'Wrestling with a Vision'; 'a kind of complicated shame', *Potter on Potter*, 6; 'Teachers love to get their hands on', *Seeing the Blossom*, 48f.; 'He never talked about', Roger Smith interview; 'I never quite worked out', Gareth Davies interview; 'Although not an outstanding player', testimonial in the archives of New College, Oxford

41 'The irrepressible Merrythought', *The Dane*, July 1951; 'rather left wing', Philip Gush letter; 'He is extremely', testimonial in the archives of New College, Oxford; 'Perce was fourteen or fifteen', Bob Christopher letter; 'At the end of his preparation', testimonial in the archives of New College, Oxford

42 'brilliant – we didn't know what to do', Jack Harvey interview; 'I used to be first', Nathan, 'Private Pottah's post-war work'; 'Yes, a teacher', *Desert Island Discs*, 1977; 'I went home', ibid.; 'They said, "You must try for Oxford"', Bakewell, 'Wrestling with a Vision'; 'a tremendous way with words', Jack Harvey interview; 'He really did shine', Bob Christopher letter; 'The Garden Scene', *The Dane*, July 1952; 'Dennis was very easy to act with', Roger Allen interview

43 'Later that day', *The Dane*, July 1952; 'We had six lectures', ibid.; 'It had more dignity', Bakewell, 'Wrestling with a Vision'; 'My . . . journey from grammar school', *Seeing the Blossom*, 10

44 'Hush, mind, our Dennis is here', *Observer*, 7 December 1986; 'My parents soon went back', *New Statesman*, 9 May 1975; 'Potter is a person of complete integrity', testimonial in the archives of New College, Oxford; 'I can see Dennis to this day', Kaye Barnes interview; 'D. C. G. Potter . . . played magnificently', *The Dane*, July 1953

45 'I am pleased to accept your offer', archives of New College, Oxford; 'its aim is to encourage', *The Dane*, July 1953; 'Our aim has been to choose', ibid.; 'Writing this article', ibid.

46 'Beauty is like the transcendent God', ibid.; 'that Art had a capital initial', *Blue Remembered Hills*, 16; 'I was in the sixth form', Lawson, 'Skin Flicks'; 'I first saw television', *Seeing the Blossom*, 55

47 'Those early grey-faced, tall nine-inch sets', *The Changing Forest*, 16f.; 'a place long buried', *The Sunday Times Magazine*, 8 January 1978; 'so shocked by the army', Bakewell, 'Wrestling with a Vision'; 'Dennis was having a rough time', Tony Baldwin interview

48 I regret the day', *Question Time*, BBC1, 22 January 1987; 'Nobody has yet been able', *The Sunday Times*, 30 October 1977; 'Transferred to the Intelligence Corps', Ministry of Defence letter; 'I can't pinpoint our first meeting', Kenith Trodd interview; 'I remember Dennis telling me', Brian Gibson interview; 'Dennis said it was the only time', Michael Grade interview; 'My father had been a crane driver', Kenith Trodd interview

50 'When I was about six', Harrison, *Dennis Potter*; 'I can remember biking round the record shops', Kenith Trodd interview

51 'As a private in the Intelligence Corps', DP to Tutor for Admissions, 31 January 1954, archives of New College, Oxford; 'Five hours' Russian', Bakewell, 'Wrestling with a Vision'; 'Dennis came across to me', Joe Melia interview; 'They were running a superior Russian course', Kenith Trodd interview

52 'The amount of work', DP to Tutor for Admissions, 3 January 1955, archives of New College, Oxford; 'which we found very boring', Joe Melia interview; 'I think we may have done some scheming', Kenith Trodd interview; 'Nell found Dennis very studious', Sidney Wale interview; 'Flo was a scream', Tony Baldwin interview; 'If I'd known', MP interview; 'I can remember Uncle Ernie', JP interview; 'wasn't entirely trivial', Nathan, 'Private Pottah's post-war work'

53 'huge office with . . . the majors', Cook, *Dennis Potter*, 70; 'had all been fighting soldiers', Nathan, 'Private Pottah's post-war work'; 'God! those long afternoons', Dickson, 'Potter back on song'; 'Discharged on termination', Ministry of Defence letter; 'rather concerned about requesting', DP to Tutor for Admissions, 27 September 1955, archives of New College, Oxford; 'He looked like a hungry animal', Peter Bayley, conversation, 26 June 1996; 'men would be trundling heavy tubs', *The Changing Forest*, 25

54 'taught himself Latin', MP interview; 'I had gone', *The Glittering Coffin*, 75f.

Chapter 5

55 'I remember that when I first arrived', *The Glittering Coffin*, 75, 77f.

56 'the talk of the scouts', Alan Coren, telephone conversation, 26 June 1996; 'we are plonked down with a bank balance', *The Glittering Coffin*, 23; 'Money wasn't a problem', Kenith Trodd interview; 'champagne parties', *The Glittering Coffin*, 82, 74ff.; 'at least more than two-thirds public school', *The Levin Interview*, BBC2, 17 May 1980; 'The few other grammar-school boys', Bakewell, 'Wrestling with a Vision'; 'I do not wish to speak with a different accent', *The Glittering Coffin*, 79; 'things seemed to become possible', Bakewell, 'Wrestling with a Vision'; 'supremely intelligent beings', Wright, 'The last acre of truth'; 'My assumption when I went up', *The Levin Interview*, BBC2, 17 May 1980

57 'what . . . shocked me about Oxford', Raven, 'Relative Values'; 'For the first time in years', *Isis*, 7 November 1956; 'the Suez abomination', *The Glittering Coffin*, 29; 'Mr Denis Potter (New College)', *Isis*, 7 November 1956; 'For the motion', *Cherwell*, 7 November 1956; 'Mr Dennis Potter . . . spoke of the broader aspects', ibid., 5 December 1956; 'I had to change buses', *The Changing Forest*, 24–6

58 'uppity', Bakewell, 'Wrestling with a Vision'; 'began asking questions', interview with Michael Dean, *Late Night Line-Up*; 'willy-nilly being pulled away', *Blue Remembered Hills*, 33; 'something of an incantation', *The Glittering Coffin*, 101; 'The fact that illiteracy', Richard Hoggart, *The Uses of Literacy*, Chatto & Windus, 1957, 278

59 'intellectual mentors', Roger Smith interview; 'speaking against the motion', *Cherwell*, 6 February 1957; 'Kenneth Trodd (University)', *Isis*, 20 February 1957; 'I think I skulked about', Kenith Trodd interview; 'The most memorable performance', *Isis*, 20 February 1957; 'rather good', Jonathan Cecil interview

60 'His interpretation, basically sound', *Isis*, 29 May 1957; 'a bad production of a good play', ibid., 13 March 1957; 'Mr Potter wishes to read modern history', report dated 9 March 1957, archives of New College, Oxford; 'used to come in a class', Sir Keith Thomas, telephone conversation, 23 September 1996; 'If anyone says Dennis had a chip', Stephen Hugh-Jones, telephone conversation, 7 July 1996

61 'I remember him sounding off', Jonathan Cecil interview; 'the great "public schools"',

The Glittering Coffin, 69; 'very, very amusing', *The Brains Trust*, 17 April 1960, BBC Written Archives; 'a membership . . . hovering between', *The Glittering Coffin*, 101; 'small and untidy office', ibid., 95; 'At twenty-five past three', *Isis*, 22 May 1957

63 'influenced and manipulated', Vance Packard, *The Hidden Persuaders*, Longmans, Green & Co., 1957, 3, 266; 'I remember thinking', Kenith Trodd interview; 'some unsuspected pride', *Woman's Hour*, 'Dennis Potter: Aspects of University Life 3', 16 April 1963, BBC Written Archives; 'There's nothing more terrifying', *Desert Island Discs*, 1988; 'a rather virulent and not very pleasant socialist', *Isis*, 13 June 1957

64 'The pale, timid and precocious child', *Blue Remembered Hills*, 33; 'depressingly busy', *Isis*, 5 March 1958; 'in difficulties', *The Changing Forest*, 110; 'sick with fear and pride', *Between Two Rivers*; 'October 5th, 1957', *Breathe on 'Um Berry!: 100 Years of Achievement by Berry Hill Rugby Football Club*, compiled by John Belcher, private publication, [c. 1993], 44; 'We used to call him Ginge', Tony Baldwin interview; 'I was . . . once kicked', *The Changing Forest*, 82; 'At Lydney . . . Town Hall', ibid., 99f.

65 'There was a band', Noreen Tye interview; 'Very slim build', SP interview; 'but Dad stole her away', JP interview; 'green eyes, the flick of her hips', Dougary, 'Potter's Weal'; 'We had a lot of fun', Noreen Tye interview; 'We weren't a bad-looking family', Mavis Wood interview; 'He was so young-looking', Noreen Tye interview

66 'But he never told her', MP interview; 'I . . . construct elaborately exhausting', *The Glittering Coffin*, 31; 'You know, left arm, as it were', *Desert Island Discs*, 1988; 'Although Dad had made his choice', SP interview; 'When he took over *Clarion*', *Isis*, 19 November 1958

67 'like being in a room', Natasha Edelman interview, Oxford, 16 November 1997; 'nearly 40 per cent agree', *Isis*, 16 October 1957

68 'horrifying picture of tweedy women', ibid., 23 October 1957; 'your correspondent is a member', ibid., 30 October 1957; 'I have been accused', ibid., 6 November 1957; 'Dennis played the part', John Fuller interview, Oxford, 8 July 1996; 'In some senses', Roger Smith interview

69 'overheard two girls in the audience', Jonathan Cecil interview; 'FILTHY SMEAR', *Cherwell*, 23 November 1957

70 'Planning done', *The Economist*, 11 June 1994; 'I would have liked', *Cherwell*, 23 November 1957; 'If Potter is in the right', *Isis*, 27 November 1957

71 'We cannot wholly divorce the fault', Gilbert, *Fight & Kick & Bite*, 56; 'Dennis had this capacity', Peter Jay interview, Woodstock, 12 July 1996; 'We [the Tories] said', Kenneth Baker, telephone conversation, 1 July 1996; 'Like an experimental machine', report in archives of New College, Oxford

72 'My stuff was absolute crap', Gilbert, *Fight & Kick & Bite*, 57; 'such sordid things as politics', *Isis*, 5 March 1958; 'I took the forms round', *The Glittering Coffin*, 106; 'I have never been ashamed', *Isis*, 12 March 1958; 'Anyone who has had the slightest contact', ibid., 30 April 1958; 'being a coalminer's son', *New Statesman*, 3 May 1958

73 'He'd set up this thing', Roger Smith interview; 'one way of not dealing with the difficulties', Kenith Trodd interview; 'When he was editor of *Isis*', Roger Smith interview

74 'She seemed to be demented', Jonathan Cecil interview; 'Dennis . . . was always The Only Person', Gilbert, *Fight & Kick & Bite*, 69; 'We all thought Dennis protested', John Fuller interview, Oxford, 8 July 1996; 'obnoxious', Alan Garner, conversation, Cheltenham, 16 October 1996; 'Talking about class', *The Glittering Coffin*, 72; 'REGARDING YOUR LETTER', BBC Written Archives, T32/533/1; 'everyone is looking at the telly', *Isis*, 12 March 1958

Chapter 6

75 'We may have heard a song or two', *Isis*, 30 April 1958

76 'there are many disturbing things', ibid.; 'Incredible though it seems', ibid., 7 May 1958; 'We're so glad', ibid., 14 May 1958; 'a prop to the pink-tinted pillars', ibid., 21 May 1958; 'medieval wrath would descend', *New Statesman*, 21 June 1958

77 'We are glad that our readers', *Isis*, 21 May 1958

78 'I thought, "My God"', Gilbert, *Fight & Kick & Bite*, 63; 'drift along', *Isis*, 11 June 1958; 'dismissed himself', ibid., 18 June 1958; 'exactly the kind of magazine', quoted in *Isis*, 15 October 1958

79 'Mr Hugh Trevor-Roper, Regius Professor', quoted *Independent on Sunday*, 12 June 1994; 'a long line of notable Oxford oddities', *The Glittering Coffin*, 83

80 'There was an unspoken rapport', Gilbert, *Fight & Kick & Bite*, 66; 'I thought he was brilliantly intelligent', Mayhew interview; 'Let's have a look', script of *Does Class Matter?* No. 2: 'Class in Private Life', broadcast 25 August 1958, BBC Written Archives, T32/533/1

82 'All the time . . . I was', *The Nigel Barton Plays*, 65; 'MINER'S SON', *Reynolds News*, 3 August 1958; Gilbert, *Fight & Kick & Bite*, 67

83 'humiliating and painful', *The Glittering Coffin*, 71; 'JACK ASHLEY AND I', BBC Written Archives, T32/533/1; 'a rare bright spot', *Isis*, 15 October 1958; 'Philip Phillips of the *Daily Herald*', *The Glittering Coffin*, 71f.; 'Of those interviewed', BBC Written Archives, T32/533/1; 'inaccurate and possibly defamatory', Roche to A.H.T.Tel. and others, 3 September 1958 BBC Written Archives, T32/533/1

84 'with an immediate generosity', *The Glittering Coffin*, 71; 'I couldn't possibly have written it', Mayhew interview; 'The book is going well', Mayhew to Philip Unwin, 15 July 1958, courtesy of Lord Mayhew; 'I am sorry to say', Gilbert, *Fight & Kick & Bite*, 68; 'I knew that the BBC', Mayhew to DP, 14 October 1958, courtesy of Lord Mayhew; 'The trouble was, Dennis kept sending', Mayhew interview; 'Dear Christopher', DP to Mayhew, 30 November 1958, courtesy of Lord Mayhew

85 'V.G. was always urging me', John Gross to HC, 7 July 1996

86 'I have been busy', DP to John Gross, 14 July 1958, Victor Gollancz archives; 'I could finish the whole book', DP to Gollancz, 21 August 1958, ibid; 'I took quite a powerful dislike', Hilary Rubinstein, telephone conversation, 21 August 1996; 'I would also appreciate', DP to Hilary Rubinstein, 1 September 1958, ibid.; 'David knew that in fact', *The Country Boy* manuscript

88 'another nine or ten days', DP to Hilary Rubinstein, 31 December 1958, Victor Gollancz archives; 'Most people take Schools', *Parson's Pleasure*, 4 December 1958; 'made a verbal agreement', report in archives of New College, Oxford

89 'I was lucky enough', *The Glittering Coffin*, 84; 'I sat opposite him', *The Sunday Times*, 26 February 1978; 'lively, interested', Anthony Quinton, telephone conversation, 6 October 1997; 'He confesses to being', *Isis*, 15 October 1958; 'Dennis dragged me out there', Smith interview

90 'Dennis Potter spoke', *Isis*, 5 November 1958; 'Dennis Potter . . . proposed the motion', *Parson's Pleasure*, 5 November 1958; 'fiery and convincing', *Cherwell*, 1 November 1958; 'Congratulations to Dennis Potter', *Cherwell*, 26 November 1958; 'I'm not buying anybody', Noreen Tye interview; 'They had the flat upstairs', Roger Smith interview

91 'Mum wasn't fazed', SP interview; 'extraordinarily impressive', Stephen Hugh-Jones, telephone conversation, 7 July 1996; 'Margaret seemed a lot older', Jonathan Cecil interview; 'there seems to be less smugness', *Isis*, 21 January 1959; 'shabby

dishonesty', *Isis*, 28 January 1959; 'Attacking ferociously', ibid., 4 February 1959; 'I knew Dennis pretty well', Paul Foot interview; 'whenever he saw a Rolls-Royce', Richard Ingrams, to HC, 27 June 1996; 'I . . . spit on a parked Rolls-Royce', *The Glittering Coffin*, 31

92 'You had all these public schoolboys', Paul Foot interview; 'Oh God, there I go again', *The Nigel Barton Plays*, 65; 'incredible popularity', Margaret Forster letters

93 'Ken Trodd once wanted', *Isis*, 25 February 1959; 'theatre, films and so on', *Cherwell*, 4 March 1959

94 'We didn't exactly get on', Margaret Forster letters; 'Gaitskell came to our play', ibid.; 'I have heard the elegantly and expensively perfumed daughter', *The Glittering Coffin*, 11; 'this could have been me', Julia McNeal, telephone conversation, 28 October 1996

95 'Technically, practically everything was wrong', *Cherwell*, 4 March 1959; 'Readers of *Isis* and *Cherwell*', *Parson's Pleasure*, 13 March 1959; 'I'm hideously distressed', Paul Foot interview; 'the three main parts', *New Statesman*, 28 March 1959; 'I have been – and still am – ill', DP to Hilary Rubinstein, 21 March 1959, Victor Gollancz archives; 'A lot of the writing', Hilary Rubinstein to DP, 1 May 1959, ibid.; 'I was too involved', Bakewell, 'Wrestling with a Vision'

96 'Why not read for a degree', *Desert Island Discs*, 1977; 'I'm proud to have failed', report in archives of New College, Oxford; 'I then stayed on a fifth year', Kenith Trodd interview

Chapter 7

97 'men and women of first-class all-round quality', BBC Written Archives, R49/731; 'from the universities', ibid.; 'Potter, looking rather farouche', P. H. Newby interview, Garsington, 24 May 1995

98 'As a general trainee', *Desert Island Discs*, 1977; 'a red-haired young man', Robin Day, *Grand Inquisitor*, Weidenfeld & Nicolson, 1989, 125; 'see the red light', BBC Written Archives, T32/1, 26/2; 'good social colour', Gilbert, *Fight & Kick & Bite*, 77f.

99 'a very sympathetic, rather shy', Robert Kee, to HC, 14 July 1996; 'I couldn't in the end', Gilbert, *Fight & Kick & Bite*, 78; 'not the kind of person to bungle', ibid.; 'one of television's great innovators', undated cutting from BBC News Information; 'first and foremost a literary man', Cook, *Dennis Potter*, 13

100 'a kind of metaphor', *Seeing the Blossom*, 13; 'It had everything I felt', Bakewell, 'Wrestling with a Vision'; 'I think I ought to begin', *The Glittering Coffin*, 5; 'I didn't actually say', *Desert Island Discs*, 1988; 'the pin-striped ethos', *The Glittering Coffin*, 7; 'appalling rigidity', ibid., 149; 'it is obvious that all the chrome', ibid., 45

101 'It seems at times', ibid., 40; 'It is impossible to be young', ibid., 31; 'We must teach people to read', ibid., 15; 'the Welfare State is to dwindle', ibid., 17; 'with people, houses and streets', ibid., 34; 'The new people's capitalism', ibid., 55; 'The one institution of power', ibid., 122; 'the comments of Angus Wilson', ibid., 135

102 'England could have become', ibid., 159; 'the anger and contempt', ibid., i; 'Unlucky Jim', quoted in the *Mail on Sunday*, 12 June 1994; 'as heartening' and 'a challenge', quoted from second-impression book jacket, Victor Gollancz archives; 'refreshingly devoid of stale language', *Times Literary Supplement*, 26 February 1960; 'he had written a less untidy', *New Statesman*, 13 February 1960

103 'twenty-one-inch televisions screens', *The Brains Trust*, 17 April 1960, BBC Written Archives, scripts; 'a young man on the make', Wright, 'The last acre of truth'; 'I am making sure', *The Glittering Coffin*, 5f.; 'I was absolutely the antithesis', Gilbert,

Fight & Kick & Bite, 80; 'That was my first meeting', *Seeing the Blossom*, 62

104 'in two lights', Gilbert, *Fight & Kick & Bite*, 80; 'Jane is my daughter', *Between Two Rivers* script, BBC Written Archives

105 'I found it fractionally distasteful', Gilbert, *Fight & Kick & Bite*, 80

107 'ordinary people didn't do documentaries', Tony Baldwin interview; 'I was what, twenty-three', *Seeing the Blossom*, 63; 'I was trying to describe', *Desert Island Discs*, 1988; 'Documentaries don't tell the truth', *Potter on Potter*, 11; 'discussing some ideas with Dennis Potter', BBC Written Archive, T32/1, 579/1

108 'Dennis Potter is at present a general trainee', ibid., R94/2, 952/1; 'because he is publishing a book', ibid., R94/2, 952/1; 'Because I was still writing things', *Desert Island Discs*, 1977; 'about mid-August', DP to J. G. Pattinson, 17 May 1960, Secker & Warburg archives, University of Reading Library; 'Clancy Sigal, an American', Mervyn Jones interview, London, 12 September 1996

109 'a detailed study of the breakdown', *The Glittering Coffin*, 44; 'almost every time I return', *The Changing Forest*, 18; 'new, well-designed council houses', ibid., 12f.; 'the external culture comes from the telly', ibid., 138; 'with the ardently youthful skill', *Blue Remembered Hills*, 22; 'Rather too large a part of the book', *Daily Herald*, 17 April 1962; 'There is . . . rather too much word-painting', *Times Literary Supplement*, 1 June 1962; 'your own "voice"', *Blue Remembered Hills*, 22

110 'working very well', BBC Written Archives, R94/2, 952/1; 'Dennis was very suspicious of me', Dick Taverne, telephone conversation; 'We had to climb all these stairs', Mavis Wood interview; 'singing "One Man Went to Mow"', JP interview; 'columnist', John McGrath interview

111 'I had to speak about *Under the Net*', Roger Smith interview; 'I don't think he read much', John McGrath interview; '*Out West* is the story', BBC Written Archives, T32/449/1

112 'I remember talking about Welshness', Jan Morris, telephone conversation, 22 August 1996; 'He isn't very good at this', Paul Foot interview; 'a happy lot who learned a good deal', Gilbert, *Fight & Kick & Bite*, 90; 'quite unworthy', BBC Written Archives, T32/1, 579/1; 'It is better to overestimate', undated cutting from *The Times*, headed 'Television's Duties to the Other Arts', with above memo, February 1961; 'he may be forced to take', BBC Written Archives, T32/1, 579/1; 'a waste of time and money', ibid., T32/1, 579/1; 'Since it was a home confinement', DP to J. G. Pattinson, 24 July 1961, Secker & Warburg archives, University of Reading Library

113 'I live on the top floor', *Daily Herald*, 18 November 1961; 'awful, a nightmare', John McGrath interview; 'Whenever I wished to be tender', *Potter on Potter*, 5; 'They've given me a "series"', BBC Written Archives, T32/1, 579/1

114 'If . . . you still want to help us', *Daily Herald*, 1 February 1962; 'in my innocence', *Desert Island Discs*, 1977; 'a Labour newspaper', Lawson, 'Skin Flicks'; 'pretty fish-and-chippy', David Nathan interview

115 'Dennis and I, along with Roger Smith', Kenith Trodd interview; 'Group 60 was Dennis's idea', Roger Smith interview, Gilbert, *Fight & Kick & Bite*, 93f.

116 'on August Bank Holiday', *Potter on Potter*, 11; 'Sid on the Railings', *Daily Herald*, 16 August 1961; 'cobwebbed attics in the middle of long corridors', *The Sunday Times*, 24 July 1977

117 'The first day I went into work', Lawson, 'Skin Flicks'; 'He wasn't what you would call a born journalist', David Nathan interview; 'I didn't enjoy the conviviality', Wade, 'Dennis Potter – rebel playwright'; 'Flanders caught polio', *Daily Herald*, 6 February 1962

118 'I was full of disappointment', *Potter on Potter*, 10; 'They wanted him for the big

series', Gilbert, *Fight & Kick & Bite*, 94; 'the self-motivation courses', *Potter on Potter*, 19; 'I hated every second', *Seeing the Blossom*, 14; 'I knew something physical', *Potter on Potter*, 12

PART TWO

Chapter 1

121 'already very pale', *Potter on Potter*, 12; 'Teams of canvassers', *Daily Herald*, 2 March 1962; 'He'd been on a selection conference', Ron and Jean Brewer interview; 'My nails were all pitted', Wapshott, 'Knowing what goes on inside people's heads'

122 'I hated being there', *Potter on Potter*, 12; 'when I was crossing the road', *Observer*, 7 December 1986

123 'I have a gluttonous appetite', *Daily Herald*, 23 March 1963; 'Addicts must have been half hoping', ibid., 9 May 1962; 'It thrives on superb camera work', ibid.; 'were watching an American cop series', John McGrath interview; 'When Troy Kennedy Martin, Allan Prior and John McGrath', *New Statesman*, 1 February 1974

124 'the under-rated Sid James', *Daily Herald*, 10 May 1962; 'Last night on BBC', 12 May 1962; 'he was unable to carry on', Dr Edmund Sever to Dr D. R. Jones, 2 July 1962, DP's medical records; 'because of the weird swiftness', *Potter on Potter*, 12

125 'a family history', Dr Edmund Sever to Dr D. R. Jones, 2 July 1962, DP's medical records; 'Yes. My grandfather', MP interview; 'suffered from a crippling arthritic disease', *Observer*, 7 December 1986; 'My father was – not like Dennis', MP interview; 'The first I remember of Dennis', ibid.

126 'without undue discomfort', Dr Edmund Sever to Dr D. R. Jones, 2 July 1962, DP's medical records; 'in the first and so most irrationally terrifying grip', *The Times*, 3 August 1968; 'Dennis saying that he had had the song', Bob Christopher letter; 'Well, if I'm going to be forced to give up', *Desert Islands Discs*, 1977; 'his psoriatic arthritis', Dr B. L. J. Treadwell to Dr D. R. Jones, 12 July 1962, DP's medical records; 'Boy, in this business', *Daily Herald*, 23 July 1962

127 'Strange that in this slick, neon-lit age', ibid., 24 July 1962; 'television reaches its peak', ibid., 7 August 1962; 'I respond to soccer', ibid., 2 March 1963; 'the bared but hesitant grin', ibid., 16 August 1962; 'fleeting shadows in a polished plate-glass window', *Daily Herald*, 26 September 1962; 'The strength of this programme', ibid., 17 August 1962; 'the gogglebox', ibid., 31 August 1962; 'was a county constituency', Ron and Jean Brewer interview

128 'caught his audience', *Independent*, 8 July 1994; 'small-scale "naturalism"', *The Nigel Barton Plays*, 10f.; '"Culture" . . . has become too suspect', *Daily Herald*, 22 September 1962; 'I hope these new programmes', ibid., 20 October 1962; 'wildly funny, dubiously improper', ibid., 26 November 1962

129 'On the way there', Gilbert, *Fight & Kick & Bite*, 101f.; 'Around this time I also did a few sketches', *Potter on Potter*, 11; 'I would be at the typewriter', David Nathan interview

130 'used to turn up done on different typewriters', Ned Sherrin, telephone conversation, 6 September 1996; 'unless there was a party', David Nathan interview; 'Never having been teenagers ourselves', BBC Written Archives, Films 47/48

131 'We weren't trying to keep', David Nathan interview; 'Here's a must for Thursday', BBC Written Archives, Films 47/48; 'What is a Mum?', ibid.; published in David Frost and Ned Sherrin (eds.), *That Was The Week That Was*, W. H. Allen, 1963, 91

132 'a cheap crook', Ron and Jean Brewer interview
133 'shrieking banality', *Daily Herald*, 25 March 1963; 'so damned "authentic"', ibid.,
30 March 1963; 'too drab', ibid., 5 April 1963; 'dismally authentic', ibid., 8 April
1963; 'infuriating, enthralling, disturbing', ibid., 29 June 1963; 'the simple,
naturalistic, tediously "authentic" drama', ibid., 30 March 1963; 'more than twenty
hours', ibid., 15 June 1963; 'Watching *Emergency – Ward 10*', ibid., 21 July 1963;
'the new occlusive technique', Dr O. L. S. Scott to Dr B. L. J. Treadwell, 8 March
1962, DP's medical records; 'What is a smoker?', BBC Written Archives, Films 47/48
134 'What is an invalid?', ibid., 18 November 1963; 'distress', Dr O. L. S. Scott to
Dr J. B. Randell, 16 August 1963, DP's medical records; 'I can't remember Dennis
telling me', Kenith Trodd interview; 'This man confused the date', Dr J. B. Randell
to Dr N. C. Mond, 16 October 1963, DP's medical records; 'Uncle Ernie was the
only one', SP to HC, 11 October 1996
135 'a total waste of time', SP interview; 'In 1962–63, when I was first in hospital', Cook,
extracts from transcript of interview with DP; 'I was staying in a friend's house',
Kenith Trodd interview; 'He'd decided that he wanted to try', ibid.; 'It was in about
1963', Roger Smith interview
136 'He said that one of the things', Kenith Trodd interview; 'I think he saw a lot of
young women', Paul Foot interview; 'I think Dennis was capable of flirting', Ron and
Jean Brewer interview; 'I don't think Dennis was particularly faithful', David Nathan
interview
137 'I'm not saying it didn't happen', SP interview; 'Mum and Dad certainly had rows',
JP interview; 'My disease is to some extent psychosomatic', *Observer*, 7 December
1986; 'If you suddenly find yourself covered in lesions', Cook, extracts from
transcript of interview with DP; 'psoriatic arthropathy is a genetic condition', *Potter
on Potter*, 12; 'paralysis became more than a metaphor', ibid.; 'My condition was
genetic', *Seeing the Blossom*, 50
138 'I've talked to dermatologists', *Potter on Potter*, 33; 'The temptation is to believe',
The Singing Detective, 56; 'If I knew what I had done', *Tender is the Night*
transmission script, episode 4; 'Actually what Dennis was', Roger Smith interview

Chapter 2

139 'slaughtered', *Daily Herald*, 21 December 1963; 'wanton destruction', ibid., 7 March
1964; 'The current shortage of writing talent', ibid., 25 January 1964
140 'I am proud', Shubik, *Play for Today*, 40; 'Troy Kennedy Martin, whom I'd met',
Roger Smith interview; 'a Scottish middle-class ex-National Service paratrooper',
ibid.; 'the brake on our wildness', Kenith Trodd interview; 'Sydney I liked', Roger
Smith interview
141 'The quantity of plays we were making', Kenith Trodd interview; 'What I wanted
to do', *Potter on Potter*, 13; 'Roger Smith . . . was a notable exception', *The Times*,
5 July 1969
142 'burst of energy', *Seeing the Blossom*, 15; 'I was depressed and ill', *The Times*,
obituary, 8 June 1994; 'through illness . . . I reinvented myself', *Seeing the Blossom*,
15; 'I had the opportunity', ibid., 50; 'strange, shadowy ally', Wapshott, 'Knowing
what goes on inside people's heads'; 'As a child I'd always thought', Lambert, 'The
thin skin of democracy'; 'Dennis was already writing', Roger Smith interview;
'I wasn't a close friend', Roger Hancock interview, London, 11 March 1997; 'The
experience of watching television', *Desert Island Discs*, 1977
143 'After *That Was The Week*', Gilbert, *Fight & Kick & Bite*, 108; 'Nothing Dennis

wrote about his background', David Nathan interview; 'really about the self-motivation courses', *Potter on Potter*, 19; 'A group of people gathered together', ibid.

144 'I got soaked through coming here tonight' and other quotations from *The Confidence Course*, from the camera script; 'So-called naturalism is by far and away', *Seeing the Blossom*, 52f.; 'Television drama at the moment', *Encore*, March–April 1964

145 'providing the dialogue is good enough', ibid., May–June 1964; 'probably dipped into one or two of the essays', *The Times*, 3 August 1968; 'responded eagerly and almost immediately', ibid.

146 'was an odd combination', *Potter on Potter*, 19–21; 'They are so wide', *Desert Island Discs*, 1977

147 'a weirdo', Roger Smith interview; 'about my experiences as a parliamentary candidate', *The Times*, 5 July 1969

148 'Although I cannot give details', *Daily Herald*, 27 June 1964' 'the fairly decent pre-Murdoch *Sun*', *Desert Island Discs*, 1988; 'deeply ashamed of the psoriasis', Dougary, 'Potter's Weal'; 'exquisitely written', *Independent*, 8 July 1994; 'At 9 p.m. on Thursday, October 15th', *Purpose in Politics*

149 'Watching the glad-handing', Bakewell, 'Wrestling with a Vision'; 'very strong streak of charlatanry', *Seeing the Blossom*, 64; 'I don't think he'd ever done', Ron and Jean Brewer interview; 'Dennis would say, "I'm the Labour candidate"', Lord Taverne, telephone conversation; 'get a sharp kick on the ankle', *Seeing the Blossom*, 64

150 'I never knew whether Dennis was disappointed', Ron and Jean Brewer interview; 'crushed, mentally and physically', Wapshott, 'Knowing what goes on inside people's heads'; 'That election just crippled me', Bakewell 'Wrestling with a Vision'; 'Politics . . . seemed the door', *Seeing the Blossom*, 14; 'I had thought that I was going to be a politician', ibid., 59; 'I wrote [*Vote, Vote*] because I thought', Dougary, 'Potter's Weal'

151 'horsey group' and other quotations from *Vote, Vote, Vote for Nigel Barton*, from *The Nigel Barton Plays*; 'some purely farcical elements', ibid., 12

152 'I'm noted for those asides', Ron and Jean Brewer interview; 'My own attitude', *The Nigel Barton Plays*, 11

155 'I mean . . . would *you* vote', *Vote, Vote, Vote for Nigel Barton* camera script, BBC Written Archives; 'explosive', Kenith Trodd interview; 'an old-timer television director', ibid.; 'Dennis's penchant for red-nose casting', Jon Amiel interview; 'Dennis Potter, the author', *Radio Times*, 18 February 1965; 'Dennis Potter is already well known', *Sun*, 25 February 1965

156 'This was former television critic', *Daily Mirror*, 15 February 1965; 'considerably puzzled', *Listener*, 4 March 1965; 'This play is about a by-election', BBC Written Archives, T48; 'a splendid piece', Gareth Davies interview; 'I would talk on the telephone', *Potter on Potter*, 33; 'The vivacity was in proportion', Kenith Trodd interview

157 'Coming from the theatre', Gareth Davies interview; 'Dennis doesn't give masses', Kenith Trodd interview; 'Some writers give you innumerable descriptions', Brian Gibson interview; 'It was like the theatre', Keith Barron interview; 'ideal', *The Nigel Barton Plays*, 17, 13

158 'Gareth phoned and said', Keith Barron interview; 'But in the meanwhile', Kenith Trodd interview; 'its own little force', Bakewell and Garnham, *The New Priesthood*, 83; 'Everyone knew they had to stay in', Keith Barron interview; 'but I don't remember seeing it', Kenith Trodd interview; 'But by that time', *The Nigel Barton Plays*, 17

159 'a terrifying building', *Daily Herald*, 6 July 1963; 'had a go', Gilbert, *Fight & Kick & Bite*, 117; 'The play . . . is very nearly a documentary', BBC Written Archives, T5/691/1; 'In place of the advertised *Wednesday Play*', ibid.; 'decided that the production as a whole', ibid.

160 'My memory is that around midday', Kenith Trodd interview; 'Mr Potter had just finished broadcasting', *Sun*, 24 June 1965; 'highly disturbing', ibid.; 'about politics', *Daily Telegraph*, 24 June 1965; 'I had a terrific row with Sydney', Roger Smith interview

161 'some kind of fascist', *The Nigel Barton Plays*, 17f.; 'appeared to be so troubled', *Seeing the Blossom*, 35; 'we were all anxious', Michael Bakewell, telephone conversation, 30 October 1996; 'We got in the car', MP interview; 'Dad was always daydreaming', JP interview; 'It took him ages', SP interview; 'Toad of Toad Hall', Mervyn James interview; 'I see you've moved again', BBC Written Archives, T48

162 'highlighted how reclusive', SP interview; 'I used to be able to get on', Lambert, 'The thin skin of democracy'; 'He is not a gregarious person', *The Sunday Times*, 23 November 1986; 'I do have a very reclusive temperament', *Desert Island Discs*, 1988; 'I remember that on the way we stopped', Kenith Trodd interview

163 'in a few important ways', *The Nigel Barton Plays*, 18; 'It takes the edge off the savagery', ibid.

164 'though I have no recollection', Ron and Jean Brewer interview; 'So poor Jack Hay', *The Nigel Barton Plays*, 18; 'what was actually shown', ibid., 19; 'stupidity', ibid., 18; 'companion piece', ibid., 19; 'I was sort of midway through a novel', *Desert Island Discs*, 1988

165 'I'm getting married tomorrow', *Wedding Night* manuscript

167 'I think [*Stand Up, Nigel Barton*] is a much better play', *The Nigel Barton Plays*, 19f.; 'probably South Nottinghamshire' and other quotations from *Stand Up, Nigel Barton* from *The Nigel Barton Plays*

168 'played by adults', ibid., 31; 'the excitement, the zest, the terror', *Seeing the Blossom*, 66

169 'to bring the play into the Sixties', Gareth Davies interview

172 'In retrospect it does look like it', *Potter on Potter*, 23f.; 'both coalminers and Oxford dons', *The Nigel Barton Plays*, 21; 'If I wanted to write', quoted in *Independent on Sunday*, 12 June 1994; 'the hierarchies of our print culture', *Potter on Potter*, 24; 'but if something is working', ibid., 122; 'the voice of the occupying power', *Seeing the Blossom*, 72; 'The women were weird', *Sun*, 9 December 1965; 'I said, "When are you going to write"', Gareth Davies interview; 'Do you think the accusations', *Potter on Potter*, 133

173 'Mr Dennis Potter, being an atheist', *Daily Mail*, 13 December 1965; 'spent some time on the telephone', *The Nigel Barton Plays*, 17; 'Mr Potter is not a promiser', *The Sunday Times*, 19 December 1965

174 'We must be growing up', *Daily Mail*, 16 December 1965; 'one of the best irreverent digs', *Daily Express*, 16 December 1965; 'enormously better than *Stand Up, Nigel Barton*', *Sun*, 16 December 1965; 'Mr Potter makes everything a bit bigger', *Guardian*, 16 December 1965; 'For the first time, I thought I could manage', Dougary, 'Potter's Weal'; 'Earl Mountbatten stood up', *Mirror Magazine*, week ending 11 October 1969

Chapter 3

175 'weren't characterized', John McGrath interview; 'with absolutely dead voice' and other quotations from *Alice* from the manuscript and the rehearsal script

176 'scarcely emerged', *Daily Mail*, 14 October 1965

177 'sad, sometimes painfully embarrassing', *The Times*, 14 October 1965; 'that haunted soul', *Potter on Potter*, 119; 'I'm fascinated, with Dodgson', *Guardian*, 6 December 1983; 'the conveyor-belt aspects', *The Nigel Barton Plays*, 21; 'Dennis was only *one*', Roger Smith interview; 'Nobody else was writing anything like', Kenith Trodd interview

178 'terrifying . . . compellingly written', *New Statesman*, 30 October 1977

179 'Ken Loach represented everything that Dennis didn't', Kenith Trodd interview; 'Dennis believed, in those days', Gareth Davies interview; 'BBC drama producers and story editors', *New Society*, 22 September 1966; 'the increasingly fashionable, hand-held camera style', ibid., 8 December 1966; 'journalism and the essay', Cook, *Dennis Potter*, 139; 'I've scarcely exchanged the time of day', Wade, 'Dennis Potter – rebel playwright'; 'like a big, black, aching tooth', *Sun*, 18 January 1968; 'Jimmy MacTaggart and his bushy-tailed acolytes', *Seeing the Blossom*, 36

180 'A walk along the corridors', ibid., 35; 'I was exceptionally fortunate', ibid., 55; 'We were keen that he should have', Michael Bakewell, telephone conversation, 30 October 1996; 'I never have a plot', *Potter on Potter*, 26, 28

181 'I doubt if he ever laboured very long', Kenith Trodd interview; 'There are writers . . . I presume', *Blue Remembered Hills*, 21; 'It doesn't feel like making an argument', *Potter on Potter*, 28; 'I don't know what my next play will be like', Paul Madden (ed.), *David Mercer: Where the difference began*, British Film Institute, 1981, 17; 'I think writing is very difficult', Lambert, 'The thin skin of democracy'

182 'Painting the portrait of a Pope' and other quotations from *Message for Posterity* from the rehearsal script

183 'There was an evasion going on', *Potter on Potter*, 31f.; 'Yes, basically it was', ibid., 32; 'The original spark was fine', Gilbert, *Fight & Kick & Bite*, 152; 'We used to discourage writers', Kenith Trodd interview; 'the result of thinking up a play', *Sunday Telegraph*, 7 May 1967

184 'I received a letter', Kenith Trodd interview; 'the half-hour play is cripplingly difficult', *New Statesman*, 23 June 1967; 'watching *Emergency – Ward 10*', *Daily Herald*, 31 July 1963; 'ramshackle London hospital' and other quotations from *Emergency - Ward 9* from DP's manuscript and the camera script.

185 'propaganda', Kenith Trodd interview

186 'Thank goodness for Dennis Potter', *Sun*, 12 April 1966; 'When writing flat out', *Karaoke*, XI

187 'Call me Shane' and other quotations from *Where the Buffalo Roam* from the rehearsal script and camera script; 'thought the language could be freed up', Gilbert, *Fight & Kick & Bite*, 141; 'When I first started writing plays', *Scan*, BBC Radio 4, 25 November 1971, BBC Written Archives, Films 41–2; 'In those days . . . I protected myself', *New Society*, 15 May 1975

188 'I am aware that I am living', *Potter on Potter*, 10f.; 'This is the play he has written', *Sun*, 3 November 1966; 'warm', Wapshott, 'Knowing what goes on inside people's heads'; 'a tiny bungalow', JP interview; 'Mothers and fathers queue outside', *New Society*, 27 October 1966

189 'This [is] to be our Christmas show', Kenith Trodd to Copyright, 8 October 1966, BBC Written Archives, T48; 'Garnett and I made a rule', Kenith Trodd interview; 'grave doubts about its suitability', BBC Written Archives, T48; 'My dislike of it went further', ibid.; 'The BBC commissioned Dennis Potter', *The Sunday Times*, 30 October 1966

190 'yelling to the press', BBC Written Archives, T48; 'I asked him if he minded', ibid.;

'best play to date', ibid.; 'The BBC knew the theme', *Sun*, 7 December 1966; 'I wrote it for grown-ups', *Daily Sketch*, 7 December 1966

191 'It wasn't very good', *Potter on Potter*, 32; 'a minuscule European monarchy' and other quotations from *Cinderella* from DP's manuscript

193 'The only scene I recall', *Potter on Potter*, 32; 'I have never written for ITV', unidentified cutting in BBC Written Archives, T5/994/1; 'strange little man' and other quotations from *Rumpelstiltskin* from DP's manuscript; 'Dennis was talking about getting Diana Dors', Roger Hancock interview, London, 11 March 1997

Chapter 4

194 'the hitherto lively *Wednesday Play*', *New Statesman*, 17 February 1967; 'I longed for a healthy belch', ibid., 3 March 1967; 'If the scriptwriters have been warned off', ibid.

195 'There is at the moment', ibid., 10 March 1967; 'has become for so many of us', ibid., 28 April 1967; 'Dennis never appeared to be nervous', Gareth Davies interview; 'We all know . . . that a lot of broadcasters', Nicholas Tomalin to DP, 28 April 1967, *New Statesman* archive, University of Sussex Library; 'Dennis Potter has delivered us', BBC Written Archives, T48; 'a sleazy, rather badly lit street' and other quotations from *The Rivers of Babylon* from DP's manuscript

203 'The pain was much too raw', Kenith Trodd interview; 'It is essential to understand', *Blue Remembered Hills*, 19; 'The closer writing approaches to therapy', Cook, *Dennis Potter*, 129; 'I don't remember feeling', Kenith Trodd interview

204 'Dennis came over to Ross', MP interview; 'There were six bedrooms', SP interview; 'We didn't have carpets', JP interview'; 'Dennis remained resolutely working class', Roger Smith interview; 'When I grow up', *The Singing Detective*, 77; 'a prosperous, placid little market town', *New Society*, 20 June 1968; 'When I started writing', *Potter on Potter*, 6

205 'Writers, actors and singers', *New Statesman*, 21 July 1967; '*Man Alive* has taken to advertising', ibid., 25 August 1967; 'writing about yourself', Nicholas Tomalin to DP, 3 October 1967, *New Statesman* archive, University of Sussex Library; 'two companion plays', BBC Written Archives, T48; 'National Theatre commitment', ibid.; 'autobiographical stage play', Clive Goodwin to Kenneth Tynan, 6 November 1968, Royal National Theatre archive; 'a play with obvious perils', to Michael Ratcliffe, 19 December 1967, News International archives

206 'thick, damp, alien' and other quotations from *A Beast with Two Backs* from DP's manuscript

207 'Every man has an inalienable right', *The Times*, 21 October 1967; 'very extensive', Dr B. S. Smith to Dr Ernest Fairburn, 7 November 1967, DP's medical records; 'emotional stress', Dr Ernest Fairburn to Dr B. S. Smith, 20 November 1967, ibid.

208 'There have been some studies', *The Times*, 9 December 1967; 'My darling, A few words', DP to MP, 4 December 1967

209 'Uncle Brian and Auntie Jean', JP interview; 'fairly acute episode', Dr B. S. Smith to Dr Ernest Fairburn, 9 January 1968, DP's medical records; 'a face worthy to launch', *Sun*, 21 January 1968; 'discovered, fully grown', ibid., 19 January 1968; 'Now I can get back', ibid., 23 February 1968; 'a purveyor of instant opinions', ibid., 11 March 1968; 'Whenever the cold winds blow', ibid., 18 March 1968

210 'like *samizdat* material', Kenith Trodd interview; 'I see that Tariq Ali', *Sun*, 25 March 1968; 'After years of bullying exploitation', ibid., 26 January 1968; 'stupid, nasty and wantonly racialist', ibid., 29 April 1968

211 'Two little girls learning how to read', ibid., 6 May 1968; 'We went to St Joseph's Convent', SP interview

212 'Millions of people will', *Sun*, 13 May 1968

213 'I think that was immediately after', *Potter on Potter*, 33; 'Uncle Sam meets King George, right?' and other quotations from *The Bonegrinder* from DP's manuscript

214 'unbelievably vulgar and spiteful', *Sunday Telegraph*, 19 May 1968; 'The Bonegrinder didn't work', *Sun*, 14 May 1968; 'queer and unbalanced', *Daily Mail*, 14 May 1968; 'The great virtue of Potter', *Guardian*, 14 May 1968; 'Their scornful unanimity', *Sun*, 20 May 1968

215 'Why be so extreme?', ibid.; 'As soon as I got out of the train', ibid., 27 May 1968; 'Even in Britain the Establishment', ibid., 20 May 1968

216 'a trendy social-butterfly figure', Kenith Trodd interview; 'not the brightest of creatures', *Hide and Seek*, 62; 'It was an odd, uninspiring occasion', *New Society*, 20 June 1968

217 'We had set up *Black Dwarf*', Tariq Ali interview, London, 23 June 1997; 'If the list . . . had been compiled', *New Society*, 20 June 1968; 'struggle, under the banner of Marxism', *Black Dwarf*, 22 September 1968; 'Roger joined the Workers' Revolutionary Party', Kenith Trodd interview; 'I joined the Socialist Labour League', Roger Smith to HC, 4 January 1997

218 'To a degree', *Potter on Potter*, 13; 'There was a fantastically fraught meeting', Paul Foot interview; 'Hush, hush, little bourgeois baby', *Sun*, 17 June 1968

219 'There was a Special Branch guy', John McGrath interview; 'Oh, I shall always remember the night', *Sun*, 17 June 1968

220 'naïve', John McGrath interview; 'I think I met Dennis', Trevor Griffiths to HC, 10 December 1996; 'He'd done that at Oxford', Roger Smith interview

221 'approximately 75 per cent control', Dr Ernest Fairburn to Dr B. S. Smith, 21 October 1968, DP's medical records

222 'an anguished sort of comedy', *Sun*, 13 May 1968; 'suitably uniformed in bowler hat' and other quotations from *Shaggy Dog* from the rehearsal script

223 'amusing and enjoyable', *The Times*, 11 November 1968; 'his best play for some time', *Daily Mail*, 11 November 1968; 'thinking he ought to get a monkey', *Sun*, 21 November 1968; '*saeva indignatio*, a terrible anger', *The Sunday Times*, 24 November 1968; 'bothered to write the play', *Guardian*, 21 November 1968; 'I saw him walking with a stick', Keith Barron interview; 'structurally rather confusing', *The Times*, 28 November 1968; 'sadly disappointing', *Bristol Evening Post*, 28 November 1968; 'I'm quite happy for any of my plays', Purser, 'A playwright comes of age'; 'The theatre is a kind of middle-class privilege', Bakewell and Garnham, *The New Priesthood*, 83; 'Television is the biggest platform', *Radio Times*, 8 October 1970

224 'The great problem was physical', Philippa Toomey, telephone conversation, 17 December 1996; 'I can't use a typewriter', *Evening Standard*, 17 November 1986; 'I often need a stick to walk', *The Times*, 7 December 1968; 'I'm not taking those things!', *The Singing Detective*, 16, 55f.; 'Five times in hospital', *The Times*, 7 December 1968

Chapter 5

225 'I first met Dennis Potter', *Daily Telegraph*, 8 June 1994; 'Dennis Potter might be the survivor', Purser, 'A playwright comes of age'

226 'so a week or two later', *Daily Telegraph*, 8 June 1994; 'It wasn't very successful as a method', SP interview

227 'Dennis was a great ringer-up', Gareth Davies interview; 'The combination of these two books', *The Times*, 25 January 1969; 'I was . . . becoming more and more reclusive', *Potter on Potter*, 32f.

228 'Towards the end of 1967', Kenith Trodd interview; 'JUST AS NO ACTOR WORTH HIS SALT' and other quotations from *Moonlight on the Highway* from Potter's manuscript

230 'between VE Day and VJ Day', *Seeing the Blossom*, 50; 'Cheap music can be so potent', *Sun*, 14 February 1968; 'Nostalgia . . . for a far-off decade', *The Times*, 13 July 1968

231 'Nostalgia is a means of forgetting the past', *Potter on Potter*, 22

234 'There was never a specifically Al Bowlly society', Kenith Trodd interview; 'it's the child that assumes guilt', Dougary, 'Potter's Weal'

235 'You know that cheap songs', *Seeing the Blossom*, 19; 'Your films and plays often present', *Potter on Potter*, 137

236 'This was an almost copybook piece', *Sun*, 14 April 1969; 'lurid', *Daily Telegraph*, 14 April 1969; 'a new play by the irritating Dennis Potter', *Guardian*, 14 April 1969

Chapter 6

237 'I know that you do not desire me', DP to Caroline Seebohm, 18 January 1969; I don't think I did meet him then', and all remaining quotations from Caroline Seebohm, Caroline Seebohm interview; 'extremely attractive – in an era of horrible clothes', Margaret Forster to HC

239 'Dinner with Clive and Dennis Potter', and all remaining quotations from Caroline Seebohm's diary, Seebohm, diary; 'Caroline, I want to write to you', DP to Caroline Seebohm, 6 May 1968

241 'heavy daily dose of steroids', *Sun*, 13 May 1968

242 'Let me *do* things with you', DP to Caroline Seebohm, 21 May 1968

243 'No – I am not destructive', ibid.; 'He definitely had crushes on people', SP interview; 'the raising of Lazarus', Roger Smith interview; 'One of my girlfriends', Kenith Trodd interview

244 'when I cried in the street', DP to Caroline Seebohm, 10–11 February 1969; 'I am well aware of the sort of fool', ibid., 11–12 January 1969; 'I have written at least ten times', ibid.; 'at this present time my own pride', ibid.

245 'drew a very firm line at any blasphemous attempt', *New Statesman*, 10 November 1972; 'Controversy has stalked every play', *Radio Times*, 10 April 1969; 'a religious revolutionary', BBC Written Archives, T48; 'Initially I thought of it being about', Bakewell, 'Wrestling with a Vision'; 'I always felt Dennis had a cunning awareness', John McGrath interview; 'No, I don't believe in throwing down gauntlets', *Potter on Potter*, 40, 38

246 'walking on eggshells and water', *The Sunday Times*, 10 April 1977; 'Of course I'd been brooding on it', Purser, 'A playwright comes of age'; 'Some of the *Son of Man* script', Gareth Davies interview; 'There's this brave, witty, sometimes oddly petulant, man', Dougary, 'Potter's Weal'

247 'Is it? Is it *me*?' and other quotations from *Son of Man* from the 'rehearsal script' (actually camera script) at BBC Written Archives; 'I had gone through a period of illness', *Radio Times*, 10 April 1969; 'We live amongst the litter of religion', Purser, 'A playwright comes of age'; 'no faith', *Church of England Newspaper*, 25 April 1969; 'a yearning for there to be something else', *Sun*, 21 April 1969; 'my christian-tinged agnosticism', DP to Caroline Seebohm, 11–12 January 1969

248 'I suppose the play represents a retreat', Purser, 'A playwright comes of age'; 'a

stocky, voluble, undogmatic, amusing and optimistic individual', *Sun*, 17 June 1968; 'Half of them couldn't strike a match', ibid.

249 'the sick and the bereft', Purser, 'A playwright comes of age'; '*Son of Man*, your play about Jesus', *Potter on Potter*, 38; 'It was so very, very nice', DP to Caroline Seebohm, 10–11 February 1969; 'I also asked for Colin Blakely', Purser, 'A playwright comes of age'; 'as the end of my apprenticeship', *Radio Times*, 10 April 1969; 'plastic and polythene', *The Times*, 5 July 1969; 'a set that looks as though it's trembling', *Potter on Potter*, 40

250 'Storm over TV Christ', Cook, *Dennis Potter*, 57; 'angered many viewers', *Daily Telegraph*, 17 April 1969; 'one indignant lady complained', *Mirror Magazine*, week ending 11 October 1969; 'Mrs Whitehouse wanted me prosecuted', *Seeing the Blossom*, 22; 'Quiet Reception for new Son of Man', *Guardian*, 17 April 1969; 'a distinct advance, a maturing', *The Sunday Times*, 20 April 1969; 'received no more telephone calls than usual', *Guardian*, 18 April 1969; 'To tell God's truth', *Sun*, 17 April 1969; 'more like a party political broadcast', *Daily Telegraph*, 17 April 1969; 'a crude, Identikit assemblage', *Listener*, 24 April 1969; 'Slang just won't work', *Sunday Telegraph*, 20 April 1969; 'This sad, clinical investigation', *Observer*, 20 April 1969

251 'It – is – ACCOMPLISHED', *Son of Man* camera script; 'now seems the only meaningful act of love', DP to Caroline Seebohm, 30 June 1969; 'the attitudes of the middle age', BBC Written Archives, T48; 'whopping great lies' and other quotations from *Lay Down Your Arms* from the rehearsal script

252 'You are probably going away soon', DP to Caroline Seebohm, 10–11 February 1969; 'revenge on persons who under-rated', *Daily Mail*, 25 May 1970; 'oddly self-indulgent', *Sunday Telegraph*, 24 May 1970

253 'the disappointment is huge', DP to Caroline Seebohm, undated

Chapter 7

254 'Dennis Potter wasn't able to shake hands', *Radio Times*, 8 October 1970; 'I can remember meetings when Dennis', Gareth Davies interview; 'He has now delivered us a play', BBC Written Archives, RCONT18, Dennis Potter, copyright file 2; 'an inheritance', Ann Scott interview

255 'He said something like', Kenith Trodd interview; 'I'd done a little bit of acting', Roger Smith interview; 'Be not forgetful to entertain strangers' and other quotations from *Angels Are So Few* from the original typescript, with manuscript additions

258 'put the fear of the devil into me', *Daily Mirror*, 6 November 1970; 'Intended, perhaps, to be painfully funny', *Guardian*, 6 November 1970; 'I think perceived that I wasn't particularly sympathetic', Gareth Davies interview; 'We did those two years at London Weekend', Kenith Trodd interview

259 'His Trotskyite convictions', *The Sunday Times*, 24 April 1977; 'But when Dennis delivered', Kenith Trodd interview; 'faithful dog faces eviction' and other quotations from *Paper Roses* from DP's manuscript; 'very, very bitter', Kenith Trodd interview; 'Providing his own review', *The Times*, 14 June 1971

260 'didn't hang together', *Daily Mail*, 15 June 1971; 'the most accurate, detailed re-creation', *Guardian*, 14 June 1971; 'It depends on the situation', Kenith Trodd interview

261 'That would be a ready-made package', *Potter on Potter*, 45; 'Roger [Smith] and his gang', Caroline Seebohm interview; 'I think . . . a feeling of betrayal', Dean, interview with DP, *Late Night Line-Up*; 'so-called patriotism' and other quotations from

Traitor from the rehearsal script; 'Flags and drums and pomp and circumstance', *Potter on Potter*, 42

262 'Bridges dips into scenes', *New Statesman*, 1 December 1972; 'Cursed with so Hamlet-like a face', *Guardian*, 15 October 1971; 'Harris emerged as a less interesting and complex character', *Daily Telegraph*, 15 October 1971; 'a superbly persuasive portrait', *The Times*, 15 October 1971; 'He was very much easier to converse with', Gilbert, *Fight & Kick & Bite*, 207; 'stayed for the weekend once or twice', Gareth Davies interview

263 'One didn't have to explain twice', Stanley Rosenthal interview, London, 30 July 1997; 'Dennis was always very practical', Frank Bloom interview, London, 2 December 1997; 'On one occasion, Dennis was very ill', Ann Scott interview; 'There was a lot of activity', Kenith Trodd interview; 'Potter lives with his wife Margaret', Oakes, 'Potter's Path'; 'Dad wasn't a practical man', SP interview

264 'were all involved in Dad's work', JP to HC, 21 February 1998; 'We didn't get taken to the studios', Raven, 'Relative Values'; 'Obviously we were aware of the fact', SP interview; 'The Corporation calls it a six-part series', Oakes, 'Potter's Path'; 'I had a weekly slot as a book critic', *Potter on Potter*, 68

265 'The credits say [*Casanova*] was "based on" them', *Potter on Potter*, 68–70; 'I simply don't believe them', Oakes, 'Potter's Path'; 'the sex was in general', John Masters, *Casanova*, Michael Joseph, 1969, 34; 'To me, the term "costume drama"', Oakes, 'Potter's Path'; 'I wanted to do a portrait', *Scan*, BBC Radio 4, 25 November 1971, BBC Written Archives, Films 41–2

266 'weeping angry sores' and other quotations from *Casanova* from the shooting scripts, and the videotapes (kindly supplied by Kenith Trodd); 'I was depressed and ill and in pain', *The Times* obituary, 8 June 1994

267 'hypnogogic images, the strangely potent montages', *Hide and Seek*, 77

268 'I assumed Casanova must have had that thing', *Potter on Potter*, 70

Chapter 8

269 'People hated it', Cook, *Dennis Potter*, 161; 'The entwining of past and present', *Daily Mail*, 17 November 1971; 'the shapely swing of the thing', *Guardian*, 17 November 1971; 'constant use of flashback', *Daily Telegraph*, 17 November 1971; 'as disorientated as Casanova', ibid., 24 November 1971; 'a six-part serial by Dennis Repeater', *The Sunday Times*, 19 December 1971; 'lewdness', *The Times*, 2 December 1971

270 'a major British car firm', BBC Written Archives, T48; 'a clergyman agrees to advertise', ibid.; 'His last days, surrounded by his confederates', ibid.; 'Dennis very much regards it', BBC Written Archives, RCONT20, Dennis Potter, 1970–74; 'It's my first really religious play', Oakes, 'Potter's Path'; 'an old London hospital and other quotations from *Follow the Yellow Brick Road* from Robert Muller (ed.), *The Television Dramatist*

275 'low point', *Blue Remembered Hills*, 19f.; 'very, very English' and other quotations from *Mushrooms on Toast* from DP's manuscript

276 'A group of people have kidnapped someone', BBC Written Archives, T48

277 'eight hours' medication a day', Oakes, 'Potter's Path'; 'Obviously he couldn't play with us', Jardine, interview with SP, *Daily Telegraph*; 'Mum was the one who did all the touching', JP interview; 'He had to learn how to do everything again', Jardine, interview with SP, *Daily Telegraph*; 'I believe that we choose our illnesses', Oakes, 'Potter's Path'; 'a movement already difficult', Dr Robert Bowers to Dr Smith,

1 March 1972, DP's medical records; 'He drinks quite a lot of alcohol', ibid.

278 'The skin closed around my fist', Wapshott, 'Knowing what goes on inside people's heads'; 'incredibly hot', Anne and Haydn Lloyd interview; 'People say they've got psoriasis', *Potter on Potter*, 13; 'We all thought he was going to die', JP interview; 'acutely painful and swollen', Dr B. S. Smith to Dr Robert Bowers, 28 March 1972, DP's medical records; 'He has borne his illness with great fortitude', ibid., 1 May 1972; 'I think the hospital didn't allow children', SP interview

279 'I saw his poor hands going', Batt, 'Man on the Moon'; 'I remember her being almost surprised', Ann Scott interview; 'I can't go on spilling out all that valuable material', *Only Make Believe* rehearsal script; 'Also, he wouldn't take responsibility', Ann Scott interview

280 'I couldn't sit up', *Desert Island Discs*, 1977; 'Most of his joints were affected', case summary by Dr Harvey Baker, 29 April 1974, DP's medical records; 'I went through everything Marlow does', *Daily Mail*, 22 November 1986; 'When I was desperately trying to get to sleep', ibid.; 'I spent the whole dreary summer', *New Statesman*, 20 October 1972; 'He gave a history of considerable tobacco intake', case summary by Dr Harvey Baker, 29 April 1974, DP's medical records

281 'I didn't actually see its first transmission', *Blue Remembered Hills*, 17; 'Pirandello effect of a real camera', *Guardian*, 5 April 1972; 'a disappointing yell of rage', *Daily Mail*, 5 July 1972; 'During his long stay', Dr Ashley Levantine to Dr Smith, 14 July 1972, DP's medical records; 'We weren't aware of Dennis Potter', Patrick Rahilly interview, Oxford, 14 July 1996

282 'His arthritis has gone on improving', Dr Harvey Baker to Dr Smith, 3 August 1972, DP's medical records; 'A writer is hired to produce', BBC Written Archives, T48; 'It was so toxic', Wapshott, 'Knowing what goes on inside people's heads'; 'His energy and muscle power are returning', Dr Harvey Baker to Dr Smith, 6 October 1972, DP's medical records

Chapter 9

283 'by pretending that it was my hobby', interview by Edward Blishen about *Hide and Seek*, 7 November 1973, BBC Sound Library, LP 37548; 'It's a stripping away', *Potter on Potter*, 127f.

284 'He knows I am trying to escape' and other quotations from *Hide and Seek*, Faber and Faber, 1990 edition

291 'read everything, and saw everything that he wrote', SP interview

292 'What I did was very consciously use', interview by Edward Blishen about *Hide and Seek*, 7 November 1973, BBC Sound Library, LP 37548; 'It was an extraordinary night', Gareth Davies interview

Chapter 10

293 'exciting, honest and strongly imagined', *The Times*, 25 October 1973; 'less than convincing', *Sunday Telegraph*, 21 October 1973; 'carefully and complexly done', *The Times Literary Supplement*, 9 November 1973; 'Pictures, crabbed pictures', ibid., 29 September 1972; 'It is now only in the rare, fiercely independent documentary', ibid., 13 October 1972; 'terribly crippled', *Guardian*, 16 February 1973

294 'I can see why she didn't like *Casanova*', ibid.; 'were meant to be part of a trilogy', *Potter on Potter*, 48, 50; 'a golden girl' and other quotations from *Only Make Believe* from DP's first draft, and the rehearsal script

295 'He was angry with me for inviting Margaret', Ann Scott interview

296 'He loved arguing', ibid.

297 'Nor has he now', *Guardian*, 12 February 1973; 'the possibility that his hero might have been faking', *Observer*, 18 February 1973; 'studio-bound and wordy', *New Statesman*, 10 May 1974; 'divided stage, with revolve', *Oxford Times*, 13 December 1974; 'Dennis was having to hold a glass', Keith Barron interview; 'foolishly stopped Methotrexate', Dr Harvey Baker to Dr R. Russell, 31 July 1973, DP's medical records; 'He writes with a pen clamped', *Los Angeles Times*, 1 January 1982

298 'We had this terrible row', Roger Smith interview; 'A hack writer discovers', BBC Written Archives, T48; 'Sometimes people approach you', *Potter on Potter*, 67; 'Hardy's world picture', ibid., 70

299 'I tell you . . . that the Church' and other quotations from *A Tragedy of Two Ambitions* from the rehearsal script; 'As yet the idea is not concrete', BBC Written Archives, T48; 'going through something of a flare-up', Dr A. S. G. Clark to Dr Harvey Baker, 11 March 1974, DP's medical records

300 'present depression and sickness', *New Statesman*, 29 March 1974; 'My own feeling is that', Dr Harvey Baker to Dr A. S. G. Clark, 11 April 1974, DP's medical records; 'a suburban Noah', BBC Written Archives, T48; 'There's no sense in it, Dan' and other quotations from *Joe's Ark* from *Blue Remembered Hills*

301 'It's not like Thomas Hardy shaking his fist', *Potter on Potter*, 48; 'The resolution makes more than a wry nod', *Blue Remembered Hills*, 20; 'the strongest, simplest and most accessible Potter play', *Daily Mail*, 15 February 1974; 'an honest attempt to articulate', *Daily Telegraph*, 15 February 1974; 'gripping and human', *Guardian*, 15 February 1974

302 'excavating the solemnity', *Blue Remembered Hills*, 90; 'We would get the irritating & increasingly ludicrous situation', DP to Elisabeth Thomas, 17 June 1974, *New Statesman* archive, University of Sussex Library; 'There is no one writing in any medium', *New Statesman*, 8 October 1974

303 'I spy with my little eye' and other quotations from *Schmoedipus* from DP's manuscript

304 'that group of plays in the early Seventies', *Potter on Potter*, 122; 'astonishing first novel', *Guardian*, 21 June 1974

305 'There came a point . . . where I just didn't like', Ann Scott interview; 'a man who decides that planned amnesia', BBC Written Archives, T48; 'Potter has obviously got a lot on his plate', ibid.; 'Wilson does not use a bludgeon', *Daily Herald*, 1 April 1963

306 'So I set all [this] among the modern furniture', *Potter on Potter*, 68; 'Angus Wilson could find himself in no better hands', *The Times*, 3 March 1975; 'An adaptation . . . must be an act', *New Statesman*, 10 January 1975; 'When asked in hospital if I wanted', ibid., 7 March 1975

307 'stiff white triangle at his top pocket', ibid.; 'The patients didn't seem to watch much television', ibid.; 'to a mute camera lens', ibid., 21 March 1975; 'Watching it is like chewing poppy seeds', ibid.; 'How many of us really believe', ibid., 4 April 1975; 'the amiable conspiracy that keeps our heads full', ibid., 24 October 1975; 'hold as many viewers as possible', ibid., 7 November 1975; 'I never saw Dad cry', JP interview

308 'and that Dad ought to make more of an effort', SP interview; 'There's so much I want to say', *The Singing Detective*, 78; 'lovely, gentle father', Lawson, 'Skin Flicks'; 'had a better relationship', *Seeing the Blossom*, 11; 'The grief has been so pitiless', *The Sunday Times Magazine*, 14 November 1976; 'I guess at those writers' struggles', *Potter on Potter*, 50

309 'I was pressuring Dennis for a script', Kenith Trodd interview; 'I don't know where

Dennis first saw me' and all other quotations from Kika Markham, Kika Markham interview; 'a not quite standard man approaching forty' and other quotations from *Double Dare* from the shooting script

314 'Kika phoned me', Kenith Trodd interview
315 'I didn't know there was anything truthful', Joe Melia, telephone conversation
316 'very menacing and dangerous', *Potter on Potter*, 113; 'Potter is one of our funniest', *New Statesman*, 9 April 1976; 'Amis is very tight, supremely skilled', *Potter on Potter*, 128
317 'This was Potter at his tantalizing best', *Daily Telegraph*, 7 April 1976; 'At times, in the presence of a play-within-a-play', *Daily Mail*, 7 April 1976

Chapter 11

318 '*Brimstone and Treacle* was delivered to the BBC', *New Statesman*, 23 April 1976; 'They have sat on the play', Gilbert, *Fight & Kick & Bite*, 216
319 'a few minor changes', *Broadcast*, 29 March 1976; 'repugnant', Alasdair Milne, *D.G.: The Memoirs of a British Broadcaster,* Hodder & Stoughton, 1988, 65; 'There resides infinitely more good' and other quotations from *Brimstone and Treacle* from the rehearsal script
322 'It's a simple flip-over', *Seeing the Blossom*, 21f.; 'forms of good can arise', *Daily Telegraph*, 5 April 1976
323 'an accusation against her father', *Seeing the Blossom*, 22; 'I have never felt the need to do that', *Seeing the Blossom*, 18; 'such was the brilliance of the acting', Milne, op. cit., 65
324 'SATAN PLAY BANNED', *Daily Mail*, 20 March 1976; 'depressing', *Guardian*, 20 March 1976; 'I wrote to Dennis', Milne, op. cit., 65; 'rape by the devil', Gilbert, *Fight & Kick & Bite*, 216f.; 'with Potter's finest work', *Daily Telegraph*, 5 April 1976; 'We had seen the tape', *Time Out*, 26 March – 1 April 1976; 'facing an open revolt', *Daily Mail*, 27 March 1976; 'this move has now been abandoned', *Daily Telegraph*, 5 April 1976
325 'What is sad is that a generation', *Daily Mail*, 27 March 1976; 'I found the play brilliantly written', *New Statesman*, 23 April 1976; 'brief and insolent', ibid.; 'the feeling that your work so totally disappears', ibid., 10 May 1974; 'Strangely enough, the argument has made me realize', Cook, *Dennis Potter*, 100
326 'I only took a few pages of it', *Potter on Potter*, 52; 'You'm *nice* boy' and other quotations from *Where Adam Stood* from the rehearsal script; 'It was just one of those things', *Potter on Potter*, 55
327 'The shape of the little drama', ibid., 54f.; 'It's probably the most complicated', ibid.
328 'not the book', *Guardian*, 22 April 1976; 'Dennis and I were due to meet', Brian Gibson interview; 'more or less coincided', *Pennies from Heaven*, vii; 'Workers' Revolutionary Party [WRP] people', Cook, *Dennis Potter*, 99; 'anxiety', ibid.; 'flirting', ibid., 98
329 'They said, "We're not making a judgement"', Kenith Trodd interview; 'finished the film I was making', *Pennies from Heaven*, viif.; 'but they came to me in a very short time', Kenith Trodd interview

PART THREE

Chapter 1

333 'six related plays', BBC Written Archives, T48; 'moonlighting', Trodd interview; 'they
were probably thinking in terms', *Pennies from Heaven*, viii; 'was only commissioned
because', *Seeing the Blossom*, 44; 'Dennis didn't know what he would write about',
Trodd interview

334 'Of course . . . *everybody* wanted to see it!', Daish interview

335 'I enter a friendly house', Bakewell, 'Wrestling with a Vision'; 'we were doing an
episode', Gilbert, *Fight & Kick & Bite*, 229

336 'No matter how skilled the acting and direction', introduction to Thomas Hardy,
The Mayor of Casterbridge, Pan Books, 1978; 'the long, unravelled consequences',
Potter on Potter, 70f.; 'miscalculation', *Times*, 23 January 1978; 'Mr Potter knows
what are the great lines', *The Sunday Times*, 5 February 1978

337 'But he kept you from me' from *The Mayor of Casterbridge* adaptation from DP's
manuscript of episode 7; 'looking for all the world', *The Times*, 23 January 1978;
'I have rewritten it considerably', *Yorkshire Post*, 6 September 1977

338 'After *Brimstone* was banned', *Observer*, 5 February 1978; '. . . the father is . . .
possibly guilty', *Daily Telegraph*, 13 October 1977; 'He came and saw it', Gilbert,
Fight & Kick & Bite, 220; 'a loving Creation [which] is in continual battle', Potter
interviewed by Mary Craig for *Sunday*, BBC Radio 4, 25 April 1976, and *Thought
for the Day*, BBC Radio 4, 30 April 1976, BBC Sound Library, LP 37129; 'surprising
invitation', *And With No Language But a Cry*, BBC Radio 3, 27 December 1976,
BBC Sound Library, LP 386009; 'evasive and uncomfortable', ibid.

339 'we got him entirely due to a letter', Godfrey Smith to HC, 4 January 1997; 'She kept
her glossy head tilted', *The Sunday Times*, 10 October 1976

340 'PERFECT POTTER PROSE', Harold Evans to DP, n.d., News International archives;
'prickly but professional', Godfrey Smith to HC, 4 January 1997; 'I was very wrong
to blame the autocue', *The Sunday Times*, 24 October 1976; 'Do you absolutely insist
on Dennis Potter', Harold Evans to Mark Boxer, 6 January 1977, News International
archives; 'from a horizontal position', *The Sunday Times*, 9 January 1977; 'the option
to come back', Harold Evans to DP, 8 January 1977, News International archives;
'I was compelled to abandon the column', DP to Harold Evans, 30 January 1977,
News International archives

342 'Dear Jane, Sarah and Robert', DP to JP, SP and RP, 24 February 1977; 'I experienced
a state of total euphoria', Wapshott, 'Knowing what goes on inside people's heads';
'The new cytotoxic drug that I'm taking', *Desert Island Discs*, 1977

343 'My hands are a bit too far gone', *The Sunday Times Magazine* 8 January 1978; 'He
has really made very satisfactory progress', Dr D. J. Atherton to Dr A. S. G. Clark,
25 March 1979, DP's medical records; 'There was one side-effect', Wapshott,
'Knowing what goes on inside people's heads'; 'It's three years since I last visited',
Batt, 'Man on the Moon'

344 'a Christ nourished on the disinfectant bottle', *The Sunday Times*, 10 April 1977

345 'After two weeks [in hospital]', ibid., 20 March 1977; 'as they were administering
Razoxane', Cook, *Dennis Potter*, 165; 'Dennis Potter has now delivered the first
play', BBC Written Archives, RCONT21; 'During that whole period', Trodd interview;
'wanted to do something about Al Bowlly', Connolly, 'When the penny dropped'; 'Al
Bowlly himself, or a fictional version', *Pennies from Heaven*, x–xi

346 'I remember one morning he rang me', Trodd interview; 'we talked about doing a

story', *Pennies from Heaven*, xi; 'a professional enabler', Trodd interview; 'He rang me again and said', ibid.; 'seized by a panic that didn't recede', *Pennies from Heaven*, xi

347 'PENNIES FROM HEAVEN' and other quotations from *Pennies from Heaven* from the published text (*Pennies from Heaven*), augmented by the rehearsal scripts

348 'It was the nature of the songs', Connolly, 'When the penny dropped'; 'I was probably half thinking of it', *Potter on Potter*, 84; 'I tried it with myself in a mirror', *Seeing the Blossom*, 20; 'Most television ends up offering its viewers', 'Realism and Non-Naturalism', in official programme of the Edinburgh International Television Festival, 1977, copy kindly lent by John Wyver

349 'It was a very difficult thing to do', *Potter on Potter*, 86, 96; 'I wanted to make quite clear', *Start the Week*, BBC Radio 4, 13 March 1978, BBC Sound Library, LP 38157; 'I find it very difficult to say exactly', Connolly, 'When the penny dropped'

350 'I picked the Thirties . . . because', *Start the Week*, BBC Radio 4, 13 March 1978, BBC Sound Library, LP 38157; 'in the last resort . . . no matter what', press handout, collection of John Wyver; 'tried to find a mode of religious drama', *The Times*, 3 February 1978; 'There is some sense in which you can actually assume', *Observer*, 5 Observer 1978; 'lacking any sense of God or faith', Nathan, 'Private Pottah's post-war work'

352 'It was almost a relief', Batt, 'Man on the Moon'; 'a straight translation of that particular psalm', *Start the Week*, BBC Radio 4, 13 March 1978, BBC Sound Library, LP 38157; 'like the Psalms of David', *Seeing the Blossom*, 43

353 'I dislike nostalgia', *Seeing the Blossom*, 67; 'after seeing the first two scripts', Trodd interview; 'he was absolutely furious with Ken', Daish interview; 'in a way, Dennis responded to my criticisms', Trodd interview

354 'Piers . . . had tremendous stamina', *Pennies from Heaven*, xii; 'I was working on a drama at Thames Television', Haggard interview; 'And there never was a musical', *Guardian*, 6 March 1978; 'Dennis was writing incredibly fast', Haggard interview

355 'the *ingénue* from the Forest of Dean', *Pennies from Heaven*, xv; 'I never write a synopsis', *The South Bank Show*, 14 February 1978, videotape lent by Kenith Trodd; 'When I'm writing, I don't have a synopsis', Wyver, transcript of unedited interview with DP, 1978

356 '*Pennies* originally ended with the hangman's hood', JP to HC, 21 February 1998

358 'I wanted to use the musical convention', Brown, 'Dollars from Hollywood'

Chapter 2

359 'Ken was very nervous of it', Piers Haggard interview; 'looked at the scripts, listened to me talk', *Seeing the Blossom*, 44; 'at least 60 per cent seriously', *Pennies from Heaven*, xiii; 'but Ken said to me', Piers Haggard interview; 'a hunch which first seemed cranky', *Pennies from Heaven*, xiii; 'about nine hours of script', Moline, *Bob Hoskins*, 91

360 'something about [Hoskins]', Cook, *Dennis Potter*, 169; 'I played a lot of myself', Moline, *Bob Hoskins*, 92; 'She read wonderfully for us', Piers Haggard interview; 'Ken and Piers had auditioned me', Cheryl Campbell interview and Gilbert, *Fight & Kick & Bite*, 239; 'initially Dennis wasn't very keen', Kenith Trodd interview; 'he gripped my arm', Gilbert, *Fight & Kick & Bite*, 236; 'I remember disliking some of the musical numbers', Piers Haggard interview

361 'They were the Odd Couple!', ibid.; 'was the sunniest and most gratifying', *Pennies from Heaven*, vii; 'When we were doing *Pennies*', Moline, *Bob Hoskins*, 93; 'even Ken was still looking very unconvinced', Judy Daish interview; 'What's on the telly

tonight?', 'Realism and Non-Naturalism', in official programme of the Edinburgh
International Television Festival, 1977; copy kindly lent by John Wyver
362 'had a row with Potter', David Hare to HC, 25 October 1996; 'I was swallowing
whisky, and shuddering', *The Sunday Times*, 6 November 1977
363 'loathing', ibid., 19 June 1977; 'David Hare is not alone', ibid., 6 November 1977;
'the sort of plot which the *Monty Python* team', ibid., 20 November 1977;
'dangerous, and subversive', ibid., 15 January 1978; 'I think you use different parts
of your imagination', *Start the Week*, BBC Radio 4, 13 March 1978, BBC Sound
Library, LP 38157; 'polemic, not abuse', ibid.
364 'the prevailing tone of contemporary high culture', *Guardian*, 15 October 1977;
'Until last summer . . . there seemed little prospect', *The Sunday Times Magazine*,
8 January 1978
365 'Just going up to London was difficult', SP interview; 'he always had to choose a
hotel', David Hare to HC, 25 October 1996; 'I was quietly debating with myself',
The Sunday Times Magazine, 8 January 1978
366 'The fear of being mugged', *Blue Remembered Hills*, 40; 'cautious walks in the Park',
The Sunday Times Magazine, 8 January 1978; 'Coming back to British television',
The Sunday Times, 2 October 1977; 'But to be perfectly honest', SP interview
367 'Six related plays using an autobiographical form', BBC Written Archives, T48; 'an
Imperial family on its last legs', ibid.; 'I'm forty-two, and going through the usual
mid-life crisis', *Desert Island Discs*, 1977; 'He's preparing to adapt his banned play',
Batt, 'Man on the Moon'; 'I knew Dennis slightly', Sir Peter Hall to HC, 19 May
1997; 'a hesitant Christian', *A Christmas Forest*
368 'it wasn't really until they'd assembled episode 1 of *Pennies*', Judy Daish interview;
'The videotape version I saw was in black and white', *The Times*, 3 February 1978;
'evangelical notions about the importance of television drama', *South Bank Show*,
14 February 1978, videotape lent by Kenith Trodd; 'I'd seen him speak the previous
summer', John Wyver interview
369 'I'm swamping it with alcohol today', transcript of unedited interview with DP, 1978;
'*Pennies from Heaven* are brilliant plays', *Time Out*, 3–9 March 1978; 'a magical
welding together', *Daily Express*, 10 February 1978; 'an enchanting musical',
Guardian, 8 March 1978; 'smashing', *The Sunday Times*, 12 March 1978; 'left me
only half engaged', *Observer*, 12 March 1978; 'a little dot-dot-dot-dot', *Start the
Week*, BBC Radio 4, 13 March 1978, BBC Sound Library, LP 38157; 'If advance
plaudits for the show', *Sunday Telegraph*, 12 March 1978
370 'At the core is [Potter's] new-found religious optimism', *Daily Telegraph*, 15 March
1978; 'The show ought to work', *Observer*, 19 March 1978; 'When Sammy Cahn
was writing songs', *Guardian*, 22 March 1978; 'Is it a hit or a miss?', *Sunday
Telegraph*, 2 April 1978; 'the series that has become compulsive viewing', *Evening
Standard*, 21 March 1978
371 'Dennis Potter is a brilliant playwright', BBC Written Archives, R92/29/1; Radio
Management Registry/Annan Report/General Part 5, July 1977 – May 1978; letter
dated 23 March 1978; 'included sex scenes', *Daily Telegraph*, 8 April 1978; 'There
cannot have been a richer television serial', ibid., 12 April 1978; 'Potter's evocation of
the Thirties', ibid., 20 February 1993; 'I was simply knocked out by it', John Wyver
interview
372 'I think it was probably my idea', Kenith Trodd interview; 'development fee', BBC
Written Archives, T48; 'a writer's dream of being in total control', *Daily Mail*,
27 January 1979; 'several small production companies', ibid., 25 May 1979; 'The
idea was that we should have a production company', Kenith Trodd interview;

'Potter . . . Haggard, and Ken Trodd', *Guardian*, 6 March 1978; 'I said to Ken', Piers Haggard interview; 'tried his hand at film writing', Connolly, 'When the penny dropped'

373 'meeting Zinnemann with Dad', SP interview

374 'I gloomily turned to Monday's *Panorama*', DP's manuscript of review; '*The Sunday Times* goes to press tonight', *Guardian*, 25 November 1978

375 'Dear Dennis, I am sorry you are resigning', Harold Evans to DP, 25 November 1978, News International archives; 'He needed to be able to drive', Judy Daish interview; 'quite (yes, *quite*)', Wyver, drafts of interview with DP, 1979; 'We were there for only a few days', Judy Daish interview

376 'exhausted us all', Batt, 'Man on the Moon'; 'After Razoxane, Dad had this enormous sense of freedom', SP interview; 'While *Pennies* was in pre-production', Kenith Trodd interview; 'Judy had been his mistress for years', Gina Bellman interview; 'Not physically', Judy Daish interview

377 'She was absolutely beautiful', Brian Gibson interview; 'She didn't dress at all glamorously', JP interview; 'She didn't want to come', Judy Daish interview; 'I know she wondered about Judy', Mavis Wood interview; 'Margaret wasn't too happy about it', Clive Lindley interview; 'I know for a fact', SP interview; 'I remember Dennis telling me', Judy Daish interview; 'at first', Wapshott, 'Knowing what goes on inside people's heads'; 'new drug', proposal for *Under My Skin*, John Wyver collection; 'did once talk to Dad directly', SP interview

378 'Dennis and Ken put some money on the table', Judy Daish interview; 'The reason I joined Judy's agency', Kenith Trodd interview; 'enormously generous, incredibly kind', Judy Daish interview; 'Margaret was an incredibly warm person', ibid.

Chapter 3

379 'leased for the scripting', Wyver, drafts of interview with DP, 1979

380 'FURTHER ADVENTURES OF THE SECRET SEVEN' and other quotations from *Blue Remembered Hills* from the published text; 'No . . . I wanted it to look', Wyver, drafts of interview with DP, 1979; 'He said there was a spiteful one', Gilbert, *Fight & Kick & Bite*, 39

381 'continual twitchy action', *Seeing the Blossom*, 19; 'I was trying to avoid twee and coy responses', *Potter on Potter*, 55; 'I used adult actors to play children', *Seeing the Blossom*, 7; 'For adults to play children', Wyver, drafts of interview with DP, 1979

382 'If you are seven', *Potter on Potter*, 55; 'The idea was that Dennis would write a piece', Brian Gibson interview; 'I just had this one image', videotape of seminar at Museum of Television & Radio, New York, 16 January 1992, Judy Daish Associates; 'Dennis and Brian and I were waiting', Judy Daish interview

383 'Ken arrived late', Gilbert, *Fight & Kick & Bite*, 243; 'Ken Trodd wanted to cast children', *Potter on Potter*, 31; 'the usual nervousness', Kenith Trodd interview; 'Dennis wanted to deliver the script', *Blue Remembered Hills*, Royal National Theatre programme; 'I don't remember telling Dennis anything', Brian Gibson interview; 'I sat down and before my apologies', *Blue Remembered Hills*, Royal National Theatre programme

384 'While Dennis was in Guy's Hospital', Judy Daish interview; 'I can't remember a time in their relationship', SP interview; 'Ken was always a great doubter', Brian Gibson interview; 'keep the adults', Gilbert, *Fight & Kick & Bite*, 243; 'A Potter work is so clearly defined', Brian Gibson interview; 'but Dennis was helpfully philistine', ibid.

385 'my task was to take the audience', *Blue Remembered Hills*, Royal National Theatre

programme; 'panic', *Seeing the Blossom*, 19; 'most satisfying', *Blue Remembered
Hills*, Royal National Theatre programme; '*Blue Remembered Hills* was the job I
have most enjoyed', ibid.; 'perfect, unflawed', *Radio Times*, 10–16 February 1979;
'one jarring line or a word out of place', *Daily Telegraph*, 31 January 1979;
'childhood is not a state of grace', *Sunday Telegraph*, 4 February 1979; 'Fear and
flight and fire', *Guardian*, 31 January 1979

386 'it begins to feel like', *Blue Remembered Hills*, Royal National Theatre programme;
'euphoric', *Time Out*, 8–14 August 1980; 'the sort of new independent producer',
Guardian, 29 July 1980; 'cocking a snook at the BBC', *Daily Telegraph*, 18 May
1979; 'Dennis making an attempt to get at the *power*', Kenith Trodd interview;
'I decided that I shouldn't be so reclusive', *Evening News*, 21 May 1979; 'Neither
Dennis nor I really had our hearts in it', Kenith Trodd interview

387 'as in a farce' and other quotations from the first version of *Rain on the Roof* from
DP's manuscript; 'I think there was quite a lot of pressure', Kenith Trodd interview

388 'I felt that the husband's death', National Film Theatre *Guardian* Lecture; 'If you did,
it would be very dangerous', ibid.; 'Janet was supposed to get out of the bath',
Gilbert, *Fight & Kick & Bite*, 250

389 'In 1970 I saw that happen', National Film Theatre *Guardian* Lecture; 'Our lot are
in', *Blade on the Feather* rehearsal script; 'convey something about my sense of
decay', *Guardian*, 29 July 1980

390 'But it emerged quite quickly', Kenith Trodd interview; 'Well, I'm not very rich',
Richard Loncraine interview; 'In my opinion he'd write a scene of genius', Gilbert,
Fight & Kick & Bite, 249; 'Dennis didn't have a clue about directors', Kenith Trodd
interview; 'I saw sod all of Dennis', Richard Loncraine interview

391 'I saw very little of Dennis', Kika Markham interview; 'When I was only about six',
JP interview; 'I was a tomboy', SP interview; 'Fast bowler', Kavanagh, 'Potter to the
Rescue'

392 'the fastest woman bowler', Raven, 'Relative Values'; 'I do not think I can ever
remember a time', *New Society*, 5 January 1966; 'My media-numbed acquaintances',
Blue Remembered Hills, 136; 'Nothing makes sense, you see', *Blade on the Feather*
rehearsal script

393 'We can pretend we're waiting', *Blue Remembered Hills*, 162; 'I believe absolutely
and without qualification', National Film Theatre *Guardian* Lecture; 'Forget that the
last several [Potter] plays', *Guardian*, 3 November 1980

394 'creating a malaise right down', Wapshott, 'Knowing what goes on inside people's
heads'; 'Recently I was buying a pen', Connolly, 'When the penny dropped';
'escalated from production to production', *Daily Telegraph*, 29 July 1980; 'PFH have
found it very difficult', *Time Out*, 8–14 August 1980

395 'the lack of budgetary control', Michael Grade interview; 'They didn't let Ken control
the whole budget', Gavin Millar, interview, London, 21 October 1997; 'I knew what
Dennis was going to do', Judy Daish interview; 'one of the things', *Daily Telegraph*,
29 July 1980; 'There was to be something about Dickens', Kenith Trodd interview;
'the fact that there were children there', *Potter on Potter*, 58; 'WHY BRITISH TV IS
GOING TO THE DOGS', *Daily Mail*, 30 July 1980

396 'instantly turned down', *Broadcast*, 6 October 1980; 'It was Nora who saw', Herbert
Ross, telephone conversation; 'shown twice in Los Angeles', *Broadcast*, 6 October
1980; 'obsessive', Kenith Trodd interview; 'I believe they thought', Herbert Ross,
telephone conversation

397 'I coaxed myself on to the Los Angeles plane', *Broadcast*, 6 October 1980; 'I went
with Dennis to Los Angeles', Judy Daish interview; 'almost like somebody from

Mars', *Late Show* interview with DP; 'Dear Jane, This is A Small Corner', DP to JP, 22 February 1980, courtesy of JP; 'By 1980, the erstwhile home', Cook, *Dennis Potter*, 185

398 'the American syntax', Kavanagh, 'Potter to the Rescue'; 'his fourth trip to the USA', *Guardian*, 29 July 1980; 'in three months I've earned', Wade, 'Dennis Potter – rebel playwright'; 'The money gained [from the film deals]', *Broadcast*, 6 October 1980; 'PFH is going to make *Brimstone and Treacle*', Wyver, transcript of unedited interview with DP, 1980; 'the first of what will be', *Broadcast*, 6 October 1980; 'The ultimate aim, obviously', *Guardian*, 29 July 1980

399 'That's average on an American script', *Potter on Potter*, 109; 'the Americans . . . continually say', Summers, 'Return of the prodigal Potter'; 'of the dozen or so drafts', Kenith Trodd interview; 'the endless drafts of *Pennies*', *Potter on Potter*, 112; 'going on safari', Grant, 'Potter's Art'; 'You're either sliding down it so fast', *Desert Island Discs*, 1988; 'I needed four or five years', Summers, 'Return of the prodigal Potter'; 'It did me good', *Desert Island Discs*, 1988

400 'I've always had an ambivalent relationship', *Potter on Potter*, 75, 109; 'I . . . sensed things were changing in England', ibid.; 'Dennis was an exquisite businessman', Judy Daish interview; 'It's alien, and you feel alien', *Desert Island Discs*, 1988; 'The longest I was ever there', *Potter on Potter*, 108

401 'Dennis fought (more than I knew at the time)', Kenith Trodd interview; 'I only met Ken after Dennis's death', Herbert Ross, telephone conversation; 'Ken Adam, the production designer', Judy Daish interview; 'I spent most of my childhood in Missouri', Rick McCallum interview; 'Rick was streetwise', SP interview; 'I'd already seen *Pennies from Heaven*', Rick McCallum interview

402 'There was a great mystique', Michael York, telephone conversation; 'Dennis would read you very quickly', Rick McCallum interview; 'I remember introducing him', Herbert Ross, telephone conversation; 'I thought *Unexpected Valleys*', *Potter on Potter*, 112

403 'about a ballet dancer', *Guardian*, 29 July 1980; 'You could lay hold of', *The Sunday Times Magazine*, 18 December 1983; 'WHAT PRICE PENNIES FROM HOLLYWOOD?', *Broadcast*, 15 September 1980

404 'It is a possible argument', ibid., 6 October 1980; 'really pissed off', Moline, *Bob Hoskins*, 98; 'There was an item', National Film Theatre *Guardian* Lecture

405 'I never claimed to be a TV critic', Miles Kington to HC, 16 April 1997; 'I do not wish to revisit them', National Film Theatre *Guardian* Lecture

406 'Compared with other TV playwrights', *New Statesman*, 7 November 1980; 'new affluence', *Daily Telegraph*, 20 October 1980; 'very tired', Wade, 'Dennis Potter – rebel playwright'; 'Good day, Parker', *Pennies from Heaven* (novelization), Quartet Books, 1981, 7

407 'When I went to visit the studio', *Potter on Potter*, 109f.; 'When you go out very late in the shoot', ibid., 111; 'Dennis was the most enthusiastic supporter', Herbert Ross, telephone conversation

408 'a stripped-down, soulless précis', *Potter on Potter*, 111; 'The audience couldn't understand', Brown, 'Dollars from Hollywood'; 'The very brilliance of the musical numbers', *Potter on Potter*, 111; 'the most emotional movie musical', *New Yorker*, 21 December 1981; 'The BBC show was an enchanted cottage', *Time*, 21 December 1981; 'one of the most hopelessly esoteric', *Variety*, 9 December 1981

409 'I like to play with the American studios', Summers, 'Return of the prodigal Potter'; 'the first response to my scripts', DP to John Hambley, Euston Films, 1 May 1987, Judy Daish Associates; 'It was the very Englishness', *Guardian*, 20 May 1982; 'started

trawling through all my old work', *Potter on Potter*, 112; 'That was a five-minute deal', Rick McCallum interview; 'about an English writer', *Potter on Potter*, 112f.

410 'Your novel, Peter, your novel!', *Love Me, True* typescript; 'with Al Pacino and Bob de Niro', Herbert Ross, telephone conversation

Chapter 4

411 'but I just didn't enjoy it', JP interview; 'When I left school', SP interview; 'appalled', Levin, 'I thought Dad was invincible'; 'He did have some guilt about it', SP interview; 'the letters that one doesn't write', *Any Questions*, 20 February 1970, BBC Written Archives, Microfilms 3/4, Talks Scripts

412 'He'd answer by phone', Judy Daish interview; 'He sacked me twelve times', Jardine, interview with SP; 'Our family wasn't like that', SP interview; 'I enjoy being part of what he's doing', Raven, 'Relative Values'; 'Rob probably had the most difficult relationship', SP interview; 'They have different sets of emotions', Raven, 'Relative Values'; 'Mum and Dad were determined', SP interview; 'Looking back, I think it was probably a mistake', RP interview

413 'Generally, he would write at night', SP interview; 'I've suffered from insomnia', Oakes, 'A suitable sleuth for treatment; 'When I'm writing', Ward, interview with DP; 'little notes for me', SP interview; 'He is obsessive about getting things just right', Ward, interview with DP; 'he wasn't any slower with a pen', SP interview

414 'He was so central to our lives', Levin, 'I thought Dad was invincible'; 'No', Kenith Trodd interview; 'It was mostly just Mervyn James', SP interview; 'I think the friendship began', Mervyn James interview; 'Dennis used to say', Anne and Haydn Lloyd interview

415 'a look', Mervyn James interview; 'We were a little bit late', Anne and Haydn Lloyd interview; 'Mervyn's wife left him', SP interview; 'He did – he was good', Mervyn James interview

416 'I think he spoke to Margaret very honestly', Anne and Haydn Lloyd interview; 'It wasn't exactly a contentious point', SP interview; 'He and his wife Margaret appear to be friends', Kavanagh, 'Potter to the Rescue'; 'a new kind of cinema', Judy Daish interview; 'It was what we called the Special Project', Herbert Ross, telephone conversation

417 'specially designed cinemas', JP interview

418 'the first crucial stages', *Brimstone and Treacle* prospectus; 'I thought, "How can I stop it?"', *Broadcast*, 25 June 1979; 'We were similar in age', Clive Lindley, telephone conversation

419 'If you caught Dennis in a bad mood', Naim Attallah interview; 'Sting wanted to do it', Kenith Trodd interview; 'I think I was sent into this world', *Wogan*, BBC1, 25 September 1987

420 'Dennis wasn't interested in being around', Gilbert, *Fight & Kick & Bite*, 221; 'definitely less successful', *Potter on Potter*, 113; 'We made naïve assumptions', ibid.; 'Dad wants me to start writing', Raven, 'Relative Values'; 'He was utterly devoted to her', Naim Attallah interview

421 'Dennis put me on a salary', Rick McCallum interview; 'It is not for me to get too close', *Potter on Potter*, 26; 'I cannot specify – except in fictional or dramatic form', *The Sunday Times*, 4 December 1977; 'something foul and terrible', *Blue Remembered Hills*, 33

422 'the most depressing place', ibid., 16; 'electric, like an old-fashioned sermon', Colm Tóibín, conversation, London, 25 February 1997; 'possible . . . that I have once

again', *Blue Remembered Hills*, 20; 'anger and frustration', ibid., 32f.; 'buried somewhere in myself', ibid., 137; 'a disappointment which never looked or sounded right', Oakes, 'A suitable sleuth for treatment'

423 'seeing what was happening to *Pennies from Heaven*', *The Sunday Times Magazine*, 18 December 1983; 'Mum and Dad spent six weeks in Provence', SP interview; 'a beach I loved to go to', Michael York, telephone conversation

424 'One day we decided to go over to Italy', Mervyn James interview; 'Dennis and I would drink outrageously every night', Anne and Haydn Lloyd interview; 'Second Draft. Third Draft', *The Sunday Times Magazine*, 18 December 1983; 'Although each change might be justified', Potter on Potter, 113–15

425 'Dustin Hoffman . . . held out for too much money', *The Sunday Times Magazine*, 18 December 1983; 'almost diametrically opposed', *Potter on Potter*, 113–15; 'Is this what you want?', *The Sunday Times Magazine*, 18 December 1983; 'severely cut, which only added to the apparent complications', *Potter on Potter*, 115; 'I saw a script gradually decline', videotape of seminar at Museum of Television & Radio, New York, 15 January 1992, Judy Daish Associates

426 'unscrupulous and appallingly sadistic', *The Sunday Times Magazine*, 18 December 1983; 'never builds up a full head of steam', *Guardian*, 5 January 1984; 'The drug seems to be giving', ibid., 5 December 1983; 'little warty growths', Grant, 'Potter's Art'; 'I don't think Dad was ever that fond of it', SP interview; 'thought it was time he attempted live theatre', *The Times*, 19 January 1984

427 'He's not very crazy about Americans' and other quotations from *Sufficient Carbohydrate* from the published text; 'I thought it was incredibly well written', Nancy Meckler interview

428 'really ill', Judy Daish interview; 'slewed on a couch', *Guardian*, 6 December 1983; 'By Christmas Eve he was immobilized', *The Times*, 14 January 1984; 'His disease . . . now hits him in periodic bursts', Grant, 'Potter's Art'; 'The chief pleasure of the evening', *Sunday Telegraph*, 11 December 1983; 'I find surreptitious Christianity', *The Sunday Times*, 11 December 1983

429 'After watching a few performances', *The Times*, 14 January 1984; 'He was giving out the usual line', Libby Purves to HC, 5 December 1996; 'perpetually on the verge of making', *The Times*, 14 January 1984; 'brewing up some kind of cancer', Dr J. R. S. Rendall to Dr Clark, n.d. [summer 1984], DP's medical records; 'With *Dreamchild* about to go into pre-production', *The Times*, 14 January 1984

430 'I read a paragraph somewhere', *Potter on Potter*, 28, 119; 'At the time, I was too young to see', *Dreamchild* first draft

431 'I'd always wanted to do *Tender is the Night*', Jonathan Powell interview; 'As he unfolded the story he wished to tell', *Guardian*, 8 June 1994; 'rushed to Michael Grade', Jonathan Powell interview; 'Set in London at the end of the Second World War', BBC Written Archives, T48

Chapter 5

432 'The more control you have', *New York Times*, 4 October 1985; 'This was the heyday', Kenith Trodd interview; 'There were two producers on *Dreamchild*', Cook, *Dennis Potter*, 206; 'If there are two producers', Kenith Trodd interview; 'a tragi-comedy', Gavin Millar interview, London, 21 October 1997

433 'a small sentimental gem of a movie', *New York Times*, 4 October 1985; 'EMI had to sell their rights', Rick McCallum interview; '[He] is good humoured and almost mellow', Summers, 'Return of the prodigal Potter'

434 'Of course Showtime did exert', *Potter on Potter*, 74; 'the packaging, lush, loving, and reeking of lucre', *Daily Telegraph*, 1 October 1985; 'I just can't help wishing', *Sunday Telegraph*, 29 September 1985; 'I did nurture the hope', Kenith Trodd interview; 'We understand that you are willing to advance', Judy Daish to Charles Denton of Black Lion Films, 6 February 1979, Judy Daish Associates

435 'proposal for new association', handwritten proposal, 1 October 1980, Judy Daish Associates; '*Under My Skin*', John Wyver collection

436 'an attempt not just to restore the relationship', KenithTrodd interview; 'Typical of Dennis to want to use something', ibid.; 'started as an idea for a sitcom', Grant, 'Potter's Art'; 'The whole thing began to take shape', Oakes, 'A suitable sleuth for treatment'

437 'Sometimes, yes, I *am* everything', *With Great Pleasure*, BBC Radio 4, 5 September 1976, BBC Sound Library, T81877; 'You'd think my mother would have had more sense' and other quotations from *The Singing Detective* from the published text; 'I don't think he really knew', SP interview; 'that sense of dread when you know', Grant, 'Potter's Art'; 'When I sat down to write *The Singing Detective*', *Daily Mail*, 22 November 1986; 'When I was working at MGM', Oakes, 'A suitable sleuth for treatment'

439 'I first used the device [of lip-synching]', ibid.

440 'There was a place in Mayfair', Clive Lindley, telephone conversation

441 'He would misinterpret people's motives', Naim Attallah interview

442 'In *The Singing Detective*,' *Seeing the Blossom*, 12; 'People say to me, you know', ibid., 70; 'Although associations abound', Oakes, 'A suitable sleuth for treatment'

443 'That's all wrong!', MP interview; 'no faith in himself', *Seeing the Blossom*, 12

444 'In a way . . . Keep going', Grant, 'Potter's Art'; 'Dennis would never let you read scripts', Jonathan Powell interview

445 'Various people turned it down', Kenith Trodd interview; 'wasn't offered *The Singing Detective*', Stephen Frears to HC, 2 June 1997; 'was asked to direct several of Dennis's scripts', *New Statesman*, 3 May 1996; 'the first fifty thousand words', Summers, 'Return of the prodigal Potter'; 'tried one novel', *The Times*, 14 January 1984; 'I wouldn't have bothered with anyone else', *Listener*, 20 November 1986; 'It could have made a play', Grant, 'Potter's Art'

446 'There it was again', *Ticket to Ride*, 31; 'echoing himself . . . as if he were quoting', Purser, 'A playwright comes of age'; 'New Cavendish Street . . .', *Ticket to Ride*, 98; 'This is one of those novels', *Guardian*, 3 October 1986; 'an electrifyingly readable book', *Evening Standard*, 1 October 1986

447 'The portrayal of psychological decay', *The Sunday Times*, 21 September 1986; 'I never had a burning ambition', Jon Amiel interview; 'sort of knew each other', Kenith Trodd interview; 'came into my office in that sidelong way', Gilbert, *Fight & Kick & Bite*, 267f.; 'But I had done everything that Dennis needed', Kenith Trodd interview; 'Ken and Dennis were in the midst', Gilbert, *Fight & Kick & Bite*, 268

448 'realized I could not and would not', Jon Amiel interview; 'just petered out', Gilbert, *Fight & Kick & Bite*, 268f.

449 'Dennis had lost interest in the thriller strand', Jon Amiel interview; 'I had to learn to trust he would get it', Gilbert, *Fight & Kick & Bite*, 269; 'once or twice', Kenith Trodd interview; 'a little austere', Jon Amiel interview; 'completely dispassionately and without any self-pity', Gilbert, *Fight & Kick & Bite*, 269; 'Margaret answered the door', Jon Amiel interview

450 'I became aware that I was holding back', *Potter on Potter*, 92f.; 'The last episode . . . though greatly improved', Gilbert, *Fight & Kick & Bite*, 270

451 'a joke Jon [Amiel] couldn't live with', Cook, *Dennis Potter*, 335; 'Rick jumped ship', Gilbert, *Fight & Kick & Bite*, 269; 'Absolute bullshit', Rick McCallum interview; 'just an in-house official', Kenith Trodd interview; 'You never knew what was really going on', Jonathan Powell interview

452 'forged in pain and conflict', Jon Amiel interview; 'Dennis felt that film downgraded', Kenith Trodd interview; 'But in the end everybody wants to use film', *Potter on Potter*, 93–5; 'felt passionately that he was the wrong choice', Jon Amiel interview; 'I remember he attended the very first read-through', *Night Waves*, BBC Radio 3, 7 June 1994; 'at the end of the read-through', Jon Amiel interview

453 'Ken Trodd had said he was very difficult', Rosemarie Whitman interview; 'I think he came to the shoot twice', Jon Amiel interview; 'Dennis came to the hospital', *Night Waves*, BBC Radio 3, 7 June 1994; 'The make-up I wore', *People*, 7 March 1993; 'I cut large chunks', Gilbert, *Fight & Kick & Bite*, 270f.

454 'last and most important rewrite of all', Cook, *Dennis Potter*, 222; 'We'd all been watching episode 2', Jon Amiel interview; 'I feel as if I've scraped out my bone marrow', *Evening Standard*, 17 November 1986; 'the tensions and difficulties of sitting down [to watch]', *Desert Island Discs*, 1988; 'It was worth the cost of a pair of opera stalls', *Guardian*, 17 November 1986; 'So extensive and intemperate', *Independent*, 17 November 1986; 'It was a startling performance', *The Sunday Times*, 23 November 1986

455 'began by laying into me', *Sunday Telegraph Magazine*, 14 April 1996; 'You will never hear a word of self-pity', *Daily Mail*, 22 November 1986; 'some BBC officials', *Today*, 30 November 1986; 'Michael Grade called a meeting', *Observer*, 7 December 1986

456 'I quizzed Ken and Jon about the scene's context', Michael Grade interview; 'not an easy decision', *The Times*, 1 December 1986; 'broadcasting must be brought under', *The Times*, 1 December 1986; 'It's always good to sprinkle a few "fucks"', Grant, 'Potter's Art'; 'the most compelling television drama', *The Times*, 1 December 1986; 'an extraordinary work of art', *Critics' Forum*, BBC Radio 3, 13 December 1986, BBC Written Archives, scripts; 'a sick joke', Gilbert, *Fight & Kick & Bite*, 272

457 'It was when he tried to turn to the next project', SP interview; 'I hadn't realized it was so close', Gilbert, *Fight & Kick & Bite*, 270; 'Although he has two projects already written', *Observer*, 7 December 1986

PART FOUR

Chapter 1

461 'a nightmare laboratory' and following quotations from the first draft of *Blackeyes*

463 'ducking from the camera', *Blitz*, November 1986

464 'I wrote it . . . between Boxing Day and St Valentine's Day', *Desert Island Discs*, 1988

465 'murder in her heart' and following quotations from the novel of *Blackeyes* from the published text

466 'something foul and terrible', *Blue Remembered Hills*, 33; 'startling number of themes', *Seeing the Blossom*, 59; 'I think any writer who keeps going over', *Potter on Potter*, 122

467 'Now that Potter is working more and more in the cinema', British Film Institute *Monthly Film Bulletin*, September 1982; 'You can feel Potter's movie experience', *Listener*, 2 October 1986; 'small cast, virtually one location', Cook, *Dennis Potter*, 259; 'Dennis was really foul to me', Piers Haggard interview

468 'We had the most blazing row', Gilbert, *Fight & Kick & Bite*, 291; '$100 million',

Cook, *Dennis Potter*, 251; 'as bad as in *The Singing Detective*', SP interview

469 'Gambon-like', *Desert Island Discs*, 1988; 'And then, bang, out of the sky!', *Wogan*, BBC1, 25 September 1987; 'Quincy Jones had a production deal', Judy Daish interview; 'the burning of Moscow by Napoleon', undated memorandum by Grio Entertainment Group, Pennies From Heaven (Overseas) Ltd; 'Martin Scorsese wanted to work with Dennis', Judy Daish interview

470 'When Michael Checkland became Director-General', Michael Grade interview; 'check on some of them to make sure', DP to Michael Grade, 23 February 1987, Kenith Trodd collection; 'It's a curiously wordy piece in places', *Did You See?*, BBC1, 25 August 1987; 'The basic theme is the humiliation of women', *Listener*, 1 October 1987

471 'both indulges and guys', unidentified cutting, dated 1 November 1988, John Wyver collection; 'In large letters', second draft of *Blackeyes* (TV serial); 'I'm just about to plunge', *Desert Island Discs*, 1988; 'monstrous, ghastly . . . cruelly ravaged', manuscript of *The Phantom of the Opera*; 'It was a brilliant idea', Jon Amiel interview

472 'ecstatic', *Potter on Potter*, 124; 'I had read a review of the book', ibid., 75

473 'There was probably a . . . need', ibid., 75, 79; 'Dennis's heart wasn't really in *Christabel*', Kenith Trodd interview; 'I *hate* politics', *Christabel*, 28; 'She's at first apolitical', *Listener*, 28 July 1988

474 'One of the things I hope people will brood upon', Lambert, 'The thin skin of democracy'; 'You don't have to buy the whole Left/Right package', ibid.; 'Have I shown unhappy marriages?', *Potter on Potter*, 77; 'I didn't connect emotionally with it', Jon Amiel interview; 'wistful and yet somehow oddly threatening', *Christabel*, 1; 'You can grasp the basics', *Listener*, 28 July 1988

475 'He was very sick', Gilbert, *Fight & Kick & Bite*, 273; 'it wasn't singing and dancing and sexy', ibid., 284; 'disappointingly transparent', Saynor, 'Black and Blue'; 'only a faint echo of Potter's authorial stamp', *Voice*, 21 February 1989; 'a mistake', Wyver, drafts of interview with DP, 1989; 'plump daughter', *Excalibur*, typescript

476 'It was just something Dad thought up', JP interview; 'His elder daughter Jane, an artist', Lambert, 'The thin skin of democracy'

477 'We bought a shop and garage', SP interview; 'a real scoop', *The Times*, 15 December 1988; 'and I let him go', Mark Shivas interview

478 'I'd had enough of his over-played petulance', *Mail on Sunday*, 16 July 1989; 'exceedingly unpleasant and exceedingly brief', ibid.; 'Never phone me again', Kenith Trodd interview; 'didn't talk to me *at all*', Cook, *Dennis Potter*, 258; 'I *have* existed outside the BBC', Kenith Trodd interview; 'which I am not particulalry interested in', Cook, *Dennis Potter*, 258; 'I think if any move', Saynor, 'Black and Blue'; 'I will miss it very much', *Mail on Sunday*, 16 July 1989; 'During 1989, I was producing', Kenith Trodd interview; 'a significant step backwards', Jon Amiel interview; 'Roeg was on the brink of doing it', *Potter on Potter*, 134; 'I decided I couldn't bear to hand it over', *American Film*, March 1989

479 'I didn't disapprove', Kenith Trodd interview; 'probably only the BBC', Cook, *Dennis Potter*, 265; 'Initially, I went through hundreds and hundreds', *Elle*, December 1989; 'a flick on some of their faces', Wyver, drafts of interview with DP, 1989; 'fantasizing, maybe?', Brooks, 'All in the dark eye of the beholder'

Chapter 2

480 'I was born in New Zealand' and all other quotations from Gina Bellman not attributed to other sources, Gina Bellman interview; 'Gina, technically speaking', *Elle*, December 1989; 'When Gina came in', Rick McCallum interview

482 'I just took "Tea for Two"', Wyver, drafts of interview with DP, 1989; 'There will be music', *Blackeyes*, BBC TV version, episode 1, manuscript

483 'an alien trying to imitate human behaviour', *Blackeyes*, BBC TV version, episode 3, draft (September 1988); 'where to put the camera', Wyver, drafts of interview with DP, 1989; 'to deal with lots of people', *Late Show*, transcript of interview with DP; 'more people . . . than I have in the last thirty years', *The Sunday Times*, 26 November 1989; 'I'd left BBC Drama', Rosemarie Whitman interview

484 'he was so embarrassed about his hands', ibid.; 'I wanted him to start off in a room', Cook, *Dennis Potter*, 267

485 'I thought, what the fuck am I doing here', Wyver, drafts of interview with DP, 1989; 'without sounding as though I was needing', *Late Show*, transcript of interview with DP; 'with a six-and-a-half-minute shot', Wyver, drafts of interview with DP, 19 89; 'wrong, it's a mistake', Cook, *Dennis Potter*, 267; 'Ten a.m. on Sound Stage 2', Saynor, 'Black and Blue'

486 'You have to keep everything *small*', *Independent*, 8 December 1989; 'setting up one of these lengthy camera ballets', Andrew, 'Dark angel'; 'a bit like a live show', Cook, *Dennis Potter*, 268, 270; 'He does ask you to do some weird things', Saynor, 'Black and Blue'; 'Dennis was always incredibly specific', Gilbert, *Fight & Kick & Bite*, 279

487 'Most directors are such wankers', Saynor, 'Black and Blue'; 'the grammar . . . of current film procedures', Wyver, drafts of interview with DP, 1989; 'bullshit', Cook, *Dennis Potter*, 267; 'In terms of direction', Rick McCallum interview; 'It wasn't that he couldn't cope', Rosemarie Whitman interview; 'Film is totally unaware', Saynor, 'Black and Blue'; 'that classic question', *Potter on Potter*, 127; 'There's probably nothing wrong', Saynor, 'Black and Blue'; 'the usual, unthinking wire-fence patterns', *Sunday Telegraph Magazine*, 26 November 1989

488 'People said that the camera was moving', Lawson, 'Skin Flicks'; 'trying to use the camera as the force of alienation', *Potter on Potter*, 130; 'With Dennis, you did it until Dennis was fed up', Cook, *Dennis Potter*, 268; 'he didn't have a lot of patience', Rosemarie Whitman interview; 'forget the writer', *Late Show*, transcript of interview with DP; 'I think the best part of directing', Wyver, drafts of interview with DP, 1989

489 'remarkably like writing', Andrew, 'Dark angel'; 'Obviously the more experienced you are', Cook, *Dennis Potter*, 266; 'It has to be a single vision', *Late Show*, transcript of interview with DP; 'The odd thing [about directing]', Wyver, drafts of interview with DP, 1989; 'you'd never see anyone drink so much', Gilbert, *Fight & Kick & Bite*, 279; 'Salmon or chicken are all right', Koenig, 'The pain of a black eye from the critics'; 'He didn't like the thought of eating', SP interview; 'paid an enormous price physically', *Potter on Potter*, 139

490 'He was unbelievably ill', Rick McCallum interview; 'I think he was mesmerized by her', ibid.; 'Dennis was a bit gobsmacked', Rosemarie Whitman interview

492 'He was always going on about being a puritan', Gilbert, *Fight & Kick & Bite*, 279

494 'On the basis of what I saw', Rick McCallum interview

495 'Now, editing, I can forget the director', *Late Show*, transcript of interview with DP; 'No, I'm looking at her *eyes*' and other quotations from DP's voice-over in *Blackeyes* from the videotapes; 'There is a line in *Blackeyes*', *Seeing the Blossom*, 23; 'Not only were you showing the manipulation', *Potter on Potter*, 132

496 'the whole thing was totally incomprehensible', Cook, *Dennis Potter*, 270

497 'to show . . . the way that people are turned into things', *Seeing the Blossom*, 23; 'how men manipulate women', Andrew, 'Dark angel'; 'men write the world', *The Late Show*, transcript of interview with DP; 'this slightly creepy character', Dougary, 'Potter's Weal'; 'to fall in love with', Cook, *Dennis Potter*, 266

498 'Potter fell in love with Blackeyes', Brooks, 'All in the dark eye of the beholder'; 'I'd rather go to a brothel', ibid.; 'Two things had to happen', Wyver, drafts of interview with DP, 1989; 'The only true passion is monogamy', *Cosmopolitan*, December 1987; 'I made touch with my younger self', Wyver, drafts of interview with DP, 1989; 'I couldn't just hand over a script', Andrew, 'Dark angel'

499 'I am not going to describe it in any way', Wyver, drafts of interview with DP, 1989; 'This was Potter's first film festival', *Observer*, 10 September 1989; 'Telluride is so politically correct', David Hare to HC, 25 October 1996 and 21 May 1997

500 'In the remnant of the first-class train', *Seeing the Blossom*, 9; 'Dennis's interview [at Telluride]', David Hare to HC, 25 October 1996 and 21 May 1997; 'laughed at how much of MGM's money', Stephen Frears to HC, 2 June 1997; 'turgid crap', *City Limits*, 30 November – 7 December 1989; 'Potter is . . . a very sick man', *Time Out*, 22–28 November 1989; 'when asked by a *Scotland on Sunday* journalist', *City Limits*, 30 November – 7 December 1989; 'THIS FOUR-HOUR PEEP SHOW', *Daily Star*, 23 November 1989

501 'The most disturbing scene in episode 1', *The Sunday Times*, 26 November 1989; 'Forget the collapse of Communism', *Evening Standard*, 27 November 1989; 'What I saw was soft porn', *Daily Mirror*, 29 November 1989

502 'Some of the single takes are as long', *Independent*, 30 November 1989; 'If you haven't seen it', *Guardian*, 30 November 1989; 'There ought to be a public outcry', *Sun*, 30 November 1989; 'Watching *Blackeyes* is about as jolly', *Daily Telegraph*, 30 November 1989; 'What keeps one viewing', *Observer*, 3 December 1989; 'It will be an Eng. Lit. A-level question', *The Sunday Times*, 3 December 1989

503 'Is *Blackeyes* just blue nonsense?', *Sunday Express*, 3 December 1989; 'immensely boring', *Daily Telegraph*, 7 December 1989; 'all very post-modern', *New Statesman*, 15 December 1989; 'to anchor itself to serious subjects', quoted in the *Independent*, 18 December 1989; 'In the end I couldn't care less', *Sunday Telegraph*, 24 December 1989; 'It was painful, beautiful and obscure', *Guardian*, 21 December 1989; 'The sadness of *Blackeyes*', *Independent*, 21 December 1989

504 'I'm in the pit of a real depression', Koenig, 'The pain of a black eye from the critics'; 'For the first time in twenty-five years', *John Dunn Show*, 13 December 1989, BBC Sound Library, T86333; 'frightened', Koenig, 'The pain of a black eye from the critics'

505 'For Dennis Potter, loss of innocence came', *Sunday Telegraph*, 31 December 1989; 'I knew from the beginning', Lawson, 'Skin Flicks'; 'Germaine Greer was very nice about it', Dougary, 'Potter's Weal'; 'should have gone out as one piece', *Potter on Potter*, 121; 'There was an edited-down movie version', Kenith Trodd interview; 'Potter . . . still feels *Blackeyes* was a failure', Wright, 'The last acre of truth'

506 'My expert would have to be Dennis Potter', *Observer Magazine*, 10 March 1990

Chapter 3

507 'Potter . . . plans to spend the next two weeks', *Daily Mail*, 30 January 1990; 'I told him I didn't think it was good', Gina Bellman interview

508 'due to begin filming next spring', Brooks, 'All in the dark eye of the beholder'; 'TV's

DIRTY DENNIS', *News of the World*, 31 December 1989

509 'stand up', Cook, *Dennis Potter*, 327f.; 'He was much taller than I expected', John R. Cook interview; 'the pain . . . was still bumping within me', Cook, extracts from transcript of interview with DP; 'body of work', Cook, *Dennis Potter*, 282; 'There is a sense in which I could abandon', Brooks, 'All in the dark eye of the beholder'; 'I'm writing one long play', videotape of seminar at Museum of Television & Radio, New York, 15 January 1992, Judy Daish Associates; 'We'd go out to restaurants', SP interview

510 'I had to go and pick his glasses for him', JP interview; 'I think that's him, yes', RP interview; 'I think I am naturally a recluse', Lawson, 'Skin Flicks'; 'I think the illness had just heightened', SP interview

511 'didn't notice anything untoward', June Thomas to HC, 11 October 1996; 'He was usually quite insulting', Graham Wale interview; 'the most fantasic program I've seen', New York *Newsday*, 21 January 1988

512 'I am amazed', *Potter on Potter*, 96; 'The [American] *Singing Detective* script', ibid., 111; 'I was asked if I was interested', Brian Gibson interview; 'it felt to me as though all the passionate and personal element', Jon Amiel interview; 'I didn't think it was a great idea', Rick McCallum interview; 'I had to do a budget to *The Singing Detective* movie', Alison Barnett interview, London, 23 October 1997

513 'Dennis was deeply committed to Gina', ibid.; 'Dennis would say, "Nobody wants you to do it"', Gina Bellman interview; 'He asked me whether I would come', Mark Shivas interview; 'Dennis phoned me up and left a message', Rosemarie Whitman interview; 'There was a time when Dennis was wobbling slightly', Kenith Trodd interview

514 'There were moments when I felt', *Mail on Sunday*, 21 April 1996; 'A high percentage of the key positions', Dougary, 'Potter's Weal'; 'Dennis was very, very insecure', Clare Douglas, telephone conversation; 'I used to see Dad a lot', JP interview

515 'almost twins in a way', Lawson, 'Skin Flicks'; 'Al Bowlly, 5 Memory Lane', *Secret Friends* draft script; 'The script was very confusing', Dougary, 'Potter's Weal'; 'It was a short shoot', Nathan, 'Private Pottah's post-war work'; 'Dennis was too ill to cope', Alan Bates, telephone conversation; 'He couldn't be bothered to wait for things', Frances Barber interview

516 'He decided that he was going to punish me', Gina Bellman interview; 'There is one particularly excruciating scene', Dougary, 'Potter's Weal'

517 'pile of psycho-twaddle', Cook, Dennis Potter, 295; 'Potter's . . . recent work has suggested', *Sight and Sound*, October 1992; 'Oh, I might . . . for ten minutes', Cook, *Dennis Potter*, 295; 'an absolute disaster', Nathan, 'Private Pottah's post-war work'; 'I think we met twice more for drinks', Gina Bellman interview; 'Dennis eventually broke the silence', Kenith Trodd interview

518 'The first evening, Alan Yentob threw Dennis softball questions', John Wyver interview; 'Was that *hommage* or plagiarism?', videotape of seminar at Museum of Television & Radio, New York, 15 January 1992, Judy Daish Associates; 'I was meant to chair the third evening', John Wyver interview

519 'When Dennis had watched the clip', Kenith Trodd interview; 'You shouldn't have ended with that clip', videotape of seminar at Museum of Television & Radio, New York, 16 January 1992, Judy Daish Associates; 'It was extremely belittling', John Wyver interview; 'What do I expect of a producer?', videotape of seminar at Museum of Television & Radio, New York, 16 January 1992, Judy Daish Associates

520 'glamour model Louise Germaine', *Daily Mail*, 21 February 1992; 'But I could feel

that things weren't right', Rosemarie Whitman interview; 'He came into my office in Charlotte Street', Peter Ansorge interview; 'One desk-light on. Gloomy', Lawson, 'Skin Flicks'

521 'Dennis became angry', Peter Ansorge interview; 'devastated', Rosemarie Whitman interview; 'He said he didn't give a shit', Gary Williamson interview; 'Dennis would phone me up at midnight', Dougary, 'Potter's Weal'

522 'Renny came in like a breath of fresh air', Rosemarie Whitman interview; 'I think they thought they'd got', Renny Rye interview

523 'How many producers have we got?', Kenith Trodd interview; 'I had long blond hair', *Daily Mail Weekend*, 5 October 1996.; 'She ran a café, and a second-hand shop', and other quotations from Louise Germaine not attributed to other sources, Louise Germaine interview; 'soft-porn model', *Daily Star*, 22 February 1993

524 'Lou had been a very gawky eighteen-year-old', Rosemarie Whitman interview; 'this delicious idea of all the colonels', John R. Cook interview; 'coincidence', *Potter on Potter*, 97f., 103f.; 'Underneath this stupid bravado', Nathan, 'Private Pottah's post-war work'

525 'I'm not interested in you', *Lipstick*, 80

526 'The notes! Think of the notes!', *Lipstick On Your Collar* videotape; 'What a wonderful world you live in!', *Lipstick*, 93–5; 'Dennis corrected all my grammar', Louise Germaine interview, and *The Times*, 24 October 1996

527 'His creation of Louise', Gina Bellman interview; 'Louise and Dennis both – on separate occasions', Renny Rye interview

528 'Dennis would give the actors notes', ibid.; 'fell in love', Gary Williamson interview; 'He is not big on eye contact', Dickson, 'Potter back on song'; 'Potter smiles, and says that he is getting better', Lawson, 'Skin Flicks'; 'But meeting Potter is never painful', Grant, 'Potter's Gold'

529 'a hurried gesture which suggests', Dougary, 'Potter's Weal'; 'Towards the end of the interview', Lawson, 'Skin Flicks'; 'in floods of tears', Rosemarie Whitman interview; 'dear, darling, tender and steadfast', Grant, 'Potter's Gold'; 'an act of public expiation', *Daily Telegraph*, 22 February 1993

530 'ennui', *Independent on Sunday*, 28 February 1993; 'it's no good pretending', *Guardian*, 8 March 1993; 'Potter is tired and clapped out', *Mail on Sunday*, 28 February 1993; 'I didn't like *Lipstick on Your Collar*', Gina Bellman interview; 'Dad was beginning to feel', SP interview; 'What I'm about to do', *Opinions*, Channel 4, 21 March 1993, videotape, Judy Daish Associates

531 'Dennis seems to have lost his magic touch', *Sun*, 22 February 1993; 'The poor devil who's abusing me', *Opinions*, Channel 4, 21 March 1993, videotape, Judy Daish Associates; 'Potter bites back to urge press reforms', *The Times*, 22 March 1993

532 'like being collared by a madman', *The Sunday Times*, 28 March 1993; 'it was almost the only time', Kenith Trodd interview; 'I've got four scripts out there', *Potter on Potter*, 74; 'I am currently having meetings', ibid., 113; '*Mesmer*'s been at the starting gate four times', ibid., 124

533 'the great problem is that Dennis's attitude', Jon Amiel interview; 'It *is* surprising', DP to D. M. Thomas, draft, n.d. [October 1983], Pennies From Heaven (Overseas) Ltd; 'He was wonderfully enthusiastic', Renny Rye interview

534 'a hairdresser!', Judy Daish interview; 'It's wonderfully Gothic', Renny Rye interview; 'I suspect nobody would now fund something', *Potter on Potter*, 134, 140; 'requested, firmly but politely', *Independent*, 8 June 1994

535 'We're finishing a film called *Midnight Movie*', *Clive Anderson Talks Back*, Channel 4, 25 June 1993, videotape, Judy Daish Associates; 'I think the package had become',

Renny Rye interview; 'Robert Altman told me he'd been offered', Jon Amiel interview; 'Dennis went berserk', *Independent*, 24 May 1996; 'I was able to put in more than half a million pounds', *Karaoke*, viii

536 'My brief was to spend', Mark Shivas interview; '*Midnight Movie* is being made with the BBC', Nathan, 'Private Pottah's post-war work'; 'Dennis made a big fuss', Renny Rye interview; '*Midnight Movie . . .* in my totally unbiased opinion', *Seeing the Blossom*, 37; 'fell between two stools', Renny Rye interview

537 'hated', Louise Germaine interview; 'We went from pillar to post', Renny Rye interview; 'Dennis was now having stomach pains', ibid.; 'Dennis kept ringing me up', ibid.

538 'I wondered if he was ever going to get through it', SP interview; 'the strange new generations of broadcasting managements' and following quotations from the MacTaggart Lecture, from *Seeing the Blossom*; 'the one British institution that really works', *Opinions*, Channel 4, 21 March 1993, videotape, Judy Daish Associates

540 'Did they like it?', Renny Rye interview; 'It was powerfully argued', *Sunday Telegraph*, 29 August 1993; 'a flamboyant distraction from the battles', *Independent*, 31 March 1993; 'a beautifully crafted piece', Michael Grade interview; 'had this aching feeling', SP interview; 'Dennis insisted that all of us came', Renny Rye interview; 'He'd talk about "my people"', SP interview; 'Like all obsessively shy people', Jon Amiel interview; 'I'd never been allowed to go down', Renny Rye interview

541 'two rich commissions', *Karaoke*, ix; 'To be honest . . . my heart sank', *Independent*, 24 May 1996; 'They'll probably get a lot of it wrong', ibid.; 'Dennis wanted to do twenty episodes', ibid.; 'Dennis was very pissed', Matthew Evans interview, London, 8 September 1997

542 'muddle', *Karaoke*, x; 'Sums it all up, really', Grant, 'Potter Gold'; 'eccentric middle-aged A-list screenwriter', *Karaoke*, episode 1, first draft

543 'truly ravaging', *Karaoke*, x; 'I couldn't function', Bragg, unedited video-recording of interview with DP; 'You know, look inside you', *Karaoke*, 67; 'He was in terrible pain', Judy Daish interview; 'What did you see down there', *Karaoke*, 79; 'a sizeable pancreatic carcinoma', Dr A. R. W. Hatfield to Dr D. Silk, 22 March 1994

544 'It is clearly distressing', ibid.; 'I remember him coming out to the car', Judy Daish interview

Chapter 4

545 '*Tuesday 15 February*', Rye, diary; 'He didn't let me get a word in', Renny Rye interview; 'When he phoned me to tell me', Rosemarie Whitman interview

546 'Margaret was on her feet again', Mavis Wood interview; 'Dad phoned me first', SP interview; 'Dad tried to make it all right', Levin, 'I thought Dad was invincible . . .' and SP interview; 'But the pounding of those cytotoxic drugs', SP interview; 'He's so worried about death', *Cosmopolitan*, December 1987; 'moment of panic', *Karaoke*, ix; 'Obviously, I had to attend to my affairs', *Seeing the Blossom*, 3

547 'imminent financial calamity', John Roberdeau and Robert Michael Geisler interview, London, 13 November 1997; 'The money *is* needed', DP to John Roberdeau and Robert Michael Geisler, 10 May 1994; 'Dennis lent me fifty thousand quid', Clive Lindley, telephone conversation; 'concoct some sort of Family Trust', *Karaoke*, vii

548 'Dad was absolutely brilliant', SP interview; 'a remake of an old but not very good movie', *Karaoke*, x–xi.

549 'I think I was the first to see Margaret' and all following quotations from Dr Paul

Downey, Paul Downey interview
550 'a path through all the opiates', *Karaoke*, xii–xv
552 'crumpled, rather pot-bellied, balding' and other quotations from *Karaoke* from the
published text
556 'I was dubbing *Chandler & Co*.', Rye, diary
557 'Judy rang me, gave me the sad news', Michael Grade interview; 'Mum didn't want
him to do the interview', SP interview; 'I think it was twenty thousand quid or
something', Michael Grade interview; 'Melvyn, I'm only doing it for the money',
Bragg, unedited video-recording of interview with DP
558 'a brilliant decision', Michael Grade interview; 'They were supposed to be there at
nine', Melvyn Bragg interview; 'We had been told that his body heat fluctuated',
Seeing the Blossom, xi–xii; 'I can't keep food down any more', ibid., 9f.; 'interested
in reassuring people', ibid.; 'Below my window in Ross', ibid., 5
559 '*Everything* feels different', *Karaoke*, vii; 'I thought, what kind of cruel old bugger is
God', *Seeing the Blossom*, 5f.; 'I'm a really cripplingly shy person', ibid., 4; '*Who
would you kill?*', ibid., 14; 'What are you writing?', ibid., 25, 27f.
560 'It was perfect Dennis!', Rick McCallum interview; 'It was a wonderful idea', Michael
Grade interview; 'I've got a GP in Ross', *Seeing the Blossom*, 27; 'I've still got bloody
psoriasis', ibid., 12; 'die four pages too soon', ibid., 28
561 'I had received the first two episodes', Rye, diary
562 'Judy rang me saying he'd like to see me', Kenith Trodd interview; 'It's very good,
brilliant', Rye, diary; 'a gesture of friendship', Kenith Trodd interview; 'He came out
with it', Louise Germaine interview
563 'impending death', *The Times*, 25 March 1994; 'extraordinary . . . vintage Potter',
Observer, 27 March 1994; 'The one thing about dying', *Desert Island Discs*, 1988;
'Thousands of people reacted', *Seeing the Blossom*, xiii; 'a long, loving letter', Jon
Amiel interview; 'Everyone said that in the final Bragg interview', Renny Rye
interview; 'I've never known a reaction to a programme', Michael Grade interview;
'I felt bitter that he could be eulogized', Gina Bellman interview
564 'Dennis walked in, straight to the bar', Rye, diary; 'Transplanted heads . . . Brains
kept alive in a bottle', *The Times*, 27 April 1968
565 'about a schizophrenic who only thought', Dougary, 'Potter's Weal'; 'look like *Dr
Who*', *Independent*, 8 June 1994; 'Dennis saying, "I've got to digest all this"', Mavis
Wood interview; 'LET ME GO!' and other quotations from *Cold Lazarus* from the
published text in *Karaoke*
566 'a comic reversal of sexual stereotyping', *Karaoke* and *Cold Lazarus* press pack
567 'to neglect those in front of me', *Karaoke*, xv–xi
568 'I got a phone call from Judy', Rye, diary; 'People did go to Dad's flat' JP to HC,
21 February 1998
569 'This isn't going to be a pleasant meeting', Rye, diary; 'A dangerous closed circuit',
Kenith Trodd interview; 'somewhat thrown', Rye, diary; 'I don't remember Dennis
throwing down a gauntlet', Kenith Trodd interview
570 'The main fray over', Rye, diary; 'Goodbye, thank you, love you', Kenith Trodd
interview
571 'hurt Dad more than his own impending fate', Levin, 'I thought Dad was invincible . . .';
'Dennis would come in to see her', Mavis Wood interview; '3 May. Weaker', and
following quotations from Dr Paul Downey's diary, Downey, 'Dealing with DP'
572 'an investment', Renny Rye interview; 'I linger on and on', DP to John Roberdeau
and Robert Michael Geisler, 10 May 1994; 'There I was, with two very ill patients',
Mavis Wood interview; 'Sadly, it was impossible to keep her at home', Levin, 'I

thought Dad was invincible . . .'

573 'Two days before Dad's birthday', SP interview; 'at precisely ten o'clock', Rosemarie Whitman interview

574 'As a fan since your television reviews', David Johnson to DP, 6 April 1994, courtesy of David Johnson; 'Dear David Johnson', DP to David Johnson, 16 May 1994, courtesy of David Johnson; 'the prospect of confronting imminent death', David Johnson to DP, 20 May 1994, courtesy of David Johnson; 'It seems I can still scrape out a word or two more', DP to David Johnson, 25 May 1994, courtesy of David Johnson

578 'How typical of Dennis', Renny Rye interview

579 'I rushed back . . . surprised at how calm I was', SP interview; 'They rang me and said they were coming in', Mavis Wood interview; 'I didn't know whether or not I wanted to be there', SP interview; 'He was devastated', Levin, 'I thought Dad was invincible . . .'; 'Dennis said, "I won't be long now"', Mavis Wood interview; 'When he was dying', MP interview

580 'Dad was determined to come', Levin, 'I thought Dad was invincible . . .'; 'It had been left as late as possible', SP interview; 'Maybe there is a present tense always', Bragg, unedited video-recording of interview with DP

581 'Judy and I sat with him', Mavis Wood interview; 'Dad had been sinking much more slowly', SP interview; 'Potter was in many ways the Jonathan Swift', The Times, 8 June 1994; 'perhaps the best television writer', Financial Times, 8 June 1994; 'He was, by common consent', Independent, 8 June 1994

582 'Dennis was his work', Daily Telegraph, 8 June 1994; 'Our relationship was stormy', Guardian, 8 June 1994; 'Merv, the crematorium', Mervyn James interview; 'Dad didn't actually care', SP interview; 'I do have one very real fear of death', Independent, 2 November 1994

583 'Michael Grade and I are delighted', Karaoke and Cold Lazarus press pack; 'The whisper from Television Centre', Daily Mail, 2 December 1994; 'That was not chiefly about Dad', SP interview; 'I haven't felt safe since Dad died', JP interview; 'Dennis had said to me', Kenith Trodd interview; 'The deal was done when Dad was alive', Levin, 'I thought Dad was invincible . . .'; 'After that . . . we all worked together', Kenith Trodd interview

584 'has secured a record payment', Daily Mail, 20 January 1995; 'He constantly reminds me of Dad', Jardine, interview with SP

585 'His reputation as the greatest dramatist', Sunday Telegraph Magazine, 14 April 1996; 'Regrettably . . . they confirm the melancholy pattern', Guardian, 15 April 1996; 'Karaoke is simply dreadful', The Sunday Times, 28 April 1996; 'Karaoke . . . must be one of the worst plays', Evening Standard, 29 April 1996; 'Frankly, in terms of writing for TV', Guardian, 4 May 1996; 'Karaoke . . . was trounced', Daily Mail, 30 April 1996; 'lost a quarter of its audience', The Sunday Times, 2 June 1996

586 'strongest drama', Daily Telegraph, 20 April 1996; 'Karaoke is not brilliant', New Statesman, 3 May 1996; 'better viewing second time around', Sunday Telegraph, 5 May 1996; 'Karaoke bears all the hallmarks', Independent on Sunday, 26 May 1996; 'lacklustre scripts', The Times, 6 May 1996; 'Maybe the Bragg interview', Renny Rye interview; 'anyone should have spent any money', Independent, 24 May 1996; 'My dear, if you thought Karaoke was bad', The Sunday Times, 2 June 1996; 'Planet of the Apes with tub-thumping', Daily Telegraph, 1 June 1996; 'flaws [Potter] would have corrected', ibid., 3 June 1996; 'Cold Lazarus is', Daily Mail, 3.6.96.; 'it teeters on the verge of ridiculous', Sunday Telegraph, 2 June 1996

587 'Cold Lazarus stands up', Financial Times, 25 May 1996; 'great fun, a futuristic

psychodrama', *Mail on Sunday*, 25 May 1996; 'a mess', *Observer*, 26 June 1996; 'To end your life with a vision', Peter Ansorge interview; 'worth their weight in plutonium', *Washington Post*, 2 June 1997; 'comic and highly disturbing', *Evening Standard*, 3 May 1996; 'a reminder of Potter at his best', *Independent*, 4 May 1996; 'I think *Blue Remembered Hills*', Piers Haggard interview; 'at his best, few modern dramatists', *Daily Telegraph*, 3 May 1996; 'Perhaps this beautiful 95-minute production', *The Sunday Times*, 12 May 1996

588 'I find it difficult to say where', *New Statesman*, 3 May 1996; 'Whether anybody would make those scripts now', Jonathan Powell interview; 'They'll usually start in the theatre', Peter Ansorge interview

589 '*EastEnders* is now probably the best-written drama', *Guardian Weekend*, 21 December 1996; 'Dennis Potter writes television plays', *Films and Filming*, April 1982; 'Hazlitt disturbed people', *The Times*, 3 August 1968; 'Now we're getting to the nub of Dennis', Gareth Davies interview; 'There's much more drama', videotape of seminar at Museum of Television & Radio, New York, 16 January 1992, Judy Daish Associates; 'Where did life-imitating-art', Gina Bellman interview

590 'Potter's loyalty to television', *Guardian*, 6 April 1994; 'I do think Dennis is a lasting phenomenon', Brian Gibson interview

Acknowledgements

My first thanks must go to Dennis Potter's executors: his agent Judy Daish, daughter Sarah Potter and accountant Stanley Rosenthal; then to his other two children, Jane and Robert; and to Dennis's mother Margaret Potter, and his sister June Thomas.

Kenith Trodd, Potter's working partner for the greater part of their careers, gave lavishly of his time, and was kind enough to make viewing copies of Potter's plays easily available to me.

Then my thanks to those who gave interviews and wrote to me about Potter: Tariq Ali, Roger Allen, Jon Amiel, Peter Ansorge, Naim Attallah, George Baker, Kenneth Baker, Michael Bakewell, Tony Baldwin, Frances Barber, Kay Barnes, Alison Barnett, Keith Barron, Alan Bates, Peter Bayley, Gina Bellman, Olwen Bick (née Birch), Frank Bloom, Melvyn Bragg, Ron Brewer, Cheryl Campbell, Jonathan Cecil, Robert Christopher, David Cocks, John R. Cook, Alan Coren, Gareth and Christine Davies, Clare Douglas, Paul Downey, Natasha Edelman, Peter Edwards, Michael Foot, Margaret Forster, Stephen Frears, Philip French, Graham Fuller, John Fuller, Robert Michael Geisler, Louise Germaine, Brian Gibson, Michael Gough, Michael Grade, Trevor Griffiths, John Gross, Philip Gush, Piers Haggard, Roger Hancock, David Hare, Jack Harvey, Stephen Hearst, Richard Hoggart, Stephen Hugh-Jones, Iris Hughes, Richard Ingrams, Mervyn James, Peter Jay, David Johnson, Mervyn Jones, Angela Lambert, Clive Lindley, Anne and Haydn Lloyd, Richard Loncraine, Rick McCallum, John McGrath, Julia McNeal (née Gaitskell), Kika Markham, Lord (Christopher) Mayhew, Nancy Meckler, Joe Melia, Gavin Millar, Christopher Morahan, David Nathan, Timothy Neal, Philip Purser, Jonathan Powell, Libby Purves, Patrick Rahilly, Michael Ratcliffe, John Roberdeau, Herbert Ross, Hilary Rubinstein, Lewis Rudd, Renny Rye, Ann Scott, Caroline Seebohm, Ned Sherrin, Mark Shivas, Clancy Sigal, Ron Simon, Greg Smith, Godfrey Smith, Roger Smith, Peter Stead, Terry Tapping, Lord (Dick) Taverne, Eddie Thomas, Colm Tóibín, Philippa Toomey,

ACKNOWLEDGEMENTS

Noreen Tye, Graham Wale, Sydney Wale, Rosemarie Whitman, Horace and Coreen Wilks, Eunice Williams, Gary Williamson, Mavis Wood, John Wyver, Alan Yentob, and Michael York.

John R. Cook and W. Stephen Gilbert, authors of previous (and immensely useful) books on Potter, were generous with their support and advice.

Other help came from Wendy Allnutt, Paul Bailey, John Belcher, Michael Billington, Christopher Burstall, Mary Craig, Alan Garner, Sir Martin Gilbert, Victoria Glendinning, Sir Peter Hall, Irving Harrison, Lady (Edna) Healey, Ron Heapy, Nicholas Hellen, Anne Henderson, Janet Henfrey, Ann Larpent, Brian Lighthill, Cassie Mayer, Stephen Morley, Julia Trevelyan Oman, Roy Porter (for a reading list on psoriasis), Jan Morris, John Rendell, the Right Reverend David Sheppard, Janet Suzman, and David Vaisey.

As to institutions and their staff, I must acknowledge the help of the late Anthony Bambridge (Managing Editor, *The Sunday Times*); Bobbie Mitchell, BBC Photo Library; Jane Blackstock, Victor Gollancz Ltd; Michael Bott, Keeper of Archives and Manuscripts, University of Reading Library; Jack Bradley, Literary Manager, The Royal National Theatre; P. Conway, Headmaster, St Clement Danes School; all the staff at Judy Daish Associates; Caroline Dalton, Archivist, New College, Oxford; G. M. Hiley, Headteacher of Berry Hill County Primary School; Sally Hine, BBC Sound Library; Jacquie Kavanagh and Gwyniver Jones, BBC Written Archives Centre; Adam Lee, Manager, BBC Document Archives; and the One-O-One photographic laboratory (special thanks to Mark for producing excellent copy prints and negatives).

At Faber and Faber, Matthew Evans made it possible for me to write the book; and Julian Loose and his assistant Luke Vinten provided valuable editorial support. My friends Nicola Bennett and Mary Jane Mowat read early drafts and gave invaluable advice. My agent Felicity Bryan has provided constant support and advice. And finally, Jill Burrows skilfully copy-edited, indexed and typeset the book, and was the best of colleagues throughout the final stage of this absorbing project.

Index

———

Main analytical references to works by DP and references to substantial quotations from his texts are indicated in **bold** type.

645